Financial Accounting

Financial
Accounting

An Introduction
To Concepts,
Methods, and Uses

Sidney Davidson, Ph.D., CPA
The University of Chicago

James S. Schindler, Ph.D., CPA
The State University of New York at Buffalo

Clyde P. Stickney, D.B.A., CPA
The University of North Carolina at Chapel Hill

Roman L. Weil, Ph.D., CPA, CMA
The Georgia Institute of Technology

The Dryden Press
· Hinsdale, Illinois

Editorial - Production Services provided
    by COBB/DUNLOP, Inc.

Whatever be the detail with which you cram your students, the chance of their meeting in after-life exactly that detail is almost infinitesimal; and if they do meet it, they will probably have forgotten what you taught them about it. The really useful training yields a comprehension of a few general principles with a thorough grounding in the way they apply to a variety of concrete details. In subsequent practice the students will have forgotten your particular details; but they will remember by an unconscious common sense how to apply principles to immediate circumstances.

Alfred North Whitehead
The Aims of Education and Other Essays

Preface

You might understandably ask, "Why another introductory financial accounting textbook? What about this book distinguishes it from the numerous others already on the market?" We feel that there is a need in the market that is not being adequately satisfied by other texts. We view the introductory course in financial accounting as having the following principal purposes or objectives:

• To help the student develop a sufficient understanding of the basic concepts underlying financial statements, so that the concepts can be applied to new and different problem situations.

• To train the student in accounting terminology and methods so that he or she can interpret, analyze, and evaluate the financial statements currently published in corporate annual reports.

Not surprisingly, most other introductory textbooks state the same, or similar, objectives. The critical differences between textbooks relate to the relative emphases on **a.** concepts, **b.** methods, and **c.** uses. In writing this book:

1. We emphasize the rationale for, and implications of, important accounting concepts. The ability to "conceptualize" material covered is an important part of the learning process. Without such conceptualization, students will have difficulty focusing on relevant issues in new and different situations. Accordingly, we have identified the important accounting concepts early in each chapter, followed by several numerical examples illustrating their application. Numerous short problems are included at the end of each chapter to check the students' ability to apply the concepts to still different problem situations.

2. We attempt to place sufficient emphasis on accounting procedures so that students can interpret, analyze, and evaluate published financial statements, but not so much emphasis on the procedures that students get bogged down in detail. The determination of just how much accounting procedure is "enough" is a problem faced by

all writers of accounting textbooks. Most feel, as we do, that the most effective way to
learn accounting concepts is the working of numerous problems and exercises. However,
when too much emphasis is placed on the accounting procedures, there is a tendency
for students to be lulled into the security of thinking they understand accounting concepts when they actually do not. The "mixture" of concepts and procedures in this book
is one with which we have experimented extensively and have found effective in class-
room use.

Our experience is that students do not understand the accounting implications of an
event until they can construct the journal entry for that event. Throughout this book,
we show journal entries in describing the nature of accounting events. Moreover, most
chapters contain questions that require the analysis of transactions with debits and
credits. Do not conclude, however, by a cursory glance through this text, that it is
primarily procedural. We are more concerned that our students learn concepts; the
procedures are required for learning concepts. Furthermore, we believe this is the most
effective way to train both professional accountants and those who wish merely to be
informed users of financial statements.

3. We attempt to bridge the gap between the preparation of financial statements
and the uses to which the statements might be put. We give extensive consideration to
the effects of alternative accounting principles on the measurement of earnings and
financial position and to the types of interpretations which should and should not be
made. Excerpts from published financial statements are used where appropriate.

■ ORGANIZATION

This book is divided into four major parts as outlined below:

Part	Topic	Chapter(s)
I	Overview of Financial Statements	1
II	Accounting Concepts and Methods	2–7
III	Measuring and Reporting Assets and Equities	8–14
IV	Synthesis	15

The four parts may be viewed as four tiers, or steps, for coverage of the material.
Part I (Chapter 1) presents a general overview of the principal financial statements and
the nature of accounting. Part II (Chapters 2 through 7) discusses the basic accounting
model used to generate the principal financial statements. Part III (Chapters 8 through
14) considers the specific accounting principles or methods used in preparing the
financial statements. Finally, Part IV (Chapter 15) serves as a synthesis for the entire
book. This organization reflects our view that learning can take place most effectively
by starting with a broad picture, then breaking up that broad picture into smaller pieces
until the desired depth is achieved, and finally synthesizing so that the relationship
between the parts and the whole can be kept in perspective.

Chapter 1 presents a brief description of the purpose and concepts underlying the
three principal financial statements: the balance sheet, the statement of net income,
and the statement of changes in financial position. The economic, social, and political
environment within which these statements are generated is also considered. Many
students, after reading Chapter 1, feel deluged with the multitude of new terms and

concepts. Most of these same students admit later, however, that the broad overview was useful in piecing material together as they later explored individual topics in greater depth.

Chapters 2 through 5 present the basic accounting model that generates the three principal financial statements. In each case, we begin with a description of the important concepts underlying each statement. The accounting procedures employed to generate the statements are then described and illustrated. One of the unique features of the book is the integration in Chapter 4 of the accounting entries for transactions during a period with the related adjusting entries at the end of the period. We have found that when these two types of entries are discussed in separate chapters, students lose sight of the fact that both kinds of entries are required to measure net income and financial position. Another unique aspect of the text is the early coverage, in Chapter 5, of the statement of changes in financial position. We have two purposes in placing it here. First, this placement elevates the statement to its rightful place among the three principal financial statements. Students can thereby integrate the concepts of profitability and liquidity more effectively and begin to understand that one does not necessarily accompany the other. When the funds statement is covered at the end of the course (in many cases, when time is running out), there is a tendency for the student to think it is less important. Our second purpose for placing this chapter early in the book is that it serves to cement understanding of the basic accounting model in Chapters 2 through 4: Preparing the statement of changes in financial position requires the student to work "backwards" from the balance sheet and income statement to reconstruct the transactions which took place. Chapter 6 discusses various issues concerning how the information generated from the basic accounting model in Chapters 2 through 5 is disclosed in the financial statements. This chapter relies heavily on excerpts from published financial statements. Chapter 7 introduces the topic of financial statement analysis. We place it here to serve as a partial synthesis of the first six chapters. Students at this point ask how information in the statements might be used. This chapter presents an opportunity to answer some of these questions, even if at only an elementary level. Effective financial statement analysis requires an understanding of the specific accounting methods discussed in Part III. Chapter 7 therefore serves as a springboard for what is to come.

Chapters 8 through 13 discuss the various "generally accepted accounting principles" employed in generating financial statements. In each chapter we not only describe and illustrate the application of the various accounting methods but also consider their effect on the financial statements. This approach reflects our view that students should be able to interpret and analyze published financial statements and to understand the effect of alternative accounting methods on such assessments. We have placed some of the more complicated topics in chapter-end appendixes to provide flexibility in coverage. Some instructors may not wish to use this more complex material. Chapter 14 discusses the methods of accounting for changing prices. We include this chapter not only because of its increasing importance but in response to students' seemingly continual questions about the relevance of accounting based on historical costs.

The students who have used the preliminary edition of this book have found that Chapter 15, which synthesizes much of the material in the first fourteen chapters, is in many ways the most useful in the book. Explicit consideration is given to the combined effects of alternative accounting methods on the financial statements, to the significance of alternative accounting methods on financial statement analysis, and to the current structure for developing "generally accepted accounting principles." Problem 13 at the end of Chapter 15 is a major review problem for the whole book. A glance at the index, at *APB* and *FASB*, will indicate that this book is up to date in using current generally accepted accounting principles.

A comprehensive glossary of financial accounting terms is included at the end of the book. This glossary serves as a useful reference tool for accounting and other business terms and provides additional descriptions of a few topics considered only briefly in the text, such as accounting changes and trade-in transactions.

The book is designed for a one-semester course. If the introductory financial accounting course is spread over two quarters, the first half might cover Chapters 1–7. If the entire course is to cover just one academic quarter, as is common at the graduate level, it may be necessary to omit some of the materials in Chapters 13 and 14.

■ RELATED MATERIALS ACCOMPANYING THE TEXT

The following materials have been prepared for use with the text:

Instructor's Manual   The instructor's manual, in addition to including responses to all questions and solutions to all exercises and problems, presents suggested course outlines for courses of varying lengths, a list of chapter objectives, helpful teaching hints, detailed lecture and discussion outlines including the numbers of particularly germane problems, and several sets of sample examination questions and problems. The instructor's manual also includes a list of check figures for various problems in the text. These check figures can be photocopied and distributed to students if the instructor so desires. A set of learning objectives for each chapter, prepared by John R. Simon, is also included in the Instructor's Manual.

Study Guide   A study guide has been prepared by LeBrone C. Harris, James E. Moon, and William L. Stephens. This study guide includes a listing of highlights from each chapter and is then followed by numerous short true/false, matching, and multiple-choice questions.

Transparency Masters   A set of masters is available for making transparencies for most of the exhibits in the text and the problems at the end of each chapter.

Working Papers   A set of forms for preparing solutions to problems is available.

■ ACKNOWLEDGMENTS

We gratefully acknowledge the helpful criticisms and suggestions of the following people who reviewed the manuscript at various stages: Harold B. Cook (Central Michigan University), Ronald M. Copeland (University of South Carolina), John C. Corless (University of Connecticut), Robert W. Findlay (University of Maine at Portland—Gorham), M. Sabry Heakal (St. Cloud State University), Gardner M. Jones (Michigan State University), Ronald M. Mano (University of Utah), Kenneth F. Martin (Pensacola Junior College), J. G. Pate (University of Texas at El Paso), Lawrence Revsine (Northwestern University), and John R. Simon (Northern Illinois University).

LeBrone C. Harris, James E. Moon, and William L. Stephens of the University of South Florida did a splendid job in preparing the Study Guide. John R. Simon of Northern Illinois University, in addition to reviewing the manuscript, prepared an excellent set of learning objectives.

Thomas Horton and Daughters, Inc. has graciously given us permission to reproduce material from *Accounting: The Language of Business*, published by them. The Sorta, Cassidy, and Julia problems were adapted from ones prepared by George Sorter. These problems involve working backwards from one financial statement to another and we have found them useful in cementing understanding.

We thank the following people for their hard work in helping us to prepare the manuscript for, and contents of, this book: Robert N. Gogel, Mary Lee Peeler, Raymonde Rousselot, K. Xenophon Rybowiak, Katherine Schipper, and Cherie B. Weil. Donna Conte supervised the production of the book and did an excellent job.

Finally, we would like to thank Jere L. Calmes, Paula Solinger, Sandy Nykerk and Blanche Duquette of The Dryden Press for their assistance and, in particular, their patience in all phases of the preparation of this book.

Contents

Overview
of Financial
Statements

Accounting Information and Resource Allocation Decisions

A major function of accounting and financial reporting is helping investors make investment decisions. For example, assume that you recently inherited $50,000 and must decide what to do with the bequest. You have narrowed the invesment decision either to depositing the money in a savings account at a local bank or to purchasing shares of common stock of Jonathan Corporation, presently selling for $20 per share. Your decision will be made in terms of the *return* anticipated from each investment and the *risk* or *uncertainty* associated with that return.

The bank is currently paying interest at the rate of 5 percent annually on savings deposits. Since it is unlikely that the bank will go out of business, you are virtually certain of earning 5 percent each year.

The return from investing in the shares of common stock of Jonathan Corporation has two components. First, the firm has been paying an annual cash dividend of $2 per share and it is anticipated that this dividend will continue in the future. Second, the market price of the stock is likely to change between the date the shares are purchased and the date in the future when they are sold. The difference between the eventual selling price per share and the $20 purchase price is also a component of the return from buying the stock.

Compared to the savings account interest, the return from the common stock investment is more uncertain or risky. Future dividends and market price changes are likely to be associated, at least partially, with the profitability of the firm. Future income might be less than that currently being earned if competitors introduce new products which erode Jonathan Corporation's share of its sales market. If a freeze on selling prices were imposed so that Jonathan Corporation could not raise its prices to compensate for the cost of replacing merchandise sold, then future income might be less than currently expected. If Jonathan Corporation makes important discoveries or introduces new products, then future income might be greater than currently anticipated.

The market price of Jonathan Corporation's shares will probably also be affected by economy-wide factors such as inflation, unemployment, and political unrest. Also, specific industry factors such as raw materials shortages or government antitrust actions may influence the market price of the shares. Since individuals generally prefer less risk to more risk, you will probably demand a higher expected return from the purchase of Jonathan Corporation's shares than if you invest the inheritance in a savings account.

There are numerous sources of information which might be consulted in assessing the return and risk of various investment alternatives. One such source is the financial statements prepared by firms and distributed periodically to stockholders and potential investors as part of the firm's annual report. In this chapter, an overview of the nature and content of the principal financial statements is presented. Some of the ways in which information contained in the statements might be used in assessing return and risk is also discussed briefly.

■ PRINCIPAL FINANCIAL STATEMENTS

The annual report to stockholders typically includes a letter from the company's president summarizing activities of the past year and assessing the company's prospects for the coming year. Also included are pictures of the firm's products and employees and similar promotional material. The section of the annual report containing the financial statements is composed of the following:

1. statement of financial position
2. statement of net income
3. statement of changes in financial position
4. various supporting statements or schedules
5. notes to the financial statements
6. opinion of the independent certified public accountant.

Statement of Financial Position

The comparative statement of financial position of the Jonathan Corporation as of December 31, 1975 and 1976, is presented in Exhibit 1.1. As its title suggests, this statement attempts to present an overall view of Jonathan Corporation's financial position as of the end of 1975 and 1976. Several aspects of this statement should be noted.

Statement at a Moment in Time   The statement of financial position presents a snapshot of the firm's financial position as of a given date. (In Exhibit 1.1, one statement reports the financial position as of December 31, 1975, and the other, as of December 31, 1976.) The statement presents amounts or levels or *stocks* of various items. (Note here that we are not referring to shares of stock.) *Stocks* are to be contrasted with *flows*. A stock is a measure of the amount of an item at a particular time, while a flow is a measure of the change in the amount of an

EXHIBIT 1.1
Jonathan Corporation
Comparative Statement of Financial Position
December 31, 1975 and 1976

ASSETS

| | December 31 | |
	1975	1976
Current Assets:[a]		
Cash	$ 75,000	$ 125,000
Accounts Receivable from Customers	75,000	200,000
Merchandise Inventory (at acquisition cost)	150,000	225,000
Total Current Assets	$ 300,000	$ 550,000
Noncurrent Assets (at acquisition cost):[a]		
Land	$ 200,000	$ 200,000
Equipment (net of accumulated depreciation)	700,000	1,000,000
Buildings (net of accumulated depreciation)	800,000	750,000
Total Noncurrent Assets	$1,700,000	$1,950,000
Total Assets	$2,000,000	$2,500,000

LIABILITIES AND STOCKHOLDERS' EQUITY

Current Liabilities:[a]		
Accounts Payable to Suppliers	$ 125,000	$ 160,000
Salaries Payable to Employees	25,000	40,000
Income Taxes Payable to Federal Government	50,000	200,000
Total Current Liabilities	$ 200,000	$ 400,000
Noncurrent Liabilities:[a]		
Bonds Payable to Lenders (due 1995)	600,000	700,000
Total Liabilities	$ 800,000	$1,100,000
Stockholders' Equity		
Common Stock	$ 500,000	$ 500,000
Retained Earnings	700,000	900,000
Total Stockholders' Equity	$1,200,000	$1,400,000
Total Liabilities and Stockholders' Equity	$2,000,000	$2,500,000

[a] The current and noncurrent classification of assets and liabilities are discussed later in this chapter.

item over a period of time. For example, to say that Jonathan Corporation had cash in the amount of $75,000 on December 31, 1975, and $125,000 on December 31, 1976, is to say something about the firm's stock of cash on these particular dates. A parallel statement about flows is to say that the firm's cash receipts and disbursements during the period were such that the cash balance increased, or changed, by $50,000.

Concepts of Assets and Equities The statement of financial position presents a listing of the firm's *assets, liabilities,* and *owners' equity*. When the corporate form of organization is used, ownership is evidenced by shares of stock, and the owners' equity is frequently referred to as *stockholders' equity*.

Assets are economic resources. An asset is an item that has the ability or potential to provide future services or benefits to a firm. For example, cash can be used to purchase merchandise inventory or equipment. Merchandise inventory can be sold to customers for an amount the firm hopes will be larger than was paid for it. Equipment can be used in transporting the merchandise inventory to customers.

Liabilities are creditors' claims on the resources, or assets, of a firm. Jonathan Corporation acquired merchandise inventory from its suppliers but has not yet paid for a portion of the purchases. As a result, these creditors have a claim on the assets of the company. Labor services have been provided by employees for which payment has not been made as of December 31 of each year. These employees likewise have a claim on the assets of the firm. Creditors' claims, or liabilities, result from benefits previously received by a firm, and typically have a specified amount and date at which they become due.

Stockholders' equity is the owners' claim on the assets of a firm. Unlike creditors, the owners have a residual interest. That is, owners have a claim on all assets in excess of those required to meet creditors' claims. The stockholders' equity is generally comprised of two parts: contributed capital and retained earnings. Contributed capital reflects the assets invested by the original stockholders in exchange for an ownership interest. Retained earnings represents the earnings, or profits, realized by a firm since its formation in excess of dividends distributed to stockholders. In other words, retained earnings are earnings reinvested by management for the benefit of the stockholders. Management directs the use of a firm's assets so that over time more assets are received than are given up in obtaining them. This increase in assets, after any claims by creditors, belongs to the firm's owners. Most firms reinvest a large percentage of their income for growth and expansion rather than distributing all of it as dividends.

Liabilities plus stockholders' equity are referred to as *total equities,* or simply *equities.*

Equality of Assets and Equities As the statement of financial position for Jonathan Corporation indicates, there is an equality between (1) assets and (2) liabilities plus stockholders' equity. That is,

$$\text{Assets} = \text{Liabilities} + \text{Stockholders' Equity.}$$

The significance of this equality can be grasped by considering the nature of each of the three components. Assets are resources of the firm. Liabilities and stockholders' equity are the claims on these resources. Thus:

Resources = Claims on Resources.

In the statement of financial position, we view the resources from two viewpoints: a listing of the assets under the control of the firm and a listing of the parties external to the firm who have a claim on these assets. Because of the equality of total assets and total equities, the statement of financial position is often called a *balance sheet*.

Balance Sheet Classification The assets and liabilities are classified in the balance sheet as being either *current* or *noncurrent*.

Current assets include cash and other assets that are expected to be turned into cash, or sold, or consumed within approximately one year from the date of the balance sheet. Cash, marketable securities, accounts receivable from customers, and merchandise inventories are the most common current assets. Current liabilities include liabilities that are expected to be paid within one year. Accounts payable to suppliers, salaries payable to employees, and taxes payable to governmental agencies are examples of current liabilities. Noncurrent assets typically are held and used for several years; they provide a firm with longer-term productive capacity. Noncurrent liabilities plus stockholders' equity are a firm's longer-term sources of capital. The usefulness of the classification of assets and equities as current or noncurrent is discussed when we consider the third principal statement, the statement of changes in financial position.

Valuation The dollar amount shown for each asset and liability listed in the statement of financial position of Jonathan Corporation is based on one of two valuation bases: (**1**) cash, or current cash-equivalent, valuation, or (**2**) acquisition, or historical, cost valuation.

Cash is stated at the amount of cash on hand or in the bank. Accounts receivable are shown at the amount of cash expected to be collected from customers. Liabilities are generally shown at the amount of cash required to discharge debts. These assets and liabilities are sometimes referred to as *monetary items* because they are valued on a cash, or current cash-equivalent, basis.

The remaining assets are shown at either unadjusted or adjusted acquisition cost. For example, merchandise inventory and land are shown at the amount of cash or other resources which the firm originally sacrificed to acquire those assets. Equipment and buildings are likewise shown at acquisition cost, but this amount is adjusted downward to reflect the portion of the assets' services that have been used since acquisition. A large proportion of Jonathan Corporation's assets are shown at either unadjusted or adjusted acquisition cost. It is unlikely that these amounts are equal to the amounts the company could realize if the assets were sold or the amounts the company would have to pay to replace them. The use of acquisition cost as the valuation method for these assets should be kept in mind when assessing the financial position of Jonathan Corporation and deciding whether the firm's stock should be purchased for its current market price of $20 per share.

Common stock is stated at the amount originally invested by owners when the firm's stock was first sold. Retained earnings is the sum of all prior years' earnings in excess of dividends. Because of its link with earnings and the valuation of assets and liabilities, retained earnings is, in effect, measured using a combination of the current cash-equivalent and acquisition-cost valuation bases.

Assets and Equities Not Shown   After having studied carefully the balance sheet of Jonathan Corporation, several possible resources of the firm are noteworthy because of their absence. Consider, for example, the value of a well-trained labor force, dynamic managerial leadership, superior technological abilities, or the good reputation of the company. These and several other intangible, but perhaps more important, resources are excluded from most firms' balance sheets. On the liability side, commitments for future payments on leased property or unresolved damage claims against the company are probably also excluded.

We have considered briefly several important asset and liability valuation and inclusion issues here to point out possible deficiencies in the balance sheet as an indicator of a firm's financial position at any moment in time. These issues are considered more fully in later chapters.

Statement of Net Income

The statement of net income of Jonathan Corporation for the year 1976 is presented in Exhibit 1.2. This statement indicates the *earnings*, or *profits*, of the

EXHIBIT 1.2
Jonathan Corporation
Statement of Net Income
For the Year 1976

Revenues:

Sale of Merchandise	$2,250,000
Sale of Engineering Services	140,000
Interest on Customers' Uncollected Accounts	10,000
Total Revenues	$2,400,000

Less Expenses:

Cost of Merchandise Sold	$ 900,000
Salaries Expense	400,000
Depreciation Expense	200,000
Selling and Administrative Expenses	350,000
Interest Expense	50,000
Income Tax Expense	200,000
Total Expenses	$2,100,000
Net Income	$ 300,000

company for the year. Note several aspects of this second principal financial statement.

Statement Reports Activities over Time   The income statement presents the results of earnings activity over time and therefore reports *flows*. In contrast, the balance sheet presents a statement of the firm's assets and equities at a specific point in time and reports *stocks*.

Concepts of Net Income, Revenue, and Expense   The terms *net income, earnings*, and *profits* are synonymous and used interchangeably in corporate annual reports and throughout this text. The generation of earnings is a primary activity of most business firms, and the income statement is intended to provide a measure of how successful a firm was in achieving this goal for a given time span. Net income is defined as the difference between revenues and expenses for a period.

Revenues are a measure of the inflows of assets (or reductions in liabilities) from selling goods and providing services to customers. During 1976, Jonathan Corporation sold merchandise and provided engineering and financing services. From its customers, Jonathan Corporation either received cash or promises to pay cash in the near future. These promises to pay are called Accounts Receivable from Customers. Thus, revenues were generated, leading to an increase in assets.

Expenses are a measure of the outflows of assets (or increases in liabilities) used up in generating revenues. The cost of merchandise sold (an expense) is measured by the acquisition cost of merchandise which was sold to customers. Salaries expense is the amount of cash payments or promises to make future cash payments (Salaries Payable) to employees for services received in helping generate revenues during the period. Depreciation expense is a measure of the services of equipment and buildings used during 1976. For each expense there is either a reduction in an asset or an increase in a liability. A firm strives to generate an excess of net asset inflows from revenues over net asset outflows or expirations from expenses required in generating the revenues. When expenses for a period exceed revenues, a firm incurs a *net loss*. The net income measure may be used as an indicator of a firm's accomplishments (revenues) relative to the efforts required (expenses) in pursuing its activities.

Relationship to Balance Sheet   The income statement articulates, or links, with the balance sheets as of the beginning and end of the period. Recall that retained earnings represents the sum of all prior earnings of a firm in excess of dividends. The amount of net income for the year helps explain the change in retained earnings between the beginning and end of the year. During 1976, Jonathan Corporation had net income of $300,000 and declared and paid dividends of $100,000. The change in retained earnings during 1976 can therefore be explained as follows:

Retained Earnings, December 31, 1975 (stock)	$700,000
Add Net Income for the Year 1976 (flow)	300,000
Subtract Dividends Declared and Paid (flow)	(100,000)
Retained Earnings, December 31, 1976 (stock)	$900,000

Net income for the period also articulates with changes in the other components of the balance sheet. If we subtract the amount for each balance sheet component at the beginning of the period from the corresponding amount at the end of the period, we get the *change* in each component during the period, as follows:

| Change in Assets | = | Change in Liabilities | + | Change in Contributed Capital | + | Change in Retained Earnings |

In explaining the change in retained earnings for 1976 of Jonathan Corporation, we saw that the change in retained earnings is equal to net income minus dividends. Thus:

| Change in Assets | = | Change in Liabilities | + | Change in Contributed Capital | + | Net Income | − | Dividends |

or:

| Net Income | = | Change in Assets | − | Change in Liabilities | − | Change in Contributed Capital | + | Dividends. |

Assets may be increased (decreased) by an increase (decrease) in liabilities, contributed capital, or net income. Net income is usually associated with an increase in assets or a decrease in liabilities. The significance of these relationships between the balance sheet and income statement is considered in more depth in later chapters. The relationships are introduced here to indicate that the amounts of assets and liabilities included in the balance sheet at the beginning and end of a period are closely related to the revenues and expenses reported in the income statement for the period.

Measurement of Revenues and Expenses As was the case with assets and equities on the balance sheet, the measurement of revenues and expenses is based on either (1) cash, or cash-equivalent, values or (2) acquisition costs. The amount reported as revenue from the sale of merchandise or services is a measure of the expected amount of cash to be received from customers. Salary, selling and administrative, interest, and income tax expenses are stated as the amount of cash the firm was required to pay for the services received. In contrast, cost of merchandise sold is measured by the acquisition cost of inventory which was sold, and depreciation expense is measured in terms of the acquisition cost of the services of the equipment and buildings which were used during the year.

Revenues and Expenses Excluded The balance sheet shows assets such as inventory, land, equipment, and buildings at acquisition cost. The income statement shows expenses such as cost of merchandise sold and depreciation expense at an appropriate portion of this acquisition cost. The income statement thus excludes any changes in the economic value of those assets. For example, land was acquired for $200,000 several years ago. Suppose that this land had a current appraised value of $500,000 at the end of 1976. This increase in value is not normally recognized as revenue on the income statement until the land is sold. The economist views changes in the market value of a firm's assets as part of its income. The accountant generally recognizes changes in the value of assets only at the time assets are sold. Thus, we see one important difference between the economist's and accountant's definitions of income.

Statement of Changes in Financial Position

The third principal financial statement of Jonathan Corporation, the statement of changes in financial position, is presented in Exhibit 1.3. This statement explains the change in *working capital* for the year. Working capital is equal to current assets less current liabilities. In the example, working capital is increased as a result of (1) generating revenues in the form of cash or accounts receivable and (2) issuing long-term bonds for cash. Working capital is decreased as a result of reporting expenses such as (1) cost of merchandise sold (which reduces merchandise inventory), (2) salaries expense (which reduces cash or increases salaries payable), and (3) selling and administrative expenses (which reduce cash or increase accounts payable). Working capital is also decreased (4) when dividends are declared and paid and (5) when equipment and buildings are purchased for cash. In the statement of changes in financial position, revenues which increase working capital and expenses which decrease working capital are grouped together

EXHIBIT 1.3
Jonathan Corporation
Statement of Changes in Financial Position
For the Year 1976

Working Capital, January 1, 1976		$100,000
Working Capital Increased by:		
Operations:		
Revenues Increasing Working Capital	$2,400,000	
Expenses Decreasing Working Capital	(1,900,000)	
Total from Operations	$ 500,000	
Proceeds from Issue of Bonds, due 1995	100,000	
Total Increases in Working Capital		600,000
Working Capital Decreased by:		
Dividends Declared and Paid	$ 100,000	
Equipment and Buildings Acquired	450,000	
Total Decreases in Working Capital		(550,000)
Working Capital, December 31, 1976		$150,000

to obtain the net increase or decrease in working capital from operations. Other sources of working capital (issuance of bonds) and uses of working capital (declaration of dividends, purchase of equipment and buildings) are then presented.

Of what significance is a statement explaining or analyzing the changes in working capital for the year? Current assets and current liabilities are the items principally involved or used in the earnings activities of a firm. For example, merchandise is purchased for cash or on credit from a supplier. The merchandise is then sold to a customer who agrees to pay within several weeks. The customer pays the account and the cash received is used to discharge current liabilities and acquire more merchandise. This sequence of activities occurs at least once each year for most firms and is termed an *earnings cycle*.

If the firm is to continue operating successfully, it must generate more working capital from revenues than it uses up for expenses. Otherwise, some link in the earnings cycle will fail to function properly. Sufficient working capital must also be generated from operations to replace equipment and buildings. In some cases the firm can borrow from long-term investors to replenish working capital, but future operations must generate sufficient working capital to repay these loans. The statement of changes in financial position, therefore, provides information that may be used in assessing the financial health of a company. Several additional aspects of this statement should be noted.

Statement Reports Activities over Time   The statement of changes in financial position indicates the increases and decreases in working capital during the year and, like the income statement, reports flows.

Relationship to Balance Sheet and Income Statement   The statement of changes in financial position helps explain the change in working capital (current assets minus current liabilities) between the beginning and end of the period. In this way, the statement articulates or links with the balance sheet. To demonstrate the relationship of this statement to the balance sheet, we again determine the change in each balance sheet component between the beginning and the end of the period as follows:

Change in Current Assets	+	Change in Noncurrent Assets	=	Change in Current Liabilities	+	Change in Noncurrent Liabilities	+	Change in Stockholders' Equity.

Rearranging:

Change in Current Assets	−	Change in Current Liabilities	=	Change in Noncurrent Liabilities	+	Change in Stockholders' Equity	−	Change in Noncurrent Assets.

As we discuss in Chapter Five, the change in working capital can be explained or analyzed by looking at changes in noncurrent liabilities (for example, long-term borrowing from creditors), changes in stockholders' equity (for example, net income and dividends), and changes in noncurrent assets (for example, purchase of equipment and buildings). Net income for the period partially explains the change in working capital, so that the income statement and the statement of changes in financial position are related.

We might summarize the relationship between the three statements as follows:

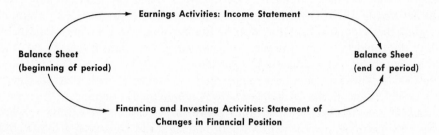

Supporting Statements or Schedules

The statements of financial position, net income, and changes in financial position shown in the annual report are usually highly condensed for easy comprehension by the average reader. Some readers are interested in details omitted from these condensed versions. The annual report, therefore, typically includes schedules that provide more detail for some of the items reported in the three main statements. For example, separate schedules may be provided to explain the change in contributed capital, retained earnings, or other items on the balance sheet.

Notes to the Financial Statements

Every set of published financial statements is supplemented with explanatory notes. These notes are an integral part of the statements. As later chapters make clear, a firm must select the accounting methods followed in preparing its financial statements from a set of generally accepted methods. The notes indicate the actual accounting methods used by the firm. The notes also disclose additional information which elaborates on items presented in the three principal statements. To understand fully a firm's balance sheet, income statement, and statement of changes in financial position, a careful reading of the notes is required. We do not present notes to the financial statements for the Jonathan Corporation because they would not mean much at this stage. Do not conclude, therefore, that the notes are unimportant merely because we have omitted them from the statements presented in this chapter.

■ USES OF FINANCIAL STATEMENTS IN INVESTMENT DECISIONS

Financial statements report the results of past transactions and events. When assessing the return and risk of investment alternatives, the decision maker is primarily interested in the future. Financial statements are useful to the investor to the extent that they provide information helpful for predicting future earnings, cash flows, or other factors of interest in the investment decision.

Future dividends and changes in the market prices of Jonathan Corporation's shares are likely to be associated with its expected future profitability, or earnings capacity. The income statement indicates that Jonathan Corporation earned $300,000 during 1976. Dividing net income by average stockholders' equity for the year (that is, one-half of the sum of the beginning stockholders' equity plus ending stockholders' equity) results in a measure of the rate of return on stockholders' equity of approximately 23 percent = $300,000/[.5 × ($1,200,000 + $1,400,000)]. This rate of return might then be compared with that of previous years to determine if the 23 percent return represented a significant increase or decrease. If there has been a significant increase or decrease in the earnings capacity of the firm, then the current period's performance could be expected to affect the market price of the firm's stock.

Since common stock represents a residual interest, or equity, in the firm after current and noncurrent liabilities have been paid, the risk or uncertainty of the return to common stockholders is influenced by the ability of the firm to pay its liabilities as they become due. Current liabilities are generally payable within the next year. Assets classified as current will normally be turned into cash within that period and may be used as a measure of the resources available to pay short-term obligations. The December 31, 1976, balance sheet of Jonathan Corporation lists current assets of $550,000 and current liabilities of $400,000. The ratio of current assets to current liabilities is 1.375 to 1.000. Thus, there are $1.375 in current assets for each dollar of current liabilities.

The statement of changes in financial position indicates that Jonathan Corporation borrowed $100,000 on a long-term basis. Since periodic interest must be paid on long-term bonds before common stockholders receive dividends, increases in debt increase the uncertainty, or risk, of the return to the common stock. If additional bonds must be issued in the future, this has implications for the relative risk of investing in Jonathan Corporation and can be expected to have an effect on the market price of the stock.

There are other sources of information that might be consulted in assessing the return and risk of investment alternatives. Daily, weekly, and monthly periodicals publish current information concerning various firms, such as major new financing, important lawsuits, and unique new products. Stock brokerage firms often provide research reports containing their assessment of particular firms. Investment advisory services publish information on the history, principal products, and similar information for most publicly held firms.

Our purpose in this section has been to suggest some of the ways in which accounting information might be used in making investment decisions. We have attempted to keep the illustration at an introductory level. As a result, more questions have probably been raised regarding the analysis and interpretation of financial statements than have been answered. As you study the concepts and procedures underlying the principal financial statements in subsequent chapters, answers to many of these questions will emerge.

■ USERS OF ACCOUNTING INFORMATION

The field of accounting has been conveniently separated into financial accounting and managerial accounting. This distinction is based on the users of accounting information.

Financial Accounting

Financial accounting is concerned with the preparation of reports which provide information to users external to the firm. The most common reports for external users are the financial statements included in annual reports to stockholders and potential investors. Other external users of accounting information are present and potential creditors, employees and labor unions, state and local tax agencies, the Internal Revenue Service, and the Securities and Exchange Commission (SEC). For each of these areas of financial accounting, the manner in which the accounting reports are prepared is largely established by external authorities. Considering the large number of users and uses of these accounting reports, there is a need for some degree of uniformity in reporting among firms. In the case of income tax returns, the accounting report is prepared in accordance with the Internal Revenue Code and Regulations. The regulations of the Securities and Exchange Commission specify the manner in which reports submitted to that governmental agency are to be prepared. Financial statements included in annual reports to stockholders and potential investors are prepared in accordance with "generally accepted accounting principles." These "principles" have evolved over time or have been granted "acceptable" status by decree from some official body within the accounting profession. Much of this text is devoted to a discussion of the underlying assumptions, rationale, and implications of specific generally accepted accounting principles. We give some consideration, though, to the Internal Revenue Code and Regulations as they relate to particular topics being discussed.

Managerial Accounting

Managerial accounting is concerned with the preparation of reports which provide information to users within the firm. For example, the corporate treasurer might use a budget of estimated cash receipts and disbursements to determine if short-term borrowing is necessary. The production manager might use a report on the productivity or efficiency of various employees in deciding how a special order is to be routed through the factory. A sales manager might use a report on the cost of producing and selling different product lines in recommending the prices which should be charged and the products which should be pushed by the sales staff. In contrast to financial accounting, there are no externally imposed procedures that must be followed in preparing these reports. Users of information within the firm are generally free to specify the type of information they want for their decisions; accounting reports are prepared to conform to these needs. Managerial accounting, then, is more flexible in nature in that it is not constrained by "generally accepted accounting principles." Since this text is an introduction to financial accounting, we do not specifically consider managerial accounting reports.

■ CRITERIA FOR EVALUATING THE USEFULNESS OF ACCOUNTING INFORMATION

Before embarking on a study of the concepts and methodology of financial accounting, it may be worthwhile first to set out some criteria for evaluating the usefulness of the information which is generated. Throughout this text, we consider various procedures for reporting the effects of a given event or transaction. It will be helpful if we are armed with some standards or criteria for choosing between alternative methods. The criteria discussed in this section are offered as possibilities.

Relevance to Decisions

To be useful, the accounting report should provide information which is helpful in answering questions which the decision maker faces in making investment decisions. For example, if investors wish to assess the return and risk from purchasing a firm's shares of common stock and desire to use accounting reports in helping to make their decisions, then financial statements should present information on the various factors affecting return and risk.

There are several practical problems in applying this criterion. One is the difficulty in determining the types of information desired by various users. The information required by bankers or security analysts is not necessarily the same as that required by the small investor. A second difficulty comes in deciding whose needs should count most. Disclosure of information on the profitability of each of the firm's product lines may be helpful to investors, but at the same time might reveal information so useful to its competitors that current stockholders would be hurt.

Accuracy of Presentation

The accuracy-of-presentation criterion suggests that we strive to present reasonably complete and accurate descriptions of the events or transactions which are disclosed in the accounting report. Accounting measurements serve as descriptions, or surrogates, for the decisions made and events which have taken place. The closer the correspondence between the event and the report, the better.

Verifiability

The criterion of verifiability suggests that the results of decisions or events should not be included in accounting reports unless they can be verified with reasonable confidence by competent, independent auditors. Verification may be helpful in reducing bias which the managers of a firm, in their own interests, might have injected into the report. Verification also serves as a check on processing and measurement errors which might have occurred.

Comparability: Through Time

The need for comparability through time suggests that the procedures or methods used by a firm in processing accounting data be followed consistently from period to period. In this way, accounting reports of a particular firm may be more easily compared from one period to the next.

Comparability: Among Firms

The need for comparability among firms suggests that the procedures or methods used by all firms within an industry or some other grouping be the same. In this way, accounting reports of various firms may be more easily compared with each other.

Efficiency

When the benefits of information to users exceed the costs of providing it, the information generating process is said to be *efficient*. This criterion might be used in determining the type of information included in accounting reports and the precision of the accounting measurements.

Timeliness

To be useful, the information must be available sufficiently early so that appropriate changes in resource allocations can be made. Application of this criterion has lead to quarterly, rather than merely annual, reporting by publicly held corporations.

Conflicts Among Criteria

In selecting the foregoing or other sets of criteria for assessing the usefulness of accounting reports, conflicts among the criteria will often arise. For example, investors might feel that the most relevant valuation basis for land, buildings, and equipment is the current selling price of each asset. If there is no ready second-hand market, however, current selling prices for used, specialized assets may be difficult to determine and verify. Trade-offs between relevancy and verifiability are therefore required. Another conflict might arise in attempting to achieve accuracy in presentation and interfirm comparability in accounting methods. The accounting methods providing the most accurate measure of performance and financial conditions for Sears may differ from those for General Motors or Paramount Pictures. These and other conflicts among the criteria are considered further in later chapters as they relate to particular accounting issues being discussed.

■ THE ROLE OF THE CPA IN CURRENT REPORTING PRACTICE

Independent audits of the financial statements of publicly held firms are made by Certified Public Accountants (CPA's). CPA's have a professional relationship with their client unlike that of physicians and lawyers. The CPA serves as an impartial auditor of the statements of the client, and must comment favorably or unfavorably on them to third parties, such as stockholders, potential investors, and governmental agencies. Because of this position of third-party trust, the CPA must strive to maintain an independent attitude with respect to the client even though the client pays the bill for the CPA's services. The physician and lawyer, on the other hand, are paid by the client and are responsible primarily for pursuing the client's best interests.

Opinion on Financial Statements

As a result of the examination of a client's accounting records and procedures, the CPA expresses an opinion on the financial statements. In unusual cases, a qualified or adverse opinion is given if something has come to the CPA's attention during the audit to indicate that the financial statements are erroneous or misleading. In most cases, though, any questionable items in the financial statements are corrected and the CPA gives an unqualified, or "clean," opinion. The unqualified opinion, which accompanies the financial statements in corporate annual reports, generally follows a standard format. An unqualified opinion covering the financial statements of Jonathan Corporation is presented below in the standard format:

> *We have examined the comparative balance sheets of Jonathan Corporation as of December 31, 1975 and 1976, and the related statements of net income and changes in financial position for the year 1976. Our examination was made in accordance with generally accepted auditing standards, and accordingly included such tests of the accounting records and such other auditing procedures as we considered necessary in the circumstances.*
>
> *In our opinion, the aforementioned financial statements present fairly the financial position of Jonathan Corporation at December 31, 1975 and 1976, and the results of its operations and changes in financial position for the year 1976 in conformity with generally accepted accounting principles applied on a basis consistent with that of the preceding year.*

Most published annual reports contain unqualified opinions. Published qualified opinions generally result from a change in accounting procedures which the CPA approves and calls to the reader's attention.

Criteria Implied in CPA's Opinion

From this standard, unqualified opinion, we can infer the criteria used to determine the information included in current accounting reports. These criteria can be compared with those discussed in the previous section.

Fair Presentation   A fair, rather than accurate, presentation has been the criterion applied in practice. Just what constitutes a "fair presentation" has been the subject of numerous disagreements and court suits. The criterion has evolved to mean the presentation of sufficient information "so as not to make the statements misleading." This negative criterion may be slightly easier to apply, but it seems to be far removed from the more positive statement about "fair presentation" made in the CPA's opinion.

Conformity with Generally Accepted Accounting Principles This criterion seeks comparability of accounting reports across firms. However, as we shall study throughout this text, there are frequently several different methods of accounting for a given transaction, all of which are within the set of generally accepted accounting principles. General acceptability, then, in most cases merely narrows the gap from many methods of accounting to a few acceptable methods.

Consistency of Methods In order to receive an unqualified opinion, a set of financial statements must be based on the same methods of accounting as in the previous year. The firm may change accounting methods, however, so long as sufficient disclosure is made of the effects of the change on the financial statements. Changes in accounting methods are relatively infrequent, but sometimes are made by publicly held firms.

Verifiability The use of the term "examined" in the first sentence of the opinion suggests that accounting data must be subject to verification with reasonable confidence by the independent auditor in order to be included in the financial statements. This criterion has been rigorously applied in defending the use of the acquisition-cost basis of valuation for assets such as inventory, land, equipment, and buildings. The acquisition cost of these assets can be verified by examining a purchase invoice, construction contract, or canceled check. The current value (selling price, replacement cost) is more difficult to verify and is subject to greater disagreement. Present accounting reports do not reflect changes in the market value of assets until they are sold and a market exchange has taken place.

Relevance to Decisions No specific mention is made in the auditor's opinion regarding the relevancy of the information to decisions. Part of the reason for such omission is that the auditor cannot know all users of the statements or their particular information needs. It is up to the potential user to assess the usefulness of information provided in the financial statements. The accounting profession has been criticized, however, for using the difficulty in specifying information needs as an excuse for basing accounting reports on easily verifiable acquisition costs, even though these amounts may not be relevant to statement users. This important criticism is considered more fully in Chapters Two and Fourteen.

■ ACCOUNTING AUTHORITIES AND LITERATURE

Frequent references are made throughout this book to "generally accepted accounting principles." These "principles" are the accounting methods used by firms in preparing their financial statements. Chapter Fifteen discusses various accounting authorities and their roles in the development of generally accepted accounting principles. The many references made to generally accepted accounting principles prior to Chapter Fifteen will not be meaningful, however, unless we devote some initial discussion to the authorities responsible for developing accounting principles.

By Congressional enactment, the Securities and Exchange Commission has been granted the legal authority to prescribe accounting principles to be followed by most corporations. The SEC has used its power sparingly, however, and the real authority over accounting principles has been vested in the financial community. Generally accepted accounting principles are not all codified, and they are not all promulgated by a single governmental, private, or professional authority. Rather they are to be found in the literature of the field, including pronouncements of interested professional organizations and security exchanges, governmental regulations, articles, and textbooks.[1] Thus the accounting profession, the users of financial statements, and the governmental agencies contribute to the continued development of generally accepted principles of accounting. Some of the leading organizations and sources of accounting literature which influence the development of accounting principles are discussed below.

The *Securities and Exchange Commission* (SEC) has a considerable responsibility assigned to it with respect to financial accounting under the Securities Act of 1933, the Securities Exchange Act of 1934, and the Public Utility Holding Company Act of 1935. The SEC has decided to rely primarily on the accounting profession for the establishment of accounting principles on most topics. The SEC prescribes the form of financial statements to be submitted to it and has issued rulings in certain areas. Among its publications are the following:

> *Regulation S-X*. A document pertaining to the form and content of financial statements required to be filed with the SEC.
>
> *Accounting Series Releases*. A series of opinions on accounting principles which together with *Regulation S-X* are the primary statements on the form and content of financial statements filed with the Commission.

Since 1973, the *Financial Accounting Standards Board* (FASB) has been the highest nongovernmental authority on generally accepted accounting principles. The FASB issues *Statements of Financial Accounting Standards* from time to time establishing or clarifying generally accepted accounting principles.

The *American Institute of Certified Public Accountants* (AICPA) is the national organization of certified public accountants. Its publications and committees are influential in the development of accounting principles and practices. It actively promulgates standards of ethics and reviews conduct within the profession. Among its influential publications are the following:

> *Journal of Accountancy*. A monthly periodical containing articles, pronouncements, announcements, and practical sections of direct interest to the practicing members of the profession.
>
> *Accounting Research Bulletins* Nos. 1–51 (1939–1959). A series of statements on accounting problems that contributed greatly to the narrowing of differences and inconsistencies in accounting practice and to the development and recognition of generally accepted accounting principles.

---

[1] A useful introduction to accounting literature is Stephen A. Zeff's "A First Guide to the Accounting Literature," in S. Zeff and T. Keller (eds.). *Financial Accounting Theory I: Issues and Controversies* (New York: McGraw-Hill, 1973), pp. 2–13.

Opinions of the Accounting Principles Board Nos. 1–31 (1962–1973). A series of statements on accounting problems and generally accepted accounting principles. These pronouncements remain in effect unless superseded by statements of the Financial Accounting Standards Board.

Accounting Research Studies. A series of monographs on accounting problems that provide a basis for further development of generally accepted accounting principles in the particular area.

Statements on Auditing Standards. No. 1 (1973) of this series is a codification of all statements on auditing standards previously issued by the AICPA. Later numbers of the series deal with specific auditing procedures. These publications form the basis of compliance with the first paragraph of the auditor's report (illustrated in this chapter) with respect to the scope of the examination.

Two publications of the American Institute of Certified Public Accountants are of special interest to students and scholars:

Accountants' Index. A series published each quarter (with annual summaries) in which the literature pertaining to the field for the period covered is indexed in detail.

Accounting Trends and Techniques. An annual publication presenting a survey of the accounting aspects of financial reports of some six hundred industrial and commercial corporations. It presents statistical tabulations on specific practices, terminology, and disclosures together with illustrations taken from individual annual reports.

In addition to the national organization, there are state societies of certified public accountants which contribute to maintaining high levels of professional performance and to developing procedures and practices.

The *American Accounting Association* is primarily an organization for accountants in academic work, but it is open to all who are interested in accounting. It participates in the development of generally accepted accounting principles and practice, and it promotes the academic phases of accounting theory, research, and instruction. Among its influential publications are the following:

The Accounting Review. A quarterly periodical containing articles and sections covering a broad span of subjects related to accounting practice, research, and instruction for purposes of both external and internal reporting.

Accounting and Reporting Standards for Corporate Financial Statements. A comprehensive presentation of accounting principles for external reporting purposes. The principles enumerated frequently indicate the direction toward which the association feels accounting reporting should be moving rather than necessarily a reflection of currently accepted accounting principles.

A *Statement of Basic Accounting Theory*. An integrated statement for educators, practitioners, and others interested in accounting. The statement seeks to identify the field of accounting, to establish standards by which accounting information can be judged, to point out possible improvements in accounting practice, and to present a useful framework for scholars who wish to extend the uses of accounting.

The *National Association of Accountants* is a national society generally open to all engaged in activities closely associated with managerial accounting. Among its publications are the following:

Management Accounting. A monthly periodical.
Research Series. A series of monographs on subjects of internal and external accounting.
Accounting Practice Reports. A series of summaries of surveys on current practice in a limited area of accounting.

The *Financial Executives Institute* is an organization of financial executives of large businesses, such as chief accountants, controllers, treasurers, and financial vice-presidents. Among its publications are the *Financial Executive*, a monthly periodical, and a number of studies on problems confronting accounting and financial management.

Income tax legislation and administration has had a substantial impact on adequate accounting and reporting. Although the income tax requirements in themselves do not establish principles and practices for general external reporting, their influence on choice of acceptable procedures is substantial. At the federal level, in addition to the *Internal Revenue Code* passed by the Congress, there are the *Regulations* and *Rulings* of the Internal Revenue Service, and the opinions of the United States Tax Court.

The *Cost Accounting Standards Board* (CASB) has been authorized by the U.S. Congress to set accounting standards for cost determination by defense contractors under federal contracts. Most of the work of the CASB does not directly affect the form of published financial statements, but the standards announced by the CASB have considerable weight in practice where the FASB has not established a standard.

■ ACCOUNTING TERMINOLOGY

A firm's Annual Report to Stockholders reaches a large group of readers. The members of this group vary in their understanding of business and accounting. If accounting is to fulfill its potential contribution, it should address this broad group of users. Thus, there is a need for a terminology based as much as possible upon that of the general citizenry.

By and large, accounting terminology follows common usage. Occasionally, however, commonly used words are given restricted technical meanings. For example, the word "reserve" in common usage indicates that a pool of something is earmarked or set aside, but in accounting terminology its meaning is altogether different. The term "surplus" may mean "too much" in commonly used terminology, but this is not its meaning when used in accounting. There are current efforts to prevent the possible confusion that can arise out of these and other similar altered usages of common terminology. Students of accounting can therefore use their vocabulary which has been developed for general communication. You will find it necessary, however, to learn a rather limited vocabulary of new technical terms and to become aware of technical meanings assigned to a few common words such as *allowance, cost, credit, expense,* and *revenue.* A glossary of accounting terms and other terms with special meanings in accounting appears at the back of this book. The first question at the end of each chapter lists the important accounting terms used in that chapter. Use the glossary to aid in reviewing the meaning of those terms.

■ SUMMARY

The purpose of this chapter has been to provide an overview of the three principal financial statements and to suggest some of the ways in which information contained in these statements might be used in making resource allocation decisions. Perhaps more questions have been raised than answered. We feel that it is helpful, though, to have an overview of the field of financial accounting before embarking on a study of the concepts and procedures employed in preparing various accounting reports.

Chapters Two to Six discuss and illustrate the concepts and procedures underlying the balance sheet, income statement, and statement of changes in financial position. Chapter Seven considers techniques for analyzing and interpreting financial statements. Chapters Eight to Thirteen explore more fully the principles of accounting for individual assets and equities, while Chapter Fourteen discusses the effects of changing prices on accounting reports. Chapter Fifteen describes the process through which accounting principles are developed and considers the effects of using alternative accounting principles on the financial statements.

Now we turn to the study of financial accounting. We recognize that most readers of this book will not choose careers in the field of accounting. Accordingly, emphasis is placed not only upon the compilation of the accounting data and preparation of reports, but also upon the uses of accounting data for those who will receive it in the form of various reports. Regardless of the reader's interest in accounting, we have found that the most effective means of comprehending the concepts and procedures discussed in this book is the careful study of the numerical examples presented in the chapters and the diligent working of several problems at the end of each chapter. This suggestion should be kept in mind as you proceed with your study of accounting.

QUESTIONS AND PROBLEMS

1. Review the meaning of the following concepts or terms introduced in this chapter:
   a. Return and risk of investment alternatives.
   b. Balance sheet.
   c. Assets.
   d. Liabilities.
   e. Stockholders' equity.
   f. Retained earnings.
   g. Income, earnings, profit.
   h. Net loss.
   i. Revenue.
   j. Expense.
   k. Working capital.
   l. Earnings cycle.
   m. Stocks and flows.
   n. Articulate.
   o. Financial accounting.
   p. Managerial accounting.
   q. Generally accepted accounting principles.
   r. Unqualified opinion.
   s. SEC.
   t. FASB.
   u. CPA.
   v. CASB.

2. Modern financial theory suggests that investment alternatives should be assessed in terms of expected return and the uncertainty or risk associated with that return. For the following personal investments, indicate how expected return might be measured, and suggest some of the factors affecting the risk or uncertainty of that return:
   a. Rental of an apartment under a 3-year rental agreement.
   b. Purchase of an automobile for cash.
   c. Purchase of a house under a 20-year mortgage agreement.

3. How would the principal financial statements of a not-for-profit hospital, library, or university differ from those presented in the chapter?

4. Prepare a balance sheet of your personal assets, liabilities, and owner's equity. How does the presentation of owner's equity on your balance sheet differ from that in Exhibit 1.1?

5. Suggest procedures you could follow in determining the amounts at which the following resources might be stated on a balance sheet if they were to be recognized as assets:
   a. Well-known trademark or other product symbol.
   b. Well-trained employee labor force.

6. Various items are classified on the balance sheet or income statement in one of the following ways:

   CA—current assets   CC—contributed capital
   NA—noncurrent assets   RE—retained earnings

CL—current liabilities   NI —income statement item (revenue or expense)
NL—noncurrent liabilities   X—item would generally not appear on a
                         balance sheet or income statement.

Using the letters above, indicate the classification of each of the following items:
- **a.** Warehouse.
- **b.** Rental revenue.
- **c.** Common stock issued by a corporation.
- **d.** Goodwill developed by a firm.
- **e.** Automobiles used by sales staff.
- **f.** Cash on hand.
- **g.** Unsettled damage suit against a firm.
- **h.** Commissions earned by sales staff.
- **i.** Supplies inventory.
- **j.** Note payable, due in 3 years.
- **k.** Increase in market value of land held.
- **l.** Dividends.
- **m.** Employee payroll taxes payable.

7. An earnings cycle might be depicted as follows:

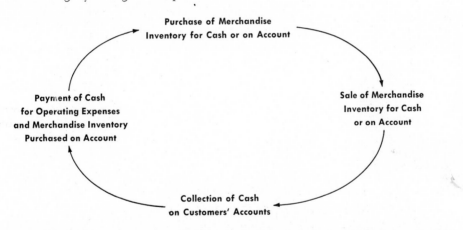

Earnings cycles are common to both the income statement and the statement of changes in financial position. The income statement reports the revenues recognized from the sale of goods and services and the expenses required in generating these revenues. The statement of changes in financial position analyzes the changes in working capital accounts such as cash, accounts receivable, merchandise inventory, and accounts payable.
- **a.** Suggest one item that would likely appear on the income statement but that does not affect the earnings cycle diagrammed above.
- **b.** Suggest three items that might appear on the statement of changes in financial position but that would not affect the earnings cycle diagrammed above.

8. Distinguish between financial accounting and managerial accounting. Suggest several ways in which the managers of a firm might use information presented in the three principal externally directed financial statements discussed in this chapter.

9. Generally accepted accounting principles are the methods of accounting used by publicly held firms in preparing their financial statements. A principle in physics, such as the law of gravity, serves as a basis for developing theories and explaining the relationships among physical objects. In what ways are generally accepted accounting principles similar to and different from principles in physics?

10. Does the unqualified or clean opinion of a certified public accountant indicate that the financial statements are free of errors and misrepresentations?

11. What sources of information other than the annual report might be consulted in assessing the return and risk from investing in a firm's common stock?

12. Assets such as buildings and equipment generally decrease in value or depreciate over time as those assets are used. Accountants measure depreciation by recognizing as an expense each period a portion of the acquisition cost of these assets based on some systematic procedure (for example, an equal amount each year of the asset's useful life). Economists measure depreciation as the decrease in the amount at which the building or equipment could be sold between the beginning and end of the period.

   You are planning to acquire the assets of a steel company and must determine the price you are willing to pay. Using either the criteria discussed in the chapter or others you consider desirable, which of these two methods of measuring depreciation and asset values do you think provides the more useful information?

13. Determine the missing balance sheet amounts in each of the four independent cases below. Only items marked "?" can be calculated.

	a	b	c	d
Noncurrent Assets	$700,000	$2,000,000	$340,000	760?000
Stockholders' Equity	450?000	1,550,000	380,000	$370,000
Total Assets	1000?000	2650?000	500,000	950?000
Current Liabilities	250,000	400,000	120*000	120**000
Current Assets	300,000	650?000	160*000	190**000
Noncurrent Liabilities	300,000	2250?000	?**	400,000
Total Liabilities and				
Stockholders' Equity	1000?000	2,650,000	500?000	950,000

* Working capital = current assets — current liabilities = $40,000.
** Working capital = current assets — current liabilities = $70,000.

14. The comparative balance sheets of the Sedwick Corporation as of December 31, 1975, and December 31, 1976, are presented below:

Sedwick Corporation
Comparative Balance Sheets
December 31, 1975 and 1976

	December 31, 1975	December 31, 1976
Total Assets	$200,000	$400,000
Liabilities	$ 40,000	$ 50,000
Capital Stock	100,000	200,000
Retained Earnings	60,000	150,000
Total Liabilities and Stockholders' Equity	$200,000	$400,000

Dividends declared and paid during 1976 were $30,000.

    a. Determine net income for the year ending December 31, 1976, by analyzing the change in retained earnings.

    b. Determine net income for the year ending December 31, 1976, by analyzing the changes in assets, liabilities, and contributed capital during the year. (Hint: Refer to the last question on p. 10.)

15. Determine the missing amount affecting retained earnings for the year 1976, in each of the independent cases below.

	a	b	c	d	e
Retained Earnings, December 31, 1975	$150,000	?	$320,000	$75,000	$40,000
Net Income	50,000	$125,000	180,000	?	(30,000)*
Dividends Declared and Paid	20,000	75,000	?	30,000	?
Retained Earnings, December 31, 1976	?	500,000	470,000	90,000	10,000

* Net loss.

16. B. Stephens, L. Harris, and G. Winkle, recent business school graduates, set up a management consulting practice on December 31, 1975, by issuing common stock for $750,000. The accounting records of the S, H, & W Corporation as of December 31, 1976, reveal the following:

Balance Sheet Items:

Cash	$ 50,000
Accounts Receivable from Clients	165,000
Supplies Inventory	5,000
Office Equipment (net of depreciation)	85,000
Office Building (net of depreciation)	500,000
Accounts Payable to Suppliers	10,000
Payroll Taxes Payable	5,000
Income Taxes Payable	20,000
Common Stock	750,000

Income Statement Items:

Revenue from Consulting Services	$300,000
Rental Revenue (from renting part of building)	30,000
Property Taxes and Insurance Expense	40,000
Salaries Expense	215,000
Depreciation Expense	25,000
Income Tax Expense	20,000

Dividend Information:

Dividends Declared and Paid	$ 10,000

    a. Prepare an income statement for S, H, & W Corporation for the year ending December 31, 1976. Refer to Exhibit 1.2 for help in designing the format of the statement.

b. Prepare a comparative balance sheet for S, H, & W Corporation December 31, 1975, and December 31, 1976. Refer to Exhibit 1.1 for help in designing the format of the statement.

c. Prepare an analysis of the change in retained earnings during 1976.

17. Indicate the effect of each of the independent transactions below on working capital (current assets minus current liabilities) using + (increase), − (decrease), 0 (no net effect). (Hint: you may want to use the equation for the change in net working capital presented in the section on the statement of changes in financial position in preparing your responses. See page 12.)

a. Issue of capital stock for cash.

b. Acquisition of land for cash.

c. Issue of 20-year bonds for cash.

d. Issue of common stock for land.

e. Purchase of merchandise inventory from suppliers by agreeing to pay within 2 months.

f. Payment of liability to supplier in e.

g. Rendering of legal services to a client and receipt from the client of a promise to pay within 3 months.

h. Collection of the client's account in g.

i. Declaration and immediate payment of a cash dividend to stockholders.

Part 2

Accounting
Concepts
and Methods

Chapter Two

Measuring Financial Position—Valuation Principles and Accounting Procedures

Chapter One introduced the balance sheet, sometimes called the statement of financial position, as one of the three principal financial statements. You will recall that the balance sheet presents a snapshot of the resources of a firm (assets) and claims on those resources (liabilities and owners' equity) as of a specific moment in time. The balance sheet derives its name from the fact that it shows the following balance, or equality:

Assets = Liabilities + Owners' Equity.

That is, a firm's resources are in balance with, or equal to, the claims on those resources by creditors and owners. In the balance sheet, we view resources from two angles: a listing of the specific forms in which they are held (for example, cash, inventory, equipment) and a listing of the persons or interests which have a claim on them (for example, suppliers, employees, governments, stockholders). Our introduction to the balance sheet in Chapter One left several important questions unanswered:

1. What limits are set in defining the business entity for which the statement is prepared?
2. Which resources of a firm are recognized as assets?
3. What valuations are placed on these assets?
4. Which claims against a firm's assets are recognized as liabilities?
5. What valuations are placed on these liabilities?
6. What valuation is placed on the owners' equity in a firm, and how is the owners' equity disclosed?

In seeking answers to these questions, we must explore briefly several accounting concepts and conventions which underlie the balance sheet. This discussion not only provides a background for understanding the statement as it is currently prepared, but also permits an assessment of alternative methods of measuring financial position. After this brief introduction to accounting theory, we describe and then illustrate the accounting procedures used in recording transactions and events for presentation in a balance sheet.

■   UNDERLYING CONCEPTS AND CONVENTIONS

Accounting Entity

Business activities are carried on through various units, or entities. The identification of the business entity is the starting point in designing an accounting system that will provide data for financial statements. Most problems of identifying the business entity are caused by differences between the definition of the entity used in accounting, or the *accounting entity*, and the definition of the entity prescribed by law, or the *legal entity*. In accounting we attempt to emphasize substance over form; that is, we focus on the unit, or entity, engaged in business activity even though it may not be recognized as a separate legal entity.

Example 1   Joan Webster operates a hardware store in her neighborhood as a sole proprietorship. According to the laws of most states, Webster's business assets and personal assets are mingled. That is, suppliers of merchandise to the hardware store can obtain payment for their claims from some or all of her personal assets if business assets are insufficient. Even so, the accounting entity is the hardware store alone, since this is the organizational unit carrying on the business activity.

Example 2   Bill White and Roger Green own and manage an apartment complex, called the Leisure Living Apartments, as a partnership. Under the laws of most states, their personal assets as well as the business assets are subject to the claims of creditors. Even so, the accounting entity is the apartment complex alone, since this is the organizational unit carrying on the business activity.

Example 3   The Domestic Corporation operates through its subsidiaries in 23 states. Each subsidiary is organized as a separate legal corporation under the laws of the state in which it is located. The accounting entity is a combination (or consolidation) of Domestic Corporation and all of its 23 subsidiary corporations, since these legally separate units operate as a single business entity. For purposes of internal performance evaluation by management, however, Domestic Corporation might treat each subsidiary as a separate reporting entity. Thus, we see that the scope of the accounting entity can be related to the purpose to be served by the financial statements.

The accounting entity for which a set of financial statements has been prepared can be determined from the heading of each statement. For the three examples above, the headings might read: Webster's Hardware Store, Leisure Living Apartments, and Domestic Corporation and Consolidated Subsidiaries.

Asset Recognition

Assets are resources which have the potential for providing a firm with future economic services or benefits. In short, an asset is a future benefit. The resources which are recognized as assets are those (1) for which the firm has acquired rights to their future use as a result of a past transaction or exchange and (2) for which the value of the future benefits can be measured, or quantified, with a reasonable degree of precision.

Example 1   Miller Corporation sold merchandise and received a note from the customer who agreed to pay $1,000 within 3 months. This note receivable is an asset of Miller Corporation, since a right has been established to receive a definite amount of cash in the future as a result of the previous sale of merchandise.

Example 2   Miller Corporation acquired manufacturing equipment costing $20,000 and agreed to pay the seller over 2 years. After the final payment, legal title to the equipment will be transferred to Miller Corporation. The equipment is an asset, even though legal title has not yet passed, since Miller Corporation has obtained the rights and responsibilities of ownership and can sustain those rights as long as the payments are made on schedule.

Example 3   Miller Corporation plans to acquire a fleet of new trucks next year to replace those wearing out. These new trucks are not now assets, since no exchange between Miller Corporation and a supplier has taken place and, therefore, no right to the future use of the trucks has been established.

Example 4   Miller Corporation has developed a good reputation with its employees, customers, and citizens of the community. This good reputation is expected to provide benefits to the firm in its future business activities. A good reputation, however, is generally *not* recognized as an asset, because the future benefits are difficult to quantify.

Most of the difficulties in deciding which items to recognize as assets are caused by uncertainties concerning the type and extent of future rights necessary to justify classification as an asset. In Example 3, suppose that Miller Corporation entered into a contract with a local truck dealer to acquire the trucks next year at a cash price of $50,000. Miller Corporation has acquired rights to future benefits, but the contract has not been executed. Unexecuted contracts of this nature are generally not recognized as assets in accounting. Miller Corporation will recognize an asset for the trucks when they are received next year.

Asset Valuation Methods

An amount must be assigned to each asset in the balance sheet. Several methods of determining this amount might be used.

Acquisition or Historical Cost   The acquisition, or historical cost, of an asset is the amount of cash payment (or cash-equivalent value of other forms of payment) made in acquiring the asset. This amount is generally determinable by referring to contracts, invoices, and canceled checks. Since a firm is not compelled to acquire a given asset, it must expect the future benefits from that asset to be at least as large as its acquisition cost. Historical cost, then, is a lower limit on the amount which a firm considered the future benefits of the asset to be worth at the time of acquisition.

Adjusted Acquisition or Historical Cost Assets such as buildings and equipment provide benefits over a period of years. At the time these assets are acquired, they might be shown at acquisition cost on the balance sheet. Throughout their useful lives, the services of these assets are used up. The acquisition cost amount should therefore be adjusted downward to reflect the remaining amount of future benefits as of the date of each balance sheet.

Current Replacement Cost Each asset might be shown on the balance sheet at the current cost of replacing it. Current replacement cost is often referred to as an *entry value*, because it represents the amount required currently to acquire, or "enter" into, the rights to receive future benefits from the asset.

For assets purchased frequently, such as merchandise inventory, current replacement cost can frequently be determined by consulting suppliers' catalogs or price lists. The replacement cost of assets purchased less frequently, such as land, buildings, and equipment, is more difficult to determine. A major problem in using current replacement cost is caused by the absence of well-organized second-hand markets for many used assets. Determining current replacement cost in these cases requires determining the cost of a similar new asset and then adjusting that amount downward somehow for the services of the asset already used. There may be difficulties, however, in finding a similar asset. With technological improvements and other quality changes, equipment purchased currently will likely be quite different from that acquired 10 years previously but that is still being used. Thus, there may be no similar equipment on the market for which replacement cost can be determined. Alternatively, the current replacement cost of an asset capable of rendering equivalent services might be substituted when the replacement cost of the specific asset is not readily available.

Net Realizable Value The net amount of cash, selling price less selling costs, which the firm would receive if it sold each asset separately might be used as the method of valuation. This value is often referred to as an *exit value*, because it reflects the amount obtainable if the firm currently disposed of the asset, or "exited" ownership. By keeping the asset rather than selling it, the firm foregoes the cash which it could have received. The net realizable value may therefore be considered one measure of the *opportunity cost* of keeping the asset. In determining net realizable value, it is generally assumed that the asset need not be sold through a forced sale at some "distress" price.

Measuring net realizable value entails difficulties similar to those in measuring current replacement cost. There may be no well-organized second-hand market for used equipment, particularly when the equipment is specially designed for a single firm's needs. In this case, the current selling price of the asset (value in exchange) may be substantially less than the value of the future benefits to the firm from using the asset (value in use).

Present Value of Future Net Cash Flows An asset is a resource that provides future benefits. This future benefit is the ability of an asset either to generate future net cash receipts or to reduce future cash expenditures. For example, accounts receivable from customers will lead directly to future cash receipts. Merchandise inventory can be sold for cash or promises to pay cash. Equipment can be used to manufacture products which can then be sold for cash. A building which is owned reduces future cash outflows for rental payments. Since these cash flows represent the future services, or benefits, of assets, they might be used in the valuation of assets. Because cash can be invested to yield interest income over time, today's value of a stream of future cash flows, called the *present value*, is worth less than the sum of the cash amounts to be received or saved over time. The balance sheet is to be prepared as of a current date. If future cash flows are to be used to measure an asset's value, then the future net cash flows must be "discounted" to find their present value as of the date of the balance sheet. The discounting methodology is described in Chapter Eleven, but the following example should help in understanding the general approach.

Example   Miller Corporation sold merchandise to a reliable customer, General Models Company, who promised to pay $10,000 one year from the date of sale. General Models Company signed a "promissory note" to that effect and gave the note to Miller Corporation. Miller Corporation judges that if it invests $9,100 today, it could earn about 10 percent on the investment in a year. At the end of one year, it would therefore receive about $10,000. Hence, the *present value* of $10,000 to be received one year from today is not $10,000, but is about $9,100. (Miller Corporation is indifferent between receiving approximately $9,100 today and $10,000 one year from today.) The asset represented by General Model Company's promissory note has a present value of $9,100. If the note was stated on the balance sheet as of the date of sale at the present value of the future cash flows, it would be shown at approximately $9,100.

If General Models Company had instead promised to pay Miller Corporation $2,000 per year for 5 years, with the first payment due one year from today, then the present value of the asset represented by the promissory note is even less than $9,100. Miller Corporation can earn 10 percent per year over the 5-year period, so the present value of General Models' promissory note is about $7,600. (This kind of calculation is explained in Appendix 11.1.)

Using discounted cash flows to determine balance sheet amounts for individual assets entails several problems. One is the uncertainty of the amounts of future cash flows. The amounts to be received can depend on whether or not competitors introduce new products, the rate of inflation, and many other factors. A second problem is allocating the cash receipts from selling a single item of merchandise inventory to all of the assets involved in its production and distribution (for example, equipment, buildings, sales staff's automobiles). A third problem is selecting the appropriate rate to be used in discounting the future cash flows back to the present. Is the interest rate at which the firm could borrow the appropriate one? Or is the rate at which the firm could invest excess cash the one that should be used? Or is the appropriate rate the firm's cost of capital (a concept introduced in managerial accounting and finance courses)?

Determining the Appropriate Valuation Method

If we use the criterion of relevancy to the decision, discussed in Chapter One, the appropriate valuation method is the one that is geared to the purpose for which the report is prepared.

Example 1 Miller Corporation is preparing its income tax return for the current year. The Internal Revenue Code and Regulations specify that acquisition or adjusted acquisition cost is the valuation method that must be used in most instances.

Example 2 A fire recently destroyed the manufacturing plant, equipment, and inventory of Miller Corporation. The firm's fire insurance policy provides coverage in an amount equal to the cost of replacing the assets which were destroyed. Current replacement cost at the time of the fire is the appropriate valuation method to be used in support of the insurance claim.

Example 3 Miller Corporation plans to dispose of one of its manufacturing divisions because it has been operating unprofitably. In deciding on the lowest price to accept for the division, the net realizable value of each asset is the valuation method which should be used.

Example 4 Brown Corporation is considering the purchase of Miller Corporation. In deciding on the highest price to be paid, Brown Corporation would be interested in the present value of the future cash flows to be realized from owning Miller Corporation. In this case, Miller Corporation's assets (and liabilities) should be stated at the net present value of the future cash flows.

Generally Accepted Accounting Asset Valuation Methods

The asset valuation method appropriate for financial statements issued to stockholders and other investors is perhaps less obvious. The financial statements currently prepared by publicly held firms are based on one of two valuation methods—one for money-like assets and one for nonmonetary assets.

Cash is stated at the amount of cash on hand or in the bank, while money-like items such as accounts receivable from customers are stated at the amount of cash expected to be collected in the future. If the period of time until a receivable is to be collected spans more than one year, then the expected future cash receipt is discounted to a present value. Most accounts receivable, however, are collected within 1 to 3 months. The amount of future cash flows is approximately equal to the present value of these flows, and the discounting process is ignored. Monetary assets, such as cash and accounts receivable, are generally shown on the balance sheet, therefore, at their current cash, or cash-equivalent, values.

Nonmonetary assets, such as merchandise inventory, land, buildings, and equipment, are stated at acquisition cost, in some cases adjusted downward for services of the assets which have been consumed.

The acquisition cost of an asset may include more than its invoice price. Cost includes all expenditures made or obligations incurred in order to put the asset into a usable condition. Transportation costs, costs of installation, handling charges, and any other necessary and reasonable costs incurred in connection with the asset up to the time it is put into service should be considered as part of the total cost assigned to the asset. For example, the cost of an item of equipment might be calculated as follows:

Invoice Price of Equipment	$8,000
Less: 2 Percent Discount for Prompt Cash Payment	160
Net Invoice Price	$7,840
Transportation Cost	232
Installation Costs	694
Total Cost of Equipment	$8,766

Instead of disbursing cash or incurring a liability, other forms of consideration (for example, common stock, merchandise inventory, land) may be given in acquiring an asset. In these cases, acquisition cost is measured by the market value of the consideration given or the market value of the asset received, depending on which market value is more readily determinable.

Accounting's use of acquisition-cost valuations for nonmonetary assets rests on three important concepts or conventions. First, a firm is assumed to be a *going concern*. Liquidation, or selling, prices of the individual assets are assumed to be largely unimportant. Second, acquisition cost is relatively easy to measure, since an *exchange* between the firm and some other entity has taken place. Third, a *common monetary measuring unit* is assumed, so that the cost of assets acquired at different times can be aggregated to determine total assets. This third assumption has questionable validity during periods of rapid price changes. We consider the effects of changing prices on accounting reports in Chapter Fourteen.

The preceding description of generally accepted accounting valuation methods is not intended to justify them. Whether the net realizable values, current replacement costs, present value of future cash flows, or acquisition costs of a firm's assets are more relevant to investors' decisions is an empirical question and one for which a definitive answer has not yet been provided.

Liability Recognition

A liability represents an obligation of a firm to make payment of a reasonably definite amount at a reasonably definite future time for benefits or services received currently or in the past.

Example 1 Miller Corporation purchased merchandise inventory and agreed to pay the supplier $5,000 within 30 days. This transaction gives rise to a liability, since the merchandise has been received and the amount and timing of payment are reasonably certain.

Example 2   Miller Corporation borrowed $2 million by issuing long-term bonds. Annual interest payments of 8 percent must be made on December 31 of each year, and the $2 million principal must be repaid in 20 years. This contractual obligation is also a liability, because cash has been received and the amount and timing of payments to the lenders are fixed.

Example 3   Miller Corporation provides 3 years of warranty service on merchandise which it sells. The charge for warranty coverage is included in the selling price of the merchandise. The firm's obligation under the warranty contract is a liability on its balance sheet. Cash has been received. Based on past experience, the amount that will be paid within the 3-year period of the contract in providing the warranty services can be estimated with reasonable certainty.

Example 4   Miller Corporation is sued by a local citizen who is injured while touring the firm's offices. The suit has not yet been brought to trial. Until a final decision is made by the court, the amount and timing of payment is highly uncertain, and no liability is recognized in the balance sheet. (Contingent liabilities of this nature are discussed in Chapter Eleven.)

Liability Valuation

Most liabilities are monetary in nature. Those due within 1 year or less are stated at the amount of cash expected to be paid to discharge the obligation. If the payment dates extend more than 1 year into the future (for example, as in the case of the bonds in Example 2 above), the liability is stated at the present value of the future cash outflows.

A liability that is discharged by delivering goods or rendering services, rather than by paying cash, is nonmonetary. For example, magazine publishers typically collect cash for subscriptions, promising delivery of magazines over many months. Cash is received currently, while the obligation under the subscription is discharged by delivering magazines in the future. Theaters and football teams receive cash for season tickets and in return incur an obligation to admit the ticket holder to future performances. Such nonmonetary obligations are included among liabilities. They are stated, however, at the amount of cash received rather than at the expected cost of publishing the magazines or of providing the theatrical or sporting entertainment.

Owners' Equity Valuation and Disclosure

The owners' equity, or interest, in a firm is a residual interest. That is, the owners have a claim on all assets not required to meet the claims of creditors. The valuation of the assets and liabilities included in the balance sheet therefore determines the valuation of total owners' equity.

The remaining question concerns the manner of disclosing this total owners' equity. From Chapter One, you will recall that a distinction was drawn between contributed capital and earnings retained by a firm. In preparing the balance sheet for a corporation, the amounts contributed directly by stockholders for an interest in the firm (that is, capital stock) are generally separated from the subsequent earnings realized by the firm in excess of dividends declared (that is, retained earnings).

In addition, the amount received from stockholders is usually further disaggregated into the *par* or *stated value* of the shares and *amounts contributed in excess of par value or stated value.* The par or stated value of a share of stock is a somewhat arbitrary amount assigned to comply with corporation laws of each state. As a result, the distinction between par or stated value and amounts contributed in excess of par or stated value is of questionable informational value, but is typically shown nonetheless. (These fine points of accounting for owners' equity are discussed in Chapter Twelve.)

Example 1 Stephens Corporation was formed on January 1, 1976. It issued 15,000 shares of $10 par value common stock for $10 cash per share. During 1976, Stephens Corporation had net income of $30,000 and paid dividends of $10,000 to stockholders. The stockholders' equity section of the balance sheet of Stephens Corporation on December 31, 1976, is as follows:

Common Stock (par value of $10 per share,	
15,000 shares issued and outstanding)	$150,000
Retained Earnings	20,000
Total Stockholders' Equity	$170,000

Example 2 Instead of issuing $10 par value common stock as in Example 1, assume that Stephens Corporation issued 15,000 shares of $1 par value common stock for $10 cash per share. (The market price of a share of common stock depends on the economic value of the firm and not on the par value of the shares.) The stockholders' equity section of the balance sheet of Stephens Corporation on December 31, 1976, is as follows:

Common Stock (par value of $1 per share,	
15,000 shares issued and outstanding)	$ 15,000
Capital Contributed in Excess of Par Value	135,000
Retained Earnings	20,000
Total Stockholders' Equity	$170,000

The balance sheets of firms that are organized as sole proprietorships or partnerships, rather than as corporations, do not distinguish between contributed capital and earnings retained in the business. The designation of par or stated value is also not used, since these forms of organization do not issue capital stock.

Example 3 Joan Webster operates her hardware store as a sole proprietorship. She contributed $20,000 on January 1, 1976, and used the cash to rent a building, acquire display equipment, and purchase merchandise inventory. During 1976, she had net income of $15,000 and withdrew $10,000 cash for personal use. The owner's equity section of the balance sheet of Webster's Hardware Store on December 31, 1976 is as follows:

Joan Webster, Capital	$25,000[a]
Total Owner's Equity	$25,000

[a] $20,000 + $15,000 − $10,000 = $25,000.

Example 4   Bill White and Roger Green own and manage an apartment complex as a partnership. Each partner contributed $50,000 cash to form the partnership on January 1, 1976. During 1976, net income from the apartment complex was $40,000, which the partners shared equally. Bill White withdrew $10,000 and Roger Green withdrew $5,000 from the partnership. The owners' equity section of the balance sheet on December 31, 1976, for the apartment complex is as follows:

Bill White, Capital	$ 60,000[a]
Roger Green, Capital	65,000[b]
Total Owners' Equity	$125,000

[a] $50,000 + (.50 × $40,000) − $10,000 = $60,000.
[b] $50,000 + (.50 × $40,000) − $ 5,000 = $65,000.

■ ACCOUNTING PROCEDURES FOR PREPARING THE BALANCE SHEET

Now that we have explored the concepts and conventions underlying the balance sheet, we are ready to consider the manner in which these concepts and conventions are applied in preparing the statement. Our objective is to develop a sufficient understanding of the accounting process that generates the balance sheet so that the resulting statement can then be interpreted and analyzed.

Dual Effects of Transactions on the Balance Sheet Equation

The equality between total assets and total equities (liabilities plus owners' equity) in the balance sheet equation is maintained by reporting the effects of *each* transaction in a way that maintains the equation. Any single transaction will have one of the following four effects or some combination of these effects:

1.   It increases both an asset and an equity.
2.   It decreases both an asset and an equity.
3.   It increases one asset and decreases another asset.
4.   It increases one equity and decreases another equity.

To illustrate the dual effects of various transactions on the balance sheet equation, consider the following selected transactions for Miller Corporation during January 1976:

TRANSACTION	ASSETS	=	LIABILITIES	+	STOCKHOLDERS' EQUITY
(1) On January 1, 1976, 20,000 shares of $10 par value common stock are issued for $200,000 cash. (Increase in both an asset and an equity)	+$200,000		0	+	$200,000
Subtotal	$200,000	=	0	+	$200,000
(2) Equipment costing $75,000 is purchased for cash on January 5, 1976. (Increase in one asset and decrease in another asset)	− 75,000 + 75,000				
Subtotal	$200,000	=	0	+	$200,000
(3) Merchandise inventory costing $20,000 is purchased from a supplier on account on January 15, 1976. (Increase in both an asset and an equity)	+ 20,000		+$20,000		
Subtotal	$220,000	=	$20,000	+	$200,000
(4) The supplier in (3) is paid $10,000 of the amount due on January 31, 1976. (Decrease in both an asset and an equity)	− 10,000		− 10,000		
Subtotal	$210,000	=	$10,000	+	$200,000
(5) The supplier in (3) accepts 500 shares of common stock at par value in settlement of $5,000 of the amount owed. (Increase in one equity and decrease in another equity)			− 5,000	+	5,000
Total—January 31, 1976	$210,000	=	$ 5,000	+	$205,000

Purpose and Use of Accounts

It would be possible to prepare a balance sheet for Miller Corporation as of January 31, 1976, using information from the preceding analysis. Total assets are $210,000. We would need to retrace the effects of each transaction on total assets to determine what portion of the $210,000 represents cash, merchandise inventory, and equipment. Likewise, the effects of each transaction on total liabilities and stockholders' equity would have to be retraced to determine which liability and stockholders' equity amounts comprise the $210,000 total. Even with just a few transactions during the accounting period, this approach to preparing a balance sheet would be cumbersome. Considering the thousands of transactions during the accounting period for most firms, some more practical approach to accumulating amounts for the balance sheet is necessary. To accumulate the changes which take place in each balance sheet item, we use a device known as an *account*.

Requirement for an Account   The requirement for a satisfactory account is simple. Since a balance sheet item that changes can only increase or decrease, all an account need do is to provide for accumulating the increases and decreases which have taken place during the period for a single balance sheet item. The balance carried forward from the previous statement is added to the total increases; the total decreases are deducted, and the result is the amount of the new balance for the current balance sheet.

Form of an Account   The account may take many possible forms, and several are commonly used in accounting practice.

Perhaps the most useful form of the account for textbooks, problems, and examinations is the skeleton account, usually called the *T-account*. This form of the account is not used in actual practice, except perhaps for memorandums or preliminary analyses. However, it satisfies the requirement of an account and it is easy to use. As the name indicates, the T-account is shaped like the letter T and consists of a horizontal line bisected by a vertical line. The name or title of the account is written on the horizontal line. One side of the space formed by the vertical line is used to record increases in the item and the other side to record the decreases. Spaces for dates and other information can, of course, be provided.

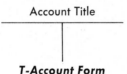

Account Title

T-Account Form

The form that the account takes in actual records depends on the type of accounting system being used. In manual systems the account may be more elaborate than a T-account; in punched-card systems the account may take the form of a group of cards; in computer systems it may be a group of similarly coded items on a tape. Whatever its form, an account contains the opening balance as well as the increases and decreases in the balance that results from the transactions of the period.

Placement of Increases and Decreases in the Account   Given the two-sided account, we must choose which side will be used to record increases and which, decreases. By long-standing custom, the following rules are used:

1.   Increases in assets are entered on the left side and decreases in assets on the right side.

ACCOUNTING PROCEDURES FOR PREPARING THE BALANCE SHEET 43

2. Increases in liabilities are entered on the right side and decreases in liabilities on the left side.
3. Increases in owners' equity are entered on the right side and decreases in owners' equity on the left side.

This custom has an element of logic. A common form of balance sheet shows assets on the left and liabilities and owners' equity on the right. Following this example, asset balances should appear on the left side of accounts; equity balances should appear on the right. But asset balances will appear on the left only if asset increases are recorded on the left side of the account. Similarly, right-hand equity balances can be produced only by recording equity increases on the right. When each transaction is properly analyzed into its dual effects on the accounting equation, and when the above three rules for recording the transaction are followed, then every transaction results in equal amounts in entries on the left- and right-hand sides of various accounts.

Debit and Credit Two terms may now be added to our vocabulary, *debit* (Dr.) and *credit* (Cr.). These terms have an interesting etymological history, but they are merely convenient abbreviations or condensations. *Debit* is an abbreviation for "record an entry on the left side of an account" when used as a verb and is an abbreviation for "an entry on the left side of an account" when used as a noun or adjective. *Credit* is an abbreviation for "record an entry on the right side of an account" when used as a verb and is an abbreviation for "an entry on the right side of an account" when used as a noun or adjective. These terms have no other meaning in accounting. More convenient abbreviations than *debit* and *credit* certainly seem possible, but these have become part of the accounting language through centuries of use and are not likely to be displaced. Often, however, the word *charge* is used instead of *debit*, both as a noun and as a verb. In terms of balance-sheet categories, a debit or charge indicates (1) an increase in an asset, (2) a decrease in a liability, or (3) a decrease in an owners' equity item. A credit indicates (1) a decrease in an asset, (2) an increase in a liability, or (3) an increase in an owners' equity item.

Any previous associations or meanings of the terms debit and credit should be disregarded in accounting. In popular parlance, to credit people with something means to give them favorable recognition for some achievement, and to debit them means to charge something unfavorable against them. These terms have, however, no such implications in accounting. The best approach is simply to accept the terms *debit* and *credit* as technical symbols meaning *left* and *right*.

In order to maintain the equality of the balance sheet equation, the amounts debited to various accounts for each transaction must equal the amounts credited to various accounts. Likewise, the sum of balances in accounts with debit balances at the end of each period must equal the sum of balances in accounts with credit balances.

Summary of Account Terminology and Procedure The conventional use of the account form and the terms debit and credit can be summarized graphically with the use of the skeleton account form, as follows:

ANY ASSET ACCOUNT		ANY LIABILITY ACCOUNT	
Beginning Balance Increases + Dr.	Decreases − Cr.	Decreases − Dr.	Beginning Balance Increases + Cr.
Ending Balance			Ending Balance

ANY OWNERS' EQUITY ACCOUNT	
Decreases − Dr.	Beginning Balance Increases + Cr.
	Ending Balance

Reflecting the Dual Effects of Transactions in the Accounts

We are now ready to illustrate the manner in which the dual effects of transactions are reflected in the accounts. We begin by creating three separate T-accounts, one for assets, one for liabilities, and one for stockholders' equity. The dual effects of the transactions of Miller Corporation for January 1976, described earlier in the chapter, are entered in the T-accounts as shown in Exhibit 2.1.

You will note that the amount entered on the left side of, or debited to, the accounts for each transaction is equal to the amount entered on the right side of, or credited to, the accounts. Recording equal amounts of debits and credits for each transaction ensures that the balance sheet equation will always be in balance. At the end of January 1976, the assets account has a debit balance of $210,000.

EXHIBIT 2.1
Summary T-Accounts Showing the Transactions of Miller Corporation

	ASSETS		=	LIABILITIES		+	STOCKHOLDERS' EQUITY	
	Increases (Dr.)	Decreases (Cr.)	Decreases (Dr.)	Increases (Cr.)		Decreases (Dr.)	Increases (Cr.)
(1) Issue of Common Stock for Cash	200,000						200,000
(2) Purchase of Equipment for Cash	75,000	75,000					
(3) Purchase of Merchandise on Account . .	20,000			20,000			
(4) Payment of Cash to Supplier in (3)		10,000	10,000				
(5) Issuance of Common Stock to Supplier in (3)				5,000			5,000
Balance	210,000		=	5,000	+		205,000

The sum of the balances in the liabilities and stockholders' equity accounts is a credit balance of $210,000.

A balance sheet could be prepared for Miller Corporation from the information in the T-accounts. As was the case in the earlier illustration, however, it would be necessary to retrace the entries in the accounts during the period to determine which individual assets, liabilities, and stockholders' equity items make up the total assets of $210,000 and the total equities of $210,000.

So that the amount of each asset, liability, and stockholders' equity item can be directly determined, a separate account is used for each balance sheet item, rather than for the three broad categories alone. The recording procedure is the same, except that we must now consider which specific asset or equity account is debited and credited.

The transactions of Miller Corporation for January 1976 are recorded in Exhibit 2.2, using separate T-accounts for each balance sheet item. The number in parentheses refers to the five transactions which we have been considering for Miller Corporation.

We can see that the total assets of Miller Corporation of $210,000, as of

EXHIBIT 2.2
Individual T-Accounts Showing the Transactions of Miller Corporation

CASH (ASSET)

Increases (Dr.)	Decreases (Cr.)
(1) 200,000	75,000 (2)
	10,000 (4)
Balance 115,000	

ACCOUNTS PAYABLE (LIABILITY)

Decreases (Dr.)	Increases (Cr.)
(4) 10,000	20,000 (3)
(5) 5,000	
	5,000 Balance

MERCHANDISE INVENTORY (ASSET)

Increases (Dr.)	Decreases (Cr.)
(3) 20,000	
Balance 20,000	

COMMON STOCK (STOCKHOLDERS' EQUITY)

Decreases (Dr.)	Increases (Cr.)
	200,000 (1)
	5,000 (5)
	205,000 Balance

EQUIPMENT (ASSET)

Increases (Dr.)	Decreases (Cr.)
(2) 75,000	
Balance 75,000	

January 31, 1976, comprise $115,000 in cash, $20,000 in merchandise inventory, and $75,000 in equipment. Total equities of $210,000 comprise $5,000 of accounts payable and $205,000 of common stock.

The balance sheet can be prepared using the amounts shown as balances in the T-accounts. The balance sheet of Miller Corporation after the five transactions of January 1976 is shown in Exhibit 2.3.

EXHIBIT 2.3
Miller Corporation
Balance Sheet
January 31, 1976

ASSETS		LIABILITIES AND STOCKHOLDERS' EQUITY	
Cash	$115,000	Accounts Payable	$ 5,000
Merchandise Inventory	20,000	Common Stock	205,000
Equipment	75,000		
		Total Liabilities and	
Total Assets	$210,000	Stockholders' Equity	$210,000

■ AN OVERVIEW OF THE ACCOUNTING PROCESS

The double-entry recording framework is employed in processing the results of various transactions and events through the accounts so that financial statements can be prepared periodically. The accounting system designed around this recording framework generally involves the following operations:

1. entering the results of each transaction in the *general journal* in the form of a *journal entry*, a process called *journalizing*
2. *posting* the journal entries from the general journal to the accounts in the *general ledger*
3. preparing a *trial balance* of the accounts in the general ledger
4. making *adjusting* and *correcting* journal entries to accounts listed in the trial balance and posting them to the appropriate general ledger accounts
5. preparing financial statements from a trial balance after adjusting and correcting entries.

Each of these operations is described further and illustrated using the transactions of Miller Corporation during January 1976.

Journalizing

Each transaction is initially recorded in the general journal in the form of a *journal entry*. The standard journal entry format is as follows:

Date	Account Debited	Amount Debited
	Account Credited	Amount Credited
	Explanation of transaction or event being journalized.	

The *general journal* is merely a book or other device containing a listing of journal entries. The general journal is often referred to as the "book of original entry," since tránsactions initially enter the accounting system through it.

The journal entries for the five transactions of Miller Corporation during January 1976 are presented below.

(1) Jan. 1, 1976	Cash		200,000	
	Common Stock			200,000
	20,000 shares of $10 par value common stock are issued for cash.			
(2) Jan. 5, 1976	Equipment		75,000	
	Cash			75,000
	Equipment costing $75,000 is purchased for cash.			
(3) Jan. 15, 1976	Merchandise Inventory		20,000	
	Accounts Payable			20,000
	Merchandise inventory costing $20,000 is purchased on account.			
(4) Jan. 31, 1976	Accounts Payable		10,000	
	Cash			10,000
	Liabilities of $10,000 are paid with cash.			
(5) Jan. 31, 1976	Accounts Payable		5,000	
	Common Stock			5,000
	500 shares of $10 par value common stock are issued in settlement of a liability of $5,000.			

In addition to their role in the processing of accounting data, journal entries are also useful tools for indicating the effects of various transactions on a firm's financial statements and in preparing solutions to the problems at the end of each chapter. You will not completely understand an accounting event until you can analyze the event into its required debits and credits and can prepare the journal entry. Consequently, journal entries are employed as tools of analysis throughout this text.

Posting

At periodic intervals (for example, weekly or monthly), the transactions journalized in the general journal are entered, or posted, to the individual accounts in the general ledger. The *general ledger* is usually a book with a separate page for each account. The general ledger may also take the form of an access number in a computer's memory bank. The skeleton, or T-account, described earlier serves as a useful surrogate for a general ledger account. The journal entries from the general journal of Miller Corporation would be posted to the general ledger accounts in the manner shown previously in Exhibit 2.2.

As with journal entries, T-accounts are useful tools in preparing solutions to accounting problems and are used extensively in this text.

Trial Balance Preparation

A trial balance is a listing of each of the accounts in the general ledger with its balance as of a particular date. The trial balance of Miller Corporation on January 31, 1976, is presented in Exhibit 2.4.

EXHIBIT 2.4
Miller Corporation
Unadjusted Trial Balance
January 31, 1976

ACCOUNT	AMOUNTS IN ACCOUNTS WITH DEBIT BALANCES	AMOUNTS IN ACCOUNTS WITH CREDIT BALANCES
Cash	$115,000	
Merchandise Inventory	20,000	
Equipment	75,000	
Accounts Payable		$ 5,000
Common Stock		205,000
Totals	$210,000	$210,000

An equality between the sum of debit and the sum of credit account balances serves as a check on the arithmetic accuracy of the manner in which the double-entry recording procedure has been carried out during the period. If the trial balance is out of balance, it is necessary to retrace the steps followed in processing the accounting data to locate the source of the error.

Trial Balance Adjustment and Correction

Any errors detected in the processing of accounting data must be corrected. Such corrections are generally few in number. A more important type of adjustment is often necessary to account for unrecorded events that help to determine financial position at the end of the period and net income for the period. This type of adjustment is considered more fully in Chapters Three and Four. Most corrections and adjustments are made by preparing a journal entry, entering it in the general journal, and then posting it to the general ledger accounts.

Financial Statement Preparation

The balance sheet and income statement can be prepared from the trial balance after adjustments and corrections. Since correcting or adjusting entries are not required for Miller Corporation, the balance sheet presented in Exhibit 2.3 is correct as presented. In subsequent chapters, we consider the accounting procedures for preparing the income statement and the statement of changes in financial position.

The accounting process might be summarized as shown in Figure 2.1. The

FIGURE 2–1
SUMMARY OF THE ACCOUNTING PROCESS

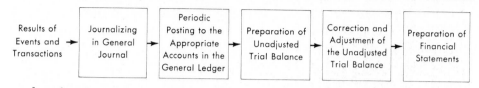

| Results of Events and Transactions | → | Journalizing in General Journal | → | Periodic Posting to the Appropriate Accounts in the General Ledger | → | Preparation of Unadjusted Trial Balance | → | Correction and Adjustment of the Unadjusted Trial Balance | → | Preparation of Financial Statements |

results of various transactions and events are processed through the accounting system following a flow beginning with the journalizing operation and ending with the financial statements.

The audit of the financial statements by the independent accountant typically flows in the opposite direction. The auditor begins with the financial statements prepared by management and then traces various items back through the accounts to the source documents (for example, sales invoices, canceled checks) which support the entries made in the general journal. Thus, it is possible to move back and forth between source documents, journal entries, general ledger postings, and the financial statements.

■ BALANCE SHEET ACCOUNT TITLES

The following list shows balance sheet account titles which are commonly used. The descriptions should help in understanding the nature of various assets, liabilities, and owners' equities as well as in selecting appropriate terms for solving problems. Alternative account titles can be easily devised. The list is not intended to exhaust all the account titles used in this book or appearing in the financial statements of publicly held firms.

Assets

Cash on Hand. Coins and currency, and such items as bank checks and money orders. The latter items are merely claims against individuals or institutions, but by custom are called "cash."

Cash in Bank. Strictly speaking, merely a claim against the bank for the amount deposited. Cash in bank consists of demand deposits, against which checks can be drawn, and time deposits, usually savings accounts and certificates of deposit. In published statements, the two items of Cash on Hand and Cash in Bank usually are combined under the title *Cash*.

Marketable Securities. Government bonds, or stocks and bonds of corporations. The word *marketable* implies that they can be bought and sold readily through a security exchange such as the New York Stock Exchange.

Accounts Receivable. Amounts due from customers of a business from the sale of goods or services. The collection of cash occurs some time after the sale. These accounts are also known as "charge accounts" or "open accounts." An alternative title is *Customers' Accounts*. The general term Accounts Receivable is used in financial statements to describe the figure representing the total amount receivable but, of course, the firm keeps a separate record for each customer.

Notes Receivable. Amounts due from customers or from others to whom loans have been made or credit extended, when the claim has been put into writing in the form of a promissory note.

Interest Receivable. Interest on assets such as promissory notes or bonds which has accrued, or come into existence, through the passing of time but which has not been collected as of the date of the balance sheet.

Merchandise Inventory. Goods on hand which have been purchased for resale, such as canned goods on the shelves of a grocery store or suits on the racks of a clothing store. This item is frequently shown simply as *Merchandise*.

Finished Goods Inventory. Completed but unsold manufactured products.

Work in Process Inventory. Partially completed manufactured products.

Raw Materials Inventory. Unused materials from which manufactured products are to be made. Sometimes combined with supplies under the title *Stores*.

Supplies Inventory. Lubricants, cleaning rags, abrasives, and other incidental materials used in manufacturing operations. Stationery, computer cards, pens, and other office supplies. Bags, twine, boxes, and other store supplies. Gasoline, oil, spare parts, and other delivery supplies. Alternative titles, such as *Factory Supplies, Office Supplies, Store Supplies,* and *Delivery Supplies,* could be used.

Prepaid Insurance. Insurance premiums paid for future coverage. An alternative title is *Unexpired Insurance*.

Prepaid Rent. Rent paid for future use of land, buildings, or equipment.

Land. Land occupied by buildings or used in operations.

Buildings. Factory buildings, store buildings, garages, warehouses, and so forth.

Machinery and Equipment. Lathes, ovens, tools, boilers, computers, motors, bins, cranes, conveyors, and so forth.

Furniture and Fixtures. Desks, tables, chairs, counters, showcases, scales, and other such store and office equipment. Other titles such as *Office Furniture and Fixtures* and *Store Furniture and Fixtures* could be used.

Office Machines. Typewriters, adding machines, bookkeeping equipment, calculators, and so forth. Sometimes combined with Furniture and Fixtures.

Automobiles. Delivery trucks, sales staff's cars, and so forth.

Organization Costs. Amounts paid for legal and incorporation fees, for printing the certificates for the shares of stock, and for accounting and any other costs incurred in organizing the business so it can begin to function. This asset is seen most commonly on the balance sheets of corporations.

Patents. A right granted for 17 years by the federal government for exclusive use of a certain process or device. Under current generally accepted accounting principles, research and development costs must be treated as an expense in the year incurred rather than being recognized as an asset with future benefits. (This treatment seems to us to be at odds with good accounting theory.) As a result, a firm which develops and owns a patent will not normally show it as an asset. On the other hand, a firm which purchases a patent from another firm or from an individual will recognize the patent as an asset. This inconsistent treatment of internally developed and externally purchased patents is discussed more fully in Chapter Ten.

Goodwill. An amount paid by one firm in acquiring another business enterprise that is greater than the sum of the values assignable to other assets. A good reputation and other desirable attributes are generally not recognized as assets by the firm which creates or develops them. However, when one firm acquires another firm, these desirable attributes are indirectly recognized as assets, since they are a factor in determining the valuation of goodwill.

Liabilities

Accounts Payable. Amounts owed for goods or services acquired under an informal credit agreement. These accounts are usually payable within 1 or 2 months. The same items appear as Accounts Receivable on the creditor's books. When an office procedure for disbursing funds known as a "voucher system" is employed, the title *Vouchers Payable* may be used. The term Accounts Payable covers the total amount due to all suppliers of goods and services, but separate records are maintained containing the amount owed to each creditor.

Notes Payable. The face amount of promissory notes given in connection with loans from the bank or the purchase of goods or services. The same item appears as Notes Receivable on the creditor's books.

Payroll Taxes Payable. Amounts withheld from wages and salaries of employees for federal and state payroll taxes. This account also includes the required employer's contributions for payroll taxes. Individual titles—Federal Insurance Contributions Act (FICA) Taxes Payable, State Unemployment Insurance Taxes Payable, and Federal Unemployment Insurance Taxes (FUTA) Payable—could be used for each of the various kinds of taxes. Common practice lumps them all under the heading Payroll Taxes Payable.

Withheld Income Taxes. Amounts withheld from wages and salaries of employees for income taxes which have not yet been remitted to the taxing authority. This is a tentative income tax on the earnings of employees, and the employer merely acts as a tax-collecting agent for the federal and state governments. A few cities also levy income taxes which the employer must withhold from wages.

Interest Payable. Interest on obligations which has accrued or accumulated with the passage of time but which has not been paid as of the date of the balance sheet. The liability for interest is customarily shown separately from the face amount of the obligation.

Income Taxes Payable. The estimated liability for income taxes, accumulated and unpaid, based upon the income of the business from the beginning of the taxable year to the date of the balance sheet. Since sole proprietorships and partnerships do not pay federal income taxes directly, this term will appear only on the books of a corporation or other taxable entity.

Rent Received in Advance. An example of a nonmonetary liability. The business owns a buildings which it rents to a tenant. The tenant has prepaid the rental

EXHIBIT 2.5
W. R. Jones Stores, Inc.
Balance Sheet
December 31, 1976

ASSETS

Current Assets

Cash:

Undeposited Cash	$ 511	
Cash in Bank	6,558	$ 7,069

Marketable Securities (Market value $12,525)		10,500

Receivables:

Accounts Receivable	$34,260	
Notes Receivable	9,000	
Interest Receivable	90	43,350

Merchandise Inventory (at acquisition cost)		85,423
Store and Office Supplies		1,550

Prepaid Costs:

Unexpired Insurance	$ 256	
Prepaid Rent	350	606

Total Current Assets	$148,498

Noncurrent Assets (at acquisition cost)

Land		$10,000
Buildings	$76,978	
Less: Accumulated Depreciation	22,556	54,422
Furniture and Fixtures	$15,102	
Less: Accumulated Depreciation	6,064	9,038
Delivery Equipment	$ 2,590	
Less: Accumulated Depreciation	1,554	1,036
Organization Costs		500
Goodwill		1,000

Total Noncurrent Assets	75,996
Total Assets	$224,494

charge for several months in advance. The amount applicable to future months cannot be considered a component of income until the rent is earned as time passes. Meanwhile the advance payment results in a liability payable in services (that is, in the use of the building). On the records of the tenant the same amount would appear as an asset, Prepaid Rent. Other similar prepaid items include deposits from customers for goods to be delivered later and payments received by a publisher for newpaper or magazine subscriptions.

LIABILITIES AND STOCKHOLDERS' EQUITY

Current Liabilities

Accounts Payable			$23,122
Notes Payable			8,000
Interest Payable			100
Wages Payable			655
Taxes Payable:			
Federal and State Income Taxes		$ 9,753	
Withheld Income Taxes		1,595	
Sales Taxes		2,533	
Payroll Taxes		555	14,436
Advances from Customers			1,000
Total Current Liabilities			$ 47,313

Noncurrent Liabilities

Contracts Payable (on fixtures)		$ 3,500	
Mortgage Payable (secured by land and buildings)		25,000	
Total Noncurrent Liabilities			28,500
Total Liabilities			$ 75,813

Stockholders' Equity

Preferred Stock—7 percent cumulative, authorized 1,000 shares, outstanding 500 shares, par value $100 per share			$50,000
Common Stock—no par, stated value $10 per share, authorized 10,000 shares, outstanding 7,500 shares		$75,000	
Capital Contributed in Excess of Stated Value of Shares		8,000	83,000
Retained Earnings			15,681
Total Stockholders' Equity			148,681
Total Liabilities and Stockholders' Equity			$224,494

Contracts Payable. Debts which involve written installment contracts usually calling for payments each month until the debt is paid. Land, automobiles, and machinery are often acquired with the use of this type of contract.

Mortgage Payable. Long-term promissory notes that have been given greater protection by the pledge of specific pieces of property as security for their payment. If the loan or interest is not paid according to the agreement, the property can be sold for the benefit of the creditor.

Bonds Payable. Amounts borrowed by the business for a relatively long period of time under a formal written contract or indenture. The loan is usually obtained from a number of lenders, each of whom receives one or more bond certificates as written evidence of his or her share of the loan.

Owners' Equity

Common Stock. Amounts received for the par or stated value of a firm's principal class of voting stock.

Preferred Stock. Amounts received for the par value of a class of a firm's stock which has some preference relative to the common stock. This preference is usually with respect to dividends and to assets in the event the corporation is liquidated.

Capital Contributed in Excess of Par or Stated Value. Amounts received from the issuance of common or preferred stock in excess of such shares' par value or stated value. This account is also referred to as *Additional Paid-In Capital* or sometimes as *Premium on Preferred* (or *Common*) *Stock.*

Retained Earnings. An account reflecting the increase in net assets since the business was organized as a result of generating earnings in excess of dividend declarations. When dividends are declared, net assets are distributed, and retained earnings are reduced by an equal amount.

A balance sheet which includes many of the accounts described in this section is presented in Exhibit 2.5. Certain items are shown for the sake of completeness even though an explanation of them is deferred to later chapters.

■ SUMMARY

The balance sheet, or statement of financial position, is composed of three major classes of items—assets, liabilities, and owners' equity.

Resources are recognized as assets when a firm has acquired rights to their future use as a result of a past transaction or exchange and when the value of the future benefits can be measured with a reasonable degree of precision. Monetary assets are, in general, stated at their current cash, or cash-equivalent, values. Nonmonetary assets are stated at acquisition cost, in some cases adjusted downward for the cost of services which have been consumed.

Liabilities represent obligations of a firm to make payments of a reasonably definite amount at a reasonably definite future time for benefits already received. Owners' equity is the difference between total assets and total liabilities and, for corporations, is typically segregated into contributed capital and retained earnings.

The equality of total assets and total equities (liabilities plus owners' equity) is maintained by recording the effects of each transaction in a dual manner in the accounts. The double-entry recording framework is summarized as follows:

ASSET ACCOUNTS		= LIABILITY ACCOUNTS		+ OWNERS' EQUITY ACCOUNTS	
Increases (Debits)	Decreases (Credits)	Decreases (Debits)	Increases (Credits)	Decreases (Debits)	Increases (Credits)

The dual effects of each transaction are initially recorded in journal entry form in the general journal. These journal entries are then posted to the appropriate asset, liability, and owners' equity accounts in the general ledger. A trial balance of the ending balances in the general ledger accounts is prepared periodically as a check on the mathematical accuracy of the double-entry recording procedure. Any necessary adjustments or corrections of the account balances in the trial balance are then made in the general journal and posted to the accounts in the general ledger. The financial statements are prepared from the adjusted and corrected trial balance. The procedures for preparing the balance sheet were considered in this chapter. The procedures for preparing the income statement are discussed in Chapters Three and Four. The statement of changes in financial position is considered in Chapter Five.

QUESTIONS AND PROBLEMS

1. Review the meaning of the following concepts or terms discussed in this chapter.
   a. Accounting entity.
   b. Legal entity.
   c. Sole proprietorship.
   d. Partnership.
   e. Corporation.
   f. Acquisition cost.
   g. Adjusted acquisition cost.
   h. Current replacement cost.
   i. Net realizable value.
   j. Present (discounted) value.
   k. Opportunity cost.
   l. Monetary assets.
   m. Nonmonetary assets.
   n. Going concern.
   o. Exchange.
   p. Common monetary measuring unit.
   q. Par value.
   r. Stated value.
   s. Debit.
   t. Credit.
   u. Journal entry.
   v. General journal.
   w. General ledger.
   x. T-account.
   y. Trial balance.
2. How can you determine from a balance sheet whether the enterprise is a corporation, partnership, or sole proprietorship?
3. Would the essential features of the double-entry recording process be affected by the deletion of the terms *debit* and *credit* from the language?

4. When a customer opens an account at a department store, the account is referred to as a *charge account*. When merchandise purchased on account is returned to the store, the customer is given *credit* for the returned merchandise. How is the use of the terms *charge* and *credit* in the department store context consistent with the definitions of *charge* and *credit* in accounting?

5. Identify the accounting entity in each of the following situations:

   a. John MacDonald owns and directs the operations of three hamburger outlets in the Chicago area.

   b. U.S. International Corporation operates through outlets located throughout the United States. Twelve foreign-held firms have been granted rights to distribute U.S. International Corporation's products in foreign countries.

   c. John Walker and Ken Wardlow have agreed to share equally the cost of constructing a fence between their properties.

   d. Residents of a nearby community have organized to lobby against a bill before the state legislature. Funds to support their endeavor have been raised from various citizens.

6. Indicate whether or not each of the following items would be recognized as assets by a firm according to the definition in the text.

   a. The cash advanced by a customer for goods to be delivered in a future accounting period.

   b. A contract signed by a customer to purchase $1,000 of goods next year.

   c. A favorable reputation.

   d. A patent on a new invention developed by a firm.

   e. A good credit standing.

   f. A delivery truck.

   g. A degree in engineering from a reputable university, awarded to the firm's chief engineer.

7. Indicate whether or not each of the following events immediately gives rise to an asset. If an asset is recognized, state the account title and amount.

   a. An investment of $8,000 is made in a government bond. The bond will have a maturity value of $10,000 in 3 years.

   b. An order for $600 of merchandise is received from a customer.

   c. Merchandise inventory with a list price of $300 is purchased, with payment being made in time to secure a 2-percent discount for prompt payment.

   d. Notice has been received from a manufacturer that materials billed at $4,000, with payment due within 30 days, have been shipped by freight. The seller retains title to the materials until they are received by the buyer.

   e. A contract is signed for the construction of a specially designed piece of machinery. The terms are $5,000 down upon signing the contract and the balance of $8,000 upon delivery of the equipment. Consider this question from the standpoint of the purchaser.

   f. A check for $900 is sent to a landlord for 2 months' rent in advance (consider from the standpoint of the tenant, often called the *lessee*).

   g. A check for $1,000 is written to obtain an option to purchase a tract of land. The price of the land is $32,500.

   h. Bonds with a face value of $100,000 are purchased for $96,000. The bonds mature in 25 years. Interest is payable by the issuer of the bonds at the rate of 8 percent annually.

8. Indicate whether or not each of the following events immediately gives rise to the recognition of an asset. If an asset is recognized, state the account title and amount.
   a. Raw materials with an invoice price of $6,200 are purchased on account from Williams Wholesalers.
   b. Defective raw material purchased in **a** for $200 is returned to Williams Wholesalers.
   c. The bill of Williams Wholesalers (see **a** and **b**) is paid promptly. A discount of 2 percent offered by the seller for prompt payment is taken.
   d. A machine is purchased for $15,000 cash.
   e. The cost of transporting the new machine in **d** to the plant site is paid in cash, $350.
   f. Material and labor costs incurred in installing the machine in **d** total $200 and are paid in cash.

9. Give an illustration, other than those in the text, of each of the following:
   a. A situation in which property is not shown as an asset on the balance sheet of the firm which has possession of the property.
   b. A situation in which property is shown as an asset on the balance sheet of a firm even though the firm does not have legal title to the property.

10. A group of investors owns an office building which they rent unfurnished to tenants. The building was purchased 5 years previously from a construction company and, at that time, was expected to have a useful life of 40 years. Indicate the procedures you might follow in determining the amount at which the building would be stated under each of the following valuation methods.
    a. Acquisition cost.
    b. Adjusted acquisition cost.
    c. Current replacement cost.
    d. Net realizable value.
    e. Present value of future cash flows.

11. Indicate whether or not each of the following items is recognized as a liability by a firm according to the definition in the text.
    a. Unpaid wages of employees.
    b. An obligation to maintain a rented office building in good repair.
    c. The amount payable by a firm for a newspaper advertisement that has appeared but for which payment is not due for 30 days.
    d. An incompetent brother-in-law of the firm's president, who is employed in the business.
    e. The reputation for not paying bills promptly.
    f. The outstanding common stock of a corporation.
    g. An obligation to deliver merchandise to a customer next year for which cash has been received.
    h. An obligation to provide rental services to a tenant who has paid 3 months' rent in advance.

12. Indicate whether or not each of the following events immediately gives rise to the recognition of a liability. If a liability is recognized, state the account title and amount.
    a. A landscaper agrees to improve land owned by the company. The agreed price for the work is $425. Consider from the standpoint of the company.
    b. Additional common stock with a par value of $50,000 is issued for $62,500.

   c. A check for $12 for a 2-year subscription to a magazine is received.

   d. A construction company agrees to build a bridge for $2 million. A down payment of $200,000 is received upon signing the contract, and the remainder is due when the bridge is completed.

   e. During the last pay period, employees earned wages amounting to $24,500 for which they have not been paid. The employer is also liable for payroll taxes of 8 percent of the wages earned.

   f. A landlord receives $900 for 3 months' rent in advance.

   g. A 60-day, 8-percent loan for $10,000 is obtained at a bank.

   h. A firm signs a contract to purchase at least $5,000 worth of merchandise during the next 3 months.

13. Some of the assets of one firm correspond to the liabilities of another firm. For example, an account receivable on the seller's balance sheet would be an account payable on the buyer's balance sheet. For each of the following items, indicate whether it is an asset or liability and give the corresponding account title on the balance sheet of the other party to the transaction.

   a. Advances by Customers.

   b. Bonds Payable.

   c. Cash in Bank.

   d. Interest Receivable.

   e. Prepaid Insurance.

   f. Rental Fees Received in Advance.

14. The assets of a business total $950,000, and liabilities total $700,000. Present the owners' equity section of the balance sheet under the following assumptions:

   a. The business is a sole proprietorship owned by William Gleason.

   b. The business is a partnership. William Gleason has a 35-percent interest, John Morgan has a 40-percent interest, and David Johnson has a 25-percent interest.

   c. The business is a corporation. Outstanding common stock was originally issued for $180,000, of which $100,000 represented par value. The remainder of the owners' equity represents accumulated, undistributed earnings.

15. Information may be classified with respect to a balance sheet in one of the following ways:

   (**1**) Asset.

   (**2**) Liability.

   (**3**) Owners' equity.

   (**4**) Item would not appear on the balance sheet as conventionally prepared.

Using the numbers above, indicate the appropriate classification of each of the following items:

   a. Salaries payable.

   b. Retained earnings.

   c. Notes receivable.

   d. Unfilled customers' orders.

   e. Land.

   f. Interest payable.

   g. Work in process inventory.

   h. Mortgage payable.

    i. Organization costs.
    j. Advances by customers.
    k. Advances to employees.
    l. Patents.
    m. Good credit standing.
    n. Common stock.

16. Information may be classified with respect to a balance sheet in one of the following ways:

(**1**) Asset.
(**2**) Liability.
(**3**) Owners' equity.
(**4**) Item would not appear on the balance sheet as conventionally prepared.

Using the numbers above, indicate the appropriate classification of each of the following items:

    a. Preferred stock.
    b. Furniture and fixtures.
    c. Potential liability under lawsuit (case has not yet gone to trial).
    d. Prepaid rent.
    e. Capital contributed in excess of par value.
    f. Cash on hand.
    g. Goodwill.
    h. Estimated liability under warranty contract.
    i. Raw materials inventory.
    j. Rental fees received in advance.
    k. Bonds payable.
    l. Unexpired insurance.

17. Indicate the effects of the transactions below on the balance sheet equation using the following format:

Transaction Number	Assets	=	Liabilities	+	Owners' Equity
(1)	+$50,000				+$50,000
Subtotal	$50,000	=			$50,000

(**1**) 5,000 shares of $10 par value common stock are issued at par value for cash.
(**2**) Merchandise is purchased on account for $18,500.
(**3**) Store equipment is purchased for $4,800. A check is drawn for $800 and the balance is payable over 3 years under an installment contract.
(**4**) Store supplies costing $450 are purchased for cash.
(**5**) A 60-day promissory note is issued to the supplier in (**2**) for the amount due.
(**6**) A check is issued for $500 covering 2 months' rent in advance on office space.

18. Indicate the effects of the transactions below on the balance sheet equation using the following format:

Transaction Number	Assets	=	Liabilities	+	Owners' Equity
(1)	+$40,000		0		+$40,000
Subtotal	$40,000	=	0	+	$40,000

(**1**) Shares of common stock are issued to stockholders for cash, $40,000.

(**2**) Equipment is purchased on an installment contract for $15,000; terms are $3,000 payable immediately and the balance in four quarterly installments.

(**3**) A check for $800 is issued to Roger White to reimburse him for costs incurred in organizing and promoting the corporation.

(**4**) A check for $900 is issued for 3 months' rent in advance for office space.

(**5**) Office equipment is purchased for $750. A down payment of $250 is made, with the balance payable in 30 days.

(**6**) A patent on a machine process is purchased for $20,000 cash.

(**7**) $275 is paid to Express Transfer Company for delivering the equipment purchased in (**2**).

(**8**) The first payment on the equipment installment contract is made.

(**9**) Supplies are purchased on account, $765.

19. Indicate the effects of the transactions below on the T-accounts for Assets, Liabilities, and Owners' Equity using the following format:

ASSETS		=	LIABILITIES		+	OWNERS' EQUITY	
Increases (Dr.)	Decreases (Cr.)		Decreases (Dr.)	Increases (Cr.)		Decreases (Dr.)	Increases (Cr.)
(1) 500,000							500,000 (1)

(**1**) The Whalen Corporation is organized with the issuance at par value of 500,000 shares of $1 par value common stock for cash.

(**2**) 250,000 additional shares are issued to a development corporation for a fully equipped factory. Of the total, $25,000 is assigned to the land, $125,000 to the equipment, and the remainder to the building.

(**3**) 5,000 shares of common stock are issued to G. W. Larsen in payment for legal services rendered in obtaining the corporate charter.

(**4**) Raw materials are purchased on account for $32,500.

(**5**) Factory supplies of $275 and office supplies of $625 are purchased for cash.

(**6**) A check is written for $1,200 for fire and general liability coverage for the next year.

(**7**) A check for $15,000 is issued to the supplier in (**4**) as partial payment on the account.

(**8**) A special order is received for $200,000 of machine parts which the firm plans to produce. A deposit of 10 percent is received with the order.

20. Set up T-accounts for the following accounts, indicate whether each account is an asset, liability, or owners' equity item, and enter the transactions described below:

Cash	Accounts Payable
Merchandise Inventory	Note Payable
Prepaid Insurance	Mortgage Payable
Building	Common Stock—Par Value
Equipment	Capital Contributed in Excess of Par Value

(**1**) 20,000 shares of $10 par value stock are issued for $15 cash per share.

(**2**) A building costing $300,000 is acquired. A cash payment of $50,000 is made, and a long-term mortgage is assumed for the balance of the purchase price.

(3) Equipment costing $2,000 and merchandise inventory costing $8,000 are acquired on account.

(4) A 3-year fire insurance policy is taken out and the $400 premium is paid in advance.

(5) A 90-day, 6-percent note is issued to the bank for a $5,000 loan.

(6) Payments of $6,000 are made to the suppliers in (3).

21. Express the following transactions of the Harris Grocery Store, a sole proprietorship, in journal entry form. You may omit explanations for the journal entries.

(1) John Harris contributes $15,000 cash to help set up the grocery store.

(2) A 60-day, 8-percent note is signed in return for a $5,000 loan from the bank.

(3) A building is rented, with the annual rental of $6,000 paid in advance.

(4) Display equipment costing $8,000 is acquired. A check is issued.

(5) Merchandise inventory costing $20,000 is acquired. A check for $4,000 is issued, with the remainder payable in 30 days.

(6) A contract is signed with a nearby restaurant under which the restaurant agrees to purchase $3,000 of groceries each week. A check is received for the first 2 weeks' orders in advance.

22. Express the following independent transactions in journal entry form. If an entry is not required, indicate the reason. You may omit explanations for the journal entries.

(1) Bonds of the Sommers Company with a face value of $40,000 and annual interest at the rate of 8 percent are purchased for $41,500 cash.

(2) A check for $2,000 is received by a fire insurance company for premiums on policy coverage over the next 2 years.

(3) A corporation issues 30,000 shares of $10 par value common stock in exchange for land, building, and equipment. The land is to be stated at $20,000, the building at $280,000, and the equipment at $100,000.

(4) A contract is signed by a manufacturing firm agreeing to purchase 100 dozen machine tool parts over the next 2 years at a price of $40 per dozen.

(5) 5,000 shares of $1 par value preferred stock are issued to an attorney for legal services rendered in organization of the corporation. The bill for the services is $7,500.

(6) A coupon book, redeemable in movie viewings, is issued for $30 cash by a movie theatre.

(7) A firm has been notified that it is being sued for $10,000 damages by a customer who incurred losses as a result of purchasing defective merchandise.

(8) Merchandise inventory costing $2,000, purchased on account, is found to be defective and returned to the supplier for full credit.

23. The transactions of the Electronics Appliance Corporation during September 1976 are as follows:

(1) The firm issues 3,000 shares of $10 par value common stock at par value for cash.

(2) A factory building is leased for the 3 years beginning October 1, 1976. Monthly rental payments are $4,000. Two months' rent is paid in advance.

(3) Factory equipment costing $17,500 is purchased. A check for $5,000 is issued, and a long-term mortgage liability is assumed for the balance.

(4) The labor costs of installing the new equipment in (3) are $250 and are paid in cash.

(**5**) Raw materials are purchased on account for $4,100.

(**6**) A check for $800 is received from a customer as a deposit on a special order for equipment which Electronics plans to manufacture. The contract price is $4,500.

(**7**) Office equipment with a list price of $850 is acquired. After deducting a discount of $25, a check is issued in full payment.

(**8**) The company hires three employees to begin work October 1. A cash advance of $100 is given to one of the employees.

(**9**) The firm's attorney is given 50 shares of common stock in payment for legal services rendered in the organization of the corporation. The bill for the services is $5,000.

a. Enter the transactions in T-accounts. Indicate whether each account is an asset, liability, or owners' equity item. Cross reference each entry to the appropriate transaction number.

b. Prepare a balance sheet for Electronics Appliance Corporation as of September 30, 1976.

24. The Standard Manufacturing Corporation is organized on January 1, 1976. During January 1976, the following transactions occur:

(**1**) The corporation issues 10,000 shares of $10 par value common stock for $150,000 in cash.

(**2**) The corporation issues 30,000 shares of common stock in exchange for land, building, and equipment. The land is to be stated at $75,000, the building at $270,000, and the equipment at $105,000.

(**3**) The corporation issues 1,000 shares of common stock to an attorney in payment of legal services rendered in obtaining the corporate charter.

(**4**) Raw materials costing $75,000 are acquired on account from various suppliers.

(**5**) Manufacturing equipment with a list price of $4,000 is acquired. After deducting a $400 discount, the net amount is paid in cash.

(**6**) Freight charges of $250 for delivery of the equipment in (**5**) are paid in cash.

(**7**) Raw materials costing $800 are found to be defective and returned to the supplier for full credit. The raw materials had been purchased on account [see (**4**)], and no payment had been made as of the time that the goods were returned.

(**8**) A contract is signed for the rental of a fleet of automobiles beginning February 1, 1976. The rental for February of $1,000 is paid in advance.

(**9**) Invoices for $30,000 of raw materials purchased in (**4**) are paid, after deducting a discount of 2 percent for prompt payment.

(**10**) Fire and liability insurance coverage is obtained from Midwest Insurance Company. The 1-year policy, beginning February 1, 1976, carries a $300 premium, which has not yet been paid.

(**11**) A contract is signed with a customer for $10,000 of merchandise which Standard plans to manufacture. The customer advanced $2,500 toward the contract price.

(**12**) A warehouse costing $40,000 is acquired. A down payment of $5,000 is made, and a long-term mortgage is assumed for the balance.

(**13**) Raw materials inventory with a list price of $2,000 is found to be defective and returned to the supplier. This inventory has already been paid for in (**9**).

The returned raw materials are the only item purchased from this particular supplier during January 1976.

(14) The firm purchased 5,000 shares of $10 par value common stock of the General Electronics Corporation for $75,000. This investment is made as a short-term investment of excess cash. The shares of General Electronics Corporation are traded on the New York Stock Exchange.

a. Enter these transactions in T-accounts. Indicate whether each account is an asset, liability, or owners' equity item. Cross reference each entry to the appropriate transaction number.

b. Prepare a balance sheet as of January 31, 1976.

Chapter Three

Income Statement—
Measurement Principles

The second principal financial statement considered is the income statement. This statement provides a measure of the earnings performance of a firm for some particular period of time. As we discussed in Chapter One and illustrated for the Jonathan Corporation in Exhibit 1.2, *net income*, or *earnings*, is equal to revenues minus expenses.

Revenues measure the inflow of net assets (assets less liabilities) from selling goods and providing services. Expenses measure the outflow of net assets which are used up, or consumed, in the process of generating revenues. As a measure of earnings performance, revenues reflect the services rendered by the firm and expenses indicate the efforts required or expended.

This chapter considers the accounting principles and conventions which underlie the income statement. We begin by discussing the concept of the accounting period, the span of time over which earnings performance is measured. We then describe and illustrate two common bases of accounting, the cash basis and the accrual basis. Finally, we discuss the criteria for recognizing and measuring revenues and expenses. Chapter Four considers the accounting procedures used in applying these principles and conventions in preparing the income statement.

■ THE ACCOUNTING PERIOD CONVENTION

The income statement is a report on earnings performance over a specified period of time. Years ago, the length of this period varied substantially among firms. Income statements were prepared at the completion of some activity, such as after the round-trip voyage of a ship between England and the colonies or at the completion of a construction project.

The earnings activities of most modern firms are not so easily separated into distinguishable projects. Instead, the income-generating activity is carried on continually. For example, a plant is acquired and used in manufacturing products for a period of 40 years or more. Delivery equipment is purchased and used in transporting merchandise to customers for 5, 6, or more years. If the preparation of the income statement were postponed until all earnings activities were completed, the report might never be prepared and, in any case, would be too late to help a reader appraise performance and make decisions. An accounting period of uniform length is used to facilitate timely comparisons and analyses across firms.

An accounting period of *1 year* underlies the principal financial statements distributed to stockholders and potential investors. Most firms prepare their annual reports using the calendar year as the accounting period. A growing number of firms, however, use a *natural business year*. The use of a natural business year is an attempt to measure performance at a time when most earnings activities have been substantially concluded. The ending date of a natural business year varies from one firm to another. For example, Sears uses a natural business year ending on January 31, which comes after completion of the Christmas shopping season. American Motors uses a year ending September 30, the end of its model year. A. C. Nielsen (producers of television ratings and other surveys) uses a year ending August 31, just prior to the beginning of the new television season.

In order to provide even more timely information, most publicly held firms also report earnings data for interim periods within the regular annual accounting period. These interim reports generally cover 3-month periods, or "quarters."

■ THE ACCOUNTING BASIS FOR RECOGNIZING REVENUES AND EXPENSES

When measuring earnings performance for the accounting period, some activities will have been started and completed within the period. For example, during a particular accounting period, merchandise might be purchased from a supplier, sold to a customer on account, and the account collected in cash. Few difficulties are encountered in measuring performance in these cases. The difference between the cash received from customers and the cash disbursed to acquire, sell, and deliver the merchandise represents earnings from this series of transactions.

Many earnings activities, however, are started in one accounting period and completed in another. Buildings and equipment are acquired in one period but used over a period of several years. Merchandise is sometimes purchased in one accounting period and sold during the next period, while cash is collected from customers during a third period. A significant problem in measuring performance for specific accounting periods concerns the determination of the amount of revenues and expenses to be recognized from earnings activities which are in process as of the beginning of the period or are incomplete as of the end of the period. Two approaches to measuring earnings performance are (1) the cash basis of accounting, and (2) the accrual basis of accounting.

Cash Basis of Accounting

Under the *cash basis of accounting,* revenues from selling goods and providing services are recognized in the period when cash is received from customers. Expenses are typically reported in the period in which expenditures are made for merchandise, salaries, insurance, taxes, and similar items. To illustrate the determination of net income under the cash basis of accounting, consider the following example.

Donald and Joanne Allens open a hardware store on January 1, 1976. They contribute $10,000 in cash and borrow $6,000 from a local bank. The loan is repayable on June 30, 1976, with interest charged at the rate of 10 percent per year. A store building is rented on January 1, and 2 months' rent of $2,000 is paid in advance. The premium of $1,200 for property and liability insurance coverage for the year ending December 31, 1976, is paid on January 1. During January, merchandise costing $20,000 is acquired, of which $13,000 is purchased for cash and $7,000 is purchased on account. Sales to customers during January total $25,000, of which $17,000 is sold for cash and $8,000 is sold on account. The acquisition cost of merchandise sold during January is $16,000, while various employees are paid $2,500 in salaries.

Exhibit 3.1 presents an income statement for Allens' Hardware Store for the month of January 1976 under the cash basis of accounting. Sales revenue of $17,000 reflects the portion of the total sales of $25,000 made during January which was collected in cash. While merchandise costing $20,000 was acquired during January, only $13,000 cash was disbursed to suppliers, and this amount is therefore recognized as an expense of the period. Expenses recognized for salaries, rent, and insurance reflect the amounts of cash disbursements during January for these services, without regard to whether or not the services were fully consumed by the end of January. The net loss for January under the cash basis of accounting is $1,700.

As a basis for measuring performance for a particular accounting period (for example, January 1976 for Allens' Hardware Store), the cash basis of accounting is subject to two important and somewhat related criticisms. First, revenues are not adequately matched with the cost of the efforts required in generating the revenues. Performance of one period therefore gets mingled with the performance of preceding and succeeding periods. The store rental payment of $2,000 provides rental services for both January and February, but under the cash basis, the full amount is recognized as an expense during January. Likewise, the annual insurance premium provides coverage for the full year, whereas under the cash basis of accounting, none of this insurance cost will be recognized as an expense during the months of February through December. The longer the period over which future benefits are received, the more serious is this criticism of the cash basis of accounting. Consider, for example, the investments of a capital-intensive firm in buildings and equipment which might be used for 10, 20, or more years. The length of time between the purchase of these assets and the collection of cash for goods produced and sold can span many years.

EXHIBIT 3.1
Allens' Hardware Store
Income Statement
For the Month of January 1976
(Cash Basis of Accounting)

Cash Receipts from Sales of Merchandise		$17,000
Less Cash Expenditures for Merchandise and Services:		
Merchandise	$13,000	
Salaries	2,500	
Rental	2,000	
Insurance	1,200	
Total Expenditures		18,700
Net Loss		($1,700)

A second, and probably less serious, criticism of the cash basis of accounting is that it postpones unnecessarily the time when revenue is recognized. In most cases, the sale (delivery) of goods or rendering of services is the critical event in generating revenue. The collection of cash is relatively routine, or at least highly predictable. In these cases, recognizing revenue at the time of cash collection may result in reporting the effects of earnings activities one or more periods after the critical revenue-generating activity has occurred. For example, sales to customers during January by Allens' Hardware Store totaled $25,000. Under the cash basis of accounting, $8,000 of this amount will not be recognized until February or later, when the cash is collected. If the credit standings of customers have been checked prior to making sales on account, it is highly probable that cash will be collected, and there is little reason to postpone recognition of the revenue.

The cash basis of accounting is principally used by lawyers, accountants, and other professional people who have relatively small investments in multiperiod assets, such as buildings and equipment, and who collect cash from their clients soon after services are rendered. Some firms use a *modified cash basis of accounting*, under which the cost of buildings, equipment, and similar items are treated as assets when purchased. A portion of the acquisition cost is then recognized as an expense when services of these assets are consumed. Except for the treatment of these long-lived assets, revenues are recognized at the time cash is received and expenses are reported when cash disbursements are made. Some physicians and dentists with relatively heavy investments in equipment use the modified cash basis of accounting.

Where inventories are an important factor in generating revenues, such as for a manufacturing or merchandising firm, the Internal Revenue Code prohibits a firm from using the cash basis of accounting in its income tax returns.

Accrual Basis of Accounting

Under the *accrual basis of accounting*, revenue is recognized when some critical event or transaction occurs which is related to the earnings process. In most cases,

EXHIBIT 3.2
Allens' Hardware Store
Income Statement
For the Month of January 1976
(Accrual Basis of Accounting)

Sales Revenue		$25,000
Less Expenses:		
Cost of Merchandise Sold	$16,000	
Salaries Expense	2,500	
Rent Expense	1,000	
Insurance Expense	100	
Interest Expense	50	
Total Expenses		19,650
Net Income		$ 5,350

this critical event is the sale (delivery) of goods or the rendering of services. The nature and significance of this critical event are discussed later in the chapter. Under the accrual basis of accounting, costs incurred are reported as expenses in the period when the revenues to which they relate are recognized. Thus, an attempt is made to *match* expenses with associated revenues. When particular types of costs incurred cannot be closely identified with specific revenue streams, they are treated as expenses of the period in which services of an asset are consumed or future benefits of an asset disappear.

Exhibit 3.2 presents an income statement for Allens' Hardware Store for January 1976 using the accrual basis of accounting. The entire $25,000 of sales during January is recognized as revenue even though cash in that amount has not yet been received. Because of the high probability that outstanding accounts receivable will be collected, the critical revenue-generating event is the sale of the goods rather than the collection of cash from customers. The acquisition cost of the merchandise sold during January is $16,000. Recognizing this amount as cost of goods sold leads to an appropriate matching of sales revenue and merchandise expense in the income statement. Of the advance rental payment of $2,000, only $1,000 applies to the cost of services consumed during January. The remaining rental of $1,000 applies to the month of February. Likewise, only $100 of the $1,200 insurance premium represents coverage for January. The remaining $1,100 of the insurance premium provides coverage for February through December and will be recognized as an expense during those months. The interest expense of $50 represents 1 month's interest on the $6,000 bank loan at an annual rate of 10 percent ($= \$6,000 \times .10 \times 1/12$). While the interest will not be paid until the loan becomes due on June 30, 1976, the firm benefited from having the funds available for its use during January and an appropriate portion of the total interest cost on the loan should be recognized as a January expense. The salaries, rental, insurance, and interest expenses, unlike the cost of merchandise sold, cannot be associated directly with revenues recognized during the period. These costs are therefore reported as expenses of January to the extent services were consumed during the month.

The accrual basis of accounting provides a better measure of earnings performance for Allens' Hardware Store for the month of January than does the cash basis, both because revenues are measured more accurately and because expenses are associated more closely with reported revenues. Likewise, the accrual basis will provide a superior measure of performance for future periods, since activities of those periods will be charged with their share of the costs of rental, insurance, and other services to be consumed.

Several important questions regarding the recognition of revenues and expenses have not yet been considered:

1. When, or at what point(s), within the earnings process is revenue recognized (that is, what is the nature of the critical revenue-generating event)?
2. How do we measure or determine the amount of revenue to be recognized?
3. When, or at what point(s), within the earnings process are expenses reported (that is, what is the nature of the matching convention)?
4. How do we measure or determine the amount of expenses to be reported?

We consider the principles employed in measuring revenues and expenses in the next two sections.

■ REVENUE RECOGNITION AND MEASUREMENT PRINCIPLES

In reporting revenue, we are concerned with *when* it arises (a timing question) and *how much* is recognized (a measurement question).

Timing of Revenue Recognition

The earnings process for the acquisition and sale of merchandise might be depicted as shown in Figure 3.1. Revenue could conceivably be recognized at the time of purchase, sale, or cash collection, at some point(s) between these events, or even continuously. To answer the timing question, we must have a set of criteria for revenue recognition.

FIGURE 3.1
EARNINGS PROCESS FOR THE ACQUISITION AND
SALE OF MERCHANDISE

Purchase of Merchandise	Sale of Merchandise	Collection of Cash

Criteria for Revenue Recognition   The criteria currently required to be met before revenue is recognized are as follows:

1. All, or a substantial portion, of the services to be provided have been performed.
2. Cash, receivables, or some other asset susceptible to objective measurement has been received.

Recognition at the Point of Sale   For the vast majority of firms involved in selling goods and services, revenue is recognized at the time of sale (delivery). This method of recognizing revenues is called the *completed sale*, or in some contexts the *completed contract*, method of revenue recognition. The goods have been transferred to the buyer or the services have been performed. Future services, such as for warranties, are likely to be insignificant, or if significant, can be estimated with reasonable precision. An exchange between an independent buyer and seller has occurred which provides an objective measure of the amount of revenue. If the sale is made on account, past experience and an assessment of customers' credit standings provide a basis for predicting the amount of cash that will be collected. The sale of the goods or services is therefore the critical revenue-generating event. Under the accrual basis of accounting, revenue is typically recognized at the time of sale.

Recognition at the Time of Production   In a few instances, revenue is recognized at the time of production. One such case is in the mining of precious metals such as silver and gold. There is a ready market for these metals. After the metals have been extracted from a mine, the only future service required is delivery to the market. Because of the ready market, current selling prices can be determined objectively. (Such a ready market is not available for most other goods and services, so future selling and delivery services are a significant part of the earnings process. In these cases, revenue is recognized at the time of sale.)

On some long-term construction projects, the buyer and the seller agree in advance on the contract price and the timing of cash payments. Revenue from these long-term contracts is often recognized during the period of production. The earnings process for a particular long-term construction project may span several years. If the firm waited until the project was completed to recognize revenue, the efforts and accomplishments of several accounting periods would be recognized in the one period when the contract was completed. This approach would give an unsatisfactory measure of performance for each period during the contract. In these cases, some firms use the *percentage of completion method* of recognizing revenue. A portion of the total contract price, based on the degree of completion of the work, is recognized as revenue each period. This proportion is determined using either engineers' estimates of the degree of completion or the ratio of costs incurred to date to the total expected costs for the contract.

While future services required on these long-term construction contracts can be substantial at any given time, the costs to be incurred in providing these services can often be estimated with reasonable precision. The existence of a contract indicates that a buyer has been obtained and a price for the construction services has been set. Cash is usually collected from the buyer as construction progresses.

Otherwise, an assessment of the customer's credit standing leads to a reasonable expectation that the contract price will be received in cash after construction is completed. Construction activities are therefore the critical revenue-generating events. The actual schedule of cash collections is *not* important to the revenue recognition process when the percentage of completion method is used.

Some firms involved with construction contracts postpone the recognition of revenue until the construction project and the sale are completed. This method is the same as the completed sale basis, but is often referred to as the *completed contract method* of recognizing revenue. In some cases, the completed contract method is used because the contracts are of such short duration (such as 3 or 6 months) that earnings reported with the percentage of completion method and the completed contract method are not significantly different. In these cases, the completed contract method is used because it is generally easier to implement. Some firms use the completed contract method in situations when a specific buyer has not been obtained during the periods while construction is progressing, as is sometimes the case in constructing residential housing. In these cases, future selling efforts are required and substantial uncertainty may exist regarding the contract price ultimately to be established and the amount of cash to be received.

The primary reason for a contractor's not using the percentage of completion method when a contract exists is the uncertainty of total costs to be incurred in carrying out the project. If total costs cannot be reasonably estimated, the percentage of total costs incurred by a given date also cannot be estimated, and the percentage of services already rendered (revenue) cannot be estimated.

Recognition at the Point of Cash Collection   Occasionally, estimating the amount of cash or other assets that will be received from customers is extremely difficult. Therefore, an objective measure of the services rendered and the benefits to be received cannot be made at the time of sale. Under these circumstances, revenue is recognized at the time of cash collection.

This basis of revenue recognition is sometimes used by land development companies. These companies typically sell undeveloped land and promise to develop it over several future years. The buyer makes a nominal down payment and agrees to pay the remainder of the purchase price in installments over 10, 20, or more years. In these cases, future development of the land is a significant aspect of the earnings process. Also, substantial uncertainty often exists as to the ultimate collectibility of the installment notes, particularly those not due until several years in the future. The critical revenue-generating event in this case is the collection of cash. When revenue is recognized as the periodic cash collections are made and costs incurred in generating the revenue are matched as closely as possible with the revenue, the firm is using the *installment method* of accounting. The installment method is similar to the cash basis of accounting, since revenue is recognized as cash is received. The installment method, however, is an accrual method of accounting, since an effort is made to match expenses with associated revenues.

For most sales of goods and services, past experience and an assessment of buyers' credit standings provide a sufficient basis for predicting the amount of cash to be received. The installment method is therefore not used in these situations, and revenue is recognized at the time of sale.

Recognition Between Purchase and Sale   The period between the acquisition, or production, and the sale of merchandise and other salable goods is referred to as a *holding period*. The current replacement cost or net realizable value of the assets could change during this holding period. Such changes are described as *unrealized holding gains and losses*, because a transaction or exchange has not taken place.

Unrealized holding gains could be recognized as they occur. In accounting practice, however, we typically wait until the asset is sold or exchanged before recognizing the gain. At that time, an inflow of net assets subject to objective measurement is presumed to have taken place. Since we assume the firm is a going concern, the unrealized gain will be recognized as revenue in a future period in the ordinary course of business. Thus, the recognition of revenue and the valuation of assets are closely associated. Nonmonetary assets are typically stated at acquisition cost until sold. At the time of sale, an inflow of net assets occurs (for example, cash, accounts receivable), and revenue reflecting the previously unreported unrealized gain is recognized. This treatment of unrealized holding gains has the effect of shifting income from periods when the asset is held and the market price increases to the later period of sale. The longer the holding period (as, for example, land used for several decades), the more is income likely to be shifted forward in time.

Current accounting practices do not treat unrealized holding losses in the same way as holding gains, particularly on inventory items. If the current replacement cost or selling price of inventory items decreases below the acquisition cost during the holding period, the asset is often written down and the unrealized loss is recognized. This treatment of losses rests on the convention that earnings should be reported conservatively. Considering the estimates and predictions required in measuring revenues and expenses, some accountants feel it is desirable to provide a conservative measure of earnings so statement users will not be misled into thinking the firm is doing better than it really is.

The inconsistent treatment of unrealized gains and unrealized losses does not seem warranted. The arguments used against recognizing unrealized gains apply equally well to unrealized losses. If gains cannot be determined objectively prior to sale, then how can losses be measured prior to sale? If losses can be measured objectively prior to sale, then why cannot gains? We consider the accounting treatment of unrealized gains and losses further in Chapters Nine and Fourteen.

Measurement of Revenue

The amount of revenue recognized is generally measured by the cash or cash-equivalent value of other assets received from customers. As a starting point, this amount is the agreed upon price between buyer and seller at the time of sale. Some adjustments to this amount may be necessary, however, if revenue is recognized in a period prior to the collection of cash.

Uncollectible Accounts If some portion of the sales for a period is not expected to be collected, the amount of revenue recognized for that period must be adjusted for estimated uncollectible accounts. Logic suggests that this adjustment of revenue should occur in the period when revenue is recognized and not in a later period when specific customers' accounts are declared to be uncollectible. If the adjustment is postponed, reported income of subsequent periods will be affected by earlier decisions to extend credit to customers. Thus, the performance of the firm for both the period of sale and the period when the account is judged uncollectible would be measured inaccurately. These problems are considered further in Chapter Eight.

Sales Discounts and Allowances Customers may take advantage of discounts for prompt payment, or allowances may be granted for unsatisfactory merchandise. In these cases, the amount of cash eventually to be received can be expected to be less than the stated selling price. Appropriate reductions should therefore be made at the time of sale in determining the amount of revenue to be recognized.

Delayed Payments If the period between the sale of the goods or services and the time of cash collection extends over several years, it is likely that the selling price includes an interest charge for the loan conveying the right to delay payment. Under the accrual basis of accounting, this interest element should be recognized as revenue during the periods between sale and collection when the loan is outstanding. To recognize all potential revenue entirely in the period of sale would be to recognize too soon the return for services rendered over time in lending money. Thus, when cash collection is to be delayed, the measure of current revenue should be the selling price reduced to account for the interest element applicable to future periods. Only the *present value* of the amount to be received should be recognized as revenue during the period of sale. For most accounts receivable, the period between sale and collection spans only 2 to 3 months. The interest element is likely to be relatively insignificant in these cases. As a result, in accounting practice no reduction for interest on delayed payments is made for receivables to be collected within 1 year or less. This procedure is a practical expedient rather than a strict following of what accounting theory suggests.

■ EXPENSE RECOGNITION AND MEASUREMENT PRINCIPLES

Analogous to the questions raised regarding revenue recognition, we are confronted with the questions of *when* expenses are recognized and at *what amount* they are stated.

Timing of Expense Recognition

Recall that assets represent resources providing future benefits to the firm. *Expenses* are a measurement of the assets consumed in generating revenue. Assets may be referred to as *unexpired costs* and expenses as *expired costs* or "gone assets." Our attention focuses on the question of when the asset expiration takes place. The critical question is "When have asset benefits expired—leaving the balance sheet—and become expenses—entering the income statement as reductions in owners' equity?" Thus:

Balance Sheet   *Income Statement*

Assets or Unexpired Costs ⟶ Expenses or Expired Costs

Expense Recognition Criteria   The criteria presently employed by accountants in making the timing decision may be summarized as follows:

1. Asset expirations, or expenses, directly associated with particular types of revenue are recognized as expenses in the period in which the revenues are recognized. This treatment is called the *matching convention,* because expenses are matched with revenues.
2. Asset expirations, or expenses, not directly or easily associated with revenues are treated as expenses of the period in which services are consumed in operations.

Product or Production Costs   The cost of goods or merchandise sold is perhaps the easiest expense to associate with revenue. At the time of sale, the asset physically changes hands. Revenue is recognized, and the cost of the merchandise transferred is treated as an expense.

A *merchandising firm* purchases inventory and later sells it without changing its physical form. The inventory is shown as an asset stated at acquisition cost on the balance sheet. Later, when the inventory is sold, the same amount of acquisition cost is shown as an expense (cost of merchandise sold) on the income statement.

A *manufacturing firm,* on the other hand, incurs various costs in changing the physical form of the goods it produces. These costs are typically of three types: (1) direct material, (2) direct labor, and (3) manufacturing overhead (sometimes called indirect manufacturing costs). Direct material and direct labor costs can be directly associated with particular products manufactured. Manufacturing overhead includes a mixture of costs which provide a firm with a capacity to produce. Examples of manufacturing overhead costs are expenditures for utilities, property taxes, and insurance on the factory, as well as depreciation on manufacturing plant and equipment. The services of each of these items are used up, or consumed, during the period while the firm is creating new assets, the inventory of goods being worked upon or held for sale. Benefits from direct material, direct labor, and manufacturing overhead are, in a sense, transferred to, or become embodied in, the asset represented by units of inventory. Since the inventory items are assets until sales are made to customers, the various direct material, direct labor, and manufacturing overhead costs incurred in producing the goods are treated as unexpired costs and included in the valuation of the inventory. Such costs, which are assets transformed from one form to another, are called *product costs.* Product costs are assets; they become expenses only when the goods in which they are embodied are sold.

Selling Costs   In most cases, the costs incurred in selling, or marketing, a firm's products relate to the units sold during the period. For example, salaries and commissions of the sales staff, sales literature used, and most advertising costs are incurred in generating revenue currently. Since these selling costs are associated with the revenues of the period, they are reported as expenses in the period when the services provided by the these costs are consumed. It can be argued that some selling costs, such as advertising and other sales promotion, provide future-period benefits for a firm and should continue to be treated as assets. However, distinguishing what portion of the cost relates to the current period to be recognized as an expense and what portion relates to future periods to be treated as an asset can be extremely difficult. Therefore, accountants typically treat selling and other marketing activity costs as expenses of the period when the services are used. These selling costs are treated as *period expenses* rather than as assets, even though they may enhance the future marketability of a firm's products.

Administrative Costs   The costs incurred in administering, or directing, the activities of the firm cannot be closely associated with units produced and sold and are, therefore, like selling costs, treated as period expenses. Examples include the president's salary, accounting and data-processing costs, and the costs of conducting various supportive activities such as legal services and corporate planning.

Summary of Cost Flows   Exhibit 3.3 summarizes the treatment of various costs incurred by a manufacturing firm.

The flow of costs for materials and services through the stages of acquisition, production, and sale can be diagrammed as shown in Figure 3.2.

Measurement of Expenses

Expenses are costs expired, or assets consumed, during the period. The amount of an expense is therefore the amount of the expired asset. Thus, the basis for expense measurement is the same as for asset valuation. Since assets are primarily stated at acquisition cost on the balance sheet, expenses are measured by the acquisition cost of the assets which were either sold or used during the period.

■ SUMMARY

Net income is determined for discrete accounting periods in order to facilitate appraisals of earnings performance among firms and over time for a given firm. Most business firms use the accrual basis of accounting for measuring earnings and financial position. A few firms use the cash basis.

Under the cash basis, revenue is recognized when cash is received, and expenses are reported when cash disbursements for merchandise, salaries, taxes, and similar items are made. The cash basis suffers from two weaknesses: (**1**) it unnecessarily defers the recognition of revenue, and (**2**) it recognizes expenses in periods which may differ from those when economic benefits are received as revenues.

EXHIBIT 3.3
Treatment of Various Costs Incurred by a Manufacturing Firm

Cost Item	Product Cost (Asset)	Period Expense Selling	Period Expense Administrative
I. Salaries			
A. President of Company			X
B. Vice-President for Sales		X	
C. Vice-President for Manufacturing	X		
D. Production Foreman	X		
E. Sales Staff		X	
F. Accountant (general office)			X
II. Materials and Supplies			
A. Raw Materials Purchased for Future Productive Use	X		
B. Raw Materials Used in the Factory	X		
C. Sales Pamphlets Distributed		X	
D. Data-Processing Supplies Used			X
E. Cleaning Supplies Used in Factory	X		
III. Other			
A. Insurance on Factory Building	X		
B. Insurance on Sales Staff's Automobiles		X	
C. Insurance on Office Building			X
D. Depreciation on Factory Equipment	X		
E. Depreciation on General Office Data-Processing Equipment			X
F. Maintenance of Sales Staff's Automobiles		X	

FIGURE 3–2
DIAGRAM OF COST FLOWS

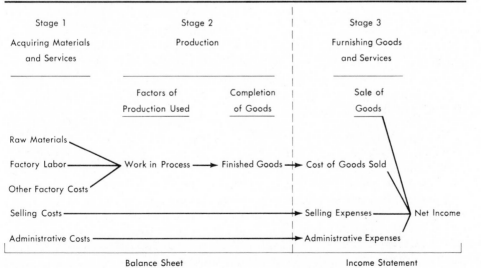

The accrual basis of accounting is not subject to these important weaknesses of the cash basis. Revenue is generally recognized when merchandise is sold or services are rendered to customers. Costs incurred in generating revenues are recognized as expenses of the period in which the associated revenues are recognized. Costs incurred which cannot be closely associated with particular revenue items are treated as expenses of the period in which the services of assets are consumed. Factory costs for labor, material, and overhead, called product costs, do not become expenses until the goods in which these costs are embodied are sold.

Firms involved in selling goods and services under long-term contracts sometimes recognize revenue on a percentage of completion, or production, basis. A portion of the contract price is recognized as revenue for each accounting period during the contract, and an appropriate amount of the costs incurred in generating the revenue is recognized as expense.

When substantial uncertainty exists regarding the amount of cash to be collected from customers for goods sold or services rendered, some firms recognize revenue on a cash collection, or installment, basis. Revenue is recognized when cash is received, and appropriate amounts of the costs incurred are recognized as expenses.

Unless information is provided to the contrary, all illustrations and problems in this book assume that the accrual basis of accounting is used and that revenue is recognized at the time goods are sold or services are rendered.

QUESTIONS AND PROBLEMS

1. Review the meaning of the following concepts or terms discussed in this chapter.
   a. Revenue.
   b. Expense.
   c. Net income.
   d. Loss.
   e. Accounting period.
   f. Natural business year.
   g. Accrual basis of accounting.
   h. Cash basis of accounting.
   i. Percentage-of-completion method.
   j. Completed sales or completed contract method.
   k. Installment method.
   l. Conservatism.
   m. Unexpired cost.
   n. Expired cost.
   o. Product cost.
   p. Period expense.
   q. Matching convention.
   r. Manufacturing overhead.
   s. Flow of costs.
2. What factors give rise to the need for generating accounting information on a time, or accounting period, basis rather than on a project basis?

3. What factors would a firm be likely to consider in its decision to use the calendar year versus a fiscal year as its accounting period?

4. If one of the purposes of the accounting period concept is to elicit more timely information for making comparisons across firms, why is the accounting period not the same for all firms (for example, a year ending on November 30 of each year)?

5. Which of the following types of businesses are likely to have a natural business year?

    a. A ski resort in Colorado.

    b. A major league baseball team.

    c. A radio and television repair firm.

    d. An automobile manufacturer.

6. Conservatism is generally regarded as a convention in accounting. Indicate who might be hurt by conservatively stated accounting reports.

7. What is the significance of complete and incomplete earnings activities in measuring performance?

8. Distinguish between a revenue and a cash receipt. Under what conditions will they be the same?

9. Distinguish between an expense and a cash disbursement. Under what conditions will they be the same?

10. Under the accrual basis of accounting, cash receipts and disbursements may precede, coincide with, or follow the period in which revenues and expenses are recognized. Give an example of each of the following:

    a. A cash receipt which precedes the period in which revenue is recognized.

    b. A cash receipt which coincides with the period in which revenue is recognized.

    c. A cash receipt which follows the period in which revenue is recognized.

    d. A cash disbursement which precedes the period in which expense is recognized.

    e. A cash disbursement which coincides with the period in which expense is recognized.

    f. A cash disbursement which follows the period in which expense is recognized.

11. Assume that the accrual basis of accounting is used and that revenue is recognized at the time goods are sold or services are rendered. How much revenue is recognized during the month of May in each of the following transactions?

    a. Collection of cash from customers during May for merchandise sold and delivered in April, $5,200.

    b. Sales of merchandise during May for cash, $3,600.

    c. Sales of merchandise during May to customers to be collected in June, $5,400.

    d. A store building is rented to a toy shop for $600 a month, effective May 1. A check for $1,200 for 2 months' rent is received on May 1.

    e. Data of **d**, except that collection is received from the tenant in June.

12. Assume that the accrual basis of accounting is used and that revenue is recognized at the time goods are sold or services are rendered. Indicate the amount of expense recognized during March, if any, in each of the following situations:

    a. Rent is paid on March 1, $1,800, for the 3 months starting at that time.

    b. An advance on the April salary is paid to an employee on March 28, $100.

    c. Property taxes on a store building for the year of $1,200 were paid in January.

    d. An employee earned $800 of commissions during March, but has not yet been paid.

    e. The cost of equipment purchased on March 26, to be put into operation on April 1, is $5,000.

f. $800 of supplies were purchased during March. On March 1, supplies were on hand which cost $300. At March 31, supplies which cost $400 were still on hand.

g. Data of **f**, except that $200 of supplies were on hand at March 1.

h. At March 1, the balance in the Prepaid Insurance account was $4,800. The insurance policy had 24 months to run at that time.

13. How would you allocate the cost of the following assets over their useful lives?

   a. A building with an estimated useful life of 30 years.

   b. A road leading to a timber tract. The road would normally last for 14 years before extensive reconstruction would be necessary, but it is expected that the timber will all be cut in 5 years.

   c. Rent prepaid for 2 years on a warehouse in Minneapolis.

   d. A truck with an estimated service life of 90,000 miles.

   e. Rent prepaid for a year on a shop used for boat repairs at a summer resort. The shop is open only from June 1 to September 1.

   f. An ore deposit owned by a mining company.

14. J. Thompson opened a hardware store on January 1, 1976. Thompson invested $5,000 and borrowed $6,000 from the local bank. The loan is repayable on March 31, 1976, with interest at the rate of 8 percent per year.

   Thompson rented a building on January 1, and paid 2 month's rent in advance in the amount of $800. Property and liability insurance coverage for the year ending December 31, 1976, was paid on January 1 in the amount of $600.

   Thompson purchased $20,000 of merchandise inventory on account on January 2 and paid $4,000 of this amount on January 25. The cost of merchandise on hand on January 31 was $12,000.

   During January, cash sales to customers totaled $7,000 and sales on account totaled $3,000. Of the sales on account, $2,000 were collected as of January 31.

   Other costs incurred and paid in cash during January were as follows: utilities, $200; salaries, $650; taxes, $150.

   a. Prepare an income statement for January, assuming that Thompson uses the accrual basis of accounting with revenue recognized at the time goods are sold (delivered).

   b. Prepare an income statement for January, assuming that Thompson uses the cash basis of accounting.

   c. Which basis of accounting do you feel provides a better indication of the operating performance of the hardware store during January? Why?

15. Management Consultants, Inc., opened a consulting business on July 1, 1976. Roy Bean and Sarah Bower each contributed $5,000 cash for shares of the firm's common stock. The corporation borrowed $6,000 from a local bank on August 1, 1976. The loan is repayable on July 31, 1977, with interest at the rate of 10 percent per year.

   Office space was rented on August 1, with 2 months' rent paid in advance. The remaining monthly rental fees of $600 per month were made on the first of each month beginning October 1. Office equipment with a 3-year life was purchased for cash on August 1 for $3,600.

   Consulting services rendered for clients between August 1 and December 31, 1976, were billed at $11,000. Of this amount, $7,000 was collected by year-end.

   Other costs incurred and paid in cash by the end of the year were as follows: utilities, $250; salary of secretary, $5,000; supplies used, $150. Unpaid bills at year-end are as follows: utilities, $50; salary of secretary, $800; supplies used, $40.

a. Prepare an income statement for the 5 months ended December 31, 1976, assuming that the corporation uses the accrual basis of accounting, with revenue recognized at the time services are rendered.

b. Prepare an income statement for the 5 months ended December 31, 1976, assuming that the corporation uses the cash basis of accounting.

c. Which basis of accounting do you feel provides a better indication of operating performance of the consulting firm for the period? Why?

16. Indicate which of the following transactions involve the immediate recognition of revenue under the accrual basis of accounting:

a. The delivery of an issue of a magazine to subscribers.

b. The sale of an automobile by an automobile agency.

c. A collection of cash from accounts receivable debtors.

d. The borrowing of money at a bank.

e. The sale of merchandise on account.

f. The collection of cash by a barber for a haircut.

g. The rendering of dry-cleaning services on account.

h. The issue of shares of preferred stock.

i. The sale of tickets for a concert to be given in 2 weeks.

17. In which of the following situations should there be an immediate recognition of revenue under the accrual basis of accounting?

a. The shipment of goods which have been paid for in advance.

b. The receipt of an order for a carload of merchandise.

c. The interest earned on a savings account between interest payment dates.

d. The issue of additional shares of common stock for cash.

e. The completion of production of a batch of shoes by a shoe factory.

f. The deduction of union dues from an employee's paycheck (from the standpoint of the employer).

g. Transaction f from the standpoint of the union when the dues are received from the employer.

h. The sale of a season ticket to a series of concerts.

18. Three ways of recognizing revenue are as follows:

(1) Recognition of revenue as production is carried on.

(2) Recognition of revenue when goods are furnished or services are rendered to customers.

(3) Recognition of revenue only when payment is collected from customers, if that time differs from (2).

Indicate the method likely to be used by each of the following types of businesses:

a. A drug store.

b. A manufacturer of umbrellas.

c. A bridge-building firm.

d. A real estate developer selling lots on long-term contracts with small down payments.

e. A wholesale tobacco distributor.

f. A dentist.

g. A clothing manufacturer.

h. A shipbuilding firm constructing an aircraft carrier.

i. A shoe store.

j. A citrus-growing firm.

19. Feltham Company acquired used machine tools costing $75,000 from various

sources. These machine tools were then sold to Mock Corporation. Delivery costs paid by Feltham Company totaled $4,500. Mock Corporation had agreed to pay $100,000 cash for these tools. Finding itself short of cash, however, Mock Corporation offered $110,000 of its par-value bonds to Feltham Company. These bonds promised 8 percent interest per year. At the time the offer was made, the bonds could have been sold in public bond markets for $98,000.

Feltham Company accepted the offer and held the bonds for 3 years. During the 3 years, it received interest payments of $8,800 per year, or $26,400 total. At the end of the third year, Feltham Company sold the bonds for $95,000.

a. What profit or loss did Feltham Company recognize on the sale of machine tools to Mock Corporation?

b. What profit or loss would Feltham Company have recognized on the sale of machine tools if it had sold the bonds for $98,000 immediately upon receiving them?

c. What profit or loss would Feltham Company have recognized on the sale of machine tools if it had held the bonds to maturity, receiving $8,800 each year for another 5 years and $110,000 at the time the bonds matured?

20. The Acme Construction Company contracted on May 15, 1976, to build a bridge for the city for $4,500,000. Acme estimated the cost of constructing the bridge would be $3,600,000. Acme incurred $1,200,000 in construction costs during 1976, $2,000,000 during 1977, and $400,000 during 1978 in completing the bridge. The city paid $1,000,000 during 1976, $1,500,000 during 1977, and the remaining $2,000,000 of the contract price at the time the bridge was completed and approved in 1978.

a. Determine the net income (revenues less expenses) of Acme on the contract during 1976, 1977, and 1978, assuming that the percentage-of-completion method is used.

b. Determine the net income of Acme on the contract during 1976, 1977, and 1978, assuming that the completed contract method is used.

c. Which method do you feel provides a better measure of Acme's performance under this contract? Why?

d. Under what circumstances would the method not selected in **c** provide a better measure of performance?

21. Carlson's Department Store had sales to customers during 1976 as follows: cash sales, $400,000; sales on account, $600,000. Based on past experience, Carlson's estimates that .5 percent of goods sold will be returned because of defects. The customers are given full credit for the returned merchandise, and the defective merchandise is scrapped. Carlson's also estimates that 2 percent of all sales on account will never be collected. Under the accrual basis of accounting, how much revenue should Carlson's report for sales during 1976?

22. What is the basic difference between a product cost and a period expense?

23. "It is easy enough to see why material and labor costs become part of the cost of manufactured goods, but it is hard to see why indirect factory costs should be considered a part of production costs, since they do not enter into the products." Comment.

24. Indicate whether each of the following types of wages and salaries are (**1**) product costs or (**2**) period expenses:

a. Cutting-machine operators.

    b. Delivery labor.
    c. Factory janitors.
    d. Factory payroll clerks.
    e. Factory superintendent.
    f. General office secretaries.
    g. Guards at factory gate.
    h. Inspectors in factory.
    i. Maintenance workers who service factory machinery.
    j. Night watch force at the factory.
    k. General office clerks.
    l. Operator of a lift truck in the shipping room.
    m. President of the firm.
    n. Sales manager.
    o. Shipping room workers.
    p. Sweepers who clean retail store.
    q. Traveling salespersons.

25. Indicate whether each of the following types of materials and supplies are (**1**) product costs, or (**2**) period expenses:
    a. Cleaning lubricants for factory machines.
    b. Paper for central office computer.
    c. Glue used in assembling products.
    d. Supplies used by factory janitor.
    e. Gasoline used by salespersons.
    f. Sales promotion pamphlets distributed.
    g. Materials used in training production workers.

26. Indicate whether each of the following costs are (**1**) period expenses, (**2**) product costs, or (**3**) some balance sheet account other than those for product costs.
    a. Office supplies used.
    b. Salary of factory supervisor.
    c. Purchase of a 3-year fire insurance policy on the store building.
    d. Expiration of 1 month's protection of the insurance in **c.**
    e. Property taxes on the factory building.
    f. Wages of truck drivers who deliver finished goods to customers.
    g. Wages of factory workers who install a new machine.
    h. Wages of mechanics who repair and service factory machines.
    i. Salary of the president of the company.
    j. Depreciation of office equipment.
    k. Construction of an addition to the factory building.
    l. Factory supplies used.

27. The Webster Corporation produces a single product at a cost of $5 each, all of which is paid in cash when the unit is produced. Selling costs total $3 a unit and are paid in cash at the time of shipment. The selling price is $10 a unit; all sales are made on account. No uncollectible accounts are expected, and no costs are incurred at the time of collection.

    During 1976, the firm produced 200,000 units, shipped 150,000 units, and collected $1 million from customers. During 1977, the firm produced 125,000 units, shipped 160,000 units and collected $2 million from customers.

    Determine the amount of net income for 1976 and 1977:

a. If revenue and expense are recognized at the time of production.

b. If revenue and expense are recognized at the time of shipment.

c. If revenue and expense are recognized at the time of cash collection.

d. A firm experiencing growth in its sales volume will often produce more units during a particular period than it sells. In this way, inventories can be built up in anticipation of an even larger sales volume during the next period. Under these circumstances, will recognition of revenue and expense at the time of production, shipment, or cash collection generally result in the largest reported net income for the period? Explain.

e. A firm experiencing decreases in its sales volume will often produce fewer units during a period than it sells in an effort to reduce the amount of inventory on hand for next period. Under these circumstances, will recognition of revenue and expense at the time of production, shipment, or cash collection generally result in the largest reported net income for a period? Explain.

Chapter Four

Income Statement—
Accounting Procedures

Chapter Three introduced the important accounting concepts underlying income measurement and reporting. Net income is measured and reported for relatively brief, discrete time periods, such as a quarter or a year, to permit timely disclosure of earnings performance and to facilitate comparisons among firms and for a given firm over time. Net income for most publicly held firms is measured on the accrual, rather than the cash, basis of accounting. Under the accrual basis, revenue is generally recognized in the period when the sale is made or services are rendered. Expenses are recognized in the period when the services of assets have been used up or consumed in generating revenue. An attempt is made to match expenses with the revenues to which they relate. In this chapter, we describe and illustrate the accounting procedures for recording the results of various events and transactions leading to the preparation of the income statement. As was the case in describing the accounting procedures underlying the balance sheet in Chapter Two, our objective is to develop a sufficient understanding of the recording process so that the income statement can then be interpreted and analyzed. We begin by providing an overview of the accounting procedures and then illustrating their application for a merchandising firm. The accounting procedures for a manufacturing firm are discussed in the appendix to this chapter.

■ OVERVIEW OF ACCOUNTING PROCEDURES

Relationship Between Balance Sheet and Income Statement

Net income, or earnings, for a period is measured by the excess of revenues over expenses. Dividends to stockholders may be declared out of earnings of the current year or of prior years. Earnings in excess of dividends declared become a component of the Retained Earnings account on the balance sheet. The following disaggregation of the balance sheet equation helps to show the relation of revenues, expenses, and dividends to the components of the balance sheet.

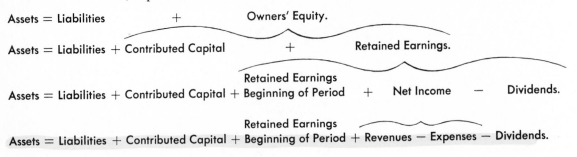

Purpose and Use of Individual Revenue and Expense Accounts

Revenue and expense amounts could be recorded directly in the Retained Earnings account. For example, the sale of merchandise on account results in an increase in assets (accounts receivable) and retained earnings (sales revenue) and a decrease in assets (merchandise inventory) and retained earnings (cost of merchandise sold). Measurement of the *amount* of net income would be relatively simple if revenues and expenses were recorded directly in the Retained Earnings account. Net income would be determined from the following equation:

$$\text{Net Income} = \frac{\text{Retained Earnings}}{\text{End of Period}} - \frac{\text{Retained Earnings}}{\text{Beginning of Period}} + \text{Dividends.}$$

In preparing an income statement, however, we are interested in the components of net income: the sources of revenue and the types of expenses. To facilitate the preparation of the income statement, individual revenue and expense accounts are maintained during the accounting period. These accounts begin the accounting period with a zero balance. During the period, revenues and expenses are recorded in the accounts as they arise. At the end of the period, the balance in each revenue and expense account represents the cumulative revenues and expenses *for the period.* These amounts are reported in the income statement, which shows the net income of the period.

Since revenues and expenses are basically components of retained earnings, the balance in each revenue and expense account is transferred at the end of the period to the Retained Earnings account. Each revenue and expense account will then have a zero balance after the transfer. Retained earnings will be increased (or decreased) by the amount of net income (or net loss) for the period.

The end result of maintaining separate revenue and expense accounts during the period and transferring their balances to the Retained Earnings account at the end of the period is the same as if revenues and expenses were initially recorded directly in the Retained Earnings account. The purpose of using separate revenue and expense accounts is to facilitate the preparation of the income statement in which specific types of revenues and expenses are disclosed. Once this purpose has been served, the usefulness of separate revenue and expense accounts *for a given accounting period* has ended. Having been reduced to a zero balance at the end of the accounting period, these accounts begin the following accounting period with a zero balance and are therefore ready for entry of the revenue and expense amounts of the following period.

The process of transferring the balances in revenue and expense accounts to retained earnings is referred to as the *closing process,* since each revenue and expense account is closed, or reduced to a zero balance. Since revenue and expense accounts accumulate amounts for only a single accounting period, they are called *temporary accounts.* On the other hand, the accounts on the balance sheet reflect the cumulative changes in each account from the time the firm was first organized, and are not closed each period. The balances in these accounts at the end of one period are carried over as the beginning balances of the following period. Balance sheet accounts are called *permanent accounts.*

Debit and Credit Procedures for Revenues, Expenses, and Dividends

Since revenues, expenses, and dividends are components of retained earnings, the recording procedures for these items are the same as for any other transaction affecting equity accounts.

OWNERS' EQUITY

Decreases (Debit)	Increases (Credit)
	Issue of Capital Stock
Expenses Dividends	Revenues

Revenue is a measure of the amount of services rendered. It is reflected in the accounts as an increase in net assets (increase in assets or decrease in liabilities) and an increase in owners' equity. The usual journal entry to record a revenue transaction is therefore:

Asset (A) Increase or Liability (L) Decrease .... Amount
    Revenue (OE) .... Amount
Typical entry to recognize revenue.

Expense is a measure of the net assets used up or consumed in generating revenue. It is reflected in the accounts as a decrease in net assets (decrease in assets or increase in liabilities) and a decrease in owners' equity. The usual journal entry to record an expense is therefore:

Expense (OE) .... Amount
   Asset (A) Decrease or Liability (L) Increase .... Amount
Typical entry to record expense.

Dividends are distributions to owners of assets generated by earnings of the current and prior years. As we will discuss in Chapter Twelve, dividends may be paid either in cash or in other assets. While the accounting procedures for dividends are similar regardless of the form of the distribution, we will assume that cash is used unless information is provided to the contrary. The usual entry to record the declaration of a dividend by the board of directors of a corporation is:

Retained Earnings (OE) .... Amount
   Dividends Payable (L) .... Amount
Typical entry to record dividend declaration.

An alternative method of recording the dividend is to debit an account, Dividends Declared. This temporary account is called an *income distribution* account. At the end of the accounting period, the balance in the Dividends Declared account is closed to the Retained Earnings account, thereby reducing the balance of Retained Earnings. The end result under both procedures is a debit to Retained Earnings and a credit to Dividends Payable for the amount of dividends declared during the period.

When the dividend is paid, the journal entry is:

Dividends Payable (L) .... Amount
   Cash (A) .... Amount
Typical entry to record dividend payment.

A conceptual error sometimes made is that of treating dividends as an expense on the income statement. *Dividends are not expenses*; rather, they represent *distributions of earnings* of the current and prior years to the owners of the firm. They are not costs incurred in *generating* earnings. Because the account, Dividends Declared, is closed in a manner similar to an expense account at the end of the accounting period, the second method of recording the dividend leads some students to regard dividends as expenses. We therefore prefer that dividends declared be debited directly to the Retained Earnings account.

Before illustrating the recording procedures for revenues and expenses, it may be helpful to review briefly the steps in the accounting process.

Review of the Accounting Process

The steps in the accounting process and the purpose of each were discussed in Chapter Two and are summarized as follows:

Journalizing   Each transaction or series of transactions during the period is recorded in journal entry form in the general journal. (In some cases, a specialized journal, such as a cash receipts journal or an accounts payable journal, may also be used.)

Posting   At periodic intervals, the entries in the general journal are posted to the accounts in the general ledger.

Trial Balance   At the end of the accounting period, the balance in each general ledger account is determined and a trial balance is prepared. A trial balance is a listing of all accounts in the general ledger. Accounts with debit balances are totaled separately from accounts with credit balances. If the recording process has been carried out properly, the total amount in accounts having debit balances must equal the total amount in accounts having credit balances.

Adjusting and Correcting Entries   During the period, some accounting events may be only partially recorded, not recorded at all, or recorded incorrectly. Before the financial statements can be prepared at the end of the period, the omissions must be accounted for and the errors corrected. The entries to do this are known as *adjusting* and *correcting* entries. These entries are made so that revenues and expenses are reported in the correct accounts and amounts and so that balance sheet accounts show appropriate amounts of assets and equities at the end of the period.

Closing Entries   The revenue and expense accounts, as well as the Dividend Declared account if used, are closed at the end of the accounting period by transferring the balance in each account to Retained Earnings.

Statement Preparation   The balance sheet, income statement, statement of changes in financial position, and any desired supporting schedules (for example, an analysis of changes in the Cash, Buildings and Equipment, or Retained Earnings accounts) are then prepared.

■ ILLUSTRATION OF THE ACCOUNTING PROCESS FOR A MERCHANDISING FIRM

Stephen's Shoe Store, Inc., has been in business since 1973. A trial balance taken from its general ledger accounts on January 1, 1976, the first day of an accounting period, is shown in Exhibit 4.1.

Note that the revenue and expense accounts are not included in this trial balance; they have zero balances at the beginning of an accounting period. Two of the accounts in the trial balance, Allowance for Uncollectible Accounts and Accumulated Depreciation, have not previously been considered. These accounts are presented on the balance sheet as deductions from Accounts Receivable and from Building and Equipment, respectively. Because of this manner of disclosure, they are referred to as *contra accounts*. A contra account accumulates amounts that are subtracted from the amount in another account. The nature and use of these contra accounts are discussed later in this illustration. An asset contra account is designated XA in the trial balance.

EXHIBIT 4.1
Stephen's Shoe Store, Inc.
Trial Balance
January 1, 1976

	Accounts with Debit Balances	Accounts with Credit Balances
Cash (A)	$ 60,000	
Accounts Receivable (A)	140,000	
Allowance for Uncollectible Accounts (XA)		$ 14,000
Merchandise Inventory (A)	350,000	
Land (A)	200,000	
Building and Equipment (A)	1,050,000	
Accumulated Depreciation (XA)		170,000
Accounts Payable (L)		270,000
Bonds Payable (L)		200,000
Common Stock (OE)		500,000
Additional Paid-in Capital (OE)		400,000
Retained Earnings (OE)		246,000
Total	$1,800,000	$1,800,000

Journalizing

The transactions of Stephen's Shoe Store during 1976 and the appropriate journal entries at the time of the transactions follow.

(1) Merchandise costing $710,000 is purchased on account.

Merchandise Inventory (A)	710,000	
Accounts Payable (L)		710,000

(2) Sales during the year are $1,250,000, of which $450,000 are for cash and the remainder are on account.

Cash (A)	450,000	
Accounts Receivable (A)	800,000	
Sales Revenue (OE)		1,250,000

(3) The cost of merchandise sold during 1976 is $780,000.

Cost of Goods Sold (OE) ..~~Expense Reduction Inventory~~....	780,000	
Merchandise Inventory (A)		780,000

(4) Salaries of $220,000 are paid in cash during the year.

Salaries Expense (OE)	220,000	
Cash (A)		220,000

(5) Customers' accounts of $650,000 are collected.

Cash (A)	650,000	
Accounts Receivable (A)		650,000

(**6**) Payments of $540,000 are made to merchandise suppliers for purchases on account.

Accounts Payable (L)	540,000	
Cash (A)		540,000

(**7**) A premium of $3,000 is paid on January 1, 1976, for a 3-year property and liability insurance policy.

Prepaid Insurance (A)	3,000	
Cash (A)		3,000

The debit in this entry, made on January 1, 1976, is to an asset account, since the insurance provides 3 years of coverage beginning on that date. The entry to reduce the Prepaid Insurance account and to record the insurance expense for 1976 is one of the adjusting entries made at the end of the accounting period.

(**8**) Warehouse space not needed in the company's operations is rented out for one year beginning December 1, 1976. The annual rental of $1,200 is received at that time.

Cash (A)	1,200	
Rental Fees Received in Advance (L)		1,200

(**9**) Annual interest on the long-term bonds outstanding at the rate of 8 percent is paid on December 31, 1976.

Interest Expense (OE)	16,000	
Cash (A)		16,000

(**10**) A 90-day note was received from a customer on December 1, 1976. The note replaced the customer's open account receivable balance of $10,000 arising from an earlier sale. The note bears interest at the rate of 9 percent per year.

Notes Receivable (A)	10,000	
Accounts Receivable (A)		10,000

(**11**) The board of directors declared a cash dividend of $30,000 on December 28, 1976. The dividend is to be paid on January 20, 1977.

Retained Earnings (OE)	30,000	
Dividends Payable (L)		30,000

Posting

The entries in the general journal are posted to the appropriate general ledger accounts. In this illustration, the posting operation takes place on December 31, 1976. The T-accounts in Exhibit 4.2 show the opening balances from the trial balance in Exhibit 4.1 and the effects of transactions (**1**) through (**11**).

EXHIBIT 4.2
Stephen's Shoe Store, Inc.
T-Accounts Showing Beginning and Ending Balances
and Transactions During 1976

CASH (A)

Bal. 1/1	60,000		
(2)	450,000	220,000	(4)
(5)	650,000	540,000	(6)
(8)	1,200	3,000	(7)
		16,000	(9)
Bal. 12/31	382,200		

NOTES RECEIVABLE (A)

Bal. 1/1	0		
(10)	10,000		
Bal. 12/31	10,000		

LAND (A)

Bal. 1/1	200,000		
Bal. 12/31	200,000		

ACCOUNTS RECEIVABLE (A)

Bal. 1/1	140,000		
(2)	800,000	650,000	(5)
		10,000	(10)
Bal. 12/31	280,000		

MERCHANDISE INVENTORY (A)

Bal. 1/1	350,000		
(1)	710,000	780,000	(3)
Bal. 12/31	280,000		

BUILDING AND EQUIPMENT (A)

Bal. 1/1	1,050,000		
Bal. 12/31	1,050,000		

ALLOWANCE FOR UNCOLLECTIBLE ACCOUNTS (XA)

		14,000	Bal. 1/1
		14,000	Bal. 12/31

PREPAID INSURANCE (A)

Bal. 1/1	0		
(7)	3,000		
Bal. 12/31	3,000		

ACCUMULATED DEPRECIATION (XA)

		170,000	Bal. 1/1
		170,000	Bal. 12/31

ACCOUNTS PAYABLE (L)

	270,000 Bal. 1/1
(6) 540,000	710,000 (1)
	440,000 Bal. 12/31

BONDS PAYABLE (L)

	200,000 Bal. 1/1
	200,000 Bal. 12/31

RETAINED EARNINGS (OE)

(11) 30,000	246,000 Bal. 1/1
	216,000 Bal. 12/31

COST OF GOODS SOLD (OE)

Bal. 1/1 0	
(3) 780,000	
Bal. 12/31 780,000	

DIVIDENDS PAYABLE (L)

	0 Bal. 1/1
	30,000 (11)
	30,000 Bal. 12/31

COMMON STOCK (OE)

	500,000 Bal. 1/1
	500,000 Bal. 12/31

SALES REVENUE (OE)

	0 Bal. 1/1
	1,250,000 (2)
	1,250,000 Bal. 12/31

SALARIES EXPENSE (OE)

Bal. 1/1 0	
(4) 220,000	
Bal. 12/31 220,000	

RENTAL FEES RECEIVED IN ADVANCE (L)

	0 Bal. 1/1
	1,200 (8)
	1,200 Bal. 12/31

ADDITIONAL PAID-IN CAPITAL (OE)

	400,000 Bal. 1/1
	400,000 Bal. 12/31

INTEREST EXPENSE (OE)

Bal. 1/1 0	
(9) 16,000	
Bal. 12/31 16,000	

Trial Balance Preparation

The trial balance prepared at the end of the accounting period before adjusting and closing entries is called an *unadjusted trial balance*. The unadjusted trial balance of Stephen's Shoe Store as of December 31, 1976, is shown in Exhibit 4.3. The amounts in the unadjusted trial balance are taken directly from the ending balances in the T-accounts shown in Exhibit 4.2.

EXHIBIT 4.3
Stephen's Shoe Store, Inc.
Unadjusted Trial Balance *same as pre trial balance*
December 31, 1976

	Accounts with Debit Balances	Accounts with Credit Balances
Cash (A)	$ 382,200	
Accounts Receivable (A)	280,000	
Allowance for Uncollectible Accounts (XA)		$ 14,000
Notes Receivable (A)	10,000	
Merchandise Inventory (A)	280,000	
Prepaid Insurance (A)	3,000	
Land (A)	200,000	
Building and Equipment (A)	1,050,000	
Accumulated Depreciation (XA)		170,000
Accounts Payable (L)		440,000
Dividends Payable (L)		30,000
Rental Fees Received in Advance (L)		1,200
Bonds Payable (L)		200,000
Common Stock (OE)		500,000
Additional Paid-in Capital (OE)		400,000
Retained Earnings (OE)		216,000
Sales Revenue (OE)		1,250,000
Cost of Goods Sold (OE)	780,000	
Salaries Expense (OE)	220,000	
Interest Expense (OE)	16,000	
Totals	$3,221,200	$3,221,200

Adjusting and Correcting Entries

The entries in the general journal made during the year result primarily from transactions between the firm and outsiders (for example, suppliers, employees, customers, and governmental units). Other events continually occur, however, for which no specific transaction signals the requirement for a journal entry, but which must be considered in measuring net income for the period and financial position at the end of the period. For example, building and equipment are continually used in the process of generating revenue. Because the services of these assets are consumed during the period, a portion of their acquisition cost must be recorded as an expense. Similarly, insurance coverage expires continually throughout the year. Because the services of the asset are gradually consumed, a portion of the asset, Prepaid Insurance, must be recorded as an expense.

Other kinds of events occur which affect the revenues and expenses of the period but for which a transaction with an outsider will not occur until a subsequent period. For example, salaries and wages are earned by employees during the last several days of the current accounting period, but they will not be paid until the following accounting period. Such salaries and wages, although payable in the next period, are expenses of the current period when the labor services are consumed. Similarly, interest accrues on a firm's notes receivable or payable. Interest will be collected or paid in a subsequent period, but a portion of the interest should be recognized as revenue or expense in the current period.

Adjusting entries are prepared at the end of the accounting period. These entries alter the balances in the general ledger accounts in order to recognize all revenues and expenses for the proper reporting of net income and financial position. Several examples of adjusting entries are illustrated for Stephen's Shoe Store in the following sections.

Recognition of Accrued Revenues and Receivables   Revenue is earned as services are rendered. For example, rent is earned as a tenant uses the property. Interest, a "rent" for the use of money, is earned as time passes on a loan. It is usually not convenient, however, to record these amounts as they accrue day by day. At the end of the accounting period, there may be some situations in which revenue has been earned but for which no entry has been made, either because cash has not been received or the time has not arrived for a formal invoice to be sent to the customer. A claim has come into existence which, although it may not be due immediately, should appear on the balance sheet as an asset and be reflected in the revenues of the period. The purpose of the adjusting entry for interest eventually receivable by the lender is to recognize on the balance sheet the right to receive cash in an amount equal to the interest already earned and to recognize the same amount as revenue on the income statement for the period.

Stephen's Shoe Store received a 90-day note from a customer on December 1, 1976. At year end, the note is included as an asset on the trial balance. Interest earned during December, however, is not reflected in the unadjusted trial balance. The note earns interest at the rate of 9 percent per year. By convention in business practice, interest rates stated on loans are almost always stated as annual interest rates. Also, by convention, a year equal to 360 days is usually assumed to simplify the calculation of interest earned. Interest of $75 is earned by Stephen's Shoe Store during December. This amount is equal to the $10,000 principal times the 9 percent annual interest rate times the elapsed 30 days divided by 360 days ($75 = $10,000 × .09 × 30/360). The adjusting entry to recognize the asset, Interest Receivable, and the interest earned, is:

(12)   Interest Receivable (A)   75
       Interest Revenue (OE)   75

OE = Revenues or Expenses in this book (handwritten margin note)

Recognition of Accrued Expenses and Payables   As various services are received, their cost should be reflected in the financial statements, whether or not payment has been made or an invoice received. Here, also, it is frequently not convenient to record these amounts day by day. It is likely that some adjustment of expenses and liabilities will be necessary at the end of the accounting period.

Salaries and wages earned during the last several days of the accounting period that will not be paid until the following accounting period illustrate this type of adjustment. According to payroll records, employees of Stephen's Shoe Store earned salaries of $12,000 during the last several days of 1976 that were not recorded at year end. The adjusting entry is:

(13)	Salaries Expense (OE)	12,000	
	Salaries Payable (L)		12,000

work done but not paid for yet (handwritten note)

Other examples of this type of adjusting entry include costs incurred for utilities, taxes, and interest.

Allocation of Prepaid Operating Costs   Another type of adjustment arises because assets are acquired for use in the operations of the firm but are not completely used during the accounting period in which they are acquired. For example, Stephen's Shoe Store paid $3,000 on January 1, 1976, for a 3-year insurance policy. During 1976, one-third of the coverage expired, so $1,000 of the premium should be reflected as insurance expense. The balance sheet on December 31, 1976, should show $2,000 of prepaid insurance among the assets, since only this portion of the premium is a future benefit—the asset of insurance coverage to be received over the next 2 years.

The nature of the adjusting entry to record an asset expiration as an expense depends on the recording of the original payment. If the payment resulted in a debit to an asset account, the adjusting entry must reduce the asset and increase the expense for the services used up during the accounting period. Stephen's Shoe Store recorded the payment of the insurance premium on January 1, 1976, as follows:

(7)	Prepaid Insurance (A)	3,000	
	Cash (A)		3,000

The adjusting entry is, therefore,

(14)	Insurance Expense (OE)	1,000	
	Prepaid Insurance (A)		1,000

Insurance expense for 1976 is $1,000, and prepaid insurance in the amount of $2,000 is shown as an asset on the balance sheet on December 31, 1976.

Instead of debiting an asset account at the time the premium is paid, some firms debit an expense account. For example, Stephen's Shoe Store might have recorded the original premium payment as follows:

(7a)	Insurance Expense (OE)	3,000	
	Cash (A)		3,000

Since many operating costs become expenses in the period in which the expenditure is made (for example, monthly rent, office supplies), this second procedure for recording expenditures during the year sometimes reduces the number of adjusting entries which must be made at year-end. In the situation with the insurance policy, however, not all of the $3,000 premium paid is an expense of 1976. If the original journal entry had been (**7a**), the adjusting entry would then be:

(**14a**) Prepaid Insurance (A) 2,000

Insurance Expense (OE) 2,000

After the original entry in (**7a**) and the adjusting entry in (**14a**), insurance expense for 1976 is reflected in the accounts at $1,000, and prepaid insurance at $2,000. The *end result* of these two approaches to recording the original payment of the premium is the same. The *adjusting entries*, however, are quite different.

Recognition of Depreciation   When assets such as buildings, machinery, furniture, and trucks are purchased, their acquisition cost is debited to appropriate asset accounts. Although these assets may provide services for a number of years, eventually their future benefits will expire. Therefore, the portion of an asset's cost which will expire is spread systematically over its estimated useful life. The charge made to the current operations for the portion of the cost of such assets consumed during the current period is called *depreciation* expense. Depreciation involves nothing new in principle; it is identical with the procedure for prepaid operating costs presented previously. For example, the most of a building is a prepayment for a series of future services, and depreciation allocates the cost of the services to the periods in which services are received and used.

Various accounting methods are used in allocating the acquisition cost of long-lived assets to the periods of benefit. One widely used method is the *straight-line method*. Under this procedure, an equal portion of the acquisition cost less estimated salvage value is allocated to each period of the asset's estimated useful life. The depreciation charge for each period is determined as follows:

$$\frac{\text{Acquisition Cost} - \text{Estimated Salvage Value}}{\text{Estimated Useful Life in Periods}} = \frac{\text{Depreciation Charge for}}{\text{Each Period}}$$

Internal records indicate that the Building and Equipment account of Stephen's Shoe Store is composed of a store building with an acquisition cost of $800,000 and a group of items of equipment with an acquisition cost of $250,000. At the time the building was acquired, it had an estimated 40-year useful life and a zero salvage value. Depreciation expense for each year of the building's life is calculated to be

$$\frac{\$800,000 - \$0}{40 \text{ years}} = \$20,000 \text{ per year.}$$

At the time the equipment was acquired, it had an estimated useful life of 6 years and an estimated salvage value of $10,000. Annual depreciation is, therefore,

$$\frac{\$250,000 - \$10,000}{6 \text{ years}} = \$40,000 \text{ per year.}$$

The adjusting entry to record depreciation of $60,000 (= $20,000 + $40,000) for 1976 is:

(15) Depreciation Expense (OE) 60,000
      Accumulated Depreciation (XA)   60,000

The credit in entry (15) could have been made directly to the Building and Equipment account, because the credit records the portion of the asset's cost which has expired, or become an expense, during 1976. The same end result is achieved by crediting the Accumulated Depreciation account, a contra-asset account, and then deducting the balance in this account from the acquisition cost of the assets in the Building and Equipment account on the balance sheet. Using the contra account enables the financial statements to show both the acquisition cost of the assets in use and the portion of that amount which has previously been recognized as an expense. Showing both acquisition cost and accumulated depreciation amounts separately provides a rough indication of the relative age of the firm's long-lived assets.

Note that the Depreciation Expense account includes only depreciation for the current accounting period, while the Accumulated Depreciation account reflects the cumulative depreciation charges on the present assets since acquisition. The Accumulated Depreciation account is sometimes referred to as Allowance for Depreciation.

Valuation of Accounts Receivable   When sales are made to customers on account, it is usually expected that some of the accounts will not be collected. In Chapter Three, we indicated that the primary objective in accounting for uncollectible accounts is to ensure that sales revenue of the period reflects only the amount of cash expected to be collected. That is, adjustments for anticipated uncollectible accounts should be charged against sales revenue *in the period of the sale*. The principal accounting problem here arises from the fact that individual accounts may not be judged uncollectible until some time after the period of sale. An estimate of the probable amount of uncollectible accounts must therefore be made in the period of sale.

Based on past experience, Stephen's Shoe Store estimates that 2 percent of sales on account during the year will ultimately become uncollectible. Since sales on account during 1976 were $800,000, the adjusting entry to provide for estimated uncollectible accounts of $16,000 (= .02 × $800,000) is:

      BAD DEBT EXPENSE
(16) Sales, Uncollectible Accounts Adjustment (OE) 16,000
      Allowance for Uncollectible Accounts (XA)   16,000

The debit entry is to an income statement account. Since revenue should be stated at the amount expected to be collected in cash, the amount in this account is preferably deducted from sales revenue on the income statement as a contra amount. Some firms, however, debit an expense account, such as Bad Debt Expense or Uncollectible Accounts Expense, which is included in the expense section rather than the revenue section of the income statement. The effect on net income is the same in either case.

The credit entry to recognize estimated uncollectible accounts is to a balance sheet account which is shown as a contra to Accounts Receivable. The net amount, accounts receivable less estimated uncollectibles, indicates the amount of cash expected to be collected from customers. Using the contra account permits the disclosure of the total receivables outstanding as well as the estimated amount that will be collected.

At periodic intervals, individual customers' accounts are reviewed to assess their collectibility. Accounts deemed to be uncollectible are eliminated or "written off." Stephen's Shoe Store determined on December 31, 1976, that specific customer's accounts totaling $15,000 would never be collected. This total represented $13,000 from sales made prior to 1976 and $2,000 from sales during 1976. The adjusting entry to write off these individual accounts is:

(17)	Allowance for Uncollectible Accounts (XA)	15,000
	Accounts Receivable (A)	15,000

Note that net income is not affected by the write-off of the specific customers' accounts. Net income is affected in the period of sale when a provision is made for uncollectible accounts [for example, entry (**16**) and similar entries made in prior years]. At the beginning of 1976, the Allowance for Uncollectibles account had a balance of $14,000. This balance resulted from making provisions for uncollectible accounts in prior years. When the $13,000 of specific customers' accounts arising from prior years' sales is written off at the end of 1976, there is no additional effect on net income. Also note that the amount, accounts receivable less estimated uncollectibles, on the balance sheet is not affected by the write-off, since both the asset and contra asset are reduced by an equal amount. We consider further the accounting treatment of uncollectible accounts in Chapter Eight.

Valuation of Liabilities   When cash is received from customers before merchandise is sold or services are rendered, the cash receipt creates a liability. For example, Stephen's Shoe Store received $1,200 on December 1, 1976, as 1 year's rent on warehouse space. When the cash was received, the liability account, Rental Fees Received in Advance, was credited. One month's rent has been earned as of December 31, 1976. The adjusting entry is:

(18)	Rental Fees Received in Advance (L)	100
	Rent Revenue (OE)	100

The remaining $1,100 of the advance rental is yet to be earned and is carried on the December 31, 1976, balance sheet as a liability.

Correction of Errors   Various errors and omissions may be discovered at the end of the accounting period as the process of checking, reviewing, and auditing is carried out. For example, the sales for one month during the year might have been recorded as $38,700 instead of $37,800. Or the sale to a specific customer might not have been recorded. Entries must be made at the end of the accounting period to correct for these errors. There were no such errors in the accounts of Stephen's Shoe Store.

Trial Balance After Adjusting Entries The adjusting entries are posted or entered in the general ledger in the same manner as entries made during the year. A trial balance of the general ledger accounts after adjusting entries are made could be prepared. Such a trial balance is called an *adjusted trial balance* and is useful in preparing the financial statements. Exhibit 4.4 presents the trial balance data before and after adjusting entries for Stephen's Shoe Store. The exhibit indicates the effect of the adjustment process on the various accounts. The number in parentheses identifies the debit and credit components of each adjusting entry.

Closing of Temporary Accounts

The purpose of the closing process is to transfer the balances in the temporary revenue and expense accounts (and income distribution accounts, if any) to retained earnings. Temporary accounts with debit balances are closed by crediting each such account in an amount equal to its balance at the end of the period and debiting Retained Earnings. The usual closing entry for temporary accounts with debit balances is:

Retained Earnings (OE)	X	
Accounts with Debit Balances (OE) (specific account titles)		X

Temporary accounts with credit balances are closed by debiting the temporary account and crediting Retained Earnings. The usual closing entry for temporary accounts with credit balances is:

Accounts with Credit Balances (OE) (specific account titles)	X	
Retained Earnings (OE)		X

After closing entries, the balances in all temporary accounts are zero. The former debit (credit) balances in temporary accounts become debits (credits) in the Retained Earnings account.

Each temporary revenue and expense account could be closed by a separate entry. Some recording time is saved, however, by closing all revenue and expense accounts in a single entry as follows:

(19) Sales Revenue (OE)	1,250,000	
Interest Revenue (OE)	75	
Rent Revenue (OE)	100	
Cost of Goods Sold (OE)		780,000
Salaries Expense (OE)		232,000
Interest Expense (OE)		16,000
Insurance Expense (OE)		1,000
Depreciation Expense (OE)		60,000
Sales, Uncollectible Accounts Adjustment (OE)		16,000
Retained Earnings (OE)		145,175

EXHIBIT 4.4
Stephen's Shoe Store, Inc.
Trial Balance Before and After Adjusting Entries[a]
December 31, 1976

Accounts	Unadjusted Trial Balance		Adjusting Entries		Adjusted Trial Balance	
	Debit	Credit	Debit	Credit	Debit	Credit
Cash (A)	$ 382,200				$ 382,200	
Accounts Receivable (A) . . .	280,000			$ 15,000 (17)	265,000	
Allowance for Uncollectible Accounts (XA)		$ 14,000	$ 15,000 (17)	16,000 (16)		$ 15,000
Notes Receivable (A)	10,000				10,000	
Interest Receivable (A)			75 (12)		75	
Merchandise Inventory (A) .	280,000				280,000	
Prepaid Insurance (A)	3,000			1,000 (14)	2,000	
Land (A)	200,000				200,000	
Building and Equipment (A)	1,050,000				1,050,000	
Accumulated Depreciation (XA)		170,000		60,000 (15)		230,000
Accounts Payable (L)		440,000				440,000
Salaries Payable (L)				12,000 (13)		12,000
Dividends Payable (L)		30,000				30,000
Rental Fees Received in Advance (L)		1,200	100 (18)			1,100
Bonds Payable		200,000				200,000
Common Stock (OE)		500,000				500,000
Additional Paid-In Capital (OE)		400,000				400,000
Retained Earnings (OE) . . .		216,000				216,000
Sales Revenue (OE)		1,250,000				1,250,000
Interest Revenue (OE)				75 (12)		75
Rent Revenue (OE)				100 (18)		100
Cost of Goods Sold (OE) . .	780,000				780,000	
Salaries Expense (OE)	220,000		12,000 (13)		232,000	
Interest Expense (OE)	16,000				16,000	
Insurance Expense (OE) . . .			1,000 (14)		1,000	
Depreciation Expense (OE) .			60,000 (15)		60,000	
Sales, Uncollectible Accounts Adjustment (OE)			16,000 (16)		16,000	
Totals	$3,221,200	$3,221,200	$104,175	$104,175	$3,294,275	$3,294,275

[a] This convenient tabular form is often called a *work sheet*. Most work sheets are more elaborate than this one, but their purpose is the same—to display data in a form for easy computations and financial statement preparation. The typical work sheet would not show just two final columns called Adjusted Trial Balance, but would show four columns: Income Statement Debit and Credit, and Balance Sheet Debit and Credit. The horizontal sum of the amounts in an income account is shown in the appropriate debit or credit income statement column of the work sheet. The horizontal sum of the amounts in a balance sheet account is shown in the appropriate debit or credit balance sheet column of the work sheet. See the glossary at *work sheet* for an example.

The amount credited to Retained Earnings is the difference between the amounts debited to revenue accounts and the amounts credited to expense and sales adjustments accounts. This amount is the net income for the period.[1]

An alternative closing procedure uses a temporary "Income Summary" account. Individual revenue and expense accounts are first closed to the Income Summary account. The income statement is prepared using information on the individual revenues and expenses in the Income Summary account. The balance in the Income Summary account, representing net income for the period, is then closed to Retained Earnings.

For example, the entry to close the Sales Revenue account under this alternative procedure is

(19a) Sales Revenue (OE) 1,250,000
       Income Summary (OE)   1,250,000

The entry to close the Cost of Goods Sold account is

(19b) Income Summary (OE) 780,000
       Cost of Goods Sold (OE)   780,000

Similar closing entries are made for the other revenue and expense accounts. The Income Summary account will have a credit balance of $145,175 after all revenue and expense accounts have been closed. The balance in the Income Summary account is then transferred to Retained Earnings:

(19c) Income Summary (OE) 145,175
       Retained Earnings (OE)   145,175

The end result of both closing procedures is the same. Revenue and expense accounts, as well as the Income Summary account if one is used, have zero balances after closing entries, and the Retained Earnings account is increased by the net income for the period of $145,175. Exhibit 4.5 shows the Income Summary account for Stephen's Shoe Store after all revenue and expense accounts have been closed at the end of the period.

Financial Statement Preparation

The income statement, balance sheet, and any desired supporting schedules can be prepared from information in the adjusted trial balance. The income statement of Stephen's Shoe Store for 1976 is presented in Exhibit 4.6. The com-

---

[1] The amount credited to Retained Earnings in the closing entry is called a *plug*. When making some journal entries in accounting, often all debits are known, as are all but one of the credits (or vice versa). Since the double-entry recording procedure requires equal debits and credits, the unknown quantity can be found by subtracting the sum of the known credits from the sum of all debits (or vice versa). This process is known as *plugging*.

EXHIBIT 4.5
Illustration of Income Summary Account for Stephen's Shoe Store, Inc.

INCOME SUMMARY ACCOUNT (OE)				RETAINED EARNINGS (OE)	
Cost of Goods Sold	780,000	1,250,000 Sales Revenue			246,000 Beginning
Salaries Expense	232,000	75 Interest Revenue			Balance
Interest Expense	16,000	100 Rent Revenue	Dividends 30,000		145,175 Net Income
Insurance Expense	1,000	1,250,175			361,175 Ending
Depreciation Expense	60,000				Balance
Sales, Uncollectible					
Accounts Adjustment	16,000				
To Close Income Summary					
Account	145,175				
	1,250,175				

EXHIBIT 4.6
Stephen's Shoe Store, Inc.
Income Statement
For the Year Ending December 31, 1976

Revenues:

Sales Revenue		$1,250,000	
Less Sales, Uncollectible Accounts Adjustment		16,000	
Net Sales Revenue		$1,234,000	
Interest Revenue		75	
Rent Revenue		100	
Total Revenues			$1,234,175

Less Expenses:

Cost of Goods Sold		$ 780,000	
Salaries Expense		232,000	
Interest Expense		16,000	
Insurance Expense		1,000	
Depreciation Expense		60,000	
Total Expenses			1,089,000
Net Income			$ 145,175

parative balance sheets for December 31, 1975 and 1976, are presented in Exhibit 4.7. An analysis of changes in retained earnings is presented in Exhibit 4.8.

■ SUMMARY

Measurement of net income *for the period* and of financial position *at the end of the period* are closely related. Revenues result from selling goods or rendering

EXHIBIT 4.7
Stephen's Shoe Store, Inc.
Comparative Balance Sheet
December 31, 1975 and 1976

ASSETS

Current Assets:	December 31, 1975		December 31, 1976	
Cash		$ 60,000		$ 382,200
Accounts Receivable	$ 140,000		$ 265,000	
Less: Allowance for Uncollectible Accounts	14,000		15,000	
Accounts Receivable—net		126,000		250,000
Notes Receivable		—		10,000
Interest Receivable		—		75
Merchandise Inventory		350,000		280,000
Prepaid Insurance		—		2,000
Total Current Assets		$ 536,000		$ 924,275
Noncurrent Assets:				
Land		$ 200,000		$ 200,000
Building and Equipment—at acquisition cost	$1,050,000		$1,050,000	
Less: Accumulated Depreciation	170,000		230,000	
Building and Equipment—net		880,000		820,000
Total Noncurrent Assets		$1,080,000		$1,020,000
Total Assets		$1,616,000		$1,944,275

LIABILITIES AND STOCKHOLDERS' EQUITY

Current Liabilities:				
Accounts Payable		$ 270,000		$ 440,000
Salaries Payable		—		12,000
Dividends Payable		—		30,000
Rental Fees Received in Advance		—		1,100
Total Current Liabilities		$ 270,000		$ 483,100
Noncurrent Liabilities:				
Bonds Payable		200,000		200,000
Total Liabilities		$ 470,000		$ 683,100
Stockholders' Equity:				
Common Stock—at par value		$ 500,000		$ 500,000
Additional Paid-in Capital		400,000		400,000
Retained Earnings		246,000		361,175
Total Stockholders' Equity		$1,146,000		$1,261,175
Total Liabilities and Stockholders' Equity.		$1,616,000		$1,944,275

EXHIBIT 4.8
Stephen's Shoe Store, Inc.
Analysis of Changes in Retained Earnings
For the Year Ending December 31, 1976

Retained Earnings, December 31, 1975		$246,000
Net Income	$145,175	
Less Dividends	30,000	
Increase in Retained Earnings		115,175
Retained Earnings, December 31, 1976		$361,175

services to customers and lead to increases in assets or decreases in liabilities. Expenses indicate that services have been consumed in generating revenue and result in decreases in assets or increases in liabilities. Since revenues represent provisional increases in owners' equity, revenue transactions are recorded by crediting (increasing) an owners' equity account for the specific type of revenue and by debiting either an asset or liability account. Expenses represent provisional decreases in owners' equity and are recorded by debiting (decreasing) an owners' equity account for the specific type of expense and crediting either an asset or a liability account. After the revenue and expense accounts have accumulated the revenues earned and expenses recognized during the period, the balances in these temporary accounts are transferred, or closed, to the Retained Earnings account at the end of the period.

Some events will not be recorded as part of the regular day-to-day recording process during the period because no explicit transaction between the firm and some external party (such as a customer, creditor, or governmental unit) has taken place to signal the requirement for a journal entry. Such events require an adjusting entry at the end of the period so that periodic income and financial position can be properly determined on an accrual basis.

Appendix 4.1
The Accounting Process for a Manufacturing Firm

The principal difference between accounting for merchandising and for manufacturing firms is the treatment of inventories. As discussed in Chapter Three, a merchandising firm acquires inventory items in finished form ready for sale. The acquisition cost of these items is reflected in the asset account, Merchandise Inventory, until the units are sold. At the time of sale, the cost of the items sold is transferred from the asset account, Merchandise Inventory, to the expense account, Cost of Goods Sold.

A manufacturing firm, on the other hand, incurs various costs in transforming raw materials into finished products. These manufacturing costs are generally classified as direct material (or raw material), direct labor, and manufacturing overhead. Until the units being produced are sold, manufacturing costs are treated as product costs—assets—and accumulated in various inventory accounts.

Separate inventory accounts are used for items at various stages of completion. The Raw Materials Inventory account includes the cost of raw materials purchased but not yet transferred to production. The balance in the Raw Materials Inventory account indicates the cost of raw materials which should be on hand in the raw materials storeroom or warehouse. When raw materials are issued to producing departments, the cost of the materials is transferred from the Raw Materials Inventory account to the Work in Process Inventory account. The Work in Process Inventory account accumulates the costs incurred in producing units during the period. The Work in Process Inventory account is debited for the cost of raw materials transferred from the raw materials storeroom, the cost of direct labor services used, and the manufacturing overhead costs incurred (for example, factory utilities, taxes, insurance, and depreciation). The Work in Process Inventory account is credited for the total manufacturing cost of units completed in the factory and transferred to the finished goods storeroom. The finished Goods Inventory account includes the total manufacturing cost of units completed but not yet sold. At the time of sale, the cost of units sold is transferred from the Finished Goods Inventory account to the Cost of Goods Sold account. This flow of manufacturing costs through the various inventory accounts is summarized in Exhibit 4.9.

Illustration of the Accounting Process for a Manufacturing Firm

The accounting process for a manufacturing firm is illustrated with information about the operations of the Moon Manufacturing Company. The Company was formed on December 31, 1975, with the issuance of 10,000 shares of $10 par value common stock for $30 per share. The firm began business on January 1, 1976. Transactions during January 1976 are described below, and the appropriate journal entries are provided:

(1) A building costing $200,000 and equipment costing $50,000 are acquired for cash.

Building (A)	200,000	
Equipment (A)	50,000	
Cash (A)		250,000

(2) Raw materials costing $25,000 are purchased on account.

Raw Materials Inventory (A)	25,000	
Accounts Payable (L)		25,000

EXHIBIT 4.9
Flow of Manufacturing Costs Through the Accounts

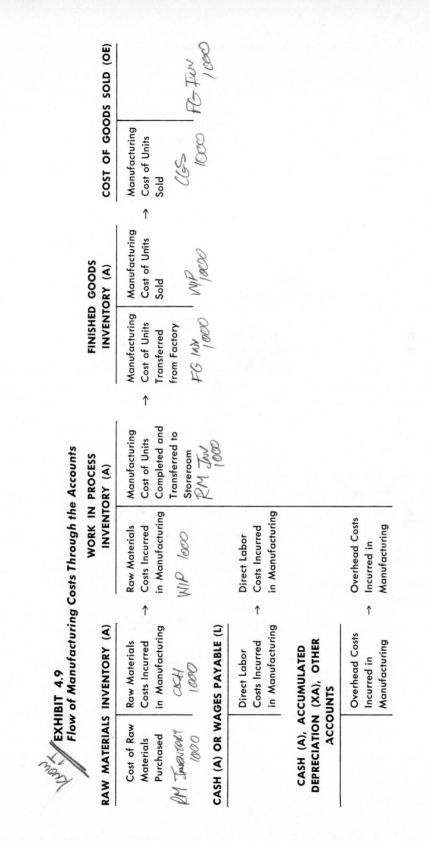

RAW MATERIALS INVENTORY (A)

Cost of Raw Materials Purchased	Raw Materials Costs Incurred in Manufacturing
RM Inventory 1000	CASH 1000

→

WORK IN PROCESS INVENTORY (A)

Raw Materials Costs Incurred in Manufacturing	Manufacturing Cost of Units Completed and Transferred to Storeroom
WIP 1000	RM Inv 1000
Direct Labor Costs Incurred in Manufacturing	
Overhead Costs Incurred in Manufacturing	

→

FINISHED GOODS INVENTORY (A)

Manufacturing Cost of Units Transferred from Factory	Manufacturing Cost of Units Sold
FG Inv 1000	WIP 1000

→

COST OF GOODS SOLD (OE)

Manufacturing Cost of Units Sold	
CGS 1000	FG Inv 1000

CASH (A) OR WAGES PAYABLE (L)

	Direct Labor Costs Incurred in Manufacturing

CASH (A), ACCUMULATED DEPRECIATION (XA), OTHER ACCOUNTS

	Overhead Costs Incurred in Manufacturing

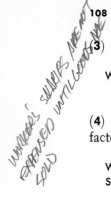

(3) Raw materials costing $20,000 are issued to producing departments.

Work in Process Inventory (A)	20,000	
Raw Materials Inventory (A)		20,000

(4) The total payroll for January is $60,000. Of this amount, $40,000 is paid to factory workers, and $20,000 is paid to selling and administrative personnel.

Work in Process Inventory (A)	40,000	
Salaries Expense (OE)	20,000	
Cash (A)		60,000

Recall from Chapter Three that nonmanufacturing costs are recorded as expenses of the period in which the services are consumed, since these costs rarely create assets with future benefits. Journal entry (4) illustrates the difference between the recording of a product cost and a period expense.

(5) The expenditures for utilities during January are $1,200. Of this amount, $1,000 is attributable to manufacturing, and $200 to selling and administrative activities.

Work in Process Inventory (A)	1,000	
Utilities Expense (OE)	200	
Cash (A)		1,200

(6) Depreciation on building and equipment during January is as follows: factory, $8,000; selling and administrative, $2,000.

Work in Process Inventory (A)	8,000	
Depreciation Expense (OE)	2,000	
Accumulated Depreciation (XA)		10,000

(7) The manufacturing cost of units completed during January and transferred to the finished goods storeroom is $48,500.

Finished Goods Inventory (A)	48,500	
Work in Process Inventory (A)		48,500

(8) Sales during January total $75,000, of which $25,000 is on account.

Cash (A)	50,000	
Accounts Receivable (A)	25,000	
Sales Revenue (OE)		75,000

(9) The manufacturing cost of the goods sold during January is $42,600.

Cost of Goods Sold (OE)	42,600	
Finished Goods Inventory (A)		42,600

EXHIBIT 4.10
Moon Manufacturing Company
T-Accounts Showing Transactions During 1976

RAW MATERIALS INVENTORY (A)

(2)	25,000	20,000	(3)
Bal. 12/31	5,000		

WORK IN PROCESS INVENTORY (A)

(3)	20,000	48,500	(7)
(4)	40,000		
(5)	1,000		
(6)	8,000		
Bal. 12/31	20,500		

FINISHED GOODS INVENTORY (A)

(7)	48,500	42,600	(9)
Bal. 12/31	5,900		

COST OF GOODS SOLD (OE)

(9)	42,600	
Bal. 12/31	42,600	

CASH (A)

Bal. 1/1	300,000	250,000	(1)
(8)	50,000	60,000	(4)
		1,200	(5)
Bal. 12/31	38,800		

ACCOUNTS RECEIVABLE (A)

(8)	25,000	
Bal. 12/31	25,000	

BUILDING (A)

(1)	200,000
Bal. 12/31	200,000

EQUIPMENT (A)

(1)	50,000	
Bal. 12/31	50,000	

ACCUMULATED DEPRECIATION (XA)

	10,000	(6)
	10,000	Bal. 12/31

SALARIES EXPENSE (OE)

(4)	20,000	
Bal. 12/31	20,000	

SALES REVENUE (OE)

	75,000	(8)
	75,000	Bal. 12/31

ACCOUNTS PAYABLE (L)

	25,000	(2)
	25,000	Bal. 12/31

UTILITIES EXPENSE (OE)

(5)	200	
Bal. 12/31	200	

DEPRECIATION EXPENSE (OE)

(6)	2,000	
Bal. 12/31	2,000	

EXHIBIT 4.11
Moon Manufacturing Company
Income Statement
For the Month of January 1976

Sales Revenue		$75,000
Less Expenses:		
Cost of Goods Sold	$42,600	
Salaries Expense	20,000	
Utilities Expense	200	
Depreciation Expense	2,000	
Total Expenses		64,800
Net Income		$10,200

The manner in which the various costs incurred flow through the accounts may be further illustrated by entering these journal entries in T-accounts as shown in Exhibit 4.10.

Exhibit 4.11 presents an income statement for Moon Manufacturing Company for January 1976.

Summary of the Accounting for Manufacturing Operations

The accounting procedures for the selling and administrative costs of manufacturing and merchandising firms are quite similar. These costs are treated as expenses of the period in which services are consumed. The accounting procedures for a manufacturing firm differ from those of a merchandising firm primarily in the treatment of inventories. A manufacturing firm incurs various costs in transforming raw materials into finished products. Until the units produced are sold, manufacturing costs are accumulated in inventory accounts—the Work in Process account or the Finished Goods Inventory account—depending on the stage of completion of each unit being produced. Product costs are therefore debited to inventory (asset) accounts until the time of sale.

QUESTIONS AND PROBLEMS

1. Review the meaning of the following concepts or terms discussed in this chapter:
   a. Revenue.
   b. Expense.
   c. Expense versus dividend.
   d. Temporary and permanent accounts.

    e. General journal entries.

    f. Adjusting entries.

    g. Closing entries.

    h. Unadjusted trial balance.

    i. Adjusted trial balance.

    j. Contra account.

    k. Accrual basis of accounting.

    l. Merchandise inventory.

    m. Raw materials inventory.

    n. Work in process inventory.

    o. Finished goods inventory.

    p. "Flow of costs."

    q. Work sheet.

2. "Revenue and expense accounts are useful accounting devices, but they could be dispensed with." What is an alternative to using them?

3. After the books have been closed, what classes of accounts will have zero balances? What classes of accounts will have nonzero balances?

4. "Despite the earnings of substantial amounts of revenue during the period, retained earnings decreased instead of increased." Explain.

5. What is the purpose of using contra accounts? What is the alternative to using them?

6. For each of the contra accounts listed below, indicate the principal account to which it is a contra:

    a. Accumulated Depreciation—Equipment.

    b. Sales, Uncollectible Accounts Adjustment.

    c. Allowance for Depreciation—Building.

    d. Allowance for Uncollectible Accounts.

7. **a.** Machine A costs $10,000, has accumulated depreciation of $4,000 as of year-end, and is being depreciated on a straight-line basis over 10 years with an estimated salvage value of zero. How old is Machine A as of year-end?

    b. Machine B has accumulated depreciation (straight-line basis) of $6,000 at year-end. The depreciation charge for the year is $2,000. The estimated salvage value of the machine at the end of its useful life is zero. How old is Machine B as of year-end?

8. Various types of adjusting entries are made at the end of each accounting period. Describe a situation and give the appropriate journal entry for each of the following types of adjustments.

    a. An asset account is debited and a revenue account is credited.

    b. A liability account is debited and a revenue account is credited.

    c. An expense account is debited and an asset account is credited.

    d. An expense account is debited and an asset contra account is credited.

    e. An expense account is debited and a liability account is credited.

    f. A revenue contra account is debited and an asset contra account is credited.

9. The particular time when various events and transactions are recorded in the accounts is often a matter of clerical efficiency. For each of the items below, describe the likely entry during each month and the adjusting entry at the end of each month, assuming that financial statements are prepared monthly.

a. The rental on buildings and equipment of $600 is paid in advance at the beginning of each month.

b. Property taxes for the calendar year of $3,600 are paid on July 1.

c. Selling and office supplies, $375, are purchased once each month but used each day in small amounts.

10. Determine the missing items in each of the independent cases below:

	a	b	c	d
Retained Earnings, January 1, 1976	$ 25,000	?	$875,000	$945,000
Retained Earnings, December 31, 1976	?	$520,000	805,000	985,000
Revenues—1976	220,000	?	460,000	680,000
Expenses—1976	165,000	480,000	?	640,000
Net Income—1976	?	355,000	?	?
Dividends—1976	20,000	75,000	5,000	?

11. Determine the missing items in each of the independent cases below:

	a	b	c	d
Stockholders' Equity January 1, 1976	?	$56,400	$21,400	$34,700
Stockholders' Equity December 31, 1976	$159,600	?	30,150	37,500
Stock Issued in 1976	18,600	15,000	0	2,500
Dividends in 1976	5,000	21,000	?	2,100
Net Income (Loss) in 1976	(7,200)	26,100	9,300	?

12. Give the journal entry that should be made upon receipt of each of the following invoices by Jake's Department Store, assuming that no previous entry has been made:

(1) The United Textile Mills, for a shipment received of women's hosiery, $3,500.

(2) Jones' Garage, for repair and servicing of a delivery truck, $180.

(3) The Manna Furniture Company, for a desk received which is to be used in the merchandise manager's office, $540.

(4) The *Daily News*, for newspaper advertising during the past month, $360.

(5) City Electricity Department, for electricity used during the past month, $68.

(6) The *Merchandise Record*, for a subscription to a trade publication which the firm has been receiving for several years. The invoice for $36 covers the 1-year period beginning next month.

(7) General Elevator Company, for a newly installed elevator, $125,000.

13. The following adjusted trial balance shows the balances in the accounts of the Luxury Place, an apartment house, after recording all of the transactions of January 1976.

Luxury Place
Adjusted Trial Balance
January 31, 1976

Accounts Payable		$ 8,508
Accumulated Depreciation		300,000
Advances by Tenants		11,400
Building	$1,800,000	
Capital Stock		1,800,000
Cash in Bank	9,600	
Cash on Hand	1,200	
Depreciation Expense	7,800	
Equipment	540,000	
Insurance Expense	900	
Land	48,000	
Prepaid Insurance	900	
Rent Receivable	8,400	
Rent Revenue		43,800
Repair Expense	2,700	
Retained Earnings		272,592
Supplies Expense	1,200	
Supplies on Hand	1,200	
Taxes Expense	3,900	
Wages Expense	10,500	
	$2,436,300	$2,436,300

a. Present the journal entry to close the revenue and expense accounts directly to Retained Earnings as of January 31, 1976.

b. Set up in T-account form the revenue, expense, and retained earnings accounts. Insert the trial balance amounts and record the closing entry from **a**.

14. Bill Wilson operates a restaurant which he has rented fully equipped from its owner. The trial balance of the restaurant on November 1, 1976, the first day of an accounting period, is as follows:

Cash on Hand	$ 675	
Cash in Bank	6,300	
Food on Hand	5,400	
Accounts Payable, Barry Meat Company		$ 2,050
Accounts Payable, Conell Wholesale Grocery		2,378
Bill Wilson, Capital		7,947
	$12,375	$12,375

A summary of the transactions for the month of November is as follows:
(1) Cash received for meals served, $26,550.
(2) Cash deposited in the bank, $26,100.
(3) November rent paid by check, $4,050.
(4) Food purchased on account from the Conell Wholesale Grocery, $7,650.
(5) Repairs to equipment paid from cash on hand, $450.

(**6**) Food purchased on account from the Barry Meat Company, $4,725.

(**7**) Payment to Barry Meat Company by check, $5,650.

(**8**) Payment to Conell Wholesale Grocery by check, $8,228.

(**9**) Salaries for the month totaling $6,273 are paid by check.

(**10**) Cost of food used, $11,925.

  a. Open T-accounts for the accounts in the trial balance and enter the beginning balances. Record the transactions for the month of November in the T-accounts, opening additional T-accounts for individual revenues and expenses as needed.

  b. Prepare an adjusted, preclosing trial balance to check the accuracy of your entries.

15. A corporation known as the Stevens Collection Agency is organized by Betty Stevens and Charles Kirby on January 1, 1976. The business of the firm is to collect overdue accounts receivable of various clients on a commission basis. The following transactions occurred during January:

(**1**) Stevens contributes office supplies worth $2,000 and cash of $13,000. She is issued stock certificates for 500 shares with a par value of $30 a share.

(**2**) Kirby contributes $2,000 in cash and office equipment valued at $10,000. He is issued stock certificates for 400 shares.

(**3**) Cash, in the amount of $9,500, is deposited in the bank.

(**4**) The Stevens agency collects $800 on an account which was turned over to it by the Giggly Market. The commission earned is 50 percent of the amount collected.

(**5**) The cash collected in (**4**) is deposited in the bank.

(**6**) The stenographer's salary during the month is paid by check, $700.

(**7**) A bill is received from Lyband and Linn, certified public accountants, for $300 to cover the cost of installing an accounting system.

(**8**) The amount due the Giggly Market [see (**4**)] is paid by check.

(**9**) An office is leased for the year beginning February 1, 1976, and the rent for 3 months is paid in advance. A check is drawn for $1,200.

(**10**) An automobile is purchased for $3,500; $2,500 is paid by check, and an installment contract, payable to the Scotch Automobile Sales Company, is signed for the balance.

  a. Open T-accounts and record the transactions during January.

  b. Prepare an adjusted, preclosing trial balance as of January 31, 1976. Indicate, by an **R** or **E**, accounts which are revenue or expense accounts.

16. The balance sheet accounts of Blake's Radio Shop at July 1, 1976, are as follows:

Cash on Hand	$ 50	
Cash in Bank	1,670	
Repair Parts on Hand	600	
Office Supplies on Hand	80	
Equipment	2,000	
Accumulated Depreciation		$ 200
Accounts Payable		2,200
Brenda Blake, Capital		2,000
	$4,400	$4,400

A summary of the transactions for July is as follows:
(1) Performed repair services, for which $600 in cash was received immediately.
(2) Performed additional repair work, $200, and sent bills to customers for this amount.
(3) Paid creditors by check, $400.
(4) Took out insurance on equipment on July 1, and issued a check to cover 1 year's premium of $72.
(5) Paid $40 out of cash on hand for a series of advertisements that appeared in the local newspaper during July.
(6) Issued check for $100 for rent of shop space for July.
(7) Paid telephone bill by check for the month, $20.
(8) Collected $80 of the amount charged to customers in item (2).
(9) Deposited $550 cash in the bank (from cash on hand).
(10) The insurance expired during July is calculated at $6.
(11) Cost of repair parts used during the month, $80.
(12) Cost of office supplies used during July, $20.
(13) Depreciation of equipment for the month is $14.

a. Open T-accounts and insert the July 1 balances. Record the transactions for the month in the T-accounts, opening additional T-accounts for individual revenue and expense accounts as needed.

b. Prepare an adjusted, preclosing trial balance at July 31, 1976.

c. Prepare an income statement for the month of July and a balance sheet as of July 31, 1976.

d. Enter closing entries in the T-accounts using an Income Summary account.

17. The trial balance of Safety Cleaners and Dyers at February 28, 1976, is shown below. The books have not been closed since December 31, 1975.

Cash on Hand	$ 360	
Cash in Bank	3,200	
Accounts Receivable	15,200	
Supplies on Hand	4,800	
Prepaid Insurance	1,040	
Equipment	65,000	
Accumulated Depreciation		$ 10,600
Accounts Payable		6,980
P. O. Grey, Capital		60,000
Sales		46,060
Salaries and Wages Expense	26,600	
Cost of Outside Work	2,040	
Advertising Expense	400	
Repairs Expense	500	
Rent Expense	1,200	
Power, Gas, and Water Expense	880	
Supplies Used	—	
Depreciation Expense	—	
Miscellaneous Expense	2,420	
	$123,640	$123,640

A summary of the transactions for the month of March 1976 is as follows:

(1) Sales: For cash, $14,000; on account, $5,800.

(2) Collections on account, $10,000.

(3) Cash deposited in the bank, $23,800.

(4) Purchases of outside work (cleaning done by wholesale cleaners), $800, on account.

(5) Purchases of supplies, on account, $2,800.

(6) Payments on account, by check, $4,000.

(7) March rent paid by check, $600.

(8) Supplies used (for the quarter), $5,340.

(9) Depreciation (for the quarter), $2,420.

(10) March salaries and wages of $11,120 are paid by check.

(11) Bills received but not recorded or paid by the end of the month: advertising, $200; repairs to equipment, $60; power, gas, and water, $380.

(12) Insurance expired (for the quarter), $400.

a. Open T-accounts and enter the trial balance amounts.

b. Record the transactions for the month of March in the T-accounts, opening additional T-accounts as needed. Cross-number the entries.

c. Prepare an adjusted, preclosing trial balance at March 31, 1976, an income statement for the 3 months ending March 31, 1976, and a balance sheet as of March 31, 1976.

d. Enter closing entries in the T-accounts using an Income Summary account.

18. The following data relate to the manufacturing activities of the Haskell Company during March 1976.

	March 1	March 31
Raw Materials Inventory	$32,400	$36,900
Work in Process Inventory	55,800	43,200
Finished Goods Inventory	44,200	46,300

Factory costs incurred during the month:

Raw Materials Purchased	$ 65,700
Labor Services Received	126,900
Heat, Light, and Power	1,260
Factory Rent	3,600

Expirations of previous factory acquisitions and prepayments:

Depreciation on Factory Equipment	$1,800
Prepaid Insurance Expired	1,440

a. Determine the cost of raw materials used during March.

b. Determine the cost of the units completed during March and transferred to the finished goods storeroom.

c. Determine the cost of goods sold during March.

19. The following data relate to the manufacturing activities of the Cornell Company during June 1976.

	June 1	June 30
Raw Materials Inventory	$22,600	$18,900
Factory Supplies Inventory	3,600	2,700
Work in Process Inventory	68,600	76,500
Finished Goods Inventory	54,300	51,900

Factory costs incurred during the month:

Raw Materials Purchased	$344,000
Factory Supplies Purchased	7,200
Labor Service Received	280,300
Heat, Light, and Power	3,300
Factory Insurance	1,800

Expirations of previous factory acquisitions and prepayments:

Depreciation on Factory Equipment	$20,800
Prepaid Rent Expired	2,400

a. Determine the cost of raw materials and factory supplies used during June.
b. Determine the cost of units completed during June and transferred to the finished goods storeroom.
c. Determine the cost of goods sold during June.

20. Melton Plastics Company was incorporated on September 16, 1976. By September 30, 1976, the firm was ready to begin operations. The trial balance at that date was as follows:

Cash in Bank	$387,200	
Raw Materials Inventory	19,200	
Factory Equipment	136,000	
Accounts Payable		$ 22,400
Capital Stock		520,000
	$542,400	$542,400

The following data relate only to the manufacturing operations of the firm during October:
(1) Materials purchased on account, $141,600.
(2) Wages and salaries earned during the month, $128,000.
(3) Raw materials requisitioned and put into process during the month, $148,800.
(4) Equipment was acquired during the month at a cost of $112,000. A check for $40,000 was issued, and an equipment contract payable in nine equal monthly installments was signed for the remainder.

(5) Additional payments by check:

Raw Materials Suppliers	$120,000
Payrolls	102,420
Repairs to Equipment	3,200
Factory Building Rent	6,000
Utilities	1,920
Insurance Premiums (for 1 year from October 1, 1976)	9,600
Miscellaneous Factory Costs	26,400
	$269,540

(6) Invoices received but unpaid at October 31, 1976:

City Water Department	$ 120
Hoster Machine Supply Company, for additional equipment	2,400

(7) Depreciation on equipment for the month, $1,200.
(8) One month's insurance expiration is recorded.
(9) The cost of parts finished during October was $291,760.
  a. Open T-accounts and enter the amounts from the opening trial balance.
  b. Record the transactions during the month in the T-accounts, opening additional accounts as needed.
  c. Prepare an adjusted trial balance at October 31, 1976.

21. This problem is a continuation of Problem **20**, Melton Plastics Company. In addition to the manufacturing activities described in that problem, the following transactions relating to selling and administrative activities occurred during October 1976.

(10) Sales, on account, $320,600.
(11) Collections from customers, $280,000.
(12) Salaries earned during the month: Sales, $20,800 office, $21,200.
(13) Payments by check:

Sales Salaries	$17,630
Office Salaries	17,550
Advertising During October	7,200
Rent of Office and Office Equipment for October	1,200
Office Supplies	1,600
Miscellaneous Office Costs	1,400
Miscellaneous Selling Costs	2,800
Total	$49,380

(14) Office supplies used during the month, $1,400.
(15) The inventory of finished goods on October 31, 1976, is $49,000.
  a. Employing the T-accounts of Problem **20** and additional accounts as needed, record the selling and administrative activities for the month in the T-accounts.
  b. Prepare a combined statement of income and retained earnings for the month.

    c. Prepare a balance sheet as of October 31, 1976.

    d. Enter closing entries in the T-accounts using an Income Summary account.

22. On July 1, 1976, the accounts of the Tampa Manufacturing Company contained the following balances:

DEBIT BALANCES		CREDIT BALANCES	
Cash on Hand	$ 10,000	Accumulated Depreciation	$ 30,000
Cash in Bank	100,000	Accounts Payable	56,000
Accounts Receivable	220,000	Wages Payable	24,000
Raw Materials Inventory	80,000	Capital Stock	1,000,000
Work in Process Inventory	230,000	Retained Earnings	200,000
Finished Goods Inventory	170,000		
Factory Supplies Inventory	20,000		
Manufacturing Equipment	480,000		
Total	$1,310,000	Total	$1,310,000

Transactions for the month of July are listed below in summary form:

  (1) Sales, all on account, were $300,000.

  (2) Labor services furnished by employees during the period amounted to $70,000. All labor is employed in the factory.

  (3) Factory supplies were purchased for $7,500; payment was made by check.

  (4) Raw materials purchased on account, $90,000.

  (5) Collections from customers, $325,000.

  (6) Cash is deposited in the bank, $322,000.

  (7) Payment of $98,000 was made to raw materials suppliers by check.

  (8) Payments to employees total $68,500.

  (9) Rent of the factory building for the month, $5,000, was paid by check.

(10) Depreciation of manufacturing equipment for the month, $10,000.

(11) Other manufacturing costs incurred and paid by check, $30,000.

(12) All selling and administrative services are furnished by Clark and Company for $8,000 per month. Their bill was paid by check.

(13) Raw materials used during month, $105,000.

(14) Factory supplies used during month, $9,000.

(15) Cost of goods completed during month, $248,000.

(16) Goods costing $251,500 were shipped to customers during the month.

    a. Open T-accounts and record the July 1, 1976, amounts. Record transactions (**1**) to (**16**) in the T-accounts, opening additional accounts as needed.

    b. Prepare an adjusted, preclosing trial balance as of July 31, 1976.

    c. Prepare a combined statement of income and retained earnings for July 1976.

    d. Prepare a balance sheet as of July 31, 1976.

    e. Enter closing entries in the T-accounts using an Income Summary account.

23. The Merchandise Supply Company received a $3,000, 3-month, 12 percent promissory note, dated December 1, 1976, from Virdon Stores to apply on its open accounts receivable.

    a. Present journal entries for the Merchandise Supply Company from December 1, 1976, through collection at maturity. The books are closed quarterly. Include the closing entry.

b. Present journal entries for Virdon Stores from December 1, 1976, through payment at maturity. The books are closed quarterly. Include the closing entry.

24. Selected transactions of the Kessinger Co. are described below. Present dated journal entries for these transactions and adjusting entries at the end of each month from January 15, 1976, through July 1, 1976. Assume that only the notes indicated were outstanding during this period. The accounting period is 1 month.

(**1**) The company issued a $1,000, 2-month, 12 percent promissory note on January 15, 1976, in lieu of payment on an account due that date to the White Wholesale Company.

(**2**) The note in (**1**) and interest were paid at maturity.

(**3**) The company issued a $2,000, 3-month, 12 percent promissory note to the White Wholesale Company on the date of purchase of merchandise, April 1, 1976.

(**4**) The note in (**3**) and interest were paid at maturity.

25. On January 1, 1976, the Office Supplies account of the Harris Company had a balance of $1,200. During the ensuing quarter, supplies were acquired on account in the amount of $6,000. On March 31, 1976, the inventory was taken and calculated to amount to $1,500.

Present journal entries to record the above acquisition and adjustments at the end of March in accordance with each of the following sets of instructions which might be established in an accounting systems manual:

a. An expense account is to be debited at the time supplies are required.

b. An asset account is to be debited at the time supplies are acquired.

26. The sales, all on account, of the Devine Company in 1976, its first year of operation, were $500,000. Collections totaled $450,000. At December 31, 1976, it was estimated that 1½ percent of sales on account during the year would likely be uncollectable. On that date, specific accounts in the amount of $2,500 were written off.

Present journal entries for the transactions and adjustments of 1976 related to sales and customers' accounts.

27. In recording the adjusting entries of the Hammond Sales Company, Inc., at the end of 1976, the following adjustments were omitted:

(**1**) Depreciation on the delivery truck of $1,500.

(**2**) Insurance expired on the delivery truck of $300.

(**3**) Interest accrued on notes payable of $75.

(**4**) Interest accrued on notes receivable of $165.

Indicate the effect (exclusive of income tax implications) of these omissions on the following items in the financial statements prepared on December 31, 1976.

a. Current assets.

b. Noncurrent assets.

c. Current liabilities.

d. Selling expenses.

e. Net income.

f. Retained earnings.

28. Present journal entries for each of the following separate sets of data:

a. On January 15, 1976, a $2,000, 2-month, 12 percent note was received by the company. Present adjusting entries at the end of each month and the entry for collection at maturity.

b. The company uses one Merchandise Inventory account to record the beginning inventory and purchases during the period. The balance in this account on December 31, 1976, was $480,000. The inventory of merchandise on hand at that time was $70,000. Present the adjusting entry.

c. The company rents out part of its building for office space at the rate of $500 a month, payable in advance for each calendar quarter of the year. The quarterly rental was received on February 1, 1976. Present adjusting and collection entries for the quarter. Assume that the books are closed monthly.

d. The company leases branch office space at $1,000 a month. Payment is made by the company on the first of each 6-month period. Payment of $6,000 was made in July 1, 1976. Present payment and adjusting entries through August 31, 1976. Assume that the books are closed monthly.

e. The balance of the Prepaid Insurance account on October 1, 1976, was $200. On December 1, 1976, the company renewed its only insurance policy for another 3 years beginning on that date by payment of $3,960. Present journal entries for renewal and adjusting entries through December 31, 1976. Assume that the books are closed quarterly.

f. The Office Supplies on Hand account had a balance of $300 on December 1, 1976. Purchases of supplies in the amount of $380 were recorded in the Office Supplies Expense account during the month. The inventory of office supplies on December 31, 1976, was $290. Present any necessary adjusting entry at December 31, 1976.

g. An office building was constructed at a cost of $250,000. It was estimated that it would have a useful life of 50 years from the date of occupancy, October 31, 1976, and a residual value of $10,000. Present the adjusting entry for the depreciation of the building in 1976. Assume that the books are closed annually at December 31.

h. Experience indicates that 1 percent of the accounts arising from sales on account will not be collected. Sales on account during 1976 were $180,000. A list of uncollectible accounts totaling $400 as of December 31, 1976, was compiled. Present journal entries for the annual provision for uncollectible accounts and the write off of specific customers' accounts as of December 31, 1976. The books are closed annually.

29. The trial balance of the Handy Hank's Hardware Store on September 30, 1976, is as follows:

Cash	$ 86,500	
Accounts Receivable	54,500	
Merchandise Inventory	136,300	
Prepaid Insurance	800	
Equipment	420,000	
Allowance for Uncollectible Accounts		$ 6,500
Accumulated Depreciation		166,000
Accounts Payable		66,300
Note Payable		10,000
Salaries Payable		2,500
Capital Stock		300,000
Retained Earnings		146,800
Total	$698,100	$698,100

Transactions during October and additional information are as follows:

(1) Sales, all on account, total $110,000.

(2) Merchandise inventory purchased on account from various suppliers is $68,400.

(3) Rent for the month of October of $12,000 is paid.

(4) Salaries paid to employees during October are $18,700.

(5) Accounts receivable of $43,800 are collected.

(6) Accounts payable of $53,200 are paid.

(7) Miscellaneous expenses of $3,200 are paid in cash.

(8) The premium on a 1-year insurance policy was paid on June 1, 1976.

(9) Equipment is depreciated over a 10-year life. Estimated salvage value of the equipment is considered to be negligible.

(10) Employee salaries earned during the last two days of October but not paid are $3,300.

(11) Based on past experience, the firm estimates that 1 percent of all sales on account will become uncollectible.

(12) Specific customers' accounts of $2,800 are determined to be uncollectible.

(13) The note payable is a 60-day, 12 percent note issued on September 30, 1976.

(14) Merchandise inventory on hand on October 31, 1976, totals $141,500.

a. Prepare general journal entries to reflect the transactions and other events during October. Indicate whether each entry records a transaction during the month (**T**) or is an adjusting entry at the end of the month (**A**).

b. Set up T-accounts and enter the opening balances in the accounts on September 30, 1976. Record the entries from **a** in the T-accounts, creating additional accounts as required.

c. Prepare an adjusted, preclosing trial balance as of October 31, 1976.

d. Prepare an income statement for the month of October.

e. Prepare a balance sheet as of October 31, 1976.

f. Enter the appropriate closing entries at the end of October in the T-accounts, assuming that the books are closed each month. Use an Income Summary account.

30. The following unadjusted trial balance is taken from the books of the Kathleen Clothing Company at July 31, 1976. The company closes its books monthly.

Accounts Payable		$ 12,695
Accounts Receivable	$ 18,000	
Accumulated Depreciation		8,240
Advances by Customers		540
Allowance for Uncollectible Accounts		1,200
Capital Stock		40,000
Cash	9,000	
Equipment	2,640	
Depreciation Expense	—	—
Dividends Payable	—	—
Furniture and Fixtures	12,000	

Income Tax Expense	—	—
Income Tax Payable		3,500
Insurance Expense	—	—
Leasehold	10,800	
Merchandise Cost of Goods Sold	—	—
Merchandise Inventory	49,500	
Miscellaneous Expenses	188	
Prepaid Insurance	450	
Rent Expense	—	—
Retained Earnings		13,068
Salaries and Commissions Expense	2,020	
Salaries and Commissions Payable		500
Sales		25,000
Sales, Uncollectible Accounts Adjustment	—	—
Supplies Inventory	145	
	$104,743	$104,743

Additional data:
  (1) Depreciation on equipment is to be calculated at 25 percent of cost per year.
  (2) Depreciation on furniture and fixtures is to be calculated at 10 percent of cost per year.
  (3) The leasehold represents long-term rent paid in advance by Kathleen. The monthly rental charge is $300.
  (4) One invoice of $240 for the purchase of merchandise from the Peoria Company on account was recorded during the month as $204.
  (5) Commissions unpaid at July 31, 1976, are $280. All salaries have been paid. The balance in the Salaries and Commissions Payable account represents the amount of commissions unpaid at July 1.
  (6) Merchandise with a sales price of $150 was recently delivered to a customer, and charged to Accounts Receivable, although the customer had paid $150 in advance.
  (7) The estimated uncollectible account rate is 1 percent of the charge sales of the month. Charge sales were 70 percent of the sales of the month.
  (8) An analysis of outstanding customers accounts indicates that two accounts totaling $140 should be written off as uncollectible.
  (9) The balance in the Prepaid Insurance account relates to a 3-year policy that went into effect on January 1, 1976.
  (10) A dividend of $1,000 was declared on July 31, 1976.
  (11) The inventory of merchandise on July 31, 1976, was $29,500.
Present adjusting journal entries at July 31, 1976. Use only the accounts listed in the trial balance.

31. (Problems **31** through **33** are adapted from problems by George H. Sorter.) Sorta Company presents the following incomplete trial balances as well as a statement of cash receipts and disbursements:

DEBITS

	1/1/76	12/31/76
Cash	$?	$?
Accounts and Notes Receivable	36,000	41,000
Merchandise Inventory	55,000	49,500
Accrued Interest Receivable	1,000	700
Prepaid Miscellaneous Services	4,000	5,200
Building, Machinery, and Equipment	47,000	47,000
Total Debits	$?	$?

CREDITS

	1/1/76	12/31/76
Accounts Payable (miscellaneous services)	$ 2,000	$ 2,500
Accounts Payable (merchandise)	34,000	41,000
Accrued Property Taxes Payable	1,000	1,500
Accumulated Depreciation	10,000	12,000
Mortgage Payable	35,000	30,000
Capital Stock	25,000	25,000
Retained Earnings	76,000	?
Total Credits	$183,000	$211,200

CASH RECEIPTS

	Year of 1976
1. Collection from Credit Customers	$144,000
2. Cash Sales	63,000
3. Collection of Interest	1,000
	$208,000

LESS: CASH DISBURSEMENTS

4. Payment to Suppliers of Merchandise	$114,000
5. Repayment on Mortgage	5,000
6. Payment of Interest	500
7. Payment to Suppliers of Miscellaneous Services	57,500
8. Payment of Property Taxes	1,200
9. Payment of Dividends	2,000
	$180,200
Increase in Cash Balance for Year	$ 27,800

Prepare a combined statement of income and retained earnings for the year 1976. (Hint: Set up T-accounts for each of the balance sheet accounts listed in the trial balance and enter the amounts shown as of January 1, 1976, and December 31, 1976. Starting with the cash receipts and disbursements for the year, reconstruct the transactions that took place during the year and enter them in the appropriate T-accounts.)

32. The Cassidy Company presents the following trial balance at the beginning of 1976 and the adjusted, preclosing trial balance at the end of 1976.

DEBITS

	1/1/76	12/31/76
Cash	$ 20,000	$ 9,000
Accounts Receivable	36,000	51,000
Merchandise Inventory	45,000	60,000
Prepayments	2,000	1,000
Land, Buildings, and Equipment	40,000	40,000
Cost of Goods Sold	—	50,000
Interest Expense	—	3,000
Operating Expenses	—	29,000
Total Debits	$143,000	$243,000

CREDITS

Accumulated Depreciation	$ 16,000	$ 18,000
Interest Payable	1,000	2,000
Accounts Payable	30,000	40,000
Mortgage Payable	20,000	17,000
Capital Stock	50,000	50,000
Retained Earnings	26,000	16,000
Sales	—	100,000
Total Credits	$143,000	$243,000

All goods and services acquired during the year were purchased on account. The Operating Expenses account includes depreciation charges and expirations of prepayments.

Prepare a schedule showing all cash transactions for the year 1976. (Hint: Set up T-accounts for each of the accounts listed in the trial balance and enter the amounts shown as of January 1, 1976, and December 31, 1976. Starting with the entries in revenue and expense accounts, reconstruct the transactions which took place during the year and enter the amounts in the appropriate T-accounts. Dividends declared during the year were debited to Retained Earnings.)

33. The following data relate to the Julia Company:

(1) Postclosing trial balance at December 31, 1976:

DEBITS

Cash	$ 10,000
Marketable Securities	20,000
Accounts Receivable	25,000
Merchandise Inventory	30,000
Prepayment for Miscellaneous Services	3,000
Land, Buildings, and Equipment	40,000
Total Debits	$128,000

CREDITS

Accounts Payable (for merchandise)	$ 25,000
Interest Payable	300
Taxes Payable	4,000
Notes Payable (6 percent, long-term)	20,000
Accumulated Depreciation	16,000
Capital Stock	50,000
Retained Earnings	12,700
Total Credits	$128,000

(**2**) Income and retained earnings data for 1976:

Sales		$200,000
Less Expenses:		
Cost of Goods Sold	$130,000	
Depreciation Expense	3,000	
Taxes Expense	8,000	
Other Operating Expenses	48,700	
Interest Expense	1,200	
Total Expenses		190,900
Net Income		$ 9,100
Less: Dividends		5,000
Increase in Retained Earnings		$ 4,100

(**3**) Summary of cash receipts and disbursements in 1976:

Cash Receipts

Cash Sales	$ 47,000	
Collection from Credit Customers	150,000	
Total Receipts		$197,000

Cash Disbursements

Payment to Suppliers of Merchandise	$128,000	
Payment to Suppliers of Miscellaneous Services	49,000	
Payment of Taxes	7,500	
Payment of Interest	1,200	
Payment of Dividends	5,000	
Purchase of Marketable Securities	8,000	
Total Disbursements		198,700
Excess of Disbursements over Receipts		$ 1,700

(**4**) Purchases of merchandise during the period, all on account, were $127,000. All "Other Operating Expenses" were credited to Prepayments.
a. Prepare a balance sheet for January 1, 1976.
b. What is the interest payment date on the long-term notes?

Chapter Five

Flows of Funds
and the Statement
of Changes
in Financial Position

Chapter One pointed out that three basic financial statements are generally deemed useful to those interested in understanding the financial activities of a business. Chapter Two discussed the balance sheet, a report on financial position at a given moment in time. Chapters Three and Four considered the income statement, a report on revenues and expenses for a period. This chapter discusses the third basic statement, the statement of changes in financial position, which reports flows of funds for a period. The discussion includes the rationale for the statement, the alternative meanings of the term *funds,* and the accounting procedures for preparing the statement.

■ RATIONALE FOR THE STATEMENT
OF CHANGES IN FINANCIAL POSITION

Solinger Electric Corporation was formed during January 1973 to operate a retail electrical supply business. The net income from operating the business has increased each year since opening, from $3,000 in 1973 to $20,000 in 1976. The firm has had increasing difficulty, however, paying its monthly bills as they become due. Management is puzzled as to how net income could be increasing while at the same time the firm continually finds itself strapped for cash.

The experience of Solinger Electric Corporation is not unusual. Many firms, particularly those experiencing rapid growth, discover that their cash position is deteriorating despite an excellent earnings record. The statement of changes in financial position provides information that is useful in assessing changes in a firm's *liquidity* (its holdings of cash and other assets that could be readily turned into cash), by reporting on the flows of funds into and out of the business during a period.

Income Flows and Cash Flows

The revenues and expenses reported in the income statement differ from the cash receipts and disbursements during a period for two principal reasons:

1. The accrual basis of accounting is used in determining net income, so that the recognition of revenues does not necessarily coincide with the receipts of cash from customers, and the recognition of expenses does not necessarily coincide with the disbursements of cash to suppliers, employees, and other creditors.
2. The firm has cash receipts and disbursements not directly related to the process of generating earnings, such as from issuing capital stock or bonds, paying dividends, or purchasing buildings and equipment.

Exhibit 5.1 shows the relationship between the revenues and expenses and the cash receipts and disbursements of Solinger Electric Corporation during 1976. While sales revenue was $125,000, only $90,000 was collected from customers. The remaining amount of sales was not collected by the end of the year and is re-

EXHIBIT 5.1
Solinger Electric Corporation
Income Statement and Statement of
Cash Receipts and Disbursements
For the Year 1976

	INCOME STATEMENT	STATEMENT OF CASH RECEIPTS AND DISBURSEMENTS	
Sales Revenue	$125,000	$ 90,000	Collections from Customers
Less Expenses:			Less Disbursements:
Cost of Goods Sold	$ 60,000	$ 50,000	To Merchandise Suppliers
Salaries	20,000	19,000	To Employees
Depreciation	10,000	0	—
Other	15,000	13,000	To Other Suppliers
Total Expenses	$105,000	$ 82,000	Total Disbursements to Suppliers and Employees
Net Income	$ 20,000	$ 8,000	Net Cash Inflow from Operations
		100,000	Receipts from Issuing Long-Term Bonds
		$108,000	Total Receipts from Operations and Bond Issue
		$ 10,000	Disbursements for Dividends
		125,000	Disbursements for Equipment
		$135,000	Total Disbursements for Dividends and Equipment
		$ 27,000	Net Decrease in Cash

flected in the Accounts Receivable account on the balance sheet. Likewise, the cost of goods sold was $60,000, but only $50,000 was disbursed to suppliers during the year. Similar differences between income flows and cash flows can be seen for salaries and for other expenses. Note that there is no specific cash flow associated with depreciation expense. While the operating activities generated $20,000 in net income, these activities led to only an $8,000 increase in cash during 1976. The firm's cash balance decreased by $27,000 between the beginning and end of 1976 because the cash inflows from operations ($8,000) and from issuing long-term bonds ($100,000) were less than the cash required to pay dividends ($10,000) and purchase equipment ($125,000).

Cash Flows and Working Capital Flows

The statement of changes in financial position reports on the flows of funds into and out of a business during a period. Funds were viewed as "cash" in Exhibit 5.1, in which the Statement of Changes in Financial Position was essentially a statement of cash receipts and disbursements. The term "funds," however, is a general one which can have different meanings, depending on the circumstances. Consider the following two questions which the management of Solinger Electric Corporation might raise:

1. Does the firm have sufficient funds to acquire new equipment tomorrow?
2. Will the firm have sufficient funds to acquire new equipment within the next 6 months?

In answering the first question, management is likely to consider the amount of cash on hand and in its bank account. It would also consider whether the equipment could be acquired on account from one of its regular suppliers. In answering the second question, management would, in addition, consider whether the firm had marketable securities or other assets which could be sold for cash during the next 6 months. It should be clear, however, that *time is the important factor* in answering the questions about available funds. When the time horizon is short, the meaning of funds is more restrictive than when the time horizon is longer.

The statements of changes in financial position of most publicly held firms use a definition of funds broader than cash. In most instances, the statements explain the change in the net current asset position, or *working capital*, of the firm. That is, funds are defined as the difference between current assets (cash, readily marketable securities, accounts receivable, inventories, and current prepayments) and current liabilities (accounts payable, salaries payable, and other short-term debt). Current assets are those assets which are either cash or are expected to be turned into cash, or sold, or consumed within the operating cycle, usually 1 year. Current liabilities are obligations expected to be discharged or paid within approximately 1 year. Thus, the amount of working capital at a particular time represents the excess of cash and near-cash assets over near-term claims on these liquid assets. This broader definition of funds is considered to provide more useful information to investors and other users of a firm's financial statements than does the more restrictive definition of funds as cash alone.[1]

Exhibit 5.2 shows the relationship between the cash receipts and disbursements and the increases (sources) and decreases (uses) of working capital of Solinger Electric Corporation during 1976. Revenues led to only a $90,000 increase in cash but to a $125,000 increase in cash and accounts receivable. Since accounts receivable are likely to be collected within a short period, the working capital definition of funds gives a better indication of the effect of revenues on liquidity. Salaries Expense and Other Operating Expenses resulted in a $32,000 (= $19,000 + $13,000) decrease in cash but a $35,000 reduction in working capital. Current liabilities (for example, Salaries Payable, Accounts Payable) must therefore have *increased* by $3,000 (= $35,000 − $32,000). The firm's liquidity is affected by the need to pay these $35,000 of obligations in the near future, and the obligation should be considered in assessing liquidity. Note that depreciation expense does not affect either cash flows or working capital flows. While operations generated a net cash inflow of $8,000, working capital from operations increased by $30,000. The $22,000 difference is due largely to an increase in accounts receivable.

Objective of the Statement of Changes in Financial Position

The statement of changes in financial position presents information on the sources (increases) and uses (decreases) of working capital during a period. The major sources and uses are depicted graphically in Figure 5.1 and are described below.

1. *Sources—operations.* The excess of revenues increasing working capital over expenses using working capital is the most important source of funds. When assessed over several years, working capital from operations indicates the extent to which the operating or earnings activities have generated more working capital than is used up. The excess from operations can then be used for dividends, acquisition of buildings and equipment, or repayment of long-term debt if necessary.

2. *Sources—issuance of long-term debt or capital stock.* In contrast to the short-term nature of working capital from operations, increases in long-term debt or capital stock represent longer-term sources of financing for a firm.

3. *Sources—sale of noncurrent assets.* The sale of buildings, equipment, and other noncurrent assets results in an increase in working capital. These sales generally cannot be viewed as a major source of financing for a firm, since the amounts received from the sales are not likely to be sufficient to replace the assets sold.

4. *Uses—dividends.* Dividends are generally a recurring use of working capital,

[1] The Accounting Principles Board, in Opinion No. 19, sanctioned the use of still a third definition of *funds* in the context of the statement of changes in financial position. This third definition is as follows: All Financial Resources = Total Assets − Total Liabilities. All Financial Resources is a reasonable and useful construct, but the implications of using it for the statement of changes in financial position raise issues of little interest for this discussion.

EXHIBIT 5.2
Solinger Electric Corporation
Statements of Cash Receipts and Disbursements
and Increases and Decreases in Working Capital
For the Year 1976

STATEMENT OF CASH RECEIPTS AND DISBURSEMENTS

Collections from Customers	$ 90,000
Less Disbursements:	
To Merchandise Suppliers	$ 50,000
To Employees	19,000
To Other Suppliers	13,000
Total Disbursements to Suppliers and Employees	$ 82,000
Net Cash Inflow from Operations	$ 8,000
Receipts from Issuing Long-Term Bonds	100,000
Total Receipts from Operations and Bond Issue	$108,000
Disbursements for Dividends	$ 10,000
Disbursements for Equipment	125,000
Total Disbursements for Dividends and Equipment	$135,000
Net Decrease in Cash	$ 27,000

STATEMENT OF INCREASES AND DECREASES IN WORKING CAPITAL

Increase in Working Capital from Operations:	
Sales Revenue	$125,000
Less Decreases in Working Capital from Operations:	
Inventory Sold	$ 60,000
Salaries Paid or Earned and Accrued	20,000
Other Expenses Paid or Accrued	15,000
Total Decreases in Working Capital from Operations	$ 95,000
Net Increase in Working Capital from Operations	$ 30,000
Increase in Working Capital from Issuing Long-Term Bonds	100,000
Total Increases in Working Capital from Operations and Bond Issue	$130,000
Decrease in Working Capital for Dividends Declared	$ 10,000
Decrease in Working Capital for Equipment Acquired	125,000
Total Decreases in Working Capital for Dividends Declared and Equipment Acquired	$135,000
Net Decrease in Working Capital	$ 5,000

FIGURE 5–1
SOURCES AND USES OF WORKING CAPITAL

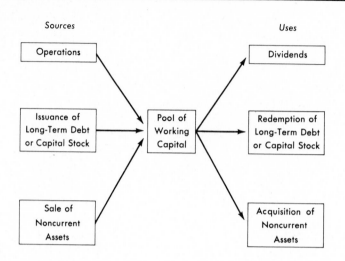

since most publicly held firms are reluctant to reduce or omit the payment of dividends, even during a year of poor earnings performance.

5. *Uses—redemption of long-term debt or capital stock.* In most instances, publicly held firms redeem or pay long-term debt at maturity with the proceeds of another bond issue. Thus, these redemptions often have little effect on the *net* change in working capital. Some firms also occasionally reacquire or redeem their own capital stock for various reasons discussed in Chapter Twelve.

6. *Uses—acquisition of noncurrent assets.* The acquisition of noncurrent assets such as building and equipment usually represents an important use of working capital. These assets must be replaced as they wear out, and additional noncurrent assets must be acquired if a firm is to grow.

Firms sometimes issue long-term debt or capital stock directly to the vendor, or seller, in acquiring buildings, equipment, or other noncurrent assets. These transactions technically do not affect a working capital account. However, the transaction is reported in the statement of changes in financial position as though two transactions took place: the issuance of long-term debt or capital stock for cash and the immediate use of the cash in the acquisition of noncurrent assets. This is called the *dual transactions assumption.* Such a transaction would normally be disclosed in the statement of changes in financial position as both a source and use of working capital of equal amounts.

Uses of Information in the Statement of Changes in Financial Position

The statement of changes in financial position provides information which may be used in:

1. assessing changes in a firm's liquidity, and
2. assessing changes in the structure of a firm's assets and equities.

Liquidity   Perhaps the most important factor not reported on the balance sheet and income statement alone is how the operations of a period affect the liquidity of a firm. It is easy to assume that increased earnings mean increased cash or other liquid assets. However, a new plant may have been acquired and other similar events could have occurred. On the other hand, increased liquidity can accompany reduced earnings, because cash is allowed to accumulate rather than being used to replace plant and equipment.

When one uses information from the statement of changes in financial position in assessing changes in liquidity, the definition of funds as working capital must be kept in mind. If near-term liquidity is of interest, then funds should be redefined as cash. The procedures for converting working capital provided by operations to cash flow provided by operations are discussed later in the chapter.

Structure of Assets and Equities   In addition to providing information about changes in a firm's liquidity during a period, the statement of changes in financial position also indicates the major transactions causing changes in the structure of a firm's assets and equities. For example, acquisitions and sales of specific types of noncurrent assets (buildings, equipment, patents) are reported. Likewise, issues and redemptions of long-term debt and capital stock are disclosed. These transactions are difficult to observe by looking at either the income statement or balance sheet alone. For example, the change in the account, "Buildings and Equipment—Net of Accumulated Depreciation," could be attributable to depreciation charges, to acquisition of new buildings and equipment, to disposition of old buildings and equipment, or to a combination of these. The income statement and comparative balance sheets do not provide sufficient information about these three items individually for the reader to disaggregate the net change in the account during the period. A statement of changes in financial position is required to report this information.

In describing the relationship of the statement of changes in financial position to the other basic financial statements, the Accounting Principles Board stated that it

> . . . is related to both the income statement and the balance sheet and provides information that can be obtained only partially, or at most in piecemeal form, by interpreting them. . . . The [statement of changes in financial position] cannot supplant either the income statement or balance sheet but is intended to provide information that the other statements either do not provide or provide only indirectly about the flow of funds and changes in financial position during a period.[2]

[2] Opinion No. 19, Accounting Principles Board, AICPA, March 1971.

■ ANALYSIS OF THE EFFECTS OF TRANSACTIONS ON WORKING CAPITAL

Algebraic Formulation

The effects of various transactions on working capital might be seen by re-examining the accounting equation. In doing so, we use the following notation:

CA	represents current assets
CL	represents current liabilities
NCA	represents noncurrent assets
NCL	represents noncurrent liabilities
OE	represents owners' equity
Δ	represents the change in an item, whether positive (an increase) or negative (a decrease) from the beginning of a period to the end of the period.

The accounting equation states that:

$$\text{Assets} = \text{Liabilities} + \text{Owners' Equity}$$
$$CA + NCA = CL + NCL + OE.$$

Furthermore, this equation must be true for balance sheets constructed at both the start of the period and the end of the period. If the start-of-the-period and end-of-the-period balance sheets maintain the accounting equation, then the following equation must also be valid:

$$\Delta CA + \Delta NCA = \Delta CL + \Delta NCL + \Delta OE.$$

Rearranging terms in this equation, we get:

$$\Delta CA - \Delta CL = \Delta NCL + \Delta OE - \Delta NCA.$$

Working capital is equal to current assets minus current liabilities; thus the left-hand side of the above equation represents the net change in working capital. The right-hand side of the equation, reflecting changes in all *nonworking* capital accounts, must also be equal in amount to the net change in working capital.

Illustration of Transactions Analysis

We can now analyze some typical transactions to demonstrate how the equation is maintained and how working capital is affected.

Assume that the following events occur during 1976 for the Solinger Electric Corporation, considered earlier in Exhibits 5.1 and 5.2.[3]

---

[3] To simplify this illustration, we have not provided information on the amounts in balance sheet accounts on January 1, 1976. As will become evident later in the chapter, however, some cash receipts and disbursements represent settlements of beginning-of-the-period receivables and payables.

1. Merchandise costing $70,000 is acquired on account.
2. Merchandise costing $60,000 is sold to customers on account for $125,000.
3. Salaries of $19,000 are paid in cash.
4. Other expenses of $13,000 are paid in cash.
5. Cash collections of customers' accounts total $90,000.
6. Cash payments to suppliers of merchandise total $50,000.
7. Salaries earned but not paid as of December 31, 1976, are accrued, $1,000.
8. Other expenses not paid as of December 31, 1976, are accrued, $2,000.
9. Depreciation for 1976 is recorded, $10,000.
10. Long-term debt is issued for cash, $100,000.
11. Dividends of $10,000 are declared and paid.
12. Equipment costing $125,000 is acquired for cash.

The effects of these transactions on the equation

$$\Delta CA - \Delta CL = \Delta NCL + \Delta OE - \Delta NCA$$

are analyzed in Exhibit 5.3. Working capital decreased by $5,000 during 1976. Both sides of the equation show this net change. The net change in working capital during a period (left-hand side of the equation) can therefore be explained, or analyzed, by focusing on the changes in nonworking capital accounts (right-hand side of the equation). For Solinger Electric Corporation, the net change in working capital of $5,000 is explained as follows:

Increases in Working Capital:
From Operations	$ 30,000
From Issuing Long-Term Debt	100,000
Total Increases	$130,000

Decreases in Working Capital:
For Dividends	$ 10,000
For Acquisition of Equipment	125,000
Total Decreases	$135,000
Net Decrease in Working Capital	$ 5,000

Note several aspects of the transactions analysis in Exhibit 5.3. First, the recording of depreciation for the period does not affect working capital. A noncurrent asset is decreased and owners' equity is decreased. No working capital accounts are affected. (Working capital was reduced in the period when the noncurrent asset was acquired.) Second, some transactions during the year have no net effect on working capital, since they merely result in transfers among working capital accounts. Several examples are the purchase of merchandise on account, the collection of accounts receivable, and the payment of accounts payable. These transactions, therefore, do not explain the *change* in working capital during the period.

The information necessary to prepare the statement of changes in financial po-

EXHIBIT 5.3
Analysis of the Effects of Solinger Electric Corporation's Transactions During 1976 on Working Capital and Nonworking Capital Accounts

TRANSACTIONS	Effect on Equation								
	Working Capital Changes			=	Nonworking Capital Changes				
	ΔCA	−	ΔCL	=	ΔNCL	+	ΔOE	−	ΔNCA
(1) Merchandise costing $70,000 is acquired on account, increasing a current asset and a current liability	$ 70,000	−	$70,000	=	0	+	0	−	0
(2) Merchandising costing $60,000 is sold to customers on account for $125,000, increasing a current asset, accounts receivable, by $125,000, decreasing the current asset, inventory, by $60,000, and increasing owners' equity by $65,000	$125,000 (−$60,000)	−	0 0	=	0 0	+	$65,000 (−$19,000)	−	0 0
(3) Salaries of $19,000 are paid in cash, decreasing a current asset and owners' equity	(−$19,000)	−	0	=	0	+	(−$19,000)	−	0
(4) Other expenses of $13,000 are paid in cash, decreasing a current asset and owners' equity	(−$13,000)	−	0	=	0	+	(−$13,000)	−	0
(5) Cash collections of customers' accounts total $90,000, increasing the current asset, cash, and decreasing the current asset, accounts receivable	$90,000 (−$90,000)	−	0	=	0	+	0	−	0
(6) Cash payments to suppliers of merchandise total $50,000, decreasing a current asset and a current liability	(−$50,000)	−	(−$50,000)	=	0	+	0	−	0
(7) Salaries of $1,000 earned but not paid as of December 31,1976, are accrued, increasing a current liability and decreasing owners' equity	0	−	$ 1,000	=	0	+	(−$1,000)	−	0
(8) Other expenses of $2,000 not paid as of December 31, 1976, are accrued, increasing a current liability and decreasing owners' equity	0	−	$ 2,000	=	0	+	(−$2,000)	−	0
(9) Depreciation for 1976 of $10,000 is recorded, decreasing owners' equity and noncurrent assets	0	−	0	=	0	+	(−$10,000)	−	(−$10,000)
Total from Operations	$ 53,000	−	$23,000	=	0	+	$20,000	−	(−$10,000)
(10) Long-term debt is issued for cash, $100,000, increasing a current asset and a non-current liability	$100,000	−	0	=	$100,000	+	0	−	0
(11) Dividends of $10,000 are declared and paid, decreasing a current asset and owners' equity	(−$10,000)	−	0	=	0	+	(−$10,000)	−	0
(12) Equipment costing $125,000 is acquired for cash, decreasing a current asset and increasing noncurrent assets	(−$125,000)	−	0	=	0	+	0	−	$125,000
Totals	$18,000	−	$23,000	=	$100,000	+	$10,000	−	$115,000
Net Change in Working Capital and Nonworking Capital	−$5,000			=					−$5,000

sition could be generated, or developed, using the transactions analysis approach illustrated in Exhibit 5.3. This approach quickly becomes cumbersome, however, as the number of transactions increases. In addition, there are numerous transactions during the year which have no net effect on working capital, (for example, collection of accounts receivable, payment of accounts payable), and can effectively be ignored in explaining the change in working capital. In the next section, we describe an alternative procedure for preparing the statement of changes in financial position which uses a variant of the T-account discussed in previous chapters.

■ PREPARATION OF THE STATEMENT OF CHANGES IN FINANCIAL POSITION

As with the balance sheet and income statement, it is not essential that you know how to prepare a statement of changes in financial position in order to use it effectively. Nevertheless, learning how to construct this statement facilitates understanding its rationale and content. In this section, we present a step-by-step procedure for preparing the statement of changes in financial position. We then illustrate this procedure using the transactions of Solinger Electric Corporation for 1976.

The Procedure and an Illustration

Step 1   Obtain balance sheets for the beginning and end of the period covered by the statement of changes in financial position and determine the net change in each account. The comparative balance sheets of Solinger Electric Corporation for December 31, 1975 and 1976, are presented in Exhibit 5.4. Properly prepared balance sheets classify both assets and equities as either current or noncurrent. The distinction between current and noncurrent items is essential to the preparation of the statement of changes in financial position when funds are defined as working capital. The net change in each balance sheet account is also indicated in Exhibit 5.4. The sum of all debit changes must equal the sum of all credit changes.

Step 2   Prepare a "double-T-account" *work sheet*. A double-T-account is an ordinary T-account with a second horizontal line—for example:

BUILDINGS AND EQUIPMENT (COST)

125,000	

The purpose of the section created between the horizontal lines is to show the net change during the period from all transactions affecting that account. For example, Exhibit 5.4 indicates that the Buildings and Equipment (Cost) account

EXHIBIT 5.4
Solinger Electric Corporation
Comparative Balance Sheets for
December 31, 1975 and 1976

ASSETS

			Net Change For Year 1976	
Current Assets	December 31, 1975	December 31, 1976	Debit	Credit
Cash	$ 30,000	$ 3,000		$ 27,000
Accounts Receivable	20,000	55,000	$ 35,000	
Merchandise Inventory	40,000	50,000	10,000	
Total Current Assets	$ 90,000	$108,000		
Noncurrent Assets				
Buildings and Equipment (Cost)	$100,000	$225,000	125,000	
Accumulated Depreciation	(30,000)	(40,000)		10,000
Total Noncurrent Assets	$ 70,000	$185,000		
Total Assets	$160,000	$293,000		

WNC = CA - CL

EQUITIES

			Net Change For Year 1976	
Current Liabilities	December 31, 1975	December 31, 1976	Debit	Credit
Accounts Payable—Merchandise Suppliers	$ 30,000	$ 50,000		20,000
Accounts Payable—Other Suppliers	10,000	12,000		2,000
Salaries Payable	5,000	6,000		1,000
Total Current Liabilities	$ 45,000	$ 68,000		
Noncurrent Liabilities				
Bonds Payable	$ 0	$100,000		100,000
Owners' Equity				
Capital Stock	$100,000	$100,000		
Retained Earnings	15,000	25,000		10,000
Total Owners' Equity	$115,000	$125,000		
Total Equities	$160,000	$293,000		
Total Changes			$170,000	$170,000

increased by $125,000 during 1976. Since increases in asset accounts are debits, the $125,000 change in the Buildings and Equipment (Cost) account is placed on the left-hand side of the double-T-account.

In preparing a double-T-account work sheet, first prepare a master account titled "Working Capital." This account is merely an aggregation of the individual current asset and current liability accounts into a single summary account. An example of this master double-T-account is shown in the top portion of Exhibit

5.5. Note that this double-T-account has sections labeled "From Operations" and "Other (Nonoperating)" Sources and Uses. Transactions affecting working capital during the period are classified under one of these headings to aid in the preparation of the statement of changes in financial position. This procedure is explained later in this section. The *net change* in working capital during the period is then

EXHIBIT 5.5
Double-T-Account Work Sheet for Solinger Electric Corporation

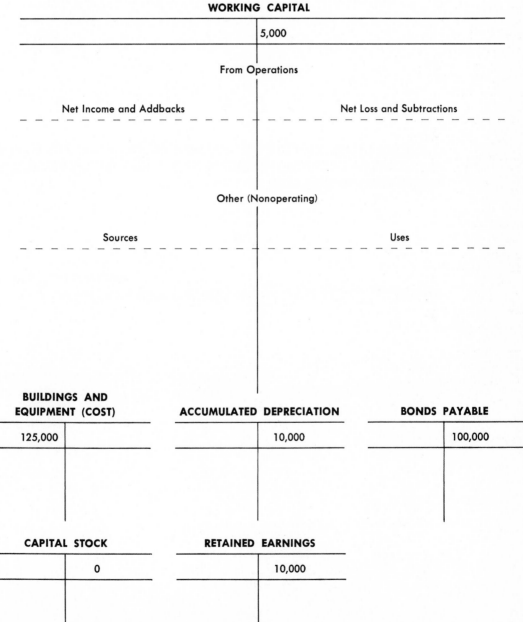

entered in the master double-T-account. The net change in working capital for Solinger Electric Corporation can be determined by subtracting the amount of working capital at the beginning of the period of $45,000 (= $90,000 − $45,000) from the amount of working capital at the end of the period of $40,000 (= $108,000 − $68,000). The net change is a decrease in working capital for the period of $5,000. Since decreases in working capital (that is, decreases in current assets or increases in current liabilities) are recorded as credits, the $5,000 net decrease is entered between the horizontal lines on the right-hand side of the master double-T-account. The net change in working capital can also be determined by using information on the net change in each current asset and current liability account in Exhibit 5.4. Working capital accounts with debit changes (Accounts Receivable and Merchandise Inventory) total $45,000. Working capital accounts with credit changes (Cash, Accounts Payable—Merchandise Suppliers, Accounts Payable—Other Suppliers, and Salaries Payable) total $50,000. There is therefore a net credit change of $5,000 for the year. Note that the master double-T-account, Working Capital, is another means of expressing the left-hand side of the equation in Exhibit 5.3.

After the master double-T-account for Working Capital has been prepared, the work sheet is completed by preparing double-T-accounts for *each* noncurrent asset and noncurrent equity account. Enter the debit or credit change during the period as determined in Exhibit 5.4 in the space between the horizontal lines. The lower portion of Exhibit 5.5 shows the double-T-accounts for each noncurrent asset and noncurrent equity. Note that these individual double-T-accounts are another means of expressing the right-hand side of the equation in Exhibit 5.3.

The double-T-account work sheet for Solinger Electric Corporation after completion of Step 2 is shown in Exhibit 5.5. At this stage, the sum of all debit changes indicated in the accounts must equal the sum of all credit changes. In this example, the debit change is $125,000. The credit changes sum is $125,000 (= $5,000 + $10,000 + $100,000 + $10,000).

Step 3   Explain or account for the change in the master working capital account by explaining or accounting for the changes in the nonworking capital accounts. This step is accomplished by *reconstructing the entries originally recorded in the accounts during the period* and entering them in the appropriate double-T-accounts. Once the net change in each of the nonworking capital accounts has been accounted for, sufficient information will have been generated to account for the net change in working capital.

The process of reconstructing the transactions during the year is usually easiest if supplementary information is accounted for first. Assume that the following information is obtained concerning the Solinger Electric Corporation for 1976:

1. Net income is $20,000.
2. Depreciation expense is $10,000.
3. Dividends declared and paid total $10,000.

The analytical entry to record the information concerning net income is:

(1) Working Capital (Operations—Net Income) 20,000
     Retained Earnings 20,000

The debit entry in (1) results in showing a provisional increase in working capital from operations in an amount equal to net income for the period. This is, however, only a provisional increase. Some portion of the items recognized as revenues and included in net income may not increase working capital accounts. Likewise, some portion of the items recognized as expenses and deducted in determining net income may not decrease working capital accounts. The portion of the revenues (or expenses) which do not affect working capital are subtracted from (or added to) the provisional increase in working capital to calculate the final amount of working capital from operations. Such an adjustment is illustrated for depreciation expense in entry (2).

(2) Working Capital (Operations—Depreciation Expense Addback) 10,000
     Accumulated Depreciation 10,000

Since depreciation expense was deducted in calculating net income but did not reduce working capital, the amount of depreciation expense must be added back to net income in determining the amount of working capital provided by operations. The results of entries (1) and (2) might be summarized as follows:

Working Capital (Operations—Net Income and Addbacks) 30,000
     Retained Earnings 20,000
     Accumulated Depreciation 10,000

This combined entry shows that the operating activities of Solinger Electric Corporation resulted in a $30,000 increase in working capital during 1976. That is, revenues increasing working capital exceeded expenses using working capital (total expenses less depreciation expense) by $30,000.

The supplementary information concerning dividends is recorded as follows:

(3) Retained Earnings 10,000
     Working Capital (Other Uses—Dividends) 10,000

Once the supplementary information has been reflected in the double-T-accounts, it is necessary to make inferences about the reasons for the remaining changes in the nonworking capital accounts. (If the statement of changes in financial position were being prepared for an actual firm, such inferences might not be necessary, since sufficient information regarding the change in each account is likely to be available from the firm's accounting records.) The Buildings and Equipment (Cost) account shows a net increase of $125,000. Without information to the contrary, we must deduce that buildings and equipment costing $125,000 were acquired during the year. The analytical entry is:

(4) Buildings and Equipment (Cost) 125,000
         Working Capital (Other Uses—Acquisitions of Buildings and
         Equipment) 125,000

The Bonds Payable account increased $100,000 during 1976. Without contrary information, we must deduce that long-term bonds were issued during the year. The analytical entry is:

(5) Working Capital (Other Sources—Long-Term Bond Issue) 100,000
         Bonds Payable 100,000

Exhibit 5.6 presents the completed work sheet for Solinger Electric Corporation for 1976. All double-T-account changes in the nonworking capital accounts have been explained. If the work has been done correctly, the change in the Working Capital account has also been explained.

Step 4 The final step is the preparation of the formal statement of changes in financial position. The statement for Solinger Electric Corporation is shown in Exhibit 5.7. Section I presents the sources and uses of working capital. This section of the statement is prepared directly from information in the master Working Capital account. In published annual reports, the amount of working capital provided by operations is typically derived by starting with net income and then adding back expenses which do not use working capital and subtracting revenues which do not provide working capital. This format is illustrated in the statement for Solinger Electric Corporation in Exhibit 5.7. Because depreciation expense is added to net income to determine working capital provided by operations, some readers of financial statements incorrectly conclude that depreciation expense is a source of working capital. As was illustrated in Exhibit 5.3, the recording of depreciation expense does not affect a working capital account. A noncurrent asset is decreased and an owners' equity account is decreased. Working capital is not affected. Working capital from operations results from selling goods and services to customers. If no sales are made, then there will be no working capital provided by operations regardless of how large the depreciation charge may be. Remember, depreciation is *not* a source of working capital. Rather, it is an expense that reduces net income, but does not use working capital. An alternative procedure for deriving working capital from operations is to list all revenue items that provide working capital and then subtract all expense items that use working capital. This approach is illustrated in the right-hand column of Exhibit 5.2 (and in Exhibit 1.3). This alternative presentation is appealing to us because depreciation expense does not appear as an element in the determination of working capital provided by operations. The latter presentation, although acceptable, is rarely used in published financial statements.

Section II of the Statement of Changes in Financial Position analyzes the

EXHIBIT 5.6
Double-T-Account Work Sheet for Solinger Electric Corporation

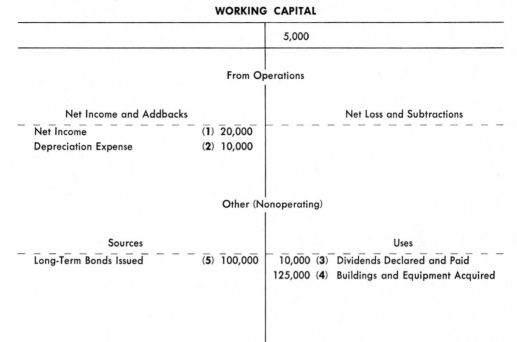

WORKING CAPITAL

	5,000

From Operations

Net Income and Addbacks

| Net Income | (1) 20,000 |
| Depreciation Expense | (2) 10,000 |

Net Loss and Subtractions

Other (Nonoperating)

Sources

| Long-Term Bonds Issued | (5) 100,000 |

Uses

| 10,000 (3) | Dividends Declared and Paid |
| 125,000 (4) | Buildings and Equipment Acquired |

BUILDINGS AND EQUIPMENT (COST)		ACCUMULATED DEPRECIATION		BONDS PAYABLE
125,000			10,000		100,000
(4) 125,000			10,000 (2)		100,000 (5)

CAPITAL STOCK		RETAINED EARNINGS	
	0		10,000
		(3) 10,000	20,000 (1)

EXHIBIT 5.7
Solinger Electric Corporation
Statement of Changes in Financial Position
For the Year 1976

SECTION I. SOURCES AND USES OF WORKING CAPITAL

Sources of Working Capital:

Operations

Net Income	$20,000	
Add Back Expenses Not Using Working Capital:		
Depreciation	10,000	
Total Sources from Operations		$ 30,000
Proceeds from Long-Term Bonds Issued		100,000
Total Sources of Working Capital		$130,000

Other Uses of Working Capital:

Dividends	$ 10,000
Acquisition of Buildings and Equipment	125,000
Total Uses of Working Capital	$135,000
Net Decrease in Working Capital during the Year (Sources Minus Uses)	$ 5,000

SECTION II. ANALYSIS OF CHANGES IN WORKING CAPITAL ACCOUNTS

Current Asset Item Increases (Decreases):

Cash	$(27,000)	
Accounts Receivable	35,000	
Merchandise Inventory	10,000	
Net Increase (Decrease) in Current Asset Items		$ 18,000

Current Liability Increases (Decreases):

Accounts Payable—Merchandise Suppliers	$20,000	
Accounts Payable—Other Suppliers	2,000	
Salaries Payable	1,000	
Net Increase (Decrease) in Current Liability Items		23,000
Net Decrease in Working Capital During the Year (Net Increase in Current Liability Items Minus Net Increase in Current Asset Items)		$ 5,000

changes in the individual current asset and current liability accounts. That is, the manner in which the net change in working capital (explained in Section I of the statement) affects the various working capital accounts is analyzed in Section II. The information needed for preparing Section II is obtained from the comparative balance sheets in Exhibit 5.4.

The information in Section II of the statement is necessary for a complete assessment of a firm's liquidity and changes in the structure of its assets and equities. The net change explained in Section I can result from the offsetting of much larger increases and decreases in individual current asset and current liability accounts.

For example, cash decreased by $27,000 while accounts receivable increased by $35,000 during the year. Together, this represents an increase of $8,000 in the firm's most liquid assets. However, most of the increased liquidity does not reflect cash immediately available to pay liabilities or to make purchases. Instead, cash must first be collected from customers. Financial statement readers interested in assessing changes in the structure of the firm's working capital would find the information in Section II of the Statement of Changes in Financial Position to be useful.

The format of the statement of changes in financial position is discussed more fully in Chapter Six.

Extension of the Illustration

The illustration for Solinger Electric Corporation considered so far in this chapter is simpler than the typical published statement of changes in financial position in at least four respects:

1. There are only a few balance sheet accounts whose changes are to be explained.
2. Several types of more complex transactions that affect the sources of working capital from operations are not involved.
3. Each transaction recorded in Step 3 involves only one debit and one credit.
4. Each explanation of a nonworking capital account change involves only one transaction, except for the Retained Earnings account.

Let us reconsider Solinger Electric Corporation with the following new information. Solinger Electric Corporation sold some equipment during 1976. This equipment cost $10,000 and was sold for $3,000 at a time when accumulated depreciation on the equipment sold was $6,000. The actual entry made during the year to record the sale of the equipment was as follows:

Cash	3,000	
Accumulated Depreciation	6,000	
Loss on Sale of Equipment	1,000	
Buildings and Equipment (Cost)		10,000

Assume that the comparative balance sheets as shown in Exhibit 5.4 are correct and thus that the net decrease in working capital for 1976 is still $5,000. The entries in the double-T-accounts must be altered to reflect this new information. The following entry in the double-T-accounts is required to recognize the effect of the sale of equipment:

(1a) Working Capital (Other Sources—Proceeds from Sale of Equipment)	3,000	
Working Capital (Operations—Loss on Sale of Equipment Addback)	1,000	
Accumulated Depreciation	6,000	
Buildings and Equipment (Cost)		10,000

The debit to Working Capital (Other Sources—Proceeds from Sale of Equipment) shows the proceeds of the sale. The debit to Working Capital (Operations—Loss on Sale of Equipment Addback) adjusts the working capital provided by operations to recognize that while the Loss on Sale of Equipment reduced net income, it did not require the use of working capital from operations. Had the firm known, when it acquired the equipment, that the selling price was going to be $3,000, the depreciation charges over the life of the equipment would have been $1,000 larger, or a total of $7,000. Thus, net income over the periods between acquisition and sale would have been $1,000 smaller. Accumulated depreciation at the time of sale would be $7,000 and there would be no loss. The loss recognized at the time of sale reduces this period's income to correct for the original misestimate. The working capital effects of acquiring, using, and selling the equipment are simply that (1) $10,000 was used when the equipment was acquired and (2) $3,000 was produced when it was sold. The addbacks to net income for depreciation (during the time the firm used the equipment) and for the loss (when the firm sold it) adjust net income to a working capital basis.

As a result of entry (1a), the double-T-accounts for Buildings and Equipment (Cost) and Accumulated Depreciation would be as follows:

BUILDINGS AND EQUIPMENT (COST)		ACCUMULATED DEPRECIATION	
125,000			10,000
	10,000 (1a)	(1a) 6,000	

When it comes time to explain the change in the account, Buildings and Equipment (Cost), the double-T-account indicates that there is a net debit change (asset increase) of $125,000 and a credit entry (1a) of $10,000 to recognize the sale of equipment. The net increase in the Buildings and Equipment (Cost) account can only be accounted for, given the decrease already entered, by assuming that new buildings and equipment have been acquired during the period for $135,000.

The reconstructed entry to complete the explanation of the change in this account would be as follows:

(4a) Buildings and Equipment (Cost) 135,000
     Working Capital (Other Uses—Acquisition of Buildings and
     Equipment) 135,000

Likewise, when the change in the double-T-account for Accumulated Depreciation is explained, there is a net credit change of $10,000 and a debit entry (1a) of $6,000 to recognize the sale. Thus, the depreciation charge for 1976 must have been $16,000. The reconstructed entry to complete the explanation of the change in the Accumulated Depreciation account would be as follows:

(2a) Working Capital (Operations—Depreciation Expense Addback) 16,000
     Accumulated Depreciation 16,000

EXHIBIT 5.8
Revised Double-T-Account Work Sheet
For Solinger Electric Corporation

WORKING CAPITAL

	5,000

From Operations

Net Income and Addbacks			Net Loss and Subtractions
Net Income	(1)	20,000	
Depreciation Expense	(2)	16,000	
Loss on Sale of Equipment	(1a)	1,000	

Other (Nonoperating)

Sources			Uses
Sale of Equipment	(1a)	3,000	
Long-Term Bonds Issued	(5)	100,000	10,000 (3) Dividends Declared and Paid
			135,000 (4) Buildings and Equipment Acquired

BUILDINGS AND EQUIPMENT (COST)		ACCUMULATED DEPRECIATION		BONDS PAYABLE	
125,000			10,000		100,000
(4) 135,000	10,000 (1a)	(1a) 6,000	16,000 (2)		100,000 (5)

CAPITAL STOCK		RETAINED EARNINGS	
	0		10,000
		(3) 10,000	20,000 (1)

A revised double-T-account work sheet for Solinger Electric Corporation incorporating the new information on the sale of equipment is presented in Exhibit 5.8.

The sale of buildings and equipment at a gain, instead of a loss, would be handled in a similar manner. However, the gain would be *subtracted* from net income to determine working capital provided by operations. The proceeds from sales of noncurrent assets are viewed as nonoperating sources of working capital rather than as sources of working capital from operations.

■ CONVERSION OF WORKING CAPITAL PROVIDED BY OPERATIONS TO CASH FLOW PROVIDED BY OPERATIONS

Most published statements of changes in financial position use working capital as the definition of funds. If the user is interested in the effects of operations on cash flows, a more restrictive definition of funds is required. A procedure for converting working capital from operations to cash flow from operations is presented below:

1. Begin with the amount of working capital provided by operations as previously determined.
2. Add the amount of the change in working capital accounts (other than cash) which experienced a net credit change during the period [that is, decreases in current asset accounts (other than cash) and increases in current liability accounts].
3. Subtract the amount of the change in working capital accounts (other than cash) which experienced a net debit change during the period [that is, increases in current asset accounts (other than cash) and decreases in current liability accounts].
4. The result is the cash flow provided by operations.

We saw in Exhibit 5.2 that the working capital provided by operations during 1976 by Solinger Electric Corporation was $30,000, while the cash flow provided by operations was $8,000. Exhibit 5.9 illustrates the procedure for converting working capital to cash flow provided by operations.

The rationale for the additions and the subtractions in this procedure may be better understood by considering Salaries Payable and Accounts Receivable.

The change in the Salaries Payable account is explained as follows:

Salaries Payable, December 31, 1975	$ 5,000
Plus Salaries Expense—1976	20,000
Less Salaries Paid in Cash—1976	(19,000)
Salaries Payable, December 31, 1976	$ 6,000

The amount of working capital provided by operations reflects a $20,000 use of working capital relating to salary expense during the period. Since only $19,000

EXHIBIT 5.9
Solinger Electric Corporation
Conversion of Working Capital Provided by Operations
to Cash Flow Provided by Operations

Working Capital Provided by Operations		$30,000
Add the Net Change in Current Asset Accounts (Except Cash) Which Decreased and Current Liability Accounts Which Increased During the Period (Credit Changes):		
Accounts Payable—Merchandise Suppliers	$20,000	
Accounts Payable—Other Suppliers	2,000	
Salaries Payable	1,000	
Total Additions		23,000
Subtract the Net Change in Current Asset Accounts (Except Cash) Which Increased and Current Liability Accounts Which Decreased During the Period (Debit Changes):		
Accounts Receivable	$35,000	
Merchandise Inventory	10,000	
Total Subtractions		(45,000)
Cash Flow Provided by Operations		$ 8,000

was disbursed to employees, $1,000 (= $20,000 — $19,000) must be added back to working capital from operations to determine cash flow from operations.

The change in the Accounts Receivable account is explained as follows:

Accounts Receivable, December 31, 1975	$ 20,000
Plus Sales on Account—1976	125,000
Less Cash Collections from Customers—1976	(90,000)
Accounts Receivable, December 31, 1976	$ 55,000

The amount of working capital provided by operations reflects a $125,000 source of working capital relating to sales on account during the period. Since only $90,000 was collected in cash, $35,000 (= $125,000 — $90,000) must be subtracted from working capital provided by operations to determine cash flow provided by operations.

■ SUMMARY

A statement of changes in financial position must be presented whenever a firm presents an income statement and a balance sheet. The statement of changes in financial position reports on flows of funds into and out of a business during a period. Funds are usually defined as working capital (current assets minus current liabilities), but occasionally funds may be defined simply as cash. The statement discloses the sources of funds from operations separately from the nonoperating sources and uses.

The primary source of funds is usually working capital provided by operations. Understanding the notion of working capital provided by operations is particularly important to understanding the statement of changes in financial position. Net income is derived from revenues and expenses computed on an accrual basis. The statement of changes in financial position converts net income from the accrual basis to a report of funds, or working capital, flows. Working capital provided by operations is rarely equal to net income provided by operations.

The statement of changes in financial position is basically derived from an analysis of changes in balance sheet accounts during the accounting period. If the double-entry recording process has been applied properly, the net change in working capital accounts during the period will equal the net change in all nonworking capital accounts. By reconstructing the entries made in nonworking capital accounts and explaining their net change during the period, the net change in the working capital accounts is also explained.

The format of the statement of changes in financial position is organized in two sections. The sources and uses of working capital are presented first, followed by an analysis of the changes in the individual working capital accounts. Most published statements of changes in financial position show the derivation of working capital provided by operations by beginning with net income and then adding expenses that do not use working capital and subtracting revenues that do not provide working capital. This format leads some statement readers to conclude incorrectly that depreciation expense is a source of working capital. To avoid this misinterpretation, we prefer a format in which the portion of revenues that provide working capital is listed and then the portion of expenses that use working capital is subtracted to obtain working capital provided by operations.

QUESTIONS AND PROBLEMS

1. Review the meaning of the following concepts or terms discussed in this chapter.
   a. Funds flow.
   b. Liquidity.
   c. Cash as funds.
   d. Working capital as funds.
   e. All financial resources as funds.
   f. Source of funds.
   g. Use of funds.
   h. Statement of changes in financial position.
   i. Working capital provided by operations.
   j. Cash flow provided by operations.
   k. Double-T-account.
   l. Analysis of changes in working capital accounts.
   m. Depreciation is not a source of funds.
   n. Liquidity may be unrelated to earnings.
   o. Dual transactions assumption.
2. What is the objective of a statement of changes in financial position?

3. Can the statement of changes in financial position substitute for the balance sheet? The income statement?

4. How would the statement of changes in financial position differ if the changes in cash, rather than working capital, were explained?

5. Refer to the problem of the Solinger Electric Corporation as summarized in Exhibit 5.4. Assume that the company sold equipment during 1976. This equipment cost $10,000 and was sold for $5,500 at a time when accumulated depreciation on the equipment sold amounted to $6,000. Net income for the year was $20,000, and dividends declared and paid were $10,000. Taking into account this additional information, prepare the following:

   a. Journal entry to be recorded at the time of sale.

   b. Double-T-account work sheet for a statement of changes in financial position. (Notice that this is the first instance of a transaction that requires a subtraction from net income to calculate working capital provided by operations. Since the entire proceeds of the sale of equipment, $5,500, are shown as a nonoperating source of working capital, the gain on sale did not produce any additional working capital from operations. If the amount of the gain were not subtracted, the amount of working capital from this transaction would be counted twice.)

   c. A statement of changes in financial position for the year 1976.

6. The statement of changes in financial position for the Alcar Company shows the following:

Sources of Funds:
   From Operations:
      Net Income $375,000
      Add Back Loss on Disposal of Factory 63,000 $438,000

In what sense is the loss on disposal of a factory a source of funds? Or is it?

7. The statement of changes in financial position indicates that the board of directors of the Calex Company declared dividends of $500,000 during the year. The comparative balance sheets show Dividends Payable of $80,000 at the start of the year and $100,000 at the end of the year. How much cash was distributed in dividends during the year?

8. Indicate the presentation, if any, of each of the following in a statement of changes in financial position:

   a. Depreciation expense.

   b. Gain on sale of machinery for cash.

   c. Declaration of a cash dividend on common stock; the dividend has not been paid at the close of the fiscal year.

   d. Issue of preferred stock for cash.

   e. Issue of common stock for cash.

   f. Gain on sale of common stock investment, a noncurrent asset, for cash.

   g. Amortization of patent, charged to production activities.

   h. Amortization of patent, treated as an expense.

   i. Acquisition of a factory site by issue of capital stock.

   j. Uninsured fire loss of a warehouse.

   k. Uninsured fire loss of merchandise stored in the warehouse.

   l. Collection of an account receivable.

    m. Issue of bonds for cash.

    n. Sale of equipment for cash, at less than book value.

9. One writer stated that:

> *Depreciation expense was the chief source of funds for growth in some industries.*

A reader criticized this statement by replying:

> *The fact remains that if the companies listed . . . had elected, in any year, to charge off $10 million more depreciation than they did charge off, they would not thereby have added one dime to the total of their funds available for plant expansion or for increasing inventories or receivables. Therefore, to speak of depreciation expense as a source of funds . . . has no significance in a discussion of fundamentals.*

Comment on these statements, including income tax effects.

10. The comparative balance sheet of the Johns Company showed a balance in the Buildings and Equipment account at December 31, 1976, of $24,645,000; at December 31, 1975, the balance was $24,150,000. The Accumulated Depreciation account showed a balance of $8,670,000 at December 31, 1976, and $7,655,000 at December 31, 1975. The president's report states that expenditures for buildings and equipment for the year totaled $1,325,000. The income statement indicates a depreciation charge of $1,205,000 for the year and a gain of $52,750 from the disposition of buildings and equipment in the determination of the periodic income.

    a. Determine the acquisition cost and accumulated depreciation of the buildings and equipment retired during the year and the proceeds from their disposition.

    b. Describe how the above information would be presented on the statement of changes in financial position for 1976.

11. The income statement of the Weller Company reports an excess of Sales over Cost of Goods Sold of $55,360,500 for 1976. Other items included in determining net income are as follows:

Dividend Revenue, Including $100,000 Not Yet Collected	$ 450,000
Gain on Sale of Depreciable Assets	80,000
Depreciation on Factory Building and Equipment	7,835,000
Uninsured Fire Loss on a Noncurrent Asset	70,000
Interest Charges	125,250
Income Taxes	17,600,000

Determine the amount of working capital made available from operations during the year. Present your calculations.

12. Condensed financial statement data of the Alberta Company for the years ending December 31, 1974, 1975, and 1976, are presented below:

Alberta Company
Postclosing Trial Balance
Comparative Data

Debits:	12/31/74	12/31/75	12/31/76
Current Assets	$ 290,160	$ 316,190	$ 326,800
Noncurrent Assets	1,616,390	1,679,220	1,874,630
Total Debits	$1,906,550	$1,995,410	$2,201,430

Credits:

Current Liabilities	$ 81,530	$ 79,860	$ 83,450
Accumulated Depreciation	697,390	720,970	746,770
Long-Term Debt	105,760	90,110	135,070
Capital Stock	376,670	423,220	513,720
Retained Earnings	645,200	681,250	722,420
Total Credits	$1,906,550	$1,995,410	$2,201,430

INCOME AND RETAINED EARNINGS STATEMENT DATA

	1975	1976
Sales	$909,690	$970,260
Cost of Goods Sold	370,170	413,810
Selling and Administrative Expenses	319,920	301,120
Depreciation	87,140	97,800
Interest and Other Revenue	4,740	7,220
Federal Income Taxes	66,370	72,350
Gain (Loss) on Disposal of Plant and Equipment	5,320	(4,680)
Dividends Declared	40,100	46,550

The book value of the noncurrent assets sold during 1975 was $43,950.

Prepare a statement of changes in financial position for the year 1975. Support the statement with a double-T-account work sheet.

13. Refer to the data of Problem **12.** Prepare a double-T-account work sheet and a statement of changes in financial position for 1976. Expenditures on noncurrent assets amounted to $317,930 during 1976.

14. Financial statement data for the Perkerson Supply Company for the years ending December 31, 1975, and December 31, 1976, are presented below:

Perkerson Supply Company
Comparative Balance Sheets

ASSETS

	12/31/75	12/31/76
	($ in 000's)	
Current Assets		
Cash	$ 267	$ 240
Accounts Receivable	223	325
Inventory	521	671
Total Current Assets	$1,011	$1,236
Noncurrent Assets		
Land	$ 142	$ 153
Buildings and Machinery	3,364	3,556
Less Accumulated Depreciation	(857)	(1,041)
Total Noncurrent Assets	$2,649	$2,668
Total Assets	$3,660	$3,904

LIABILITIES AND STOCKHOLDERS' EQUITY

Current Liabilities

Accounts Payable	$ 138	$ 231
Taxes Payable	117	104
Other Short-Term Payables	301	392
Total Current Liabilities	$ 556	$ 727

Noncurrent Liabilities

Bonds Payable	995	971
Total Liabilities	$1,551	$1,698

Stockholders' Equity

Common Stock	$ 807	$ 827
Retained Earnings	1,302	1,379
Total Stockholders' Equity	$2,109	$2,206
Total Liabilities and Stockholders' Equity	$3,660	$3,904

Additional Information:

(1) Net income for the year was $159,000; dividends declared and paid were $82,000.

(2) Depreciation expense for the year was $210,000 on buildings and machinery.

(3) Machinery originally costing $53,000 and with accumulated depreciation of $26,000 was sold for $30,000.

Prepare a statement of changes in financial position for the Perkerson Supply Company for 1976. Support the statement with a double-T-account work sheet.

15. Condensed financial statement data for the Edwards Construction Company for the end of years 1975, 1976, and 1977 are presented below:

Edwards Construction Company
Comparative Balance Sheets

ASSETS

	12/31/77	12/31/76	12/31/75
Current Assets	$302,060	$262,230	$245,040
Noncurrent Assets (at Cost)	511,470	483,550	439,470
Accumulated Depreciation	(185,710)	(167,230)	(146,790)
Total Assets	$627,820	$578,550	$537,720

LIABILITIES

	12/31/77	12/31/76	12/31/75
Current Liabilities	$103,690	$ 87,810	$ 96,720
Bonds Payable	84,390	97,610	63,410
Total Liabilities	$188,080	$185,420	$160,130

STOCKHOLDERS' EQUITY

Common Stock	$150,560	$150,000	$150,000
Additional Paid-In Capital	6,870	6,870	6,870
Retained Earnings	282,310	236,260	220,720
Total Stockholders' Equity	**$439,740**	**$393,130**	**$377,590**
Total Liabilities and Stockholders' Equity	**$627,820**	**$578,550**	**$537,720**

Additional Information:

(1) In 1977, noncurrent assets originally costing $50,040 were sold for their book value of $6,150.

(2) In 1977, net income to stockholders was $117,330 and dividends on common stock were $71,280.

From the above information, prepare a statement of changes in financial position for the year 1977. Support the statement with a double-T-account work sheet.

16. Refer to the financial statement data for the Edwards Construction Company in Problem 15 and to the additional information below:

(1) Net income to stockholders in 1976 was $86,650, which included a loss of $5,120 on disposition of noncurrent assets.

(2) Depreciation expense in 1976 amounted to $57,880; acquisitions of noncurrent assets totaled $146,230.

(3) Dividends declared in 1976 were $71,110.

Prepare a statement of changes in financial position for the year 1976. Support the statement with a double-T-account work sheet.

17. The Quinta Company presents the following postclosing trial balance and statement of changes in financial position for the year 1976.

Quinta Company
Postclosing Trial Balance, December 31, 1976

Debit Balances:

Working Capital	$200,000
Land	40,000
Buildings and Equipment	500,000
Investments (Noncurrent)	100,000
Total Debits	$840,000

Credit Balances:

Accumulated Depreciation	$200,000
Bonds Payable	100,000
Common Stock	200,000
Retained Earnings	340,000
Total Credits	$840,000

Quinta Company
Statement of Changes in Financial Position for the Year 1976

SOURCES OF WORKING CAPITAL

		($ in 000's)
A. From Operations:		
Net Income		$200
Addbacks for Expenses and Losses Not Using Working Capital:		
Depreciation	$60	
Loss on Sale of Investments	10	
Total Addbacks		$70
Subtractions for Gains Not Producing Working Capital:		
Gain on Sale of Buildings and Equipment	5	
Net Expense, Loss, and Gain Adjustments		65
Total Sources from Operations		$265
B. Proceeds from Issues of Securities and Debt:		
Capital Stock Issue	$50	
Bond Issue	50	
Total Proceeds		100
C. Proceeds of Disposition of Noncurrent Assets:		
Sale of Investments	$40	
Sale of Buildings and Equipment	15	
Sale of Land	10	
Total Proceeds		65
Total Sources of Working Capital		$430

USES OF WORKING CAPITAL

A. Dividends	$200
B. Acquisition of Buildings and Equipment	130
Total Uses of Working Capital	$330
Increase in Working Capital During the Year	
(Sources Minus Uses)	$100

Net Increase in Working Capital Items

(Net Current Asset Item Increases Minus Net Current Liability Item Increases) ... $100

The accumulated depreciation of the equipment sold was $20,000. Current liabilities were $75,000 at the start of the year and $125,000 at the end of the year. Prepare a balance sheet for the beginning of the year, January 1, 1976.

18. Condensed financial statement data for the Harris Company are shown below.

Harris Company
Comparative Balance Sheets

ASSETS

	January 1, 1976	December 31, 1976
Cash	$ 12,000	$ 14,000
Receivables (Net)	36,000	40,000
Inventory	63,000	64,000
Land	11,000	11,000
Building and Equipment (Cost)	300,000	313,000
Less Accumulated Depreciation	(160,000)	(167,000)
Total Assets	$262,000	$275,000

LIABILITIES AND STOCKHOLDERS' EQUITY

Accounts Payable	$ 45,000	$ 48,000
Notes Payable (Current)	14,000	13,000
Mortgage Payable	40,000	40,000
Common Stock	100,000	104,000
Retained Earnings	63,000	70,000
Total Liabilities and Stockholders' Equity	$262,000	$275,000

Harris Company
Partial Statement of Income and Retained Earnings
For the Year 1976

Net Income	$17,000
Dividends on Common Stock	10,000
Addition to Retained Earnings for Year	$ 7,000
Retained Earnings, January 1, 1976	63,000
Retained Earnings, December 31, 1976	$70,000

Supplementary Information:
(1) Depreciation expense during the year amounted to $11,000.
(2) Equipment costing $5,000 and with $4,000 of accumulated depreciation was sold for $1,000.
   a. Prepare a double-T-account work sheet for the statement of changes in financial position for the year 1976.
   b. Prepare a statement of changes in financial position for the year 1976.
19. Refer to Problem 14 concerning Perkerson Supply Company. Convert working capital provided by operations to cash flow provided by operations.
20. Refer to Problem 18 concerning Harris Company. Convert working capital provided by operations to cash flow provided by operations.
21. The purpose of this problem is to convince you that gains from dispositions of previously acquired noncurrent assets require a subtraction from net income to

derive funds provided by operations in the statement of changes in financial position. To carry out this exercise, get one writing pen and a dollar's worth of nickles and dimes (or pieces of paper to represent this amount). Clear off some space on your desk. Put 40 cents and the writing pen on the other side of the desk and put 60 cents on your side of the desk.

(1) Your balance sheet now looks like the one shown below.

My Balance Sheet as of Now

ASSETS		EQUITIES	
Cash	$0.60	Contributed Capital	$0.60

(2) You are about to acquire a noncurrent asset, one long-lived writing pen. The pen costs 40 cents.

(3) Acquire the pen by exchanging 40 cents for the pen which is now across the desk. You record the following journal entry:

Noncurrent Assets.......................................	0.40	
Cash		0.40

(4) Because of scarce supplies, the price of pens has just increased to 70 cents each, and you decide to sell your pen. Dispose of your pen to the other side of the desk for 70 cents. Record the following journal entry:

Cash	0.70	
Noncurrent Assets		0.40
Gain on Disposition of Noncurrent Assets		0.30

  a. Ignore income taxes. Prepare an income statement for the period just ended and a balance sheet as of the end of the period.

  b. Prepare a statement of changes in financial position for the period just ended. Start with net income and adjustments thereto. You should also show a non-operating source of funds from the disposition of noncurrent assets ($0.70) and a nonoperating use of funds for the acquisition of noncurrent assets ($0.40).

    Note: Observe that net income produced no funds not otherwise counted in the nonoperating sources and uses. Funds were provided by selling one pen. If you were to add net income to the proceeds of the sale of the pen, you would double-count your sources of funds. If this is not clear, then repeat steps **a** and **b** until it is.

22. The purpose of this problem is to convince you that depreciation expense uses no funds and that depreciation is not a source of funds. To carry out this exercise, get one writing pen, a dollar's worth of change, and a piece of paper. Put 40 cents, the writing pen, and the piece of paper on the other side of the desk and put 60 cents on your side of the desk.

(1) Your balance sheet now looks like the one shown below.

My Balance Sheet as of Now

ASSETS		EQUITIES	
Cash	$0.60	Contributed Capital	$0.60

(2) You are about to acquire a *noncurrent* asset, one long-lived writing pen. The pen costs 40 cents.

(3) Acquire the pen by exchanging 40 cents for the pen which is now across the desk. Record the following journal entry:

Noncurrent Assets	0.40	
Cash		0.40

(4) Acquire the piece of paper, a current asset item, by trading 5 cents for the paper which is now across the desk. Record the following journal entry:

Current Asset—Paper Inventory	0.05	
Cash		0.05

(5) Sign your name on the piece of paper you now have with the pen you acquired. (No journal entry required.)

(6) Because of a sudden surge in your popularity, your autograph has become valuable. Sell your autograph to the other side of the table for 80 cents. Record the following journal entry:

Cash	0.80	
Sales		0.80

(7) The accounting period is over. Record an adjusting entry to recognize 10 cents depreciation for the period on the writing pen:

Depreciation on Noncurrent Assets	0.10	
Accumulated Depreciation on Noncurrent Assets		0.10

(8) Depreciation on Noncurrent Assets is, in this case, a cost of work in process inventory which is to be counted as part of Cost of Goods Sold. Record the following journal entry to measure Cost of Goods Sold.

Cost of Goods Sold	0.15	
Depreciation on Noncurrent Assets		0.10
Current Asset—Paper Inventory		0.05

(9) Close all temporary accounts with the following entry:

Sales	0.80	
Cost of Goods Sold		0.15
Retained Earnings		0.65

a. Ignore income taxes. Prepare an income statement for the period just ended and a balance sheet as of the end of the period.

b. Prepare a statement of changes in financial position for the period just ended. Start with net income and adjustments thereto.

Note: Observe that depreciation used no funds not otherwise counted in the nonoperating sources and uses. Funds were provided by selling one autograph. Notice that your funds on hand at the end of the period do not depend on the amount of depreciation on the pen for the period. If this is not clear, repeat **a** and **b** assuming depreciation of $0.30 or $0.00 in step (**7**).

Chapter Six

Financial Statement Format and Disclosure

Our study of accounting thus far has focused on the concepts underlying the balance sheet, income statement, and statement of changes in financial position, as well as on the procedures for preparing each statement. In this chapter, we consider the manner in which information about the firm's operations and financial position is presented, or disclosed, in these accounting reports. The discussion and illustrations concentrate on the financial statements presented in annual reports to stockholders, although similar reporting practices are followed in preparing financial statements for creditors, stock exchanges, and governmental agencies.

■ COMPONENTS OF ANNUAL REPORTS

Where the capital stock of a corporation is widely held and its affairs are of interest to the general public, the annual report becomes a matter of public relations. Modern annual reports are often elaborate brochures containing a great deal of art work, photographs, charts, and even advertisements for the firm's products.

The section of the annual report presenting the firm's financial statements generally includes the following items:

1. auditor's opinion
2. comparative financial statements and supporting schedules
3. a summary of significant accounting policies
4. a series of notes elaborating more fully on items reported upon in the financial statements.

Auditor's Opinion

An important section of the annual report to the stockholders is the opinion of the independent Certified Public Accountant on the financial statements, supporting schedules, and notes. The accountant's opinion is frequently described as the *Accountant's Report,* or sometimes merely as the *Opinion* or *Certificate.* It is often called the report of the *Auditor* or *Certified Public Accountant.*

The auditor's opinion generally follows a standard format, with some variations to meet specific circumstances. A recent opinion of the auditor for Ford Motor Company is shown in Exhibit 6.1.

EXHIBIT 6.1
An Unqualified Auditor's Opinion

Auditors' Opinion

To the Board of Directors and Stockholders of Ford Motor Company:

We have examined the consolidated balance sheet of Ford Motor Company and Consolidated Subsidiaries as of December 31, 1974 and the related consolidated statements of income, stockholders' equity and changes in financial position for the year then ended. Our examination was made in accordance with generally accepted auditing standards, and accordingly included such tests of the accounting records and such other auditing procedures as we considered necessary in the circumstances. We previously examined and reported upon the financial statements of Ford Motor Company and Consolidated Subsidiaries for the year ended December 31, 1973.

In our opinion, the aforementioned financial statements present fairly the consolidated financial position of Ford Motor Company and Consolidated Subsidiaries at December 31, 1974 and 1973, and the consolidated results of operations and the changes in financial position for the years then ended, in conformity with generally accepted accounting principles applied on a consistent basis.

Coopers & Lybrand

Coopers & Lybrand
211 West Fort Street, 23rd Floor
Detroit, Michigan 48226
February 14, 1975

The opinion usually contains two paragraphs—a *scope* paragraph and an *opinion* paragraph. The scope paragraph indicates the financial presentations covered by the opinion and affirms that auditing standards and practices generally accepted by the accounting profession have been adhered to unless otherwise noted and described. Exceptions to the statement that the auditor's "examination was made in accordance with generally accepted auditing standards" are seldom, if ever, seen in published annual reports. There are occasional references to the auditor's having relied on financial statements examined by other auditors, particularly for subsidiaries or for data from prior periods.

The opinion expressed by the auditor in the second paragraph is the heart of the accountant's report. The opinion may be *unqualified* or *qualified.* The great majority of opinions are unqualified; that is, there are no exceptions or qualifications to the auditor's opinion that the statements "present fairly the financial position . . . and the results of operations and the changes in financial position . . .

in conformity with generally accepted accounting principles applied on a consistent basis."

Qualifications to the opinion result primarily from material uncertainties regarding valuation or realization of assets, outstanding litigation or tax liabilities, or accountng inconsistencies between periods caused by changes in the application of accounting principles. An opinion qualified as to fair presentation is usually noted by the phrase *subject to*; an opinion qualified as to consistency in application of accounting principles is usually noted by *except for*, with an indication of the auditor's approval of the change. A qualified ("except for") opinion in the accountant's report on the financial statements of S. S. Kresge Company is presented in Exhibit 6.2.

A qualification so material that the auditor feels an opinion cannot be expressed as to the fairness of the financial statements as a whole must result in either a *disclaimer of opinion* or an *adverse opinion*. Adverse opinions and disclaimers of opinion are extremely rare in published reports.

A member of the American Institute of Certified Public Accountants (AICPA) is expected to adhere to the pronouncements of the body designated by the AICPA as the official source of generally accepted accounting principles.[1] The official authoritative body from 1938 to 1959 was the Committee on Accounting Procedure and from 1959 to 1973 was the Accounting Principles Board. Since 1973, the Financial Accounting Standards Board has been given the authority for specifying generally accepted accounting principles. A Certified Public Accountant may not, in general, attest that statements are in conformity with generally accepted accounting principles when the statements contain material departures from rulings of those bodies. If, however, the CPA can demonstrate that, because of unusual circumstances, departures are required so that the statements are not misleading, then the CPA may attest to statements with material departures from generally acceped accounting principles. The grounds for justifying departures are so stringent, however, that such departures are seldom, if ever, seen in published financial statements.

Comparative Statements and Notes

With few exceptions, the primary financial statements are presented in comparative form, usually for the current year and the preceding year. It is generally recognized that comparative reports make clearer the nature and trend of changes in operations, assets, and financing than would a single set of statements. The principal financial statements also contain a series of notes which explain more fully various items in the body of the statement.

Consolidated Statements

Most large, publicly held corporations conduct their activities through numerous, legally separate, subsidiary corporations. Since the parent corporation generally

---

[1] Rule 203, Code of Professional Ethics, AICPA, March 1973.

EXHIBIT 6.2
A Qualified Auditor's Opinion

To the Stockholders and Board of Directors of S. S. Kresge Company

We have examined the accompanying consolidated balance sheets of S. S. Kresge Company and its subsidiaries as of January 29, 1975 and January 30, 1974, and the related consolidated statements of income, income retained for use in the business and changes in financial position for the years then ended. Our examinations were made in accordance with generally accepted auditing standards and accordingly included such tests of the accounting records and such other auditing procedures as we considered necessary in the circumstances.

As described in Note B to the financial statements, in 1974, the Company changed to the last-in, first-out method of determining costs for a substantial amount of its domestic inventories.

In our opinion, the accompanying consolidated financial statements examined by us present fairly the financial position of S. S. Kresge Company and its subsidiaries at January 29, 1975 and January 30, 1974, the results of their operations and the changes in financial position for the years then ended, in conformity with generally accepted accounting principles consistently applied during the period except for the change, with which we concur, referred to in the preceding paragraph.

Price Waterhouse & Co.

211 West Fort Street
Detroit, Michigan
March 14, 1975

owns a sufficient voting interest in these subsidiaries to exert control over their activities, consolidated financial statements are prepared for this group of entities essentially as if the group were a single entity. The preparation and interpretation of consolidated financial statements are discussed in Chapter Thirteen.

Summary of Significant Accounting Policies

A summarized statement of significant accounting policies is required as an integral part of the financial statement presentation.[2] The disclosure of accounting policies identifies the accounting principles adopted by the reporting enterprise and the methods of applying the principles which substantially affect the determination of income, financial position, and changes in financial position. The summary statement may be given either in a separate "Summary of Significant Accounting Policies" preceding the notes to the financial statements, or in the first note to the statements. A summary of accounting policies from the financial statements of Ford Motor Company is shown in Exhibit 15.1.

The following list indicates the areas of accounting principles and methods of application frequently presented in a summary statement of accounting principles:

Basis for consolidation
Basis for foreign currency translation
Method of recognizing income on long-term construction contracts
Method of recognizing revenue from franchising and leasing operations
Basis for valuation of inventory
Methods of accounting for:
    investments
    property, plant, and equipment
    research and development costs
    intangibles, such as patents and goodwill
    retirement and pension plans
    leases and rentals
    income taxes and investment tax credits
    earnings per share.

All of these items are not likely to appear in any one annual report.

Much of the remainder of this text is devoted to a description and illustration of the accounting principles, or procedures, which a firm might adopt in preparing its financial statements.

■ THE BALANCE SHEET

Format of the Balance Sheet

Most published balance sheets follow the conventional procedure of presenting the balance sheet accounts in two groups. Assets are typically displayed in one group at the left and liabilities and stockholders' equity in another group at the

[2] Opinion No. 22, Accounting Principle Board, AICPA, April 1972.

right. Exhibit 6.3 presents a recent balance sheet for Ford Motor Company. (You are not now able to understand some of the accounts shown in that balance sheet, but you should understand all of them by the time you have completed this book.) If the statement is sufficiently condensed, a vertical arrangement is used, with assets shown at the top of the page and liabilities and stockholders' equity shown at the bottom. Some corporations have adopted a variation of the basic balance

EXHIBIT 6.3
Ford Motor Company and Consolidated Subsidiaries
Consolidated Balance Sheet
December 31, 1974 and 1973
(in millions of dollars)

Assets	1974	1973
Current Assets		
Cash (Note 7)...	$ 234.2	$ 434.4
Marketable securities, at cost, which approximates market......................	371.7	647.8
Receivables—(including $63.4 million in 1974 and $139.2 million in 1973 from unconsolidated subsidiaries)...................................	1,457.1	1,078.8
Inventories..	4,253.0	3,592.7
Income taxes allocable to the following year...................................	221.4	206.5
Other current assets...	303.8	229.3
Total current assets...	6,841.2	6,189.5
Investments and Other Assets		
Equities in net assets of unconsolidated subsidiaries and affiliates (Note 8)........	1,140.1	1,069.1
Other investments, at cost, and other assets....................................	229.1	223.5
Total investments and other assets......................................	1,369.2	1,292.6
Property		
Land, plant and equipment, at cost (Note 9).....................................	9,476.4	8,836.7
Less accumulated depreciation...	4,834.5	4,460.1
Net land, plant and equipment..	4,641.9	4,376.6
Unamortized special tools..	1,042.1	816.1
Net property...	5,684.0	5,192.7
Excess of Cost of Investments in Consolidated Subsidiaries over Equities in Net Assets......................................	279.2	279.2
Total Assets..	$14,173.6	$12,954.0

sheet form. Current liabilities are deducted from current assets to determine working capital; other assets are added to this figure, and the long-term liabilities are deducted from the total. The balance is the total of stockholders' equity. The components of stockholders' equity are then presented. This format focuses on the stockholders' interest in the net assets position of the firm and on the stockholders' equity.

Liabilities and Stockholders' Equity	1974	1973
Current Liabilities		
Accounts payable and accrued liabilities....................................	$ 3,932.3	$ 3,537.1
Income taxes...	127.8	158.9
Short-term debt of consolidated subsidiaries (Note 10).......................	1,219.3	651.8
Long-term debt payable within one year....................................	61.5	181.2
Total current liabilities...	5,340.9	4,529.0
Long-Term Debt (Note 10)...	1,476.7	977.0
Other Liabilities and Reserves		
Accrued liabilities, noncurrent..	396.5	368.9
Deferred supplemental compensation awards..................................	47.4	43.5
Unawarded supplemental compensation......................................	1.0	61.6
Deferred income taxes...	376.0	284.9
Deferred investment tax credits...	128.1	98.9
Reserve for foreign operations (Note 2).....................................	26.2	60.0
Total other liabilities and reserves....................................	975.2	917.8
Minority Interests in Net Assets of Consolidated Subsidiaries..................	139.5	125.1
Stockholders' Equity		
Capital stock, par value $2.50 a share, 1974—93.6 million shares and 1973—99.2 million shares (Notes 11 and 12)...............................	234.0	248.0
Capital account in excess of par value of stock.............................	361.9	380.5
Earnings retained for use in the business....................................	5,645.4	5,776.6
Total stockholders' equity...	6,241.3	6,405.1
Total Liabilities and Stockholders' Equity....................................	$14,173.6	$12,954.0

Classification Within the Balance Sheet

The classification of items within asset, liability, and stockholders' equity sections varies widely in published annual reports. The greatest uniformity in annual reports is in the classification of current assets and current liabilities. The principal balance sheet categories currently used are described below.

Current Assets   The term *current assets* "is used to designate cash and other assets or resources commonly identified as those which are reasonably expected to be realized in cash or sold or consumed during the normal operating cycle of the business."[3] Included in this category are cash, marketable securities held as short-term investments, accounts and notes receivable net of allowance for uncollectible accounts, inventories of merchandise, raw materials, supplies, work in process, and finished goods and prepaid operating costs. Prepaid costs, or prepayments, are current assets in the sense that if they were not paid in advance, then current assets would be required to be used to acquire them within the next operating cycle.

Investments   The section of the balance sheet labeled "Investments" includes primarily the investments in securities of other firms where the purpose of the investment is long term in nature. For example, shares of common stock of a supplier might be purchased to help assure continued availability of raw materials. Or shares of common stock of a firm in another area of business activity might be acquired to permit the acquiring firm to diversify its operations. When one corporation (the parent) owns greater than 50 percent of the voting stock in another corporation (the subsidiary), consolidated financial statements are usually prepared. That is, the specific assets, liabilities, revenues, and expenses of the subsidiary are merged, or consolidated, with those of the parent corporation. When consolidated financial statements are prepared, the account, Investment in Subsidiary, is eliminated as part of the consolidation process. Intercorporate investments in securities shown in the Investments section of the balance sheet are therefore investments in firms whose financial statements have not been consolidated with the parent or investor firm. Consolidated financial statements are discussed in Chapter Thirteen.

The holders of a firm's long-term bonds may require that cash be set aside periodically so that sufficient funds will be available to retire, or redeem, the bonds at maturity. The funds are typically given to a trustee, such as a bank or insurance company, which invests the funds received. Funds set aside for this purpose are debited to a Sinking Fund account and classified under Investments on the balance sheet.

Property, Plant, and Equipment   Property, plant, and equipment (sometimes called plant assets or fixed assets) includes the tangible, long-lived assets used in a firm's operations over a period of years and generally not acquired for resale. This category includes land, buildings, machinery, automobiles, furniture, fixtures, computers, and other equipment. The amount shown on the balance sheet for

[3] Accounting Research Bulletin No. 43, Chapter 3.A, AICPA, June 1953.

each of these items (except land) is acquisition cost less accumulated depreciation. Frequently, only the net balance, or book value, is disclosed on the balance sheet. Land is presented at acquisition cost.

Intangible Assets   Intangible assets include such items as patents, trademarks, franchises, and goodwill. When presented on the balance sheet, these items are sometimes referred to as *deferred charges*. The expenditures made by the firm in developing intangible assets are often recognized as an expense as incurred, because of the difficulty of determining the existence of future benefits necessary to warrant treatment of the costs as assets.

Current Liabilities   The term *current liabilities* "is used principally to designate obligations whose liquidation is reasonably expected to require the use of existing resources properly classified as current assets, or the creation of other current liabilities."[4] Included in this category are liabilities to merchandise suppliers, employees, and governmental units. Notes and bonds payable are also included to the extent that they will require the use of current assets within a relatively short period of time, typically during the next 12 months.

Long-Term Debt   Obligations having due dates, or maturities, more than 1 year after the balance sheet date are generally classified as long-term debt. Included are bonds, mortgages, and similar debts, as well as some obligations under long-term leases.

Other Long-Term Liabilities   Obligations not properly considered as current liabilities or long-term debt are classified as *other long-term liabilities*, or *indeterminate-term liabilities*. Included are such items as deferred pension obligations and deferred income taxes.

Stockholders' Equity   Stockholders' equity is classified as to capital contributed by shareholders and retained earnings. Contributed capital is further classified into the par or stated value of the outstanding shares and the amounts received from shareholders in excess of par or stated value. As we discuss in Chapter Twelve, this latter subclassification is of questionable value to statement users.

■ THE INCOME STATEMENT
Format and Classification
Within the Income Statement

The income statement might contain some or all of the following sections or categories, depending on the nature of the firm's income for the period:

1. income from continuing operations
2. income, gains, and losses from discontinued operations
3. adjustments for changes in accounting principles
4. extraordinary gains and losses.

The great majority of income statements include only the first section. The other sections are added if necessary.

4 *Ibid.*

Income from Continuing Operations   Revenues, gains, expenses, and losses from the continuing areas of business activity of a firm are presented in the first section of the income statement. A heading such as "Income from Continuing Operations" is used if there are other sections in the income statement.

This first section follows one of two general formats: the single-step form or the multiple-step form. In the single-step form, all revenues and gains are listed and totaled, then all expenses and losses are listed and totaled; a single subtraction of all expenses from all revenues is then made to show Income from Continuing Operations. A modified single-step form frequently adopted separates federal income taxes from all other expenses, with an intermediate income amount shown for Income from Continuing Operations Before Federal Income Taxes. All income statements shown so far in this book are single-step.

In the multiple-step form, various intermediate income subtotals, such as Gross Margin (sales revenue minus cost of goods sold), Operating Income (operating revenues minus operating expenses), and Income Before Federal Income Taxes, are disclosed. With the increasing condensation of financial statements, use of the multiple-step form is decreasing. An example of one kind of multiple-step income statement is shown for Ford Motor Company in Exhibit 6.4.

Income, Gains, and Losses from Discontinued Operations   If a firm sells a major division or segment of its business during the year or contemplates its sale within a short time after the end of the accounting period, Accounting Principles Board Opinion No. 30 requires that any income, gains, and losses related to that segment be disclosed separately from ordinary, continuing operations in a section of the income statement entitled "Income, Gains, and Losses from Discontinued Operations."[5] This section follows the section presenting income from continuing operations.

Adjustments for Changes in Accounting Principles   A firm which changes its principles, or methods, of accounting during the period is required in some cases to disclose the effects of the change on current and prior years' net income.[6] This information is presented in a separate section, after Income, Gains, and Losses from Discontinued Operations. Changes in accounting principles are discussed further in Chapter Twelve.

Extraordinary Gains and Losses   Extraordinary gains and losses are presented in a separate section of the income statement. For an item to be classified as *extraordinary*, it must generally meet all three of the following criteria (one exception—gain or loss on bond retirement—is discussed in Chapter Eleven):

1. unusual in nature
2. infrequent in occurrence
3. material in amount.[7]

---

[5] Opinion No. 30, Accounting Principles Board, AICPA, June 1973.
[6] Opinion No. 20, Accounting Principles Board, AICPA, July 1971.
[7] Opinion No. 30, Accounting Principles Board, AICPA, June 1973.

EXHIBIT 6.4
Ford Motor Company and Consolidated Subsidiaries
Consolidated Statement of Income
For the Years Ended December 31, 1974 and 1973
(in millions of dollars)

	1974	1973
Sales...	$23,620.6	$23,015.1
Costs and Expenses		
Costs, excluding items listed below...........................	20,668.0	19,069.3
Depreciation...	530.8	485.1
Amortization of special tools.................................	392.7	463.1
Selling and administrative....................................	1,032.0	1,047.4
Employe retirement plans (Note 3).............................	385.3	335.9
Provision for supplemental compensation......................	0	60.5
Total costs and expenses.................................	23,008.8	21,461.3
Operating Income...	611.8	1,553.8
Equity in net income of unconsolidated subsidiaries and affiliates..............	58.5	48.5
Other income (deductions), net (Note 4)......................	(82.9)	30.4
Income Before Income Taxes..............................	587.4	1,632.7
Provision for income taxes (Note 5)..........................	201.5	702.1
Income Before Minority Interests.........................	385.9	930.6
Minority interests in net income of consolidated subsidiaries...................	25.0	24.1
Net Income...	$ 360.9	$ 906.5
Average number of shares of capital stock outstanding (in millions).............	93.4	99.3
Net Income a Share (Note 6)..............................	$3.86	$9.13
Net Income a Share Assuming Full Dilution (Note 6)........	$3.69	$8.57
Cash Dividends a Share...................................	$3.20	$3.20

These criteria are applied as they relate to a specific firm and similar firms in the same industry, taking into consideration the environment in which the entities operate. Thus, an item might be extraordinary for some firms and ordinary for others. Examples of items likely to be extraordinary for most firms are losses from hurricanes and tornadoes, and expropriation or confiscation of assets by foreign governments. Since 1973, when Accounting Principles Board Opinion No. 30 was issued, extraordinary items are seldom seen in published annual reports.

Earnings per Share

Earnings per share data must be shown in the body of the income statement in order to receive an unqualified accountant's opinion.[8] Earnings per common share is conventionally calculated by dividing net income minus preferred stock dividends by the average number of outstanding common shares during the accounting period. For example, assume that Champion Corporation had net income of $500,000 during the year 1976. Dividends declared and paid on outstanding preferred stock were $100,000. The average number of shares of outstanding common stock during 1976 was 1 million shares. Earnings per common share is $.40 [= ($500,000 — $100,000)/1,000,000].

If a firm has securities outstanding which can be converted into or exchanged for common stock, it may be required to present two earnings-per-share amounts: *primary earnings per share* and *fully diluted earnings per share*. For example, some firms issue convertible bonds or convertible preferred stock which can be exchanged directly for shares of common stock. Also, many firms have employee stock option plans under which shares of the company's common stock may be acquired by employees under special arrangements. If these convertible securities were converted or stock options were exercised and additional shares of common stock were issued, the amount conventionally shown as earnings per share would probably decrease, or become *diluted*. When a firm has outstanding securities which, if exchanged for shares of common stock, would decrease earnings per share by 3 percent or more, a dual presentation of primary and fully diluted earnings per share is required.[9]

Primary Earnings per Share   Adjustments may be made in the determination of earnings per share for securities which are nearly the same as common stock. These securities are called *common stock equivalents*. Common stock equivalents are securities whose principal value arises from their capability of being exchanged for, or converted into, common stock rather than for their own periodic cash yields over time. Stock options and warrants are always common stock equivalents. Convertible bonds and convertible preferred stock may or may not be common stock equivalents. A test is employed to determine whether the yield, or return, from these convertible securities at the date of their issue is substantially below the yield otherwise available from other debt or preferred stock investments. If so, the presumption is that the securities derived their value primarily from their

---

[8] Opinion No. 15, Accounting Principles Board, AICPA, May 1969.
[9] *Ibid.*

conversion privileges and are therefore common stock equivalents. Adjustments are made in calculating primary earnings per share for the dilutive effects of securities classified as common stock equivalents.

Fully Diluted Earnings per Share   As the title implies, fully diluted earnings per share indicates the maximum possible dilution which would occur if all options, warrants, and convertible securities outstanding at the end of the accounting period were exchanged for common stock. This amount, therefore, represents a lower limit on possible dilution which could take place on the date of the balance sheet. All securities convertible into or exchangeable for common stock, whether or not classified as common stock equivalents, enter into the determination of fully diluted earnings per share.

Firms which do not have convertible or other potentially dilutive securities outstanding compute earnings per share in the conventional manner. Firms with outstanding securities which have the potential for materially diluting earnings per share as conventionally determined must present dual earnings per share amounts.

An income statement in the modified single-step form which includes primary and fully diluted earnings per share amounts is presented in Exhibit 6.4 for Ford Motor Company.

■ STATEMENT OF CHANGES IN FINANCIAL POSITION

Format of the Statement of Changes in Financial Position

As discussed in Chapter Five, the statement of changes in financial position usually explains and discloses the changes in working capital (current assets minus current liabilities) during the period. The statement also discloses other significant changes in financial position, even though the transactions or events do not affect working capital directly. For example, the issue of capital stock in the acquisition of land would be an event disclosed in the statement.

The statement of changes in financial position is typically divided into two sections: (1) sources and uses of working capital or financial resources, and (2) an analysis of changes in the individual current asset and current liability accounts.

Classification Within the Statement of Changes in Financial Position

The sources and uses of working capital or financial resources presented in the first section of the statement of changes in financial position might be classified as being related to

1. earnings activities
2. financing activities
3. income distributions of the firm, and
4. investing activities.

The first item generally reported on the statement is the amount of working capital provided (or used) by operations. This item indicates whether the earnings activities of the firm (that is, acquiring and selling goods or services) have resulted in an increase or decrease in working capital. If a firm is to continue operating effectively over a period of years, the operating activities must generate sufficient working capital so that inventory can be replaced and creditors' claims can be paid. Operations must also generate, or provide, working capital so that plant and equipment can be replaced as they wear out. Working capital provided (or used) by operations is therefore an important indicator of the firm's financial health, particularly when working capital flows are assessed over several years.

The derivation of the amount of working capital provided (or used) by operations is typically shown in the statement by beginning with the amount of net income for the period and adjusting net income for expenses not using working capital and revenues not providing working capital. As we discussed in Chapter Five and illustrated for Jonathan Corporation in Exhibit 1.3, the amount of working capital provided or used from operations might better be disclosed by listing revenues that provide working capital and then subtracting only those expenses that use working capital. The end result is the same under both methods of presentation. The first procedure leads some statement readers to conclude mistakenly that depreciation expense is a source of working capital.

If a firm reports an extraordinary gain or loss in the income statement, then the effects of the extraordinary item (net of income tax effects) on working capital must be disclosed separately in the statement of changes in financial position. For example, the uninsured loss of merchandise inventory as a result of a tornado would likely represent an extraordinary loss on the income statement and an extraordinary use of working capital on the statement of changes in financial position.

The sources and uses of working capital from financing activities include the issuance and redemption of common or preferred stock or long-term bonds. The sources and uses of working capital from investing activities include the purchase and sale of land, buildings, equipment, and other noncurrent assets. The declaration of dividends (income distribution) is a use of working capital.

While the first section of the statement of changes in financial position presents the sources and uses of working capital or financial resources, the second section summarizes the change in each of the working capital accounts.

An example of a Statement of Changes in Financial Position for Lehigh Portland Cement Company is presented in Exhibit 6.5.

■ OTHER ITEMS IN ANNUAL REPORTS

Several additional schedules or statements, which supplement the three principal financial statements, are often presented in the annual report. In most cases, these items are covered by the auditor's opinion.

Reconciliation of Retained Earnings

The beginning and ending balances in retained earnings must be reconciled in the financial statements. The reconciliation can appear either in a separate

EXHIBIT 6.5
Lehigh Portland Cement Company
Consolidated Statements of Changes in Financial Position
For the Years Ended December 31, 1974 and 1973

	Year Ended December 31,	
	1974	**1973***
SOURCES OF WORKING CAPITAL		
Provided by Operations		
Net earnings...	$ 7,599,000	$ 10,841,000
Add (deduct) items not affecting working capital in the period:		
Depreciation and cost depletion...	8,717,000	8,498,000
Amortization of intangible assets.......................................	247,000	290,000
Write-off of excess of cost over net assets of acquired companies and other intangible assets.....................................	2,420,000	—
Income tax deferred..	2,536,000	1,544,000
Net gain on sales of real estate and plants, net of taxes.................	(895,000)	(393,000)
Total Funds Provided by Operations.....................................	20,624,000	20,780,000
Proceeds from loans and refinancing agreements...........................	10,375,000	—
Effect of tax settlement on accumulated income tax deferments............	3,119,000	—
Proceeds from sales of property, plant and equipment, net of taxes........	4,850,000	2,175,000
Decrease in non-current receivables and investments......................	1,177,000	920,000
Increase in other non-current items..	225,000	650,000
Total Sources of Working Capital..	40,370,000	24,525,000
APPLICATIONS OF WORKING CAPITAL		
Additions to property, plant and equipment................................	16,961,000	12,491,000
Reduction in long-term debt..	4,428,000	8,264,000
Dividends declared...	2,720,000	2,836,000
Increase in non-current receivables and investments......................	625,000	263,000
Reduction in non-current pension and related obligations.................	3,303,000	1,515,000
Purchase of treasury stock...	—	13,400,000
Other	97,000	204,000
Total Applications of Working Capital....................................	28,134,000	38,973,000
INCREASE (DECREASE) IN WORKING CAPITAL...........................	$ 12,236,000	$(14,448,000)
INCREASE (DECREASE) IN ELEMENTS OF WORKING CAPITAL		
Cash	$ 3,016,000	$ (78,000)
Certificates of deposit and commerical paper..............................	(10,932,000)	(13,250,000)
Receivables	4,541,000	1,826,000
Inventories	4,912,000	111,000
Prepaid expenses..	699,000	(354,000)
Accumulated income tax prepayments......................................	(224,000)	(249,000)
	2,012,000	(11,994,000)
Current maturities of long-term debt......................................	(2,697,000)	(575,000)
Accounts payable and accrued expenses...................................	(2,854,000)	2,284,000
Dividends payable..	—	57,000
Income taxes...	(4,673,000)	688,000
	(10,224,000)	2,454,000
INCREASE (DECREASE) IN WORKING CAPITAL...........................	$ 12,236,000	$(14,448,000)

*Reclassified to conform to 1974 presentation.

statement or as the lower section in a combined statement of income and retained earnings. In most instances, net income and dividends are the only reconciling items. Occasionally an adjustment or correction of prior years' income statements will appear as a charge or credit to the beginning balance in retained earnings. Examples of such items are settlements of litigation and income tax disputes, corrections of accounting errors in past reports, and retroactive restatements for certain changes in accounting principles or procedures. These items are called *prior period adjustments* and are discussed in Chapter Twelve.

Statement of Changes in Contributed Capital

As with retained earnings, a reconciliation of changes in the capital stock and additional paid-in capital accounts must be presented. This reconciliation includes the effects of financing by issuing capital stock, conversion of debt or preferred stock into common stock, issuance of stock to employees under stock option plans, issue of stock to shareholders as a stock dividend, and reacquisitions of the firm's shares on the market to be held as treasury stock. A statement analyzing the changes in the stockholders' equity accounts of Ford Motor Company is presented in Exhibit 12.2.

Historical Summary

It is common reporting practice to include a 5- or 10-year historical summary of important financial statement information in the annual report. Items usually included in the historical summary are net sales revenue, income taxes, net income, earnings per share, dividends per share, working capital, total assets, long-term debt, and stockholders' equity. To enhance comparability of the data, restatements of previously reported amounts may be required for changes in accounting procedures, acquisitions of other companies, and changes in the number of outstanding shares caused by stock dividends and stock splits.

Line of Business or Segment Reports

The growing number of conglomerate firms which have segments or divisions operating in widely different industries has led to the desire for information concerning the performance of each segment. Most firms provide information for lines, or segments, of business in the annual report. The segments are typically classified by product or industry groupings. Other definitions of segments include geographical location of markets (domestic and foreign) and type of customer (consumer, industry, government). In most cases, only net sales and net income (or income before allocation of certain common corporate-wide costs) are reported for each segment. A complete set of segmented financial statements is generally not provided.

Two common accounting problems encountered in preparing segment earnings reports concern the treatment of sales and other transactions between divisions and the allocation of central corporate expenses. Should sales between divisions be included in the segment sales, or should only sales to parties outside the firm be

EXHIBIT 6.6
General Electric Company and Consolidated Affiliates
Income Statement and Segment Report on Operations
For the Years Ended December 31, 1974 and 1973
(dollar amounts in millions; per-share amounts in dollars)

Summary of operating results	1974	1973
Sales of products and services	$13,413	$11,575
Operating costs		
Employee compensation, including benefits	5,223	4,710
Materials, supplies, services and all other operating costs	7,195	5,910
	12,418	10,620
Operating margin	995	955
Other income	186	184
Interest and other financial charges	(180)	(127)
Earnings before income taxes and minority interest	1,001	1,012
Provision for income taxes	(383)	(419)
Minority interest	(10)	(8)
Net earnings	$ 608	$ 585
Earnings per common share	$3.34	$3.21
Dividends declared per common share	$1.60	$1.50
Operating margin as a percentage of sales	7.4%	8.2%
Earned on share owners' equity	17.2%	18.1%

Operating results by major categories	Sales		Net earnings		Earnings as a percentage of sales	
	1974	1973	1974	1973(a)	1974	1973(a)
Industrial Power Equipment	$ 2,787	$ 2,477	$101	$129	3.6%	5.2%
Consumer	3,214	3,097	86	148	2.7	4.8
Industrial Components and Systems	4,529	3,728	254	181	5.6	4.9
Aerospace	1,916	1,611	75	44	3.9	2.7
International	3,218	2,318	174	139	5.4	6.0
General Electric Credit Corporation	—	—	43	42	—	—
Corporate eliminations	(2,251)	(1,656)	(125)	(98)	—	—
Total Company	$13,413	$11,575	$608	$585	4.5	5.1

(a) Amounts for 1973 and prior years have been reclassified, consistent with refinements of corporate interest allocation procedures implemented in 1974. This reclassification's principal effect on previously reported earnings was to increase the Industrial Power Equipment and decrease the International categories.

Sales and net earnings by major category throughout this Report include intercategory transactions. To the extent that sales and earnings are recognized in more than one category, appropriate elimination is made at corporate level. Net earnings for each major category are after allocation of corporate items such as expenses of headquarters personnel, corporate research and development, interest and other financial charges and income as well as income taxes. Unless otherwise indicated by the context, the terms "General Electric" and "Company" are used on the basis of consolidation described on page 30.

disclosed? If sales or transfers to other divisions are included, what transfer price should be used (for example, cost to the selling division, outside market price, negotiated price between the segments)? Likewise, should central corporate expenses recognized during the period (for example, the president's salary, research and development or data-processing expenses, interest, and income tax expenses) be allocated to each segment, or left unallocated? If these expenses are allocated, what basis should be used (for example, number of employees, square feet of floor space used, segment sales revenue)? The accounting profession has not yet developed a definitive set of responses to these questions. Therefore, each segment report must be read carefully to determine the treatment of intersegment transfers and central corporate expenses. An example of a segment earnings report for the General Electric Company is presented in Exhibit 6.6.

■ INTERIM REPORTS

Most publicly held corporations issue condensed financial statements more often than once a year. Such financial statements issued at regular intervals during the company's annual accounting period are called *interim reports*. Interim reports are most often issued quarterly.

The principal problems involved in preparing and interpreting interim reports arise for businesses that have relatively seasonal trends in revenues. Professional sports teams, vacation resorts, and most department stores, for example, sell their goods and services at a nonuniform rate throughout the year. Many operating costs, however, are incurred at a relatively uniform rate throughout the year. Examples include rent, property taxes, insurance, and most salaries. The principal accounting question is how these operating costs are to be assigned to each of the quarters during the year. Suppose that a summer resort generates 80 percent of its revenues during the third quarter of the year. Should the interim report for the first quarter of the year, January through March, which shows little or no revenue, show one-fourth of the year's property taxes, insurance, and other similar costs and thereby report a loss? Alternatively, should the interim report for the third quarter, which shows 80 percent of the year's revenues, show 80 percent of the year's costs as expenses and thereby report 80 percent of the anticipated net income for the year?

Before these questions can be answered, some consensus must be reached regarding the purpose of interim reports. Some adopt the view that the interim report is a report on performance during a discrete time period whose income is independent of other interim periods during the year. Others adopt the view that the purpose of the interim report is to help users predict net income for the year. The manner in which annual operating costs are assigned to interim periods during the year depends on which purpose the interim report is presumed to serve. Accounting Principles Board Opinion No. 28 states "that each interim period should be viewed primarily as an integral part of an annual period."[10] This implies a preference for

[10] Opinion No. 28, Accounting Principles Board, AICPA, May 1973.

the viewpoint of annual earnings prediction. There is, however, no uniform agreement as to which methods of recognizing revenues and expenses during each quarter lead to the best predictions of annual net income. The reader of interim reports must ascertain the methods used in constructing the report so that valid interpretations can be made. Exhibit 6.7 presents an interim earnings report for AVX Corporation.

■ ASSESSING CURRENT REPORTING PRACTICES

In Chapter One, we discussed several possible criteria for assessing the usefulness of accounting information, including relevance to decisions, fairness in presentation, and others. In recent years, the usefulness of the financial statements has been questioned on three broad fronts.

EXHIBIT 6.7
AVX Corporation
Interim Income Statement and Balance Sheet
For the Thirteen Weeks Ended March 29, 1975, and March 30, 1974

AVX CORPORATION
FINANCIAL SUMMARY
(Unaudited)

	(In Thousands) Thirteen Weeks Ended	
	March 29, 1975	March 30, 1974
Sales	$6,863	$9,271
Income From Continuing Operations	170	682
Loss From Operations Of Opcoa Division Less Income Tax Credit Of $176	—	(174)
Extraordinary Income	—	52
Net Income	$ 170	$ 560

INCOME (LOSS) PER SHARE OF COMMON STOCK

Income From Continuing Operations	$.15	$.47
Loss From Discontinued Operations	—	(.12)
Extraordinary Item	—	.04
Net Income	$.15	$.39
Average Shares Outstanding	1,139	1,438

AVX CORPORATION
CONDENSED BALANCE SHEET
(Unaudited)   ($ In Thousands)

	March 29, 1975	March 30, 1974
ASSETS		
Current Assets	$ 9,101	$10,482
Fixed Assets — Net	6,306	6,269
Other Assets	1,100	887
	$16,507	$17,638
LIABILITIES & STOCKHOLDERS' EQUITY		
Current Liabilities	$ 2,937	$ 4,496
Long-term Liabilities	2,381	2,391
Stockholders' Equity	11,189	10,751
	$16,507	$17,638

Some critics have complained that the information disclosed is too aggregated, or condensed, to be of much help to readers in assessing operating performance and financial position. The presentation of earnings data by segments or lines of business is one response to this criticism. Another response is in the expanded use of notes to the financial statements, providing further elaboration on items in the body of the statements.

Perhaps the easiest way to satisfy these critics is to provide more data and let each user decide what is or is not relevant information. The incremental benefits of more data must be compared, though, with the incremental costs of generating the data. Some point will be reached where the incremental costs will exceed the incremental benefits. Further, the managers of some firms argue that expanded disclosure will help competitors and thus will harm stockholders.

A second major criticism is aimed at the diversity of generally accepted accounting principles and the flexibility permitted firms in choosing the accounting methods used in preparing financial statements. The use of different accounting procedures, it is suggested, makes it difficult to compare performance and financial position among firms. The counterargument is that alternative accounting methods are necessary so that the firm can select the methods which most fairly present the underlying transactions or events to which it is a party. The various generally accepted accounting principles or procedures for individual assets and equities are the central theme of Chapters Eight through Thirteen. The effect of using alternative accounting principles on the financial statements and on investors' decisions to commit resources is discussed in Chapter Fifteen.

A third criticism of current accounting reports is that too much emphasis is placed on verifiability, or auditability, and not enough on relevancy to the user. This criticism has been directed primarily at the use of acquisition cost as the valuation basis for many assets rather than some type of current valuation, such as replacement cost or net realizable value. The interest among accountants in disclosing current values for assets as supplements to acquisition cost amounts has been increasing in recent years. We consider this topic further in Chapter Fourteen.

■ SUMMARY

This chapter has provided an overview of the manner in which information generated as part of the accounting process and discussed in Chapters Two through Five is disclosed in published accounting reports. Perhaps the most effective overview is obtained by reading and studying carefully the annual reports of several publicly held companies. Such an overview serves not only as a synthesizing device for the material covered thus far, but as an introduction to the analysis of financial statements to be considered next in Chapter Seven.

In reading corporate annual reports at this stage in your study of accounting, it will quickly become apparent that your background is not yet adequate for understanding many items reported in the financial statements. In Chapters Eight through Thirteen, we explore more fully the generally accepted accounting principles or procedures for measuring and disclosing individual assets, equities, and net income in the financial statements.

QUESTIONS AND PROBLEMS

1. Review the meaning of the following concepts or terms discussed in this chapter.
    a. Accountant's opinion.
    b. Unqualified opinion.
    c. Fixed assets.
    d. Deferred charges.
    e. Single-step income statement.
    f. Multiple-step income statement.
    g. Income from continuing operations.
    h. Income from discontinued operations.
    i. Extraordinary items.
    j. Primary earnings per share.
    k. Fully diluted earnings per share.
    l. Common stock equivalent.
    m. Working capital provided by operations.
    n. Prior period adjustment.
    o. Historical summary.
    p. Segment report.
    q. Transfer price.
    r. Central corporate expenses.
    s. Interim earnings report.
2. What is the advantage of presenting comparative financial statements in a corporation's annual report?
3. What is the purpose of presenting schedules of comparative statistics in the annual report? What are some of the limitations of using comparative statistics?
4. What is the purpose of the independent accountant's audit and expression of opinion on a firm's financial statements?
5. Under what circumstances are qualified opinions expressed on a set of financial statements?
6. If an item is considered important enough to warrant disclosure in a note to the financial statements, why is it not disclosed in the body of the statement?
7. Why are investments in the securities of some companies shown among current assets and those in other companies included among long-term investments?
8. In what sense is the term "fixed assets" a misnomer?
9. Why is the term "deferred charges" undesirable in describing intangibles and similar assets?
10. Why are current maturities of some long-term debt obligations classified under current liabilities, while current maturities of other long-term debt obligations are classified under long-term debt?
11. Since the Allowance for Uncollectible Accounts and Accumulated Depreciation accounts normally have credit balances, why are they not classified as liabilities?
12. Define dilution and describe its significance in measuring earnings per share.

13. What is the purpose of interim earnings reports? Are there any problems unique to interim reports which are not encountered in preparing annual earnings reports?

14. Consolidated financial statements essentially represent an aggregation of the financial statements of a parent company and its subsidiaries. Segment reports represent a disaggregation of financial statement information for various units or divisions of the firm. Explain the apparent paradox of aggregating financial information and then disaggregating it.

15. Explain the difference, if any, between the items referred to by the following pairs of terms:
    a. Accountant's report and auditor's opinion.
    b. Qualified opinion and unqualified opinion.
    c. "Subject to" opinion and "except for" opinion.
    d. Statement of financial position and statement of changes in financial position.
    e. Income from continuing operations and income from discontinued operations.
    f. Extraordinary items and prior-period adjustments.
    g. Primary earnings per share and fully diluted earnings per share.
    h. Income from continuing operations and working capital provided by operations.
    i. Statement of changes in financial position and funds statement.
    j. Consolidated income statement and segment earnings report.

16. Refer to a recent edition of *Accounting Trends and Techniques*, published by the American Institute of Certified Public Accountants, and respond to the following questions:
    a. What title is used most frequently for the statement which presents the firm's assets and equities at the beginning and end of the period? What other titles are also used?
    b. What title is used most frequently for the statement reporting revenues, gains, expenses, and losses for the period? What other titles are used?
    c. What proportion of the statements of changes in financial position use cash as the definition of funds instead of working capital?
    d. Approximately how frequently are qualified opinions rendered by the independent accountant on the financial statements of the sample firms?

17. Accounts might be classified in the balance sheet and income statement in one of the following categories:
    (1) Current assets.
    (2) Investments.
    (3) Fixed assets.
    (4) Intangibles.
    (5) Current liabilities.
    (6) Long-term liabilities.
    (7) Stockholders' equity.
    (8) Income statement items.
    (9) Items excluded from the balance sheet and income statement under present generally accepted accounting principles.

    Various accounts which might be presented in the financial statements are listed below. Using the numbers above, indicate the appropriate classification of each account. Use an **X** before the number if the account is a contra account. For example, Allowance for Uncollectible Accounts is **X-1**. State any assumptions which you feel are necessary.

    a. Accounts payable.
    b. Accounts receivable.
    c. Accumulated depreciation.
    d. Advances by customers.
    e. Advances to suppliers.
    f. Advertising expense.
    g. Allowance for uncollectibles.
    h. Bond sinking fund.
    i. Building.
    j. Cash.
    k. Certificate of deposit.
    l. Common stock.
    m. Construction in progress.
    n. Current maturities of bonds payable (to be paid from general cash account).
    o. Current maturities of bonds payable (to be paid from cash in bond sinking fund).
    p. Customers' deposits.
    q. Deposits on equipment purchases.
    r. Depreciation expense.
    s. Dividends payable.
    t. Estimated liabilities under warranty contracts.
    u. Finished goods inventory.
    v. Furniture and fixtures.
    w. Gain on sale of equipment.
    x. General and administrative expenses.
    y. Goodwill.

18. Accounts might be classified in the balance sheet and income statement in one of the following categories:
    (1) Current assets.
    (2) Investments.
    (3) Fixed assets.
    (4) Intangibles.
    (5) Current liabilities.
    (6) Long-term liabilities.
    (7) Stockholders' equity.
    (8) Income statement items.
    (9) Items excluded from the balance sheet and income statement under present generally accepted accounting principles.

Various accounts which might be presented in the financial statements are listed below. Using the numbers above, indicate the appropriate classification of each account. Use an **X** before the number if the account is a contra account. For example, Allowance for Uncollectible Accounts is **X-1**. State any assumptions which you feel are necessary.
    a. Income taxes withheld.
    b. Interest expense.
    c. Interest payable.
    d. Interest receivable.
    e. Investment in General Motors stock.

    f. U.S. Treasury Notes.

    g. Investment in unconsolidated subsidiary.

    h. Land.

    i. Machinery.

    j. Marketable securities.

    k. Merchandise inventory.

    l. Mortgage payable (noncurrent).

    m. Notes payable (due in 3 months).

    n. Notes receivable (due in 6 months).

    o. Patents.

    p. Plant.

    q. Preferred stock.

    r. Prepaid insurance.

    s. Raw materials inventory.

    t. Rental revenue.

    u. Retained earnings.

    v. Sales discounts and allowances.

    w. Tools and dies.

    x. Unexpired insurance.

    y. Work in process.

19. The results of various transactions and events are classified within the income statement in one of the following three sections: (**1**) income from continuing operations, (**2**) income, gains, and losses from discontinued operations, and (**3**) extraordinary items. Using the appropriate number, identify the classification of each of the transactions or events below. State any assumptions which you feel are necessary.

    a. Depreciation expense for the year on a company's automobile used by its president.

    b. Uninsured loss of a factory complex in Louisiana as a result of a hurricane.

    c. Gain from the sale of marketable securities.

    d. Loss from the sale of a delivery truck.

    e. Loss from the sale of a division that conducted all of the firm's research activities.

    f. Earnings during the year up to the time of sale of the division in **e**.

    g. Loss in excess of insurance proceeds on an automobile destroyed during an accident.

    h. Loss of plant, equipment, and inventory held in a South American country when confiscated by the government of that country.

20. The trial balance of the Morton Manufacturing Company at December 31, 1976, is as follows:

Accounts Payable		$ 91,000
Accounts Receivable	$ 262,000	
Accumulated Depreciation—Buildings		24,000
Accumulated Depreciation—Machinery and Equipment		72,000
Allowance for Uncollectible Accounts		7,000
Administrative Expenses	340,000	
Advances on Special Orders		6,900

Buildings	110,000	
Cash in Bank	13,500	
Common Stock—$10 par value		350,000
Cost of Goods Sold	1,467,500	
Dividend Revenue from Stock of Subsidiary		4,000
Dividends Payable		14,750
Factory Supplies Inventory	2,800	
Federal Income Tax Expense	41,200	
Federal Income Tax Payable		41,200
First Mortgage Bonds Payable (10 percent)—Par		50,000
Finished Goods Inventory	91,000	
Interest Expense on Notes	1,680	
Interest Expense on Bonds	4,500	
Interest Revenue from Notes		220
Interest Payable		2,600
Interest Receivable	100	
Investment in Stock of Subsidiary	60,000	
Land	24,000	
Machinery and Equipment	260,000	
Notes Payable (due 7/1/77)		26,600
Notes Receivable (due 2/15/77)	45,000	
Patents	25,000	
Payroll Taxes Payable		11,700
Preferred Stock—$100 par value		200,000
Raw Materials Inventory	84,000	
Retained Earnings		176,940
Royalty Revenue from Patents		5,000
Sales		2,461,700
Sales, Uncollectible Accounts Adjustment	84,000	
Selling Expenses	480,000	
Sinking Fund	57,500	
Undeposited Cash	850	
Unexpired Insurance	1,400	
Withheld Income Tax		15,420
Work in Process Inventory	105,000	
Total	$3,561,030	$3,561,030

Additional data:
(1) There were 2,000 shares of preferred stock outstanding throughout 1976.
(2) There were 35,000 shares of common stock outstanding throughout 1976.
(3) Dividends declared and paid during 1976 were $12,000 on preferred stock and $17,500 on common stock.

a. Prepare a statement of income and retained earnings for the year ending December 31, 1976.

b. Prepare a balance sheet as of December 31, 1976.

21. The adjusted trial balance of the Herman Manufacturing Company as of December 31, 1976, is as follows:

Accounts Payable		$ 142,100
Accounts Receivable	$ 231,600	
Accumulated Depreciation—Buildings		129,000
Accumulated Depreciation—Machinery and Equipment		333,000
Allowance for Uncollectible Accounts		6,100
Bonds Payable (10 percent)—Par		300,000
Buildings	306,000	
Capital Contributed in Excess of Stated Value		250,000
Cash in Bank	32,450	
Common Stock—$10 par value		400,000
Cost of Goods Sold	1,907,500	
Dividend Revenue from Investment in Common Stocks		20,000
Factory Supplies Inventory	19,700	
Federal Income Tax Expense	80,200	
Finished Goods Inventory	239,200	
General and Administrative Expenses	205,800	
Goodwill	20,000	
Interest Expense on Bonds	30,600	
Interest Expense on Notes	3,600	
Interest Revenue		3,800
Interest Payable		6,600
Interest Receivable	610	
Investment in Common Stocks	250,000	
Land	50,000	
Loss on Sale of Plant Assets	3,700	
Machinery and Equipment	774,000	
Marketable Securities	32,000	
Notes Payable		66,000
Notes Receivable	22,500	
Preferred Stock—$100 par value		300,000
Raw Materials Inventory	146,500	
Refund of Prior Year (1972) Income Taxes		6,200
Retained Earnings		260,880
Sales		2,531,100
Sales, Uncollectible Accounts Adjustment	69,300	
Selling and Delivery Expenses	156,300	
Sinking Fund	75,000	
Taxes Payable		83,200
Undeposited Cash	670	
Unexpired Insurance	1,450	
Wages Payable		10,100
Work in Process Inventory	189,400	
Total	$4,848,080	$4,848,080

Additional data:

(1) There were 3,000 shares of preferred stock outstanding throughout 1976.

(2) There were 40,000 shares of common stock outstanding throughout 1976.

(3) Dividends declared and paid during 1976 were $18,000 on preferred stock and $40,000 on common stock.

a. Prepare a statement of income and retained earnings for the year ending December 31, 1976.

b. Prepare a balance sheet as of December 31, 1976.

22. Comment on any unusual features of the following balance sheet of the Western Sales Corporation.

Western Sales Corporation
Balance Sheet
For the Year Ended December 31, 1976

ASSETS

Current Assets:

Cash and Certificates of Deposit	$ 86,500	
Accounts Receivable—Net	193,600	
Merchandise Inventory	322,900	$ 603,000

Investments (substantially at cost):

Investment in U.S. Treasury Notes	$ 60,000	
Investment in Eastern Sales Corp.	196,500	256,500

Fixed Assets (at cost):

Land	$225,000	
Buildings and Equipment—Net	842,600	1,067,600

Intangibles and Deferred Charges:

Prepaid Insurance	$ 1,200	
Prepaid Rent	1,500	
Goodwill	2	2,702
Total Assets		$1,929,802

LIABILITIES AND STOCKHOLDERS' EQUITY

Current Liabilities:

Accounts Payable	$225,300	
Accrued Expenses	10,900	
Income Taxes Payable	89,200	$ 325,400

Long-Term Liabilites:

Bonds Payable	$500,000	
Pensions Payable	40,600	
Contingent Liability	100,000	640,600

Stockholders' Equity:

Common Stock—$10 par value, 50,000 shares		
issued and outstanding	$625,000	
Earned Surplus	338,802	963,802
Total Liabilities and Stockholders' Equity		$1,929,802

23. Comment on any unusual features of the following income statement of Nordic Enterprises, Inc.

Nordic Enterprises, Inc.
Income Statement
December 31, 1976

Revenues and Gains:

Sales Revenue	$1,964,800	
Rental Revenue	366,900	
Interest Revenue	4,600	
Gain on Sale of Equipment	2,500	
Gain on Sale of Subsidiary	643,200	$2,982,000

Expenses and Losses:

Cost of Goods Sold	$1,432,900	
Depreciation Expense	226,800	
Salaries Expense	296,900	
Interest Expense	6,600	
Loss of Plant Due to Fire	246,800	
Additional Income Taxes for Prior Years (1974–1975)	122,000	
Income Tax Expense	200,000	
Dividends Expense	100,000	2,632,000
Net Income		$ 350,000

24. The segment earnings report for Norton Products, Inc., for the years 1972–1976 appears below:

Norton Products, Inc.
Segment Earnings Statement
For the Years Ending December 31, 1972 to 1976

The following table reflects the respective contributions in excess of 10 percent of certain product lines to sales and net income before taxes. The compilation has been prepared by management, predicated on the present marketing pattern for the various groups of products and has not been subject to independent verification by the Company's auditors.

	Percent				
	1972	1973	1974	1975	1976
Sales and Net Income Before Taxes by Product Lines					
Sales					
Domestic					
Drugs and Cosmetics	26%	27%	26%	26%	25%
Household Products	20	21	23	22	22
Food Products	20	19	19	19	17
Specialty Chemicals	12	12	11	11	11
Industrial and Ice Control Salt	8	7	8	7	8
International	14	14	13	15	17
	100%	100%	100%	100%	100%

Net Income Before Taxes

Domestic

Drugs and Cosmetics	52%	64%	56%	55%	55%
Household Products	7	6	12	10	2
Food Products	18	15	16	13	12
Specialty Chemicals	(4)	(7)	(5)	–	5
Industrial and Ice Control Salt	11	9	9	9	9
International	16	13	12	13	17
	100%	100%	100%	100%	100%

What questions might be raised regarding the manner in which the segment earnings data are disclosed in this report?

25. Each of the following describes the contents of interim reports or a policy used by a company in preparing its interim reports. On the basis of this information, does it appear that the company is (1) treating the interim period as a discrete accounting period, or (2) treating the interim period as a component of the annual period and reporting in such a way that valid inferences about annual net income can be made?

   a. A department store makes 40 percent of its sales in the months of October through December and allocates 40 percent of the annual depreciation charge on the store building to that quarter.

   b. Payroll taxes are levied on the first $15,000 of the salary earned by an individual during the year. Many of the company's employees earn more than $15,000 per year. The company reports payroll tax expense for employees in interim reports as the salaries are earned and the liability to the government arises.

   c. The income tax expense was computed as 22 percent of the income before taxes in the first quarter's interim report and 48 percent of the income before taxes in the third quarter's interim report.

   d. An appliance manufacturer sells most of its television sets in the second half of the year. The company pays bonuses to executives based on income before taxes for the year. The amount of executive bonuses shown as expenses on each of the four quarterly reports for the year is the same.

   e. A cereal company reports that income for the quarter is 60 percent larger than for the comparable quarter of the preceding year. The increase is attributable to a reduction in advertising expenditures this quarter, relative to expenditures in the corresponding quarter last year. The company expects its advertising expense for this year to be about the same as for last year.

26. Brown Tax Services, Inc., provides income tax preparation services to its customers. Fee revenues are highly seasonal during the four quarters of the calendar year and occur in the following proportions: .60, .20, .10, .10. That is, 60 percent of the firm's revenues are usually generated during the months of January through March. The following operating costs were anticipated and actually incurred evenly throughout the year ended December 31, 1976.

Salaries	$250,000
Rent	125,000
Insurance	25,000
Total	$400,000

During the first quarter of 1976, fee revenues totaled $360,000.

a. Determine net income for the first quarter assuming that operating costs are assigned equally to each of the four quarters during the year.

b. Determine net income for the first quarter assuming that operating costs are assigned to each quarter in proportion to the percentage of the anticipated year's revenues recognized during each quarter.

c. If the pattern of fee revenues during 1976 occurs as anticipated (that is, .60, .20, .10, .10), what is the anticipated net income for the year?

d. Which of the interim earnings measures determined in **a** and **b** will lead to the more accurate prediction of the annual net income calculated in **c**?

Chapter Seven

Introduction
to Financial
Statement Analysis

Previous chapters have introduced the concepts and procedures underlying the principal financial statements prepared by business firms for external users. One of the major purposes of accounting is to provide information useful for making investment decisions. Financial statement analysis embraces the methods used in assessing and interpreting the results of past performance and current financial condition as they relate to particular factors of interest in investment decisions. Comprehensive analysis and interpretation require an understanding of the accounting measurement principles discussed in Chapters Eight through Fourteen. Our purpose here is to introduce some of the basic concepts and methods of financial statement analysis and, thereby, provide a bridge between the preceding introductory chapters and the more advanced ones which follow.

■ OBJECTIVES OF FINANCIAL STATEMENT ANALYSIS

When comparing investment alternatives, the decision maker is interested in the expected return to be realized from each investment and the risk or uncertainty of that return. The decision maker is concerned with the future. Financial statements, based on the results of past activities, are analyzed and interpreted as a basis for predicting future rates of return and for assessing risk.

The factors affecting the assessment of rates of return and risk depend on the type of investment. For example, an investor might purchase a firm's common or preferred stock, acquire its long-term bonds, or extend short-term credit through an open account, note, or similar debt instrument.

The return from an investment in common or preferred stock consists of dividends plus capital gains (or minus capital losses) from changes in market prices of the shares. One of the principal factors affecting future dividends and market price changes is the expected *profitability* of a company. The past profitability of a firm is, therefore, assessed as a basis for predicting future profitability and rates of return.

An investor in long-term bonds is interested in a firm's ability to make periodic interest and principal payments as they become due. A firm that is unable to make its required payments is insolvent. An investor in long-term debt is therefore interested in assessing the long-term *solvency* of a firm.

A bank which makes a 3- or 6-month loan to a firm is more interested in short-term *liquidity*. That is, the bank is concerned with whether the firm will have sufficient cash available to repay the loan and interest within a few months.

To summarize, investors in common or preferred stock are concerned primarily with a firm's profitability. Investors in a firm's bonds are more interested in assessing long-term solvency; short-term investors in the liquidity of a firm.

■ USEFULNESS OF RATIOS

The various items in financial statements may be difficult to interpret in the form in which they are presented. For example, the profitability of a firm may be difficult to assess by looking at the amount of net income alone. It is useful to compare earnings with the assets or capital required to generate those earnings. This relationship, and other important ones between various items in the financial statements, can be expressed in the form of ratios. Some ratios compare items within the income statement only; some compare only balance sheet data; others compare items from both statements. Ratios are useful tools of financial statement analysis because they conveniently summarize data in a form which is more easily understood, interpreted, and compared.

Ratios are, by themselves, difficult to interpret. For example, does a rate of return on common stock of 8.6 percent reflect a good performance? Once calculated, the ratios must be compared with some criterion or standard. Several possible criteria might be used:

1. the planned or budgeted ratio for the period being analyzed
2. the corresponding ratio during the preceding period for the same firm
3. the corresponding ratio for a similar firm in the same industry
4. the average ratio for other firms in the same industry.

Difficulties encountered in using each of these bases for comparison are discussed later in the chapter.

The number of ratios which could be calculated between various items in the financial statements is quite large. Many of these ratios have limited usefulness. In the sections which follow, we describe several ratios which have been found to provide useful information for assessing profitability, liquidity, and solvency. Some of the ratios, however, may be used in assessing more than one of these factors. The balance sheet, income statement, and statement of changes in financial position of the Horrigan Corporation, presented in Exhibits 7.1, 7.2, and 7.3,

EXHIBIT 7.1
Horrigan Corporation
Comparative Balance Sheets

ASSETS

	($ in Thousands) December 31	
	1976	1975
Current Assets		
Cash	$ 1,300	$ 1,100
Marketable Securities	300	300
Accounts Receivable (Net)	2,600	2,500
Inventories	7,300	6,900
Total Current Assets	$11,500	$10,800
Noncurrent Assets		
Plant and Equipment	$ 5,200	$ 4,500
Less Accumulated Depreciation	1,300	1,000
Net Plant and Equipment	$ 3,900	$ 3,500
Land	1,200	1,200
Total Noncurrent Assets	$ 5,100	$ 4,700
Total Assets	$16,600	$15,500

LIABILITIES AND STOCKHOLDERS' EQUITY

	1976	1975
Current Liabilities		
Accounts Payable	$ 1,600	$ 1,700
Accrued Payables	800	900
Income Taxes Payable	300	200
Notes Payable	1,900	1,200
Total Current Liabilities	$ 4,600	$ 4,000
Long-Term Liabilities		
Bonds Payable (8 percent)	$ 2,000	$ 2,100
Mortgage Payable	200	200
Total Long-Term Liabilities	$ 2,200	$ 2,300
Total Liabilities	$ 6,800	$ 6,300
Stockholders' Equity		
Preferred Stock (6 percent, $100 par)	$ 2,000	$ 2,000
Common Stock ($1 par)	500	500
Additional Paid-in Capital	2,500	2,500
Total Contributed Capital	$ 5,000	$ 5,000
Retained Earnings	4,800	4,200
Total Stockholders' Equity	$ 9,800	$ 9,200
Total Liabilities and Stockholders' Equity	$16,600	$15,500

EXHIBIT 7.2
Horrigan Corporation
Statement of Income and Retained Earnings
Year of 1976

	($ in Thousands)	Percent of Total Revenues
Revenues		
Sales	$26,500	101.5%
Less Sales Allowances, Returns, and Discounts	600	2.3
Net Sales	$25,900	99.2
Interest and Other Revenues	200	.8
Total Revenues	$26,100	100.0
Expenses		
Cost of Goods Sold	$20,500	78.5
Selling and Administrative Expenses:		
Selling Expenses	$2,120	8.1
Administrative Expenses	1,000	3.8
Depreciation	300	1.1
Total Selling and Administrative Expenses	3,420	13.1[a]
Interest Expense	180	.7
Income Tax Expense	800	3.1
Total Expenses	$24,900	95.4
Net Income to Stockholders	$ 1,200	4.6%
Dividends		
Dividends on Preferred Stock	$ 120	
Dividends on Common Stock	480	
Total Dividends	600	
Addition to Retained Earnings for Year	$ 600	
Retained Earnings, January 1, 1976	4,200	
Retained Earnings, December 31, 1976	$ 4,800	
Earnings Per Share of Common Stock (in dollars)[b]	$2.16	

[a] Sum of three figures above does not equal 13.1 percent because of rounding.
[b] ($1,200,000 — $120,000)/500,000 shares.

respectively, are used in illustrating the calculation of the ratios and in describing the general approach to financial statement analysis.

■ MEASURES OF PROFITABILITY

Usually the most important question asked about a business is: How profitable is it? Most financial statement analysis is directed at various aspects of this question. Some measures of profitability relate earnings to resources or capital em-

EXHIBIT 7.3
Horrigan Corporation
Statement of Changes in Financial Position
Year of 1976
($ in thousands)

Sources of Working Capital:

Net Income $1,200

Add Back Expenses Not Using Working Capital:

Depreciation Expense 300

Working Capital Provided by Operations $1,500

Uses of Working Capital:

Preferred Stock Dividend .... $ 120

Common Stock Dividend 480

Purchase of Plant and Equipment 700

Redemption of Bonds Payable 100   1,400

Increase in Working Capital for the Year .... $ 100

Analysis of Increases (Decreases) in Working Capital Amounts

Cash .... $ 200

Marketable Securities 0

Accounts Receivable (Net) 100

Inventories 400

Accounts Payable 100

Accrued Payable 100

Income Taxes Payable .... (100)

Notes Payable .... (700)

Increase in Working Capital for the Year .... $ 100

ployed, other computations relate earnings and various expenses to sales, while a third group seeks to explain profitability by measuring the efficiency with which inventories, receivables, or other assets have been administered.

Rate of Return on Total Capital

One of the most important profitability ratios, particularly in assessing management's performance, is the *rate of return earned on total capital* or resources employed by the firm. The "capital employed" is indicated by the total of either side of the balance sheet, the total assets or the total equities. Since the earnings rate *during the year* is being determined, the denominator should reflect the average of invested capital during the year. A crude, but usually satisfactory, figure for average invested capital is the sum of the total assets, or equities, at the beginning and end of the year divided by two.

In order to assess management's operating performance independently of financing decisions, the earnings figure to be compared with total capital employed should be net income before deducting any distributions to the furnishers of capital. Since interest is a payment to a source of capital, interest expense should be added back to net income to measure the return on total capital employed. The amount added back to net income, however, is not equal to interest expense shown on the income statement. Since interest expense is deductible in determining taxable income, interest expense does not reduce *aftertax* net income by the full amount of interest charges. The amount added back to net income is, therefore, interest expense net of income tax effects.

For example, interest expense of Horrigan Corporation in Exhibit 7.2 is $180,000. To determine the reduction of income taxes obtained by deducting this $180,000 in calculating taxable income, observe that the income tax rate is 40 percent [= $800,000/($1,200,000 + $800,000)]. The income tax saved because interest is deductible in determining taxable income is $72,000 (= .40 × $180,000). The interest charge (net of income tax savings) which is added back to net income is, then, $108,000 (= $180,000 − $72,000).

The rate of return on total capital for Horrigan Corporation is

$$\frac{\text{Net Income} + \text{Aftertax Interest Expense}}{\text{Average Total Assets or Equities for the Period}}$$

$$= \frac{\$1,200,000 + \$108,000}{(\$15,500,000 + \$16,600,000)/2} = 8.1 \text{ percent.}$$

The rate of return on total capital is sometimes called the *all-capital earnings rate.*

Rate of Return on Common Stock Equity

The investor in a firm's common stock is probably more interested in the *rate of return on common stock equity* than in the all-capital earnings rate. To determine the amount of earnings assignable to common stock equity, the earnings allocable to preferred stock equity, usually dividends on preferred stock declared during the period, must be deducted from net income. The capital provided during the period by common stockholders can be determined by averaging the aggregate par value of common stock, capital contributed in excess of par value on common stock, and retained earnings (or by deducting the equity of preferred stockholders from total stockholders' equity) at the beginning and end of the period.

The rate of return on common stock equity of Horrigan Corporation is

$$\frac{\text{Net Income} - \text{Preferred Stock Dividends}}{\text{Average Common Stock Equity for the Period}}$$

$$= \frac{\$1,200,000 - \$120,000}{(\$7,200,000 + \$7,800,000)/2} = 14.4 \text{ percent.}$$

The rate of return on the common stock equity (14.4 percent) is larger in this case than the rate of return on the total capital (8.1 percent). The return to the common stock equity is larger than the rate of return on all capital because the required rate to the other suppliers of capital is less than 8.1 percent of the amount of capital they provided. The current liabilities carry no explicit interest payment, the bonds were issued to yield 8 percent, and the preferred stock requires only a 6 percent annual dividend. The common stock equity group benefited because capital contributed by these other groups earned 8.1 percent but required a lower rate of interest payments or income distributions. Financing with debt and preferred stock to increase the return to the residual common stock equity is referred to as *leverage*.

Earnings per Share of Common Stock

As we discussed in Chapter Six, generally accepted accounting principles require the presentation of *earnings per common share* amounts in the income statement. Earnings per common share is determined by dividing net income applicable to common stock by the average number of shares outstanding during the period. Earnings per share of common stock of Horrigan Corporation is

$$\frac{\text{Net Income} - \text{Preferred Stock Dividends}}{\text{Average Number of Common Shares Outstanding During the Period}} = \frac{\$1,200,000 - \$120,000}{500,000 \text{ shares}}$$

$$= \$2.16 \text{ per share.}$$

A firm with outstanding convertible bonds, convertible preferred stock, or stock options and warrants has committed itself to issuing common shares at the discretion of the owners of these securities. Accounting Principles Board Opinion No. 15 requires the firm to present amounts for primary and fully diluted earnings per share if these securities have the potential for materially diluting, or reducing, the earnings-per-share amount.[1] The Horrigan Corporation did not have any such securities outstanding.

Earnings-per-share amounts are often compared with the market price of the stock to determine the rate of return currently being earned on the investment. This return is the starting point in investors' estimates of the rate that may be earned in the future. For example, assume that the common stock of Horrigan Corporation is selling for $25.00 per share at the end of 1976. The earnings yield is 8.6 percent (= $2.16/$25). The *price-earnings ratio* (called the P/E ratio) is the reciprocal of the earnings yield: 11.6 to 1. The latter ratio is often presented in tables of stock market prices and in financial periodicals. The relationship is sometimes expressed by saying that "the stock is selling at 11.6 times earnings."

Percentages of Revenue

One method of measuring profitability and efficiency is to compare net income and various expenses to total revenues for the period. These amounts are usually calculated in percentage form as shown in Exhibit 7.2. Most published income

[1] Opinion No. 15, Accounting Principles Board, AICPA, May 1969.

statements do not, however, disclose these percentages directly on the income statement.

The *operating ratio*, the percentage of total expenses to total revenues, is often considered an important basis for judging the general effectiveness of operations. The *profit margin ratio*, the percentage of net income to total revenue, serves a similar role. The profit margin ratio is the complement of the operating ratio (that is, the operating ratio plus the profit margin ratio equals 1.0 or 100 percent). Several of the expense percentages are watched closely by management on a weekly or monthly basis in an effort to note the trend of expenses and to take prompt action to control expenses that appear to be getting out of line.

In making comparisons and interpretations of these percentages, however, the fact that not all expenses vary with revenues must be taken into account. For example, if revenues increase, a relatively fixed expense such as real estate taxes should show a decline in percentage while a relatively variable expense, such as delivery costs, should remain at approximately the same percentage. Also, caution must be exercised in comparing operating and profit margin ratios for different firms, particularly if the firms are in different industries. A profit margin ratio of 10 percent might be high in some industries, but normal or low in others. For example, the profit margin ratio of American Telephone and Telegraph Company in a recent year was 12.8 percent, while that of Sears was 5.5 percent. Since significantly different amounts of capital were required per dollar of sales by the two companies, these differences in profit margin rates are not necessarily indicative of differing managerial effectiveness.

Total Assets Turnover

The profit margin ratio discussed in the preceding section focuses on the firm's ability to control expenses in relation to sales revenues. The profit margin ratio does not recognize explicitly, however, the capital or assets required to generate a particular level of sales. The *total assets turnover*, the ratio of total revenue to average total assets during the period, provides a measure of the revenue generated for each dollar invested in assets. The total assets turnover for Horrigan Corporation is calculated as follows:

$$\frac{\text{Total Revenue}}{\text{Average Total Assets}} = \frac{\$26,100,000}{(\$15,500,000 + \$16,600,000)/2} = 1.63.$$

On average, each dollar invested in assets by Horrigan Corporation yielded \$1.63 in revenue during 1976.

Disaggregated Rate of Return Measures

The profit margin ratio and total assets turnover ratio, when used separately, do not measure profitability completely. When combined, these ratios are useful tools in analyzing and interpreting measures of rate of return. For example, the all-capital earnings rate might be disaggregated into a profit margin ratio (before interest expense and related tax effects) and total assets turnover ratio as follows:

$$\begin{array}{ccc} \text{All-Capital} \\ \text{Earnings Rate} \end{array} = \begin{array}{c} \text{Profit Margin Ratio} \\ \text{(before interest ex-} \\ \text{pense and related} \\ \text{income tax effects)} \end{array} \times \begin{array}{c} \text{Total Assets} \\ \text{Turnover Ratio.} \end{array}$$

$$\frac{\text{Net Income Plus After-tax Interest Expense}}{\text{Average Total Assets}} = \frac{\text{Net Income Plus After-tax Interest Expense}}{\text{Total Revenue}} \times \frac{\text{Total Revenue}}{\text{Average Total Assets.}}$$

The all-capital earnings rate for Horrigan Corporation is 8.1 percent. This rate of return can be disaggregated as follows:

$$\frac{\$1,200,000 + \$108,000}{(\$15,500,000 + \$16,600,000)/2} = \frac{\$1,308,000}{\$26,100,000}$$

$$\times \frac{\$26,100,000}{(\$15,500,000 + \$16,600,000)/2}$$

or

$$8\% = 5\% \times 1.63.$$

Improving the all-capital earnings rate can be accomplished by increasing the profit margin ratio, the rate of asset turnover, or both. Some firms, however, may have little flexibility in altering one or the other, or both, of these components. For example, a firm committed under a 3-year labor union contract may have little control over the wage rate paid. Or a firm operating under market- or government-imposed price controls may not be able to increase the prices of its products. In these cases, the opportunities for improving the profit margin ratio are limited. In order to increase the rate of return on capital employed, the level of investment in assets such as inventory, plant, and equipment must be reduced or, to put it another way, revenues per dollar of assets must be increased.

Inventory Turnover

In an effort to judge the efficiency of using various classes of assets, the turnover of these assets can be calculated. For example, a significant indicator of the efficiency of the operations of many businesses is the *inventory turnover ratio*, or the number of times the average inventory has been sold during the period. The calculation involves dividing cost of goods sold by the average inventory during the period. The inventory turnover ratio for Horrigan Corporation is

$$\frac{\text{Cost of Goods Sold}}{\text{Average Inventory}} = \frac{\$20,500,000}{(\$6,900,000 + \$7,300,000)/2} = 2.9 \text{ times per year.}$$

The interpretation of the inventory turnover figure involves two opposing considerations. Management would like to sell as many goods as possible with a minimum of capital tied up in inventories. An increase in the rate of inventory turnover between periods would seem to indicate more profitable use of the investment in inventory. On the other hand, management does not want to have so little inventory on hand that shortages result and customers become dissatisfied. An increase in the rate of inventory turnover in this case may mean a loss of customers and thereby offset any advantage gained by decreased investment in inventory. Some trade-offs are therefore required in deciding the optimum level of inventory for each firm and thus the desirable rate of inventory turnover.

A variation in the inventory turnover calculation indicates the average number of days that merchandise is held during the period. The number of days in the period, such as 365 days for a year, is divided by the inventory turnover ratio. For Horrigan Corporation, the inventory was on hand an average of 126 days ($= 365/2.9$). Expressing the inventory turnover ratio in terms of average number of days inventory is held is frequently considered to be a more useful form for appraising the liquidity of the inventory. The turnover of accounts receivable is also used as an indicator of liquidity and is discussed in the next section on measures of liquidity.

■ MEASURES OF SHORT-TERM LIQUIDITY

Investors or creditors whose claims will become payable in the near future are interested in the liquidity or "nearness to cash" of a firm's assets. One tool for predicting whether or not cash will be available when the claims become due is a budget of cash receipts and disbursements for several months or quarters in the future. Such budgets are often prepared for management and used internally for planning cash requirements. At the present time, budgets of cash receipts and disbursements are not generally available for use by persons outside a firm. Investors must therefore use other tools in assessing liquidity.

The statement of changes in financial position is one published source of information for assessing liquidity. The amount of working capital provided by operations indicates the extent to which the operating activities have generated sufficient working capital to replace fixed assets and pay dividends. The statement also discloses the extent to which additional financing has been required for these purposes. For Horrigan Corporation, working capital provided by operations of $1.5 million exceeds the uses of working capital needed for paying dividends, replacing plant and equipment, and redeeming long-term debt. Therefore, additional long-term financing was not necessary during the period.

Several ratios are also useful in assessing the current liquidity of the firm. They include the current ratio, quick ratio, and the rate of accounts receivable turnover.

Current Ratio

The *current ratio* is calculated by dividing current assets by current liabilities. It is commonly expressed as a ratio such as "2 to 1" or "5 to 1," meaning that current assets are twice or five times as large as current liabilities. The current ratio of Horrigan Corporation on December 31, 1976, is:

$$\frac{\text{Current Assets}}{\text{Current Liabilities}} = \frac{\$11,500,000}{\$4,600,000} = 2.5 \text{ or a ratio of 2.5 to 1.}$$

This ratio is presumed to indicate the ability of the concern to meet its current obligations, and is therefore of particular significance to short-term creditors.

Although an excess of current assets over current liabilities is generally considered desirable from the creditor's viewpoint, changes in the trend of the ratio may be difficult to interpret. For example, when the current ratio is larger than 1 to 1, an increase of equal amount in both current assets and current liabilities results in a decline in the ratio, while equal decreases result in an increased current ratio. Assume, for example, first that each of the amounts used in the preceding calculation increased $2 million and then that each amount decreased $2 million. The resulting current ratios are as follows:

$$\frac{\$13,500,000}{\$6,600,000} = 2.0 \text{ to } 1; \quad \frac{\$9,500,000}{\$2,600,000} = 3.7 \text{ to } 1.$$

If a corporation has a particularly profitable year, the large current liability for income taxes may cause a decline in the current ratio. In a recession period, business is contracting, current liabilities are paid, and even though the current assets may be at a low point, the ratio will often go to high levels. In a boom period, just the reverse effect might occur. In other words, a very high current ratio may reflect unsatisfactory business conditions, while a falling ratio may accompany profitable operations.

Furthermore, the current ratio is susceptible to "window dressing"; that is, management can take deliberate steps to produce a financial statement which presents a better current ratio at the balance sheet date than the average or normal current ratio. For example, toward the close of a fiscal year normal purchases on account may be delayed. Or loans to officers, classified as noncurrent assets, may be collected and the proceeds used to reduce the current liabilities. These actions may be taken so that the current ratio will appear as favorable as possible in the annual financial statements.

While the current ratio is probably the most common ratio presented in statement analysis, there are limitations in its use as discussed above. Its trends are difficult to interpret and, if overemphasized, it can easily lead to undersirable business practices as well as misinterpretation of financial condition.

Quick Ratio

A variation of the current ratio, usually known as the *quick ratio* or *acid-test ratio*, is computed by including in the numerator of the fraction only those current assets which could be converted quickly into cash. The items customarily included are cash, marketable securities, and receivables, but it would be better to make a study of the facts in each case before deciding whether or not to include receivables and to exclude inventories. In some businesses the inventory of merchandise might be converted into cash more easily than the receivables of other businesses.

Accepting the customary procedure of including accounts receivable and excluding inventories, the quick ratio of Horrigan Corporation is as follows.

$$\frac{\text{Cash} + \text{Marketable Securities} + \text{Accounts Receivable}}{\text{Current Liabilities}} = \frac{\$1,300,000 + \$300,000 + \$2,600,000}{\$4,600,000} = .9.$$

Accounts Receivable Turnover

The rate at which certain assets turn over, particularly accounts receivable and inventory, gives some indication of the current liquidity of the firm. The rates of turnover are particularly useful when expressed as the average number of days that receivables are outstanding or inventory items are held.

The *accounts receivable turnover* for Horrigan Corporation, assuming that all sales are on account, is calculated as follows:

$$\frac{\text{Net Sales on Account}}{\text{Average Accounts Receivable}} = \frac{\$25,900,000}{(\$2,500,000 + \$2,600,000)/2}$$

$$= 10.2 \text{ times per year.}$$

The average number of days that accounts receivable are outstanding is 35.8 days ($= 365/10.2$). Thus, on average, accounts receivable are collected approximately 36 days after the date of the sale. The interpretation of this average collection period depends on the terms of sale. If the terms of sale are "net 30 days," the accounts receivable turnover indicates that collections are not being made in accordance with the stated terms. Such a condition would warrant a review of the credit and collection activity for an explanation and for possible corrective action. If, however, the firm offers terms of "30 days EOM" (due in 30 days from the end of the month of sale), the results indicate that the accounts receivable are being handled well.

To take a real example, the notes to the financial statements in a recent annual report of the General Electric Company remark that a twenty-percent increase in the amount of accounts receivable during the year "was due principally to the increase in sales" during the year. We can check for ourselves that this is a valid explanation of the unusual increase in the accounts receivable balance by computing the accounts receivable turnover for both this year and the preceding one. In both years the accounts receivable turnover was about 5.6 times, so we can judge that GE's collections on accounts receivable have not significantly deteriorated.

■ MEASURES OF LONG-TERM SOLVENCY

Measures of long-term solvency are used in assessing the firm's ability to meet interest and principal payments on long-term debt and similar obligations as they become due. If the payments cannot be made on time, the firm becomes *insolvent* and may have to be reorganized or liquidated.

Perhaps the best indicator of long-term solvency is a firm's ability to generate profits over a period of years. If a firm is profitable, it will either generate sufficient capital from operations or be able to obtain needed capital from creditors and owners. The measures of profitability discussed previously are therefore applicable for this purpose as well. Two other commonly used measures of long-term solvency are equity ratios and the number of times that interest charges are earned.

Equity Ratios

There are several variations in the equity ratio, but the one most commonly encountered is the *debt-equity* ratio. This ratio is calculated by dividing total liabilities (current and noncurrent) by total liabilities plus stockholders' equity. For Horrigan Corporation, the debt equity ratio at December 31, 1976, is as follows:

$$\frac{\text{Total Liabilities}}{\text{Total Equities}} = \frac{\$6,800,000}{\$16,600,000} = .41.$$

This ratio indicates the proportion of total capital supplied by creditors. In general, the higher the ratio, the higher the likelihood the firm may be unable to meet fixed interest and principal payments in the future. The decision for most firms is how much financial risk they can afford to assume. Funds obtained from issuing bonds or borrowing from a bank have a relatively low interest cost but require fixed, periodic payments.

In assessing the debt-equity ratio, the analyst customarily varies the standard in direct relation to the stability of the firm's earnings. The more stable the earnings, the higher the debt-equity ratio which is considered acceptable or safe. The debt-equity ratios of public utilities are customarily high, on the order of 60 percent to 70 percent. The stability of public utility earnings makes the ratios acceptable to many investors who would be dissatisfied with such debt-equity ratios for firms with less stable earnings.

One variation of the equity ratio relates total stockholders' equity to total equities. This is, of course, the complement of the debt-equity ratio. For Horrigan Corporation, this ratio is 59 percent (= $9,800,000/$16,600,000). Another variation of the equity ratio relates total long-term debt to total long-term financing (long-term debt plus stockholders equity). For Horrigan Corporation, this ratio is 18 percent [= $2,200,000/($2,200,000 + $9,800,000)]. Since several variations of the equity ratio appear in corporate annual reports, careful comparisons of equity ratios among firms are necessary.

Times Interest Charges Earned

Another measure of long-term solvency is the *number of times that interest charges are earned*, or covered. This ratio is calculated by dividing net income before interest and income tax expenses by interest expense. The number of times that interest charges were earned during 1976 for Horrigan Corporation is calculated as follows:

$$\frac{\text{Net Income + Interest Expense + Income Tax Expense}}{\text{Interest Expense}} = \frac{\$1,200,000 + \$180,000 + \$800,000}{\$180,000}$$

$$= 12.1 \text{ times.}$$

The purpose of this ratio is to indicate the relative protection of bondholders and to assess the probability that the firm will be forced into receivership by a failure to meet required interest payments. If periodic repayments of principal on long-term liabilities are also required, they might also be included in the denominator of the ratio. The ratio would then be described as the *number of times that fixed charges were earned,* or covered.

The times interest or fixed charges earned ratios can be criticized as measures for assessing solvency because the ratios use earnings rather than cash flows in the numerator. Interest and other fixed payment obligations are paid with cash, and not with earnings. When the value of the ratio is relatively low (for example, two to three times), some measure of cash flows, such as cash flows from operations, may be preferable in the numerator.

For convenient reference, Table 7.1 summarizes the calculation of the ratios discussed in this chapter.

■ LIMITATIONS OF RATIO ANALYSIS

The analytical computations discussed in this chapter have a number of limitations which should be kept in mind by anyone preparing or using them. Several of the more important limitations are given below:

1. The ratios are based on financial statement data and are therefore subject to the same criticisms as the underlying financial statements (for example, use of acquisition cost rather than current replacement cost or net realizable value, latitude permitted firms in selecting from among various generally accepted accounting principles).
2. Changes in many ratios are highly associated, or correlated, with each other. For example, the changes in the current ratio and quick ratio between two different times are generally in the same direction and approximately proportional. It is therefore not necessary to compute more than two or three ratios to assess a particular factor being considered in the analysis.
3. When comparing the size of a ratio during the current period with the corresponding ratio during a previous period for the same firm, one must recognize conditions which have changed between the periods being compared (for example, different product lines or geographical markets served, changes in economic conditions, changes in prices).
4. When comparing ratios of a particular firm with those of similar firms, one must recognize differences between the firms (for example, use of different methods of accounting, differences in the method of operations, type of financing, and so on).

Not many results of financial statement analyses can be used by themselves as direct indications of good or poor management. Such analyses merely indicate probabilities or matters which might be investigated further. For example, a

TABLE 7.1
Summary of Important Financial Ratios

Ratio	Numerator	Denominator
Rate of return on total capital	Net income + interest expense (net of tax effects) [a]	Average total assets or equities during the period
Rate of return on common stock equity	Net income − preferred stock dividends	Average common stockholders' equity during the period
Earnings per share of common stock [b]	Net income − preferred stock dividends	Weighted average number of common shares outstandnig during the period
Operating ratio	Total expenses	Total revenues
Profit margin ratio	Net income	Total revenues
Total assets turnover	Total revenues	Average total assets during the period
Inventory turnover	Cost of goods sold	Average inventory during the period
Average number of days inventory on hand	365	Inventory turnover ratio
Accounts receivable turnover	Net sales on account	Average accounts receivable during the period
Average collection period for accounts receivable	365	Accounts receivable turnover ratio
Current ratio	Current assets	Current liabilities
Quick or acid-test ratio	Highly liquid assets (ordinarily, cash, marketable securities, and receivables) [c]	Current liabilities
Debt-equity ratio	Total liabilities	Total equities (liabilities plus stockholders' equity)
Times interest charges earned	Net income before interest and income taxes	Interest expense

[a] If a consolidated subsidiary is not owned entirely by the parent corporation, the minority interest share of earnings must also be added back to net income. Procedures for accounting for minority interests are discussed in Chapter Thirteen.

[b] See Chapters Six and Twelve for possible complications when there are convertible securities, options, or warrants outstanding.

[c] Receivables could conceivably be excluded for some firms and inventories included for others. Such refinements are seldom employed in practice.

decrease in the turnover of raw materials inventory, ordinarily considered to be an undesirable trend, may reflect the accumulation of scarce materials which will keep the plant operating at full capacity during shortages when competitors have been forced to restrict operations or to close down. Ratios derived from financial statements must be combined with an investigation of the facts before valid conclusions can be drawn.

■ SUMMARY

Financial statement analysis embraces the methods used in assessing past performance and current financial position as a basis for predicting future rates of return and for assessing the risk or uncertainty of that return. Ratios are useful tools for expressing important financial relationships between items in the financial statements.

The relative weight given to assessments of profitability, liquidity, and solvency in assessing return and risk differs, though, depending on the nature of the investment. For many investors, the firm's profitability is the most important concern. The rate of return on total capital or on common stock equity, turnovers of total assets, accounts receivable and inventory, and various percentages of expenses or net income to revenues provide useful measures of profitability. For relatively short-term lenders, liquidity is of paramount interest. The current and quick ratios are useful tools in this situation, although an analysis of cash or working capital flows is also helpful. Relatively long-term lenders are more concerned with a firm's ability to meet its obligations for fixed payments as they come due. The debt-equity ratio and the times interest (fixed charges) earned ratio are useful for assessing long-term solvency.

The potential limitations inherent in ratio analysis cannot be overemphasized. Ratios are used principally for detecting significant changes or unusual relationships between financial statement items. They serve as signals of the need for further investigation. Particular caution must be exercised when comparing the size of a ratio with the corresponding ratio of an earlier period or with that of a similar firm in the same industry. Changed conditions or different operating environments may limit the comparability of the ratios in these and other cases. Different methods of accounting, to be discussed in Chapters Eight through Thirteen, and summarized in Chapter Fifteen, may also reduce the comparability of ratios among firms.

QUESTIONS AND PROBLEMS

1. Review the meaning of the following concepts or terms discussed in the chapter.
   a. Return and risk.
   b. Profitability.
   c. Liquidity.

    d. Solvency.

    e. Rate of return on total capital.

    f. Rate of return on common stock equity.

    g. Leverage.

    h. Earnings per share.

    i. Price-earnings ratio.

    j. Operating ratio.

    k. Profit margin ratio.

    l. Inventory turnover.

    m. Accounts receivable turnover.

    n. Total assets turnover.

    o. Current ratio.

    p. Quick ratio.

    q. Debt-equity ratio.

    r. Times interest charges earned.

2. Financial statements report the results of past performance and current financial condition. An investor is interested primarily in a firm's future performance. How can financial statement analysis be useful in investment decisions?

3. In what ways are ratios useful tools for analyzing and interpreting financial statements?

4. Is rate of return on common stock equity a measure for assessing the return from investing in a firm's common stock or for assessing the risk or uncertainty of that return? Explain.

5. Distinguish between liquidity and solvency.

6. Describe several factors which might limit the comparability of a firm's current ratio over several years.

7. Describe several factors which might limit the comparability of one firm's current ratio with that of another firm in the same industry.

8. Net income attributable to common stockholders' equity of Florida Corporation during 1976 was $250,000, while earnings per share were $.50 during the period. The average common stockholders' equity during 1976 was $2,500,000, while the market price at year end was $6.00 per share.

    a. Determine the rate of return on common stockholders' equity for 1976.

    b. Determine the rate of return currently being earned on the market price of the stock (the ratio of earnings per share to market price per share).

    c. Why is there a difference between the rates of return determined in **a** and **b**?

9. Under what circumstances will the rate of return on the common stock equity be more than the return on total capital? Under what circumstances will it be less?

10. The following comparative percentages were obtained from the financial statements of Companies M and N:

	CO. M	CO. N
Net Income to Sales	4%	6%
Net Income to Stockholders' Equity	13%	10%

On the basis of this limited data, which company would appear to be more profitable? Explain.

11. The following data are taken from the 1976 annual reports of the Alabama Company and Carolina Company:

	ALABAMA CO.	CAROLINA CO.
Sales	$2,000,000	$2,400,000
Net Income	120,000	120,000
Average Total Assets During the Year	1,500,000	1,000,000

   a. Determine the rate of return on total assets for each company (assume that interest expense and preferred dividends are zero).
   b. Disaggregate the rate of return in **a** into profit margin percentages and asset turnover ratios.
   c. Comment on the relative performance of the two companies.
12. In calculating the inventory turnover, when might the use of the average of the beginning and ending inventories lead to an inaccurate result?
13. Illustrate with amounts how a decrease in the amount of working capital between two dates can accompany an increase in the current ratio.
14. Merchandise inventory costing $30,000 is purchased on account. Indicate the effect (increase, decrease, no effect) of this transaction on (**1**) working capital and (**2**) the current ratio, assuming current assets and current liabilities immediately prior to the transaction were as follows:
   a. Current assets, $120,000; current liabilities, $120,000.
   b. Current assets, $120,000; current liabilities, $150,000.
   c. Current assets, $120,000; current liabilities, $80,000.
15. Assuming an excess of current assets over current liabilities, indicate the effect of the following upon the current ratio:
   a. Collection of an account receivable.
   b. Payment of an account payable.
   c. Acquisition of merchandise on account.
   d. Acquisition of merchandise for cash.
   e. Acquisition of machinery on account.
   f. Acquisition of machinery for cash.
   g. Sale of marketable securities at less than book value.
   h. Sale of an investment at less than book value.
16. Assuming an excess of current assets over current liabilities, indicate the effect of the following upon the current ratio:
   a. The acquisition of government bonds for cash.
   b. The borrowing of funds from a bank on a noninterest-bearing note.
   c. The issuance of bonds for cash.
   d. The payment of a short-term note at the bank.
   e. The recording of accrued interest on a note receivable.
   f. The receipt of a noninterest-bearing, 2-month note from a customer to apply to an account receivable.
   g. The sale of machinery and equipment at less than book value.
17. Following is a schedule of the current assets and current liabilities of the Lewis Company:

Current Assets	Dec. 31, 1976	Dec. 31, 1975
Cash	$ 355,890	$ 212,790
Accounts Receivable	389,210	646,010
Inventories	799,100	1,118,200
Prepayments	21,600	30,000
Total Current Assets	$1,565,800	$2,007,000
Current Liabilties		
Accounts Payable	$ 152,760	$ 217,240
Accrued Payroll, Taxes, etc.	126,340	318,760
Notes Payable	69,500	330,000
Total Current Liabilities	$ 348,600	$ 866,000

The Lewis Company operated at a loss during 1976.
- **a.** Calculate the current ratio for each date.
- **b.** Explain how the improved current ratio is possible under the 1976 operating conditions.

18. The following data are taken from the financial statements of the Press Company:

	Dec. 31, 1976	Dec. 31, 1975
Current Assets	$210,000	$180,000
Noncurrent Assets	275,000	255,000
Current Liabilities	78,000	85,000
Long-Term Liabilities	75,000	30,000
Common Stock (10,000 shares)	300,000	300,000
Retained Earnings	32,000	20,000

	1976 Operations
Net Income	$72,000
Interest Expense	3,000
Income Taxes (40% rate)	48,000
Dividends Declared	60,000

Calculate the following ratios:
- **a.** Rate of return on total capital.
- **b.** Rate of return on stockholders' equity.
- **c.** Earnings per share of common stock.
- **d.** Current ratio (both dates).
- **e.** Times interest earned.
- **f.** Debt-equity ratio (both dates).

19. Refer to the financial statements of Jonathan Corporation in Chapter One and calculate the following:
- **a.** Rate of return on total capital. The income tax rate is 40 percent.
- **b.** Rate of return on stockholders' equity.
- **c.** Earnings per share. (500,000 shares were outstanding throughout the year.)
- **d.** Profit margin ratio.
- **e.** Inventory turnover.

    f. Current ratio (both dates).

    g. Debt-equity ratio (both dates).

    h. Times interest earned.

20. Indicate the effects (increase, decrease, no effect) of each of the indepedent transactions below on (**1**) rate of return on common stock equity, (**2**) current ratio, and (**3**) debt-equity ratio. State any necessary assumptions.

    a. Merchandise inventory costing $120,000 is sold on account for $150,000.

    b. Collections from customers on accounts receivable total $100,000.

    c. A provision is made for estimated uncollectible accounts, $15,000.

    d. Specific customers' accounts totaling $10,000 are written off as uncollectible.

    e. Merchandise inventory costing $205,000 is purchased on account.

    f. A machine costing $40,000 and on which $30,000 depreciation had been taken is sold for $8,000.

    g. Dividends of $80,000 are declared. The dividends will be paid during the next accounting period.

21. Indicate the effects (increase, decrease, no effect) of the independent transactions below on (**1**) earnings per share, (**2**) working capital, and (**3**) quick ratio, where accounts receivable are *included* but merchandise inventory is *excluded* from "quick assets." State any necessary assumptions.

    a. Merchandise inventory costing $240,000 is sold on account for $300,000.

    b. Dividends of $160,000 are declared. The dividends will be paid during the next accounting period.

    c. Merchandise inventory costing $410,000 is purchased on account.

    d. A machine costing $80,000 and on which $60,000 depreciation had been taken is sold for $16,000.

    e. Merchandise inventory purchased for cash in the amount of $7,000 is returned to the supplier because it is defective. A cash reimbursement is received.

    f. 10,000 shares of $10 par value common stock were issued on the last day of the accounting period for $15 per share. The proceeds were used to acquire the assets of another firm composed of the following: accounts receivable, $30,000; merchandise inventory, $60,000; plant and equipment, $100,000. The acquiring firm also agreed to assume current liabilities of $40,000 of the acquired company.

    g. Marketable securities costing $16,000 are sold for $20,000.

22. The following information relates to the activities of Tennessee Corporation and Kentucky Corporation for 1976.

	Tennessee Corp.	Kentucky Corp.
Sales on Account, 1976	$4,050,000	$2,560,000
Accounts Receivable, December 31, 1975	960,000	500,000
Accounts Receivable, December 31, 1976	840,000	780,000

    a. Compute the accounts receivable turnover of each company.

    b. Determine the average number of days that accounts receivable are outstanding for each company.

    c. Which company is managing its accounts receivable most efficiently?

23. The income statements and balance sheets of Illinois Corporation and Ohio Corporation are presented below:

Income Statements
For the Year 1976

	Illinois Corp.	Ohio Corp.
Sales	$4,300,000	$3,000,000
Less Expenses:		
Cost of Goods Sold	$2,800,000	$1,400,000
Selling and Administrative Expenses	330,000	580,000
Interest Expense	100,000	200,000
Income Tax Expense	428,000	328,000
Total Expenses	$3,658,000	$2,508,000
Net Income	$ 642,000	$ 492,000

Balance Sheets
December 31, 1976

ASSETS

	Illinois Corp.	Ohio Corp.
Cash	$ 100,000	$ 50,000
Accounts Receivable (Net)	700,000	400,000
Merchandise Inventory	1,200,000	750,000
Plant and Equipment (Net)	4,000,000	4,800,000
Total Assets	$6,000,000	$6,000,000

EQUITIES

	Illinois Corp.	Ohio Corp.
Accounts Payable	$ 572,000	$ 172,000
Income Taxes Payable	428,000	328,000
Long-Term Bonds Payable (10 percent)	1,000,000	2,000,000
Capital Stock	2,000,000	2,000,000
Retained Earnings	2,000,000	1,500,000
Total Equities	$6,000,000	$6,000,000

Assume that the balances in asset and equity accounts at year-end approximate the average balances during the period. The income tax rate is 40 percent. On the basis of this information, which company is:

   a. More profitable?

   b. More liquid?

   c. More secure in terms of long-term solvency?

24. The following information is taken from the financial statements of the Eastern Oil Company for the year ending December 31, 1975 and 1976:

Eastern Oil Company
Consolidated Statement of Financial Position

ASSETS

	(in millions of dollars)	
	December 31, 1976	December 31, 1975
Cash	$ 921.0	$ 866.1
Receivables (Net)	1,198.3	1,173.2
Inventories	1,676.0	1,566.0
Plant and Equipment (Net)	11,930.4	11,305.3
Other Noncurrent Assets	4,589.5	4,331.2
Total Assets	$20,315.2	$19,241.8

EQUITIES

	(in millions of dollars)	
Current Liabilities	$ 3,329.7	$ 3,240.1
Long-Term Liabilities	5,392.6	5,051.0
Capital Stock (average shares outstanding in 1976: 224,100,000; in 1975: 221,000,000)	2,640.5	2,608.4
Retained Earnings	8,952.4	8,342.3
Total Equities	$20,315.2	$19,241.8

Eastern Oil Company
Statement of Income for the Years 1976 and 1975

	(in millions of dollars)	
Revenues	1976	1975
Sales	$20,361.7	$18,143.3
Other Revenue	801.4	553.4
Total Revenues	$21,163.1	$18,696.7
Expenses		
Crude Oil and Product Costs	$ 6,283.8	$ 5,520.7
Selling and Administrative Expenses	11,806.8	10,415.2
Interest Expenses	261.7	241.6
Income Taxes Expense	1,349.2	1,209.2
Total Expenses	$19,701.5	$17,386.7
Net Income to Stockholders	$ 1,461.6	$ 1,310.0

On the basis of this information, assess the relative (**a**) profitability, (**b**) liquidity, (**c**) solvency of the firm as between 1975 and 1976. Assume the balances in the asset and equity accounts at year-end approximate the average balances during the period. Also assume an income tax rate of 48 percent.

Part 3

Measuring
and Reporting
Assets
and Equities

Chapter Eight

Cash,
Marketable Securities,
and Receivables

By now, you have been exposed to all of the basic concepts and procedures of financial accounting. We have discussed the purpose of accounting, its theoretical framework, some of its procedures, and introduced financial statement analysis. From this point onward, we will deal with specific and specialized problems in financial accounting. This chapter and the next five discuss various extensions of financial accounting. The chapters are organized essentially in balance sheet order. Current assets is the subject of Chapters Eight and Nine. The emphasis of this chapter is on liquid, cash-like, or "quick" assets, and the emphasis of Chapter Nine is on inventories. Chapter Ten discusses noncurrent assets. Chapters Eleven and Twelve discuss the right-hand side of the balance sheet—liabilities and owners' equity. Chapter Thirteen, somewhat out of "balance sheet order," focuses on accounting for long-term investments in securities of other companies.

As Chapter Seven pointed out, the liquidity of the business is essential to its continuing success—an insolvent company, one that cannot pay its bills and meet its committments in the short run, will not survive no matter how large its owners' equity. Most bankrupt companies show positive owners' equity on the books at the time of bankruptcy. Bankruptcy is usually caused by insolvency, the inability to meet debts when they come due. One of the largest bankruptcies of recent times occurred in 1970 when the Penn Central Transportation Company was placed into bankruptcy by its parent holding company, the Penn Central Company. At that time, Penn Central Transportation Company had almost $2 billion of stockholders' equity, including some $500 million of retained earnings. Nevertheless, the company was insolvent because it could not meet "only" a few hundred million dollars in current obligations at that time.

Money-like assets are an important determinant of a firm's liquidity. Cash, marketable securities, accounts receivable, and notes receivable are a business's liquid assets. This chapter discusses each of these.

■ CASH

The most liquid asset is cash. Four issues in accounting for cash are: determination of cash items, their valuation, disclosure in the financial statements, and control. Cash includes cash on hand and cash in the bank. Cash on hand may be in petty cash or change funds, or may represent cash not yet deposited in the bank. Cash in the bank may be in checking accounts, called demand deposits, in savings accounts, called time deposits, or in certificates of deposit. Valuing cash presents few problems. Since most accounting is based on monetary measurement and since cash is a monetary item, the measure of cash is its stated amount. When a business holds substantial amounts of foreign currencies, however, there can be a problem of determining the U.S. dollar equivalent value of that cash. This valuation problem and the related ones are discussed in Chapter Thirteen. In most published balance sheets, these items are generally grouped together under the title Cash, and the amount is nearly always shown as the first item among the assets on the balance sheet.

Cash is a firm's most vulnerable asset because of its susceptibility to theft or embezzlement. Hence, cash is the asset most difficult to control physically. The appendix to this chapter describes some accounting procedures for controlling cash.

■ MARKETABLE SECURITIES

A business may temporarily find itself with more cash than it needs for current and near-term business purposes. Rather than allow excess cash to remain unproductive in a checking account, the business may invest some of its currently excess cash in income-yielding securities such as bonds or stocks of other companies. Such uses of liquid assets are known as investments in *marketable securities* or *temporary investments* and are alternatives to putting cash in time deposits or certificates of deposit. Securities are identified as "temporary investments" or "marketable securities" so long as they can be readily converted into cash *and* management intends to do so when it needs cash.

When a business buys stock in another company, intending to hold the securities for long periods of time, the asset is called an investment and different accounting methods are used. The various purposes of such acquisitions of securities and the accounting for them are discussed in Chapter Thirteen. The discussion here concentrates on purchases of securities with excess cash, where the intent is to convert the securities back into cash as it is needed.

Valuation of Marketable Securities

Marketable securities are classified on the balance sheet as a current asset and are typically reported at acquisition cost. Dividends declared and interest earned on marketable securities are revenues of the period. Increases in market value of marketable securities still held (that is, gains that have not been realized in actual market transactions by selling the securities) are not reported in income and are not subject to income tax.

There is perhaps no other generally accepted accounting principle more at odds with economic reality than showing marketable securities at cost rather than at current market value. Since at least 1939, accounting theorists have argued that marketable securities should be shown at market value, whether greater or less than cost. Their very marketability makes valuing them on a current basis reasonably objective. Showing marketable securities at cost fails to recognize the easily measurable changes in a firm's economic position and also gives management an opportunity to manipulate reported income for a period. Management can increase reported income for a period by selling securities that are recorded at cost but that have appreciated in value since acquisition in an earlier period. To lower reported income, securities that have declined in value since acquisition would be sold. In current practice, many firms show the current market value of their marketable securities *parenthetically* on the balance sheet or in notes to the financial statements. Other firms use the lower-of-cost-or-market procedure (also discussed in Chapter Nine in the context of inventories), which recognizes the effects of price declines below current book value, but not those of increases above current book value. Permitting or requiring departures from the cost basis for marketable securities that have increased in value has been considered several times by the official bodies of the accounting profession, but no final action has been taken. The case for departure from the acquisition-cost basis of valuation for marketable securities is so strong that this is likely to be the first area where upward revaluations from the acquisition cost will become acceptable.[1] *Please read footnote.*

Transactions and Journal Entries for Marketable Securities

If marketable securities are acquired for $10,000, the entry is:

Marketable Securities	10,000	
Cash		10,000

If dividends of $125 are declared, then received, on these securities, the entry is:

Cash	125	
Dividend Revenue		125

If the lower-of-cost-or-market method is being used and the market value of the securities at the next balance sheet date is $8,000, the following adjusting entry is made:

Loss on Holding Marketable Securities	2,000	
Marketable Securities		2,000

[1] See Robert R. Sterling, "Accounting Research, Education, and Practice," *The Journal of Accountancy* (September 1973), pp. 44–52. **Note.** Since 1976 most firms *are required* to use lower-of-cost-or-market for certain marketable securities. See FASB Statement No. 12.

Finally, when the securities are sold, say for $11,000, one of the following entries is made, depending upon whether the securities are carried at acquisition cost or at the lower-of-cost-or-market valuation.

1. Assuming that marketable securities are carried at acquisition cost:

Cash	11,000	
Marketable Securities		10,000
Gain on Sale of Marketable Securities		1,000
To recognize gain on sale of securities carried on the books at $10,000.		

2. Assuming the use of lower-of-cost-or-market:

Cash	11,000	
Marketable Securities		8,000
Gain on Sale of Marketable Securities		3,000
To recognize gain on sale of securities carried on the books at $8,000.		

Notice that the total, or net, gain is $1,000 in either case. Carrying the marketable securities at acquisition cost results in recognizing all gains at the time of sale. When the lower-of-cost-or-market procedure is used, a loss of $2,000 is recognized in the first, holding, period and a gain of $3,000 in the second period when the securities are sold. Still, the net gain from acquiring and disposing of the securities is $1,000.

If dividends have been declared by the end of an accounting period but not yet recorded by the stockholder, then journal entries are required to recognize both the revenue and the receivable not yet recorded in the accounts. Furthermore, if interest-bearing securities are held at the end of an accounting period, journal entries are required to recognize the interest earned but not recorded in the accounts.

■ NOTES RECEIVABLE

Many business transactions involve written promises to pay sums of money at a future date. These written promises are called promissory notes. The holder of a promissory note has a liquid asset, notes receivable. A promissory note is a written contract in which one person, known as the *maker*, promises to pay to another person, known as the *payee*, a definite sum of money. The money may be payable either on demand or at a definite future date. The maker may be a group of individuals and there may also be more than one payee. The amount is usually payable to the order of the payee, so that the note can readily be transferred from one holder to another. A note may or may not provide for the payment of interest in addition to the principal amount.

Promissory notes are used most commonly in connection with obtaining loans at banks or other institutions, the purchase of various kinds of property, and as a temporary settlement of an open or charge-account balance when payment cannot be made within the usual credit period. A note may be *secured* by a mortgage on real estate (land and buildings) or personal property (machinery and merchandise), or by the deposit of specific collateral (stock certificates, bonds, and so forth). If the secured note is not collected at maturity, the lender can take possession of the real estate, personal property, or other collateral, sell it, and apply the proceeds to the repayment of the note. Any proceeds in excess of the amount due under the note are then paid to the borrower. Alternatively, the note may be *unsecured*, in which case it has about the same legal position as an account receivable.

The Nature of Interest

Interest is the price paid for the use of borrowed funds. From the lender's point of view, it is a type of revenue. The interest price is usually expressed as a percentage rate of the principal, with the rate being stated on an annual basis. Thus, a 2-month, 12-percent note would have interest equal to 2 percent of the principal; a 3-month, 6-percent note would have interest equal to 1½ percent of principal, and so on. Since interest is a payment for the use of borrowed funds for a period of time, it accrues with the passage of time. Although interest accrues every day (indeed, every time the clock ticks), firms usually record interest only at the time payments are made or received or at the end of an accounting period.

Simple Interest Calculations

The general formula for the calculation of simple interest is

$$\text{Interest} = \text{Base (Principal or Face)} \times \text{Interest Rate} \times \text{Elapsed Time.}$$

The calculation of simple interest for a year or for any multiple or fraction of a year is an elementary arithmetic computation. For example, the interest at the rate of 8 percent a year on $2,000 is $160 for 1 year, $320 for 2 years, $80 for 6 months, and so on. The calculation for shorter periods, while still not an involved mathematical problem, is complicated by the odd number of days in a year and the variations in the number of days in a month. Simple interest at the rate of 8 percent a year on $2,000 for 90 days would be $2,000 × .08 × 90/365, or $39.45, if an exact computation were made. For many purposes, especially the calculation of accrued interest, a satisfactory approximation of the correct interest can be obtained by assuming that the year has 360 days and that each month is one-twelfth of a year. Thus, 30 days is the equivalent of 1 month, and 60 days is the equivalent of 2 months or one-sixth of a year. Under this method, the interest at 8 percent on $2,000 for 90 days would be the same as the interest for 3 months or one-quarter of a year, or $40. Keep in mind that nearly all quotations of simple interest rates state the rate per year, unless some other period is specifically mentioned. In the formula for simple interest, Principal × Rate × Elapsed Time, "time" should be expressed in terms of years, since the rate is the rate per year. Most long-term loans involve *compound interest*, which is explained in Chapter Eleven.

Determination of Elapsed Time

For the sake of uniformity and simplicity, we shall use the following rules in connection with the calculation of interest throughout the text and problems:

1. When the maturity terms are given in months, consider 1 month to be one-twelfth of a year; 3 months to be one-fourth of a year; 6 months to be one-half of a year, and so on, regardless of the actual number of days in the period. This is equivalent to regarding any 1-month period as being 30 days in a 360-day year.
2. When the maturity terms are given in days, use the 360-day year. Consider 30 days to be one-twelfth of a year, 60 days to be one-sixth of a year, 17 days to be 17/360 of a year, and so on. Determine maturity dates and elapsed time by using the actual number of days.
3. When the maturity terms are given in actual dates, such as 60 days from April 1, the first day is not counted and the last day is. That is, all transactions are assumed to occur at the close of a business day. Thus, 60 days from April 1 is May 31.

Accounting for Interest-Bearing Notes Receivable

The notes to be discussed in this section, so-called interest-bearing notes, are those which indicate a face, or principal, amount together with explicit interest at a stated rate for the time period stated in the note. For example, the basic elements of such a note might read: "Sixty days after date (June 30, 1976), the Suren Company promises to pay to the order of the Mullen Company $3,000 with interest from date at the rate of 12 percent per annum." At the maturity date, August 30, 1976, the maturity value would be the face amount of $3,000 plus interest of $60 calculated in accordance with the preceding discussion ($60 = $3,000 \times .12 \times 60/360$), or a total of $3,060.

Among the types of transactions related to a note receivable discussed in this section are the following: receipt of note, interest recognition at an interim date, transfer prior to maturity, and collection at maturity dates.

Receipt of Note and Collection at Maturity   Promissory notes usually are received from customers in connection with sales or with the settlement of an open account receivable. The customer is usually the maker, but the customer may transfer a note which has been received from another. It is common practice to allow the customer full credit for the face value and accrued interest, if any, although a different value might be agreed upon in some instances.

If, on June 30, 1976, the Mullen Company were to receive a 60-day, 12-percent note for $3,000, dated July 1, 1976, from the Suren Company, to apply on its account, the entry would be:

June 30   Notes Receivable   3,000
          Accounts Receivable—Suren Company   3,000

Assuming the accounting period of the Mullen Company to be the calendar year, the entry upon collection at maturity would be:

Aug. 30	Cash on Hand	3,060	
	Notes Receivable		3,000
	Interest Revenue		60

Assuming the accounting period of the Mullen Company to be 1 month, the interest adjustment at the interim date, July 31, would be:

July 31	Interest Receivable	30	
	Interest Revenue		30
	($3,000 × .12 × 30/360 = $30)		

The entry upon collection at maturity would then be:

Aug. 30	Cash on Hand	3,060	
	Notes Receivable		3,000
	Interest Receivable		30
	Interest Revenue		30

At the maturity date, the note may be collected, as illustrated above, renewed, partially collected with renewal of the balance, or dishonored by the maker. These other possibilities involve more advanced accounting procedures and are not discussed in this book.

Transfer of Notes Receivable   A note may be transferred to another party *without recourse*. This procedure is tantamount to a sale of the note, because the transferor has no further liability even if the maker fails to pay at maturity.

If Mullen Company transferred without recourse the 60-day, 12-percent, $3,000 note to Lane Trust Company for $3,030 one month after the date of the note, the entry would be:

July 31	Cash	3,030	
	Notes Receivable		3,000
	Interest Revenue		30
	To record transfer of note without recourse.		

Most businesses that "purchase" notes are, however, unwilling to acquire them without recourse. Such firms do not want to be responsible for investigating the credit worthiness of the maker or for any collection efforts required for dishonored notes. Consequently, most notes that are transferred are done so *with recourse*.

A transfer with recourse places a potential or "contingent" liability upon the transferor if the maker fails to pay at maturity. This contingent liability is assumed when the transferor signs or "endorses" the note with only a signature or with a signature together with wording such as "pay to the order of. . . ." Such a transfer is not a closed, or completed, transaction because of the possibility that the endorser will have to pay the note in case the maker defaults at maturity.

Contingent liabilities, such as those for notes transferred with recourse or for the potential loss arising from an unsettled damage suit, are discussed in Chapter Eleven. Contingent liabilities are not shown directly in the accounts, but are merely disclosed in notes to the balance sheet.

If Mullen Company transferred with recourse the 60-day, 12-percent $3,000 note to Lane Trust Company 1 month after the date of the note, the entry would be the same as if the note was transferred without recourse. If Mullen Company prepared financial statements before Lane Trust Company collected from the maker, however, the notes to Mullen's balance sheet would contain a statement such as the following:

> Contingent Liabilities. *The firm is contingently liable for a note transferred and accrued interest thereon to the Lane Trust Company. The face value of the transferred note is $3,000.*

■ ACCOUNTS RECEIVABLE

The last liquid asset to be considered in this chapter is accounts receivable. The entry when a sale is made on account has been illustrated in earlier chapters. It is[2]

Accounts Receivable	250	
Sales		250

The accounting problems associated with sales arnd accounts receivable include uncollectible accounts, cash discounts, returns, and allowances.

Uncollectible Accounts

Whenever credit is extended to customers, there will almost certainly be some accounts that will never be collected. The uncollectible amount will vary among different types of enterprises both as to its relative significance and as to its regularity. In recording uncollectible accounts, the practice is sometimes followed of waiting until a customer's account has clearly been demonstrated to be uncollectible and then recognizing a loss when the account is written off. If it is decided that the account receivable of Robert S. Thomley for $135 has become uncollectible, the entry would be:

Bad Debt Expense	135	
Accounts Receivable—Robert S. Thomley		135
To record loss from account receivable which has become uncollectible.		

[2] In practice, a sale on account leads to another notation in the accounting records. The firm must keep track of who owes the $250. The individual customers' accounts are recorded in a *subsidiary ledger*. The Accounts Receivable account is a *controlling account*, which merely shows the aggregate balance of all individual customers' accounts receivable. In general, *a controlling account shows summarized data about a related group of accounts kept in a separate ledger, called a subsidiary ledger*. (In a large business, controlling accounts with backup subsidiary ledgers might be kept for Notes Receivable, Inventory, Land, Equipment, Accounts Payable, Capital Stock, and the like.)

This "direct write-off" method is not appropriate when such losses are significant in amount and occur frequently, as in retail stores. The direct write-off method usually fails to recognize an uncollectible amount in the accounting period when the sale occurs and revenue from it is recognized. Too much income is reported in the period of sale and too little in the period of write-off. The time of the sale on account to customers is the appropriate time for the adjustment, not the later time when the firm discovers that a specific account is uncollectible.

A better procedure is known as the *allowance method*. This method involves:

1. estimating the amount of uncollectible accounts which will occur at some time in connection with the sales of each period
2. making an adjusting entry reducing the reported revenue of the period for the estimated uncollectible amount
3. making a corresponding adjustment to the amount of accounts receivable so that the balance sheet figure reports the amount expected to be collected.

The entry involves a debit to Sales, Uncollectible Accounts Adjustment, which is an account contra to Sales, and a credit to Allowance for Uncollectible Accounts, which is an account contra to the total of Accounts Receivable. The credit must be made to a contra account rather than to Accounts Receivable because no specific, individual account is being written off at the time of entry. Since the Allowance for Uncollectible Accounts is a contra to Accounts Receivable, its balance at the end of the period appears on the balance sheet as a deduction from Accounts Receivable. The Sales, Uncollectible Accounts Adjustment account, as a revenue contra, is deducted from sales revenue on the income statement. The presentation of these accounts in the financial statements is shown later in Exhibits 8.2 and 8.3.

Use of the Allowance Method

To illustrate the allowance method, assume that 2 percent of the credit sales made during the present period will never be collected. If sales on account are $35,000, then the entry to reduce revenue and reduce the amount of Accounts Receivable to the amount expected to be collected would be:

Sales, Uncollectible Accounts Adjustment 700
    Allowance for Uncollectible Accounts 700
To record estimate of uncollectible accounts arising from current period's sales
(.02 × $35,000).

When a particular customer's account is judged uncollectible, it is written off against the Allowance for Uncollectible Accounts. If, for example, it is decided that a balance of $135 due from Robert S. Thomley will not be collected, the entry to charge off the account is:

Allowance for Uncollectible Accounts 135
    Accounts Receivable 135
To write off Robert S. Thomley's account.

Under the allowance method, the revenue for the period of sale is reduced by the amount of uncollectibles that is estimated to arise from that period's sales. Some time later, when the attempts at collection are finally abandoned, the specific account is written off. Net assets are not affected by writing off the specific account. The reduction in net assets took place earlier, when the Allowance for Uncollectibles was credited in the entry recognizing the estimated amount of eventual uncollectibles.

Rationale for the Revenue-Contra Presentation

In practice, many firms do not treat the adjustment for estimated uncollectibles as a reduction in revenue. Instead the adjustment is treated as an administrative or selling expense, reported in the income statement as Bad Debt Expense. Net income for the period is the same whether the uncollectibles charge is treated as a revenue contra or as an expense provided that the same method for estimating the *amount* of uncollectibles is used.

We prefer to treat the adjustment for estimated uncollectibles as a reduction in revenue, not as an expense. To justify this preference, we ask, "What is the optimal amount of uncollectible accounts for a firm?" For most firms, the optimal amount of uncollectibles is not zero. If a firm is to have no uncollectible accounts, it must screen credit customers carefully, which is costly. Furthermore, the firm would deny credit to many customers who would pay their bills even though they could not pass a most stringent credit check. Some of the customers who are denied credit will take their business elsewhere and sales will be lost. So long as the revenue collected from credit sales to a given class of customers exceeds the cost of goods sold and the selling expenses to that class of customers, the firm will be better off selling to that class rather than losing the sales. The rational firm should prefer granting credit to a class of customers who have a high probability of paying their bills, rather than losing their business, even though there may be some uncollectible accounts.

For example, if gross margin—selling price less cost of goods sold—on new credit sales is 20 percent of credit sales, then a firm could afford uncollectible accounts of up to 20 percent of the new credit sales and still show increased net income, so long as selling and administrative expenses remain constant.

An expense is a "gone asset." Accounts that prove uncollectible are not assets, because the rational firm made credit sales expecting that a small percentage of those sales would never be collected. Hence, the amount of uncollectibles was never an asset or revenue in the first place. Thus we reach the conclusion that the amount of the uncollectible accounts should be treated as an adjustment in determining revenue, not as a "gone asset" or expense.

We do not suggest, of course, that a firm grant credit indiscriminately or ignore collection efforts for uncollected accounts receivable. We do suggest that a cost/benefit analysis of credit policy will probably dictate a strategy that results in some amount of uncollectible accounts.

Estimating Uncollectibles

There are two basic methods used for calculating the amount of the adjustment for uncollectible accounts. These are the *percentage of sales method* and the *aging of accounts receivable method.*

Percentage of Sales Method   The easiest method in most cases is to multiply the total sales on account during the period by an appropriate percentage, because it seems reasonable to assume that uncollectible account amounts will vary directly with the volume of credit business. (The example on page 223 used the percentage of sales method.) The percentage to be used can be determined by a study of the experience of the business or by an inquiry into the experience of similar enterprises. The rates found in use will generally be within the range of ¼ percent to 2 percent of credit sales.

To illustrate, assume that sales on account total $150,000, and experience indicates that the appropriate percentage of uncollectible accounts is 2 percent. The entry is:

Sales, Uncollectible Accounts Adjustment 3,000
   Allowance for Uncollectible Accounts   3,000
To provide for estimate of uncollectibles as determined by a percentage of sales.

If cash sales occur in a relatively constant proportion to credit sales, the percentage, proportionately reduced, can be applied to the total sales for the period. The total sales amount may be more readily available than that for sales on account.

Aging of Accounts Receivable Method   Another method of calculating the amount of the adjustment, often called *aging the accounts,* involves classifying each customer's account as to the length of time during which the accounts have been uncollected. Common intervals used for classifying individual acounts receivable are

1.   not yet due
2.   past due 30 days or less
3.   past due 31 to 60 days
4.   past due 61 to 180 days
5.   past due more than 180 days.

The presumption is that the balance in the Allowance for Uncollectible Accounts should be large enough to cover substantially all accounts receivable past due for more than 6 months and smaller portions of the more recent accounts. The actual portions are estimated from past experience.

As an example of the adjustment to be made, assume that the present balance in the Accounts Receivable account is $85,000 and the balance in the Allowance for Uncollectible Accounts is $3,600. An aging of the accounts receivable balances ($85,000), shown in Exhibit 8.1, results in an estimate that $6,800 of the accounts will probably become uncollectible. The adjustment requires that the Allowance

EXHIBIT 8.1
Illustration of Aging Accounts Receivable

CLASSIFICATION OF ACCOUNTS	AMOUNT	ESTIMATED UNCOLLECTIBLE PERCENTAGE	ESTIMATED UNCOLLECTIBLE AMOUNTS
Not yet due	$68,000	0.5%	$ 340
1–30 days past due	6,000	6.0	360
31–60 days past due	3,000	25.0	750
61–180 days past due	5,000	50.0	2,500
Over 180 days past due	3,000	95.0	2,850
	$85,000		$6,800

for Uncollectible Accounts balance be $6,800, an increase of $3,200, at the end of the period. The adjusting entry is:

Sales, Uncollectible Accounts Adjustment	3,200	
Allowance for Uncollectible Accounts		3,200

To increase Allowance account to $6,800 as determined by an aging analysis.

Even when the percentage method is used, aging the accounts should be done periodically as an occasional check upon the accuracy of the percentage being used. If the aging analysis shows that the balance in the Allowance for Uncollectible Accounts is apparently too large or too small, the percentage of sales to be charged to the contra-revenue account can be raised or lowered so that the apparent error will work itself out through future adjustments.

When the percentage of sales method is used, the periodic provision for uncollectible accounts (for example, $3,000), is merely added to the amounts provided in previous periods in the account, Allowance for Uncollectible Accounts. When the aging method is used, the balance in the account, Allowance for Uncollectible Accounts, is adjusted (for example, by $3,200) to reflect the desired ending balance. If the percentage used under the percentage of sales method is reasonably accurate, the *balance* in the allowance account should be approximately the same at the end of each period under these two methods of estimating uncollectible accounts.

Sales Discounts

Often the seller of merchandise offers a reduction from its invoice price for prompt payment. Such reductions are called *sales discounts* or *cash discounts*.[3] Discounts should be considered as a reduction in sales revenue in the period of the

[3] See the glossary for the definition of a *discount* and a summary of the various contexts where this word is used in accounting.

sale. There is nothing incongruous in the proposition that goods may have two prices: a cash price or a higher price if goods are sold on credit. The cash discount is offered, not only as an interest allowance on funds paid before the bill is due—the implied interest rate is unreasonably large—but also as an incentive for prompt payment so that additional bookkeeping and collection costs can be avoided. To state it more realistically, the goods are sold for a certain price if prompt payment is made, and a penalty is added in the form of a higher price if the payment is delayed. The bills rendered by many public utilities illustrate this more realistic approach. The amount of sales discount made available to customers, then, should be considered as one of the adjustments in the determination of net sales revenue.

The need to prepare operating statements for relatively short periods leads to alternative possibilities for recording sales discounts and determining the amount of sales discounts reported for a period. The theoretical issue is whether the amount of cash discount should be deducted from sales revenue in the period when the sales revenue is recognized or in the period of cash collection. In determining the amount of sales discounts recognized for a period, the major alternatives are the following:

1. to recognize discounts when taken by the customer, without regard to the period of sale (called the *gross price method*)
2. to estimate the total amount of discounts which will be taken on the sales which were made during the period (called the *allowance method*)
3. to record sales amounts reduced by all discounts made available to customers and to recognize additional revenue when a discount lapses (called the *net price method*).

These methods are discussed in advanced accounting texts.

Sales Returns

When a customer returns merchandise, the sale has, in effect, been canceled, and an entry which reverses the recording of the sale would be appropriate. In analyzing sales activities, however, management may be interested in the amount of goods returned. If so, a Sales Returns account, a contra to Sales, is used to accumulate the amount of returns for a particular period.

A cash refund, such as might be made in a retail store when a customer returns merchandise which had been purchased for cash, would be entered as:

Sales Returns	23	
Cash on Hand		23

If the cost of the returned goods had previously been debited to cost of goods sold and credited to inventory, then that entry must be reversed:

Inventory	16	
Cost of Goods Sold		16
To reduce Cost of Goods Sold for returned goods which cost $16.		

Return of goods by a customer who buys "on account" would usually involve the preparation of a credit memorandum which is, in effect, the reverse of a sales invoice. The credit memorandum lists the goods which have been returned and indicates the amount which is to be allowed the customer. The entry to record the issuance of the credit would normally be a debit to the Sales Returns account and a credit to the Accounts Receivable account.

Sales returns represent a reduction in sales revenue, and the net amount of sales for the period will reflect the amount of such returns. See, for example, Exhibit 8.2.

Sale and Return in Different Periods Somewhat misleading sales and income amounts can result if goods are returned in a period after the one of sale. If there is no adjustment, the sales and income amounts for the period of sale are overstated, since they reflect transactions which are later canceled. Further, sales and revenue amounts are correspondingly understated in the period when the goods are returned. It would be possible to use the same type of estimated allowance procedure for returns that was illustrated for uncollectible accounts, but since the amounts involved are usually relatively small, it is not customary to do so.

Another type of distortion may occur: the costs which have been incurred in making the sale, other than the cost of the goods, constitute a loss to the business and should not, strictly speaking, be charged against other completed sales. Occasionally, a charge is made to the customer for delivery costs both ways on returned goods or a deduction is made for loss in value of the goods from handling and shipment, but usually the privilege of return without penalty is granted as a part of the service of the merchant. It would be difficult, if not impossible, to isolate the costs relating to a particular returned sale. Further, some accountants argue that these costs are normal—necessary for ongoing business operations—and can

EXHIBIT 8.2
INCOME STATEMENT ILLUSTRATION OF
SALES AND SALES ADJUSTMENTS
Caral Company
Partial Income Statement
For the Month Ended June 30, 1976

Revenues			
Sales—Gross			$51,523
Less Sales Adjustments:			
Discounts Taken[a]	$2,367		
Allowances	1,126		
Uncollectible Accounts Adjustment	1,030		
Returns	857		
Total Sales Adjustments		5,380	
Net Sales			$46,143

[a] The gross price method is used. If the net price method were used, discounts taken would not be shown and there would be an *addition* to revenue for the amount of sales discounts which lapsed.

therefore logically be absorbed as costs of making the sales which are not returned. There are techniques for meeting some of the foregoing considerations, but they are beyond the scope of this discussion.

Sales Allowances

A *sales allowance* is a reduction in price granted to a customer, usually after the goods have been delivered and found to be unsatisfactory or damaged. Again, as in the case of sales returns, the effect is a reduction in the sales revenue, but it may be desirable to accumulate the amount of such adjustments as a separate item. A revenue contra account, Sales Allowances, may be used for this purpose, or a combined account title, Sales Returns and Allowances, may be employed. The bookkeeping problems are similar to those caused by sales returns.

Presentation of Sales Adjustments in the Income Statement

In discussing the complications that accompany accounts receivable, we have introduced several adjustments to sales which are accumulated in revenue contra accounts. All these adjustments—for uncollectible accounts, for discounts, for returns, and for allowances—are illustrated in the Caral Company's income statement, Exhibit 8.2, for the month of June 1976. Caral Company uses the gross price method for recording sales-related transactions.

EXHIBIT 8.3
DETAILED ILLUSTRATION OF CURRENT ASSETS ON THE BALANCE SHEET
Caral Company
Partial Balance Sheet
June 30, 1976

Current Assets

Cash on Hand (Change and Petty Cash Funds)		$ 1,000
Cash in Bank		13,000
Certificates of Deposit		8,000
Marketable Securities (At Cost, Less than Market Value of $20,000)		16,000
Notes Receivable (Note A)		8,000
Interest Receivable on Notes		200
Accounts Receivable	$50,000	
Less: Allowance for Uncollectible Accounts	3,000	47,000
Merchandise Inventory		72,000
Prepaid Rent		3,000
Prepaid Insurance		1,800
Total Current Assets		$170,000

Note A. The amount of Notes Receivable does not include notes with a face amount of $2,000 which have been discounted with recourse at the Harris Bank. The Company is contingently liable for these notes should the makers not honor the notes at maturity. The estimated amount of our liability is zero.

■ ILLUSTRATION OF BALANCE SHEET PRESENTATION

The balance sheet accounts discussed in this chapter include Cash, Certificates of Deposit, Marketable Securities, Notes Receivable, and Accounts Receivable. The presentation of these items in the balance sheet is illustrated in Exhibit 8.3, which includes all of the current assets, not just the liquid assets, for the Caral Company as of June 30, 1976.

■ SUMMARY

This chapter has examined the accounting for cash and other liquid, or cash-like, assets. Liquid assets are usually stated on the balance sheet at face amount or at their current cash-equivalent value. Balance sheet classifications used for liquid assets should indicate any restrictions on the use of these resources. *Flows* of cash and other liquid assets are reported in the statement of changes in financial position.

Estimates of future amounts of uncollectible accounts receivable should be recorded in accounts contra to the Sales account on the income statement and contra to the Accounts Receivable account on the balance sheet. The reductions for estimated uncollectibles are required so that the amounts reported as revenue in the income statement and the amounts reported as assets on the balance sheet accurately reflect the amounts of cash expected to be received. (Similar adjustments for sales allowances, discounts, and returns may also be required for accurate reporting of revenues and assets.) Aging of accounts receivable helps in determining the likely amount of uncollectibles and in spotting particular accounts receivable for which collection efforts may be required.

Internal control procedures for protecting cash are discussed in the appendix to this chapter.

Appendix 8.1
Controlling Cash

Of all assets, cash is the most difficult to control—to safeguard from theft. This appendix discusses the usual procedures of accounting for and controlling cash.

■ CONTROLLING CASH RECEIPTS AND DISBURSEMENTS

The system for controlling cash receipts should be designed to ensure that all money collected for the firm ends up in the firm's treasury. In most businesses, collections are received primarily through the mail in the form of bank checks or in currency and coins for cash sales. The need to control the collections of currency and coins is obvious. All collections for cash sales should be recorded promptly, either in a cash register or some other device that both records the receipts and locks in the amount of the collection. Other kinds of collections are more susceptible to mishandling because they occur less often. These include receipts from the sale of assets not normally intended to be sold, receipts from dividends and interest on investments, collections on notes receivable, proceeds of bank loans, and proceeds of stock or bond issues.

One way to provide effective control of cash receipts would be to maintain duplicate sets of records, each under separate supervision. But doing so would be expensive. The business need not undertake this expensive control device, however, if it (1) designs its cash-handling techniques so that the monthly statement received from its bank effectively serves as a duplicate record and (2) separates the functions of cash handling and record keeping. To use the bank statement as an effective cash-controlling device requires daily depositing of all receipts and making all disbursements by check.

Undeposited Cash

If a firm follows the desirable plan of depositing all receipts intact, disbursements will usually be made only from checking accounts. Any balance in the Cash on Hand account will represent cash received since the last deposit, which usually will have been made the previous business day. A daily record of cash on hand is usually necessary. Cash registers facilitate the accumulation of cash data. There are many types, but the usual cash register is a combination of a cash drawer and a multiple-register adding machine. The transactions are entered by hand. Then they are recorded and accumulated by the register so that at the end of the day the totals are available for each of several divisions of the day's activities—the total cash sales (sometimes classified according to products or departments), total collections on account, and total sales of each salesperson.

Cash in Bank—Deposits

A deposit ticket provides the information for preparing the journal entry to record the deposit of cash funds in the checking account. The deposit ticket should be prepared in duplicate; the bank keeps the original and the firm keeps the duplicate. The duplicate is often initialed by the bank teller and used as a receipt for the deposit of the funds. The total on the deposit ticket is entered in a journal as a debit to Cash in Bank and a credit to Cash on Hand.

Cash in Bank—Issuance of Checks

The information for the entry to record checks drawn in payment of bills comes from the document authorizing the disbursement. The customary entry will be a debit to Accounts Payable and a credit to Cash in Bank.

Control of Disbursements by Check

All cash payments except for those of very small amounts should be made by check. The firm can thereby restrict the authority for payments to a few employees.

Firms often provide further control by requiring that all checks be signed by two employees. Another control device is the use of a Cash Disbursements Journal or Check Register in which all checks issued are recorded. Using such a journal provides control because a single person, who is not allowed to authorize payments or to sign checks, is responsible for recording all payments.

In any case, control over disbursements should ensure that:

1. Disbursements are made only by authorized persons.
2. Adequate records support each disbursement. Such records attest that disbursement was for goods and services procured by proper authority and actually received by the business. The records attest that payment is made in accordance with the purchase contract.
3. The transaction is entered properly in the formal accounting records.
4. Authority for authorization of payment is separate from authority to pay, and record keeping is separate from both.

■ THE BANK STATEMENT

At the end of each month (or other regular interval), the bank sends a statement together with the canceled checks which have been paid and deducted from the depositor's account, and memorandums of any other additions or deductions which have been made by the bank. When the bank statement is received, it should be compared promptly with the record of deposits, checks drawn, and other bank items on the records of the firm.

The balance shown on the bank statement will rarely correspond to the balance of the Cash in Bank account. The two basic causes of the difference are time lag and errors. In the normal course of business activities, some items will have been recorded by either the bank or the firm without having reached the recording point on the other set of records, hence a *time lag* difference. Causes of such differences include: checks outstanding (that is, checks recorded by the drawing firm but not yet received by the bank on which they were drawn), deposits made just before the bank statement date which do not appear on the bank statement, and transactions (such as service charges and collections of notes or drafts) that have not been recorded on the firm's books. The other basic difference is caused by errors in record keeping by either the firm or the bank. The process of comparing the bank statement with the books is known as *reconciling* the bank account, and the schedule which is prepared to demonstrate the results of the comparing is called a *bank reconciliation*. A typical reconciliation schedule is shown in Exhibit 8.4. The preparation of the bank reconciliation schedule is explained below.

Preparing the Bank Reconciliation Schedule

The purpose of the bank reconciliation is to explain the difference between the book balance of Cash in Bank and the bank's statement of the firm's cash on deposit and to indicate the required adjustments of the firm's accounts. If the

EXHIBIT 8.4
Young Spring Company
Bank Reconciliation Schedule—Citizens National Bank
April 1, 1976

Balance shown on bank statement, April 1, 1976		$2,323.36
Deposits of March 30 and 31, not yet recorded by bank		643.16
Check of Young Wire Co. deducted by bank in error		10.00
		$2,976.52
Outstanding checks:		
#367	$ 69.67	
#470	142.53	
#471	131.26	
#472	131.44	
#474	243.55	
#475	305.52	
Less: Total outstanding checks		1,023.97
Adjusted bank balance[a]		$1,952.55
Balance shown on books, April 1, 1976		$1,453.55
Items unrecorded on books:		
Collection of note of J. T. Munn—		
Face amount of note	$500.00	
Less collection charge	(5.00)	495.00
Less bank service charge for March		(14.00)
Adjusted book balance before correction of errors		$1,934.55
Check #467 for $168.81 was entered in the check register as $186.81. It was issued in March 1976, to pay a bill for office equipment		18.00
Adjusted book balance[a]		$1,952.55

[a] This is the amount that would be shown in the Cash in Bank account if a balance sheet were prepared as of April 1, 1976.

bank statement is used as a control device, as we suggest it should, the bank reconciliation is the final step in the monthly procedures for controlling cash receipts and disbursements. The bank reconciliation provides a convenient summary of the adjusting entries that must be made by the firm to account for previous errors in recording cash-related transactions or for cash transactions that have not yet been recorded.

Preparing the bank reconciliation schedule typically involves the following steps.

1. Enter at the top of the reconciliation schedule the balance as shown on the bank statement.
2. Enter next any deposits that have not been recorded on the bank statement. Such items usually occur because the bank has prepared the statement before the deposits for the last day or two have been recorded. If there are any time

or date breaks in the list of deposits for the period, the bank should be notified promptly.

3. Enter any other adjustments of the bank's balance such as errors in recording canceled checks or deposits, or the return of checks belonging to some other customer of the bank. Errors on bank statements are infrequent.

4. Obtain a total.

5. List the outstanding checks. A list should be prepared, beginning with the checks still outstanding from the previous period and continuing with the checks outstanding which were drawn during the current period.

6. Deduct the sum of the outstanding checks from the total obtained in step 4. The balance is the adjusted bank balance—the balance that would be shown on the bank statement if all deposits had been entered, all checks written had been returned, and no errors had been made; it is the final figure for this first section of the statement.

These steps will frequently conclude the reconciliation because this balance should correspond to the balance of the Cash in Bank account as of the bank statement date when there are no unrecorded transactions or errors. If these two amounts are not equal at this point, the following steps must be taken and shown in a second section of the reconciliation schedule.

7. Enter the Cash in Bank account balance as shown on the books as of the bank statement date.

8. Add or deduct any errors or omissions that have been disclosed in the process of reviewing the items returned by the bank. These will include such items as errors in recording deposits or checks, unnumbered checks that have not been entered in the check register, and service charges and collection fees deducted by the bank.

9. The net result is the adjusted book balance, and it must correspond to the adjusted bank balance derived in the first section. If it does not, the search must be continued for other items that have been overlooked.

Adjusting Entries from Bank Reconciliation Schedule

The bank reconciliation schedule shows two distinct kinds of differences:

1. differences between the balance shown on the bank statement and the adjusted bank balance and

2. differences between the account balance in the firm's books and the adjusted book balance.

Only the second type of difference requires entries on the firm's books. Any deposits not credited by the bank will presumably have been recorded by the time the reconciliation is prepared and, in any event, represent funds that the depositor may assume are in the bank and available for disbursement by check.

Entries must be made for all of the differences between the firm's account balance on the books and the adjusted book balance, since they represent errors or omissions that must be corrected. The reconciliation illustrated in Exhibit 8.4 requires adjustments for bank service charges, for the collection of a note, and for the check whose amount was incorrectly recorded.[4] The entries would be

Bank Service Charge Expense	14	
Cash in Bank		14
Service charges for month of March.		
Cash in Bank	495	
Collection Expense	5	
Note Receivable, J. T. Munn		500
Note collected by bank.		
Cash in Bank	18	
Accounts Payable		18
To correct entry of check #467.		

■ SUMMARY OF ACCOUNTING FOR CASH

Management is always concerned about getting the best and safest use of its resources, and an enterprise's most valuable resource, cash, is also its most vulnerable. An internal control system is essential to the proper management of cash. One way to provide control is to maintain duplicate and independent records of cash flows, but this is not necessary if an enterprise uses the monthly bank statement as a duplicate record. Using the bank statement as an effective control device requires depositing receipts daily and making all disbursements by check or through petty cash funds. By this means the bank reconciliation serves as a control device because the bank record will reflect the cash inflows and outflows of the enterprise.

QUESTIONS AND PROBLEMS

1. Review the meaning of the following concepts or terms discussed in this chapter.
   a. Monetary assets.
   b. Quick assets.
   c. Insolvency.
   d. Cash.
   e. Time deposits, demand deposits.
   f. Certificate of deposit.
   g. Bank statement.

[4] The bank must, of course, correct any error on its books when the mistake is called to its attention. The entry on the bank's books to correct the error shown on the reconciliation in Exhibit 8.4 is:

Deposits—Young Wire Company	10	
Deposits—Young Spring Company		10
To correct posting of check charged to Young Spring Company account in error.		

    h. Bank reconciliation.
    i. Marketable securities.
    j. Notes, secured and unsecured.
    k. Maker.
    l. Payee.
    m. Principal.
    n. Maturity.
    o. Interest.
    p. With recourse.
    q. Without recourse.
    r. Contingent liability.
    s. Controlling account.
    t. Gross price, net price, and allowance methods.
    u. Sales, Uncollectible Accounts Adjustment account.
    v. Aging of accounts receivable.
    w. Sales discounts.
    x. Sales returns.
    y. Sales allowances.

2. What evidence of cash control have you observed in a cafeteria? A department store? A theater? A gasoline service station?

3. A store is running short of change during a busy day, so the cashier takes some of the undeposited checks to the bank and exchanges them for small bills and coins. Is any journal entry necessary? Do you see anything objectionable in the practice?

4. The Tastee Delight ice cream stores prominently advertise on signs in the stores that the customer's purchase is free if the clerk does not present a receipt. Oakland's Original hot dog stand says that the customer's purchase is free if the cash register receipt contains a red star. What control purposes do such policies serve?

5. How does the accounting for marketable securities differ from the accounting for the same securities held as investments?

6. Calculate simple interest on a base of $6,000 for the following intervals and rates, using a 360-day year.
    a. 60 days at 12 percent.
    b. 60 days at 8 percent.
    c. 90 days at 9 percent.
    d. 60 days at 16 percent.
    e. 15 days at 16 percent.
    f. 6 months at 9 percent.
    g. 5 months, 15 days at 12 percent.
    h. 4 months, 12 days at 9 percent.

7. Which of the two methods for treating uncollectible accounts implies recognizing revenue reductions earlier rather than later? Why?

8.   **a.** An old wisdom in tennis holds that if your first serves are always good, then you are not hitting them hard enough. An analogous statement in business might be that if you have no uncollectible accounts, then you probably are not selling enough on credit. Comment on the validity of this statement.
    b. When are more uncollectible accounts better than fewer uncollectible accounts?
    c. When is a higher percentage of uncollectible accounts better than a lower one?

9.   **a.** The Feldman Company has a gross margin on credit sales of 30 percent. That is, cost of goods sold on account is 70 percent of sales on account. Uncollectible accounts amount to 2 percent of credit sales. If credit is extended to a new class of customers, credit sales will increase by $10,000, 8 percent of the new credit sales will be uncollectible, and selling expenses will increase by $1,000. Would Feldman Company be better or worse off if it extends credit to the new class of customers and by how much?

b. How would your answer to **a** differ if $2,000 of the $10,000 increase in credit sales would have been made anyway as sales for cash? (Assume that the uncollectible amount on new credit sales is $800.)

c. The Norman Company has credit sales of $100,000, a gross margin on those sales of 25 percent, and 3 percent of the credit sales are uncollectible. If credit is extended to a new class of customers, sales will increase by $40,000, selling expenses will increase by $1,500, and uncollectibles will be 5 percent of *all* credit sales. Verify that Norman Company will be $4,500 better off if it extends credit to the new customers. What percentage of the new credit sales are uncollectible?

10. The customary method of accounting for sales returns results in adequate reporting for the returned sales when the goods are returned in the same period in which they are sold. If the goods are returned in a period subsequent to that of the sale, distortion of the reported revenue figures results. Explain how sales returns may produce each of the described effects.

11. Under what circumstances will the Allowance for Uncollectible Accounts have a debit balance during the accounting period? The balance sheet figure for the Allowance for Uncollectible Accounts at the end of the period should never show a debit balance. Why?

12. **a.** Arrange the following data related to the Ayer Company in bank reconciliation form.

Adjusted bank balance	$6,453
Adjusted book balance	6,453
Balance per bank statement, October 31, 1976	7,532
Balance per books, October 31, 1976	5,873
Error in deposit of October 28; $457 deposit entered on books as $475	18
Outstanding checks	1,133
Payroll account check deducted from this account in error	54
Proceeds on note of W. Y. Jones, taken by the bank for collection, less collection fee of $2	598

b. Present journal entries on the books of the Ayer Company to record the adjustments indicated in the bank reconciliation schedule.

13. **a.** Prepare a bank reconciliation schedule at July 31, 1976, for the Home Appliance Company from the following information:

Balance per bank statement, July 29	$1,211
Balance per ledger, July 31	663
Deposit of July 30 not recorded by bank	180
Debit memo—service charges	6
Credit memo—collection of note by bank	250

An analysis of the canceled checks returned with the bank statement reveals the following:

Check #901 for purchase of supplies was drawn for $58 but was recorded as $85.

The manager wrote a check for traveling expenses of $85 while out of town. The check was not recorded. The following checks are outstanding:

#650	$180
#721	162
#728	200
	$542

b. Journalize the adjusting entries required by the information revealed in the bank reconciliation schedule.

14. On May 31, 1976, the books of the Locus Land Company show a debit balance in the Cash in Bank account of $3,977. The bank statement at that date shows a balance of $4,758. The deposit of May 31 of $302 is not included in the bank statement. Notice of collections made by the bank on mortgages of the company in the amount of $123, including interest of $8, and of bank service charges of $4 have not previously been received. Outstanding checks at May 31 total $964.
    a. Prepare a bank reconciliation for the Locus Land Company at May 31, 1976.
    b. Journalize the entries required upon preparation of the bank reconciliation schedule.

15. The following items are taken from the April 30, 1976, bank reconciliation schedule of the Porter Company. Present a journal entry required on the books of the company for each item; indicate if no adjustment is required.
    (1) Outstanding checks total $1,650.
    (2) A check drawn as $196 for office supplies was recorded in the appropriate journal as $169.
    (3) Included among the checks returned by the bank was one for $150 drawn by the Peter Company and charged to this company in error.
    (4) The deposit of April 3 of $420 was not included on the bank statement.
    (5) A debit memorandum was included for service charges for April in the amount of $10.
    (6) The bank collected a note of $1,750, including $50 of interest, for the company.
    (7) Checks for traveling expenses of $250 had not been entered in the journal.
    (8) A check was written and recorded on April 29 for the regular monthly salary of an office employee who had resigned on March 31. The check has been voided, but an entry to record the voiding has not been made. The monthly salary was $600; deductions of 8 percent for FICA taxes and $120 for withheld income taxes were made.

16. The bank reconciliation of the Clark Company at March 31, 1976, was as follows:

Balance per bank statement, March 31, 1976	$ 3,850
Unrecorded deposit	475
	$ 4,325
Outstanding checks	820
Adjusted bank and book balance, March 31, 1976	$ 3,505

The bank statement, returned checks, and other documents received from the bank at the end of April provide the following information:

Balance, April 29, 1976	$ 3,685
Deposit of March 31, 1976	475
Deposits of April 1–29 including a credit memo for a collection of a note, $808	16,160
Canceled checks issued prior to April 1, 1976	600
Canceled checks issued during April, 1976	16,200

The Cash in Bank account of the Clark Company for the month of April shows deposits of $16,190 and checks drawn of $17,015. The credit memo has not as yet been recorded on the books of the company; it represents the collection of a note with $800 face value on which $5 interest had been accrued as of March 31, 1976.

a. Prepare a bank reconciliation for the Clark Company at April 30, 1976.

b. Present in journal entry form any adjustment of the company's books resulting from the information determined in the bank reconciliation.

17. Accar Corporation purchased 100 shares of KXR Company stock on January 2 as a temporary investment. The acquisition price was $23 a share plus $65 brokerage commission and postage. The following information relates to Accar's investment in KXR Company's stock.

February 10	Quarterly dividend of $.50 per share is received by KXR Company.
March 31	KXR Company's stock closed the month at $20.
May 10	KXR Company skips the quarterly cash dividend but declares a 10 percent stock dividend—10 shares for Accar. Accar receives its 10 shares of stock. (Stock dividends are not treated as revenue under generally accepted accounting principles. No entry is required.)
June 30	KXR Company's stock closed the month at $27.
August 10	Quarterly dividend of $.40 a share is received by KXR Company.
September 1	Accar sells its 110 shares in KXR Company. The selling price is $25 a share; commissions and postage amount to $70.

Accar Company closes its books quarterly, at the end of March, June, September, and December.

a. Present journal entries for Accar Company's temporary investment in the stock of KXR Company assuming that Accar carries the investment at acquisition cost.

b. Repeat **a** assuming that Accar carries the investment at the lower of cost or market.

c. What was Accar Company's rate of return on its investment (total income from January 2 through September 1 divided by the amount of the investment) in KXR Company, assuming that the investment is carried at acquisition cost? At lower of cost or market? Ignore income taxes.

d. Compare the answers in **c**. Explain the similarity or difference.

18. On May 10, 1976, the Pacific Supply Company receives a note from one of its customers, Silk Builders, Inc., to apply on its account. The 6-month, 12-percent note for $6,600, issued on May 10, 1976, is valued at its face amount.

On July 25, 1976, the Pacific Supply Company endorses the note and transfers it with recourse to the Cobb Steel Products Company to settle an account payable. The note is valued at its face amount plus accrued interest.

On November 12, 1976, the Pacific Supply Company was notified that the note was paid at maturity.

a. Present dated entries on the books for the Pacific Supply Company, assuming that it closes its books quarterly on March 31, June 30, and so on.

b. Present dated entries on the books of the Cobb Steel Products Company, assuming that it closes its books quarterly on March 31, June 30, and so on.

19. The following journal entries, shown in chronological order, represent transactions with a single customer with respect to a single sale. Describe the event that led to each entry.

a. Accounts Receivable—J. Sveda	300	
Sales		300
b. Sales Contra	15	
Accounts Receivable—J. Sveda		15
c. Notes Receivable	285	
Accounts Receivable—J. Sveda		285
d. Cash	295	
Notes Receivable		285
Interest		10

20. The data in the following schedule pertain to the first 8 years of the Gordon Company's credit sales and experiences with uncollectible accounts.

YEAR	CREDIT SALES	RELATED UNCOLLECTIBLE ACCOUNTS	YEAR	CREDIT SALES	RELATED UNCOLLECTIBLE ACCOUNTS
1.....	$100,000	$2,550	5.....	$250,000	$3,000
2.....	150,000	3,225	6.....	275,000	2,700
3.....	200,000	3,725	7.....	280,000	2,875
4.....	225,000	4,000	8.....	290,000	2,925

Gordon Company has not previously used an Allowance for Uncollectible Accounts but has merely charged accounts written off directly to Uncollectible Accounts Expense.

What percentage of credit sales for a year would you recommend that Gordon Company charge to the sales adjustment account if one were to be set up at the end of year 8?

21. Lave Company's accounts receivable show the following balances by ages:

AGE OF ACCOUNTS	BALANCE RECEIVABLE
0–30 days	$150,000
31–60 days	50,000
61–120 days	25,000
more than 120 days	10,000

The credit balance in the Allowance for Uncollectible Accounts is now $5,075.

Lave Company's independent auditors suggest that the following percentages be used to compute the estimates of amounts that will eventually prove uncollectible; 0–30 days: .5 of 1 percent; 31–60 days: 1 percent; 61–120 days: 10 percent; more than 120 days: 60 percent.

Prepare a journal entry that will carry out the auditor's suggestion.

22. The sales, all on account, of the Nelson Company in 1975, its first year of operation, were $500,000. Collections totaled $450,000. On December 31, 1975, it was estimated that 1.5 percent of sales on account would probably be uncollectible. On that date, specific accounts in the amount of $2,500 were written off.

The company's trial balance before adjustment on December 31, 1976, included the following accounts and balances:

Accounts Receivable (Dr.)	$60,000
Allowance for Uncollectible Accounts (Dr.)	3,000
Sales, Uncollectible Accounts Adjustment	—
Sales (Cr.)	$600,000

It was concluded that the estimated uncollectible account rate of 1.5 percent of sales should be applied to 1976 operations.

Present journal entries to portray the following:
a. Transactions and adjustments of 1975 related to sales and customers' accounts.
b. Transactions of 1976 resulting in the above trial balance amounts.
c. Adjustment for estimated uncollectibles for 1976.

23. The trial balance of the Wagner Company at the end of 1975, its first year of operations, included $18,000 of outstanding customers' accounts. An analysis reveals that 90 percent of the total credit sales of the year had been collected and that no accounts had been charged off as uncollectible.

The auditor estimated that 1 percent of the total credit sales would be uncollectible.

On January 31, 1976, it was concluded that the account of H. J. Williams, who had owed a balance of $200 for 6 months, was uncollectible and should be written off at that time.

On July 1, 1976, the amount owed by H. J. Williams, previously written off, was collected in full.

Present dated journal entries to record the following:
a. Adjustment for estimated uncollectible accounts on December 31, 1975.
b. Write-off of the H. J. Williams account on January 31, 1976.
c. Collection of the H. J. Williams account on July 1, 1976, assuming that it is felt that there is evidence that the account should not have been written off as uncollectible.

24. The following data summarize transactions involving marketable securities of the Nurnberg Company.

SECURITY	DATE ACQUIRED	ACQUISITION COST	DIVIDENDS DECLARED DURING 1977	MARKET VALUE ON JAN. 1, 1977	MARKET VALUE ON DEC. 31, 1977
A Company	11/1/76	$10,000	$1,000	$11,000	$13,000
B Company	12/1/76	20,000	1,500	18,000	17,000
C Company	2/1/77	30,000	2,000	—	26,000
D Company	4/1/77	40,000	3,000	—	42,000

Neither A Company nor B Company declared dividends in the last 2 months of 1976. C Company and D Company dividends were declared in the second half of 1977.

a. Present all journal entries for 1976 and 1977 required for marketable securities, assuming that the acquisition-cost valuation method is used.

b. Present all journal entries for 1976 and 1977 required for marketable securities, assuming that the lower-of-cost-or-market valuation method is used.

c. What amounts would be shown on the balance sheet for December 31, 1977, assuming that marketable securities are carried at acquisition cost? At lower of cost or market?

d. What amounts of revenue, gains, and losses would be shown on the income statement for 1977, assuming that marketable securities are carried at acquisition cost? At lower of cost or market?

25. A recent annual report of Northwest Industries, Inc., reports net income of $57 million. The balance sheet discloses holdings of marketable securities of $42 million, which are shown in a separate section below current assets. The notes to the financial statements contain the following:

> Marketable Securities. *Marketable securities are stated at . . . cost. . . . Management considers their aggregate quoted market value [about $26 million] to be unrealistically low and, accordingly, has removed them from current assets. . . .*

a. What purpose do you suppose Northwest Industries, Inc., had in mind in removing marketable securities from current assets?

b. Ignoring income taxes, how much lower or higher would reported income for the year have been if marketable securities were classified as current assets and were valued at lower of cost or market? What percentage change in net income would result?

c. How do you react to management's judgment that the aggregate quoted market value is unrealistically low?

Inventories
and Cost
of Goods Sold

In 1974, many major U.S. corporations changed their method of accounting for inventories and cost of goods sold. As a result of the change in methods, these corporations altogether reported about $4 billion less net income for 1974 than had been anticipated for the year. Paradoxically, these firms were actually better off as a result of the change. This chapter attempts to resolve the apparent paradox of how a firm could be better off despite the reporting of less net income than had been anticipated. We introduce the choices that any firm must make in accounting for inventories and show how the decisions made can affect reported expenses and net income for the period. The choices made in accounting for inventories can make two companies that are basically alike appear to be quite different.

■ INVENTORY TERMINOLOGY

The term *inventory*, as used in accounting and in this chapter, means a stock of goods or other items owned by the firm. Goods held for sale by a retail or whole-sale business are referred to as *merchandise* or *merchandise inventory*; goods held for sale by a manufacturing concern are referred to as *finished goods*. The inventories of manufacturing firms also include *work in process* (partially completed products in the factory) and *raw materials* (materials being stored which will become part of goods to be produced). Various types of supplies which will be consumed in administrative, selling, and manufacturing operations are also frequently included in inventories on the balance sheet.

The term *inventory* is sometimes used as a verb. To inventory a stock of goods means to prepare a list of the items on hand at some specified date, to assign a unit price to each item, and to calculate the total cost of the inventory.

■ SIGNIFICANCE OF ACCOUNTING FOR INVENTORIES

A major objective of financial accounting is the determination of periodic income. The role of accounting for inventories in that process is to determine the proper assignment of cost to various accounting periods as expenses. The total cost of goods available for sale or use during a period must be allocated between the current period's usage (cost of items sold—expense) and the amounts carried forward to future periods (the end-of-period inventory—asset).

One equation, or identity, applies to all inventory situations and will facilitate our discussion of accounting for inventory:

$$\text{Beginning Inventory} + \text{Additions} - \text{Withdrawals} = \text{Ending Inventory.}$$

If we begin a period with 1,000 pounds of salt (beginning inventory), if we purchase (add) 1,500 pounds during the period, and if we use (withdraw) 1,300 pounds during the period, there should be 1,200 pounds of salt left at the end of the period (ending inventory). More important for accounting purposes, the inventory equation can be rewritten as

$$\text{Beginning Inventory} + \text{Additions} - \text{Ending Inventory} = \text{Withdrawals.}$$

If we begin the period with 1,000 pounds of salt, if we purchase 1,500 pounds of salt, and if we observe 1,200 pounds of salt on hand at the end of the period, then we know that 1,300 pounds of salt were used, or otherwise withdrawn from inventory, during the period.

If accounting were concerned merely with keeping a record of physical quantities, there would be few problems in accounting for inventories. But, of course, accounting reports are stated in dollar amounts, not physical quantities. If all prices remained constant, inventory accounting problems would be minor, because any variation in values of inventories would be attributable solely to changes in quantities. The major problems in inventory accounting arise from fluctuations over time in the unit acquisition costs of inventory items.

Consider the inventory of goods for sale in a merchandising firm. The inventory equation can be written as

$$\text{Beginning Inventory} + \text{Net Purchases} - \text{Cost of Goods Sold} = \text{Ending Inventory}$$

or, rearranging terms,

$$\text{Beginning Inventory} + \text{Net Purchases} - \text{Ending Inventory} = \text{Cost of Goods Sold.}$$

The valuation for the ending inventory will appear on the balance sheet as the asset, Merchandise Inventory; the amount of Cost of Goods Sold will appear on the income statement as an expense of generating the sales revenue. To illustrate, suppose that the beginning inventory had been one toaster, which shall be called Toaster 1 and which cost $25. Suppose further that two toasters were purchased during the period, Toaster 2 for $29 and Toaster 3 for $30, and that one toaster was sold during the period. The three toasters are alike in every physical respect, so there is no way of determining which toaster was the one sold during the period. Some assumption about which toaster was sold must therefore be made. The total cost of the three toasters available for sale is $84, and the average cost of the toasters is $28 (= ($25 + 29 + 30)/3). There are at least four ways to apply the inventory equation to determine the Cost of Goods Sold expense for the income statement and the Ending Inventory for the balance sheet:

ASSUMED ITEM SOLD	COST OF GOODS AVAILABLE FOR SALE (BEGINNING INVENTORY PLUS PURCHASES)	=	COST OF GOODS SOLD (FOR INCOME STATEMENT)	+	ENDING INVENTORY (FOR BALANCE SHEET)
Toaster 1	$84		$25		$59
Toaster 2	84		29		55
Toaster 3	84		30		54
"Average" toaster ..	84		28		56

As the equation and the example both show, the higher is the Cost of Goods Sold, the lower must be the Ending Inventory. The choice of which particular pair of numbers to use—one for the income statement and one for the balance sheet—is determined by the *cost-flow assumption*. Making a cost-flow assumption is just one problem, but it is the major one, in accounting for inventories.

Problems of Inventory Accounting

Discussion of inventory accounting can be conveniently split into consideration of individual problems, treated more or less separately. The rest of this chapter discusses six such problems:

1. acquisition of inventory
2. choice of periodic or perpetual inventory methods
3. valuation bases
4. cost-flow assumptions
5. inclusion problems
6. income tax considerations.

These problems are not equally difficult nor equally important. The sections on valuation bases (3), cost-flow assumptions (4), and inclusion problems (5) merit particular attention.

There are other inventory management problems which require attention by a successful business, but these problems are considered in management science and managerial accounting courses. For example, the physical size of inventories can significantly influence the profitability of the firm. A firm whose inventory is too small may lose customers because of "stockouts," while one whose inventory is too large will incur extra costs of holding and storing unnecessary quantities.

Most inventory accounting problems are essentially identical for merchandising and manufacturing firms. In the following discussion, we concentrate on merchandishing firms, but the lessons apply as well to manufacturing firms. Only in the discussion of inclusion problems (absorption and direct costing) does the distinction between merchandising and manufacturing firms assume significance.

■ ACQUISITION OF INVENTORY

Cost Components of Merchandise Inventory

All costs incurred in connection with acquiring goods and preparing them for sale may appropriately enter into the valuation of the goods as assets. Such costs include purchasing, transportation, receiving, unpacking, inspecting, and shelving costs as well as that portion of the bookkeeping and office cost which relates to the recording of purchases. Since the amounts involved are often relatively small, and especially since it is extremely difficult to assign a definite dollar amount for many of these costs to specific purchases, the tendency in practice is to restrict the actual additions to a few significant items which can easily be identified with particular goods, such as transportation costs. The costs of operating a purchasing department, the salaries and expenses of buyers, the costs of the receiving and warehousing departments, and the costs of handling and shelving are usually treated as expenses of the period in which they are incurred, although they logically are part of the total cost of merchandise made ready for sale.

The Purchase Transaction

The procedures for recording purchases of merchandise, raw materials, and supplies vary a great deal from one business to another. Purchase transactions culminate, of course, when the goods are received and inspected and the purchase is entered into the records. From the legal point of view, purchases should be recorded in the formal accounting records when title to the goods passes. The question of when title passes is often a technical, legal matter, and the precise answer depends upon a consideration of all of the circumstances of the transaction. As a convenience, therefore, the accountant usually recognizes purchases only after both the invoice and the goods are received and inspected. Adjustments may be made at the end of the accounting period in order to reflect the legal formalities at that time.

Merchandise Purchases Account

During the accounting period, acquisitions of merchandise can be debited either to the appropriate inventory account, such as Merchandise Inventory, or to a Merchandise Purchases account. (The shorter title Purchases is used in practice, but the full title is occasionally used here to avoid ambiguity.) The Merchandise Purchases account is a temporary, asset adjunct account. That is, the balance in Merchandise Purchases is closed at the end of each accounting period to the appropriate inventory account and does not appear in the balance sheet. The typical entry to record a specific purchase of merchandise is:

Merchandise Purchases   350
    Cash (or Accounts Payable)   350
To record purchase of merchandise.

At the end of the period the closing entry, assuming merchandise costing $1,675 was purchased during the period, would be:

Merchandise Inventory   1,675
    Merchandise Purchases   1,675
To close purchases account to the inventory account.

The special account to record purchases is used to give more complete information about purchase transactions during the period than is provided when all purchases are debited directly to the Merchandise (or Raw Materials) Inventory accounts.

Merchandise Purchases Adjustments

The invoice price of goods purchased will seldom be the correct measure of the total acquisition cost. Additional costs may be incurred in transporting and handling the goods, and deductions may be required for cash discounts, goods returned, and other allowances or adjustments of the invoice price. All of these adjustments could be handled through the one Merchandise Purchases account. Frequently, however, a number of contra and adjunct accounts are used for these adjustments so that a more complete analysis of the cost of purchases is available. Freight-In, Purchase Returns, Purchase Allowances, and Purchase Discounts (or Purchase Discounts Lost) are used to provide the needed detail. The treatment of purchase discounts and purchase allowances by the purchaser is analogous to the treatment of sales discounts and sales allowances by the seller as discussed in Chapter Eight.

Merchandise Purchases Discounts

The largest adjustment to the invoice price of merchandise purchases is likely to be that for purchase discounts. The amount of discounts taken during a period is sometimes shown as a special or "other" revenue item on the income statement. Some supporters of this treatment argue that the discounts represent interest earned on cash and so should be viewed as a revenue item.

The more appropriate interpretation, however, is to treat purchase discounts as a reduction in the purchase price. We explained in Chapter Eight that there is a cash price for purchases, and if payment is delayed, there is an additional charge for the right to delay payment and for the other additional services the seller is compelled to render. To view purchase discounts as revenue would indicate that revenue may be earned simply by buying goods and paying for them with cash within a specified time even though the goods have not been sold to others. It seems more reasonable to treat discounts as a reduction in the cost of merchandise purchased and thereby to defer their effect on net income until the goods have been sold.

Some accountants who recognize the logic of treating purchase discounts as a reduction in price nevertheless suggest that purchase discounts should be treated as "other" revenue for reasons of expediency. These accountants would treat discounts on major purchases, such as equipment, as reductions in the purchase price. They would not, however, deduct purchase discounts from the gross price of merchandise when the amounts involved are too small to justify the additional record-keeping effort. There is merit in the view that precision in accounting may cost more than the benefits received from greater accuracy. Whenever the amounts involved are not material or significant, the most convenient, rather than the logically correct, procedure may be satisfactory because the effects on net income are approximately the same.

Purchase discounts are often a material item; for some firms, the total of purchase discounts has been greater than net income. In this day of electronic calculating devices and machine record keeping, there should be little inconvenience or extra cost incurred in treating purchase discounts as a reduction in purchase price rather than as "other" revenue.

Two alternatives for treating discounts on merchandise purchases are often used in practice: (1) recognize the amount of discounts taken on payments made during the period, without regard to the period of purchase (gross price method), or (2) deduct all discounts made available from the gross purchase invoice prices at the time of purchase (net price method).

Recording Purchase Discounts

Alternative 1: Gross Price Method   The gross price method of accounting for purchases records invoices at the gross price and accumulates the amount of discounts taken on payments made. Suppose that goods with a gross invoice price of $1,000 are purchased, 2/10, net/30. (That is, a 2-percent discount from invoice price is offered if payment is made within 10 days and the full invoice price is due, in any case, within 30 days.) The entries to record the purchase and the payment (1) under the assumption that the payment is made in time to take the discount, and (2) under the assumption that the payment is too late to take advantage of the discount, are as follows:

GROSS PRICE METHOD	(1) DISCOUNT TAKEN		(2) DISCOUNT NOT TAKEN	
Purchases	1,000		1,000	
Accounts Payable		1,000		1,000
To record purchase.				
Accounts Payable	1,000		1,000	
Cash		980		1,000
Purchase Discounts		20		—
To record payment.				

The balance in the Purchase Discounts account is deducted from the balance in the Purchases account in calculating net purchases for a period. Such a deduction merely approximates the results achieved by treating purchase discounts as a reduction in purchase price at the time of purchase. It is only an approximation because the total adjustment includes discounts taken on payments made this period, without regard to the period of purchase.

An accurate adjustment would require eliminating the discounts taken related to purchases of previous periods while including the amount of discounts available at the end of the accounting period which are expected to be taken during the following period. This refinement in the treatment of purchase discounts is seldom employed in practice.

Alternative 2: Net Price Method The net price method for handling purchase discounts is clearly superior to the gross price method for measuring periodic performance. As we pointed out in the discussion of sales discounts, the interest rate implied by sales discounts is much too high to be simply a payment for receiving money sooner. From the point of view of the buyer, prompt payment to receive the benefit of discounts is usually so profitable that nearly all firms will want to take advantage of all purchase discounts. Management of such firms will want to know the amount of discounts lapsed or lost for whatever reason. Management assumes that all discounts will be taken, and sees no point in reporting the amount of discounts taken. Under the net price method, the amount of the discounts lost rather than the amount taken is recorded. The net price method also results in an important recording advantage. Since purchases and liabilities are initially recorded at the amount of cash currently payable, the need for adjustments as invoices are paid is eliminated and the adjustments at the end of the accounting period are eliminated or simplified. This advantage is fully realized only if the firm follows the policy, as most successful firms do, of taking practically all purchase discounts.

In recording purchases, the purchase discount is deducted from the gross purchase price immediately upon receipt of the invoice, and the net invoice price is used in the entries. The example used previously of a $1,000 invoice price for goods subject to a 2-percent cash discount would be recorded as follows under the net price method:

NET PRICE METHOD	(1) DISCOUNT TAKEN		(2) DISCOUNT NOT TAKEN	
Purchases	980		980	
Accounts Payable		980		980
To record purchase.				
Accounts Payable	980		980	
Purchase Discounts Lost	—		20	
Cash		980		1,000
To record payment.				

The balance in the Purchase Discounts Lost account could be added to the cost of the merchandise purchased and, therefore, viewed as an additional component of goods available for sale. It is sometimes suggested, and with a good deal of logic, that discounts lost should be shown as a financial or general operating expense rather than as an addition to the cost of purchases, since lost discounts may indicate an inefficient office force or inadequate financing. In this text, we treat purchase discounts lost as an expense unless an explicit contrary statement is made.

■ INVENTORY METHODS

There are two principal methods of determining the physical quantity and dollar amount of an inventory. One is known as the *periodic* inventory method and the other as the *perpetual* inventory method.

Periodic Inventory Method

The periodic inventory method determines the ending inventory figure as the physical count of units multiplied by the cost per unit. Then the inventory equation is used to determine the withdrawals which represent the cost of goods sold expense (or the cost of manufacturing materials, a product cost, or of supplies used, either a product cost or a general and administrative expense).

When the periodic inventory method is used, no record or entry is made for withdrawals (cost of goods sold or used) until the end of the accounting period. If sales during the period amounted to $123,500, then entries to record sales would be made which have the combined effect of the following entry:

Cash and Accounts Receivable	123,500	
Sales		123,500

At the end of the period, a physical count is taken, an inventory valuation is made, and the cost of the withdrawals is determined from the inventory equation. For example,

Merchandise Inventory, Jan. 1, 1976	$ 10,000
Plus Merchandise Purchases (Net) During 1976	100,000
Goods Available for Sale During 1976	$110,000
Less Merchandise Inventory, Dec. 31, 1976	15,000
Cost of Goods Sold During 1976	$ 95,000

The cost of goods sold expense is recognized in a single entry:

Cost of Goods Sold	95,000	
Merchandise Inventory		95,000

The principal disadvantage of the periodic inventory method is the assumption that all goods not accounted for by the physical inventory count have been sold or used. Any "shrinkages" or losses from such causes as theft, evaporation, and waste are buried in the cost of goods sold or the cost of materials or supplies used. Furthermore, physically counting the inventory at the end of the accounting period is apt to interfere seriously with normal business operations for several days. Some firms using the periodic inventory method even close down and engage practically the entire staff on the physical count and measurement of the items on hand. Preparing operating statements more frequently than once a year is seldom possible when the inventory figures are obtained only by physically counting inventories.

Perpetual Inventory Method

Under the *perpetual* (or *continuous*) inventory method, the system of records is designed so that the cost of withdrawals is recorded at the time these assets are withdrawn from inventory. The perpetual inventory method determines the withdrawals by physical observation and uses the inventory equation to determine what should be in the ending inventory after each acquisition or withdrawal.

Such entries as the following may be made from day to day.

Cost of Goods Sold	546	
Merchandise Inventory		546
To record the cost of goods withdrawn from inventory and sold.		
Work in Process Inventory	1,075	
Raw Material Inventory		1,075
To record the cost of raw material withdrawn from the storeroom and used in production.		

The balance in the Merchandise Inventory account or in the Raw Materials Inventory account, when postings for a period have been completed, is the cost of the goods still on hand. Operating statements can be prepared without a physical count of inventory.

Using a perpetual inventory system does not entirely eliminate the need to take physical inventories. A physical count of the goods on hand must be taken from time to time to check the accuracy of the book figures and to gauge the loss from shrinkages. Some businesses make a complete physical check at the end of the accounting period, in the same way as when the periodic inventory method is used. Frequently, however, a more effective procedure can be employed. Rather than taking the inventory of all items at one time, the count may be staggered throughout the period. For example, an attempt may be made to check an individual item when the supply of that item reaches a low point. All items should be counted at least once during every year. Certain items may be checked more frequently, either because of their high value or because of a high probability of errors in recording their withdrawals.

Choosing Between Periodic and Perpetual Inventory Methods

The perpetual method helps maintain up-to-date information on quantities actually on hand. Thus, its use is justified when being "out of stock" may lead to costly consequences, such as customer dissatisfaction or the need to shut down production lines. In such cases, the perpetual inventory system might keep track of the physical quantities of inventory but not the dollar amounts.

Further, controlling losses or shrinkages is difficult if they cannot be measured. The periodic inventory method usually costs less to administer than the perpetual inventory method, but it provides no data on losses, shrinkages, and deterioration. To gather data on losses from inventory requires both a continuous record of withdrawals and periodic counts so that the amounts that the books indicate should be on hand can be compared with the actual amounts. As with other choices that have to be made in accounting, the costs of any system have to be compared with its benefits. The periodic inventory method is likely to be cost-effective when being out of stock will not be extremely costly, when there is a large volume of items with a small value per unit, or when items are hard to steal or pilfer. Perpetual methods are cost-effective when there is a small volume of high-value items or when running out of stock is costly.

■ BASES OF INVENTORY VALUATION

The basis of valuation for inventories significantly affects periodic income. At least four bases of valuation are in current use. The two most common are (1) acquisition cost and (2) lower of (acquisition) cost or market. Two other bases, used less frequently, are (3) standard cost and (4) net realizable value.

Acquisition-Cost Basis

When the cost basis is used, units in inventory are carried at their acquisition cost until sold. Thus, there is no effect on income until a sale takes place. The figure shown in the balance sheet is more or less out of date, depending upon intervening price changes and how long the units have been on hand.

"Cost" includes "the sum of the applicable expenditures and charges directly or indirectly incurred in bringing an article to its existing condition and location."[1] As discussed earlier, the cost of inventory includes the quoted invoice price of merchandise, materials, and supplies plus the cost of transportation, less the sum of discounts, allowances, and returns. Other costs such as those of purchasing, receiving, handling, and storage could be included. These other costs, however, are usually charged to expense (or manufacturing overhead) in the period of the incurrence. If the business is a manufacturing enterprise, this definition of cost would apply to its raw materials and supplies; cost also includes all of the other

---

[1] *Accounting Research Bulletin No. 43*, American Institute of Certified Public Accountants, 1953, Chapter 4, Statement 3.

manufacturing costs which may have been incurred in producing the goods in process or the finished products.

The acquisition-cost basis should be used only for goods which are undamaged and can be used effectively in current operations. If materials or goods have become damaged, shopworn, or obsolete, they should be written down to a figure below cost, such as "net realizable value," which is explained below.

Lower-of-Cost-or-Market Basis

The-lower-of-cost-or-market (in general, acquisition cost or current replacement cost, whichever is lower) valuation basis has received wide acceptance in principle, but there is reason to believe that its practical use has not been as extensive as the attention which it has received. The American Institute of Certified Public Accountants justified the need for the lower-of-cost-or-market valuation basis as follows:

> A departure from the cost basis of pricing the inventory is required when the utility of the goods is no longer as great as its cost. Where there is evidence that the utility of goods, in their disposal in the ordinary course of business, will be less than cost, whether due to physical deterioration, obsolescence, changes in price levels, or other causes, the difference should be recognized as a loss of the current period. This is generally accomplished by stating such goods at a lower level commonly designated as market.[2]

Use of the lower-of-cost-or-market basis involves the determination of both acquisition cost and "market" information for each item in the inventory and, as the name implies, using the lesser of these two amounts as the inventory value. The difficulty of gathering the necessary information for each of the hundreds or thousands of items in an inventory, to say nothing of the difficulty of calculating the market value of work in process and finished goods on the basis of present material prices, present labor rates, and present prices for each of the other costs of production operations, certainly lends much support to our opinion that the method is limited in application. It is used frequently for valuable items and for other items where the change in price has been significant.

The lower-of-cost-or-market basis for inventory valuation is thought to be a "conservative" policy because (1) losses from decreases in market value are recognized before goods are sold, but gains from increases in market value are never recorded before a sale takes place[3] and (2) inventory figures on the balance sheet are never greater, but may be less, than acquisition cost. An examination of the effects of using the lower-of-cost-or-market basis over a series of accounting periods shows why the "conservatism" argument is questionable. For any one unit, there is only one gain or loss figure—the difference between its selling price and its

---

[2] Accounting Research Bulletin No. 43, American Institute of Certified Public Accountants, 1953, Chapter 4, Statement 5.
[3] To use the terms introduced in Chapter Three and discussed further in Chapter Fourteen, holding losses are reported currently, while holding gains are not reported until the goods are sold.

acquisition cost; the valuation rule merely determines how this amount of gain or loss is to be spread over the accounting periods between acquisition and final disposition. When the lower-of-cost-or-market basis is used, the net income of the present period may be lower than if the acquisition cost basis were used, but if so, the net income of a later period, when the unit is sold, will be higher. (Refer to the example in Chapter Eight of gain and loss recognition on marketable securities accounted for on a lower-of-cost-or-market basis.)

Standard Costs

Standard cost is a predetermined estimate of what items of manufactured inventory *should* cost. Studies of past and estimated future cost data provide the basis for standard costs. Standard cost systems are frequently used by manufacturing firms for internal performance measurement and control. These are discussed in managerial and cost accounting texts. Standard cost is also occasionally used as the valuation basis for preparing financial statements. Units in inventory may be valued at standard cost, especially in the preparation of monthly or quarterly statements. If so, any excess of actual cost over standard cost (called an *unfavorable variance*) is usually debited to cost of goods sold or to other expenses of the period. If actual cost is less than standard cost, the variance is usually credited to cost of goods sold.

Net Realizable Value

Net realizable value is occasionally used in inventory valuation. *Net realizable value* is defined as the estimated selling price less costs to complete the item and to sell it. Agricultural products on hand at the close of an accounting period, for example, are often stated at net realizable value. When this method is used, income is recognized in the period of production rather than in the period of sale. By-products of manufacturing operations are usually valued on a similar basis. Net realizable values are appropriate for this purpose when cost figures are difficult to obtain, or when an established market virtually eliminates both the necessity for sales effort and any uncertainty about selling price.

■ COST-FLOW ASSUMPTIONS

Specific Identification and the Need for a Cost-Flow Assumption

If the individual units of an item can be physically identified as coming from a specific purchase, there is no special problem of ascertaining the acquisition cost of the unit withdrawn and of the units still on hand. The cost can be marked on the unit or on its container, or the unit can be traced back to its purchase invoice or cost record. In most cases, however, new items are mixed with old units on shelves, in bins, or in other ways, and physical identification is impossible or impractical. Recall the problem in allocating the costs of the toasters discussed earlier in this chapter.

The inventory valuation at any date is the cost of the goods on hand which is to be carried forward to future periods. The inventory valuation problem arises because there are *two* unknowns in the inventory equation:

Beginning Inventory + Net Purchases − Cost of Goods Sold = Ending Inventory.

The values of the beginning inventory and net purchases are known; the values of the cost of goods sold and of ending inventory are not known. The question is whether to value the ending inventory using the most recent costs, the oldest costs, the average cost, or some other alternative. Of course, the question could have been put in terms of valuing the cost of goods sold, for once we determine the value of one unknown quantity, the inventory equation automatically determines the value of the other. The relation between the two unknowns, Cost of Goods Sold and Ending Inventory, in the inventory equation is such that the higher the value assigned to one of them, the lower must be the value assigned to the other.

There is no historical cost-based accounting method for valuing both inventories and cost of goods sold that allows the accountant to show current values on both the income statement and the balance sheet during a period of changing prices. For example, in a period of rising prices, if current, higher prices are used in measuring cost of goods sold shown on the income statement, then older, lower prices must be used in valuing the ending inventory shown on the balance sheet, and vice versa. As long as cost of goods sold and ending inventory are based on acquisition costs, financial statements can present current values in one account, but not in both. Of course, combinations of current and out-of-date information can be shown in both accounts.

If more than one purchase is made of the same item at different prices, and specific identification is not feasible or possible, then some assumption must be made as to the flow of costs in order to estimate the acquisition cost applicable to the units remaining in the inventory. One of three cost-flow assumptions is typically used for this purpose. These cost-flow assumptions are

1. first in, first out (FIFO)
2. last in, first out (LIFO)
3. weighted average.

The demonstrations of each of these methods which follow are based upon the data shown in Exhibit 9.1, which reports beginning inventory, additions, withdrawals, and ending inventory of Item X for the month of June.

First In, First Out

The first-in, first-out cost-flow assumption, abbreviated FIFO, assigns the cost of the earliest units acquired to the withdrawals and the cost of the most recent acquisitions to the ending inventory. The oldest materials and goods are assumed to be used first. This assumption conforms to good business practice, especially in the case of items which deteriorate physically or which become obsolete.

When the periodic inventory method is used, the unit prices to be applied to

EXHIBIT 9.1
Data for Illustration of Inventory Cost-Flow Assumptions

ITEM X

	Units	Unit Price	Total Cost
Beginning Inventory, June 1	100	$1.00	$100
Purchases, June 7	300	1.10	330
Purchases, June 12	100	1.25	125
Total Available for Sale	500		$555
Withdrawals, June 5	25		?
Withdrawals, June 10	10		?
Withdrawals, June 15	200		?
Withdrawals, June 25	150		?
Total Withdrawals	385		?
Ending Inventory, June 30	115		?

quantities on hand are usually determined by working backward through the purchases until a sufficient quantity is accumulated to cover the inventory at the end of the month. If a physical count reveals that there are 115 units on hand at June 30, the prices paid for the most-recently acquired 115 units must be determined. The most recent purchase is the one of June 12, which accounts for 100 units at a cost of $125.00. The next most recent purchase is that of June 7. The remaining 15 units are priced at the $1.10 unit price of that purchase transaction. The total value of the inventory is, then, $141.50 as shown in Exhibit 9.2. FIFO has been appropriately characterized as the "most-recent-invoice method" of valuing inventories when the periodic inventory method is used. Under FIFO, perpetual and periodic

EXHIBIT 9.2
Ending Inventory and Cost of Goods Sold Determination Adopting the Periodic Inventory Method and a FIFO Cost-Flow Assumption

ITEM X

100 units @ $1.25	$125.00
15 units @ $1.10	16.50
Ending Inventory, June 30	**$141.50**
Cost of Goods Available for Sale	$555.00
Less Ending Inventory	141.50
Cost of Goods Sold	**$413.50**

inventory systems lead to identical cost of goods sold and ending inventory amounts.

Last In, First Out

The last-in, first-out cost-flow assumption, abbreviated LIFO, has attracted a good deal of attention since 1939 when it first became acceptable for income tax determinations. In a period of consistently rising prices, LIFO results in a lower reported periodic income—and lower current income taxes—than either FIFO or weighted-average cost-flow assumptions.

LIFO assumes that the business carries a certain number of units on hand and that current operations and sales are carried on with the use of units purchased most recently.[4] There are some situations where the physical conditions justify such an assumption, such as where material is kept in a bin and new purchases are dumped in before the supply is exhausted completely. The quantity at the bottom of the bin may have been purchased many months or years ago. Most often, however, LIFO cannot be justified in terms of physical flows but is used because, in a period of rising prices, it produces a cost of goods sold figure that is based on more up-to-date prices and thereby reduces reported income and income taxes.

When the periodic inventory method is used, the value of ending inventory is determined by starting with the beginning inventory and then working forward through the purchases until sufficient units have been priced to cover the ending inventory. In the illustration, ending inventory is valued as shown in Exhibit 9.3.

The type of calculation shown in Exhibit 9.3 is realistic only when the quantity on hand never dropped below the number of units in the beginning inventory, 100 units in the illustration. This would not be known unless perpetual inventory records were kept. This doubtful assumption weakens the logic of LIFO when a

EXHIBIT 9.3
Ending Inventory and Cost of Goods Sold Determination Adopting the Periodic Inventory Method and a LIFO Cost-Flow Assumption

ITEM X

100 units @ $1.00 (from beginning inventory)	$100.00
15 units @ $1.10 (from first purchase, June 7)	16.50
Ending Inventory at Cost	**$116.50**
Cost of Goods Available for Sale	$555.00
Less Ending Inventory	116.50
Cost of Goods Sold	**$438.50**

[4] The LIFO assumption in the strict sense can be applied only to physically identical items such as tons of ore or pounds of cotton. LIFO can be used for style goods (for example, dresses and suits) or annual models of appliances by using a variant known as *dollar-value LIFO* or *retail-method LIFO*. These methods are beyond the scope of this discussion.

periodic inventory system is used. On the other hand, when a periodic inventory system is used, LIFO usually requires less pricing of inventory items at the end of the period. Because the quantity in the ending inventory is apt to be somewhat larger than the quantity in the beginning inventory, only the increase in units need be priced. (This increase in physical quantities with its own set of prices is often called a *LIFO inventory layer.*) Few firms use a LIFO cost-flow assumption with a perpetual inventory method. The cost of goods sold and ending inventory amounts are usually different with a perpetual system than with a periodic system.

Weighted Average

To use a weighted-average periodic inventory method, a weighted average of the costs of all goods available for use during the month, including the cost applicable to the beginning inventory, must be calculated. The weighted-average cost is applied to the units on hand at the end of the month, as shown in Exhibit 9.4. The method is physically appropriate for liquids and not unreasonable for other types of products where distinguishing different lots is difficult. The result shown in Exhibit 9.4 is correct, strictly speaking, only if no units were used or sold until after the firm makes the last purchase which enters the computations of the weighted average. Seldom do all additions to inventory precede any withdrawals and, therefore, the logic of the method is somewhat weakened.

The weighted-average cost-flow assumption is often the easiest to apply with a perpetual inventory system, especially where the number of purchases is less than the number of withdrawals. The technique requires the calculation of a new average unit cost after each purchase, and this unit-cost figure is used to price all withdrawals until the next purchase is made. Hence, this method is often called the *moving-average method* when it is used in a perpetual inventory system. The illustration in Exhibit 9.5 indicates how the moving-average method operates with the use of perpetual inventory records. The inventory at the end of the month is

EXHIBIT 9.4
Ending Inventory and Cost of Goods Sold Determination Adopting the Periodic Inventory Method and a Weighted-Average Cost-Flow Assumption

ITEM X

6/1 100 units @ $1.00	$100.00
6/7 300 units @ $1.10	330.00
6/12 100 units @ $1.25	125.00
500 units @ $1.11 (= $555/500)	$555.00
Ending Inventory (115 units @ $1.11)	$127.65
Cost of Goods Available for Sale	$555.00
Less Ending Inventory	127.65
Cost of Goods Sold	$427.35

EXHIBIT 9.5
Ending Inventory and Cost of Goods Sold Determination Adopting the Perpetual Inventory Method and a Moving-Average Cost-Flow Assumption

ITEM X

Date	Received			Issued			Balance		
	Units	Price	Amount	Units	Price	Amount	Units	Price	Amount
6/1							100	$1.00	$100.00
6/5				25	$1.00	$ 25.00	75	1.00	75.00
6/7	300	$1.10	$330.00				375	1.08	405.00
6/10				10	1.08	10.80	365	1.08	394.20
6/12	100	1.25	125.00				465	1.1166	519.20
6/15				200	1.1166	223.32	265	1.1166	295.88
6/25				150	1.1166	167.49	115	1.1166	128.39

Cost of Goods Sold $426.61

ALTERNATIVE COST-OF-GOODS-SOLD COMPUTATION

Cost of Goods Available for Sale	$555.00
Less Ending Inventory	128.39
Cost of Goods Sold	**$426.61**

valued at the last amount shown on the perpetual inventory form, $128.39. The unit price of $1.1166 is used only for determining the amount of subsequent withdrawals. The ending inventory of $128.39 is calculated as $295.88 less $167.49 ($= 150 \times \$1.1166$), not as $115 \times \$1.1166$.

Comparison of Cost-Flow Assumptions

FIFO results in balance sheet figures which are closest to current cost, since the latest purchases dominate the ending inventory valuation. The cost-of-goods-sold expense tends to be out of date, however, since it assumes that the earlier prices of the beginning inventory and the earliest purchases are charged to expense. When prices change, FIFO usually leads to the highest reported net income of the three methods when prices are rising and the smallest when prices are falling. When FIFO is used, both the perpetual and periodic inventory methods lead to the same figure for the cost of goods sold and, hence, to the same figure for the ending inventory.

LIFO leads to opposite results. LIFO produces balance sheet figures that may be far removed from current costs and a cost of goods sold figure close to current costs. The net income under LIFO is usually the smallest of the three when prices are rising (highest cost of goods sold), and the largest when prices are falling (lowest cost of goods sold). Also, LIFO ordinarily results in the least fluctuation in reported income, since selling prices tend to be changed as current prices of inventory items change. Under LIFO, the perpetual and periodic inventory methods usually lead to different figures for cost of goods sold and, hence, for ending inventory. Such a difference occurs when it is necessary to dip into the beginning LIFO inventory layers during the period, even though the quantities are replaced by the end of the period.

A major objective of using LIFO is to reduce current taxes in periods of rising prices and rising inventory quantities. Usually LIFO produces this result, but if inventory quantities decline, the opposite effect can occur in the year of the decline. For example, if under LIFO, a firm must for some reason reduce end-of-period physical inventory quantities below what they were at the beginning of the period, then the older and lower costs will enter the cost of goods sold. Such a firm will have larger reported income and income taxes in that period than if the firm had been able to maintain its inventory at beginning-of-period levels. Suppose that LIFO inventory at the beginning of 1976 consists of 46 units with a total cost of $342, as follows:

NUMBER OF UNITS	YEAR PURCHASED	COST PER UNIT	TOTAL COST
10	1972	$ 5	$ 50
11	1973	6	66
12	1974	8	96
13	1975	10	130
46			$342

Assume that the price per unit at the end of 1976 is $12 per unit. If 1976 ending inventory is more than 46 units, then the cost of goods sold will be roughly $12 per unit. If, however, the 1976 ending inventory drops to 10 units, then all the 36 units purchased in 1973 through 1975 will enter cost of goods sold. These 36 units cost $292 (= $66 + $96 + $130), but the current cost of comparable units is $432 (= 36 units × $12 per unit). Cost of goods sold will be $140 (= $432 − $292) smaller because of the "dip into old LIFO layers" of inventory. Income before taxes will be $140 larger than if inventory quantities had not declined from 46 to 10 units. In reality, many LIFO firms have inventory layers built up over several decades, and the costs of the early units are often as little as 10 percent of the current cost. For these firms, a dip into old layers will substantially increase income. A footnote from a recent annual report of the U.S. Steel Corporation illustrates this phenomenon:

> *Because of the continuing high demand throughout the year, inventories of many steel-making materials and steel products were unavoidably reduced and could not be replaced during the year. Under the LIFO system of accounting, used for many years by U.S. Steel, the net effect of all the inventory changes [reductions] was to increase income for the year by about $16 million.*

The weighted-average cost-flow assumption falls between the other two in its effect both upon the balance sheet and the income statement. It is, however, much more like FIFO than like LIFO in its effects on the balance sheet. When inventory turns over rapidly, the weighted-average inventory values are almost as close to present prices as FIFO. Weighted averages reflect all of the prices during the period in proportion to the quantities purchased at those prices as well as beginning inventory costs carried over from the previous period.

Both the FIFO and the weighted-average cost-flow assumptions seem satisfactory from the viewpoint of accounting theory, particularly if an attempt is made to select the one which corresponds more closely to the physical flow of the items. On the other hand, LIFO usually presents a cost-of-goods-sold figure more closely related to current costs. It may also have the practical advantage of deferring income taxes. LIFO may reduce fluctuations in reported income and, thereby, please some stockholders. To say that LIFO's less variable income estimates are more accurate is meaningless and ignores balance sheet effects. No method is more "accurate" than any other, because each is based on an assumption made for some reporting purpose. In historical cost accounting for inventory, "truth" is a matter of definition. LIFO may cause reported income to appear stable, but it leads to a balance sheet figure for inventory so far removed from current values as possibly to delude and confuse readers of financial statements. For example, consider the current ratio (= current assets/current liabilities) introduced in Chapter Seven. The current ratio is often used by readers of financial statements to assess the liquidity of a company. If LIFO is used in periods of rising prices while inventory quantities are increasing, the amount of inventory counted in the numerator will be much smaller than if the inventory were valued at current prices. Hence, the unwary reader may underestimate the liquidity of a company which uses a LIFO cost-flow assumption.

Finally, if matching physical flows with cost flows is considered important, then LIFO is unsatisfactory because it assumes an order of consumption that is not likely to conform to reality or to good business practice. Oldest materials are rarely sold or used last.

Identifying Operating Margin and Holding Gains

The reported net income under FIFO is generally larger than under LIFO during periods of rising prices. This higher reported net income is caused by the *recognition* of a larger *holding gain* under FIFO than under LIFO. The significance of holding gains in the determination of net income under FIFO and LIFO is illustrated in this section. The conventionally reported gross margin (sales minus cost of goods sold) is split into (**1**) an operating margin and (**2**) a realized holding gain. In addition, there is usually an unrealized holding gain that is not reported.

The difference between the selling price of an item and its replacement cost at the time of sale is called an *operating margin.* This operating margin gives some indication of the relative advantage which a particular firm has in the market for its goods, such as a reputation for quality or service. The difference between the current replacement cost of an item and its acquisition cost is called a *holding gain* (or *loss*). The holding gain (or loss) reflects the change in cost of an item during the period while the inventory item is held.

To illustrate the calculation of the operating margin and holding gain, consider the example for Item X discussed in this chapter. The acquisition cost of the 500 items available for sale during the period is $555. If 385 units were sold for, say, $1.50 each, the total revenue would be $577.50. The replacement cost of the items at the time they were sold can be determined from information in Exhibit 9.1 to be $473.50 [= (25 × $1.00) + (10 × $1.10) + (350 × $1.25)]. The current replacement cost at the end of the month for each item in ending inventory is $1.25. The top portion of Exhibit 9.6 illustrates the separation of the conventionally reported gross margin into the operating margin and the realized holding gain.

EXHIBIT 9.6
*Reporting of Operating Margins
and Holding Gains for Item X*

PERIODIC INVENTORY METHOD

	Cost-Flow Assumption	
	FIFO	LIFO
Sales Revenue from Item X (385 × $1.50)	$577.50	$577.50
Less Replacement Cost of Goods Sold [(25 × $1.00) + (10 × $1.10) + (350 × $1.25)][a]	473.50	473.50
Operating Margin on Sales of Item X	$104.00	$104.00
Realized Holding Gain on Item X:		
Replacement Cost of Goods Sold[a]	$473.50	$473.50
Less Acquisition Cost of Goods Sold (FIFO—Exhibit 9.2; LIFO—Exhibit 9.3)	413.50	438.50
Realized Holding Gain on Item X	60.00	35.00
Conventionally Reported Gross Margin	$164.00	$139.00
Unrealized Holding Gain on Item X:		
Replacement Cost of Ending Inventory (115 × $1.25)[a]	$143.75	$143.75
Less Acquisition Cost of Ending Inventory (FIFO—Exhibit 9.2; LIFO—Exhibit 9.3)	141.50	116.50
Unrealized Holding Gain on Item X	2.25	27.25
Economic Profit on Sales and Holding Inventory of Item X	$166.25	$166.25

[a] The Securities and Exchange Commission (SEC) requires (as of 1976) disclosure of these two items, replacement cost of goods sold and replacement cost of ending inventory, in notes to the financial statements. If these disclosures are made, readers of financial statements will be able to make calculations like those shown in this Exhibit. The SEC refers to the "Realized Holding Gains" as *Inventory Profit.* See the glossary at *inventory profit.*

The operating margin is the difference between the $1.50 selling price and the replacement cost for Item X at the time of sale. The total operating margin of $104 is the same under both the FIFO and LIFO cost-flow assumptions. The *realized holding gain* is the difference between cost of goods sold based on replacement cost and cost of goods sold based on acquisition cost. The realized holding gain under FIFO is larger than under LIFO, since the earlier purchases at lower costs are assumed to be in cost of goods sold under FIFO. This larger realized holding gain under FIFO is the principal reason why net income under FIFO is typically larger than under LIFO during periods of rising prices.

The calculation of an unrealized holding gain on units in ending inventory is also shown in Exhibit 9.6. The *unrealized holding gain* is the difference between the current replacement cost of the ending inventory and its acquisition cost. This unrealized holding gain on ending inventory is not reported in the income statement as presently prepared. The unrealized holding gain under LIFO is larger than under FIFO, since earlier purchases with lower costs are assumed to remain in ending inventory under LIFO. The sum of the operating margin plus all holding gains (both realized and unrealized) is the same under FIFO and LIFO. Most of the holding gain under FIFO is recognized in determining net income each period, whereas most of the holding gain under LIFO is not currently recognized. Instead, under LIFO the unrealized holding gain remains unreported, so long as the older acquisition costs are shown on the balance sheet as ending inventory.

LIFO Versus FIFO Impact
on Financial Statements: An Illustration

A recent report of the General Electric Company (GE) states, in part:

> *Substantially all these [inventories] are valued on a last-in, first-out (LIFO) basis. . . . If the FIFO method of inventory accounting had been used by the Company, inventories would have been $783.7 million higher [at year end] and $429.7 million higher [at the beginning of the year]. . . .*

GE's beginning inventories amounted to $1,986.2 million. GE's ending inventories amounted to $2,257.0 million. Cost of goods sold was $10,137.6 million and sales were $13,413.1 million.

Let us see what we can deduce from this information about GE's reported income as it is affected by the choice of a flow assumption. The data from the annual report quoted above is shown in Exhibit 9.7 along with other amounts that can be computed from the given information.

Recall the inventory equation:

Cost of Goods Sold = Beginning Inventory + Purchases − Ending Inventory.

FIFO's higher beginning inventory increases reported cost of goods available for sale and the cost of goods sold by $429.7 million, relative to LIFO. FIFO's higher ending inventory decreases cost of goods sold by $783.7 million, relative to LIFO. Hence the cost of goods sold is $783.7 million minus $429.7 million, or $354.0

EXHIBIT 9.7
General Electric Company Inventory Data from Financial Statements and Footnotes

(Amounts shown in **boldface** are given in GE's financial statements. Other amounts are computed as indicated.)

Dollar Amounts in Millions

	LIFO Cost Flow Assumption (Actually Used)	+	Excess of FIFO over LIFO Amount	=	FIFO Cost-Flow Assumption (Hypothetical)
Beginning Inventory	**$ 1,986.2**		**$429.7**		**$ 2,415.9**
Purchases	10,408.4[a]		0		10,408.4
Cost of Goods Available for Sale	$12,394.6		**$429.7**		$12,824.3
Less Ending Inventory	**2,257.0**		**783.7**		3,040.7
Cost of Goods Sold	**$10,137.6**		($354.0)[b]		$ 9,783.6
Sales	**$13,413.1**		0		**$13,413.1**
Less Cost of Goods Sold	**10,137.6**		($354.0)		9,783.6
Gross Margin on Sales	**$ 3,275.5**		$354.0		$ 3,629.5

Order of computations of amounts not presented in GE's financial statements.

a. Purchases = Cost of Goods Sold + Ending Inventory − Beginning Inventory
   $10,408.4 =   **$10,137.6**   +   **$2,257.0**   −   **$1,986.2**

b. ($354.0) = **$429.7 − $783.7**

million less under FIFO than it was under LIFO. GE's pretax income would be $354.0 million more under FIFO than it was under the LIFO flow assumption actually used. GE's reported pretax income for the year was about $1 billion, so GE's reported income would have been about 35 percent larger if it had used a FIFO, rather than a LIFO, flow assumption.

Many investors and financial analysts look not merely at net income amounts, but at the rate of growth of these amounts. GE's reported pretax income in the previous year was also about $1 billion. The rate of growth of income using the LIFO flow assumption was zero, but would have been about 20 percent had GE used a FIFO flow assumption in both years. (See Problem **20** at the end of this chapter.) The rate of growth in income under FIFO would have been much larger than it appears with a LIFO flow assumption. GE has a substantial unreported holding gain (in excess of $780 million) in inventory because it uses the LIFO cost-flow assumption. Had it been using FIFO, the unreported holding gain would be much smaller. GE is not exceptional in this regard.

The moral is clear: The choice of inventory-flow assumption can have an important effect on financial statements and their interpretation. There is no other choice between generally accepted financial accounting principles that affects financial statements for most companies as much as the inventory-flow assumption during periods of substantial price change.

■ AN INCLUSION PROBLEM: ABSORPTION AND DIRECT COSTING

In the illustrations considered so far in this book for manufacturing firms, *all* production costs are debited to Work in Process Inventory. This procedure, called *absorption* (or *full*) *costing*, is the one most commonly used in accounting practice. An alternative procedure, known as *direct costing* (or more properly, *variable costing*), has received substantial attention in recent years.

In the direct costing procedure, production costs are classified into variable manufacturing costs (those that tend to vary with output) and fixed manufacturing costs (those that tend to be relatively unaffected by the number of units produced). Fixed manufacturing costs are treated in the same way as selling and administrative costs; that is, they are treated as expenses assigned to the period of incurrence rather than as costs assignable to the product produced. Fixed manufacturing costs are charged in their entirety against revenues in determining net income for the period. In the direct costing procedure, only variable manufacturing costs are classified as product costs, to be assigned to Work in Process Inventory and, later, to Finished Goods Inventory. Direct labor and direct materials are variable costs. Most manufacturing overhead items, such as property taxes and depreciation of equipment, are fixed costs.

When the absorption costing method is used, reported net income from one year to the next can display some strange patterns if the number of units produced differs from the number of units sold. These unusual changes in net income could lead some statement users to make incorrect interpretations about the operating performance of a firm. The direct costing procedure does not produce these unusual patterns of income. It has been suggested, therefore, that the direct costing method should be used so that more useful information will be provided for assessing operating performance.

Generally accepted accounting principles, however, do not permit a firm to use direct costing procedures in preparing financial statements. We suspect that direct costing is not generally acceptable for financial reporting primarily because it is not allowed for tax reporting. If it were allowed for tax purposes, we think that financial accounting authorities would permit direct costing for financial reporting. For these reasons, we defer to managerial accounting courses the discussion of the criticism of the absorption costing method and the suggested benefits of the direct costing method for internal management uses.

■ INCOME TAX CONSIDERATIONS

As we have seen, the differences between LIFO and FIFO cost-flow assumptions can lead to substantial differences in reported income. Similarly, the choices made on tax returns can lead to substantial differences in taxable income and, hence, in income tax payments. Other things being equal, the rational manager prefers lower taxes to higher taxes and would probably choose those accounting methods for tax purposes that minimize current taxes. Accounting choices for financial reporting and for tax returns can often be made independently of one another, but generally not with respect to inventory-flow assumptions.

Cost-Flow Assumption

There is only one major area in accounting where the Internal Revenue Service requires firms to use the same method for reports to stockholders as for tax returns. When the LIFO flow assumption is elected for tax returns, it must also be used in financial reports to stockholders. Once a firm has chosen to adopt LIFO, it must request permission to change back to FIFO or weighted average, and may incur a tax liability if it does so.

During the 1960's, some firms which had adopted LIFO during the mid-1950's so that income taxes would be lower (at the cost of reporting lower net income in the financial statements) switched back to FIFO so that net income reported to investors would be higher (at the cost of paying larger current income taxes). This seems to us to have been a questionable action by management of these firms. Recently, however, many firms, including Du Pont and Eastman Kodak, have switched from FIFO to LIFO. Given the rapid rate of price increases over the past several years, the switch from FIFO to LIFO has resulted in substantially lower cash payments for income taxes. For example, when Du Pont switched from FIFO to LIFO for its tax return filed in 1974, it lowered current income taxes by about $150 million.[5] In spite of our questioning of LIFO on theoretical grounds, we think that most company managements will best serve their stockholders by using a LIFO cost-flow assumption for tax, and hence, necessarily, for financial reporting, purposes. Moreover, the LIFO flow assumption should be coupled with the periodic rather than the perpetual inventory method, because using the periodic method reduces the probability of older, less expensive items entering the cost of goods sold.

Valuation Basis

The Internal Revenue Service does not permit the lower-of-cost-or-market valuation basis to be used with a LIFO cost-flow assumption. Consider the effect of allowing LIFO with lower of cost or market. When prices are rising, the LIFO cost-flow assumption results in a lower ending inventory amount and lower reported income than does FIFO. When prices are falling, the lower-of-LIFO-cost-or-market basis leads to an ending inventory amount approximately equal to that of the lower-of-FIFO-cost-or-market basis. The Internal Revenue Service is unwilling to allow a cost-flow assumption that, when compared to FIFO, results in lower taxable income when prices are rising and no higher taxable income when prices are falling. If LIFO coupled with the lower-of-cost-or-market basis were allowed, it would result in a guarantee of no worse tax position (falling prices) and the hope of a better tax position (rising prices) when compared to FIFO used with lower

---

[5] Thus, the apparent "paradox" in the introduction to this chapter is resolved.

of cost or market. If a firm selects the LIFO cost-flow assumption for income tax purposes, therefore, it must use the acquisition-cost basis of inventory valuation.

If a firm chooses the FIFO or average cost-flow assumption for income tax purposes, it can use either the acquisition cost or lower-of-acquisition-cost-or-market valuation basis. These firms should select the lower-of-cost-or-market basis, since it results in the immediate recognition of a loss whenever market price at the end of the year is less than acquisition cost.

Cost Inclusions

Where a choice exists, a firm should exclude as many elements of the cost of inventory items from their valuation. In this way, these costs can be deducted immediately in determining taxable income rather than waiting until the inventory is sold. Some choice exists with respect to the treatment of storage, special handling, and similar costs. Since direct costing is not permitted for income tax purposes, fixed manufacturing costs must be included in the cost of inventory items.

■ SUMMARY

Inventory measurements affect both the cost-of-goods-sold expense on the income statement for the period and the amount shown for the asset, inventory, on the balance sheet at the end of the period. The sum of the two must be equal to the beginning inventory plus the cost of purchases, at least in accounting based on acquisition costs and actual transactions. The allocation between expense and asset depends on four factors:

1. the inventory method used
2. the valuation basis used
3. the cost-flow assumption used
4. the types of manufacturing and other costs included in inventory.

The first factor involves a choice between periodic and perpetual inventory methods. The second factor involves a choice essentially between the cost basis and the lower-of-cost-or-market basis. The third factor concerns a choice among the FIFO, LIFO, and weighted-average cost-flow assumptions. The fourth factor involves consideration of absorption and direct costing as well as the disposition of purchasing costs.

QUESTIONS AND PROBLEMS

1. Review the meaning of the following concepts or terms discussed in this chapter.
   a. Inventory (both as a noun and as a verb)
   b. Finished goods.
   c. Inventory equation.
   d. Cost of goods sold (merchandising and manufacturing).

    e. Purchases.

    f. Freight-in.

    g. Purchase returns, allowances, and discounts.

    h. Gross price method of accounting for purchase discounts.

    i. Net price method of accounting for purchase discounts.

    j. Shrinkages.

    k. Periodic inventory method.

    l. Perpetual inventory method.

    m. Acquisition-cost basis.

    n. Lower-of-cost-or-market basis.

    o. Standard cost.

    p. Net realizable value.

    q. Cost flow assumption

    r. FIFO.

    s. LIFO.

    t. Weighted average.

    u. LIFO inventory layer.

    v. Realized holding gain.

    w. Unrealized holding gain.

    x. Absorption (full) costing.

    y. Direct (variable) costing.

    z. Inventory profit.

2. Department Store X regularly deducts available cash discounts from the gross invoice price when purchases are entered in the books, while Department Store Y enters the gross invoice price and credits discounts taken to a discount account. Discuss the relative advantages and disadvantages of the two methods and state what variations, if any, would occur in the valuation of inventories under the two methods.

3. Two television dealers may have identical stocks of goods on hand, and yet their inventories as stated in their respective balance sheets may be different in amount. Explain how this might occur.

4. "Acquisition cost for inventory valuation is reasonable from the standpoint of the income statement but misleading for balance sheet purposes." Comment on this statement.

5. Which of the two inventory methods, periodic or perpetual, would you expect to find used in each of the following situations?

    a. The greeting card department of a retail store.

    b. The fur coat department of a retail store.

    c. Supplies storeroom for an automated production line.

    d. Grocery store.

    e. College bookstore.

    f. Diamond ring department of a jewelry store.

    g. Ballpoint pen department of a jewelry store.

6. Under what circumstances would the perpetual and periodic inventory methods both yield the same inventory amount if the weighted-average flow assumption were used?

7. What is the underlying reason for the difference in net income under direct costing and absorption costing?

8. Goods which cost $800 are sold for $1,000 cash. Present the normal journal entries at the time of sale:

   a. When a periodic inventory method is used.

   b. When a perpetual inventory method is used.

9. During a period of rising prices, will the FIFO, LIFO, or weighted-average cost-flow assumption result in the highest ending inventory amount? The lowest inventory amount? Assume no changes in physical quantities during the period.

10. Refer to the preceding question. Which cost-flow assumption will result in the highest ending inventory amount during a period of declining prices? The lowest inventory amount?

11. During a period of rising prices, will the FIFO, LIFO, or weighted-average cost-flow assumption result in the highest cost of goods sold? The lowest cost of goods sold? Assume no changes in physical quantities during the period.

12. Refer to the preceding question. Which method will result in the highest cost of goods sold during a period of declining prices? The lowest cost of goods sold?

13. The following are selected transactions of the Wearever Shoe Store:

   (1) A shipment of shoes is received from the Standard Shoe Company, $2,100. Terms 2/30, n/60.

   (2) Part of the shipment of (**1**) is returned. The gross price of the returned goods is $200, and a credit memorandum for this amount is received from the Standard Shoe Company.

   (3) The invoice of the Standard Shoe Company is paid in time to take the discount.

   a. Give entries on the books of the Wearever Shoe Store, assuming that the net price method is used.

   b. Give entries on the books of the Wearever Shoe Store, assuming that the gross price method is used.

14. The inventory footnote to the 1976 annual report of the Cheral Company reads in part as follows:

> *Because of continuing high demand throughout the year, inventories were unavoidably reduced and could not be replaced. Under the LIFO system of accounting, used for many years by Cheral Company, the net effect of all the inventory changes was to increase pretax income by $60,000 over what it would have been had inventories been maintained at their physical levels at the start of the year.*

The price of Cheral Company's merchandise purchases was $22 per unit during 1976 after having risen steadily for many years. Cheral Company uses a periodic inventory method. Cheral Company's inventory positions at the beginning and end of the year are summarized below.

DATE	PHYSICAL COUNT OF INVENTORY	LIFO COST OF INVENTORY
January 1, 1976	30,000 units	$?
December 31, 1976	20,000 units	$260,000

   a. What was the average cost per unit of the 10,000 units removed from the January 1, 1976, LIFO inventory?

   b. What was the January 1, 1976, LIFO cost of inventory?

15. The LIFO Company and the FLCM Company both manufacture paper and cardboard products. Prices of timber, paper pulp, and finished paper products have generally increased by about 5 percent per year through the *start of this year.* Inventory data for the beginning and end of the year are shown below.

	JANUARY 1	DECEMBER 31
LIFO Company Inventory (last in, first out)	$19,695,000	$15,870,000
FLCM Company Inventory (first in, first out, lower of cost or market)	46,284,000	38,250,000

Income statements for the two companies for the year ending December 31 are as follows:

	LIFO COMPANY	FLCM COMPANY
Sales	$57,000,000	$129,000,000
Expenses:		
Cost of Goods Sold	$44,580,000	$108,000,000
Depreciation	5,400,000	12,000,000
General Expenses	2,220,000	5,400,000
Income Taxes (40 percent of pretax income) ..	1,920,000	1,440,000
Total Expenses	$54,120,000	$126,840,000
Net Income	$ 2,880,000	$ 2,160,000

a. Assuming that the prices for timber, paper pulp, and finished paper had remained unchanged during the year, how would the two companies' respective inventory valuation methods affect the interpretation of their financial statements for the year?

b. How would the answer to **a** differ if prices at the end of the year had been lower than at the beginning of the year?

c. How would the answer to **a** differ if prices at the end of the year had been higher than at the beginning of the year?

16. Prepare a journal form with two pairs of columns, one headed Net Price Method and the other headed Gross Price Method. Using this journal form, show summary entries for the following events in the history of Evans and Foster, furniture manufacturers.

(1) During the first year of operations, materials with a gross invoice price of $60,000 are purchased. All invoices are subject to a 2-percent cash discount if paid within 10 days.

(2) Payments to creditors during the year amount to $53,000, settling $54,000 of accounts payable at gross prices.

(3) Of the $6,000, gross, in unpaid accounts at the end of the year, the discount time has expired on one invoice amounting to $400. It is expected that all other discounts will be taken. This expectation is reflected in the year-end adjustment.

(4) During the first few days of the next period, all invoices are paid in accordance with expectations.

17. The Harding Company was formed on July 1. It decided to use the net price method of recording purchases and to close the books semiannually on June 30 and

December 31. During the first 6 months of operations, merchandise with a gross invoice price of $57,000 was purchased. All suppliers offered terms of 2/10, n/30. The company returned $3,000 (gross price) of goods as being unsatisfactory, and checks for $48,775 were sent to suppliers in settlement of bills with a gross amount of $49,700. Discounts are still available on all bills outstanding at December 31, except one for $400, gross. The inventory of merchandise at December 31 is $9,210.

Journalize the foregoing on the books of the Harding Company, including entries to recognize cost of goods sold.

18. Indicate the position of each of the following accounts in the financial statements by the use of the following key.

(**1**) Revenue section of the income statement.

(**2**) Expense section of the income statement.

(**3**) Asset section of the balance sheet.

(**4**) Liability section of the balance sheet.

Not all the accounts would be found on one set of books. Place an **X** after the appropriate number if the account is a contra, that is, to be deducted from some other account on the financial statements.

a. Purchase Discounts Lost.

b. Allowance for Sales Discounts.

c. Purchase Returns.

d. Sales Tax on Purchases.

e. Freight-In (on Purchases).

f. Purchase Discounts.

g. Sales Allowances.

h. Federal Excise Tax Payable.

i. Customers' Deposits.

j. Merchandise Purchases.

k. Merchandise Purchase Allowances.

l. Sales Discounts Lapsed.

19. On December 30, 1976, merchandise amounting to $750 was received by the Perrin Company and was included in its December 31 inventory. The invoice was not received until January 4, at which time the acquisition was recorded. Assume that the error was not discovered by the firm when the invoice was received, and that Perrin Company uses the periodic inventory method. Indicate the effect (overstatement, understatement, none) on each of the following amounts: (**1**) Inventory, 12/31/76; (**2**) Inventory, 12/31/77; (**3**) Cost of goods sold, 1976; (**4**) Cost of goods sold, 1977; (**5**) Net income, 1976; (**6**) Net income, 1977; (**7**) Accounts payable, 12/31/76; (**8**) Accounts payable, 12/31/77; (**9**) Retained earnings, 12/31/76; (**10**) Retained earnings, 12/31/77.

20. Refer to the LIFO versus FIFO illustration for the General Electric Company given in Exhibit 9.7. The beginning inventory for the year preceding the one discussed in the chapter was $1,759.0 million computed under a LIFO flow assumption and would have been $2,063.1 million computed under a FIFO flow assumption.

a. Pretax income for this preceding year was reported under a LIFO flow assumption at about $1 billion. What would that pretax income have been if a FIFO flow assumption had been used?

b. Verify the statement in the text that income did not increase from the previous year under a LIFO flow assumption but would have increased about 20 percent under a FIFO flow assumption.

21. The inventory at September 1 and the purchases during September of a certain item of raw material were as follows:

9/1	Inventory	1,000 lbs.		$ 4,000
9/5	Purchased	3,000 lbs.		13,500
9/14	Purchased	3,500 lbs.		17,500
9/27	Purchased	3,000 lbs.		16,500
9/29	Purchased	1,000 lbs.		6,000

The inventory at September 30 is 1,800 pounds.

Compute the cost of the inventory on September 30 under each of the following cost flow assumptions:
  a. FIFO.
  b. Weighted average.
  c. LIFO.

22. This problem tries to make clear the difference between the impact on financial statements of the choice between a FIFO and a LIFO flow assumption. Take twelve pieces of paper and mark each one with a number between 1 and 12 inclusive. Sort the pieces of paper into a pile with the numbers in consecutive order facing up, so that number 1 is on top and number 12 is on bottom. These twelve pieces of paper are to represent twelve identical units of merchandise purchased at prices increasing from $1 to $12. Assume that four of the units are purchased each period for three periods, that three units are sold each period, and that the periodic inventory method is used.
  a. Compute the cost of goods sold and ending inventory amounts for each of the three periods under a FIFO flow assumption.
  b. Compute the cost of goods sold and ending inventory amounts for each of the three periods under a LIFO flow assumption.
  c. Re-sort the twelve pieces of paper into decreasing order to represent declining prices for successive purchases. Compute the cost of goods sold and ending inventory amounts for each of the three periods under a FIFO flow assumption.
  d. Repeat **c** using a LIFO flow assumption.
  e. If you are not convinced that the following are all true statements, then repeat parts **a–d** until you are.
    (1) In periods of rising prices, FIFO implies higher reported income than does LIFO.
    (2) In periods of declining prices, LIFO implies higher reported income than does FIFO.
    (3) Under FIFO, current prices are reported on the balance sheet and old prices are reported on the income statement.
    (4) Under LIFO, current prices are reported on the income statement and very old prices are reported on the balance sheet.
    (5) The difference between FIFO and LIFO balance sheet amounts for inventory at the end of each period after the first one is larger than the differences between FIFO and LIFO reported net income for each period after the first one.

23. The following information concerning an item of raw materials is available:

Nov. 2	Inventory	4,000 lbs. @ $5
9	Issued	3,000 lbs.
16	Purchased	7,000 lbs. @ $6
23	Issued	3,000 lbs.
30	Issued	3,000 lbs.

Compute the value of the inventory at November 30 and the cost of withdrawals during the month, assuming that the company uses periodic inventory records under the following cost-flow assumptions: (**1**) FIFO, (**2**) weighted-average, and (**3**) LIFO. Carry unit-cost calculations to the nearest tenth of a cent.

24. The Central Supply Company has in its inventory on May 1 three units of Item K, all purchased on the same date at a price of $60 per unit. Information relative to Item K is as follows:

DATE	EXPLANATION	UNITS	UNIT COST	TAG NUMBER
May 1	Inventory	3	$60	K—515,516,517
3	Purchase	2	65	K—518,519
12	Sale	3		K—515,518,519
19	Purchase	2	70	K—520,521
25	Sale	1		K—516

Compute the cost of units sold in accordance with the following:
a. Specific identification of units sold.
b. FIFO cost-flow assumption and periodic inventory method.
c. LIFO cost-flow assumption and periodic inventory method.
d. Weighted-average cost-flow assumption and perpetual inventory method.
e. Weighted-average cost-flow assumption and periodic inventory method.

25. The Salem Company began business on January 1, 1975. The information concerning merchandise inventories, purchases, and sales for the first 3 years of operations is as follows:

	1975	1976	1977
Sales	$300,000	$330,000	$450,000
Purchases	280,000	260,000	350,000
Inventories, Dec. 31:			
At cost	80,000	95,000	95,000
At market	75,000	80,000	100,000

a. Compute the gross margin on sales (sales minus cost of goods sold) for each year (**1**) using the lower-of-cost-or-market basis in valuing inventories and (**2**) using the acquisition-cost basis.
b. Indicate your conclusion whether the lower-of-cost-or-market basis of valuing inventories is "conservative" in all situations where it is applied.

26. The Burch Corporation began a merchandising business on January 1, 1975. It acquired merchandise costing $100,000 in 1975, $125,000 in 1976, and $135,000 in 1977. Information about Burch Corporation's inventory, as it would appear on the balance sheet under different inventory methods, is shown below:

Burch Corporation
Inventory Valuations for Balance Sheet
Under Various Assumptions

DATE	LIFO COST	FIFO COST	LOWER OF FIFO COST OR MARKET
12/31/75	$40,800	$40,000	$37,000
12/31/76	36,400	36,000	34,000
12/31/77	41,200	44,000	44,000

In answering each of the following questions, indicate how the answer is deduced. Keep in mind for parts **c–f** the form of the equation relating gross profits and inventories that says, for comparing any inventory Method A against any other Method B:[6]

$$\text{Income}_{\text{Method A}} - \text{Income}_{\text{Method B}} = \text{Increase in Inventory}_{\text{Method A}}$$
$$- \text{Increase in Inventory}_{\text{Method B}}$$

a. Did prices go up or down in 1975?
b. Did prices go up or down in 1977?
c. Which inventory method would show the highest income for 1975?
d. Which inventory method would show the highest income for 1976?

---

[6] Some readers may prefer an algebraic derivation of this result. In symbols, the inventory equation says that

$$BI + P - EI = COGS. \qquad (1)$$

The equation relating income from sales to cost of goods sold is

$$\text{Margin} = \text{Revenues} - \text{Cost of Goods Sold}$$

or, in symbols,

$$M = R - COGS. \qquad (2)$$

Substituting from equation (**1**) into equation (**2**) yields

$$M = R - (BI + P - EI). \qquad (3)$$

Since purchases and revenues are what they are independent of the flow assumption, the difference between FIFO and LIFO margins, denoted ΔM, is

$$\Delta M = \Delta R - (\Delta BI + \Delta P - \Delta EI)$$
$$= 0 - (\Delta BI + 0 - \Delta EI)$$
$$= \Delta EI - \Delta BI. \qquad (4)$$

Equation (**4**) says that the difference between FIFO and LIFO margins on sales during a period is equal to the difference between the increases of FIFO and LIFO inventory amounts. The difference between FIFO and LIFO margins is reflected in the difference between FIFO and LIFO net incomes.

e. Which inventory method would show the lowest income for all three years combined?

f. For 1977, how much higher or lower would income be on the FIFO cost basis than it would be on the lower-of-cost-or-market basis?

g. The notes to the financial statements in a recent annual report of the Westinghouse Electric Corporation contain the following statement. "The excess of current cost [of inventories] . . . over the cost of inventories valued on the LIFO basis was $230 million at [year end] and $163 million at [the beginning of the year]." How much higher or lower would Westinghouse's pretax reported income have been if its inventories had been valued at current costs, rather than with a LIFO cost-flow assumption? Westinghouse reported $28 million net income for the year and tax expense equal to 48 percent of pretax income. By what percentage would Westinghouse's net income increase if a FIFO flow assumption had been used?

27. The Sanlex Company started the year with no inventories on hand. It manufactured two batches of inventory which were identical, except that the variable costs of producing the first batch were $120 and the variable costs of producing the second batch were $200 because of rising prices. By the end of the year, Sanlex Company had sold three-fourths of the first batch for $300 and none of the second batch. The ending inventory had a market value of $305. Total fixed manufacturing costs for the year were $160. Under the absorption costing procedure, $100 of fixed manufacturing costs allocated to units produced remained in inventory at the close of the year. Selling and administrative expenses for the year were $30.

Prepare a statement of pretax income for the Sanlex Company for the year under each of the following sets of assumptions.

a. FIFO, acquisition-cost basis
b. LIFO, acquisition-cost basis
c. FIFO, lower-of-cost-or-market basis.

28. The Wilson Company sells chemical compounds made from expensium. The company has used a LIFO inventory-flow assumption for many years. The inventory of expensium on January 1, 1970, consisted of 2,000 pounds from the inventory bought in 1966 for $30 a pound. The following schedule shows purchases and physical ending inventories of expensium for the years 1970 through 1975.

YEAR	PURCHASE PRICE PER POUND DURING YEAR	COST OF UNITS PURCHASED	END-OF-YEAR INVENTORY IN POUNDS
1970	$48	$240,000	2,000
1971	46	296,000	2,200
1972	48	368,000	3,000
1973	50	384,000	3,600
1974	50	352,000	2,600
1975	52	448,000	4,000

Because of temporary scarcities, expensium is expected to cost $62 per pound during 1976, but to fall back to $52 per pound in 1977. Sales for 1976 are expected to require 7,000 pounds of expensium. The purchasing agent suggests that the inventory of expensium be allowed to decrease from 4,000 to 600 pounds by the end of 1976 and to be replenished to the desired level of 4,000 pounds early in 1977.

The controller argues that such a policy would be foolish. If inventories are allowed to decrease to 600 pounds, then the cost of goods sold will be extraordinarily low (because the older LIFO purchases will be consumed) and income taxes will be extraordinarily high. Furthermore, he points out that the diseconomies of smaller orders during 1976, as required by the purchasing agent's plan, would lead to about $1,000 of extra costs through lost quantity discounts. He suggests that 1976 purchases should be planned to maintain an end-of-year inventory of 4,000 pounds.

Assume that sales for 1976 do require 7,000 pounds of expensium, that the prices for 1976 and 1977 are as forecast, and that the income tax rate for Wilson Company is 40 percent.

Calculate the cost of goods sold and end-of-year LIFO inventory:

a. For each of the years 1970 through 1975.

b. For 1976, assuming that the controller's advice is followed so that inventory at the end of 1976 is 4,000 pounds.

c. For 1976, assuming that the purchasing agent's advice is followed and inventory at the end of 1976 is 600 pounds.

Assuming that the controller's, rather than the purchasing agent's, advice is followed, calculate:

d. The tax savings for 1976.

e. The extra cash costs for inventory.

f. Using the results derived so far, what should Wilson Company do?

g. Would your advice be different if Wilson Company used a FIFO inventory-flow assumption?

29. The Harrison Corporation was organized and began retailing operations on January 1, 1976. Purchases of merchandise inventory during 1976 and 1977 were as follows:

	QUANTITY PURCHASED	UNIT PRICE	ACQUISITION COST
1/10/76	100,000	$ .10	$10,000
6/30/76	40,000	.15	6,000
10/20/76	20,000	.16	3,200
Total 1976	160,000		$19,200
2/18/77	30,000	$ .18	$ 5,400
7/15/77	10,000	.20	2,000
12/15/77	50,000	.22	11,000
Total 1977	90,000		$18,400

The number of units sold during 1976 and 1977 was 90,000 units and 110,000 units, respectively. Harrison Corporation uses a periodic inventory method.

a. Determine the cost of goods sold during 1976 under the FIFO cost-flow assumption.

b. Determine the cost of goods sold during 1976 under the LIFO cost-flow assumption.

c. Determine the cost of goods sold during 1976 under the weighted-average cost-flow assumption.

d. Determine the cost of goods sold during 1977 under the FIFO cost-flow assumption.

e. Determine the cost of goods sold during 1977 under the LIFO cost-flow assumption.

f. Determine the cost of goods sold during 1977 under the weighted-average cost-flow assumption.

g. For the 2 years, 1976 and 1977, taken as a whole, will FIFO or LIFO result in reporting the largest net income? What is the difference in net income for the 2-year period under FIFO as compared to LIFO? Assume an income tax rate of 40 percent for both years.

h. Which method, LIFO or FIFO, should Harrison Corporation probably prefer and why?

30. (This problem should not be attempted until the previous one has been done.) Assume the same data for the Harrison Corporation as given in the previous problem and that the current cost of a unit of merchandise inventory is $.17 on December 31, 1976, and $.22 on December 31, 1977.

a. Compute the unrealized holding gain as of December 31, 1976, under each of the three cost-flow assumptions.

b. Compute the unrealized holding gain as of December 31, 1977, under each of the three cost-flow assumptions.

c. Demonstrate that over the 2-year period, the economic profits of the Harrison Corporation are independent of the cost-flow assumption.

Long-Lived Assets and Amortization Expense

In everyday language, the term *asset* means something good, something that is beneficial and that will provide benefits in the future. This definition of asset applies in accounting as well. Assets are either short-lived or long-lived. A business acquires a short-lived asset, such as cash, in one period and can use up its benefits in the same period. A long-lived asset is different: to enjoy all its benefits, the owner must use it for many years. In these cases, the accountant must apportion, or allocate, the cost of the asset over the several accounting periods of benefit. This general procedure is called *amortization*. Amortization of *plant assets*, which include the fixtures, machinery, equipment, and physical structures of a business, is called *depreciation*.

In addition to its plant assets, a company such as Gulf Oil has other long-lived assets. Oil companies own natural gas and oil wells. These natural resources are called *wasting assets*. Oil wells, coal mines, uranium deposits, and other natural resources are eventually used up, and amortization of the cost of these wasting assets is called *depletion*.

Businesses may also acquire nonphysical assets. These include *intangible assets* and, while there are many examples of them, some of the best-known ones are probably close at hand. A local operator may pay several thousand dollars to acquire a McDonald's or Kentucky Fried Chicken franchise. Such franchises do not generally have a perpetual life, so the accountant must amortize their costs.

Most of this chapter is devoted to depreciation because plant assets are the most common long-lived assets, and depreciation problems are typical of almost all other amortization problems.

The problems of plant asset valuation and depreciation expense measurement can be conveniently separated into the consideration of four separate kinds of events:

1. recording the acquisition of the asset
2. recording its use over time
3. recording adjustments for changes in capacity or efficiency and for repairs or improvements
4. recording its retirement or other disposal.

■ ACQUISITION OF PLANT ASSETS

The cost of a plant asset includes all charges necessary to prepare it for rendering services, and it is often recorded in a series of transactions. Thus, the cost of a piece of equipment will be the sum of the entries to recognize the invoice price (less any discounts), transportation costs, installation charges, and any other costs necessary before the equipment is ready for use. When a firm constructs or fabricates its own buildings or equipment, many entries to record the labor, material, and overhead costs will normally be required before the total cost is recorded on the books. When a firm acquires a new asset in exchange for an old one, such as in a trade-in transaction or a bartered transaction, the fair market value of the assets given up plus any cash disbursed in the transaction should be used as the cost of the new asset. Trade-in transactions are discussed later in this chapter.

Repair and maintenance *costs* will almost certainly occur during the life of the asset. These costs are required to *maintain* the service level anticipated from the asset and are treated as expenses of the period. Once an asset is in service, certain costs are incurred to *improve* the asset and should be "capitalized" or added to its cost. Improvements are defined as those costs that extend the life of the asset, increase the asset's output, or reduce the cost of operating the asset. It is often difficult to decide whether a particular expenditure is a repair to be treated as a period expense or as an improvement to be treated as an asset. The line between maintaining service and improving or extending it is not a distinct one. Some expenditures seem to meet the criteria to be either a repair expense or an improvement cost. There is frequent disagreement between Internal Revenue Service and taxpayers, as well as among accountants, over this question in specific situations.

■ PLANT ASSETS AND DEPRECIATION: FUNDAMENTAL CONCEPTS

Plant Assets

The terms *plant assets* and *fixed assets* are often used interchangeably. They refer to long-lived assets used in the operations of trading, service, and manufacturing enterprises, and include land, buildings, machinery, and equipment. The ordinary usage of the terms *plant assets* and *fixed assets* often does not adequately encompass the class of long-lived assets that includes all land, buildings, machinery, and equipment. *Plant assets* is sometimes used too narrowly to mean only items in a factory or plant. *Fixed assets* is sometimes used too narrowly to mean only items such as land and buildings which are immovable and tend to have very long service lives.

Most plant assets except land can be kept intact and in usable operating condition for more than a year, but eventually they must be retired from service. The central purpose of the depreciation accounting process is to allocate the cost of these assets to the periods of their use in a reasonable and orderly fashion.

Depreciation

Through a process of evolution in accounting terminology, the use of the term depreciation is restricted to the expiration of the cost of plant assets. Although in popular speech *depreciation* is often associated with a decline in market value of any kind of property, special terms have been developed in accounting usage for the decline in recorded costs of assets other than plant assets. As was suggested earlier, *depletion* refers to the allocation of costs of wasting assets, or natural resources, over time. The general term *amortization* is used for the process of allocating the costs of intangibles over time. On the other hand, merchandise and materials may become shopworn or obsolete, but the accounting recognition of this fact is described as an "inventory adjustment" rather than as depreciation.

It is useful to think of the cost of an asset with a limited life as the price paid for a series of future services—a purchase of so many hours or other units of service. When deciding to purchase a building or machine, the purchaser need not make elaborate calculations to arrive at the present value of a series of precisely appraised future benefits, but the purchaser must at least roughly approximate those procedures. One machine is preferred because its cost of operation per hour or unit of product will be less than another machine. It would be irrational to purchase an asset if the present value of the services expected to be received from it were known to be less than the required investment.

The investment in a depreciating asset is the price paid for a series of future services. The asset account may well be considered as a prepayment, similar in many respects to prepaid rent or insurance—a payment in advance for services to be received. As the asset is used in each accounting period, an appropriate portion of the investment in the asset is treated as the cost of the service received and is treated as an expense of the period or as part of the cost of goods produced during the period.

The Causes of Depreciation

The causes of depreciation are the causes of decline in an asset's service and of its ultimate retirement. Unless the asset must eventually be retired from its planned use, there is no depreciation. The services or benefits provided by land do not ordinarily diminish over time, so land is not depreciated. Many factors lead to the retirement of assets from service, but the causes of decline in service potential can be classified as either *physical* or *functional*. The physical factors include such things as ordinary wear and tear from use, chemical action such as rust or electrolysis, and the effects of wind and rain. The most important functional or nonphysical cause is *obsolescence*. Inventions, for example, may result in new equipment, the use of which reduces the unit cost of production to the point where continued operation of the old asset is not economical, even though it may be relatively unimpaired physically. Retail stores often replace display cases and store fronts long before they are worn out in order to keep the appearance of the store as attractive as their competitors'. Changed economic conditions may also become functional causes of depreciation, such as when an old airport becomes inadequate and must be abandoned, and a new, larger one built to meet the requirements of heavier traffic, or when an increase in the cost of gasoline causes a reduction in demand for automobile products, which results in a reduced scale of operations in automobile manufacturing.

Identifying the specific causes of depreciation is not essential for considering the fundamental problem of its measurement. It is enough to know that almost any physical asset will eventually have to be retired from service and that in some cases the retirement will become necessary at a time when physical deterioration is negligible. The specific causes become important only when the attempt is made to predict the useful life of an asset.

Depreciation as a Decline in Value

Depreciation is frequently characterized as a decline in the market value of assets. Such an interpretation is fundamentally sound when applied to the entire service life—there certainly is a decline in the value of an asset from the time it is acquired until it is retired from service. However, a decline in asset values is an unsatisfactory description of the charge made to the operations of each accounting period. One incorrect inference from such a description is that if, in a given period of time, there has been an increase in the value of an asset, such as an increase arising from increasing prices for the asset, then there has been no depreciation during that period. Rather, there have been two partially offsetting processes: (1) a holding gain on the asset, which usually is not recognized in historical cost-based accounting, and (2) depreciation of the asset's historical cost. (A holding gain is an increase in the market price of an asset since the time the asset was acquired. These issues are discussed further in Chapter Fourteen.)

Further, the word *value* has so many uses and connotations that it is not a serviceable term for a definition. (The noun *value* should seldom be used in accounting without a qualifying adjective.) If depreciation is defined as a decline in value and the undepreciated balance of an asset account as a "present" value, it is usually necessary to explain that under generally accepted accounting principles, it is value to the going concern based on historical cost, not on selling price, not on second-hand value, nor on replacement cost. The word *value* is not entirely inappropriate in defining depreciation, but it is not helpful in isolating its essence.

Summary of Depreciation Concepts

Depreciation is a process of cost allocation, not one of valuation. This chapter discusses the problems of *allocating* assets' costs to the periods of benefits. Chapter Fourteen discusses the problems of *valuation* for assets. A depreciation problem will exist whenever (1) capital is invested in services to be rendered by a plant asset, and (2) at some reasonably predictable date in the future the asset will have to be retired from service with a residual value less than its cost because of a decline in service potential. The problem is to interpret and account satisfactorily for this diminution of capital investment.

Note especially that replacing the asset is *not* essential to the existence of depreciation. Depreciation is the expiration or disappearance of investment from the time the plant asset is put into use until the time it is retired from service. Whether or not the asset is replaced is completely independent of the amount or treatment of its depreciation.

■ DEPRECIATION ACCOUNTING PROBLEMS

There are three principal accounting problems in allocating the cost of an asset over time:

1. calculating and recording the depreciation charge which is made to operations of each accounting period for its share of the total cost of the asset
2. revising the depreciation charge during the life of the asset because of changes in the estimated useful life or salvage value of the asset and recording the effects of the revised estimates
3. handling the retirement of the asset from service.

Calculating the Periodic Charge

Determining the amount of the periodic charge for depreciation is not an exact process. The cost of the plant asset is a *joint cost* of the several benefited periods. That is, each of the periods of the asset's use benefits from its services. There is usually no logically correct way to allocate a joint cost. The depreciation process seeks to assign reasonable periodic charges that reflect a careful and systematic method of calculation.

Whenever it is feasible to do so, depreciation should be computed for individual items such as a single building, machine, or truck. Where many similar items are in use and each one has a relatively small cost, individual calculations may be impractical and the depreciation charge is usually calculated for the group as a whole. Furniture and fixtures, tools, and telephone poles are examples of assets that are usually depreciated in groups. Group depreciation techniques are treated in advanced financial accounting courses. The basic principles of depreciating individual items discussed here apply in a similar manner, however, to group depreciation situations.

The calculation of the periodic depreciation charge is based upon

1. the acquisition cost of the depreciating asset
2. the estimate of its net residual value
3. the estimate of its useful service life
4. the pattern of expiration of its services.

Recording the acquisition of assets was discussed in the first section of this chapter.

Estimating Net Residual Value   The total depreciation of an asset over its life is the difference between its cost and the amount which can be received for the asset when it is retired from service. The amount received on retirement is described as the asset's *net residual value* or *salvage value*, and it is necessary to estimate it in making the depreciation calculation. (The terms *net residual value* and *salvage value* refer to estimated proceeds on disposition of an asset less all transaction and removal costs. Salvage value must be an estimate at any time before the asset is retired. Hence, before retirement, the terms *salvage value* and *estimated salvage value* are synonymous.)

For buildings, common practice assumes a zero salvage value. This treatment rests on the assumption that the cost to be incurred in tearing down the building will approximate the sales value of the scrap materials recovered. For other assets, however, the salvage value may be substantial, and should be estimated and taken into account in making the periodic depreciation charge. This is particularly true where it is planned to retire an asset which is worth something to another user. For example, a car rental firm will replace its automobiles at a time when other owners can use the cars for several years more. The rental firm will be able to realize a substantial part of acquisition cost from the sale of used cars. Past experience usually forms the best basis for estimating salvage value.

Estimates of salvage value are necessarily subjective. Disputes over estimated salvage value have led to many disagreements between Internal Revenue Service agents and taxpayers. Partly to reduce such controversy, the Internal Revenue Code was amended to provide that, starting in 1962, salvage value of up to 10 percent of the cost of assets such as machinery and equipment may be ignored in depreciation calculations for tax purposes. The same rule is frequently followed in making calculations for financial records; however, the entire salvage value is to be taken into account for working problems in this text unless explicit contrary instructions are given.

Estimating Service Life   The third factor in the depreciation calculation is the estimated service life of the asset. In making the estimate, both the physical and the functional causes of depreciation must be taken into account. Experience with similar assets, corrected for differences in the planned intensity of use or alterations in maintenance policy, is usually the best guide for this estimate.

In 1962, the Internal Revenue Service published guidelines of suggested useful lives. The guidelines provide estimated useful lives based on categories of assets by broad classes. Examples of guideline lives are as follows:

Warehouses	60 years
Factory Buildings	45 years
Land Improvements	20 years
Office Furniture, Fixtures, Machines, and Equipment	10 years
Heavy Trucks	6 years
Light Trucks	4 years
Automobiles	3 years

In 1971, the Internal Revenue Service ruled that the guideline lives need not be strictly followed. Rather, the IRS said that taxpayers may use a life anywhere in the range from 80 percent to 120 percent of the guideline life. Such ranges are called *asset depreciation ranges.*

Despite the abundance of data from experience, estimation of service lives is the most difficult task in the entire depreciation calculation. Making proper allowances for obsolescence is particularly difficult because obsolescence results for the most part from forces external to the firm. Unless the estimator possesses prophetic powers, it is likely that the estimates will prove to be incorrect. For this reason, it is wise to reconsider the estimates of useful service life of important assets or groups of assets every few years.

Pattern of Expiration of Services   Once the cost has been determined and both salvage value and service life have been estimated, the total of depreciation charges for the whole life of the asset has been determined. There then remains the problem of selecting the pattern for allocating those charges to the specific years of the life. There are five basic patterns for such allocations. They are labeled **E, A, S, D,** and **N** in Figure 10.1.

FIGURE 10–1
PATTERNS OF DEPRECIATION: BOOK VALUE OVER LIFE OF ASSET

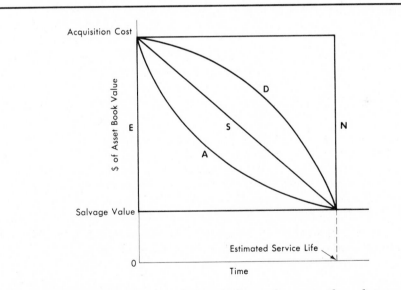

If salvage value is assumed to be zero, then, of course, the salvage value line coincides with the horizontal axis and the entire cost will be depreciated.

The patterns are discussed in more detail in the next section. **A** represents *accelerated* depreciation; **S,** *uniform* or *straight-line* depreciation; **D,** *decelerated* depreciation. (Understanding the term "accelerated" and "decelerated" is easier if you compare the depreciation charges in the early years to straight-line depreciation.) Patterns **A** and **S** are much more commonly used than **D**. Pattern **E**, of course, represents immediate expensing of the item. All costs are charged to the period when the cost is incurred. This pattern is discussed further in the section on intangibles. Pattern **N** represents the situation, such as for land, where there are no periodic amortization charges. The asset is shown on the books at acquisition cost until it is sold or otherwise retired.

■ DEPRECIATION METHODS

All depreciation methods should aim to allocate, reasonably and systematically, the cost of the asset minus its estimated salvage value, to the periods in which it is used. The methods discussed here are as follows:

1. straight-line (time) method
2. production or use (straight-line use) method
3. declining-balance methods
4. sum-of-the-years'-digits method.

When a depreciable asset is acquired or retired during an accounting period, depreciation should be calculated only for that portion of the period during which the asset is used.

The Straight-Line (Time) Method

The allocation method that is used most commonly for financial reporting is known as the straight-line method, represented by Pattern **S** in Figure 10.1. It was used almost exclusively until 1954, when the income tax laws were revised specifically to recognize other depreciation methods. Under the straight-line method, the cost of the asset, less any estimated salvage value, is divided by the number of years of its expected life in order to arrive at the annual depreciation:

$$\text{Annual Depreciation} = \frac{\text{Cost Less Estimated Salvage Value}}{\text{Estimated Life in Years}}.$$

For example, if a machine costs \$12,000, has an estimated salvage value of \$1,000, and has an expected useful life of 5 years, the annual depreciation will be \$2,200 [= (\$12,000 − \$1,000)/5]. Occasionally, instead of a positive salvage value, the cost of removal exceeds the gross proceeds on disposition. This excess of removal costs over gross proceeds should be added to the cost of the asset in making the calculation. Thus, if a building is constructed for \$37,000, and it is estimated that it will cost \$5,000 to remove it at the end of 25 years, the annual depreciation would be \$1,680 [= (\$37,000 + \$5,000)/25].

A common practice, especially when the salvage value is assumed to be zero, is to apply an appropriate percentage, known as the depreciation rate, to the *acquisition cost* in order to calculate the annual charge. The rate is chosen so that it will charge the entire acquisition cost off over the estimated life. A rate of 10 percent will write off the cost of an asset in 10 years, a rate of 25 percent in 4 years, and so on. The building referred to in the preceding paragraph would be depreciated at the rate of 4 percent of acquisition plus removal costs for 25 years.

Production or Use (Straight-Line Use) Method

Although the straight-line (time) method is widely used, it is justifiable only because it frequently corresponds roughly to the amount of use which is made of the asset and because it requires only simple arithmetic. Many assets are not, however, used uniformly over time. Manufacturing plants often have seasonal variations in operation so that certain machines may be used 24 hours a day at one time and 8 hours or less a day at another time of year. Trucks are not likely to receive the same amount of use in each month or year of their lives. The straight-line (time) method of depreciation may, then, result in an illogical depreciation charge for such assets.

When the rate of usage varies from period to period and when the total usage of an asset over its life can be reliably estimated, a depreciation charge based on actual usage during the period may be justified. For example, depreciation of a truck for a period could be based upon the ratio of miles driven during the period to total miles expected to be driven over the truck's life. The depreciation cost per unit (mile) of use is

$$\text{Depreciation Cost per Unit} = \frac{\text{Cost Less Estimated Salvage Value}}{\text{Estimated Number of Units}}.$$

The arithmetic of the calculation is simple, but it is necessary to keep a special record of the units of opertaion of each asset or of the number of units produced. If a truck which costs $9,000 and has an estimated salvage value of $600 is expected to be driven 100,000 miles before it is retired from service, then the depreciation per mile is $.084 [= ($9,000 − $600)/100,000]. Then, if the truck is operated 1,000 miles in a given month, the depreciation charge for the month is 1,000 × $.084 = $84.

Accelerated Depreciation

The efficiency and earning power of many plant assets decline as the assets grow older. Cutting tools lose some of their precision; printing presses are shut down more frequently for repairs; rentals in an old office building are lower than those in its gleaming new neighbor. These examples show the tendency of some assets to provide more and better services in the early years of their lives while requiring increasing amounts of maintenance as they grow older. Where this is the case, methods that recognize progressively smaller depreciation charges in successive periods may be justified. Such methods are referred to as *accelerated depreciation* methods because the depreciation charges in the early years of the asset's life are larger than in later years. Accelerated depreciation leads to a pattern such as **A** in Figure 10.1.

For convenience, the depreciation charges for a year, however they are determined, are allocated on a straight-line basis to periods *within* the year.

Declining-Balance Methods

The *declining-balance method* is one accelerated depreciation method. In this method, the depreciation charge is calculated by multiplying the *net book value* of the asset (cost less accumulated depreciation) at the start of each period by a fixed rate. The estimated salvage value is not subtracted from the cost in making the depreciation calculation, as is the case with other depreciation methods. Since the net book value declines from period to period, the result is a declining periodic charge for depreciation throughout the life of the asset.[1] The rate most commonly used is the maximum one permitted for income tax purposes, which ordinarily is twice the straight-line rate. When this rate is used, the method is called the *double-declining-balance* method. Thus, for example, an asset with an estimated 10-year life would be depreciated at a rate of 20 percent ($= 1/10 \times 2$) per year of the book value at the start of the year. To take another example, if a machine costing $5,000 is purchased on January 1, 1976, and it is estimated to have a 5-year life, a 40 percent ($= \frac{1}{5} \times 2$) rate would be used. The depreciation charges would be calculated as shown in Exhibit 10.1.

The undepreciated cost as of December 31, 1980, is $389 ($= \$648 - \$259$), but is not likely to equal the salvage value at that time. The problem is usually anticipated and solved by adjusting the depreciation charge in one or more of the later years. Under income tax rules, the asset cannot be depreciated below salvage value if that value is large; if the salvage value is small, the undepreciated cost minus salvage value can be written off in straight-line fashion over the last years of life. Refer again to Exhibit 10.1. If the asset had an estimated salvage value of $200, the depreciation charges in 1979 and 1980 could be $440 a year (net book value at January 1, 1979, of $1,080 less the estimated salvage value of $200 divided by the 2 years of remaining life). In general, the switch to the straight-line method for the remaining life is made when the switch will produce a greater depreciation charge than the one resulting from continued application of the double-declining-balance method. For assets with zero scrap value, this ordinarily occurs just after the midpoint of the service life.

---

[1] Under the declining-balance method, as strictly applied, the fixed depreciation rate used is one that will charge the cost less salvage value of the asset over its service life. The formula for computing the rate is

$$\text{Depreciation Rate} = 1 - \sqrt[n]{\frac{s}{c}} = 1 - \left(\frac{s}{c}\right)^{1/n}.$$

In this formula $n =$ estimated periods of service life, $s =$ estimated salvage value, and $c =$ cost.

Estimates of salvage value have a profound effect upon the rate. Unless a positive salvage value is assumed, the rate is 100 percent—that is, all depreciation is charged in the first period. For an asset costing $10,000, with an estimated life of 5 years, the depreciation rate is 40 percent per period if salvage value is $778, but it is 60 percent per period if salvage value is $102.

The effect of small changes in salvage value on the rate and the seeming mathematical complexity of the formula have resulted in widespread use of approximations or rules of thumb instead of the formula.

EXHIBIT 10.1
Double-Declining-Balance Depreciation

Year	Acquisition Cost (1)	Accumulated Depreciation as of Jan. 1 (2)	Net Book Value as of Jan. 1 (1) − (2) (3)	Depreciation Rate (4)	Depreciation Charge for the Year = (3) × (4) (5)
1976	$5,000	$ 0	$5,000	.40	$2,000
1977	5,000	2,000	3,000	.40	1,200
1978	5,000	3,200	1,800	.40	720
1979	5,000	3,920	1,080	.40	432
1980	5,000	4,352	648	.40	259
1981	5,000	4,611	389	—	—

Sum-of-the-Years'-Digits Method

The other accelerated depreciation method mentioned in the Internal Revenue Code is the *sum-of-the-years'-digits method*. Under this method, the depreciation charge is determined by applying a fraction, which diminishes from year to year, to the cost less estimated salvage value of the asset. The numerator of the fraction is the number of periods of remaining life at the beginning of the year for which the depreciation calculation is being made. The denominator is the sum of all such numbers, one for each year of estimated service life; if the service life is n years, the denominator for the sum-of-the-years'-digits method[2] is $1 + 2 + \cdots + n$.

The method is illustrated by again considering an asset costing $5,000 purchased January 1, 1976, which has an estimated service life of 5 years and an estimated salvage value of $200. The sum of the years' digits[3] is 15 (= 1 + 2 + 3 + 4 + 5). The depreciation charges are calculated in Exhibit 10.2.

Compound Interest Methods

Compound interest methods are not widely used in financial accounting, but they are theoretically sound for certain management decisions. For plant assets producing equal annual net inflows of cash, compound interest depreciation leads to a pattern like **D** in Figure 10.1. Compound interest methods are not illustrated in this text.

---

[2] A useful formula for summing the numbers 1 through n is $1 + 2 + \cdots + n = n(n + 1)/2$.
[3] That is, according to the formula given in the previous footnote. $1 + 2 + 3 + 4 + 5 = 5 \times 6/2 = 15$.

EXHIBIT 10.2
Sum-of-the-Years'-Digits Depreciation

Year	Acquisition Cost Less Salvage Value (1)	Remaining Life in Years (2)	Fraction = (2)/15 (3)	Depreciation Charge for the Year = (3) × (1) (4)
1976	$4,800	5	5/15	$1,600
1977	4,800	4	4/15	1,280
1978	4,800	3	3/15	960
1979	4,800	2	2/15	640
1980	4,800	1	1/15	320
				$4,800

Factors to Consider in Choosing the Depreciation Method

To the individual firm, depreciation is a factor in the determination of income reported on the financial statements as well as a deduction from otherwise taxable income on tax returns. The firm need not choose the same depreciation method for both financial and tax reporting purposes. If it chooses different methods for the two purposes, the difference in taxable income requires a reconciliation in the financial statements. This reconciliation leads to a liability for deferred taxes which is discussed in the next chapter.

Financial Reporting   The goal in financial reporting for long-lived assets is to seek a statement of income that realistically measures the expiration of these assets. The only difficulty is that no one knows, in any realistic or logical sense, just what portion of the service potential of a long-lived asset expires in any one period. All that can be said is that financial statements should report depreciation charges based on reasonable estimates of asset expirations. The firm's selection from alternative accounting principles, including the choice of depreciation methods, is discussed more fully in Chapter Fifteen.

Tax Reporting   We are relatively confident about the nature of depreciation for tax purposes. It seems clear that the goal of the firm should be to maximize the present value of the reductions in tax payments from claiming depreciation. When tax rates remain constant over time and are independent of the amount of taxable income, the goal can be characterized by saying that a firm should maximize the present value of the cash savings of depreciation deductions from otherwise taxable income. That is, for tax purposes the asset should be written off as quickly as possible. Of course, a firm can deduct only the acquisition cost, less salvage value, from otherwise taxable income over the life of the asset. Earlier deductions are, however, worth more than later ones because a dollar saved today is worth more than a dollar saved tomorrow, so long as interest rates are positive.

Congress has presented business firms with several permissible alternatives to follow in determining the amount of depreciation to be deducted each year. The firm can choose double-declining-balance, sum-of-the-years'-digits, straight-line, or various combinations of these methods. It seems clear to us that the firm should choose that alternative which meets the general goal of paying the least amount of tax, as late as possible, within the law. (This goal is sometimes called the *least and latest rule*.)

We can put this more strongly by saying that management has an affirmative obligation in a competitive economy to carry on operations so as to minimize all costs—that is, to minimize the present value of those costs over the long run. Failure to minimize costs hinders the attempt of the competitive market economy to allocate resources efficiently. Management's obligation to reduce costs applies to taxes as well as to all other costs, and, except in a highly unusual circumstance, the present value of taxes is minimized by taking depreciation as rapidly as is legally possible. It is clear that either the double-declining-balance or the sum-of-the-years'-digit method will give a more rapid rate of charge-off than the straight-line method. However, the choice between the two accelerated methods depends upon the specific circumstances of the firm. In general, the method that will maximize the present value of the depreciation charges is to start with the double-declining-balance method and to switch to the sum-of-the-years'-digits method sometime during the asset's life. There are, however, some limitations on the kinds of changes in methods a firm can make for income tax purposes. The intricacies of the optimal depreciation method are beyond the scope of an introductory accounting course.[4] All problems in this text that require an accelerated depreciation method specify which method is to be used.

Accounting for Periodic Depreciation

The debit made in the entry to record periodic depreciation is usually either to an expense account or to a production cost account. In a manufacturing concern, the depreciation of factory buildings and equipment is a production cost, a part of the work in process and finished product cost. Depreciation on sales equipment is a selling expense. Depreciation on office equipment is a general or administrative expense. The matching credit for periodic depreciation could logically be made directly to the asset account affected, such as buildings or equipment. While such an entry is sometimes made, it is customary to credit a special contra-asset account so that the acquisition cost of the asset will be left undisturbed and so that the total amount written off through depreciation can be readily observed. The effect, however, is precisely the same as a direct credit to the asset account. We have used Accumulated Depreciation as the title of the account to be credited.

[4] For a complete analysis of these problems, see Clyde P. Stickney and Jeffrey B. Wallace, "A Guide to Increasing the Maximum Available Depreciation Deduction Under the ADR System," *Taxation for Accountants*, July 1975, pp 42-48.

The entry to record periodic depreciation of selling office facilities, a period expense, is:

Depreciation Expense	1,500	
Accumulated Depreciation		1,500

The entry to record periodic depreciation of manufacturing facilities, a product cost, is:

Work in Process Inventory	1,500	
Accumulated Depreciation		1,500

The Depreciation Expense account is closed at the end of the accounting period as a part of the regular closing-entry procedure. The Work in Process Inventory account is an asset. Product costs, such as depreciation on manufacturing facilities, are accumulated in the Work in Process account until the goods being produced are completed and transferred to Finished Goods Inventory. The Accumulated Depreciation account remains open at the end of the period and is shown on the balance sheet as a deduction from the asset account to which it refers. The balance in the Accumulated Depreciation account usually represents the total charges to accounting periods prior to the balance sheet date for the depreciation on assets currently in use. The difference between the balance of the asset account and the balance of its accumulated depreciation account (with possibly an adjustment for salvage value) represents the amount that will presumably be charged to future accounting periods. This difference is called the *book value* of the asset. (Problem **3** at the end of this chapter involves another benefit of recording the asset's cost and its accumulated depreciation separately in the balance sheet accounts.)

■ CHANGES IN PERIODIC DEPRECIATION

The depreciation charge for a particular asset may require changing. The original or previous estimates of useful life (and possibly of salvage value as well) may have been incorrect as judged in the light of new information. To change the depreciation plan because of previous misestimates of useful life or salvage value is a common and desirable accounting practice.

Misestimates of the useful life of an asset may become apparent at any time during its life. It is usually possible to improve the degree of accuracy of the estimates as the time of retirement approaches. If it appears that the misestimate will be relatively minor, an adjustment usually is not made. If the misestimate appears to be material, corrective action must be taken if the effect of the previous estimation error is to be kept at a minimum. The generally accepted procedure for handling this problem is to make no adjustment for the past misestimate, but to spread the undepreciated balance less the revised estimate of salvage value over the new estimate of remaining service life of the asset. A second, and perhaps more logical, possibility is to make an adjustment of past periods' earnings for the misestimate of the past periods, and use the revised rate of depreciation for the remaining portion of the life of the asset. (Adjustments of the past periods' earnings, when allowed, are called *prior-period adjustments*. Prior-period adjustments, discussed in Chapter Twelve, are *not* allowed for changes in estimates for depreciable assets.)

The following data will be used in the discussion of revised estimates. An office machine is purchased on January 1, 1971, for $9,200. It is estimated that the machine will be operated for 20 years with a salvage value of $200. On December 31, 1976, before the books are closed for the year, it is decided that, in view of the evidence then available, a total useful life of 30 years with the same salvage value of $200 would be a more accurate estimate. The depreciation charge for each of the years from 1971 through 1975 under the straight-line method would initially have been $450 [= ($9,200 − $200)/20].

No Change in Depreciation Charges

If the revised estimate of service life were ignored, the original annual depreciation charge of $450 would be continued through 1990. The years 1991 to 2000 would receive no charge to operations for the use of the machine. The Accumulated Depreciation account would remain undisturbed for those years until the machine was retired from service. Thus, during the last 10 years that the machine was in service, no charge for depreciation would be made.

Revise Only Future Depreciation Charges

The accepted procedure for recognizing this substantial increase in service life is to revise the future depreciation so that the correct total will presumably be accumulated in the Accumulated Depreciation account at the end of the revised service life. In our example, the total amount of acquisition cost yet to be depreciated before the 1976 adjustments is $6,750 (= $9,000 − $2,250). The new estimate of the *remaining* life is 25 years, so the new annual depreciation charge is $270 (= $6,750/25). The only change in the accounting procedure is to substitute the new amount of $270 for the former annual depreciation of $450. The depreciation entry on December 31, 1976, and each year thereafter would be:

Depreciation Expense	270	
Accumulated Depreciation		270

This method avoids adjusting retained earnings for the past misestimate.

This generally accepted method can only be defended, however, as an expedient procedure, for it merely offsets misestimates made in past operating charges by creating errors in the other direction for future operating charges.

Revise Past and Future Depreciation Charges

An attempt to correct past misestimates through an adjustment to Retained Earnings and to apply a corrected depreciation rate to the remaining life of the asset is a third possible approach. In this illustration, $2,250 has been charged off for depreciation through the year 1975 under the straight-line method. Based on the revised service life, use of the correct annual depreciation of $300 [= ($9,200 − $200)/30] would have amounted to only $1,500 for the years 1971 to 1975, so that $750 too much depreciation has been recognized during this 5-year period. The entry to correct for the overdepreciation, ignoring income tax effects, would be:

Accumulated Depreciation	750	
Retained Earnings (January 1, 1976)		750

Then, beginning in 1976, the annual depreciation charge would be $300 each year [= ($9,200 − $200)/30]. This procedure is not permitted by generally accepted accounting principles. Changes in estimated useful lives and salvage values are corrected by adjusting only future depreciation charges.[5]

■ RETIREMENT OF ASSETS

When an asset is retired from service, the cost of the asset and the related amount of accumulated depreciation must be removed from the books. As part of this entry, the amount received from the sale or trade-in and the difference between that amount and book value must be recorded. The difference between the proceeds received on retirement and book value is a gain (if positive) or a loss (if negative). Before making the entry to write off the asset and its accumulated depreciation, an entry should be made to bring the depreciation up to date; that is, the depreciation that has occurred between the start of the current accounting period and the date of disposition must be recorded.

To illustrate the retirement of an asset, assume that sales equipment which cost $5,000, was expected to last 4 years, and had an estimated salvage value of $200, is depreciated on a straight-line basis. The equipment is sold 2 years and 7 months after it was acquired. Assume that the date of sale is 3 months after the start of the current accounting period. The depreciation from the start of the accounting period to the date of sale of $300 [= 3/12 × ($5,000 − $200)/4] is recorded:

Depreciation Expense	300	
Accumulated Depreciation		300

The book value of the asset is now its cost less 31 months of straight-line depreciation of $100 per month or $1,900 (= $5,000 − $3,100). The entry to record the retirement of the assets depends on the amount of the selling price.

[5] Opinion No. 9, Accounting Principles Board, AICPA, December 1966; Opinion No. 20, Accounting Principles Board, AICPA, July 1971.

1. Suppose that the equipment were sold for $1,900 cash. The entry to record the sale would be:

Cash	1,900	
Accumulated Depreciation	3,100	
Equipment		5,000

2. Suppose that the equipment were sold for $2,500 cash. The entry to record the sale would be:

Cash	2,500	
Accumulated Depreciation	3,100	
Equipment		5,000
Gain on Retirement of Equipment		600

3. Suppose that the equipment were sold for $1,500. The entry to record the sale would be:

Cash	1,500	
Accumulated Depreciation	3,100	
Loss on Retirement of Equipment	400	
Equipment		5,000

Trade-In Transactions

Instead of selling the asset when it is retired from service, it is far more common for the asset to be traded in on a new unit. This is a particularly common practice for automobiles. The trade-in transaction can best be viewed as a sale of the old asset followed by a purchase of the new asset. The accounting for trade-in transactions in financial reporting and income tax reporting is surprisingly complicated. Most of the details are discussed in more advanced accounting books, but an introduction to the methods is described in the glossary at *trade-in transaction*.

■ DEPRECIATION AND REPAIRS

Depreciation is not the only cost of using a depreciating asset. There will almost always be some repair and maintenance costs during the life of the asset. The repair policy adopted by the business will often affect the depreciation rate. If, for example, machinery, trucks, and other plant assets are checked frequently and repaired as soon as any difficulty develops, such assets will have a longer useful life, and therefore, a lower depreciation rate than otherwise. The more commonly used estimates of service life and depreciation rates assume that normal repairs will be made during the life of an asset.

Although some major parts of an asset may have shorter lives than the asset as a whole, it is frequently impracticable to account for them with separate depreciation accounts. Thus, the cost of a replacement set of tires is usually charged to repairs expense, although it would be possible to treat the tires as a separate asset subject to depreciation. It may be useful, though, to disaggregate assets for the purposes of depreciation. For example, using single machines instead of a group of machines, or dealing with motors in aircraft separately from the rest of the asset, may be a practicable and logical procedure.

Repairs must be distinguished from improvements and from rehabilitation. *Repairs* are the small adjustments and replacements of parts whose effect does not extend estimated service life materially beyond a year or two. *Improvements* involve adding a part or installing a new part that is substantially better than the old one. The benefit from the improvement will be received for a significant time over the future, but the total useful life of the asset will not ordinarily be extended. *Rehabilitation* involves major construction so that the asset can provide a broader range of services or so that the life of the asset is extended considerably beyond the originally estimated date of retirement.

For example, the replacement of shingles which have blown off a roof would be treated as a repair. The replacement of a shingled roof with a metal roof, or the construction of an addition to the building, would be an improvement. The reconstruction of the interior, the construction of a new front, or the reinforcement of the foundation would in most cases come under the definition of rehabilitation.

Repairs are charged to expense as expenditures are made. Improvements are customarily debited to the asset account. Rehabilitations are merely extensive improvements and are normally treated in the same way as improvements. Rehabilitation could logically be viewed, however, as a replacement of the old asset and entries made just as though the old asset were retired from service and a new one acquired. In any case, the accounting for improvements and rehabilitations results in a debit to the asset account. The total depreciation for the remaining life of the original asset is increased accordingly.

■ WASTING ASSETS AND DEPLETION

The costs of finding natural resources and preparing to extract them from the earth should be capitalized and amortized. Amortization of wasting assets, or natural resources, is called *depletion*. The depletion method most often used is the *units-of-production* method. For example, if $4.5 million in costs are incurred to discover and to prepare pumping equipment for an oil well that contains an estimated 1.5 million barrels of oil, then the costs of $4.5 million would be amortized at the rate of $3 (= $4,500,000/1,500,000) for each barrel of oil removed from the well. The major accounting problem of extractive industries stems from the uncertainty of the benefits from exploratory efforts.

Percentage Depletion Allowances

In some special circumstances, the tax laws permit computation of depletion for measuring taxable income by methods that are not acceptable for financial accounting. In financial accounting, depletion allocates the cost of natural resources to the periods when the resources are used. The "percentage depletion allowances" granted by the U.S. Congress for tax purposes to certain companies exploring for natural resources have little relation to the amortization of costs of developing the natural resources as shown in the financial statements. The percentage depletion allowances are a device instituted by the Congress to make some companies' search for natural resources more attractive than it otherwise would be. The effect of percentage depletion is to allow some firms to deduct on income tax returns over the life of the asset amounts larger than the total of expenses recognized in financial statements. Financial statement expense over the life of the asset must be equal to the acquisition cost of the asset.

◼ INTANGIBLE ASSETS AND AMORTIZATION

Assets can provide future benefits without having physical form. Such assets are called *intangibles*. Examples are research costs, advertising costs, patents, trademarks, and copyrights. The first problem with intangibles is to decide whether the expenditures have future benefits and should be "capitalized" (set up as assets) and amortized over time, or whether they have no future benefits and thus are expenses of the period in which the costs are incurred. In this latter case, the immediate expensing of the asset's cost is represented by Pattern **E** in Figure 10.1. The second problem to solve is how to amortize the costs if they have been capitalized. Amortization of capitalized intangibles is usually recorded using the straight-line method, but other methods can be used if they seem appropriate. This section discusses some common intangibles and the issues involved in deciding whether to expense or to capitalize their costs.

Research and Development

Some of the more common intangible costs are for research and development (R & D). This type of cost is incurred for various reasons. Perhaps the firm seeks to develop a technological or marketing advance in order to have an edge on competition. Or it might wish to explore possible applications of existing technology to design a new product or improve an old one. Other research may be undertaken in response to a government contract, in preparing for bids on potential contracts, or in pursuit of "discoveries," with no specific product in mind. Whatever the reason, practically all research costs will yield their benefits, if any, in future periods. Herein lies the accounting issue: to expense research and development costs immediately when they are incurred (Pattern **E** in Figure 10.1), or to capitalize and amortize them over future periods.

Generally accepted accounting principles[6] require immediate expensing of research and development costs. This requirement is based on arguments that the future benefits from most R & D efforts are too uncertain to warrant capitalization,

---

[6] Statement of Financial Accounting Standards No. 2, Financial Accounting Standards Board, October 1974.

and that writing them off as soon as possible is more conservative. Nevertheless, others feel that there must be future benefits in many cases or else R & D efforts would not be pursued. Theoretically, R & D costs should be matched with the benefits produced by the R & D expenditures through the capitalization procedure with amortization over the benefited periods.

If R & D costs were to be capitalized, there would be a number of problems. The first would be to determine and analyze R & D costs. Direct costs for each research project would have to be segregated for management control purposes. General R & D overhead costs could either be expensed in total, or spread to specific projects and treated just as the rest of the specific project costs are treated. The second problem would be deciding which projects should be capitalized. Where it is obvious that no foreseeable benefits are forthcoming from a certain line of research, its costs should be expensed. Costs of projects that result in future benefits should be capitalized. A third accounting problem would be to determine the period over which capitalized R & D costs should be amortized. Usually, the life span of benefits is uncertain, and the benefits are unevenly distributed over the years. As a consequence, it would usually be necessary to select an arbitrary time period, such as 5 years, over which to amortize the costs.

Advertising

The case for capitalizing and then amortizing advertising cost is not so strong as that for R & D. Advertising expenditures are normally designed to increase sales of the period in which they are made, but there is an obvious lag between the incurrence of these costs and their impact. Often the primary impact of advertising will extend into the following period, and a secondary impact will extend much longer.

Common practice immediately expenses (Pattern **E** in Figure 10.1) all advertising and sales promotion costs, regardless of the timing of their impact. Those supporting this practice argue that: (1) it is more conservative to do so; (2) it is almost impossible to quantify the future effects and timing of benefits derived from these costs; and (3) when these costs remain stable from year to year, income is not affected by the capitalization policy after the first few years. Nevertheless, there is still some support for capitalization treatment. Doing so will better match costs and resulting benefits.

Goodwill

Goodwill is an intangible asset that will be mentioned here only briefly. A more detailed discussion follows in Chapter Thirteen. Goodwill arises from the purchase of one company or operating unit by another company and is measured as the difference between the amount paid for the acquired company as a whole and the current value of its individual assets. Thus, goodwill will appear in the financial statements of the company making the acquisition. Under present practice, the amount of goodwill acquired is recognized only when it is acquired in the purchase of another operating unit and then is amortized over a time period not longer than 40 years. It is generally not recognized by a company that develops the goodwill itself, even though the stock market may indicate a current market value for a firm which must include some amount of goodwill.

Patents

A patent is an exclusive right obtained from the federal government to the benefits from an invention. The legal life of patent protection is 17 years, although the economic life of the patent may be considerably less. The accounting for patent costs depends upon whether the patent was purchased from another party or developed internally. If the former, the purchase price is capitalized. If the latter, the total cost of product development and patent application is expensed as required for all R & D costs. Purchased patent costs are usually amortized over the shorter of: (1) 17 years—the legal patent life, or (2) its estimated economic life. If for some reason the patent becomes worthless, the remaining capitalized cost is immediately recognized as an expense of that period.

■ SUMMARY

Although there are three major classes of long-lived operating assets—fixed assets, wasting assets (natural resources), and intangibles—the major accounting problems for each class are the same: (1) determine the cost of the asset to be amortized, (2) estimate the total period of benefit or the amount of expected benefits, and (3) assign the cost among the benefited periods or units of benefit in a systematic and reasonable fashion.

We have focused our attention on depreciable fixed assets and their depreciation. For these assets, the cost figure to be charged off is frequently reduced by salvage value. The period (or number of units) of benefit is determined by judgment based upon experience or by relying on guidelines set down by the Internal Revenue Service. The pattern of depreciation charges over the asset's life is usually based on some conventional method—the most common methods in practice are straight-line, double-declining-balance, and sum-of-the-years'-digits.

If the asset is retired before the end of the estimated service life for an amount different from its book value, a gain or loss may be recognized. If the asset is traded in on another asset, a gain or loss may or may not be recognized depending on whether the asset received is similar to the asset traded in. The accounting procedures for trade-in transactions are discussed in the glossary.

QUESTIONS AND PROBLEMS

1. Review the meaning of the following concepts or terms discussed in this chapter.
   a. Amortization.
   b. Plant assets and depreciation.
   c. Wasting assets and depletion.
   d. Percentage depletion allowance.
   e. Intangibles.
   f. Capitalize.

    g. Improvements.
    h. Repairs.
    i. Maintenance.
    j. Joint cost.
    k. Value.
    l. Residual value.
    m. Salvage value.
    n. Service life.
    o. Depreciable life.
    p. Asset depreciation ranges.
    q. Straight-line (time and use) methods.
    r. Accelerated depreciation methods.
    s. Declining- and double-declining-balance methods.
    t. Sum-of-the-years'-digits method.
    u. Book value.
    v. Treatment of changes in estimates of useful lives and salvage values of long-lived assets.
    w. Trade-in transaction.
    x. Research and development.
    y. Goodwill.

2.   **a.** "Accounting for depreciating assets would be greatly simplified if accounting periods were only long enough or the life of the assets short enough." What is the point of the quotation?

    b. "The major purpose of depreciation accounting is to provide funds for the replacement of assets as they wear out." Do you agree? Explain.

3. Chapter Four contains the following statement: "Showing both acquisition cost and accumulated depreciation amounts separately provides a rough indication of the relative age of the firm's long-lived assets."

    a. Assume that the Abril Company acquired an asset with a depreciable cost of $100,000 several years ago. Accumulated depreciation as of December 31, 1976, recorded on a straight-line basis, is $60,000. The depreciation charge for 1976 is $10,000. What is the asset's depreciable life? How old is the asset?

    b. Assume straight-line depreciation. Devise a formula that, given the depreciation charge for the year and the asset's accumulated depreciation, can be used to determine the age of the asset.

4. For each of the following expenditures or acquisitions, indicate the type of account —asset other than production cost, production cost, or expense—debited. If the account debited is an asset account, then specify whether it is current or noncurrent.

    a. $150 for repairs of office machines.
    b. $1,500 for emergency repairs to an office machine.
    c. $250 for maintenance of delivery trucks.
    d. $5,000 for a machine acquired in return for a 3-year note.
    e. $4,200 for research and development staff salaries.
    f. $3,100 for newspaper ads.
    g. $6,400 for wages of factory workers engaged in production.
    h. $3,500 for wages of factory workers engaged in installing equipment.
    i. $2,500 for salaries of office work force.
    j. $1,000 for legal fees in acquiring an ore deposit.

k. $1,200 for a 1-year insurance policy beginning next month.

l. $1,800 for U.S. Treasury Notes, to be sold to pay the next installment due on income taxes.

5. In 1971 the Internal Revenue Service Code was amended to provide for depreciable lives for tax purposes from 20 percent less of the guideline lives previously established to 20 percent more of the guideline lives. The Secretary of the Treasury announced that depreciable lives had been extended by 40 percent. A noted accountant remarked that the government could have extended depreciable lives by 100 percent (from 20 percent less to 80 percent more) with the same effects on tax collections as the 40 percent extension. What did the accountant mean?

6. On April 30, 1976, the Tico Wholesale Company acquired a new machine with a fair market value of $14,000. The seller agreed to accept the company's old machine, $7,000 in cash, and a 12-percent, 1-year note for $4,000 in payment.

The old machine was purchased on January 1, 1971, for $10,000. It was estimated that the old machine would be useful for 8 years, after which it would have a salvage value of $400. It is estimated that the new machine will have a service life of 10 years and a salvage value of $800.

Assuming that the Tico Company uses the straight-line method of depreciation and closes its books annually on December 31, give the entries that were made in 1976.

7. On July 1, 1953, a building and site were purchased for $96,000 by a retail clothing store. Of this amount, $40,000 was allocated to the land and the remainder to the building. The building is depreciated on a straight-line basis.

On July 1, 1975 (no additions or retirements having been recorded in the meanwhile), the net book value of the building was $25,200. On March 31, 1976, the building and site were sold for $60,000. The fair market value of the land was $50,000 on this date.

The firm closes its books annually at June 30. Give the entries required on March 31, 1976. (Hint: First compute what the annual depreciation charges must be, based on the facts given.)

8. The Alexander Company acquired three used machine tools for a total price of $49,000. Costs to transport the machine tools from the seller to Alexander Company's factory were $1,000. The machine tools were renovated, installed, and put to use in manufacturing the firm's products. The costs of renovation and installation were as follows:

	MACHINE TOOL A	MACHINE TOOL B	MACHINE TOOL C
Renovation Costs	$1,700	$800	$950
Installation Costs	300	550	250

The machine tools have the following estimated remaining lives: Tool A—4 years; Tool B—10 years; Tool C—6 years.

a. Assume that each machine tool is capitalized in a separate asset account and that the remaining life of each machine tool is used as the basis for allocating the joint costs of acquisition. Compute the depreciable cost of each of the three machine tools.

b. Present journal entries to record depreciation charges for years 1, 5, and 8, given the assumption in **a**. Use the straight-line method.

c. Assume that the three machine tools are treated as one composite asset in the accounts. If management decides to depreciate the entire cost of the composite asset on a straight-line basis over 10 years, what is the depreciation charge for each year?

d. Which treatment, **a** or **c**, should management of the Alexander Company probably prefer for tax purposes and why?

9. Give the journal entries for the following selected transactions of the Eagle Manufacturing Company. The company uses the straight-line method of calculating depreciation and closes its books annually on December 31.

(1) A machine is purchased on November 1, 1976, for $15,000. It is estimated that it will be used for 10 years and that it will have a salvage value of $300 at the end of that time. Give the journal entry for the depreciation at December 31, 1976.

(2) Record the depreciation for the year ending December 31, 1977.

(3) In August, 1982, it is decided that the machine will probably be used for a total of 12 years and that its scrap value will be $200. Make a correction of prior years' earnings and record the depreciation for the year ending December 31, 1982.

(4) What procedure should have been followed for the information in **(3)** according to generally accepted accounting principles?

(5) The machine is sold for $500 on March 31, 1987. Record the entries of that date, assuming that depreciation is recorded as indicated in **(3)**.

10. On March 1, 1976, one of the buildings owned by the Metropolitan Storage Company was destroyed by fire. The cost of the building was $100,000; the balance in the Accumulated Depreciation account at January 1, 1976, was $38,125. A service life of 40 years with a zero salvage value had been estimated for the building. The company uses the straight-line method. The building was not insured.

a. Give the journal entries made at March 1.

b. If there have been no alterations in the service life estimate, when was the building acquired?

11. Journalize the following transactions:

(1) A piece of office equipment is purchased for $850 cash.

(2) Depreciation for 1 year of $85 is recorded.

(3) The equipment is sold for $400. At the time of the sale, the Accumulated Depreciation account shows a balance of $425. Depreciation of $85 for the year of the sale has not yet been recorded.

12. A building which cost $150,000 has a book value (acquisition cost less accumulated depreciation) of $75,000 after having been in use for 20 years. The building is depreciated on a straight-line basis. The assumption is that removal costs will equal salvage value. In the twenty-first year it is decided that the total life of the building will be 50 years. Calculate the amount of the depreciation charge **(1)** in the twenty-first year and **(2)** in the forty-second year of use:

a. If depreciation charges continue to be based on the original estimates.

b. If the undepreciated cost after 20 years is to be spread over the estimated remaining life.

c. If a correction of prior periods' earnings is made and depreciation charges thereafter are based on the new estimates.

13. Give correcting entries for the following situations. In each case, the firm uses the straight-line method of depreciation and closes its books annually on December 31. Recognize all gains and losses currently.

   a. A cash register was purchased for $300 on January 1, 1971. It was depreciated at a rate of 10 percent. On June 30, 1976, it was sold for $200 and a new cash register was acquired for $500. The bookkeeper made the following entry to record the transaction:

Store Equipment	300	
Cash in Bank		300

   b. A used truck was acquired in May 1976 for $4,000. Its cost when new was $6,000, and the bookkeeper made the following entry to record the purchase:

Truck	6,000	
Accumulated Depreciation		2,000
Cash		4,000

   c. A testing mechanism was purchased on April 1, 1974, for $600. It was depreciated at a 10-percent annual rate. On June 30, 1976, it was stolen. The loss was not insured, and the bookkeeper made the following entry:

Theft Loss	600	
Testing Mechanism		600

14. Give the journal entries for the following transactions:

   (1) An office building is constructed at a cost of $36,000. It is estimated that it will be unsable for 45 years, at which time it will have a salvage value of $2,250. It is put into operation on September 1, 1942. Give the entry for depreciation for the last 4 months of 1942. The straight-line method of depreciation is used.

   (2) Record the depreciation for the year 1943.

   (3) In 1976 it is decided that the total life of the building will be only 40 years, and that its salvage value will be $3,000. Make a retained earnings adjustment to correct the depreciation charges for the period 1942–1975, although such adjustments are not sanctioned by generally accepted accounting principles. Then record the depreciation for the year of 1976.

   (4) The building is abandoned for operational reasons on March 1, 1978. It is sold to wreckers for $2,000. Record the journal entries at March 1, 1978.

15. The Grogan Manufacturing Company started business on January 1, 1975. At that time it acquired Machine A for $20,000, payment being made by check.

   Due to an expansion in the volume of business, Machine B, costing $25,000, was acquired on September 30, 1976. A check for $15,000 was issued, with the balance to be paid in annual installments of $2,000 plus interest at the rate of 6 percent on the unpaid balance. The first installment is due on September 30, 1977.

   On June 30, 1977, Machine A was sold for $13,000 and a larger model, Machine C, was acquired for $30,000.

   All installments are paid on time.

   All machines have an estimated life of 10 years with an estimated salvage value equal to 10 percent of acquisition cost. The company closes its books on December 31. The straight-line method is used.

Prepare dated journal entries to record all transactions through December 31, 1977, including year-end adjustments but excluding closing entries.

16. The Chisholm Manufacturing Company purchased a plot of land for $50,000 as a plant site. There was a small office building on the plot, conservatively appraised at $8,000, which the company will continue to use with some modification and renovation. The company had plans drawn for a factory and received bids for its construction. It rejected all bids and decided to construct the plant itself. Below are listed additional items which management feels should be included in plant asset accounts.

(1) Cement block, bricks, and tile	$ 77,345
(2) Cement, sand, and gravel	39,864
(3) Lumber, sash, and plumbing	84,392
(4) Other materials and supplies	47,204
(5) Cellar excavation	12,000
(6) Labor on construction	138,639
(7) Cost of remodeling old building into office building	9,473
(8) Interest on money borrowed by Chisholm	4,592
(9) Interest on Chisholm's own money used	11,394
(10) Cash discounts on materials used	6,439
(11) Supervision by management	9,500
(12) Compensation insurance premiums	8,000
(13) Payment of claim for injuries not covered by insurance	2,500
(14) Clerical and other expenses of construction	7,943
(15) Paving of streets and sidewalks	4,879
(16) Architect's plans and specifications	3,000
(17) Legal costs of conveying land	1,300
(18) Legal costs of injury claim	900
(19) Income credited to Retained Earnings account, being the difference between the foregoing cost and the lowest contractor's bid	12,345

Show in detail the items to be included in the following accounts: Land, Factory Building, Office Building, and Site Improvements. Explain why you excluded items not included in the four accounts.

17. Calculate the depreciation charge for the first and second years of the asset's life in the following cases.

Asset	Cost	Estimated Salvage Value	Life (Years)	Depreciation Method
a. Blast Furnace	$800,000	$25,000	20	Double-Declining-Balance
b. Hotel	500,000	50,000	45	Straight-Line
c. Typewriter	400	40	8	Sum-of-the-Years'-Digits
d. Tractor	6,000	500	10	Double-Declining-Balance
e. Ferris Wheel	7,600	400	12	Straight-Line
f. Delivery Truck	5,500	1,300	6	Sum-of-the-Years'-Digits

18. On January 1, 1976, the Central Production Company acquired a new turret lathe for $36,000. It was estimated to have a useful life of 4 years and no salvage value. The company closes its books annually on December 31. Indicate the amount of the depreciation charge for each of the 4 years under:
   a. The straight-line method.
   b. The declining-balance method at twice the straight-line rate.
   c. The sum-of-the-years'-digits method.
19. Give the annual or unit depreciation charge in the following cases. The firm uses straight-line (time and use) methods.

Asset	Cost	Estimated Salvage Value	Estimated Life
a. Adding Machine	$ 400	$ 40	12 Years
b. Taxicab	5,000	100	100,000 Miles
c. Building	37,000	1,000	18 Years
d. Desk	280	30	20 Years
e. Aircraft Engine	25,000	500	2,000 Flying Hours
f. Bakery Oven	6,800	350	16 Years
g. Display Counter	2,000	400	12 Years

20. A machine is acquired for $8,900. It is expected to last 8 years and to be operated for 25,000 hours during that time. It is estimated that its salvage value will be $1,700 at the end of that time. Calculate the depreciation charge for each of the first 3 years using:
   a. The straight-line (time) method.
   b. The sum-of-the-years'-digits method.
   c. The declining-balance method using a 25 percent rate (the maximum rate allowed).
   d. The units-of-production method. Operating times are as follows: first year, 3,500 hours; second year, 2,325 hours; third year, 4,895 hours.
21. The Slowpoke Shipping Company buys a new truck for $10,000 on January 1, 1975. It is estimated that it will last 6 years and have a salvage value of $1,000. Early in 1977, it is determined that the truck will last only an additional 2 years, or 4 years in total. The company closes its books on December 31.
   a. Present a table showing the depreciation charges for each year from 1975 to 1978 and give the adjusting entry made in 1977. Assume that the company desires to follow the theoretically sound, but disapproved, method of correcting the past misestimates in depreciation so that the future depreciation charges will not be in error. Follow the instructions for each of the following methods:
      (1) The straight-line method.
      (2) The sum-of-the-years'-digits method.
      (3) The declining-balance method with depreciation at twice the straight-line rate. The remaining undepreciated cost less salvage value is to be written off in the last year.

   b. Present a table showing the depreciation charges for each year from 1975 to 1978 under each of the methods in part **a**. Assume that the company follows the policy of charging off the undepreciated cost less salvage over the remaining life when service life estimates are revised. (This is the method currently required.)

22. The Linder Manufacturing Company acquires a new machine for $7,200 on July 1, 1975. It is estimated that it will have a service life of 6 years and then have a salvage value of $900. The company closes its books annually on June 30.

   a. Compute the depreciation charges for each year of the asset's life assuming the use of:

     (**1**) The straight-line method.

     (**2**) The sum-of-the-years'-digits method.

     (**3**) The declining-balance method, with a rate twice the straight-line rate.

   b. If the machine were sold for $700 on October 30, 1980, give the journal entries that would be made on that date under each of the methods in part **a**.

23. Starting in 1976, Equilibrium Company plans to spend $3,000 per year on advertising the company's brand names and trademarks. The controller wonders what the effect on the financial statements will be of (**1**) expensing the advertising costs each year or (**2**) capitalizing them and amortizing them over 3 years on a straight-line (time) basis.

   a. Prepare a 4-year summary, showing for each year both the amount of expenses resulting from advertising that would appear on the income statement and the amount of advertising asset that would appear on the balance sheet under each method, (**1**) and (**2**).

   b. What will be the affect on net income and on the balance sheet in succeeding years under each of the policies if Equilibrium Company continues to spend $3,000 each year?

   c. In what sense is expensing the advertising costs, policy (**1**), a conservative policy?

24. In each of the following situations, compute the amounts of revenue, gain, expense, and loss to be shown on the income statement for the year and the amount of asset to be shown on the balance sheet as of the end of the year. Show the journal entry or entries required, and provide reasons for your decisions. Straight-line amortization is used. The reporting period is the calendar year. The situations are independent of each other, except where noted.

   a. Because of a new fire code, a department store must install additional fire escapes on a building leased from its owner. The fire escapes are acquired for $28,000 cash on January 1. The lease on the building has 7 years to run as of January 1.

   b. Many years ago, a firm acquired shares of stock in the General Electric Company for $100,000. On December 31, the firm acquired a building with an appraised value of $1 million. The company paid for the building by giving up its shares in the General Electric Company at a time when equivalent shares traded on the New York Stock Exchange for $1,050,000.

   c. Same data as **b**, except that the shares of stock represent ownership in Small Timers, Inc., whose shares are traded on a regional stock exchange. The last transaction in shares of Small Timers, Inc., occurred on December 27. Using the prices of the most recent trades, the shares of stock of Small Timers, Inc., given in exchange for the building have a market value of $1,050,000.

d. A company decides that it can save $3,500 a year for at least a decade by switching from small panel trucks to larger delivery vans. To do so requires remodeling costs of $18,000 for various garages. The first fleet of delivery vans will last for 5 years, and the garages will last for 20 years. The garages are remodeled on January 1.

e. A company drills for oil. It sinks ten holes during the year at a cost of $1 million each. Nine of the holes are dry, but the tenth is a gusher. By the end of the year, the oil known to be recoverable from the gusher has a net realizable value of $40 million. No oil was extracted during the year.

f. A company manufactures aircraft. During the current year, all sales were to the government under defense contracts. The company spent $400,000 on institutional advertising to keep its name before the business community. It expects to resume sales of small jet planes to corporate buyers in 2 years.

g. A company runs a large laboratory which has, over the years, found marketable ideas and products worth tens of millions of dollars. On average, the successful products have a life of 10 years. Expenditures for the laboratory this year were $1,500,000.

25. In each of the following situations compute the amounts of revenue, gain, expense, and loss to be shown on the income statement for the year, as well as the amount of asset to be shown on the balance sheet as of the end of the year. Show the journal entry or entries required, and provide reasons for your decisions. Straight-line amortization is used. The reporting period is the calendar year. The situations are independent of each other, except where noted.

a. A textile manufacturer gives $250,000 to the Textile Engineering Department of a local university for basic research in fibers. The results of the research, if any, will belong to the general public.

b. A film producer incurred costs of $12 million during the year to produce a movie for television. A television network paid the film producer $10 million during the year for the rights to show the film once. The contract with the network specifies that the film will be shown during the summer of the next accounting period, and that the network will pay the producer another $5 million at the time of that showing.

c. Same data as in **b**, but the network has the additional option to show the film still a third time 2 years from now for an additional fee of $5 million, payable only if the option is exercised.

d. The same film producer mentioned above incurred costs of $3 million to produce an *avant garde* film. No network has yet purchased rights to show the film. In the past, the producer has generally sold less than half of such speculative films.

e. On January 1, an automobile company incurs costs of $6 million for specialized machine tools necessary for producing a new model automobile. Such tools last for 6 years, on average, but the new model automobile is expected to be produced for only 3 years.

f. A company wishes to acquire a 5-acre site for a new warehouse. The land it wants is part of a 10-acre site that the owner insists be purchased as a whole for

$18,000. The company purchases the land, spends $2,000 in legal fees for rights to divide the site into two 5-acre plots, and immediately offers half of the land for resale. The two best offers are:

(1) $12,000 for the east half, and

(2) $13,000 for the west half.

The company sells the east half.

g. Same data as in **f**, except the two best offers are

(1) $5,000 for the east half, and

(2) $12,000 for the west half.

The company sells the west half.

Chapter Eleven

Liabilities

This chapter and the next examine the accounting concepts and procedures for the right-hand side of the balance sheet, which shows the sources of a firm's financing. Business capital comes from two sources: owners and nonowners. Owners' equity is the subject of Chapter Twelve. This chapter discusses capital provided to a business by nonowners. Banks or creditors providing debt on a long-term basis are aware of their role as providers of capital, but suppliers, employees, and customers usually do not think of themselves as contributing to a firm's capital, even though they do. The obligation that a business incurs to these nonowning contributors of capital is called a liability.

A reasonable definition of a liability, as the term is used in accounting, is a definite legal obligation to make a payment of a definite (or reasonably certain) amount at a definite (or reasonably certain) time in return for a current benefit. There are usually four operable constraints on an obligation before it is recognizable as a liability: legal obligation, certainty of amount, certainty of due date, and receipt of a current benefit. Most of the liabilities discussed in this chapter meet all four criteria; any item designated as a liability that does not meet all four criteria is noted in the discussion of that item.

A thorough understanding of long-term liabilities requires some knowledge of compound interest and present-value computations. In these computations, payments made at different times are made comparable by taking into account the interest that cash can earn over time. Appendix 11.1 of this chapter introduces the computations. While Appendix 11.1 can be omitted without losing continuity with the rest of the book, much of the discussion in this chapter will be easier to follow if you understand the concepts, but not necessarily the procedures, of present-value analysis.

■ CURRENT LIABILITIES

Current liabilities are normally those due within 1 year. They include accounts payable to creditors, payroll accruals, taxes payable, short-term notes payable, and a few others. Current liabilities are continually discharged and replaced with new ones in the course of business operations.

Accounts Payable to Creditors

Companies seldom pay for goods and services when received. Payment is usually deferred until a bill is received from the supplier. Even then, the bill might not be paid immediately, but instead, accumulated with other bills until a specified time of the month when all bills are paid. Since explicit interest is not paid on these accounts, management tries to obtain as much capital as possible from its creditors. Nevertheless, failure to pay creditors according to schedule can lead to poor credit ratings and to restrictions on future credit.

Payroll Accruals

Deductions are taken from an employee's gross pay to cover federal income taxes, payroll (FICA[1] or social security) taxes, medical plans, pension plans, insurance plans, and other items. The accounting for these deductions is relatively simple, although time consuming. Instead of showing the gross pay as being entirely payable to employees, the employer shows the net, or "take-home," pay as being payable to employees, and deductions, or withholdings, as being payable to the various recipients. For example, gross wages of $2,000 in a merchandising firm might be shown as

Labor Expense		2,000
Wages Payable		1,460
Federal Withholding Taxes Payable		240
State Withholding Taxes Payable		80
Payroll Taxes Payable		160
Medical Plan Payable		20
Pension Plan Payable		30
Insurance Plan Payable		10

In addition, the employer is required to match the FICA contributions of the workers. Assuming in this example that the labor contract requires the employer also to match the medical and pension plan contributions of the workers, and those contributions are judged to be a component of labor expense, the additional journal entry would be

[1] FICA is the Federal Insurance Contribution Act. The actual deduction depends on several factors and has steadily increased over time. For the purpose of illustrations and problems in this text, it will be assumed that the tax is calculated at 8 percent of the first $15,000 of gross income for each employee.

Labor Expense	210	
Payroll Taxes Payable		160
Medical Plan Payable		20
Pension Plan Payable		30

Short-Term Notes and Interest Payable

Businesses obtain interim financing for less than a year from banks or other creditors in return for a short-term note called a *note payable.* Such notes are discussed in Chapter Eight from the point of view of the lender, or note holder. The treatment of these notes by the borrower is the mirror image of the treatment by the lender. Where the lender records an asset, the borrower records a liability. When the lender records interest receivable and revenue, the borrower records interest payable and expense.

Income Taxes

The corporation is the only form of business organization on which a separate federal income tax is levied. An income tax must be paid each year by corporations on their taxable income from business activities. In contrast, business entities organized as partnerships or sole proprietorships do not pay income taxes. Instead, the income of the business entity is taxed to the individual partners or sole proprietor. Each partner or sole proprietor adds his or her share of business income to income from all other (nonbusiness) sources in preparing individual income tax returns.

Accounting for Income Taxes

The details of the income tax on corporations are subject to change. The rates and schedules of payments mentioned below should not be taken as an indication of the exact procedure in force at any particular time, but rather as an indication of the type of accounting procedures which are involved.[2] The accounting for state and local income taxes follows the same general pattern as that for federal income taxes, except for rates and dates of payment.

Corporations must make an estimate of the amount of taxes that will be due for the year and make quarterly payments equal to one-fourth of the estimated tax. This is frequently described as "pay-as-you-go" taxation. For a corporation on a calendar-year basis, and using 1976 as an example, 25 percent of the estimated tax for 1976 must be paid by April 15, 1976; 50 percent by June 15, 1976; 75 percent by September 15, 1976; and the entire estimated tax for 1976 must be paid by December 15, 1976.

The estimated income and, hence, the estimated tax may change as the year passes. The corporation must report such changed estimates quarterly. The

[2] The discussion in this section is based on the law and regulations in effect January 1, 1976. Most corporate income is taxed at a rate of 48 percent. Throughout the remainder of the text, an income tax rate of 40 percent is used in almost all illustrations for ease of calculation.

amount of the quarterly payment is revised to reflect the new estimated tax and takes into account the cumulative payments made during previous quarters of the year. The final income tax return for the year is due by March 15, 1977. Any difference between the actual tax liability for 1976 and the cumulative tax payments during 1976 must be paid, one-half by March 15, 1977, and one-half by June 15, 1977. The law provides for penalties if the amount estimated is substantially less than the actual tax liability.

If income statements are prepared more often than quarterly, or if the end of the reporting period does not coincide with the tax payment period, it is necessary to estimate the income tax for the reporting period so that a more accurate measurement can be made of the net income for the period. Monthly or other short-period estimates of the tax are likely to be far from dependable, because the tax rate is graduated, and early estimates of taxable income for the year are likely to be in error. All that can be done is to set up the best possible estimate of tax in the light of earnings of the year to date and the prospects for the remainder of the year.

Deferred Performance Liabilities

Another current liability arises from advance payments by customers for goods or services. This liability, unlike the preceding ones, is discharged by delivering goods or services, rather than by paying cash. This liability represents "unearned" and, therefore, unrecognized, revenue; that is, cash is received before the goods or services are furnished to the customer.

An example of this type of liability is the advance sale of theater tickets, say for $200. Upon the sale, the following entry will be made:

Cash	200	
Liability for Advance Sales		200

Note that in these cases, the due date is not definite but is reasonably certain. Hence the deferred performance obligations qualify as liabilities. After the theater performance, or after the tickets have expired, revenue would be recognized and the liability would be removed:

Liability for Advance Sales	200	
Performance Revenue		200

Other examples of deferred performance liabilities are magazine subscriptions, transportation tickets, and service contracts.

A related type of deferred performance liability arises when a firm provides a warranty for free service or repairs for some period after the sale. At the time of sale, the firm can only estimate the likely amount of warranty liability. If sales during the accounting period were $28,000, and the firm estimated that 4 percent of the sales amounts would eventually be used to satisfy warranty claims, the entry would be:

Accounts Receivable	28,000	
Warranty Expense	1,120	
Sales		28,000
Deferred Warranty Liability		1,120

Note that this entry recognizes the warranty expense in the period when revenue is recognized, even though the repairs may be made in a later period. Because the expense is recognized, the liability is created. In this case, neither the amount due nor the due date of the liability are definite, and they may not even be "reasonably certain." The accountant, however, attempts to recognize the related expense in the same period when revenue is recognized.

When expenditures of, say, $675 are made at a later date for repairs under the warranty, the entry would be:

Deferred Warranty Liability	675	
Cash (or other assets consumed for repairs)		675

With experience, the firm will adjust the percentage of sales it charges to Warranty Expense so that the credit balance in the Deferred Warranty Liability account stays within a reasonable range. This treatment of warranty costs is much like the "allowance" method introduced in Chapter Eight for uncollectible accounts.

■ LONG-TERM LIABILITIES

The principal long-term liabilities are mortgages and bonds. The significant differences between long-term and short-term, or current, liabilities are that: (1) interest on long-term liabilities is ordinarily paid at regular intervals during the life of a long-term obligation while interest on short-term debt is usually paid in a lump sum at maturity; (2a) the principal of long-term obligations is often paid back in installments, or (2b) special funds are often accumulated by the borrower for retiring long-term liabilities.

Mortgages

A *mortgage* is a contract in which the lender is awarded legal title to certain property of the borrower, with the provision that the title reverts to the borrower when the loan is repaid in full. (In a few states the lender merely acquires a lien on the borrower's property rather than legal title to it.) The mortgaged property is security for the loan. The customary terminology designates the lender as the *mortgagee* and the borrower as the *mortgagor*.

As long as the mortgagor meets the obligations under the mortgage agreement, the mortgagee does not have the ordinary rights of an owner to possess and use the property. If the mortgagor defaults on either the principal or interest payments, the mortgagee can foreclose the mortgage or arrange to have the property sold for his or her benefit. The mortgagee has first rights to the proceeds from the foreclosure sale for satisfying any unpaid claim. If there is an excess, it is paid to the mortgagor.

If the proceeds are insufficient to pay the remaining loan, the lender becomes an unsecured creditor for the unpaid balance.

Accounting for Mortgages

Some of the more common problems in accounting for mortgages are presented in the following illustration.

On October 1, 1975, the Midwestern Products Company borrows $30,000 for 5 years from the Home Savings and Finance Company to obtain funds for additional working capital. As security, Midwestern Products Company gives Home Savings and Finance Company title to several parcels of land that it owns and that are on its books at a cost of $50,000. The interest rate is 8 percent per year compounded semiannually, with payments due on April 1 and October 1. Midwestern agrees to make ten equal payments of $3,700 each over the 5 years of the mortgage so that when the last payment is made on October 1, 1980, the loan and all interest will have been paid. The Midwestern Products Company closes its books annually on December 31. (The derivation of the semiannual payment of $3,700 is shown in Example 9 of Appendix 11.1 of this chapter.)

The entries from the time the mortgage is issued through December 31, 1976, would be:

10/1/75	Cash	30,000	
	Mortgage Payable		30,000
	Loan obtained from Home Savings and Finance Company for 5 years at 8 percent compounded semiannually.		
12/31/75	Interest Expense	600	
	Interest Payable		600
	Interest expense on mortgage from 10/1/75 to 12/31/75 (.08 × $30,000 × 3/12).		
4/1/76	Interest Expense	600	
	Interest Payable	600	
	Mortgage Payable	2,500	
	Cash		3,700
	Interest expense on mortgage from 1/1/76 to 4/1/76, payment of 6 months' interest, and reduction of loan by the difference, $3,700 − $1,200 = $2,500.		
10/1/76	Interest Expense	1,100	
	Mortgage Payable	2,600	
	Cash		3,700
	Payment of interest for the period 4/1/76 to 10/1/76. Interest expense for the period is $1,100 [= .08 × ($30,000 − $2,500) × 1/2].		
12/31/76	Interest Expense	498	
	Interest Payable		498
	Interest expense from 10/1/76 to 12/31/76 [.08 × ($30,000 − $2,500 − $2,600) × 3/12].		

Bonds

Mortgages or notes are used whenever the funds being borrowed can be obtained from a small number of sources. When large amounts are needed, the firm may have to borrow from the general investing public through the use of a bond issue. Bonds are used primarily by corporations and governmental units. The distinctive features of a bond issue are as follows:

1. A *bond indenture,* or agreement, is drawn up which shows in detail the terms of the loan and the rights and duties of the borrower and other parties to the contract.

2. *Bond certificates* are used. Engraved certificates are prepared, each one representing a portion of the total loan. The usual minimum denomination in business practice is $1,000, although smaller denominations are sometimes used. Government bonds are issued in denominations as small as $25.

3. A *trustee* is named to hold title to any property serving as security for the loan and to act as the technical representative of the bondholders. The trustee is usually a bank or trust company.

4. An agent is appointed, usually a bank or trust company, to act as *registrar* and *disbursing agent.* The borrower deposits interest and principal payments with the disbursing agent, who distributes the funds to the bondholders.

5. Most bonds are *coupon bonds.* Coupons are attached to the bond certificate covering the interest payments throughout the life of the bond. When a coupon comes due, the bondholder cuts it off and deposits it with a bank. The bank sends the coupon through the bank clearing system to the disbursing agent.

6. Bonds are commonly *registered as to principal*, which means that the holder's name appears on the bond certificate and on the records of the registrar. Sometimes both the principal and interest of bonds are registered, in which case the interest payments are mailed directly to the bondholder and coupons are not used. Registered bonds are easily replaced if lost, but the transfer from one holder to another is cumbersome. Unregistered bonds may be transferred merely by delivery, while registered bonds have to be assigned formally from one holder to another.

7. The entire bond issue is usually issued by the borrower to an investment banking firm, or to a group of investment bankers known as a *syndicate,* which takes over the responsibility of reselling the bonds to the investing public.

Types of Bonds

Real estate bonds, sometimes called *mortgage bonds,* carry a mortgage on real estate as security for the repayment of the loan. *Collateral trust bonds* are usually secured by stocks and bonds of other corporations. The most common type of corporate bond, except in the railroad and public utility industries, is the *debenture bond.* This type carries no special security or collateral; instead, it is issued on the general credit of the business. To give added protection to the bondholders, provisions are usually included in the bond indenture that limit the amount of subsequent long-term debt that can be incurred. *Convertible bonds* are debentures that the holder can exchange, possibly after some specific period of time has elapsed, for a specific number of shares of capital stock.

Almost all bonds provide for the payment of interest at regular intervals, usually semiannually. The amount of interest is typically expressed as a percentage of the principal. For example, an 8-percent, 10-year semiannual coupon bond with face or principal amount of $1,000 promises to pay $40 every six months, with the first payment occurring 6 months after the bond issue date, until a total of twenty payments are made. At the time of the final $40 coupon payment, the $1,000 principal is also due. The principal amount of a bond is its face, or par value. The terms *face value* and *par value* are used synonymously in this context. A bond can be issued for, and can subsequently be traded in the marketplace, below par, at par, or above par.

Proceeds of a Bond Issue

The amount received by the borrower may be more or less than the par value of the bonds issued. The difference arises primarily because there is a difference between the coupon rate printed on the bond certificates and the interest rate the market requires the firm to pay to borrow under the circumstances. If the coupon rate is less than the rate the market, in aggregate, requires the firm to pay, then the bonds will sell for less than par and the difference between par and selling price is called the *discount* on the bond. If the coupon rate is larger than the rate the market requires, then the bonds will sell above par and the difference between selling price and par is called the *premium* on the bond.

The presence of a discount or premium in and of itself indicates nothing about the credit standing of the borrower. A firm with a credit standing that would enable it to borrow funds at 7¼ percent might issue 7-percent bonds that would sell at a discount, while another firm with a lower credit standing that would require it to pay 7¾ percent on loans might issue bonds at 8 percent which would sell at a premium.

The following illustrations cover the calculations of the proceeds of a bond issue when the effective interest rate is equal to, more than, and less than the coupon rate.

The Macaulay Corporation issues $100,000 face value of 8-percent semiannual coupon debenture bonds. The bonds are dated July 1, 1976, and are due July 1, 1986. Coupons are dated July 1 and January 1. The coupon payments promised at each interest payment date total $4,000. Assuming that the issue was taken by L. Fisher and Company, investment bankers, on July 1, 1976, at a rate to yield 8 percent compounded semiannually, the calculation of the proceeds to Macaulay would be as follows. (The present-value calculations are explained in Appendix 11.1 of this chapter.)

(a) Present value of $100,000 to be paid at the end of 10 years . . . . $ 45,639
  (Appendix Table 2 at the back of the book shows the present value of $1
  to be received in twenty periods at 4 percent per period to be $.45639;
  $100,000 × .45639 = $45,639).

(b) Present value of $4,000 to be paid each 6 months for 10 years   54,361
(Appendix Table 4 shows the present value of an ordinary annuity of $1
per period for twenty periods discounted at 4 percent to be $13.59033;
$4,000 × 13.59033 = $54,361.)

Total Proceeds $100,000

The issue price would be stated as 100 (that is, 100 percent of par), which implies that the market rate was 8 percent compounded semiannually, the same as the coupon rate.

Assuming that the bonds were issued at a price to yield 9 percent compounded semiannually, the calculation of the proceeds would be

(a) Present value of $100,000 to be paid at the end of 10 years . . . . $ 41,464
(Present value of $1 to be received in twenty periods at 4½ percent per
period is $0.41464; $100,000 × 0.41464 = $41,464.)

(b) Present value of $4,000 to be paid each 6 months for 10 years   52,032
(Present value of an ordinary annuity of $1 per period for twenty periods,
discounted at 4½ percent per period = $13.00794; $4,000 × 13.00794 =
$52,032.)

Total Proceeds . . . . $ 93,496

If the issue price were stated on a conventional pricing basis in the market at 93.50 (93.50 percent of par), the issuing price would be $93,500. This amount implies a market yield of slightly less than 9 percent compounded semiannually.

Assuming that the bonds were issued at a price to yield 7 percent compounded semiannually, the calculation of the proceeds would be

(a) Present value of $100,000 to be paid at the end of 10 years . . . . $ 50,257
(Present value of $1 to be received in twenty periods at 3½ percent per
period is $0.50257; $100,000 × 0.50257 = $50,257.)

(b) Present value of $4,000 to be paid each 6 months for 10 years   56,850
(Present value of an ordinary annuity at $1 per period for twenty periods,
discounted at 3½ percent per period = $14.2124; $4,000 × 14.2124 =
$56,850.)

Total Proceeds $107,107

If the issue price were stated on a conventional pricing basis in the market at 107.11 (107.11 percent of par), the issuing price would be $107,110.[3] This price

[3] In many contexts, bond prices are quoted in dollars plus thirty-seconds of a dollar. A bond selling for about 117.107 percent of par would be quoted at 107³⁄₃₂, which would be written as 107.3. In order to read published bond prices, you must know whether the information after the "decimal" point refers to fractions expressed in one-hundredths or in thirty-seconds. (If you are reading published bond prices and see any number larger than 31 after the decimal point, then you can be sure that one-hundredths are being used. If you see many prices, but none of the numbers shown after the point is larger than 31, then you can be reasonably sure that thirty-seconds are being used.) In this book, we use decimal fractions, that is, one-hundredths.

would imply a market yield of slightly less than 7 percent compounded semi-annually.

Bond Tables

Fortunately, a firm does not have to make these tedious calculations every time it wants to issue a bond. Special bond tables have been prepared to show the results of calculations like those just described. Examples of such tables are included in the Appendix at the end of the book. Appendix Table 5 shows for 6-percent, semiannual coupon bonds the price as a percent of par for various market interest rates (yields) and years to maturity. Appendix Table 6 shows market rates and implied prices for 8-percent, semiannual coupon bonds. (Some modern electronic calculators are capable of making these calculations in a few seconds.)

The percentages of par shown in these tables represent the present value of the bond indicated. Since the factors are expressed as a percent of par, they have to be multiplied by 10 to find the price of a $1,000 bond. If you have never used bond tables before now, turn to Appendix Table 6 and find in the 10-year column the three different prices for the three different effective yields used in the preceding example. Notice further that a bond will sell at par if and only if it has an effective yield equal to its coupon rate.

These tables are useful whether a bond is being issued by a corporation or resold later by an investor. The approach to determining the market price will be the same in either case, although the years to maturity will be less than the original term of the bond when it is resold. The following generalizations can be made regarding bond prices:

1. When the effective yield equals the coupon rate, the market price will equal par.
2. When the effective yield is greater than the coupon rate, the market price will be less than par.
3. When the effective yield is less than the coupon rate, the market price will be greater than par.

Accounting for Bonds Issued at Par

The following illustration covers the more common problems associated with bonds issued at par.

We use the data presented in the previous sections for the Macaulay Corporation, where the bonds were issued at par and we assume that the books are closed semiannually on June 30 and December 31. The entry at the time of issue would be

```
7/1/76  Cash ...............................................  100,000
          Debenture Bonds Payable .......................        100,000
        $100,000 of 8-percent, 10-year bonds issued at par.
```

The entries for interest would be made at the end of the accounting period and on the interest payment dates. Entries through January 2, 1977, would be

12/31/76	Interest Expense on Bonds	4,000	
	Interest Payable		4,000
	To record accrual of interest for 6 months.		

1/2/77	Interest Payable	4,000	
	Cash		4,000
	To record payment of 6 months' interest.		

Accounting for Bonds Issued at a Discount

The following illustration covers the more common problems associated with bonds issued at a discount.

Assume the data presented for the Macaulay Corporation where the bonds were issued for $93,500 and the books are closed on June 30 and December 31. The entry at the time of issue would be

7/1/76	Cash	93,500	
	Discount on Debenture Bonds Payable	6,500	
	Debenture Bonds Payable		100,000
	$100,000 of 8-percent, 10-year bonds issued at a discount.		

The discount is primarily an indication that 8 percent is not a sufficiently high rate of interest for the bonds to bring their face value in the open market. Because the market requires approximately 9 percent compounded semiannually, Macaulay actually acquires the use of only $93,500. Macaulay agrees to pay to bondholders the face value of $100,000 when the bond matures as well as the twenty semiannual payments of $4,000 each. The difference between the par value and the amount of proceeds, $6,500, represents additional interest which will be paid as a part of the face value at maturity. Thus the total interest that must be charged to the periods during which the loan is outstanding is $86,500 (periodic payments totaling $80,000 plus the $6,500 included in the principal payment at maturity).

The periodic interest expense includes the coupon payment *plus* an expense representing an allocation of an appropriate part of the discount. This process of allocating the discount as extra interest expense over the life of the bond is called *amortization.* The simplest approach to discount amortization involves the straight-line allocation of discount over the life of the bond. The straight-line method is illustrated in this section. Although the straight-line method is permitted under generally accepted accounting principles, the more technically correct and preferred approach involves compound-interest calculations and is known as the *effective-interest method.* The effective-interest method is illustrated below.

Under the straight-line method, the amount of discount to be amortized each 6 months is the total discount to be amortized over the life of the bond divided by the number of half-years of the bond's life. In this illustration, the semiannual straight-line amortization of bond discount is $325 (= $6,500/20) per 6 months until the discount is fully amortized at the maturity date.

The entries to record the interest expense through January 2, 1977, would be

12/31/76	Interest Expense on Bonds	4,325	
	Interest Payable		4,000
	Discount on Debenture Bonds Payable		325
	To record the accrual of interest and amortization of discount for 6 months.		
1/2/77	Interest Payable	4,000	
	Cash in Bank		4,000
	To record payment of 6 months' interest.		

The bond and interest accounts would appear as follows:

DEBENTURE BONDS PAYABLE		DISCOUNT ON DEBENTURE BONDS PAYABLE	
	7/1/76 100,000	7/1/76 6,500	12/31/76 325

INTEREST EXPENSE ON BONDS		INTEREST PAYABLE	
12/31/76 4,325	(Closing Entry) 12/31/76 4,325	1/2/77 4,000	12/31/76 4,000

This series of entries will continue until July 1, 1986, when the bond discount will be completely amortized and the face value of the bonds will be paid.

The Discount on Debenture Bonds Payable account is a contra-liability account, since the discount represents additional interest that will be paid as part of the face value at maturity. The Discount on Debenture Bonds Payable should be shown on the balance sheet as a deduction from the liability account, Debenture Bonds Payable. The balance sheet for December 31, 1976, would show

Debenture Bonds Payable		$100,000	
Less: Discount on Debenture Bonds Payable		6,175	$93,825

Amortization of Bond Discount in the Statement of Changes in Financial Position

The amortization of discount requires special treatment in the statement of changes in financial position. Interest expense reported for the first 6 months is $4,325: $4,000 of coupon payments and $325 of discount amortization. Notice that only $4,000 of working capital was used for the expense. There was an increase in Interest Payable of $4,000 followed by discharge of that current liability with cash payment. The remainder of the interest expense, $325, is an increase in the net noncurrent liability, Debenture Bonds Payable less Discount on Debenture Bonds Payable. Consequently, there must be an addback to net income in determining "working capital provided by operations" in the statement of changes in financial position. The amount of the addback is the amount of the expense which did not use working capital, $325.

Amortization of Discount by the Effective-Interest Method

The amortization of discount by the straight-line method results in periodic interest expenses that are constant over the life of the loan. Since the effective liability, par value less unamortized discount, is changing, straight-line amortization results in a changing *rate* of interest each period. To calculate an interest charge each period that results in a constant interest *rate*, as implied by the present-value calculations of the proceeds from issue, the *effective-interest* method of amortization is used. The total interest charges over the life of the bonds will be the same as when the straight-line method is used, but the charge will increase each period for bonds issued at a discount.

Assume the data presented for the Macaulay Corporation, where the bonds were issued for $93,500 to yield approximately 9 percent compounded semiannually. An amortization schedule like the one shown in Exhibit 11.1, which assumes an

EXHIBIT 11.1
Effective-Interest Discount Amortization Schedule for $100,000 of 8-Percent, 10-Year Bonds Issued for 93.5 Percent of Par to Yield 9 Percent, Interest Payable Semiannually

					End of Period	
Period (6-month intervals) (1)	Liability at Start of Period (2)	Effective Interest: 4½ Percent per Period[a] (3)	Coupon Rate: 4 Percent of Par (4)	Discount Amorti-zation[b] (5)	Unamor-tized Discount[c] (6)	Net Liability[d] (7)
0					$6,500.00	$ 93,500.00
1	$93,500.00	$ 4,207.50	$ 4,000.00	$ 207.50	6,292.50	93,707.50
2	93,707.50	4,216.84	4,000.00	216.84	6,075.66	93,924.34
3	93,924.34	4,226.60	4,000.00	226.60	5,849.06	94,150.94
4	94,150.94	4,236.79	4,000.00	236.79	5,612.27	94,387.73
	(calculations continued for twenty periods)					
20	99,521.53	4,478.47	4,000.00	478.47	0	100,000.00
Total		$86,500.00	$80,000.00	$6,500.00		

[a] .045 × (2).
[b] (3) — (4).
[c] (6), previous period, minus (5), current period.
[d] $100,000 — (6) = (2) + (5).

annual effective yield of 9 percent with interest compounded and payable semi-annually, would be prepared.

The effective interest for a period, shown in column 3, is determined by multiplying the net liability at the start of the period (column 2) by the effective yield rate on the bond issue *at the time of issue*. Since the effective yield at issue is 9 percent compounded semiannually, the effective rate for the 6-month period is 4½ percent. The net liability (column 7) is increased at the end of each 6-month period by the amount of discount amortization for the period.

The interest-related entries through June 30, 1977, would be as follows:

12/31/76	Interest Expense on Bonds	4,207.50	
	Discount on Debenture Bonds Payable		207.50
	Interest Payable		4,000.00
	To record accrual of interest and amortization of discount for 6 months.		
1/2/77	Interest Payable	4,000.00	
	Cash		4,000.00
	To record payment of interest for 6 months.		
6/30/77	Interest Expense on Bonds	4,216.84	
	Discount on Debenture Bonds Payable		216.84
	Interest Payable		4,000.00
	To record accrual of interest and amortization of discount for the second 6 months.		

This series of entries will continue with an increasing amortization each 6-month period until the entire discount is amortized by the maturity date, July 1, 1986.

Accounting for Bonds Issued at a Premium

The following illustration covers the more common problems associated with bonds issued at a premium.

Assume the data presented for the Macaulay Corporation, where the 8-percent coupon, 10-year bonds are issued for $107,100 to yield approximately 7 percent and the books are closed on June 30, and December 31 of each year. The entry at time of issue would be:

7/1/76	Cash	107,100	
	Debenture Bonds Payable		100,000
	Premium on Debenture Bonds Payable		7,100
	$100,000 of 8-percent, 10-year bonds issued at a premium. The premium is recorded in a separate liability-adjunct account.		

The Premium on Debenture Bonds Payable, like discounts on bonds, represents an adjustment of the cost of borrowing. When the premium is amortized, either at an interest-payment date or at the end of an accounting period, the effect of amortization will be to *reduce* the interest expense below the cash actually paid for coupons. (Consequently, there will be a subtraction from working capital provided by operations in the statement of changes in financial position. More working capital is used than the amount of the expense reported.) The true interest expense on the loan each period will be the difference between the amount paid or payable to bondholders and the amortization of premium. The total interest that must be charged to the periods during which the loan is outstanding is $72,900 (periodic payments totaling $80,000 less the premium of $7,100). As in the case of amortization of discount, the premium can be amortized by the straight-line or the effective-interest method.

The amount of premium amortization each 6 months using the straight-line method is the total premium divided by the number of 6-month periods of the loan. In this illustration, the total premium to be amortized is $7,100, or $355 (= $7,100/20) each 6 months until the bonds mature and the premium is fully amortized.

The entries to record the interest expense and premium amortization through January 2, 1977, would be:

12/31/76	Interest Expense on Bonds	3,645	
	Premium on Debenture Bonds Payable	355	
	Interest Payable		4,000
	To record the accrual of interest and amortization of premium for 6 months.		
1/2/77	Interest Payable	4,000	
	Cash		4,000
	To record payment of 6 months' interest.		

This series of entries will continue until July 1, 1986, when the bond premium will be completely amortized and the face value of the bonds will be paid.

The Premium on Debenture Bonds Payable account is an adjunct to a liability account. It should be shown on the balance sheet as an addition to the liability account, Debenture Bonds Payable.

Amortization of premium under the effective interest method would follow the same principles used in discount amortization. A partial *premium* amortization schedule for the Macaulay Corporation's 8-percent, semiannual coupon bonds assumed to have been issued for $107,100 to yield approximately 7 percent compounded semiannually is shown in Exhibit 11.2.

Special Provisions for Bond Retirement

If the issuing firm is required to make a special provision for retiring the bond issue, the details of that requirement will be spelled out in the bond indenture. There are two major types of retirement provisions. One provides that certain portions of the principal amount will come due on a succession of maturity dates; the bonds of such issues are known as *serial bonds*. (The bonds considered so far

EXHIBIT 11.2

Effective-Interest Premium Amortization Schedule for $100,000 of 8-Percent, 10-Year Bonds Issued for 107.1 Percent of Par to Yield 7 Percent, Interest Payable Semiannually

Period (6-month intervals) (1)	Liability at Start of Period (2)	Effective Interest: $3\frac{1}{2}$ Percent per Period[a] (3)	Coupon Rate: 4 Percent of Par (4)	Premium Amortization[b] (5)	End of Period	
					Unamortized Premium[c] (6)	Net Liability[d] (7)
0					$7,100.00	$107,100.00
1	$107,100.00	$3,748.50	$4,000.00	$ 251.50	6,848.50	106,848.50
2	106,848.50	3,739.70	4,000.00	260.30	6,588.20	106,588.20
3	106,588.20	3,730.59	4,000.00	269.41	6,318.79	106,318.79
4	106,318.79	3,721.16	4,000.00	278.84	6,039.95	106,039.95
(calculations continued for twenty periods)						
20	100,483.09	3,516.91	4,000.00	483.09	0	100,000.00
Total	$72,900.00	$80,000.00	$7,100.00			

[a] $.035 \times (2)$.
[b] $(4) - (3)$.
[c] (6), previous period minus (5), current period.
[d] $100,000 + (6) = (2) - (5)$.

in this chapter are not serial bonds.) The other major type of retirement provision stipulates that the firm must accumulate a fund of cash or other assets that will be used to pay the bonds when the maturity date arrives or to reacquire and retire portions of the bond issue from time to time. Funds of this type are commonly known as *sinking funds*, although *bond retirement funds* would be a more descriptive term. The sinking fund is usually held by the trustee of the bond issue.

Some bond issues make no provision for installment repayment or for accumulating funds for the payment of the bonds when they come due. Such bonds are usually well protected with property held by the trustee as security or by an exceptionally high credit standing of the issuer. Under these circumstances, the entire bond liability may be paid at maturity out of cash in the bank at that time. Quite commonly, however, this procedure is not followed. Instead the bond issue is *refunded*—a new set of bonds is issued to obtain the funds to retire the old ones when they come due.

A common provision gives the issuing company the right to retire portions of the bond issue if it so desires, but does not require it do so. In order to facilitate such reacquisition and retirement of a part of the bond issue, the bond indenture usually provides that the bonds shall be *callable*. That is, the issuing company will have the right to reacquire its bonds at prices specified in the bond indenture. The *call price* is usually set a few percentage points above the par value and declines as the maturity date approaches.

A firm might wish to call the bonds because the current market rate of interest is less than the coupon rate on the bonds. Assume, for example, that the firm had issued 8-percent semiannual coupon bonds at par, but market interest rates and the firm's credit standing at a later date would currently allow it to borrow at 6 percent. The firm would be paying more to borrow the face value than it would have to pay if the bonds were issued currently. If $100,000 par value bonds issued at par are called at 105, the entry, in addition to the one to record the accrued interest expense, would be:

Bonds Payable	100,000	
Loss on Retirement of Bonds	5,000	
Cash		105,000

Financial Accounting Standards Board Statement No. 4 requires that this loss, or an analogous gain, recognized on bond retirement be classified as an extraordinary item in the income statement.

If the bonds were originally issued at a discount (or premium), then the appropriate portion of the unamortized discount (or premium) must also be retired when the bonds are called or otherwise retired. Suppose that $100,000 par value bonds were issued at a premium several years ago and that the unamortized premium is now $3,500. If $10,000 par value bonds are called at 105, the entry to record the retirement would be:

Bonds Payable	10,000	
Premium on Bonds Payable	350	
Loss on Retirement of Bonds	150	
Cash		10,500

The market rate of interest a firm must pay depends upon two factors: the general level of interest rates and its own credit worthiness. If the market rate of interest has risen since bonds were issued (or the firm's credit rating has declined), the bonds will sell in the market at less than issue price. A firm that wanted to retire such bonds would not *call* them, because the call price is typically greater than the issue price. Instead the firm could purchase its bonds in the open market and realize a gain on the retirement of bonds. This gain would be shown on the income statement as an extraordinary item.

Contracts and Long-Term Notes

Real estate is often purchased on a *land contract*. Equipment is frequently acquired on the installment plan, and the liability is called an *equipment contract*. Payments on such contracts are usually made monthly. Sometimes an explicit interest rate is provided in the contract, while in other cases so-called *carrying charges* are added to the purchase price, and the total is divided over a certain number of months without any specific charge being indicated for interest. A common arrangement, particularly in the case of real estate, is to have a regular monthly payment which is applied first to interest accrued since the last payment, with the balance of the payment reducing the principal.

When there is no explicit mention of interest on such a long-term contract or note, generally accepted accounting principles require that the liability be shown at its present value.[4] The difference between the present value and the face value of the liability is a discount that must be treated much the same as the discount on bonds payable. The discount must be amortized over the life of the liability and periodic interest expenses must be shown.

There are two acceptable ways to determine the present value of the liability. The first is to use the market value of the assets acquired. For example, if equipment, which has a list price of $12,000 but can be bought for $10,500 cash, is purchased in return for a note with face amount $13,500 payable in 3 years, the entry would be:

Equipment	10,500	
Discount on Long-Term Note Payable	3,000	
Long-Term Note Payable		13,500

If undeveloped land had been purchased with the same 3-year note, the firm might not be able to establish the current market value of the asset acquired. The firm would then use the interest rate it would have to pay for a similar loan in the open market to find the present value of the note. This is the second acceptable method for quantifying the amount of the liability. Suppose that the market rate for notes such as the one above is 8 percent compounded annually. The present value at 8 percent per year of the $13,500 note due in 3 years is $10,716 ($= \$13,500 \times .7938$; see Example 4 in Appendix 11.1 of this chapter). The entry to record the purchase of land and payment with the note would be:

Land	10,716	
Discount on Long-Term Note Payable	2,784	
Long-Term Note Payable		13,500

A note that is the long-term liability of the borrower is a long-term asset of the lender. Generally accepted accounting principles require the lender to show the asset in the Long-Term Note Receivable Account at its present value. The rate at which the lender discounts the note should in theory be the same as that used by the borrower, but in practice the two rates often differ.

Pension Plans

Most firms have pension plans that, in one form or another, provide for payments to its retired former employees. The actuarial and accounting details of pension

---

[4] Opinion No. 21, Accounting Principles Board, AICPA, August 1971.

liabilities are beyond the scope of introductory accounting. You can, however, get some insight into the variables of corporate pension plans by referring to the following terms in the glossary: *defined benefit plan* and *money-purchase plan; contributory* and *noncontributory; vested, partially vested,* and *graded vesting; funded* and *partially funded.* The accounting aspects of pension plans are discussed in the glossary at *normal costs, past service costs,* and *prior service costs.*

Leases

There is one business obligation that meets all of the criteria for a liability but is sometimes not treated as a liability. That obligation is a long-term noncancelable lease. Many firms are currently acquiring rights to use assets through long-term noncancelable leases. A company might, for example, agree to lease an airplane for 15 years, or a building for 40 years, promising to pay a fixed periodic fee for the duration of the lease. Promising to make an irrevocable series of lease payments commits the firm just as surely as a bond indenture or mortgage, but generally accepted accounting principles allow firms not to show some obligations as liabilities as they would have to do if they issued either bonds or mortgages. This mode of financing is often referred to as *off-balance sheet* financing because the implicit liability is not shown on the balance sheet. Perhaps the possibility of not having to show the debt for these leases on the balance sheet helps to explain why so many firms choose to acquire such services through lease arrangements.

Let us examine the accounting for noncancelable leases, how it may differ from the usual accounting treatment for similar commitments, and the effects on the financial statements of both treatments. Suppose that the Myers Company wants to acquire a computer that has a 3-year life and costs $30,000, and assume that Myers Company can borrow money for 3 years at 8 percent per year. The computer manufacturer is willing to sell the computer for $30,000 or to lease it for 3 years on a noncancelable basis. That is, Myers Company must make payments for 3 years no matter what. Myers Company is responsible for property taxes, maintenance, and repairs of the computer under either the purchase or leasing plans.

Assume that the lease is signed on January 1, 1976, and that payments on the lease are due on December 31, 1976, 1977, and 1978. In practice, lease payments are usually made in advance, but the computations in the example are simpler if we assume payments at the end of the year. Compound-interest computations show that each lease payment must be $11,641. (The present value of $1 paid at the end of this year and each of the next 2 years is $2.5771 when the interest rate is 8 percent per year. See Appendix Table 4 at the end of the book. Since the lease payments must have present value of $30,000, each payment must be $30,000/2.5771 = $11,641).

Operating-Lease Method In an *operating lease,* the owner, or lessor, merely sells the rights to use the property to the lessee for specified periods of time. The telephone company leases telephones by the month, and car rental companies lease cars by the day or week on an operating basis. If the Myers Company lease was accounted for as an operating lease, then no entry would be made on January

1, 1976, when the lease is signed, and the following entry is made on each of the dates December 31, 1976, 1977, and 1978:

Leasing (Rental) Expense	11,641	
Cash		11,641
To recognize annual expense of leasing computer.		

Financing-Lease Method If this lease were judged to be a form of borrowing to purchase the computer, then it would be accounted for as a *financing lease.** This treatment recognizes the signing of the lease as the simultaneous acquisition of a long-term asset, called a *leasehold,* and the incurring of a long-term liability for lease payments. At the time the lease is signed, both the leasehold and the liability are recorded on the books at the present value of the liability, $30,000 in the example.

The entry made at the time Myers Company signed its 3-year noncancelable lease would be:

Asset—Computer Leasehold	30,000	
Liability—Present Value of Lease Obligations		30,000
To recognize acquisition of asset and the related liability.		

At the end of the year, two separate entries must be made. The leasehold is an asset and, like most assets, it must be amortized over its useful life. The first entry made at the end of each year recognizes the amortization of the leasehold asset. Assuming that Myers Company uses straight-line amortization of its leasehold, the entry made at the end of 1976, 1977, and 1978 would be:

Amortization Expense (on Computer Leasehold)	10,000	
Asset—Computer Leasehold		10,000

(An alternative treatment would be to credit a contra-asset account, Accumulated Amortization of Computer Leasehold.) The second entry made at the end of each year recognizes the lease payment, which is part payment of interest on the liability and part reduction in the liability itself. The entries made at the end of each of the 3 years would be:

December 31, 1976:		
Interest Expense	2,400	
Liability—Present Value of Lease Obligations	9,241	
Cash		11,641
To recognize lease payment, interest on liability for year (.08 × $30,000 = $2,400) and the plug for reduction in the liability. The present value of the liability after this entry is $20,759 = $30,000 − $9,241.		

---

* As this book goes to press, the FASB proposes calling this a "capital lease."

December 31, 1977:

Interest Expense	1,661	
Liability—Present Value of Lease Obligations	9,980	
Cash		11,641

To recognize lease payment, interest on liability for year (.08 × \$20,759 = \$1,661) and the plug for reduction in the liability. The present value of the liability after this entry is \$10,779 = \$20,759 − \$9,980.

December 31, 1978:

Interest Expense	862	
Liability—Present Value of Lease Obligations	10,779	
Cash		11,641

To recognize lease payment, interest on liability for year (.08 × \$10,779 = \$862) and the plug for reduction in the liability. The present value of the liability after this entry is zero (= \$10,779 − \$10,779).

Notice that in this method, the total expense over the 3 years is \$34,923, consisting of \$30,000 (= \$10,000 + \$10,000 + \$10,000) for amortization expense and \$4,923 (= \$2,400 + \$1,661 + \$862) for interest charges. This is exactly the same as the total expense recognized under the operating-lease method described above. The difference between the operating-lease method and the financing-lease method is the *timing* of the expense recognition and the entries in balance sheet accounts. The operating-lease method requires no entries in balance sheet accounts and is often described as "off-balance-sheet financing" because it recognizes neither the asset nor the liability. The financing-lease method recognizes both the asset and the liability, and also recognizes expense sooner than does the operating-lease method, as summarized in Exhibit 11.3.

In this simple example, expense under the financing-lease method is only slightly larger than expense under the operating-lease method in the first year. In more realistic cases where the lease extends over 20 years, the expense in the first year

EXHIBIT 11.3
Comparison of Expense Recognized Under Operating and Financing Lease Methods

Year	Expense Recognized Each Year under	
	Operating-Lease Method	Financing-Lease Method
1976	\$11,641	\$12,400 (= \$10,000 + \$2,400)
1977	11,641	11,661 (= 10,000 + 1,661)
1978	11,641	10,862 (= 10,000 + 862)
Total	\$34,923[a]	\$34,923 (= \$30,000[b] + \$4,923[c])

[a] Leasing expense.
[b] Amortization expense.
[c] Interest expense.

under the financing-lease method may be twenty-five percent larger than under the operating-lease method.

Most firms prefer to use the operating-lease method whenever they can, because the reported income is higher in the earlier years of the lease than it would be under the financing-lease method. Starting in 1974, however, the Securities and Exchange Commission requires that if the operating-lease method is used in financial reports when the lease qualifies as a financing lease under SEC definitions, then the footnotes to the financial statements must disclose how much lower net income would have been if the financing-lease method had been used. A recent annual report of UAL, Inc. (United Air Lines), illustrates this supplementary disclosure. A footnote to the financial statement states, in part,

> Assuming the companies were to have capitalized their financing leases, amortized the cost of the rights to the leased assets on a straight-line basis and reflected interest expense on the basis of the outstanding lease liability, net earnings [of $101 million] would have been reduced by $6,940,000 [or about 6.8 percent]. . . . This reduction in net earnings is caused by the aggregate of the assumed amortization ($66,587,000) . . . and interest expense ($58,750,000) . . . being greater than the actual rentals paid.

Within the near future, we expect the Financial Accounting Standards Board to require that the financing-lease method be used for most noncancelable leases in computing and reporting net income.

■ DEFERRED INCOME TAXES

As we have indicated at various points in this book, there are some areas where there are alternative generally accepted accounting principles. The tax laws and regulations similarly allow a choice of alternative treatments for the same event. One example is in the calculation of depreciation charges. Both generally accepted accounting principles and the tax law allow the firm to choose from among straight-line, sum-of-the-years'-digits, and double-declining-balance methods of depreciation.

In selecting among alternative methods for tax purposes, management often tries to minimize the present value of the firm's tax liabilities for a given set of operating results. (The principles of income tax management are summarized conveniently by the expression "Pay the least amount of tax, as late as possible, within the law." This is sometimes known as the *least* and *latest* rule. It is difficult to generalize about which of the alternative accounting principles management selects, or should select, for financial reporting. This question is discussed more fully in Chapters Ten and Fifteen.

Suppose that, for whatever reasons it deems appropriate, management decides to use straight-line depreciation for a given plant asset for financial reporting. Suppose, further, that management has calculated that the present value of taxes paid will be smallest if the sum-of-the-years'-digits method is used for tax purposes. The firm is allowed to use straight-line for financial reporting and sum-of-the-years'-digits for taxes. The firm will thereby show a higher pretax income in its financial reports than in its tax return in the early years of the asset's life. This is permissible, but the firm must show in its income statement *deferred income tax expense* for the difference between the tax payment that results from using the accelerated method and the tax payment that *would have* resulted had it used the straight-line method for tax reporting.[5] Since the expense is recognized but payment is deferred, a liability is created.

The problems of deferred income tax liabilities can perhaps be best understood by examining an example. Assume that Drake, Inc., pays income taxes at the rate of 40 percent of taxable income. Suppose that Drake purchased a plant asset for $170,000 that has a 5-year life and an estimated salvage value of $20,000. Suppose further that this asset produces net cash flows of $44,000 a year. That is, after paying for the cash costs of running and maintaining the asset, the firm enjoys a $44,000 per year excess of receipts over expenditures from it. Drake uses straight-line depreciation for financial reporting and the sum-of-the-years'-digits method for calculating its taxes. Thus, in the first year the new plant asset is used, depreciation on the financial records will be $30,000 ($= \$150,000/5$) and on the tax return will be $50,000 ($=\$150,000 \times 5/15$). Suppose that in addition to the $44,000 of net cash flow from the plant asset, other pretax income for each year is $80,000. Exhibit 11.4 summarizes the computation of taxes for financial reporting and for tax purposes. By using the accelerated method for tax purposes, Drake is able to pay $8,000 less in taxes in the first year than the financial reports will show as the income tax expense for the year. The entry to record the income tax transaction would be:

Income Tax Expense	37,600	
Income Tax Payable		29,600
Deferred Income Tax Liability		8,000
First year income tax entry.		

Notice that $8,000 of tax expense did not use working capital, so that an addback to net income is required in the statement of changes in financial position in deriving "working capital provided by operations." The $8,000 of expense merely increases the noncurrent liability for deferred income taxes. The statement of changes in financial position of Lehigh Portland Cement Company (Exhibit 6.5), Ford Motor Company (Exhibit 12.3), and Westinghouse Electric Corporation (Exhibit 13.3) all illustrate the addback to net income for deferred taxes in arriving at working capital provided by operations.

If only one asset is considered, the $8,000 difference does not represent taxes forgiven but merely taxes delayed. Later, in the fourth and fifth years of this example, the financial records will show larger depreciation and smaller income than the tax return will show. Consequently, the income tax expense will be lower than

[5] Opinion No. 11, Accounting Principles Board, AICPA, December 1967.

EXHIBIT 11.4
*Deferred Income Tax Computations
For Drake, Inc.*

FIRST YEAR

	Financial Reports	Tax Return
Other Pretax Income	$80,000	$ 80,000
Cash Flow from Plant Asset	44,000	44,000
Depreciation	(30,000)	(50,000)
Income Before Taxes	$94,000	$ 74,000
Income Tax Expense (at 40 percent)	$37,600	
Income Tax Currently Payable (at 40 percent)		$ 29,600

FIFTH YEAR

	Financial Reports	Tax Return
Other Pretax Income	$80,000	$ 80,000
Cash Flow from Plant Asset	44,000	44,000
Depreciation	(30,000)	(10,000)
Income Before Taxes	$94,000	$114,000
Income Tax Expense (at 40 percent)	$37,600	
Income Tax Currently Payable (at 40 percent)		$ 45,600

the income taxes payable in those years and Drake will debit the Deferred Income Tax Liability. Exhibit 11.4 also shows the tax computations for the fifth year of Drake's plant asset, assuming that nothing has changed except for the passage of time. The entry to record the fifth year's tax transaction would be:

Income Tax Expense	37,600	
Deferred Income Tax Liability	8,000	
Income Tax Payable		45,600
Fifth year income tax entry.		

More working capital ($45,600) is used than the amount of the expense ($37,600) reported in the income statement. Consequently, there must be a subtraction of $8,000 in the statement of changes in financial position to derive "working capital provided by operations."

Exhibit 11.5 shows a summary of the entries in Drake's Deferred Income Tax Liability account for the 5 years during which it uses the plant asset. Observe that the total tax expense shown on the financial statements over the asset's life is the same as the total taxes payable, but that the accelerated method used on the tax returns defers payment and thus leads to a lower present value of taxes paid.

In general, the deferred income tax liability arises from differences in timing

EXHIBIT 11.5
Summary of Deferred Income Tax Liability Account for Drake, Inc.

Year (1)	Financial Statements				Tax Returns			Deferred Income Tax Liability Account		
	Income Before Depreciation and Tax Expenses (2)	Depreciation Expense (3)	Pretax Income (4)	Tax Expense (5)[a]	Depreciation Deduction (6)[b]	Pretax Income (7)[c]	Taxes Payable (8)[d]	Debit (9)	Credit (10)	Credit Balance at Year-End (11)
1	$124,000	$ 30,000	$94,000	$ 37,600	$ 50,000	$ 74,000	$ 29,600		$8,000	$ 8,000
2	124,000	30,000	94,000	37,600	40,000	84,000	33,600		4,000	12,000
3	124,000	30,000	94,000	37,600	30,000	94,000	37,600	—	—	12,000
4	124,000	30,000	94,000	37,600	20,000	104,000	41,600	$4,000		8,000
5	124,000	30,000	94,000	37,600	10,000	114,000	45,600	8,000		0
		$150,000		$188,000	$150,000		$188,000			

a .40 × $94,000.
b ($170,000 − $20,000) × t/15, where t = 5, 4, 3, 2, 1 for the years, in order.
c $124,000 − (6).
d (7) × .40.

333

between financial reporting of revenues and expenses and tax reporting of these items. The following list shows some of the ways in which the timing differences can arise.

1. Depreciation for tax purposes is different from that shown in the financial records in a given period either because different asset lives or different depreciation patterns, or both, are used for the two purposes.
2. Revenues from installment sales are recognized in the financial records on the date of sale, but are recognized for tax purposes in the periods when payments are received.
3. Revenues from long-term construction projects are recognized in financial records on the percentage-of-completion basis but on tax returns under the completed-contract basis.

Some differences between reported income and taxable income can never reverse. An example is interest revenue on tax-exempt municipal bonds held as asset. Such tax-exempt interest is part of reported income but not of taxable income. Differences between reported income and taxable income that can never reverse are called *permanent differences*. Permanent differences do not require an entry for deferred income taxes.

Weaknesses of Accounting for Deferred Income Taxes

As the Drake example shows, if the deferred tax liability is considered to arise from the depreciation of any one asset, it will eventually be paid. In reality, a growing firm may be able to defer payment of the so-called liability indefinitely. If a firm acquires plant assets each year in a dollar amount equal to, or more than, it acquired in the preceding year, then tax payments will never exceed reported tax expense. Moreover, in no year will there be net debits to the Deferred Tax Liability account arising from different depreciation patterns. Tax payments can exceed tax expense reported in the financial statements only when the firm stops acquiring new assets while it continues to earn positive taxable income. (If there is no taxable income, there is no income tax expense.) We find it hard to visualize a company that both stops replacing assets and continues to earn profits. Thus, the deferred tax liability is likely never to be discharged.

The deferred income tax liability clearly does not meet the four criteria suggested for liabilities. It fails three of the tests: contractual obligation, certainty of amount, and certainty of due date. Nevertheless, generally accepted accounting principles wish to match the reported income tax expense with the reported pretax income of a period and, thus, require the firm to recognize the deferred income tax expense in the usual case. The account credited when the deferred income tax expense is recognized has a special nature which Accounting Principles Board Opinion No. 11 says is a "deferred credit" and not a liability.[6] Since we feel that

---

[6] Opinion No. 11, Accounting Principles Board, AICPA, December 1967.

the right-hand side of the balance sheet logically contains only liabilities and owners' equity items, we classify the Deferred Income Tax Liability as an *indeterminate-term liability*.

■ CONTINGENT LIABILITIES—POTENTIAL OBLIGATIONS

One of the criteria used by the accountant to recognize a liability is that there be a legal obligation. The world of business and law is full of uncertainties. At any given time the firm may find itself potentially liable for events that have occurred in the past. A *contingent liability* is not a current legal obligation but a potential future obligation. It arises from an event that has occurred in the past but whose outcome is not now known. Whether or not the item becomes an obligation, and how large an obligation it will become, depends on a future event, such as the outcome of a lawsuit.

Suppose that the company is sued for damages in a formal court proceeding for an accident involving a customer who was visiting the company. The suit is not scheduled for trial until after the close of the accounting period. If the company's lawyers and auditors agree that the outcome is likely to be favorable for the company or that if unfavorable, the amount of the damage settlement will not be large, then no obligation or liability will be recognized in the accounts. The footnotes to the financial statements must disclose, however, significant contingent liabilities.

If either the company's lawyers or auditors expect that the outcome will be unfavorable and the amount of damages awarded by the court will be significant, then the item should not be a contingent liability but an *estimated liability* which should be reported as a liability in the balance sheet. If an estimated liability were recognized for the expected amount of the court's award of damages, then the journal entry would be:

Loss on Damage Claim	50,000	
Estimated Liability for Damages		50,000
To recognize estimated liability for expected damage arising from lawsuit.		

The debit in the above entry is to a loss account (presented among other expenses on the income statement), and the credit is to an estimated liability which should be treated as a current liability, similar to the Deferred Warranty Liability account, on the balance sheet. In practice, an account with the title "Estimated Liability for Damages" would seldom, if ever, appear in published financial statements, since it would be perceived as an admission of guilt. Such an admission is likely to adversely affect the outcome of the trial. The liability account would be combined with others for financial statement presentation.

The term *contingent liability* is used only when the item is not recognized in the accounts but, rather, in the footnotes. (Notes receivable sold *with* recourse, described in Chapter Eight, are another example of a contingent liability.) A recent annual report of General Motors illustrates the disclosure of contingent liabilities as follows.

Note 15. Contingent Liabilities

There are various claims and pending actions against the Corporation and its subsidiaries in respect of taxes, product liability, alleged patent infringements, warranties, alleged air pollution, and other matters arising out of the conduct of the business. Certain of these actions purport to be class actions, seeking damages in very large amounts. The amounts of liability on these claims and actions at . . . [year-end] were not determinable but, in the opinion of management, the ultimate liability resulting will not materially affect the consolidated financial position or results of operations of the Corporation and its consolidated subsidiaries.

■ SUMMARY

Liabilities generally are legal obligations of definite or reasonably certain amounts due at definite or reasonably certain times incurred in return for current benefits. Some obligations of the firm do not meet all these criteria but are, nevertheless, treated as liabilities. An example of such a liability is that for deferred income taxes. We suggest that deferred income taxes be viewed as a liability of indeterminate term. Often, obligations under long-term noncancelable leases and pension plans meet the criteria to be liabilities but are not accounted for as liabilities.

Accounting for long-term liabilities is accomplished by recording these obligations at their present value at the date the obligation is incurred and then showing the change in that present value as the maturity date of the obligation approaches. Retirement of long-term liabilities can be brought about in a variety of ways, but in each case, the process is the same. The net obligation is offset against what is given in return, usually cash, with gain or loss on retirement recognized as appropriate.

Appendix 11.1
Compound-interest and Present-value Computations

Money is a scarce resource, and its owner can use it to command other resources. Like owners of other scarce resources, owners of money can permit others (borrowers) to rent the use of their money for a period of time. Payment for the use of money differs little from other rental payments, such as those made to a landlord for the use of property or to a car rental agency for the use of a car. Payment for the use of money is called *interest*. Accounting is concerned with interest because it must record transactions where the use of money is bought and sold.

Accountants are concerned with interest calculations for another, equally important, reason, Expenditures for an asset most often do not occur at the same time as the receipts for services produced by that asset. Money received sooner is more valuable than money received later. The difference in timing can affect whether or not acquiring an asset is profitable. Amounts of money received at different times are different commodities. Accountants use interest calculations to make amounts of money to be paid or received at different times comparable. For example, an analyst might compare two amounts to be received at two different times by using interest calculations to find the equivalent value of one amount at the time the other is due. Money contracts involving a series of money payments over time, such as bonds, mortgages, notes, and leases, are evaluated by finding the *present value* of the stream of payments. The present value of a stream of payments is a single amount of money due at the present time that is the economic equivalent of the entire stream.

■ COMPOUND INTEREST

The quotation of interest "cost" is typically specified as a percentage of the amount borrowed per unit of time. Examples are 6 percent per year, 1 percent per month, and, for discounts on purchases, 2/10, net/30, which is equivalent to 2 per-cent for 20 days because if the discount is not taken, the money can be used for an extra 20 days. The amount borrowed or loaned is called the *principal*. To *compound* interest means either to pay to the lender at the end of the period the in-terest accumulated during the period or, at the end of the period, to add the interest to the principal so that the principal for the next interest period is larger. The period between interest calculations, during which the principal accumulates interest, is called the *compounding* period.

If you deposit $1,000 in a savings account that pays compound interest at the rate of 6 percent per year, you will be credited with $60 at the end of a year. (The bank's credit is your debit.) Thus, $1,060 will be earning interest during the second year. During the second year your principal of $1,060 will earn $63.60 in-terest, $60 on the initial deposit of $1,000 and $3.60 on the $60 earned the previous year.

The "force," or effect of compound interest is more substantial than many people realize. For example, compounded annually at 6 percent, money "doubles itself" in less than 12 years. Put another way, if you invest $49.70 in a savings ac-count that pays 6 percent compounded annually, you will have $100 in 12 years. If the Indians who sold Manhattan Island for $24 in May 1626 had been able to invest that principal at 8 percent compounded annually, the principal would have grown to almost $12 trillion by May 1976, 350 years later. The rate of interest affects the amount of accumulation more than you might expect. If the Indians invested at 6 percent rather than 8 percent, the $24 would have grown to "only" $16 billion in 350 years.

When only the original principal earns interest during the entire life of the loan, the interest due at the time the loan is repaid is called *simple* interest. Simple interest is computed as the principal multiplied by the rate multiplied by the elapsed time. At simple interest of 6 percent per year, the Indians' $24 would have grown to only $528 in 350 years, $24 of principal and $504 of simple interest ($24 × .06 × 350). Nearly all economic calculations involve compound interest.

Problems involving compound interest fall into two groups with respect to time: first, there are the problems for which we want to know the future value of money invested or loaned today; second, there are the problems for which we want to know the present value, or today's value, of money to be received or paid later.

Future Value

When $1.00 is invested today at 6 percent is compounded annually, it will grow to $1.0600 at the end of 1 year, $1.1236 at the end of 2 years, $1.1910 at the end of 3 years, and so on according to the following formula:

$$F_n = P(1 + r)^n,$$

where

F_n represents the accumulation, or future value
P represents the initial investment today
r is the interest rate per period
n is the number of periods from today.

The amount F_n is the future value of the present payment, P, compounded at r percent per period for n periods. Table 1 in the Appendix at the back of the book shows the future values of $P = \$1$ for various numbers of periods and for various interest rates. Extracts from that table, rounded to four decimal places, are shown here in Table 11A.1.

TABLE 11A.1 (Appendix Table 1)
Future Value of $1 at 6 Percent and 8 Percent per Period
$$F_n = (1 + r)^n$$

Number of Periods = n	Rate = r	
	6 Percent	8 Percent
1	1.0600	1.0800
2	1.1236	1.1664
3	1.1910	1.2597
10	1.7908	2.1589
20	3.2071	4.6610

Example Problems in Determining Future Value
1. How much will $1,000 deposited today at 6 percent compounded annually be worth 10 years from now?

One dollar deposited today at 6 percent will grow to $1.7908; therefore $1,000 will grow to $1,000(1.06)^{10} = $1,000 × 1.7908 = $1,790.80.

2. How much will $500 deposited today at 8 percent compounded annually be worth 23 years from today?

The tables do not show values for 23 periods. Interpolation between the numbers shown in tables in in imprecise; rather, notice that $F_{23} = P(1.08)^{23} = P(1.08)^{20} \times (1.08)^3$. Calculate the future value for 23 years in two steps: first, determine the amount that $1 will grow to in 20 years at 8 percent or $4.6610. Then let $4.6610 be the principal that grows for 3 (more) years. One dollar invested for 3 years at 8 percent grows to $1.2597. Therefore, $4.6610 invested for 3 years grows to $4.6610 × 1.2597 = $5.8715. (Note that factors for any two periods that sum to 23 can be used and produce the same answer. For example, factors from the tables in the Appendix at the end of the book can be used to compute: $(1.08)^{23} = (1.08)^{11} \times (1.08)^{12}$ = 2.33164 × 2.51817 = 5.8715.) So $1 invested for 23 years at 8 percent has a future value of $5.8715, and $500 invested for 23 years at 8 percent grows to $500 × 5.8715 = $2,935.75.

A rule of thumb worth remembering for rough calculations is the *Rule of 72.* For interest rates between 3 percent and 12 percent per period, the number of periods required for an amount to double in value when invested at i percent per period is $72/i$. The Rule of 72 says, for example, that money invested at 4 percent per period doubles in $72/4 = 18$ periods; the exact answer is slightly more than 17.67 periods. At 10 percent, the Rule of 72 suggests that money doubles in 7.2 periods, which is reasonably close to the correct answer, approximately 7.27 periods.[7]

Present Value

The preceding section developed the tools for computing the future value, F_n, of a sum of money, P, deposited or invested today. P is known; F_n is calculated. This section deals with the problems of calculating how much principal P has to be invested today in order to have a specified amount, F_n, at the end of n periods. The future amount, F_n, the interest rate, r, and the number of periods, n, are known; P is to be found. In order to have $1 one year from today when interest is earned at 6 percent, P of $.9434 must be invested today. That is, $F_1 = P(1.06)^1$ or $1 = $.9434 × 1.06$. Since $F_n = P(1 + r)^n$, dividing both sides of the equation by $(1 + r)^n$ yields

$$\frac{F_n}{(1 + r)^n} = P$$

or

$$P = \frac{F_n}{(1 + r)^n} = F_n (1 + r)^{-n}.$$

[7] An even better rule, one that works for interest rates between ¼ percent and 100 percent, is the Rule of 69: compounded at i percent per period, money doubles in $69/i + .35$ periods. See John P. Gould and Roman L. Weil, "The Rule of 69," *Journal of Business,* 47 (July, 1974), 397–398.

To have $F_2 = \$1$ two years from today, the amount P that must be invested at 6 percent is $P = \$1/(1.06)^2$. The value of $(1.06)^2$ can be read from Table 11A.1 (2-period row, under the $r = 6$ percent column) as 1.1236. The quotient is $1/1.1236 = .8900$. In order to accumulate $1 at the end of two periods, $.89 must be invested when the interest rate is 6 percent.

The number $(1 + r)^{-n}$ is the present value of $1 to be received after n periods when interest is earned at r percent per period. The term *discount* is used in this context as follows: the *discounted* present value of $1 to be received n periods in the future is $(1 + r)^{-n}$ when the *discount* rate is r percent per period for n periods. The number r is the discount *rate* and the number $(1 + r)^{-n}$ is the discount *factor* for n periods. A discount factor $(1 + r)^{-n}$ is merely the reciprocal, or inverse, of a number, $(1 + r)^n$, in Table 11A.1. Therefore, tables of discount factors are not necessary for present-value calculations if tables of future values are at hand. But present-value calculations are so frequently needed, and division is so onerous, that tables of discount factors are as widely available as tables of future values. Portions of Appendix Table 2 (at the back of the book), which shows discount factors or, equivalently, present values of $1 for various interest (or discount) rates for various numbers of periods, are shown in Table 11A.2.

TABLE 11A.2 (Appendix Table 2)
Present Value of $1 at 6 Percent and 8 Percent per Period
$P = F_n (1 + r)^{-n}$

Number of Periods = n	Rate = r	
	6 Percent	8 Percent
1	.9434	.9259
2	.8900	.8573
3	.8396	.7938
10	.5584	.4632
20	.3118	.2145

Example Problems in Determining Present Values
3. What is the present value of $1 due 10 years from now if the interest (equivalently, the discount) rate r is 6 percent per year?

From Table 11.A.2, 6-percent column, 10-period row, the present value of $1 to be received ten periods hence at 6 percent is $.5584.

4. You issue a noninterest-bearing note that promises to pay $13,500 three years from today in exchange for undeveloped land. How much is that promise worth today if the discount rate is 8 percent per period?

One dollar received 3 years hence discounted at 8 percent has a present value of $.7938. Thus the promise is worth $13,500 × .7938 = $10,716.

5. What is the present value of $5,000 to be received 23 years hence when the discount rate is 6 percent per year?

The tables do not show values for 23 periods. Interpolation is not precise; rather, note that $P = F_{23}(1.06)^{-23} = F_{23}(1.06)^{-20}(1.06)^{-3}$. Calculate the present value in two steps: first, find the present value of $1 received 20 years later discounted at 6 percent, $.3118. Then let $.3118 represent the amount to be received 3 years later. The present value of $1 received 3 years later discounted at 6 percent is $.8396. Therefore the present value of $.3118 to be received 3 years later is $.3118 $\times$ .8396 = $.2618. [Factors for any two periods that sum to 23 could be used: for example, $(1.06)^{-23} = (1.06)^{-11} \times (1.06)^{-12} = .52679 \times .49697 = .2618$.] So $1 received 23 years from now is currently worth $.2618, and $5,000 received 23 years from now is worth $5,000 $\times$ .2618 = $1,309 today, when the discount rate is 6 percent per year.

■ ANNUITIES

An *annuity* is a series of equal payments made at the beginning or end of equal periods of time. Examples of annuities include monthly rental payments, semiannual corporate bond coupon (or interest) payments, and annual payments to a retired employee under a pension plan. Armed with an understanding of the tables for future and present values, you can solve any annuity problem. Annuities arise so often, however, and their solution is so tedious without special tables, that annuity problems warrant special study and the use of special tables.

Terminology

An annuity whose payments occur at the *end* of each period is called an *ordinary annuity* or an *annuity in arrears*. Corporate bond coupon payments are usually paid in arrears or, equivalently, the first payment does not occur until after the bond has been outstanding for 6 months.

An annuity whose payments occur at the *beginning* of each period is called an *annuity due* or an *annuity in advance*. Rent is usually paid in advance, so a series of rental payments is an annuity in advance.

A *deferred* annuity is one whose first payment is at some time later than the end of the first period.

Annuities can be paid forever. Such annuities are called *perpetuities*. Bonds that promise payments forever are called *consols*. The British and Canadian governments have, from time to time, issued consols. A perpetuity can be in arrears or in advance. The only difference between the two is the timing of the first payment.

Annuities can be confusing. Their study is made easier with a time line such as the one shown below.

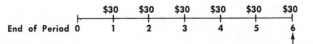

A time line marks the end of each period, numbers the periods, shows the payments to be received or paid, and shows the time at which the annuity is valued. The time line just pictured represents an ordinary annuity for six periods of $30 to be valued at the end of period 6. The end of period 0 is "now." The first payment is to be made one period from now.

Ordinary Annuities

The future values of ordinary annuities are shown in Appendix Table 3, portions of which are reproduced in Table 11A.3.

TABLE 11A.3 (Appendix Table 3)
Future Value of an Ordinary Annuity of $1 per Period at 6 Percent and 8 Percent

Number of	Rate = r	
Periods = n	6 Percent	8 Percent
1	1.0000	1.0000
2	2.0600	2.0800
3	3.1836	3.2464
5	5.6371	5.8666
10	13.1808	14.4866
20	36.7856	45.7620

Consider an ordinary annuity for three periods at 6 percent. The time line for the future value of such an annuity is

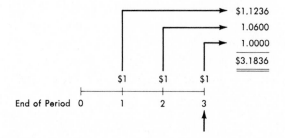

The $1 received at the end of the first period earns interest for two periods, so it is worth $1.1236 at the end of period 3. The $1 received at the end of the second period grows to $1.06 by the end of period 3, and the $1 received at the end of period 3 is, of course, worth $1 at the end of period 3. The entire annuity is worth $3.1836 at the end of period 3. The mathematical expression for the future value, F, of an annuity of A per period, compounded at r percent per period for n periods, is

$$F = \frac{A[(1 + r)^n - 1]}{r}.$$

The present values of ordinary annuities are shown in Appendix Table 4, portions of which are reproduced in Table 11A.4.

TABLE 11A.4 (Appendix Table 4)
Present Value of an Ordinary Annuity of $1 per Period at
6 Percent and 8 Percent

Number of Periods $= n$	Rate $= r$	
	6 Percent	8 Percent
1	0.9434	0.9259
2	1.8334	1.7833
3	2.6730	2.5771
5	4.2124	3.9927
10	7.3601	6.7101
20	11.4699	9.8182

The time line for the present value of an ordinary annuity of $1 per period for 3 periods, discounted at 6 percent, is

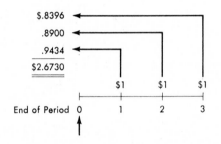

The $1 to be received at the end of period 1 has a present value of $.9434, the $1 to be received at the end of period 2 has a present value of $.8900, and the dollar to be received at the end of the third period has a present value of $.8396. Each of these numbers comes from Table 11A.2. The present value of the annuity is the sum of these individual present values, $2.6730, shown in Table 11A.4.

The present value of an ordinary annuity for n periods is the sum of the present values of $1 received 1 period from now plus $1 received two periods from now . . . , plus $1 received n periods from now. The mathematical expression for the present value, P_A, of an annuity of A per period, for n periods, compounded at r percent per period, is

$$P_A = \frac{A[1 - (1 + r)^{-n}]}{r}.$$

Example Problems in Determining Values of Ordinary Annuities
6. What is the present value of an ordinary annuity of $4,000 to be received each 6 months for 10 years at 8 percent compounded semiannually?

Eight percent compounded semiannually for 10 years is equivalent to 4 percent per period compounded for twenty periods. From Appendix Table 4, 4-percent column and 20-period row, $1 received at the end of each period has a present value of $13.59033. So the $4,000 semiannual annuity has a present value of $4,000 × 13.59033 = $54,361.

7. What is the future value of $1 invested per year compounded at 6 percent for 23 years if the first dollar is invested 1 year from now (an ordinary annuity for 23 periods)?

The time line is

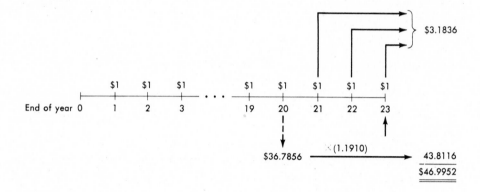

The tables do not show future values for 23 years. At the end of year 20, the annuity will have grown to $36.7856 (Table 11A.3). That accumulation will grow for 3 more years at 6 percent, so (from Table 11A.1, future value of $1 compounded at 6 percent for 3 periods) it will grow to $36.7856 × 1.1910 = $43.8116. In addition, as of the end of year 20, the payments from the ends of years 21, 22, and 23 are an ordinary annuity for 3 years with a future value of $3.1836. The entire annuity has a future value of $43.8116 + $3.1836 = $46.9952.

8. What is the present value of an ordinary annuity of $1 per year for 23 years at 6 percent?

The time line for this problem is

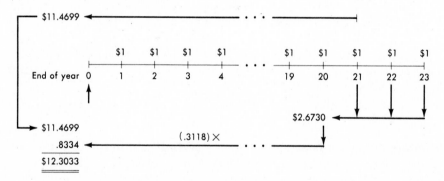

The first twenty payments have a present value of $11.4699, as shown in Table 11A.4. As of the end of year 20, the final three payments have a present value of $2.6730. One dollar received in 20 years is worth $.3118 at the start of year zero, so $2.6730 due at the end of year zero is worth $.8334 (= $2.6730 × .3118). The entire annuity is worth $11.4699 + $.8334 = $12.3033.

9. What semiannual payment must the Midwestern Products Company make to discharge its $30,000 mortgage obligation? Recall from the discussion of mortgages that Midwestern borrowed $30,000 on October 1, 1975, and promised to make ten semiannual payments commencing April 1, 1976. Each payment includes both accrued interest and a principal repayment. The interest rate is 8 percent per year compounded semiannually, or 4 percent per 6 months.

The time line for this problem is

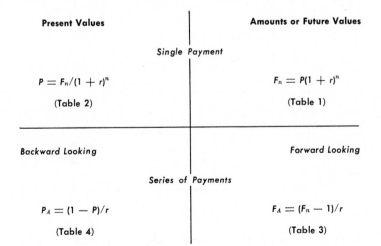

We need to know the periodic annuity payment that has a present value of $30,000 when paid for ten periods at a discount rate of 4 percent per period. From Appendix Table 4, the present value of a $1 annuity for 10 periods at 4 percent per period is $8.1109. Therefore, the semiannual payment that has a present value of $30,000 is $30,000/8.1109 = $3,699.

■ SUMMARY OF COMPOUND INTEREST

Accountants typically use one of four kinds of compound interest calculations: the present or future value of a single payment or a series of payments. These four calculations are pictured in the following diagram.[8]

Present Values	Amounts or Future Values
Single Payment	
$P = F_n/(1 + r)^n$	$F_n = P(1 + r)^n$
(Table 2)	(Table 1)
Backward Looking	*Forward Looking*
Series of Payments	
$P_A = (1 - P)/r$	$F_A = (F_n - 1)/r$
(Table 4)	(Table 3)

[8] David O. Green of the University of Chicago was, to our knowledge, the first to present this diagram.

The table numbers shown correspond to the table numbers in the Appendix which give the appropriate factors. As is apparent from a study of the formulas, all the compound interest factors in Tables 2, 3, and 4 can be derived from numbers in Table 1. Nevertheless, the other tables are given because the calculations are done relatively often, and having all the tables saves much calculating time.

In working annuity problems, drawing a time line will be helpful in deciding which particular kind of annuity is involved. The following time lines depict annuities. In both cases, an ordinary annuity for four periods is illustrated.

		Present Value					Future Value			
		$1	$1	$1	$1		$1	$1	$1	$1
Ordinary Annuity (in arrears)	End of Period									
		0	1	2	3	4	0	1	2	3	4

QUESTIONS AND PROBLEMS

(All questions and parts thereof that require compound-interest or present-value computations are marked with an asterisk. For these questions or parts, round all interest factors to three places after the decimal point.)

1. Review the meaning of the following concepts or terms discussed in this chapter.
   a. Liability.
   b. FICA.
   c. Contingent liability and estimated liability.
   d. Mortgage, mortgagee, mortgagor.
   e. Bond indenture.
   f. Coupon bond.
   g. Debenture bond.
   h. Convertible bond.
   i. Discount from and premium over par value of bond.
   j. Yield or effective rate on bond.
   k. Bond tables.
   l. Amortization of bond discount or premium using the straight-line and effective-interest methods.
   m. Sinking fund.
   n. Serial bonds.
   o. Bond refunding.
   p. Call price.
   q. Noncancelable lease.
   r. Financing lease.
   s. Operating lease.
   t. Deferred income tax expense and liability.
   u. Timing difference.
   v. Permanent difference.

2. Review the meaning of the following concepts or terms discussed in the appendix to this chapter:

    a. Compound interest.
    b. Principal.
    c. Simple interest.
    d. Future value.
    e. Present value.
    f. Discounted value.
    g. Discount factor.
    h. Discount rate.
    i. Rule of 72.
    j. Ordinary annuity (annuity in arrears).
    k. Annuity in advance.

3. For each of the following items indicate:
    (1) Does the item meet all of the criteria of the accountant's usual definition of a liability?
    (2) If the item does not meet all the criteria to be a liability, is it nevertheless shown on the balance sheet as a liability? Why?
    (3) If the item is recognized as a liability, how is the amount of the liability determined?
    a. Interest accrued but not paid on a note.
    b. Advances from customers for goods and services to be delivered later.
    c. Firm orders from customers for goods and services to be delivered later.
    d. Mortgages payable.
    e. Bonds payable.
    f. Product warranties.
    g. Fifteen-year cancelable lease on an office building.
    h. Twenty-year noncancelable lease on a factory building.
    i. Deferred taxes.
    i. Damages the company must pay if a pending lawsuit is lost.
    k. Cost of restoring strip mining sites after mining operations are completed.

4. What factors determine the amount of money a firm actually receives when it offers a bond issue to the market?

5. Why do noninterest-bearing notes have a smaller value at time of issue than at time of maturity?

6. What are the relative advantages and disadvantages of the straight-line method versus the effective-interest method of bond discount (or premium) amortization?

*7. The terms of sale "2/10, net/30" mean that a discount of 2 percent from gross invoice price can be taken if the invoice is paid within 10 days and that otherwise the full amount is due within 30 days.
    a. Write an expression for the implied annual rate of interest being offered, if the entire discount is viewed as being interest for funds received sooner rather than later. (Note that 98 percent of the gross invoice price is being borrowed for 20 days.)
    b. The tables at the back of the book do not permit the exact evaluation of the expression derived in **a**. The rate of interest implied is 44.59 percent per year. Use the tables to convince yourself that this astounding (to some) answer must be close to correct.

8. A call premium is the difference between the call price of a bond and its par value. What is the purpose of such a premium?

9. If a company borrows $1,000,000 by issuing at par, 20-year, 8-percent bonds with semiannual coupons, the total interest expense over the life of the issue is $1,600,000 (= 20 × .08 × $1,000,000). If a company undertakes a 20-year financing lease or mortgage with an implicit borrowing rate of 8 percent, the annual lease payments are $1,000,000/9.81815 = $101,852. The total lease payments are $2,037,040 (= 20 × $101,852), and the total interest expense over the life of the lease or mortgage is $1,037,040 (= $2,037,040 − $1,000,000). Why are the amounts of interest expense different for these two means of borrowing for the same length of time at identical interest rates?

10. Under what circumstances may a deferred tax liability arise? If a firm is growing, what does this imply about when the liability is likely to be paid?

11. Does the present value of a given amount to be paid in 10 years increase or decrease as the interest rate increases? Suppose that the amount were due in 5 years? 20 years? Does the present value of an annuity to be paid for 10 years increase or decrease as the discount rate decreases? Suppose that the annuity were for 5 years? 20 years?

12. Rather than pay you $100 a month for the next 20 years, the person who injured you with a car is willing to pay a single amount now to settle your claim for injuries. Would you rather an interest rate of 6 percent or 12 percent be used in computing the present value of the lump sum settlement?

13. Why is a noncancelable lease accounted for by the lessee as an operating lease often called "off-balance-sheet" financing? Why might firms prefer off-balance-sheet financing?

14. In what sense is the expense from a noncancelable lease independent of the method of accounting for it by the lessee?

15. How should the deferred tax liability be treated by an analyst who wishes to study the debt-equity ratio of a business?

*16. State the rate per period and the number of periods, in each of the following:
   a. 12 percent per annum, for 5 years, compounded annually.
   b. 12 percent per annum, for 5 years, compounded semiannually.
   c. 12 percent per annum, for 5 years, compounded quarterly.
   d. 12 percent per annum, for 5 years, compounded monthly.

*17. Compute the future value of
   a. $100 invested for 5 years at 4 percent compounded annually.
   b. $500 invested for 15 periods at 2 percent compounded once per period.
   c. $200 invested for 8 years at 3 percent compounded semiannually.
   d. $2,500 invested for 14 years at 8 percent compounded quarterly.
   e. $600 invested for 3 years at 12 percent compounded monthly.

*18. Compute the present value of
   a. $100 due in 33 years at 4 percent compounded annually.
   b. $50 due in 27 years at 6 percent compounded semiannually.
   c. $250 due in 8 years at 8 percent compounded quarterly.
   d. $1,000 due in 2 years at 12 percent compounded monthly.

*19. Compute the amount (future value) of an ordinary annuity of
   a. 13 rents of $100 at 1½ percent per period.
   b. 8 rents of $850 at 6 percent per period.
   c. 27 rents of $375 at 4 percent per period.
   d. 35 rents of $1,400 at 3 percent per period.

*20. Compute the present value of an ordinary annuity of
   a. $1,000 for 29 years at 4 percent per year.
   b. $1,500 for 31 years at 6 percent per year.
   c. $400 for 41 years at 8 percent per year.
   d. $750 for 75 years at 10 percent per year.

*21. Mr. Adams has $500 to invest. He wishes to know how much it will amount to if he invests it at
   a. 6 percent per year for 21 years.
   b. 8 percent per year for 33 years.

*22. Ms. Black wishes to have $15,000 at the end of 8 years. How much must she invest today to accomplish this purpose if the interest rate is
   a. 6 percent per year?
   b. 8 percent per year?

*23. Mr. Case plans to set aside $4,000 each year, the first payment to be made on January 1, 1976, and the last on January 1, 1981. How much will he have accumulated by January 1, 1981, if the interest rate is
   a. 6 percent per year?
   b. 8 percent per year?

*24. Ms. David wants to have $450,000 on her sixty-fifth birthday. She asks you to tell her how much she must deposit on each birthday from her fifty-eighth to sixty-fifth, inclusive, in order to receive this amount. Assume an interest rate of
   a. 4 percent per year.
   b. 6 percent per year.

*25. If Mr. Edwards invests $900 on June 1 of each year from 1976 to 1986, inclusive, how much will he have accumulated on June 1, 1987 (note that 1 year elapses after last payment) if the interest rate is
   a. 5 percent per year?
   b. 10 percent per year?

*26. Mr. Frank has $145,000 with which he purchases an annuity on February 1, 1976. The annuity consists of six annual payments, the first to be made on February 1, 1977. How much will he receive in each payment? Assume an interest rate of
   a. 4 percent per year.
   b. 6 percent per year.

*27. Ms. Grady agrees to lease a certain property for 10 years, at the following annual rentals, payable in advance:
   years 1 and 2—$1,000 per year.
   years 3 to 6—$2,000 per year.
   years 7 to 10—$2,500 per year.
   What single immediate sum will pay all of these rents if they are discounted at
   a. 6 percent per year?
   b. 8 percent per year?
   c. 10 percent per year?

*28. If you promise to leave $25,000 on deposit at the Quarter Savings Bank for 4 years, the bank will give you a new car and your $25,000 back at the end of 4 years. How much are you, in effect, paying today for the car if the bank pays 8 percent interest compounded quarterly (2 percent paid four times per year)?

*29. The Roberts Dairy Company switched from delivery trucks with regular gasoline engines to ones with diesel engines. The diesel trucks cost $2,000 more than the ordinary gasoline trucks, but $600 per year less to operate. Assume that the operating costs are saved at the end of each month. If Roberts Dairy uses a discount rate of 1 percent per month, approximately how many months, at a minimum, must the diesel trucks remain in service for the switch to save money?

*30. On January 1, 1975, Outergarments, Inc., opened a new textile plant for the production of synthetic fabrics. The plant is on leased land; 20 years remain on the nonrenewable lease.

The cost of the plant was $2 million. Net cash flow to be derived from the project is estimated to be $300,000 per year. The company does not normally invest in such projects unless the anticipated yield is at least 12 percent.

On December 31, 1975, the company finds cash flows from the plant to be $280,000 for the year. On the same day, farm experts predict cotton production to be unusually low for the next 2 years. Outergarments estimates the resulting increase in demand for synthetic fabrics to boost cash flows to $350,000 for each of the next 2 years. Subsequent years' estimates remain unchanged. Ignore tax considerations.

  a. Calculate the present value of the future expected cash flows from the plant when it was opened.

  b. What is the present value of the plant on January 1, 1976, after the reestimation of future incomes?

  c. On January 1, 1976, the day following the cotton production news release, Overalls Company announces plans to build a synthetic fabrics plant to be opened in 3 years. Outergarments, Inc., keeps its 1976–1978 estimates, but reduces the estimated annual cash flows for subsequent years to $200,000. What is the value of the Outergarments present plant on January 1, 1976, after the new projections?

  d. On January 2, 1976, an investor contacts Outergarments about purchasing a 20-percent share of the plant. If the investor expects to earn at least a 12-percent annual return on the investment, what is the maximum amount that the investor can pay? Assume that the investor and Outergarments, Inc., use the same estimates of annual cash flows.

*31. A group of investors has decided to purchase a large herd of beef cattle, to sell cattle as calves are born, and to sell the entire herd after 6 years. They have also agreed that no investment of the syndicate should return less than 10 percent per year. They purchase the cattle on January 1, 1975, for a price of $1,200,000, and they expect to sell the herd remaining on December 31, 1980, for the same price. The projected net cash flows from sale of beef during the 6 years is $200,000 per year.

On December 31, 1975, the syndicate finds that its cash flow from the herd is $210,000. But during December, the herd was stricken with a disease and 20 percent of the cattle died. The syndicate wants to rebuild the herd, and they decide to sell only enough beef to cover expenses until the herd grows to its original size. They anticipate that this process will result in zero cash flow for 1976, and $200,000 for each of the remaining 4 years.

Ignore tax considerations in your calculations.

  a. Calculate the present value of the herd to the syndicate at time of purchase.

  b. If there had been no disease, what would have been the value of the herd on January 1, 1976? Use only future cash flows for this and subsequent computations.

c. What was the value of the herd on January 1, 1976, after the disease and the decision to rebuild?

d. What was the cost to the syndicate of the disease?

e. On January 1, 1976, Mr. Bovine, who has a 25-percent interest in the herd, decides to sell his share. What is the least amount that he should be willing to accept for his share? Assume that he is looking at alternative investments which would yield 10 percent per year.

32. On December 1, 1975, the Percival Company obtained a 90-day loan for $12,600 from the Twin City State Bank at an annual interest rate of 10 percent. On the maturity date the note was renewed for another 30 days, with a check being issued to the bank for the accrued interest. The Percival Company closes its books annually at December 31.

a. Present entries on the books of the Percival Company to record the issue of the note, the year-end adjustment, the renewal of the note, and the payment at maturity of the renewed note.

b. Present entries at maturity date of the original note for the following variations in the settlement of the note of the Percival Company.

(1) The original note is paid at maturity.

(2) The note is renewed under the same terms, except that the new note bears interest at 12 percent per annum.

33. The Myrtle Lunch sells coupon books that patrons may use later to purchase meals. Each coupon book sells for $17 and can be used to purchase meals with menu prices of $20. On July 1, redeemable unused coupons with face value of $1,500 were outstanding. During July, 250 coupon books were sold; during August, 100; during September, 100. Cash receipts exclusive of coupons were $1,200 in July, $1,300 in August, and $1,250 in September. Coupons with a face value of $2,700 were redeemed by patrons during the 3 months.

a. If the Myrtle Lunch had a net income of $500 for the quarter ending September 30, how large were expenses?

b. What effect, if any, do the July, August, and September coupon sales and redemptions have on the right-hand side of the September 30 balance sheet?

34. The Jones Company sells service contracts to repair copiers at $300 per year. When the contract is signed, the $300 fee is collected and Service Contract Fees Received in Advance is credited. Revenues on contracts are recognized on a quarterly basis during the year in which the coverage is in effect. On January 1, 1976, 1,000 service contracts were outstanding. Of these, 500 expired at the end of the first quarter, 300 at the end of the second quarter, 150 at the end of the third quarter, and 50 at the end of the fourth quarter. Sales and service during 1976 came to these amounts (assume that all sales occurred at the beginning of the quarter):

	SALES OF CONTRACTS	SERVICE EXPENSES
First Quarter	$120,000 (400 contracts)	$50,000
Second Quarter	240,000 (800 contracts)	60,000
Third Quarter	90,000 (300 contracts)	45,000
Fourth Quarter	60,000 (200 contracts)	55,000

a. Prepare journal entries for the first three quarters of 1976 for the Jones Company. Assume that quarterly reports are prepared on March 31, June 30, and September 30.

b. What is the balance in the Service Contract Fees Received in Advance account on December 31, 1976?

35. The Holmes Sales Company sells a building lot to Ruth Watson on September 1, 1976, for $27,000. The down payment is $3,000, and minimum payments of $266.64 a month are to be made on the contract. Interest at the rate of 12 percent per annum on the unpaid balance is deducted from each payment, and the balance is applied on the principal. Payments are made as follows: October 1, $266.64; November 1, $266.64; December 1, $600; January 2, $266.64. Prepare a table showing payments, interest and principal, and remaining liability at each of these dates.

36. Lynne Michals secures a mortgage loan of $27,000 from the Oakley National Bank. The terms of the mortgage require monthly payments of $413.10. The interest rate to be applied to the unpaid balance is 9 percent per annum. Calculate the distribution of payments for the first 4 months between principal and interest and present the new balance figures. Prepare a table showing payments, interest and principal, and remaining liability at each of these dates.

37. On June 1, 1976, the Southern Oil Company purchases a warehouse from F. S. Brandon for $60,000, of which $10,000 is assigned to the land and $50,000 to the building. There is a mortgage on the property payable to the Dixie National Bank, which, together with the accrued interest, will be assumed by the purchaser. The balance due on the mortgage is $24,000. The mortgage provides that interest at the rate of 10 percent per annum on the unpaid balance, and $2,000 of the principal will be paid on April 1 and October 1 of each year. A 10-year second mortgage for $15,000 is issued to F. S. Brandon; it bears interest at the rate of 12 percent per annum, payable on June 1 and December 1. A check is drawn to complete the purchase. Prepare journal entries for the Southern Oil Company for June 1, October 1, and December 1, 1976.

38. On September 1, 1976, Howell Stores, Inc., issues 20-year, first mortgage bonds with a face value of $1,000,000. The proceeds of the issue are $1,060,000. The bonds bear interest at the rate of 8 percent per annum, payable semiannually at March 1 and September 1. Howell Stores, Inc., closes its books annually at December 31.

a. Present dated journal entries related to the bonds from September 1, 1976, through September 1, 1977, inclusive. Assume that Howell Stores, Inc., uses the straight-line method to amortize the bond premium.

b. Repeat instructions for part **a**, but assume that the company uses an effective-interest method. The effective-interest rate to be used is 7.4 percent, compounded semiannually.

39. On April 1, 1976, the Oliver Company acquired $1,000,000 par value of bonds of the Bret Company for $1,350,000. Costs of acquisition amounted to an additional $50,000. The bonds bear interest at 9 percent payable on March 31 and September 30 and mature on March 31, 1986. Use straight-line amortization of premium.

a. Present journal entries on the books of the Oliver Company from April 1, 1976, through March 31, 1977, inclusive. Assume the books are closed annually on December 31.

b. Present the journal entry (or entries) for the sale of the bonds on July 1, 1979, at 103.5 plus accrued interest.

40. In 1975, the Central Power Company issued $2 million of bonds in two series, A and B. Each series had face amount of $1 million and was issued at prices to yield 7 percent. Issue A contained semiannual 6-percent coupons. Issue B contained 8-percent semiannual coupons. In 1976, Central Power issued series C, with face amount of $1 million. This issue contained 8-percent semiannual coupons; the effective yield at time of issue was 8.6 percent. Issues A, B, and C all mature 30 years from issue date.

Answer the following questions for each of the issues A, B, and C:

a. What is the issuing price of the bonds?

b. Make the journal entry for the date of bond issue.

c. Using the effective-interest method, show the journal entries made on the first semiannual interest payment date.

d. Repeat **c** for the second and third payment dates.

e. Show the semiannual entry if straight-line amortization of discount (or premium) is used.

41. The following events are recorded on the books of the K. Schipper Company during 1976:

(1) Machinery costing $100,000 is acquired. Estimated service life is 5 years with no salvage value.

(2) Installment sales of $800,000 are made; cost of goods sold is $600,000. During 1976, $500,000 of this amount is collected.

(3) The estimated future warranty liability on sales is charged to warranty expense for the year and amounts to $100,000. Actual expenditures for warranty repairs under the agreements during 1976 total $25,000. Tax regulations require that deductions from revenues for warranty expense cannot exceed actual expenditures for that purpose.

(4) Outlays for research and development are $50,000. Management estimates that benefits of this R & D outlay will accrue to the company over a 5-year period.

Recall the "least and latest rule," and make the unrealistic assumption that only these four events occurred during 1976. Compute the income before taxes, tax liabilities, and income after taxes for the K. Schipper Company. If there is a difference between tax expense and tax currently payable, indicate how this difference is recorded. Assume a tax rate of 40 percent. Use straight-line depreciation and completed-sales revenue recognition for financial reports. Use the sum-of-the-years'-digits method of depreciation and cash-collection revenue recognition for tax purposes.

42. The Carom Company plans to acquire, as of January 1, 1976, a computerized cash register system that costs $100,000 and that has a 5-year life and no salvage value. The company is considering two plans for acquiring the system.

(1) Outright purchase. To finance the purchase, $100,000 of par value 10-percent semiannual coupon bonds will be issued January 1, 1976, at par.

(2) Lease. The lease requires five annual payments to be made on December 31, 1976, 1977, 1978, 1979, and 1980. The lease payments are such that they have a present value of $100,000 on January 1, 1976, when discounted at 10 percent per year.

Straight-line amortization methods will be used for all amortization computations.

*a. Verify that the amount of each lease payment is $26,380.

b. What balance sheet accounts will be affected if plan (**1**) is selected? If plan (**2**) is selected and the operating-lease treatment is used? If plan (**2**) is selected and the financing-lease treatment is used?

c. What will be the total depreciation and interest expenses for the 5 years under plan (**1**)?

d. What will be the total expenses for the 5 years under plan (**2**) if the lease is accounted for as an operating lease? As a financing lease?

e. Why are the answers in **d** the same? Why are the answers in **c** different from those in **d**?

f. What will be the total expenses for the first year, 1976, under plan (**1**)? Under plan (**2**) accounted for as an operating lease? Under plan (**2**) accounted for as a financing lease?

g. Repeat part **f** for the fifth year, 1980.

43. In the years 1976 and 1977, the Golden Que Company undertook rapid expansion. The firm purchased $300,000 of plant assets at the start of 1976 and $460,000 at the start of 1977. These assets were purchased with the proceeds of an $800,000 bond issue that pays semiannual coupons of 8 percent for 15 years. The issue sold for $760,000 on January 1, 1976. The assets are expected to last 10 years, with no salvage value. Assume that the management of the Golden Que follows the "least and latest rule."

a. Compute the net income to stockholders, assuming a 40-percent tax rate, and present journal entries to account for the accrual of the income tax liability for 1976. Income before depreciation and interest was $800,000 in both 1976 and 1977. Use straight-line depreciation for plant assets in financial reports and sum-of-the-years'-digits depreciation in tax returns. Use the effective-interest method of bond discount amortization in financial reports and the straight-line method in tax returns.

b. Repeat **a** for 1977.

c. Compute the difference in the tax payment for 1976 and 1977 if double-declining-balance depreciation had been used for plant assets, rather than sum-of-the-years'-digits depreciation, in tax returns. Round off all answers to the nearest dollar.

44. Equilibrium Company adopted a program of purchasing a new grinding machine each year under the income tax provision which permits the use of the sum-of-the-years'-digits method of depreciation. Each machine costs $15,000 installed. The estimated service life is 5 years with no expected salvage value. Calculate:

a. Depreciation for each of the first 7 years in accordance with the sum-of-the-years'-digits method of depreciation.

b. Depreciation for each year in accordance with the straight-line method of depreciation.

c. Annual difference in depreciation calculated in **a** and **b**.

d. Annual increase or decrease in the Deferred Income Tax Liability account. Assume a 40-percent tax rate and straight-line depreciation in financial reports.

e. Year-end balances of Deferred Income Tax Liability account.

f. If Equilibrium Company continues to follow its policy of buying a new machine every year, what will happen to the balance in the Deferred Income Tax Liability account?

Chapter Twelve

Owners' Equity

The economic resources of a firm come essentially from two major sources. Nonowners provide funds to a firm; the sources of these funds are shown on the balance sheet as *liabilities*, which were discussed in Chapter Eleven. Owners provide funds; the sources of these funds are shown on the balance sheet as *owners' equity*. Owners' equity is discussed in this chapter.

The accounting equation states

$$\text{Assets} = \text{Liabilities} + \text{Owners' Equity}$$

or

$$\text{Assets} - \text{Liabilities} = \text{Owners' Equity}.$$

Many readers of financial statements think of owners' equity as being calculated from the excess of assets over liabilities. Double-entry record keeping, however, provides for the continuous, independent computation of owners' equity.

Our emphasis in this chapter is on the corporation. The corporation is the most common form of business organization in the United States for at least three reasons:

1. The corporate form provides the owner, or stockholder, with limited liability. That is, should the corporation become insolvent, creditors' claims are limited to the assets of the corporate entity. The assets of the individual owners are not subject to the claims of the corporation's creditors. On the other hand, creditors of partnerships and sole proprietorships have a claim on both the owners' personal and business assets in settlement of such firms' debts.
2. The corporate form facilitates the raising of large amounts of funds through

the issue of shares of capital stock by the corporation which the general public can acquire in varying amounts.

3. The corporate form makes transfer of ownership interests relatively easy, because individual shares can be sold by current owners to others without interfering with the ongoing operations of the business. The continuity of the management and of operations is not affected by these ongoing changes in ownership.

This chapter discusses three separate kinds of problems in accounting for owners' equity in corporations: the accounting for capital contributed by owners, the accounting for income earned by the firm which may be retained or distributed to owners, and other changes in owners' equity accounts. The last section of the chapter discusses the treatment of capital contributions as well as the determination and distribution of earnings in partnerships.

■ CAPITAL CONTRIBUTIONS: CORPORATIONS

The corporation is viewed in the law as a legal entity separate from its owners, and it therefore has a separate legal existence. Capital contributions are made by individuals or other entities under a contract between themselves and the corporation. Because those who contribute capital funds are usually issued certificates for share of stock, they are known as stockholders or shareholders.[1] The rights and obligations of a stockholder are determined by:

1. The corporation laws of the state in which incorporation takes place.
2. The articles of incorporation or *charter*. This is the agreement between the firm and the state in which the business is incorporated. The enterprise is granted the privilege of operating as a corporation for certain stated purposes and of obtaining its capital through the issue of shares of stock.
3. The bylaws of the corporation. Bylaws are adopted by the board of directors and act as the rules and regulations under which the internal affairs of the corporation are conducted.
4. The stock contract. Each type of capital stock has its own provisions as to such matters as voting, sharing in earnings, distribution of earnings, and sharing in assets in case of dissolution.

Some "closely held" corporations have a small number of stockholders and operate much the same as a partnership. The few people involved agree to the amount of capital to be contributed, elect each other to be members of the board of directors and officials of the firm, and agree upon policies regarding dividends and salaries. They may restrict the transfer of shares to outsiders, and may even become liable for debts of the corporation by endorsing its notes and bonds.

In the case of large, widely owned corporations, the effect of the separate legal

---

[1] In accounting for owners' equity, the term *contribution* rarely means a gift; capital given to the corporation as a gift is specifically called *donated capital*.

entity of the corporation becomes more pronounced. Officials and directors may own little or no stock in the corporation. Actual control is likely to be in the hands of a few individuals or a group who own or control enough shares to elect a majority of the board of directors. Most "minority" stockholders think of their stock holdings merely as investments, and they participate little, if at all, in the conduct of the affairs of the corporation. The stockholders assume no obligation for the debts of the business. Shares of stock change hands at the will of the stockholders, and the record may not show the change for some time after it has occurred. The record of who owns shares is usually kept by a bank or trust company.

Issue of Shares of Stock

The accounting for the initial issue of shares of stock is normally a routine matter. The usual entry, where the shares are issued for cash, is

Cash	1,250,000	
Capital Stock		1,250,000

In addition to exchanges for cash, stock is sometimes issued in exchange for property, for personal services rendered, or in settlement of a liability. The form of the entry in these cases is the same as the one illustrated above, but the debit will be made to the accounts for property or services received or the liability settled. The amount for the entry should be the fair market value of the stock issued, or, if this amount is not reasonably determinable, the fair market value of the product, property, or services received.

Classes of Stock

Corporations are often authorized to issue more than one class of stock, each representing ownership in the business. Most stock issued is either *common* or *preferred*. Occasionally, there may be several classes of common or preferred stock. Each share of stock has the same rights and privileges as every other share of the same class. All corporations must have common stock (although the stock may be designated by another name, such as Class A stock); preferred stock need not be authorized or issued by a corporation.

Common stock has the claim to earnings of the corporation after commitments to preferred stockholders have been satisfied. Frequently, common stock is the only voting stock of the company. In the event of corporate dissolution, all of the proceeds of asset disposition, after settling the claims of creditors and required distributions to preferred stockholders, are distributable to the common stockholders.

Preferred stock is granted special privileges. While these features vary considerably from issue to issue, preferred stock usually entitles its holder to dividends at a certain rate which must be paid before dividends can be declared and paid to common stockholders. Sometimes, though, these dividends may be postponed or omitted, according to the provisions of the issue. If the preferred dividends are *cumulative*, then all current and previously postponed dividends must be paid before common stock dividends can be distributed.

Most preferred stock issued by corporations in recent years has been *callable*. Callable preferred stock may be reacquired by the corporation at a specified price, which may vary according to a predetermined time schedule. Callability is provided primarily for the benefit of the corporation. If sufficient financing is otherwise available, especially if that alternative financing is available at a lower cost than the rate previously fixed for the preferred stock, a corporation may wish to reduce the relatively fixed commitment of preferred dividends (as compared to common) by calling the preferred stock.

Preferred stock with a conversion feature has become increasingly popular. Convertible preferred stock may be converted into a specified amount of common stock at specified times by its owner. The conversion privilege may appear advantageous to both the individual stockholder and the corporation. The preferred stockholder enjoys the security of a relatively assured dividend as long as the stock is held. The stockholder also has the opportunity to realize capital appreciation by converting the shares into common stock if the market price of the common stock has risen sufficiently. Because of this feature, the change in the market price of convertible preferred stock will often parallel a rise in the market price of the common stock.

The firm may also benefit from the conversion option. By including it in the issue, the company is usually able to specify a lower dividend rate on the preferred than otherwise would have been required to issue the stock for a given price.

A major consideration in the issue of preferred stock is that preferred stock dividends are not deductible in calculating taxable income. However, bond interest is deductible, which reduces the aftertax cost of borrowing as compared to issuing preferred stock.

Separate accounts are used for each class of stock. On the balance sheet, each class of stock is shown separately, many times with a short description of the major features of the stock. Customarily, preferred stock is listed before common stock on the balance sheet.

Par Value and No-Par Stock

Shares of capital stock often have a *par*, or nominal, value per share specified in the articles of incorporation and printed on the face of the stock certificates. The par value of common stock has some legal significance but little economic significance, although accountants meticulously separate par value from other contributed capital amounts. Stock assigned a certain par value will almost always sell on the stock market at a price different from par. Also, *the book value of a share of common stock*—the total common stock equity divided by the number of shares outstanding—is almost always greater than the par value of the stock, in part because retained earnings are usually positive. The par value rarely denotes the worth of the stock, except perhaps at the date of original issue. The par value of common stock is used primarily to record shares of stock outstanding in the capital stock account. It is the amount which the creditors can usually rely upon as the minimum investment that has been made by the shareholders in the corporation. Par value of preferred stock is more meaningful. The dividend rate specified in the preferred stock contract (for example, 8 percent) is almost always based upon par value. Any preference as to assets in liquidation that preferred stockholders may have is usually related to the par value of the preferred shares.

Although preferred stock usually has a par value, common stock without a par value is widely used. When no-par-value shares are issued, there need be no problem of assigning a nominal value to the shares issued, because the amount actually contributed can be credited directly to the capital stock account. However, customary practice assigns a *stated* value to the no-par shares, which has much the same effect as assigning the shares a par value. Some state corporation laws require the directors to assign a stated value to each no-par share. The stated value can usually be changed from time to time at the discretion of the directors, but par value is usually fixed by the articles of incorporation and can be altered only by formal legal process.

Contributions in Excess of Par or Stated Value

One awkward convention in accounting is that the capital stock account is usually credited with the par or stated value of the shares issued. Shares are usually issued for amounts greater than par. For example, stockholders who invest in stock of the corporation some time after it is organized normally should pay a higher price per share to compensate current stockholders for the additional capital that has been accumulated by the retention of earnings in the business. The excess of issue proceeds over par (or stated) value is credited to an account called Additional Paid-in Capital. The title Capital Contributed in Excess of Par (Stated) Value is probably a more appropriate one, but is too cumbersome to be used extensively. Sometimes the title used is Premium on Capital Stock.

The entries to record additional paid-in capital involve nothing new. If par value shares are used, the credit to the Additional Paid-in Capital account is always the difference between the amount received and the par value of the shares issued to the stockholders. For shares with no par value, the additional paid-in capital is the excess of the amount received over the stated value. Thus, the entry to record the issue of 100 shares of no-par-value stock, with a stated value of $1 per share, for $10,000, would be the same as the entry to record the issuance of a like number of $1 par-value shares for the same proceeds:

Cash	10,000	
Capital Stock—Stated (or Par) Value		100
Additional Paid-in Capital		9,900

Since stock has no maturity date, the Additional Paid-In Capital, or Premium on Capital Stock account remains on the books indefinitely as a partial measure of contributions by stockholders. This account differs from Premium on Bonds, considered in Chapter Eleven, in two important respects. Premium on Capital Stock appears in the stockholders' equity section of the balance sheet, while Premium on Bonds is shown in the long-term liability section; Premium on Capital Stock is not amortized, while Premium on Bonds is amortized over the life of the bonds to which it relates.

Treasury Stock

Shares of stock reacquired by the issuing corporation are called *treasury stock* or *treasury shares.* Treasury stock may be acquired for a variety of purposes. The firm may reacquire its own shares for later distribution under stock option plans or for stock dividends. (Stock option plans and stock dividends are discussed later in this chapter.) The firm may also consider treasury stock as a worthwhile use for idle funds. Treasury shares are not entitled to dividends nor to vote, since they are not considered to be "outstanding" shares for these purposes.

When common stock is reacquired, a Treasury Stock—Common account is debited with the total amount paid to reacquire the shares.

Treasury Stock—Common	11,000	
Cash		11,000

$11,000 paid to reacquire 1,000 shares of $5 par-value common stock.

If the treasury shares are later reissued by the corporation, Cash is debited with the amount received and the Treasury Stock account is credited. It is unlikely, of course, that the reissue price will precisely equal the amount paid to acquire the treasury shares. Generally accepted accounting principles do not permit a company to recognize any "gain" or "loss" on its dealings in treasury stock in the income statement. If the reissue price is greater than the acquisition price, the Additional Paid-In Capital account is credited to make the entry balance. Assuming that the 1,000 shares reacquired in the entry illustrated above were reissued for $14,000, the entry would be:

Cash	14,000	
Treasury Stock—Common		11,000
Additional Paid-in Capital		3,000

Reissue of 1,000 shares of treasury stock.

If the reissue price is less than the amount paid, the debit to make the entry balance is usually to Additional Paid-In Capital, as long as there is a sufficient credit balance in that account. If there is not, the additional balancing debit is made directly to Retained Earnings. This debit represents an income distribution, not an expense or loss.

Treasury stock is shown on the balance sheet as a deduction from the total of the other accounts of stockholders' equity. The Treasury Stock account is a contra owners' equity account. A balance sheet of the Firestone Tire and Rubber Company illustrates this disclosure:

Stockholders' Equity

Preferred Stock (Cumulative), Par Value $100 per share, Authorized
150,000 shares, none issued

Common Stock, Authorized 36,000,000 shares, 29,522,465 issued without

par value	$ 61,505,135
Additional [Paid-in] Capital	177,540,817
Retained Earnings	783,269,451
Total	$1,022,315,403
Less: Treasury Stock (217,617 shares) at Cost	11,836,071
Total Stockholders' Equity	$1,010,479,332

■ RETENTION OF EARNINGS: CORPORATIONS

After a new business has established itself and is profitable, it usually generates additional owners' equity from undistributed earnings. These undistributed earnings are the accumulated periodic net income that remains after dividends have been declared. Retention of earnings increases owners' or stockholders' equity and often provides the main source of capital for expansion.

Net Income and Cash Position

One misconception about net income is that it represents a fund of cash available for distributions or expenditures. Earnings from operations usually involve cash at some stage—goods are sold to customers, the cash is collected, more goods are acquired, bills are paid, more sales are made, and so on—but assets generated by earnings do not remain in the form of cash. Only under most unrealistic conditions, with net plant and equipment, inventories, receivables, and liabilities remaining at constant figures, would it be reasonable to presume that the earnings, or net income, resulted in a corresponding increase in cash during the period. The statement of changes in financial position shows how the funds provided by operations and other sources are used during a period. An interesting paradox is that for many businesses an increased net income is frequently associated with decreased cash, while contraction of net income may be accompanied by an increase in cash. In the first stages of a business decline, cash may start to build up from the liquidation of inventories and receivables that have not been replaced, as well as from postponing replacement or expansion of plant. When conditions improve, inventories and receivables are expanded, new plant acquired, and a cash shortage may develop.

A well-managed firm keeps its cash at a reasonable minimum. If cash starts to accumulate, the firm may pay some obligations, increase its stock of goods, buy more equipment, declare dividends, or use the funds in some other way. This process of cash management goes on continuously. Thus, there is no way of predicting how the retention of earnings will be reflected in the individual asset and liability accounts at any particular time. The only certain statement that can be made about the effect of an increase in retained earnings is that it results in increased *net assets* (that is, an increase in the excess of all assets over all liabilities).

The stockholders of a corporation do not directly control distributions of corporate net income. The corporation bylaws almost always delegate the authority to declare dividends to the board of directors. When a dividend is declared, the entry is:

Retained Earnings	150,000	
Dividends Payable		150,000

To record declaration of dividends. (Sometimes an account called Dividends or Dividends Declared would be debited. The Dividends account is a temporary income distribution account and is closed to Retained Earnings at the end of the period.)

Once the board of directors declares a dividend, the dividend becomes a legal liability of the corporation. Dividends Payable is shown as a current liability on the balance sheet if the dividends have not been paid at the end of the accounting period. When the dividends are paid, the entry is:

Dividends Payable	150,000	
Cash		150,000

The directors, in considering whether or not to declare dividends, must conclude both (1) that the declaration of a dividend is legal and (2) that it would be financially expedient.

■ OTHER CHANGES IN OWNERS' EQUITY ACCOUNTS

Stock Dividends

The previous section has indicated that through the retention of earnings there may be a substantial increase in the amount of stockholders' equity that is more or less permanently committed to the business. To indicate such a permanent commitment of reinvested earnings, a *stock dividend* may be issued. When a stock dividend is issued, stockholders receive additional shares of stock in proportion to their existing holdings without making any additional contributions. If a 20-percent stock dividend is issued, each stockholder receives one additional share for every five shares held before the dividend. In the accounts, a stock dividend requires a transfer from retained earnings to the contributed capital accounts. Generally accepted accounting principles require that the amount transferred from retained earnings be equal to the market value of the shares issued. For example, the directors of a corporation may decide to issue a stock dividend of 10,000 additional shares of common stock with a par value of $10 per share at a time when the market price of a share is $38. The entry would be:

Retained Earnings	380,000	
Common Stock—Par		100,000
Additional Paid-in Capital		280,000

The most significant internal effect of the stock dividend is to convert a portion of the retained earnings which had been legally available for dividend declarations to a more permanent form of capital. A stock dividend logically shows that the funds represented by past earnings have been used for plant expansion, used to replace assets at higher price levels, or used to retire bonds or other debt and are therefore more or less permanently unavailable for cash dividends.

Stockholders should not feel particularly gratified upon receiving a stock dividend. If the shares are of the same type as those held before, each stockholder's proportionate interest in the capital of the corporation and proportionate voting power have not changed. The book value per common share (total common stockholders' equity divided by number of common shares outstanding) will have decreased, but the total book value of each stockholder's interest will remain unchanged, since a proportionately larger number of shares will be held. The market value per share should decline, but, all else being equal, the total market value of the stockholders' holdings will not change. Stockholders cannot dispose of the additional shares without affecting their proportionate interests in the corporation. They could have achieved that result by selling a portion of their original holdings. To describe such a distribution of shares as a "dividend" is, therefore, misleading but is, nevertheless, generally accepted terminology.

If the stockholder receives shares of a different class from those held before, the situation may be slightly different. For example, if a corporation has preferred stock outstanding and issues preferred shares to common stockholders as a stock dividend, then the position of the common stockholders is altered in relation to that of the other preferred stockholders.

The distribution of shares of stock issued by another, unrelated corporation to stockholders as a dividend is not a stock dividend. It is described as a *dividend in kind* or a *property dividend*. Another dividend in kind would be a systematic distribution of a corporation's products to its shareholders.

Stock Splits

Stock splits (or, more technically, *split-ups*) are similar to a stock dividend. Additional shares of stock are issued to shareholders in proportion to existing holdings. No additional capital is raised and assets are unaffected. In a stock split, the par or stated value of all the stock in the issued class is reduced in proportion to the additional shares issued. A corporation may, for example, have 1,000 shares of $100 par-value stock outstanding, and, by a stock split, exchange those shares for 2,000 shares of $50 par-value stock (a two-for-one split), or 4,000 shares of $25 par-value stock (a four-for-one split), or any number of shares of no-par stock. If the stock outstanding has no par nor stated value, then the shareholders are merely issued additional stock certificates.

A stock split generally does not require a journal entry. The amount of retained earnings is not reduced. The amount shown in the capital stock account is merely represented by a larger number of shares. Of course, the additional number of shares held by each stockholder must be recorded in the subsidiary capital stock ledger. It is customary to limit stock dividends to a maximum of 20 or 25 percent (that is, one share for every five or four shares held). Distributions in a greater ratio (for example, one share for every two shares held) are treated as stock splits.

A stock split (or a stock dividend) usually reduces the market value per share, all other factors remaining constant, in inverse proportion to the split (or dividend). Thus a two-for-one split could be expected to result in a 50-percent reduction in the market price per share. Stock splits and stock dividends have, therefore, usually been used to prevent the market price per share from rising to a price level unacceptable to management. For example, if it is thought that a market price of $30 to $40 is an effective trading range for its stock (this is purely a subjective estimate, and is almost never supported by convincing evidence) and the stock has risen to $60 in the market, then the board of directors may declare a two-for-one split. Stock splits and stock dividends are seldom used by corporations whose stocks are not currently or soon to be traded on a stock exchange or in a public over-the-counter market.

Stock Options

Stock options are often a part of employee compensation plans. Under such plans, employees are granted an option to purchase, at some time within a specified number of years in the future, shares in their company at a specified price, usually the market price of the stock on the day the option is granted. Frequently, shares acquired through exercise of stock options must be held for a specified length of time before they can be sold. Stock option plans are *qualified* if they meet requirements that make the options nontaxable to the recipient-employee at time of exercise. Stock options present two kinds of accounting problems: (**1**) recording the granting of the option and (**2**) recording its exercise or lapse.

Granting the Option   The generally accepted accounting treatment[2] for options usually results in no entry being made at the time the options are granted. If the exercise price is equal to the market price at the date the option is granted, the prevailing view is that the grant of the option does not result in compensation to the employee or expense to the employer.

A better treatment in our opinion, but one not generally acceptable, would be to record the granting of an option as the compensation that it must be. If an option has value, as most options do, why would employers grant the option other than as a form of compensation? We suspect that the reason that employee stock options are not treated as an expense at the time of grant is that ascertaining an objective, easily auditable measure of its value can be difficult. Although valuing such options is difficult, recently created public options markets may give some

---

[2] Opinion No. 25, Accounting Principles Board, AICPA, October 1972.

clues about appropriate valuations. In any case, valuation at zero is inappropriate, but is nevertheless assumed under generally accepted accounting principles. If, at the time options were granted, the market value of those options were quantified at $7,500, the entry which we assert should be made is:

Salary Expense	7,500	
Additional Paid-in Capital		7,500

Exercise or Lapse When the option is exercised, both the conventional entry and the one that would be made if salary expense were recognized at the time of grant treat the transaction simply as an issue of stock at the option price.

Cash	35,000	
Common Stock—Par		5,000
Additional Paid-in Capital		30,000

To record issue of 1,000 shares of $5 par value stock upon exercise of options and receipt of $35,000 cash.

If the option lapses or expires without being exercised, no entry is required.

Stock options are designed to attract and retain qualified employees. Salary increases for well-paid executives can be largely absorbed by personal income taxes. Stock options may provide an opportunity for management personnel to obtain long-term capital gains that are taxed at lower rates than ordinary (salary) income. Stockholders, though, may have mixed feelings about stock option plans. Options can result in higher reported corporate income if they are granted in lieu of salary increments for employees, because no explicit salary expense is recorded. Options may also provide special motivation to executives who hold them and thus benefit all stockholders. Yet when options are exercised, the equity of existing stockholders is reduced, or diluted, because the price at exercise date is less than the current market price. (If the exercise price were not lower than the market price at the time of exercise, the options would not be exercised.)

Disclosure of Options Generally accepted accounting principles require that the terms of options granted, outstanding, and exercised during a period be disclosed in text or notes accompanying the financial statements. For example, the notes to the 1975 annual report of Sears, Roebuck and Co. contains the information shown in Exhibit 12.1. The note explains that each of the options outstanding at January 31, 1975, is exercisable at the market prices prevailing on the date of the grant. Thus Sears recognized no compensation expense for these options.

Convertible Bonds

Chapter Eleven briefly mentioned convertible bonds. These bonds are typically semiannual coupon bonds like the ones discussed in Chapter Eleven but with one added feature. The holder of the bond can *convert* or "trade in" the bond into shares of capital stock. The number of shares to be received when the bond is

EXHIBIT 12.1
Sears, Roebuck and Co. Disclosure of Employee Stock Options

6. Employe stock options

Options under Sears plans are granted at the fair market value on the date of the grant. Generally options become exercisable in four annual and cumulative installments beginning one year after the date of grant and expire 10 years after the date of grant.

In October 1974, options for 3,077,288 shares, at a price range of $85.94 to $89.82 per share, were cancelled at the election of the optionees.

On January 22, 1975, options for 3,489,070 shares were granted to 15,727 employes at $52.19 per share.

Outstanding options at year end ranged in price from $52.19 to $116.44 per share, aggregating $187,820,000. At January 31, 1975, 51,392 shares were exercisable and 1,522,572 shares were available for future grants under the 1967 and 1972 Employe Stock Plans.

A summary of option shares outstanding is:

	Year Ended January 31	
(thousands of shares)	1975	1974
Beginning balance.........	3,211	3,076
Cancelled................	(3,147)	(2,489)
Granted..................	3,489	2,629
Exercised................	—	(5)
Ending balance.	3,553	3,211

converted into stock, the dates when conversion can occur, and other details are specified in the bond indenture. Convertible bonds are usually callable.

Investors often find convertible bonds attractive. The owner is promised a regular interest payment. In addition, should the company business be so successful that its capital stock rises in price on the stock market, then the holder of the bond can convert the investment from debt into equity and share in the good fortune of the company. Of course, an investor does not get something for nothing. Because of the potential participation in the earnings of the company once the bonds are converted into common shares, an investor in the bonds must accept a lower interest rate than would be received if the bonds were not convertible into stock. From the company's point of view, convertible bonds allow borrowing at lower rates of interest than is required on ordinary debt, but the company must promise to give up an equity interest if the bonds are converted. The purchaser of the convertible bond is paying something for the option to acquire common stock later. Thus, a portion of the proceeds from the issue of convertible bonds actually represents a form of capital contribution.

Suppose, for example, that the Johnson Company's credit rating would allow it to issue $100,000 of ordinary 10-year, 11-percent semiannual coupon bonds at par. The firm prefers to issue convertible bonds with a lower coupon rate. Assume that Johnson Company issues at par $100,000 of 10-year, 8-percent semiannual coupon bonds, but each $1,000 bond is convertible into 50 shares of Johnson Company $5 par value common stock. (The entire issue is convertible into 5,000 shares.) Appendix Table 6 (for 8-percent coupon bonds) indicates that 8-percent, 10-year semiannual (nonconvertible) coupon bonds sell for about 82 percent of par when the market rate of interest is 11 percent. Thus, if the 8-percent convertible bonds can be issued at par, then the conversion feature must be worth 18 percent of par. Then 18 percent of the proceeds from the bond issue is actually a capital contribution by the bond buyers for the right to acquire common stock later. The logical entry to record the issue of these 8-percent convertible bonds at par would be:

Cash	100,000	
Discount on Convertible Bonds	18,000	
Convertible Bonds Payable		100,000
Additional Paid-in Capital		18,000

Issue of 8-percent semiannual coupon convertible bonds at a time when ordinary 8-percent bonds could be issued for 82 percent of par.

Notice that the determination of the amounts for this entry requires that we know what the proceeds would be of an issue of nonconvertible bonds which are otherwise similar to the convertible bonds. Because auditors are often unable to ascertain this information in a reasonably objective manner, generally acceptable accounting principles do not allow the logical journal entry above. Instead, the following, simpler entry is required:[3]

| Cash | 100,000 | |
| Convertible Bonds Payable | | 100,000 |

Issue of convertible bonds at par.

This entry effectively treats convertible bonds just like ordinary, nonconvertible bonds and records the value of the conversion feature at zero. (Generally accepted accounting principles do recognize the potential issue of common stock implied by the conversion feature in the calculations of earnings-per-share figures.)

Conversion of Bonds To carry the illustration further, assume that the common stock of the Johnson Company increases in the market to $30 a share so that one $1,000 bond, which is convertible into 50 shares of stock, can be converted into stock with a market value of $1,500. If the entire convertible bond issue were converted into common stock at this time, then 5,000 shares of $5 par value stock would be issued on conversion.

The usual entry to record the conversion of bonds into stock ignores current market prices in the interest of simplicity and merely shows the swap of stocks for bonds at their book value.

Convertible Bonds Payable	100,000	
Common Stock—$5 Par		25,000
Additional Paid-in Capital		75,000

To record conversion of 100 convertible bonds with book value of $100,000 into 5,000 shares of $5 par value stock.

An allowable alternative treatment recognizes that market prices provide information useful in quantifying the market value of the shares issued. Under the alternative treatment, when the market price of a share is $30 and the fair market value of the 5,000 shares issued on conversion is $150,000, then the journal entry made would be:

[3] Opinion No. 14, Accounting Principles Board, AICPA, March 1969. The Accounting Principles Board stated that, in reaching its conclusions, less weight was given to the practical difficulties than to some other considerations, spelled out in the Opinion. We concur with the dissent to this Opinion expressed by several members of the Board.

Convertible Bonds Payable	100,000	
Loss on Conversion of Bonds	50,000	
Common Stock—$5 Par		25,000
Additional Paid-in Capital		125,000

To record conversion of 100 convertible bonds into 5,000 shares of $5 par value stock at a time when the market price of a share is $30.

The alternative entry is the equivalent of the following two entries:

Cash	150,000	
Common Stock—$5 Par		25,000
Additional Paid-in Capital		125,000

To record issue of 5,000 shares of $5 par value stock at $30 per share.

Convertible Bonds Payable	100,000	
Loss on Retirement of Bonds	50,000	
Cash		150,000

Retirement by purchase for $150,000 of 100 convertible bonds carried on the books at $100,000.

Earnings per Share Chapter Six explained that earnings per share of common stock is conventionally calculated by dividing net income attributable to the common stockholders by the weighted-average number of shares of common stock outstanding during the period. When a firm has outstanding securities which, if exchanged for common stock, would decrease earnings per share as conventionally calculated, then the earnings-per-share calculations become somewhat more complicated. Stock options, stock rights, warrants, and convertible bonds all have the potential of reducing earnings per share and must be taken into account in calculating earnings per share. To review the concepts involved, refer to the discussion in Chapter Six and to the following terms in the glossary: *potentially dilutive, common stock equivalent, primary earnings per share,* and *fully diluted earnings per share.*

Retained Earnings Adjustments

Nearly all items that cause the total of retained earnings to change during a period result from transactions reported in the income statement for that period. One exception to this general rule—dividend declarations—has been mentioned throughout the text and this chapter. Dividend declarations are income distributions which reduce the balance in the Retained Earnings account but which do not affect the determination of net income. There are two other exceptions to the general rule that changes in retained earnings arise from transactions reported on the income statement. These are *corrections of errors* and *prior-period adjustments* for items significant enough that they are not reported as part of, or "buried in," the current year's income statement.

Errors result from such actions as miscounting inventories, arithmetic mistakes, and misapplications of accounting principles. Such errors, if they are material, are corrected with debits or credits to the Retained Earnings account. If, for example, merchandise inventory is discovered to be $10,000 less than was reported at the end of the previous period, then the following entry (ignoring income tax effects) would be made this period.

Retained Earnings 10,000
    Merchandise Inventory 10,000
Correction of inventory error.

A prior-period adjustment results in an entry directly to the Retained Earnings account, such as the following entry recording the payment of additional income taxes assessed on the income tax return of a prior year.

Retained Earnings 35,000
    Cash 35,000
Prior-period adjustment for income taxes.

Prior-period adjustments are extremely rare in accounting because, for a transaction to qualify as a prior-period adjustment, it must meet all four of the following criteria specified in Accounting Principles Board Opinion No. 9.[4] A transaction is classified as a *prior-period adjustment* only if

1. It relates directly to business operations of a specific prior period.
2. It is not attributable to economic events subsequent to the close of that prior period.
3. It depends primarily upon determinations by persons other than management of the business recording the transaction.
4. The economic effect of the transaction was not susceptible to reasonable estimation in the prior period.

Examples of events that are generally treated as prior-period adjustments include settlement of a lawsuit initiated in a prior year and adjustments of income tax of a prior year.

Recall from Chapter Ten that when the estimate of the remaining life or salvage value of a depreciating asset is changed, we suggested that the logical procedure would be to correct the earnings of prior periods and to make the correct depreciation entries based on the new information in subsequent periods. Such treatment would require a prior-period adjustment. This transaction does not qualify as a prior-period adjustment, however, because it violates conditions 2 and 3 above: depreciable lives and salvage values are classified as management estimates and not as economic events. (This is not considered to be an arithmetic error.) As Chapter Ten pointed out, the generally accepted method for handling changes in estimates of the lives or salvage values for depreciable assets does nothing about the effects of the misestimates on earnings of prior periods, but changes the amounts of depreciation to be charged to earnings during the remaining years of the asset's depreciable life.

Corrections of errors and prior-period adjustments must be reported in the

[4] Opinion No. 9, Accounting Principles Board, AICPA, December 1966.

financial statement that reconciles the beginning and ending balances of retained earnings. Both error corrections and prior-period adjustments are rarely seen in published financial statements.

■ DISCLOSURE OF CHANGES IN OWNERS' EQUITY

The changes in all owners' equity accounts must be explained in the annual reports to stockholders.[5] As previous chapters have pointed out, the reconciliation of retained earnings may appear in the balance sheet, in a statement of income and retained earnings, or in a separate statement. A recent annual report of the Ford Motor Company contained the Consolidated Statement of Stockholders' Equity reproduced in Exhibit 12.2. The 2-year comparative statement shows sepa-

EXHIBIT 12.2
Ford Motor Company and Consolidated Subsidiaries
Consolidated Statement of Stockholders' Equity
(in millions of dollars)

Line Number[a]		Capital Stock		Capital Account in Excess of Par Value of Stock	Earnings Retained for Use in the Business	Total Stockholders' Equity
		Shares	Amount			
	Balance, January 1, 1973	101.5	$253.7	$379.5	$5,328.1	$5,961.3
(1)	Net income				906.5	906.5
(2)	Cash dividends				(317.1)	(317.1)
(3)	Common stock issued under certain employe stock plans	0.2	0.5	9.9		10.4
(4)	Conversion of debentures (Note 11)			0.6		0.6
(5)	Capital stock retired	(2.5)	(6.2)	(9.5)	(140.9)	(156.6)
	Balance, December 31, 1973	99.2	248.0	380.5	5,776.6	6,405.1
(1)	Net income				360.9	360.9
(2)	Cash dividends				(298.1)	(298.1)
(3)	Common stock issued under certain employe stock plans	0.1	0.2	1.8		2.0
(4)	Conversion of debentures (Note 11)			1.4		1.4
(5)	Capital stock retired	(5.7)	(14.2)	(21.8)	(194.0)	(230.0)
	Balance, December 31, 1974	93.6	$234.0	$361.9	$5,645.4	$6,241.3

[a] This caption and the line numbers do not appear on the original statement. The line numbers correspond to the journal entries in the text.

[5] Opinion No. 12, Accounting Principles Board, AICPA, December 1967.

rate columns for capital stock at par, capital contributed in excess of par value, retained earnings, and total stockholders' equity. The statement shows opening balances, net income, cash dividends, stock issued under employee option plans, capital stock retired, and capital stock issued on conversion of convertible bonds. Ford made no prior-period adjustments during the 2 years reported on in Exhibit 12.2, so none are shown.

Journal Entries for Changes in Owners' Equity

To review the accounting for owners' equity, we reconstruct the journal entries made by Ford Motor Company which resulted in the changes in owners' equity disclosed in Exhibit 12.2. The following entries summarize all entries made by Ford Motor Company in the owners' equity accounts during the 2 years covered by Exhibit 12.2. The amounts shown represent millions of dollars, and the journal entries are numbered in the same way as the lines in Exhibit 12.2 to which the entries apply.

	(MILLIONS OF DOLLARS)			
	1973		1974	
(1) Income Summary	906.5		360.9	
Earnings Retained for Use in Business		906.5		360.9
Net income for the year, recorded assuming that an Income Summary account is used.				
(2) Earnings Retained for Use in Business	317.1		298.1	
Cash (or Dividends Payable)		317.1		298.1
Cash dividends declared.				
(3) Cash	10.4		2.0	
Capital Stock		0.5		0.2
Capital Account in Excess of Par Value of Stock		9.9		1.8
Common stock issued under certain employee stock plans.				
(4) Convertible Debentures (Bonds)	X + 0.6		Y + 1.4	
Treasury Stock		X		Y
Capital Account in Excess of Par Value of Stock		0.6		1.4
Common stock issued on conversion of convertible debentures (bonds). The shares "issued" on conversion were shares *reissued* from a block of treasury shares. Thus, the par value of these shares is already shown in the capital stock account and does not appear in Exhibit 12.2. X and Y represent the cost of the Ford Motor Company of the treasury shares at the time of acquisition.				
(5) Capital Stock	6.2		14.2	
Capital Account in Excess of Par Value of Stock	9.5		21.8	
Earnings Retained for Use in the Business	140.9		194.0	
Cash		156.6		230.0
Retirement of capital stock acquired for cash.				

Changes in Owners' Equity Reported in the Statement of Changes in Financial Position

Each of the transactions affecting owners' equity is reported in the statement of changes in financial position of the Ford Motor Company, which is shown in Exhibit 12.3. The lines of the statement of changes in financial position that are affected by the owners' equity transactions are identified with the numbers used for the journal entries reconstructed above. The working capital produced by operations shows net income as the first item (**1**). Dividends are the first use ("disposition") of working capital (**2**). The proceeds of the common stock issues are shown as a source of ("an addition to") working capital (**3** and **4**). For entry (**4**), only the amount credited to Capital Account in Excess of Par Value of Stock is shown on the Issuance of Common Stock and Reductions in Long-Term Debt lines. The exchange of treasury stock for the convertible debt is viewed as an exchange not involving working capital. Finally, the acquisition and retirement of capital stock which was retired is reported in the statement of changes in financial position as a use of working capital (**5**).

■ PARTNERSHIPS

A partnership is a contractual arrangement between individuals to share resources and operations in a jointly owned business. The partnership form is generally used by small businesses and groups of professionals such as lawyers, accountants, or doctors. (A partnership need not be "small"; some of the large public accounting partnerships and law firms are multimillion dollar businesses.) The partnership is governed by a partnership contract and by state laws. The partnership contract specifies matters such as division of income, management responsibilities, and procedures to be followed upon dissolution of the partnership or withdrawal of a partner. Partnerships are used as a business form because

1. They are simple to organize.
2. There are no income taxes on partnership earnings comparable to the corporate income tax. Rather, income is allocated to the individual partners who include their share of the income as part of their personal taxable income for the year.

The debts of the partnership are the residual responsibility of the general partners. Partnerships may have limited partners who are not personally responsible for partnership debts, but every partnership must have at least one general partner who is fully liable for all debts. The accounting for partnerships is based upon the same underlying principles as for the corporation except for the entries that affect owners' equity.

For all practical purposes, a sole proprietorship is accounted for like a partnership with a single partner. Thus, the following discussion applies to sole proprietorships except that there is no need to separate the interest of the several partners.

EXHIBIT 12.3
Ford Motor Company and Consolidated Subsidiaries
Consolidated Statement of Changes in Financial Position
(in millions of dollars)

Line Number[a]		1974	1973
	Working Capital, January 1	$1,660.5	$1,684.5
	Additions to Working Capital		
	From operations		
(1)	Net income	360.9	906.5
	Depreciation	530.8	485.1
	Amortization of special tools	392.7	463.1
	Deferred income taxes and investment tax credits	120.3	113.2
	Other	(44.0)	58.0
	Total from operations	1,360.7	2,025.9
	Issuance of long-term debt	578.4	186.7
	Increase in minority interests in net assets	14.4	18.4
(3 and 4)	Issuance of Common Stock	3.4	11.0
	Total additions	1,956.9	2,242.0
	Dispositions of Working Capital		
(2)	Cash dividends	298.1	317.1
	Net additions to property	1,414.8	1,403.0
(5)	Capital stock purchased	230.0	156.6
(4)	Reductions in long-term debt	78.7	203.6
	Additional investments in unconsolidated subsidiaries and affiliates	33.2	120.7
	Other	62.3	65.0
	Total dispositions	2,117.1	2,266.0
	Decrease in Working Capital	(160.2)	(24.0)
	Working Capital, December 31	$1,500.3	$1,660.5

Changes in the Components of Working Capital	Increase (Decrease) in Working Capital	
Cash and marketable securities	$ (476.3)	$ (387.0)
Receivables	378.3	232.0
Inventories	660.3	811.9
Currently payable and deferred income taxes	46.0	125.6
Accounts payable and accrued liabilities	(395.2)	(419.2)
Debt payable within one year	(447.8)	(439.5)
Other current assets	74.5	52.2
Net Change	$ (160.2)	$ (24.0)

[a] This caption and the line numbers do not appear on the original statement. The line numbers correspond to the journal entries in the text.

Capital Contributions: Partnerships

The amount and the form of the capital contribution of each partner are determined by the partnership agreement. The property contributed may be in the
form of cash or other property, or it may be in the form of goodwill—above-normal
earnings expected to be derived from the reputation or experience of a particular
partner. A separate capital account is opened for each partner. This account is
credited with the amount of each partner's original investment and with any
additional amounts subsequently contributed to the business.

The capital account balances may be increased by the investment of additional
funds or by the retention of earnings; they may be decreased by partners' withdrawals or by losses. The understanding between the partners as to the provisions
for making additional investments or withdrawing funds should be covered by the
partnership agreement. The partners may, for example, agree to keep the ratios
of capital accounts constant, which implies that withdrawals by partners must be
in proportion to the ownership percentage of each partner.

The amount appearing in each partner's capital account is significant for a
number of purposes. Its proportion to the total partners' capital indicates his or
her *interest in the capital of the business*. For example, if the total capital is
$40,000 and one partner's capital account has a balance of $10,000, then that
partner has a one-quarter, or 25-percent interest, in the partnership at that time.
The capital balances are often a factor in the distribution of net income, as when
an "interest" allowance is made on capital balances or when profits are distributed
in proportion to capital balances. In case of dissolution, the balance in the partners' accounts indicates their share in the net assets (assets less liabilities) of the
partnership. Any profits or losses incurred in the disposition of the assets would,
of course, change the capital account balances.

The legal features of partnerships may require a partner to make additional
contributions in order to meet the liabilities of the firm. General partners usually
are "jointly and severally" liable for partnership obligations, so that one partner
may not only lose his or her entire investment in the enterprise but also may have
to pay the debts of the business from personal resources. Such a partner would
then try to collect from the other partners their proportionate shares of the debts.

Formation of a Partnership

Accounting for the formation of a partnership is demonstrated in the following
illustration.

Lois L. Baker and John A. Stone start business as partners. Each partner is to
contribute $20,000 of capital. Baker, who has been in business before, contributes
some installment notes receivable from her customers with a face value of $7,000
but valued at $6,000, office equipment worth $3,000, cash of $1,000, and her cus-
tomer relationships valued at $10,000 as goodwill. Stone's contribution consists
of $8,000 cash, office equipment valued at $5,000, an automobile valued at $3,600,
and his promissory 8-percent demand note for $3,400. In transactions of this sort,

it is necessary for the partners to agree on the valuation that is to be assigned to each asset; this is especially true in the case of goodwill. The entries would be:

Installment Notes Receivable	7,000	
Office Equipment	3,000	
Cash	1,000	
Goodwill	10,000	
Allowance for Uncollectible Notes		1,000
L. L. Baker, Capital		20,000
Cash	8,000	
Office Equipment	5,000	
Automobile	3,600	
Notes Receivable—Partners	3,400	
J. A. Stone, Capital		20,000

The opening balance sheet of the partnership would appear as shown in Exhibit 12.4.

EXHIBIT 12.4
Opening Balance Sheet for Partnership
Baker & Stone
(Date)

ASSETS			LIABILITIES AND CAPITAL	
Cash		$ 9,000	L. L. Baker, Capital	$20,000
Installment Notes			J. A. Stone, Capital	20,000
Receivable	$7,000			
Less: Allowance for Un-				
collectible Notes	1,000	6,000		
Notes Receivable—Partners		3,400		
Office Equipment		8,000		
Automobile		3,600		
Goodwill		10,000		
Total Assets		$40,000	Total Liabilities and Capital	$40,000

Allocation of Partnership Net Income

In a partnership, the increase in ownership equity shown in each partner's capital account is determined in two steps: (**1**) allocating net income of the period among the partners, and (**2**) deducting partners' drawings during the period.

At the end of each accounting period, the net income of the period is allocated among the partners. The partnership agreement determines the fraction to which each partner is entitled. If the partnership agreement does not specify the sharing arrangements, the Uniform Partnership Act provides that profits and losses are to be shared equally.

There are many variations in the arrangements that may be specified by the partnership agreement. The more common types of arrangements for the allocation of profits and losses are as follows:

1. a fixed percentage allocation
2. allocation in proportion to capital balances
3. allocation on a combination of bases to reflect various aspects of the partners' contribution of services and capital to the business.

The allocation of net income is usually recorded in the final closing entry: the Income Summary account is debited with an amount which reduces its balance to zero and each of the partners' capital accounts is credited as appropriate. (If there is a loss for the period, the accounts debited and credited in the previous sentence are, of course, reversed.)

The simplest form of net income or loss distribution is the allocation to each partner of a fixed fraction or percentage of the total net income or net loss. For example, if there are three partners, each may be entitled to one-third or some other proportion of net income. If the net income of the Baker and Stone partnership for the year is $60,000, and the profits and losses are to be distributed 60 percent to Baker and 40 percent to Stone, the closing entry would be:

Income Summary	60,000	
L. L. Baker, Capital		36,000
J. A. Stone, Capital		24,000

Partners' Withdrawals

A partnership may legally adopt any desired policy with regard to the retention or distribution of net income. The withdrawal of assets by the partners is guided only by the wishes of the partners and the provisions of the partnership agreement. These withdrawals seldom present accounting complications, and do not merit extended discussion.

Partners' Capital Accounts

One capital account for each partner will often be sufficient. It will be credited with the partner's share of the net income as well as with capital contributions and debited with the partner's share of any losses and the amount of any withdrawals. The balance of such an account may be withdrawn at any time, subject to the restrictions imposed by the partners themselves in their partnership agreement.

Although a single capital account for each partner is usually sufficient, a second account, known as a *drawing* or *personal* account is often used. The drawing account records each partner's withdrawals for personal use and other current charges. The balance in the drawing account at the end of the period is then closed into the capital account.

The monthly entry to record withdrawals of $1,250 by partner Baker might be:

L. L. Baker, Drawings	1,250	
Cash		1,250

At the end of the year the drawing account would have a debit balance of $15,000 (= 12 × $1,250). If Baker's share of income for the year is $36,000, the combined closing entries for her might be:

Income Summary	36,000	
L. L. Baker, Drawings		15,000
L. L. Baker, Capital		21,000

■ SUMMARY

Accounting for owners' equity in a corporation is based on the premise that there should be a separate account for each source of capital contributed by owners. The sources of capital from stockholders include

1. receipts from issues of stock at par or stated value
2. receipts in excess of par or stated value of stock issues
3. earnings retentions.

Owners' equity is reduced when the corporation declares dividends, acquires treasury stock, or experiences losses from business operations.

In a partnership, capital is either contributed directly by the owners or indirectly through earnings retentions. Since there is no capital stock, there is no need to differentiate contributions by classes of stock or between contributions made at par value and in excess of par value. Rather, the accounting for partnership owners' equity attempts to disclose separately the interest of each partner. Partnership owners' equity is increased by capital contributions and periodic income; owners' equity is reduced by partners' drawings and losses.

QUESTIONS AND PROBLEMS

1. Review the meaning of the following concepts or terms discussed in this chapter.
   a. Corporation.
   b. Corporate charter.
   c. Corporate bylaws.
   d. Capital stock, common stock, preferred stock.
   e. Cumulative preferred stock.
   f. Callable preferred stock.
   g. Convertible preferred stock.
   h. Par value.
   i. Stated value.
   j. Additional paid-in capital.
   k. Treasury stock.

l.   Earnings are not cash.

m.   Convertible bond.

n.   Stock dividend.

o.   Stock split.

p.   Stock option.

q.   Stock right.

r.   Stock warrant.

s.   Correction of error.

t.   Prior-period adjustment.

u.   Partnership.

v.   General and limited partners.

w.   Drawings.

2.   Under what circumstances would you expect par-value stock to be issued at a price in excess of par? What is the entry to record such an issue?

3.   A construction corporation is attempting to borrow money on a note secured by some of its property. A bank agrees to accept the note, provided that the president of the corporation will personally endorse it. What is the point of this requirement? Would the bank be likely to require a similar endorsement if the firm were a partnership?

4.   "Par value of preferred stock is frequently a significant figure, but par value of common stock possesses little significance." Why may par value of preferred stock be significant? In what way is the par value of common stock with a par value different from the stated value of no-par common stock?

5.   What is treasury stock? How is it reported on the balance sheet?

6.   A certain corporation retained almost all of its earnings, only rarely paying a cash dividend. When some of the stockholders objected, the reply of the chairman of the board of directors was: "Why do you want cash dividends? You would just have to go to the trouble of reinvesting them. Where can you possibly find a better investment than our own company?" Comment.

7.   Compare the position of a stockholder who receives a cash dividend with one who receives a stock dividend.

8.   At the 1976 stockholders' meeting, the president of the Santa Cris Corporation made the following statement: "The net income for the year, after taxes, was $1,096,000. The directors have decided that the corporation can only afford to distribute $500,000 as a cash dividend." Are the two sentences of this statement compatible?

9.   Distingiush between a potentially dilutive security and a common stock equivalent.

10.   What is the difference between primary earnings per share and fully diluted earnings per share?

11.   Indicate whether each of the following statements is true or false.

a.   Cash dividends reduce the book value per share of capital stock.

b.   The allocation of partnership income is governed by the terms of the partnership agreement.

c.   A stock dividend does not affect the Retained Earnings account.

d.   Investing 50 percent of net income in government bonds has no effect upon the amount legally available for dividends.

12. Indicate whether each of the following statements is true or false, ignoring income taxes:

   a. Stock dividends reduce the book value per share of capital stock.

   b. The declaration of a cash dividend does not reduce the amount of the stock-holders' equity.

   c. The distribution of a stock dividend tends to reduce the market value per share of capital stock.

   d. A stock split generally does not affect the Retained Earnings account.

   e. A stock-dividend declaration is usually accompanied by a reduction in par or stated value per share.

   f. Declaration and payment of a stock dividend does not affect the amount of stockholders' equity.

13. Indicate the effect of each of the following transactions upon (**1**) the balance in the Retained Earnings and (**2**) the total stockholders' equity.

   a. Bonds are issued at a discount.

   b. A check is written to the Internal Revenue Service for additional income taxes levied on past years' income (no previous entry).

   c. A stock split is voted by the directors. The par value per share is reduced from $200 to $50 and each shareholder is given four new shares in exchange for each old share.

   d. The manager is voted a bonus of $3,500 by the directors.

   e. Notes payable in the face amount of $50,000 are paid by check.

   f. A dividend in preferred stock is issued to common stockholders (no previous entry).

   g. Securities held as a long-term investment are sold at book value.

   h. A building site is donated to the company by the local chamber of commerce.

   i. A building is sold for less than its book value.

14. For each of the following transactions, present the journal entries in two-column form. These transactions do not relate to the same set of records.

   a. The shares of no-par stock of a corporation are selling on the market at $200 a share. In order to bring the market value down to a "more popular" figure, the board of directors votes to issue five shares to stockholders in exchange for each share already held by them. The shares are issued.

   b. The treasurer of the corporation reports that cash on hand exceeds normal requirements by $200,000. Pending a decision by the board of directors on the final disposition of the funds, investments in marketable securities in the amount of $198,640 are made.

   c. The net income for the year is $150,000. The directors vote to issue 500 shares of 6-percent, $15 par value preferred stock as a stock dividend on the 2,500 shares of no-par common stock outstanding. The preferred's market price is $20 a share. The common's market price is $5 a share.

   d. After the books are closed, it is discovered that an arithmetic error was made in calculating depreciation on equipment for the preceding period. The depreciation charged was $900 too high.

15. For each of the following events, indicate whether or not an adjustment of retained earnings is required. If an adjustment is required, then indicate if the adjustment qualifies as a prior-period adjustment or as a correction of an error.

If it does not require an adjustment, then indicate why not and the accounting procedures required, if any.

a. Additional depreciation charges for last year resulting from a change in the estimate of the salvage value of the asset.

b. Additional depreciation charges for last year resulting from the mistake of deducting salvage value in computing double-declining-balance depreciation charges.

c. During last year, total debits to Sales, Uncollectible Accounts Adjustment account for last year's sales amount to $10,000. This year, $15,000 of last year's sales on account—$5,000 more than had been planned for—proved to be uncollectible and were written off.

d. A damage suit brought 2 years ago against the company for selling defective products is settled for $20,000.

e. An income tax refund of $12,000 was received this year because the Internal Revenue Service decided the company had overstated its taxable income 3 years ago.

f. Inventory was understated in last year's balance sheet because items in a corner of the warehouse were overlooked.

g. Advertising costs of $40,000 were incurred 2 years ago and were capitalized as an asset to be amortized over a 5-year period. This year the company decides that the advertising will not have future benefits because of a change in brand names used, and the entire unamortized portion of the costs is written off.

16. The comparative balance sheet of the Forty-Misty Company shows the following data:

	DEC. 31, 1976	DEC. 31, 1977
Common Stock	$1,200,000	$1,320,000
Retained Earnings	460,000	400,000
Total Stockholders' Equity	$1,660,000	$1,720,000

During 1977, common stockholders received $50,000 in cash dividends and $120,000 in stock dividends. A refund on 1975 taxes of $30,000 was received on March 1, 1977, and was credited to Retained Earnings. A loss on retirement of plant assets of $5,600 occurred during the year and was incorrectly charged to Retained Earnings.

What net income is reported to stockholders for 1977? What net income should have been reported for 1977? Show your calculations.

17. The comparative balance sheet of the Royal Corporation shows the following information:

	DEC. 31, 1976	DEC. 31, 1977
Preferred Stock (6%)	$ 750,000	$ 600,000
Common Stock	1,400,000	1,540,000
Retained Earnings	324,000	372,000
Total Stockholders' Equity	$2,474,000	$2,512,000

During 1977 stock dividends of $140,000 were issued to common stockholders. In addition, common stockholders received $70,000 in cash dividends; the preferred stockholders received $40,500 in cash dividends. On July 1, 1977, preferred stock with a par value of $150,000 was called at 104; that is, $156,000 was paid to retire the shares. What net income is reported to stockholders for 1977?

18. The Chelex Company began business on January 1, 1976. Its balance sheet for December 31, 1976, contains the stockholders' equity section shown below.

Chelex Company
Stockholders' Equity as of December 31, 1976

Capital Stock ($10 par value)	$ 50,000
Additional Paid-in Capital	77,000
Retained Earnings	10,000
Less: 300 Shares Held in Treasury	(6,000)
Total Stockholders' Equity	$131,000

During the year, Chelex Company engaged in the following capital stock transactions:

(**1**) Issued shares for $25 each.
(**2**) Acquired a block of 500 shares for the treasury in a single transaction.
(**3**) Reissued some of the treasury shares.

Assuming that these were all the capital stock transactions during the year, answer the following questions.

  a. How many shares were issued for $25?
  b. What was the price at which the treasury shares were acquired?
  c. How many shares were reissued from the block of treasury shares?
  d. What was the price at which the treasury shares were reissued?
  e. What journal entries must have been made during the year?

19. The Worman Company began business on January 1, 1976. Its balance sheet for December 31, 1976, contains the stockholders' equity section shown below.

Worman Company
Stockholders' Equity as of December 31, 1976

Capital Stock ($5 par value)	$ 50,000
Additional Paid-in Capital	252,800
Retained Earnings	25,000
Less: 600 Shares Held in Treasury	(16,800)
Total Stockholders' Equity	$311,000

During the year, Worman Company engaged in the following capital stock transactions:

(**1**) Issued shares for $30 each.
(**2**) Acquired a block of 1,000 shares for the treasury in a single transaction.
(**3**) Reissued some of the treasury shares.

Assuming that these were the only capital stock transactions during the year, answer the following questions.

a. How many shares were issued for $30 each?

b. What was the price at which the treasury shares were acquired?

c. How many shares were reissued from the block of treasury shares?

d. What was the price at which the treasury shares were reissued?

e. What journal entries must have been made during the year?

20. On March 1, 1976, William A. Strover, Larry J. Martin, and Roberta R. Dawson form a partnership to conduct a retail business. The partnership agreement provides for the following contributions by the partners:

(**1**) William A. Strover, who has been conducting a retail business as a sole proprietor, is to turn over all the assets of his business except the cash to the partnership and the partnership is to assume all its liabilities. The store's condensed balance sheet at February 28, 1976, showed the following assets and liabilities:

Assets:

Cash, $8,000

Accounts Receivable, $7,600

Merchandise, $30,200

Store Furniture and Fixtures (net), $7,800

Liabilities:

Accounts Payable, $3,800.

The partners agree that an allowance for uncollectible accounts of $1,000 should be set up for the receivables and that the store furniture and fixtures should be valued at $7,000.

(**2**) Larry J. Martin is to contribute a delivery truck valued at $3,000, his 6-month, 8-percent note for $10,000, and cash of $7,000.

(**3**) Roberta R. Dawson is to contribute $16,000 in cash and office equipment valued at $4,000.

All capital contributions are made as set forth in the partnership agreement.

a. Prepare journal entries for Strover's books to show his investment in the partnership.

b. Prepare journal entries for the partners' contributions on the new set of books that is opened for the partnership.

c. Present a balance sheet of the partnership on March 1, 1976, after the contributions have been made.

21. S. Walter, R. Ron, and K. Kelvin are partners engaged in a retail business under the name of Prosperity Company. Their partnership agreement provides that net income or loss is to be shared in the following manner:

(**1**) Interest at the rate of 8 percent per annum is to be allowed on the partners' average capital balances during the year.

(**2**) The following salary allowances are to be provided: Ron $17,000 and Kelvin $14,400. Walter is no longer active in the business and receives no salary allowance.

(**3**) Any remaining income or loss is to be divided 40 percent to Walter, 35 percent to Ron, and 25 percent to Kelvin.

The partners' capital accounts during 1976 show the following data:

S. WALTER, CAPITAL	
3/31/76 2,000	1/ 1/76 80,000
6/30/76 2,000	
9/30/76 2,000	

R. RON, CAPITAL	
6/30/76 2,000	1/ 1/76 36,000
8/31/76 4,000	4/30/76 14,000
10/31/76 6,000	

K. KELVIN, CAPITAL	
1/31/76 6,000	1/ 1/76 24,000
10/31/76 3,000	9/30/76 4,000

The net income from operations for 1976, before deducting any salary or interest allowances, was $54,960.

  a. Show the calculation of the partners' average capital balances.
  b. Prepare a schedule showing the distribution of 1976 net income to the partners.
  c. Prepare a schedule of partners' capital accounts for 1976.

22. The following data are selected from the records of capital stock and retained earnings of the Wheellock Company. Present journal entries for these transactions.

  a. July 5, 1976. Articles of incorporation are filed with the secretary of state. The authorized capital stock consists of 1,000 shares of 6-percent preferred stock with a par value of $100 per share and $10,000 shares of no-par common stock.
  b. July 8, 1976. The company issues 3,000 shares of common stock for cash at $50 per share.
  c. July 9, 1976. The company issues 6,000 shares of common stock for the assets of the partnership of Wheellock and Wheellock. Their assets are valued as follows: accounts receivable, $30,000; inventories, $60,000; land, $20,000; buildings, $90,000; and equipment, $100,000.
  d. July 13, 1976. 750 shares of preferred stock are issued at par for cash.
  e. December 31, 1976. The balance in the Income Summary account after closing all expense and revenue accounts is $200,000. That account is to be closed to the Retained Earnings account.
  f. January 4, 1977. The regular semiannual dividend on the preferred stock and a dividend of $2 per share on the common stock are declared. The dividends are payable on February 1.
  g. February 1, 1977. The dividends declared on January 4 are paid.
  h. July 2, 1977. The regular semiannual dividend on the preferred stock is declared. The dividend is payable on August 1.
  i. August 1, 1977. The dividend declared on July 2 is paid.

23. The following events relate to stockholders' equity transactions of the Richardson Copper Company during the first year of its existence. Present journal entries for each of the transactions.

  a. January 2. Articles of incorporation are filed with the State Corporation Commission. The authorized capital stock consists of 5,000 shares of $100 par value, preferred stock which offers a 5-percent annual dividend, and 50,000 shares of no-par common stock. The original incorporators are issued 100 shares of common stock at $20 per share; cash is collected for the shares. A stated value of $20 per share is assigned to the common stock.

b. January 6. Fifteen thousand shares of common stock are issued for cash at $20 per share.

c. January 8. 2,800 shares of preferred stock are issued at par.

d. January 9. Certificates for the shares of preferred stock are issued.

e. January 12. The tangible assets and goodwill of Richardson Copper Works, a partnership, are acquired in exchange for 600 shares of preferred stock and 10,000 shares of common stock. The tangible assets acquired are valued as follows: inventories, $40,000; land, $45,000; buildings, $80,000; and equipment, $95,000.

f. July 3. The semiannual dividend on the preferred stock outstanding is declared, payable July 25, to stockholders of record on July 12.

g. July 5. Operations for the first 6 months have been profitable, and it is decided to expand. The company issues 20,000 shares of common stock for cash at $23 per share.

h. July 25. The preferred stock dividend declared July 3 is paid.

i. October 2. The directors declare a dividend of $1 per share on the common stock, payable October 25, to stockholders of record on October 12.

j. October 25. The dividend on common stock declared on October 2 is paid.

24. Journalize the following transactions:

(**1**) A cash dividend of $2 a share is declared on the outstanding preferred stock. There are 5,000 shares authorized, 3,000 shares issued, and 100 shares reacquired and held in the treasury.

(**2**) A cash dividend of $1 a share is declared on the no-par common stock of which there are 10,000 shares authorized, 7,000 shares issued, and 1,000 shares reacquired and held in the treasury.

(**3**) The dividend on the preferred stock is paid.

(**4**) The dividend on the common stock is paid.

25. Give journal entries for the following transactions.

a. Outstanding shares of stock are acquired by the issuing corporation for its treasury at a cost of $500,000.

b. Dividends are declared on preferred stock, $120,000.

c. A dividend is paid to common stockholders consisting of shares of preferred stock in the same corporation with a par value of $200,000.

d. A dividend is paid to common stockholders consisting of shares of no-par common stock in the same corporation. The amount assigned to these shares of stock is $600,000.

e. The building is mortgaged for $100,000, and this amount is distributed to the common stockholders as a cash dividend.

26. Give journal entries, if required, for the following transactions, which are unrelated unless otherwise specified:

a. The regular quarterly dividend is declared on the 5-percent, $100 par value preferred stock. There are 10,000 shares authorized, 8,000 shares issued, and 1,600 shares reacquired and held in the treasury.

b. The dividend on the preferred stock (see **a**) is paid.

c. A stock dividend of $250,000 of no-par common stock is issued to common stockholders.

d. A building replacement fund of $125,000 is created. The fund is to be used to purchase a new building when the present one becomes inadequate.

e. Bonds with $500,000 par value are retired at par out of the sinking fund created for that purpose.

f. The shares of no-par stock of the corporation are selling on the market at $300 a share. In order to bring the market value down to a more popular price and thereby broaden the distribution of its stockholdings, the board of directors votes to issue four extra shares to stockholders for each share already held by them. The shares are issued.

27. The following transactions all relate to the same set of records. Use the straight-line method for amortizing bond discount and premium. Journalize these transactions.

a. The company issues 23,000 shares of common stock (par value, $100 per share) for cash at $105 per share.

b. Twenty-year, 8-percent bonds with $500,000 par value are issued for $492,000.

c. Interest expense on the bond is recognized at the time the first semiannual interest payment is made.

d. The bond indenture requires a sinking fund to be built up to pay the principal of the bonds at maturity. The company deposits $18,600 with the sinking fund trustee.

e. A cash dividend of $2 per share of common stock is declared.

f. At the end of the twentieth year of the life of the bonds, the final semiannual interest payment is made and the bonds are retired. There are sufficient funds in the sinking fund to accomplish the retirement.

g. A fund of $50,000 is created for future expansion.

h. An additional 7,000 shares of common stock are issued for cash at $110 a share.

28. Refer to the schedule reproduced here which shows employee stock option data for the General Products Company (GP). At December 31, 1976, there were 2.7 million options outstanding to purchase shares at an average of $54 per share. Total stockholders' equity at December 31, 1976, was about $3,370 million.

General Products Company Disclosure of Employee Stock Options

Stock Options	Shares Subject to Option	Average per Share Option Price	Average per Share Market Price
Balance at Dec. 31, 1974	2,388,931	$45.70	$62.62
Options granted	475,286	67.62	67.62
Options exercised	(297,244)	42.71	65.79
Options terminated	(90,062)	45.52	—
Balance at Dec. 31, 1975	2,476,911	50.27	72.88
Options granted	554,965	64.75	64.75
Options exercised	(273,569)	42.84	63.69
Options terminated	(58,307)	52.50	—
Balance at Dec. 31, 1976	2,700,000	54.00	63.00

a. If GP were to issue 2.7 million shares in a public offering at the market price per share on December 31, 1976, what would be the proceeds of the issue?

b. If GP were to issue 2.7 million shares to employees who exercised all outstanding stock options, what would be the proceeds of the issue?

c. Are GP's stockholders better off under **a** or under **b**?

d. The text accompanying the stock option data in the GP annual report reads, in part, as follows:

> *Option price under these plans is the full market value of General Products common stock on date of grant. Therefore, participants in the plans do not benefit unless the stock's market price rises, thus benefiting all share owners. . . .*

GP seems to be saying that stockholders are not harmed by these options, whereas your answers to parts **a** and **b** show stockholders are worse off when options are exercised than when shares are issued to the public. Attempt to reconcile GP's statement with your own analysis in parts **a** and **b**.

29. On January 2, 1976, the Oklahoma Corporation issues $1 million of 20-year, $1,000 par value 6-percent semiannual coupon bonds at par. Each $1,000 bond is convertible into 40 shares of $1 par value common stock. The Oklahoma Corporation's credit rating is such that it would have to issue 8-percent semiannual coupon bonds if the bonds were not convertible and if they were to be issued at par. On January 2, 1980, the bond issue is converted into common stock. The common stock has a market price of $45 a share on January 2, 1980. Present the journal entries made on January 2, 1976 and 1980, under generally accepted accounting principles, to record the issue and conversion of the issue.

30. The net income of the firm of Donald, Marvin, and Patron for the year 1976 is $54,000. The partnership agreement provides that the net profits shall be divided in the following manner:

(1) Interest at 8 percent per annum on the average investment of each partner during the year shall be computed and credited to their respective capital accounts.

(2) The partners' capital accounts shall be credited with special salary allowances as follows: Donald, $30,000; Marvin, $20,000; Patron, $10,000.

(3) The balance of the net income or loss shall be divided equally among the respective partners' capital accounts.

The capital accounts of the partners show the following data:

	DONALD	MARVIN	PATRON
Balance, January 1, 1976	$20,000	$10,000	$10,000
Withdrawals, June 30, 1976	(10,000)	(4,000)	(6,000)
Invested, September 30, 1976		4,000	4,000
Balance December 31, 1976 before Distributing Income for 1976	$10,000	$10,000	$ 8,000

Calculate and present in a schedule the division of the net income among the three partners. Neither partners' salary allowances nor interest on capital contributions are treated as expenses in the determination of net income.

31. Gordon and Ginn are partners with capital balances of $90,000 and $120,000, respectively, on January 1, 1976. Their partnership agreement provides:

(1) Salaries are to be allowed to Gordon, $15,000 per year; to Ginn, $14,000 per year.

(2) Each partner is to be credited with an interest allowance at the rate of 8 percent per annum on his capital balance at the beginning of the year.

(3) The balance of profits or losses is to be distributed 60 percent to Gordon and 40 percent to Ginn.

During 1976, both partners drew their full salary allowances. What would the balances in the partners' capital accounts be at December 31, 1976, under the following alternative conditions? Assume that net income figures are calculated before salary and interest allowances are deducted.

a. Net income during 1976 was $30,000.

b. Net income during 1976 was $70,000.

c. Net income during 1976 was $120,000.

32. The stockholders' equity section of the balance sheet of the Conte Corporation at December 31, 1976, is as follows:

Stockholders' Equity

Common Stock—$10 Par Value, 500,000 Shares Authorized and 100,000 Shares Outstanding	$1,000,000
Additional Paid-in Capital	500,000
Retained Earnings	2,000,000
Total Stockholders' Equity	$3,500,000

a. Determine the total book value and the book value per common share as of December 31, 1976.

b. For each of the following transactions or events, give the appropriate journal entry and determine the total book value and the book value per common share of the Conte Corporation after the transaction. The transactions and events are independent of each other, except where noted.

(1) A 10-percent stock dividend is declared when the market price of Conte Corporation's common stock is $50 per share.

(2) A two-for-one stock split is declared and the par value of the common stock is reduced from $10 to $5 per share. The new shares are issued immediately.

(3) Ten thousand shares of Conte Corporation's common stock are purchased on the open market for $50 per share and held as treasury stock.

(4) Ten thousand shares of Conte Corporation's common stock are purchased on the open market for $30 a share and held as treasury stock.

(5) The shares acquired in (**3**) are sold for $60 per share.

(6) The shares acquired in (**3**) are sold for $40 per share.

(7) The shares acquired in (**3**) are sold for $30 per share.

(8) Options to acquire 10,000 shares of Conte Corporation stock are exercised by officers for $20 per share.

(9) Same as (**8**), except that the exercise price is $40 per share.

(10) Convertible bonds with a book value of $300,000 and a market value of $340,000 are exchanged for 10,000 shares of common stock having a market value of $34 per share. No gain or loss is recognized on the conversion of bonds.

(11) Same as (10), except that gain or loss is recognized on the conversion of bonds into stock. Ignore income tax effects.

c. Using the results from **b**, summarize the transactions and events that result in a reduction in

(1) total book value

(2) book value per share.

Chapter Thirteen

Investments
in Corporate
Securities

For a variety of reasons, corporations often acquire the capital stock of other corporations. First, a corporation may hold excess cash, and its management may think that an investment in another corporation is the most profitable use that can be made of the excess funds. Relatively short-term investments of excess cash in corporate securities are usually classified as Marketable Securities and are shown in the Current Assets section of the balance sheet. Chapter Eight discusses the methods of accounting for marketable securities.

Second, a corporation may acquire another corporation's stock to gain control of the acquired company's operations or to make easier the integration of separate operations. These investments, which have a more long-term purpose, are typically classified on the asset side of the balance sheet in a separate section called "Investments." This chapter discusses the accounting procedures for these long-term investments. We focus on the problems of

1. recording the acquisition
2. recognizing income subsequent to acquisition
3. reporting the nature and effect of the relationship between the corporation acquiring the stock and the one whose stock is acquired.

Some consideration is also given to the special problems in accounting for corporate acquisitions under the *purchase* and *pooling of interests* methods and in reporting the results of foreign operations.

The method of accounting for long-term investments depends primarily on the percentage of the voting stock that one corporation owns of another. If the acquiring company owns less than 20 percent of the stock of the acquired company, it accounts for its investment by the *cost method*. If it owns from 20 to 50 percent of the acquired company, it must use the *equity method*. If the acquiring company owns more than 50 percent of the stock of the acquired company, the *consolidation method* is usually used in reports to stockholders, but the equity method may be used under special circumstances. The three methods are discussed in the following sections.

Throughout this chapter, we call the acquiring corporation P for *purchaser* or for *parent*, depending on the context, while S stands for *seller* or for *subsidiary*.

■ MINORITY INVESTMENTS

When a stockholder owns less than 50 percent of the voting shares of another company, the stockholder is called a *minority* investor. Minority investments are accounted for using one of two methods, depending upon the fraction of shares owned. These two methods are the *cost method* and the *equity method*.

Cost Method

When a corporation, P, holds less than 20 percent of the stock of another corporation, S, P will use the cost method to account for its investment under current generally accepted accounting principles. Chapter Eight presented the accounting for marketable securities. The accounting under the cost method is virtually identical with the accounting for marketable securities. The only important difference is that marketable securities are classified as current assets on the balance sheet, while investments accounted for on the cost method are classified as noncurrent assets.

Suppose that P acquires 1,000 shares of S for $40,000. The entry to record the acquisition would be:

Investment in S	40,000	
Cash		40,000

If the purpose of the purchase were merely a short-term investment to use idle cash, the debit would be to Marketable Securities.

If, while P holds this stock, S declares a dividend of $2 per share, P would make the following entry:

Dividends Receivable	2,000	
Dividend Revenue		2,000

When the dividend is collected, P will debit Cash and credit Dividends Receivable.

If P sells all of its stock of S, P will debit Cash for the proceeds, credit the Investment in S account to reduce the balance in that account to zero, and credit Gain on Sale of Stock (or debit Loss on Sale of Stock) to complete the entry. If P sells its 1,000 shares of S for $40,500, the entry would be:

Cash	40,500	
Investment in S		40,000
Gain on Sale of Stock		500

If, under these same conditions, P sells half its investment in stock, the entry would be:

Cash	20,250	
Investment in S		20,000
Gain on Sale of Stock		250

To summarize, when Company P accounts for its investment in Company S using the cost (actually, lower-of-cost-or-market; FASB Statement No. 12) method:

1. Company P reports as income each period its share of the dividends declared by Company S.
2. Company P reports on the balance sheet the lower-of-cost-or-market value of the shares in Company S. Declines in market value below cost are debited directly to an owners' equity account such as "Unrealized Losses on Investments."
3. Company P recognizes gains or losses on the income statement from holding the stock of Company S at the time the shares are sold.

Equity Method

Under the cost method, P makes entries only when it buys stock, becomes entitled to receive a dividend, collects the dividend, or sells stock. Suppose that S follows a policy of financing its own growing operations through retention of earnings, so that S consistently pays dividends substantially less than its net income. The market price of a share of S's stock may increase. Under the cost method, P will continue to show the Investment in S account at acquisition cost. Suppose further that P holds a substantial fraction of the shares of S so that P is able to influence the financial policy of S. Under these conditions, the cost method may not reasonably reflect the earnings generated under P's influence or control. The equity method is designed to provide a better measure of earnings and asset valuations for investments in securities where there are substantial holdings and where P is able to influence the operations of S because of the substantial holdings.

When Company P can exercise significant influence over operating and financial policies of Company S, generally accepted accounting principles require that the investment by P in S be reported using the *equity method*.[1] To determine when significant influence can be exercised involves judgment. For the sake of objectivity, generally accepted accounting principles require that the equity method be used when Company P owns 20 percent or more of the common stock of Company S, but not more than 50 percent of it.

Under the equity method, the purchase and sale of stock is recorded just as under the cost method; however, P treats as income (or revenue) each period its proportionate share of the periodic earnings, not merely the dividends, of S. Dividends paid by S are then treated by P as a reduction in its Investment in S.

[1] Opinion No. 18, Accounting Principles Board, AICPA, March 1971.

Suppose that P acquires 30 percent of the outstanding shares of S for $600,000. The entry to record the acquisition would be:

(1) Investment in S 600,000
    Cash 600,000

Between the time of the acquisition and the end of P's next accounting period, S reports income of $80,000. P, using the equity method, would record:

(2) Investment in S 24,000
    Revenue from Investments 24,000
    To record 30 percent of income earned by investee accounted for
    using the equity method.

If S declares a dividend of $30,000 to holders of common stock, P would be entitled to receive $9,000 and would record:

(3) Dividends Receivable 9,000
    Investment in S 9,000
    To record dividends receivable from investee accounted for using
    the equity method and the resulting reduction in the investment
    account.

Notice that the credit is to the Investment in S account. P records income earned by S as an *increase* in investment. The dividend becomes an income distribution which is a return of capital or a *decrease* in investment. Note that this method produces the same result, revenues of $24,000, as treating the dividends ($9,000) as investment income and recognizing P's share of S's *undistributed* earnings for the year [30 percent of ($80,000 − $30,000) or $15,000] as additional income.

Suppose that S subsequently reports earnings of $100,000 and also declares dividends of $40,000. P's entries would be

(4) Investment in S 30,000
    Revenue from Investments 30,000
(5) Dividends Receivable 12,000
    Investment in S 12,000
    To record revenue and dividends from investee, accounted for
    using equity method.

P's Investment in S account now has a balance of $633,000 as follows:

INVESTMENT IN S

(1)	600,000	9,000	(3)
(2)	24,000	12,000	(5)
(4)	30,000		
Bal.	633,000		

Suppose that P now sells one-fourth of its shares for $152,500, reducing its holdings. P's entry to record the sale would be:

(6) Cash 152,500
    Loss on Partial Liquidation of Investment in S 5,750
      Investment in S 158,250
    (¼ × $633,000 = $158,250.)

The equity method as described above is simple enough to use. To make financial reports using the equity method more realistic, generally accepted accounting principles require some modification of the entries under certain circumstances.[2]

Even though S does not declare all of its earnings in dividends, P reports its proportionate share of S's earnings as income. But this income to P is not currently taxable. Consequently, there will often be an entry in the deferred tax account. Determination of the amount of the deferred tax charge presents issues too complex for this introductory text.

An additional complication in using the equity method arises when the acquisition cost of P's shares exceeds P's proportionate share of the book value of the net assets (= assets minus liabilities), or stockholders' equity of S, at the date of acquisition. For example, assume that P acquires 25 percent of the stock of S for $400,000 when the total stockholders' equity of S is $1 million. The excess of P's cost over book value acquired is $150,000 (= $400,000 − .25 × $1,000,000) and is called *goodwill*. Accounting for goodwill is also a problem in the consolidation method and is discussed later in this chapter.

On the balance sheet, an investment accounted for on the equity method is shown in the Investments section. The amount shown will generally be equal to the acquisition cost of the shares plus P's share of S's undistributed earnings since the date the shares were acquired. On the income statement, P shows its share of S's income as a revenue each period. (The financial statements of the investee, S, are not affected by the accounting method used by the investor, P.)

The Cost and Equity Methods and the Statement of Changes in Financial Position

When Company P uses the cost method to account for its investment in Company S, all dividend revenues recognized in determining net income also produce working capital. No adjustments to net income are required in determining Working Capital Provided by Operations.

Accounting for investments using the equity method, however, requires an adjustment to net income to determine Working Capital Provided by Operations in the statement of changes in financial position. Suppose that Company P prepares its financial statements at the end of a year during which transactions (1)–(5), above, occurred. P's revenue from its investment in S is $54,000. This amount is the sum of the revenue recognized in transactions (2) and (4). P's income

[2] Opinion No. 18, Accounting Principles Board, AICPA, March 1971.

(ignoring income tax effects) increased $54,000 because of its investment. However, P's working capital increased by only $21,000 [transactions (**3**) and (**5**)] as a result of S's dividend declarations. Consequently, there must be a *subtraction* from net income of $33,000 (= $54,000 — $21,000) to show that working capital did not increase by as much as the amount of revenue recognized under the equity method.

In preparing P's statement of changes in financial position using the double-T-account method, the following change in a noncurrent asset account would have to be explained:

INVESTMENT IN S

633,000

The entries to explain this debit change of $633,000 would be:

Investment in S	600,000	
Working Capital (Use—Acquisition of Investment)		600,000
To recognize use of funds for an investment in a noncurrent asset.		
Investment in S	33,000	
Working Capital (Subtraction—Undistributed Income Under Equity Method)		33,000
To recognize that working capital was not increased by the full amount of revenue recognized under the equity method.		

Keep in mind that these two entries are not formally made in the accounting records, but are made only in the work sheet used for preparing the statement of changes in financial position under the double-T-account method.

Minority Investments Illustrated

Exhibits 13.1, 13.2, and 13.3 show the income statement, balance sheet, and statement of changes in financial position of the Westinghouse Electric Corporation. The balance sheet, Exhibit 13.2, shows investments of approximately $226 million as of year-end 1974. The income statement for 1974, Exhibit 13.1, shows $32,285,000 of loss from the investments accounted for on the equity method as "Equity in income (loss) from non-consolidated subsidiaries and affiliated companies." This loss did not use working capital, so the statement of changes in financial position, Exhibit 13.3, shows an addback of $32,285,000 to net income in deriving "Working capital provided by continuing operations" for 1974. For 1973, income from non-consolidated subsidiaries of $3,341,000 is shown in Exhibit 13.1. The statement of changes in financial position, Exhibit 13.3, shows a subtraction of the same amount in deriving "Working capital provided by continuing operations."

EXHIBIT 13.1
From the Annual Report of Westinghouse Electric Corporation
Consolidated Statements of Income and Retained Earnings

Westinghouse Consolidated Statements of Income and Retained Earnings

Income Statement	Year Ended December 31 1974	Year Ended December 31 1973
Income:		
Sales	$5,798,513,000	$5,101,123,000
Equity in income (loss) from non-consolidated		
subsidiaries and affiliated companies	(32,285,000)	3,341,000
Other income	71,890,000	63,567,000
	5,838,118,000	5,168,031,000
Costs and expenses:		
Cost of sales	4,669,745,000	3,960,412,000
Distribution, administration and general	727,426,000	698,775,000
Depreciation	123,518,000	107,564,000
Interest	111,261,000	69,317,000
Income taxes	63,970,000	145,933,000
Minority interest in net income of		
consolidated subsidiaries	3,261,000	2,516,000
	5,699,181,000	4,984,517,000
Income from continuing operations	138,937,000	183,514,000
Discontinued operations:		
Loss from operations of discontinued businesses	(39,805,000)	(21,586,000)
Loss on disposal of discontinued businesses	(71,000,000)	—
Net income	$ 28,132,000	$ 161,928,000
Earnings per common share:		
Continuing operations	$1.57	$2.06
Discontinued operations:		
Loss from operations	(.45)	(.24)
Loss on disposal	(.81)	—
Net income per common share	$ .31	$1.82

Retained Earnings	Year Ended December 31 1974	Year Ended December 31 1973
Retained earnings at beginning of year	$1,220,914,000	$1,145,711,000
Plus:		
Net income	28,132,000	161,928,000
Less:		
Dividends paid on preferred stock	1,158,000	1,158,000
Dividends paid on common stock	85,332,000	85,567,000
Retained earnings at end of year	$1,162,556,000	$1,220,914,000

EXHIBIT 13.2
From the Annual Report of Westinghouse Electric Corporation
Consolidated Balance Sheet

Westinghouse
Consolidated
Balance Sheet

Assets	At December 31 1974	At December 31 1973
Current assets:		
Cash and marketable securities	$ 137,806,000	$ 129,289,000
Customer receivables	1,247,121,000	1,308,232,000
Inventories and recoverable costs	758,354,000	983,911,000
Prepaid and other current assets	184,417,000	186,346,000
Total current assets	2,327,698,000	2,607,778,000
Investments	226,209,000	185,935,000
Estimated realizable value – discontinued businesses ..	202,442,000	—
Plant and equipment, net	1,298,576,000	1,324,913,000
Other assets	246,879,000	289,039,000
Total assets	$4,301,804,000	$4,407,665,000

Liabilities and Stockholders' Equity		
Current liabilities:		
Short-term loans and current portion of long-term debt ..	$ 236,063,000	$ 475,301,000
Accounts payable – trade	392,835,000	405,307,000
Accrued payrolls and payroll deductions	180,473,000	175,154,000
Income taxes currently payable	47,172,000	19,182,000
Deferred current income taxes	31,146,000	140,009,000
Estimated future costs – discontinued businesses	46,394,000	—
Other current liabilities	382,122,000	287,272,000
Total current liabilities	1,316,205,000	1,502,225,000
Non-current liabilities	62,360,000	87,131,000
Deferred non-current income taxes	97,270,000	80,955,000
Revolving credit notes payable	200,000,000	—
Debentures and other debt	643,123,000	671,727,000
Minority interest	58,775,000	69,490,000
Stockholders' equity:		
Capital	761,515,000	775,223,000
Retained earnings	1,162,556,000	1,220,914,000
Total stockholders' equity	1,924,071,000	1,996,137,000
Total liabilities and stockholders' equity	$4,301,804,000	$4,407,665,000

EXHIBIT 13.3
From the Annual Report of Westinghouse Electric Corporation
Consolidated Statement of Changes in Financial Position

Westinghouse Consolidated Statement of Changes in Financial Position

Changes in Financial Position	Year Ended December 31 1974	Year Ended December 31 1973
Resources provided:		
Net income from continuing operations	$138,937,000	$183,514,000
Income charges (credits) not affecting working capital:		
Depreciation	123,518,000	107,564,000
Deferred income taxes	21,222,000	38,768,000
Minority interest in net income of consolidated subsidiaries	3,261,000	2,516,000
Equity in income from non-consolidated subsidiaries and affiliated companies	32,285,000	(3,341,000)
Working capital provided by continuing operations	319,223,000	329,021,000
Losses applicable to discontinued operations	(110,805,000)	(21,586,000)
Income charges (credits) not affecting working capital:		
Depreciation	10,143,000	7,597,000
Deferred income taxes	(4,907,000)	—
Loss on disposal (less $46,394,000 current estimated future costs)	24,606,000	—
Working capital absorbed by discontinued operations	(80,963,000)	(13,989,000)
Revolving credit notes payable	200,000,000	—
Increase in debentures and other debt	19,747,000	69,185,000
Issuance of common stock to employes	25,467,000	26,278,000
Total resources provided	483,474,000	410,495,000
Resources applied:		
Expenditures for new and improved facilities	213,274,000	202,414,000
Dividend payments	86,490,000	86,725,000
Reduction in debentures and other debt	48,351,000	26,567,000
Increase in investments	40,479,000	14,273,000
Purchase of common stock for treasury	39,442,000	36,296,000
Reclassification of working capital to estimated realizable value – discontinued businesses	143,379,000	—
Other – net	6,119,000	15,682,000
Total resources applied	577,534,000	381,957,000
Net change in working capital	$(94,060,000)	$ 28,538,000

Analysis of Changes in Working Capital

Increase (decrease) in working capital:		
Cash and marketable securities	$ 8,517,000	$ (9,938,000)
Customer receivables	(61,111,000)	292,041,000
Inventories and recoverable costs	(225,557,000)	117,010,000
Prepaid and other current assets	(1,929,000)	36,177,000
Short-term loans and current portion of long-term debt	239,238,000	(266,955,000)
Accounts payable – trade	12,472,000	(54,262,000)
Income taxes (including deferred income taxes)	80,873,000	(13,659,000)
Estimated future costs – discontinued businesses	(46,394,000)	—
All other current liabilities	(100,169,000)	(71,876,000)
Net change in working capital	$(94,060,000)	$ 28,538,000

■ MAJORITY INVESTMENTS

When a firm owns more than 50 percent of the voting stock of another company, the firm is called the *majority* investor, or *parent*. In most cases, the financial statements of the majority-owned *subsidiary* are combined, or *consolidated*, with those of the parent. In some instances, however, consolidated financial statements are not prepared. Instead, the investment is reported using the equity method. Whether consolidated statements are prepared or the equity method is used depends on the consolidation policy of the firm.

Purpose of Consolidated Statements

Consolidated financial statements present the results of operations, financial position, and changes in financial position of an affiliated group of corporations under the control of a parent essentially as if the group of corporations were a single entity. The parent and each subsidiary corporation are legally separate entities, but they operate as one centrally-controlled *economic entity*. Consolidated financial statements generally provide more useful information to the stockholders of the parent corporation than would separate financial statements of the parent and each subsidiary. Consolidated financial statements generally provide more useful information than does using the equity method. The parent, because of its voting interest, can effectively control the use of the subsidiary's assets. Consolidation of the individual assets and equities of both the parent and the subsidiary provides a more realistic picture of the operations and financial position of the single economic entity.

In a legal sense, consolidated statements merely supplement, and do not replace, the separate statements of the individual corporations, although it is common practice to present only the consolidated statements in published annual reports.

Consolidation Policy

Consolidated financial statements are generally prepared when all of the following three criteria are met:

1. The parent owns more than 50 percent of the voting stock of the subsidiary.
2. There are no important restrictions on the ability of the parent to exercise control of the subsidiary.
3. The asset and equity structure of the subsidiary is not significantly different from that of the parent.

Ownership of more than 50 percent of the subsidiary's voting stock implies an ability to exert control over the activities of the subsidiary. For example, the parent can control the subsidiary's corporate policies and dividend declarations. There may be situations, however, where control of the subsidiary's activities cannot be carried out effectively, despite the ownership of a majority of the voting stock. For example, the subsidiary may be located in a foreign country that has severely restricted the withdrawal of funds from that country. Or the subsidiary may be in bankruptcy and under the control of a court-appointed group of trustees. In these cases, the financial statements of the subsidiary probably will not be consolidated with those of the parent. The parent would use the equity method or even, perhaps, the cost method in unusual circumstances.

If the asset and equity structure of the subsidiary is significantly different from that of the parent, the subsidiary's financial statements are frequently not consolidated with those of the parent and the equity method is used. For example, a consolidated statement would probably not be prepared if the parent is a manufacturing concern with heavy investments in property, plant, and equipment, while the subsidiary is a finance or insurance company with large holdings of cash, receivables, and marketable securities. The presentation of consolidated financial statements of corporations with significantly different asset and equity structures generally submerges potentially important information about the individual corporations. This is particularly true when the assets of the subsidiary are not, by law, fully available for use by the parent, such as when the subsidiary is a bank or an insurance company. For example, Sears, Roebuck and Company owns 100 percent of the stock of Allstate Insurance Company, but accounts for Allstate in its financial statements using the equity method.

The consolidated income statement of Westinghouse Electric Corporation, Exhibit 13.1, refers to "Equity in income (loss) from non-consolidated subsidiaries and affiliated companies." Westinghouse explains in the notes to its financial statements that:

> The financial statements include the consolidation of all significant wholly and majority owned subsidiaries except Westinghouse Credit Corporation and Urban Systems Development Corporation. The equity method of accounting is followed for non-consolidated subsidiaries and for investments in significant affiliates (20 to 50 percent owned).

Reasons for Legally Separate Corporations

The parent could, in many instances, bring the legal existence of the subsidiary to an end by merging it into the parent. However, using several corporations, instead of one, may serve several purposes. From the standpoint of the parent, the more important reasons for the existence of legally separate subsidiary companies are as follows:

1. To reduce the financial risk. Separate corporations may be used for mining raw materials, transporting them to a manufacturing plant, producing the product, and selling the finished product to the public. If any one part of the total process proves to be unprofitable or inefficient, the corporation performing the particular step can be dissolved and the required goods or services be purchased from other sources without seriously interfering with the operations of other corporations in the group. Losses from insolvency will fall only on the owners and creditors of the one subsidiary corporation.

2. To meet more effectively the requirements of state corporation laws and tax legislation. If an organization does business in a number of states, it is often faced with overlapping and inconsistent taxation, regulations, and requirements. It may be more economical to organize separate corporations to conduct the operations in the various states.

3. To expand with a minimum of capital investment. A firm may absorb another company by acquiring a controlling interest in its voting stock. The result may be accomplished with a substantially smaller capital investment, as well as with less difficulty and inconvenience, than if a new plant had been constructed or a complete merger were arranged.

Understanding Consolidated Statements

The remainder of this section discusses the following four concepts essential for understanding published consolidated statements:

1. the need for intercompany eliminations
2. the meaning of consolidated income and retained earnings
3. the nature of the minority interest
4. the consolidated statement of changes in financial position.

Appendix 13.1 discusses the procedures for preparing consolidated statements.

Need for Intercompany Eliminations The items on consolidated statements are little more than the sum of the items on the financial statements of the corporations being consolidated. Consolidated statements are intended to reflect the results that would be achieved if the affiliated group of companies were a single company. The amounts resulting from a summation of the accounts of the companies being consolidated must therefore be adjusted to eliminate double counting and intercompany transactions.

For example, the parent's balance sheet shows an asset, Investment in Subsidiary. The subsidiary's balance sheet shows its individual assets. If the two balance sheets were merely added together, the sum would show both the parent's investment in the subsidiary's assets and the assets themselves. The parent's balance sheet item, Investment in Subsidiary, must therefore be eliminated from the sum of the balance sheets. Since the consolidated balance sheet must maintain the accounting equation, corresponding eliminations must be made on the right-hand side as well. To understand the eliminations from the right-hand side of the balance sheet, recall that the right-hand side shows the sources of the firm's financing. The subsidiary is financed by creditors (liabilities) and by owners (stockholders' equity). Assume that the parent owns 100 percent of the subsidiary's stock. Then the assets on the consolidated balance sheet of the single economic entity are financed by the creditors of both companies and by the parent's stockholders. That is, the equities of the consolidated entity are the liabilities of both companies but the stockholders' equity of the parent alone. If the stockholders' equity accounts of the subsidiary were added to those of the parent, then the financing from the parent's stockholders would be counted twice. Hence, when the parent's investment account is eliminated from the sum of the two companies' assets, the accounting equation is maintained by eliminating the stockholders' equity accounts of the subsidiary.

A parent may lend funds to its subsidiary. If the separate balance sheets were merely added together, those funds would be counted twice: once as the notes receivable on the parent's books and again as the cash or other assets on the subsidiary's books. Consolidated balance sheets eliminate intercompany transactions that would not be reported for a single, integrated enterprise. Thus, the note receivable of the parent and the note payable of the subsidiary are eliminated in preparing the consolidated balance sheet.

Similarly, certain intercompany transactions must be eliminated from the sum of income statement accounts so that the operating performance of the consolidated entity can be meaningfully presented. For example, if a manufacturing parent sells goods to a subsidiary which, in turn, sells the goods to the public, then the sum of individual income statements would double-count sales and costs of goods sold. Suppose that the parent sells to the subsidiary but that the subsidiary has not yet sold the goods to the public. The parent will have recorded profits on the sale, but from the standpoint of the overall economic entity, no profits for stockholders have actually been realized because the items are still in the inventory of the overall economic entity. Consequently, profits from the parent's sales to subsidiaries that have not been realized by subsequent sales to outsiders are eliminated from consolidated net income amounts. The consolidated income statement attempts to show sales, expenses, and net income figures that report the results of operations of the group of companies as though it were a single company.

Consolidated Income and Retained Earnings The amount of consolidated net income for a period is the same as the amount that would be reported if the parent company used the equity method of accounting for the intercorporate investment. That is, consolidated net income is equal to

| Parent Company's Net Income | + | Parent's Share of Subsidiary's Net Income | − | Profit (or Plus Loss) on Intercompany Transactions. |

The principal difference between the consolidated income statement and the income statement where the subsidiary is accounted for under the equity method is the components of income presented. When a consolidated income statement is prepared, the individual revenues and expenses of the subsidiary (less intercompany adjustments) are combined with those of the parent. When the equity method is used for an unconsolidated subsidiary, the parent's share of the subsidiary's net income minus gain on intercompany transactions is shown on a single line of the income statement with a title such as "Equity in Earnings (Loss) of Unconsolidated Subsidiary." (See, for example, the income statements of Westinghouse Electric Corporation in Exhibit 13.1 and of Ford Motor Company in Exhibit 6.4. Those income statements are consolidated income statements. Both companies have, however, "subsidiaries and affiliates" that are not consolidated but are accounted for with the equity method.)

The amount shown on the consolidated balance sheet for retained earnings is likewise the amount that would be reported if the parent company used the equity method of accounting for the intercorporate investment. That is, consolidated retained earnings is equal to

Parent's Retained Earnings	+	Parent's Share of the Change in Subsidiary's Retained Earnings Since Acquisition	−	Profit (or Plus Loss) on Intercompany Transactions.

If the parent actually used the equity method of accounting for the investment on its books, the second and third terms above would already be included in the parent's retained earnings. In this case, consolidated retained earnings equals the parent's retained earnings. The parent may, however, use the cost method of accounting for the investment on its own, single-company books if it intends to publish consolidated statements. If the parent uses the cost method, the parent's share of the subsidiary's retained earnings since acquisition less any profit on intercompany transactions must be combined with the parent's retained earnings in preparing the consolidated balance sheet. The mechanics of the required adjustments are discussed in Appendix 13.1.

Minority Interest in Consolidated Subsidiary In many cases, the parent will not own 100 percent of the voting stock of a consolidated subsidiary. The owners of the remaining shares of voting stock are called *minority shareholders*, or the *minority interest*. These shareholders continue to have a proportionate interest in the net assets (= total assets minus total liabilities), or stockholders' equity, of the subsidiary as shown on the subsidiary's separate corporate records. They also have a proportionate interest in the earnings of the subsidiary.

An issue in the generally accepted accounting principles for consolidated statements is whether the statements should show only the parent's share of the assets and equities of the subsidiary or whether they should show all of the subsidiary's assets and equities along with the minority interests in them. The generally accepted accounting principle is to show all of the assets and equities of the subsidiary, since the parent, with its controlling voting interest, can effectively direct the use of all the assets and liabilities, not merely an amount equal to the parent's percentage of ownership. The consolidated balance sheet and income statement in these instances must, however, disclose the interest of the minority shareholders in the subsidiary which has been consolidated.

The amount of the minority interest shown on the balance sheet is generally the result of multiplying the common stockholders' equity of the subsidiary by the minority's percentage of ownership. For example, if the common stockholders' equity (that is, assets minus liabilities, or common stock, additional paid-in capital, and retained earnings) of a consolidated subsidiary totals $500,000 and the minority owns 20 percent of the common stock, then the minority interest shown on the consolidated balance sheet is $100,000 (= .20 × $500,000).

The minority interest is typically presented among the equities on the consolidated balance sheet between the liabilities and stockholders' equity. See, for example, the Westinghouse consolidated balance sheet in Exhibit 13.2. Note that "Minority interest" is shown on a line separate from either liabilities or stockholders' equity. To take another example, refer to the consolidated balance sheet of Ford Motor Company in Exhibit 6.3. Notice there that "Minority Interests in Net Assets of Consolidated Subsidiaries" is shown on a separate line and that its amount is excluded from both the total of liabilities and the total of stockholders' equity. We think that the right-hand side of the balance sheet should contain only liabilities and owners' equity items, so that the minority interest should be classified as one or the other. The minority interest does not meet the definition of a liability discussed in Chapter Eleven, because there is no maturity date. The minority interest might be classified as an indeterminate-term liability, much the same as deferred taxes. We think it probably better to view the minority interest as a form of owners' equity, much the same as preferred stock is viewed as owners' equity.

The amount of the minority interest in the subsidiary's income shown on the consolidated income statement is generally the result of multiplying the subsidiary's net income by the minority's percentage of ownership. The consolidated income is allocated to show the portions applicable to the parent company and the portion of the subsidiary's income applicable to the minority interest. Refer again to Westinghouse's consolidated income statement shown in Exhibit 13.1. Notice the deduction of $3,261,000 for the "Minority interest in net income of consolidated subsidiaries" before the derivation of the consolidated net income figure. The consolidated net income includes that portion of net income of subsidiary companies allocable to the stockholders of Westinghouse. Typically, the minority interest in the subsidiary's income is shown as a deduction before the net income of the parent's stockholders.

Statement of Changes in Financial Position The consolidated statement of changes in financial position is constructed from the consolidated balance sheet, income statement, and supplementary information in the same way as explained in Chapter Five for a single company. Two items may appear in the consolidated statement, however, that do not usually appear on single-company statements of changes in financial position.

The first item in consolidated statements of changes in financial position that does not appear in single-company statements is the addback to net income for the minority interest in earnings. As we pointed out in the discussion of minority interest above, Westinghouse shows a deduction of $3,261,000 for the minority's share of earnings before the final net income figure in Exhibit 13.1. This deduction did not require the use of any working capital. Consequently, there must be an addback to derive "Working capital provided by continuing operations" in the consolidated statement of changes in financial position. Westinghouse shows the addback of $3,261,000 in its statement of changes in financial position, Exhibit 13.3, as "Minority interest in net income of consolidated subsidiaries." (Ford

Motor Company shows the minority interest in its statement of changes in financial position, reproduced in Exhibit 12.3, as another source of working capital, rather than as an addback in determining working capital provided by operations.)

Second, the amortization of goodwill may appear in consolidated income statements. Goodwill was introduced in Chapter Ten, and is explained in more detail later in this chapter. Just like other amortization charges, amortization of goodwill causes a reduction in reported net income without using any working capital. Therefore, there must be an addback to net income in the amount of that amortization in order to derive the amount of working capital provided by operations. Often, however, as in the case of the consolidated statement of changes in financial position of Westinghouse Electric Corporation shown in Exhibit 13.3 (and Ford Motor Company shown in Exhibit 12.3), the amount of this amortization is so small that it does not warrant separate disclosure and is included with "Other" items. The notes to the Westinghouse annual report include the following statement:

> **Other Assets** *include goodwill of $88 million in 1974 and $91 million in 1973. Goodwill acquired prior to November 1, 1970, is not being amortized. Goodwill of $15.1 million at December 31, 1973, and $13.9 million at December 31, 1972, resulting from business combinations subsequent to November 1, 1970, remained to be amortized over the estimated period to be benefited, not to exceed 40 years.*

Limitations of Consolidated Statements

The consolidated statements do not replace those of individual corporations; rather, they supplement those statements and aid in their interpretation. Creditors must rely upon the resources of one corporation and may be misled if forced to rely entirely upon a consolidated statement that combines the data of a company in good financial condition with that of one verging on insolvency. Dividends can legally be declared only from the retained earnings of one corporation. Where the parent company does not own all of the stock of the subsidiary, the outside or minority stockholders can judge the dividend constraints, both legal and financial, only by an inspection of the subsidiary's statements.

In the best of all possible worlds, parent corporations would report on their own and their subsidiaries' operations in both single-company and consolidated statements. Generally accepted accounting principles do not require the publication of both single-company and consolidated reports. Only the consolidated report need be published and, in fact, we know of no major U.S. corporation that publishes separate financial statements for both the parent and each of the subsidiaries as single companies.

■ CORPORATE ACQUISITIONS

There are essentially three ways that Company P can acquire control of Company S:

1. Company P can organize Company S. The majority of companies consolidated in financial statements are companies that have been organized by the parent.
2. Company P can acquire the shares of an existing Company S from its current owners by paying cash or by issuing securities other than common stock for the common stock of Company S.
3. Company P can issue its common stock to the current owners of Company S in exchange for their shares of common stock in Company S.

The first two ways of acquiring Company S are both accounted for by the *purchase method,* and the third is generally accounted for by the *pooling of interests method.* The remainder of this section discusses the differing implications of the two methods of accounting for the combination, both at the time of acquisition and, later, when consolidated statements are prepared.

Purchase Method

The purchase method treats the acquisition of a group of assets in much the same way as historical-cost accounting treats the acquisition of a single asset. That is, the assets acquired are recorded at the amount of cash (or market value of other consideration) given in exchange for them. For example, assume that at the time the stock of the subsidiary is purchased, its books show Capital Stock plus Additional Paid-In Capital of $600,000 and Retained Earnings of $200,000. The book value of the stockholders' equity of the acquired company is, therefore, $800,000. If the fair market value of the subsidiary's individual net assets (assets minus liabilities) is $800,000 and the parent paid $800,000 cash for its 100-percent interest, the parent would merely record the purchased assets at their book value, which equals current market value.

Acquisition Price Exceeds Book Value Acquired   If the parent paid $900,000 for its 100-percent interest, the excess of cost over book value acquired is $100,000. This excess could arise for several reasons. For example, the assets of the subsidiary might be undervalued on its books, having a larger current market value than the historical cost less accumulated depreciation. In addition, perhaps the subsidiary has built up good relations with its employees, customers, and suppliers, so that as a going concern the whole is worth more than the sum of the parts. The assets of the subsidiary must be revalued to current fair market values at the date of the acquisition. If cost exceeds book value acquired after all tangible assets of the subsidiary are shown at their current market values, the excess is called *goodwill* and is formally recognized in the consolidated statements.

The goodwill arising from a purchase is a long-lived asset, and generally accepted accounting principles require that this asset be amortized over a period of no more than 40 years.[3] Some theorists disagree with this treatment and argue that goodwill ought never be recognized. Others disagree in the opposite direction; they contend that the future benefits can have an indefinite life, and therefore that amortization is not appropriate in all cases. (Goodwill arising from the pur-

[3] Opinion No. 17, Accounting Principles Board, AICPA, August 1970.

chase of an interest in another company accounted for on the equity method must similarly be amortized over a period not to exceed 40 years.[4])

If less than 100 percent of the subsidiary's stock is acquired, the goodwill recognized is calculated as the acquisition price minus the product of the fraction of the outstanding stock acquired times the fair market value of the net assets. Consider the preceding example, where the fair market value of S's net tangible assets is $800,000. If a 60-percent interest is acquired for $600,000, the goodwill recorded by P is $120,000 [= $600,000 − (.60 × $800,000)].

When the parent pays more than book value for the subsidiary's assets, these assets are shown in the consolidated statements at higher costs than the costs shown on the subsidiary's books before the purchase. Insofar as these assets have limited useful lives, they must be amortized. The goodwill that is formally recognized on the consolidated statements must also be amortized. Therefore, under these circumstances, the amortization charges on the consolidated statements must necessarily be larger than the sum of amortization charges on the parent's and the subsidiary's statements before combination.

Acquisition Price Is Less Than Book Value Acquired   The parent could conceivably pay less than book value, $800,000 in the example, for its 100-percent interest in the subsidiary. This suggests that the asset amounts shown on the subsidiary's books are overvalued or the liabilities are undervalued or both. If the parent paid only $700,000 for its 100-percent interest, then the excess of cost over book value acquired would be negative. The amounts shown for unrealistically valued assets and liabilities must be changed so that book value (assets less liabilities) is equal to $700,000.

Pooling of Interests Method

The pooling of interests method of accounting for corporate acquisitions seeks to reflect a continuity of ownership interests in the combined companies by the stockholders of P and S. The rationale for the use of this method is that there is not a purchase by P nor a sale by S but, rather, a pooling or combining or merging of the interests of both the existing ownership groups. The combination is viewed as a change in form but not a change in substance. The amount recorded on the books of the combining companies for each asset and liability is carried over to the consolidated statements of the new, combined entity. The pooling of interests method makes possible P's acquiring S without altering the reported amounts of S's assets in the consolidated balance sheet.

Generally accepted accounting principles[5] allow pooling of interests only under a set of restrictive conditions, all of which must be met. One of the conditions requires that P must issue voting common stock for S rather than purchase S for cash. The acquisition by stock issue must occur in a single transaction rather than being spread over a period of time. Another restriction requires that P acquire

---

[4] Opinion No. 18, Accounting Principles Board, AICPA, March 1971.
[5] Opinion No. 16, Accounting Principles Board, AICPA, August 1970.

at least 90 percent of S's stock. Under pooling of interests accounting, no assets are revalued, so no extra amortization expenses are required. The balance sheet resulting from a pooling of interests is little more than a summation of the single-company balance sheets.

Comparison of Purchase and Pooling of Interests Methods

This section illustrates the consolidated statements resulting from a pooling of interests and compares them to those where the acquisition is treated as a purchase.[6] Companies P and S decide to combine operations. Management estimates that the combination will save $50,000 a year in expenses of running the combined businesses. Columns 1 and 2 in Exhibit 13.4 show abbreviated single-company financial statements for P and S before combination. S has 20,000 shares of stock outstanding that sell for $84 per share in the market. The market value of S as a going concern is, then, $1,680,000. As shown in column 3, S's stockholders have $1,230,000 of equity not recorded on the books. Of this $1,230,000, $400,000 is determined to be attributable to undervalued noncurrent assets and $830,000 is assigned to goodwill. P has 100,000 shares outstanding, which have a $5 par value and sell for $42 each in the market. The illustration ignores income taxes throughout.

Purchase Assume that P purchases S to combine their operations. P issues (sells) 40,000 additional shares on the market for $42 each, or $1,680,000 in total, and uses the proceeds to purchase all shares of S for $84 each. (Each share of S is, in effect, "sold" for two shares of P.) P has acquired 100 percent of the shares of S and now owns S.

P's acquisition of S would be accounted for as a purchase. P decides to amortize the revalued asset costs over 5 years and to amortize the goodwill over 40 years. Consolidated financial reports, similar to those shown in column 4, will be issued for the combined entity accounted for under the purchase method. The consolidated balance sheet is the sum of columns 1 and 3 except for the stockholders' equity section. Since P issued 40,000 new shares for $42 each, the Common Stock account shows 140,000 shares at $5 par value. The Additional Paid-In Capital account shows P's former Additional Paid-in Capital plus the addition arising from the new stock issue: $200,000 + [40,000 \times ($42 - $5)] = $1,680,000. The retained earnings of the consolidated enterprise are equal to P's retained earnings.

The consolidated income statement, when the acquisition is treated as a purchase, starts with the combined incomes before consolidation. To that amount is added the cost savings of $50,000 resulting from the more efficient operations of

---

[6] The illustration is adapted from one by Hugo Nurnberg and Corwin Grube, "Alternative Methods of Accounting for Business Corporations," *The Accounting Review* 45 (October 1970), 783–789. See also Hugo Nurnberg, Clyde P. Stickney, and Roman L. Weil, "Combining Stockholders' Equity Accounts Under the Pooling of Interests Method," *The Accounting Review* 50 (January 1975), 179–183.

EXHIBIT 13.4
*Consolidated Statements Comparing Purchase
and Pooling of Interests Methods*

	Historical Cost		S Shown at Current Values	P & S Consolidated at Date of Acquisition	
	P	S		Purchase	Pooling of Interests
	(1)	(2)	(3)	(4)	(5)

BALANCE SHEETS

Assets

Current Assets	$1,500,000	$450,000	$ 450,000	$1,950,000	$1,950,000
Long-Term Assets Less Accumulated Depreciation	1,700,000	450,000	850,000	2,550,000[1+3]	2,150,000 [1+2]
Goodwill	—	—	830,000	830,000	—
Total Assets	$3,200,000	$900,000	$2,130,000	$5,330,000	$4,100,000

Equities

Liabilities	$1,300,000	$450,000	$ 450,000	$1,750,000	$1,750,000
Common Stock ($5 par)	500,000	100,000	100,000	700,000[a]	700,000[a]
Additional Paid-in Capital PLUS	200,000	150,000	150,000	1,680,000[b]	250,000[e]
Retained Earnings	1,200,000	200,000	200,000	1,200,000[c]	1,400,000[d]
Unrecorded Equity at Current Valuation	—	—	1,230,000	—	—
Total Liabilities and Stockholders' Equity	$3,200,000	$900,000	$2,130,000	$5,330,000	$4,100,000

INCOME STATEMENTS (IGNORING INCOME TAXES)[h]

Precombination Income	$ 300,000	$160,000		$ 460,000	$ 460,000
From Combination					
Cost Savings (projected)	—	—		50,000	50,000
Extra Depreciation Expense	—	—		(80,000)[f]	—
Amortization of Goodwill	—	—		(20,750)[g]	—
Net Income	$ 300,000	$160,000		$ 409,250[h]	$ 510,000[h]
Number of Common Shares Outstanding	100,000	20,000		140,000	140,000
Earnings Per Share	$3.00	$8.00		$2.92	$3.64

Assumptions: (1) Company S has 20,000 shares outstanding that sell for $84 each in the market.

(2) Company P's shares sell for $42 each in the market. Company P issues 40,000 shares for the purpose of acquiring Company S.

[a] P's 100,000 original shares plus 40,000 new shares at $5 par.
[b] P's $200,000 original additional paid-in capital plus 40,000 × ($42 − $5).
[c] P's retained earnings.
[d] Sum of P's and S's retained earnings.
[e] Plug to equate pooled stockholders' equity to the sum of all the stockholders' equity accounts of the combining companies before combination.
[f] 1/5 × ($850,000 − $450,000).
[g] 1/40 × $830,000.
[h] As projected.

the combination. Then both the additional depreciation expense arising from the asset revaluations and the goodwill amortization expense are subtracted. The reported consolidated net incomes, as projected, is $409,250.

Pooling of Interests Now, examine the accounting for the acquisition, as shown in column 5, assuming that it qualifies for the pooling of interest method. Assume that P issued the 40,000 shares of stock directly to the owners of S in return for their shares. The balance sheet items, except for the individual stockholders' equity accounts, are merely the sum of the single-company amounts shown in columns 1 and 2. The stockholders' equity after pooling must then equal total stockholders' equity before pooling.

The capital stock of the pooled enterprise must, of course, equal the par value of the shares outstanding after pooling. After pooling there are 140,000 shares outstanding with a par value of $700,000. The general rule is that the pooled retained earnings balance is the sum of the retained earnings before pooling. The example illustrates the general rule. The total paid-in capital (par value plus additional paid-in capital) after pooling will generally equal the sum of the paid-in capital accounts of the firms before pooling. Thus, the additional paid-in capital of the pooled firm is, ordinarily, the plug to equate the pooled paid-in capital with the sum of the paid-in capital accounts before pooling.

The income statement resulting from a pooling of interests shows the same revenues and cost savings as those following a purchase. There are, however, no extra depreciation and amortization expenses resulting from increased asset valuations and the recognition of goodwill. Consequently, the pooled enterprise projects net income of $510,000 and stockholders' equity of $2,350,000 (a rate of return on stockholders' equity of 22 percent), whereas the identical acquisition accounted for using the purchase method projects smaller income, $409,250, and larger stockholders' equity of $3,580,000 (a rate of return on stockholders' equity of 11 percent). Notice that the earnings-per-share figure—one often scrutinized by financial analysts—under the pooling of interests method is 25 percent larger than under the purchase method.

This example, if anything, understates the difference between the purchase and pooling methods. Notice that S's market value before the merger is less than four times ($1,680,000/$450,000 = 3.7) its book value. In practice, poolings of interests have occurred when the ratio of market value to book value was as high as ten or more to one. Thus, the amortization charges of the "purchased" subsidiary's assets can be many times larger than the amortization of the "pooled" subsidiary's assets.

Managing Earnings Pooling of interests not only keeps reported expenses from increasing after the merger, it may also allow management of the pooled companies to manage the reported earnings in an arbitrary way. Suppose, as has happened, that Company P merges with an old, established firm, Company F, which has produced commercial movie films. These films were made in the 1940's and 1950's and were amortized so that by the early 1970's the book value of these films is close to zero. But the market value of the films is much larger than zero, because television stations find that old movies please their audiences. If Company P purchases Company F, then the old films will be shown on the consolidated balance sheet at the films' current fair market value. If Company P merges with Company F using the pooling of interests method, the films will be shown on the consolidated balance sheet at their near-zero book values. Then, when Company P wants to bolster reported earnings for the year, all it need do is sell some old movies to a television network, and a handsome gain can be reported. Actually, of course, the owners of Company F enjoyed this gain when their stock was "sold to" (or exchanged with) Company P for current asset values, not the obsolete book values.

Those who defend pooling of interests accounting argue that the management of the pooled enterprise has no more opportunity to manage earnings than did the management of Company F before the pooling. Management of Company F can sell old movies any time it chooses and then report handsome gains. The fault lies ultimately in the historical-cost basis of accounting, which recognizes gains only when there has been a market transaction. Defenders of pooling argue that there is no reason to penalize the management of a merged company relative to the management of an established company with many assets undervalued on its books. Opponents of pooling reply that it was the management of Company F which earned the holding gains, whereas the management of Company P will be able to report them as realized gains under pooling.

In summary, if the acquisition qualifies as a purchase, then the reported income of the combined enterprise may be reduced by additional depreciation and amortization expenses. The extra depreciation and amortization expenses result from recognizing increased asset valuations and, perhaps, goodwill. If the acquisition qualifies as a pooling of interests, reported income for the consolidated enterprise will ordinarily be larger than for the same consolidated enterprise accounted for as a purchase. In our opinion, every business combination is, in reality, a purchase of some sort. There is no logical reason, we think, for the pooling of interests method of accounting.

■ ACCOUNTING FOR FOREIGN OPERATIONS

In order to carry on operations in a foreign country, a company may establish a division, branch, or a corporation in a foreign country, or it may acquire the capital stock of an existing foreign company. Generally accepted accounting principles require special techniques for reporting assets and liabilities carried on the books in foreign currencies and for reporting the results of operations carried on in foreign countries.[7] The two major problems in accounting for foreign subsidiaries are discussed briefly below. These problems are as follows:

[7] *Statement of Financial Accounting Standards No. 1*, Financial Accounting Standards Board, December 1973.

1. Should the operations and the assets and liabilities of the foreign unit be consolidated with the parent company's statements?
2. How should the amounts of assets, liabilities, revenues, and expenses originally expressed in foreign currencies be translated into dollars?

Consolidating Foreign Operations

In general, a parent consolidates a subsidiary when the parent exercises control over the subsidiary and the nature of the subsidiary's asset and equity structure is not substantially different from that of the parent. These criteria apply to foreign subsidiaries as well. Most U.S. companies consolidate their foreign operations. In recent years, about half of the 600 companies surveyed in *Accounting Trends and Techniques*[8] had foreign subsidiaries. More than two-thirds of these companies consolidated their foreign subsidiaries, and that portion has been growing steadily.

When assets are held in a foreign country, however, there may exist conditions that inhibit the exercise of effective control over the subsidiary. Foreign governments may restrict the use of assets or the flow of capital and currency across international borders. When there is sufficient uncertainty about the parent's ability to control foreign operations, the foreign unit's net assets and results of operations should not be consolidated in the parent's statements. Rather, the equity method or even, in unusual circumstances, the cost method would be used.

In some cases, earnings of foreign units operating under severe restrictions on operations or on currency flows may not be reported by the parent until cash has been transferred between countries. That is, the cost method is used.

Currency Translation

Accounting seeks to report assets, liabilities, and the results of operations using a single, common measurement unit. The measurement unit used by U.S. corporations is, of course, the U.S. dollar. Once the decision has been made to combine foreign operations with domestic operations in the financial statements, a decision must be made as to how to translate foreign currency amounts into dollars so that items can be meaningfully added together.

The translation of foreign currency items into dollars is accomplished by multiplying the foreign currency amount by an exchange rate. An *exchange rate* indicates the number of currency units of one currency (for example, U.S. dollars) which is equivalent to, or could be exchanged for, one unit of another currency (for example, a French franc or a German mark). If we lived in a world of fixed, unchanging exchange rates, where there was never any doubt about the number of dollars required to purchase a given amount of foreign currency or vice versa, there would be no problem. All foreign currency amounts could be translated into dollars by using a multiplier that is constant over time for a given currency. But, of course, exchange rates do vary. The major problem in accounting for foreign

[8] Annual publication of the American Institute of Certified Public Accountants; see description in Chapter One.

units arises because the exchange rate between foreign currencies and the dollar can vary substantially over time. The exchange rate between the dollar and the German mark or the Japanese yen has varied by as much as 25 percent within a single year. Exchange rates between the dollar and some South American currencies have varied even more.

Once we recognize that exchange rates can vary, the problem arises in accounting for the gains and losses in dollars that occur just because of exchange rate fluctuations, independent of any operating results. Suppose, for example, that a U.S. company converts $50,400 into 21,000 British pounds at a time when the exchange rate is £1 = $2.40. Assume that the £21,000 are merely deposited in a checking account in London. One year later, assume that the exchange rate has changed so that £1 is worth only $2.10, and that the U.S. company converts its pounds back into dollars. The U.S. company would receive only $44,100 (= £21,000 × $2.10 per £). The U.S. company would have suffered a *foreign exchange translation loss* of $6,300 (= $50,400 − $44,100). To make the example more realistic, suppose that a foreign subsidiary makes sales on account for £21,000 at a time when the exchange rate is £1 = $2.40 and collects cash after the pound has fallen to $2.10. Some recognition will have to be given to the difference in the dollar value of the revenue at the time of sale and the dollar value of the cash collected at the later date.

In translating foreign currency amounts into dollars, there are basically two different rates which can be used. The exchange rate used can be either the historical rate—the rate in effect at the time of a given transaction—or the current rate—the rate in effect as of the date of the financial statements. Generally accepted accounting principles favor the use of the current rate for all *monetary items*, and the historical rate for all other items.

A *monetary item* in foreign currency analysis is any asset or liability requiring settlement in specific amounts of foreign currency. Examples include payables and receivables denominated in foreign currencies, whether current or noncurrent, as well as amounts of foreign cash. Monetary items are translated into dollars using the exchange rate in effect as of the date of the financial statements.

Nonmonetary items include all other accounts, that is, all of the balance sheet accounts that are not specifically monetary items, as well as all revenue and expense accounts recorded in foreign currencies. Nonmonetary items are translated at the rate in effect at the time of the transaction that brought the item onto the books.

These two general procedures imply, for example, that the translated dollar amount of a bond denominated in a foreign currency will vary from one financial statement date to another as the exchange rate varies, but the cost of a foreign plant asset will always be reported on the parent's books in dollars at the exchange rate applicable to the time of acquisition. All depreciation charges are then based on historical costs translated into dollars at historical rates.

The method of translating foreign statements into dollars and computing the amount of foreign exchange gain or loss is described in advanced accounting textbooks.

■ SUMMARY

Businesses acquire stock in other businesses for a variety of reasons and in a variety of ways. Accounting for the acquisition and subsequent events depends both on the amount of stock involved and the manner of acquisition. The cost method is used when the parent owns less than 20 percent of the stock of another company. The equity method is used when the parent owns at least 20 percent but not more than 50 percent. Consolidated statements are generally prepared when the parent owns more than 50 percent of the voting stock of another company but, under certain circumstances, the equity method may be used.

Under the cost method, income is recognized only when dividends become receivable by the investor. Consolidated statements and the equity method both have the same effect on net income: the parent shows as income its proportional share of the acquired firm's periodic income after acquisition. Income statement amounts of revenues and expenses will be larger under the consolidation method, however, because the revenues and expenses of the acquired company are combined with those of the parent. Balance sheet components will be larger under the consolidation method than under the equity method, since the individual assets and liabilities of the acquired company will be substituted for the investment balance on the parent company's books.

Recording an acquisition as a pooling of interests, rather than as a purchase, produces different results in the consolidated income statement and balance sheet. Under pooling, assets and equities will generally be shown at lower values on the balance sheet, and the income statement will generally report a higher net income.

Investments in foreign operations are accounted for in much the same way as domestic ones. Foreign investments do raise the problems of accounting for fluctuating exchange rates and the resulting gains or losses from these fluctuations.

Appendix 13.1
Illustration of Consolidated Financial Statement Preparation

This appendix illustrates the preparation of consolidated financial statements for Company P and Company S. The situation illustrated here is simplified. The section following the illustration indicates some of the omitted complications and how these would affect the preparation of the statements. Knowing how to construct consolidated financial statements is not essential for learning how to interpret and to analyze them. Nevertheless, we think it helps.

Data for the Illustration

The single-company financial statements of Company P and Company S are shown in Exhibit 13.5. The following additional information is to be considered in preparing the consolidated financial statements.

EXHIBIT 13.5
*Illustrative Data for Preparation of Consolidated
Financial Statements*

	Single-Company Statements	
	Company P	Company S

CONDENSED STATEMENT OF INCOME AND INCOME DISTRIBUTIONS FOR 1976

Revenues:

	Company P	Company S
Sales	$ 900,000	$ 250,000
Dividend Revenue	13,000	—
Total Revenues	$ 913,000	$ 250,000

Expenses:

	Company P	Company S
Cost of Goods Sold (excluding depreciation)	$ 440,000	$ 80,000
Depreciation Expense	120,000	50,000
Administrative Expenses	80,000	40,000
Income Tax Expense	104,000	32,000
Total Expenses	$ 744,000	$ 202,000
Net Income	$ 169,000	$ 48,000
Dividend Declarations	50,000	13,000
Increase in Retained Earnings for the Year	$ 119,000	$ 35,000

CONDENSED BALANCE SHEETS AS OF DECEMBER 31, 1976

Assets:

	Company P	Company S
Accounts Receivable	$ 200,000	$ 25,000
Investment in Stock of Company S (at cost)	650,000	—
Other Assets	2,150,000	975,000
Total Assets	$3,000,000	$1,000,000

Equities:

	Company P	Company S
Accounts Payable	$ 75,000	$ 15,000
Other Liabilities	70,000	280,000
Capital Stock	2,500,000	500,000
Retained Earnings	355,000	205,000
Total Equities	$3,000,000	$1,000,000

CONDENSED (PARTIAL) STATEMENT OF CHANGES IN FINANCIAL POSITION FOR 1976

Sources of Working Capital:

	Company P	Company S
Net Income	$ 169,000	$ 48,000
Add Back Depreciation Expense	120,000	50,000
Total Sources	$ 289,000	$ 98,000

Uses of Working Capital:

	Company P	Company S
Dividends Declared and Paid	50,000	13,000
Net Increase in Working Capital	$ 239,000	$ 85,000

1. Company P acquired 100 percent of the outstanding shares of Company S for $650,000 cash on January 1, 1973. At the time of acquisition, the book value of the stockholders' equity of Company S was $650,000 comprised of the following balances.

COMPANY S, JANUARY 1, 1973

Capital Stock	$500,000
Retained Earnings	150,000
Total Stockholders' Equity	$650,000

Since the purchase price was exactly equal to the book value of Company S, there is apparently no need for asset revaluations and there is no goodwill to be recognized. Company P made the following journal entry at the time of acquisition:

Investment in Stock of Company S (at cost)	650,000	
Cash		650,000

2. Company P accounts for its investment in the stock of Company S under the cost method. (The equity method need not be used in the parent's single-company accounts when consolidated statements are to be prepared.)

3. At December 31, 1976, $12,000 of Company S's accounts receivable represent amounts payable by Company P.

4. During 1976 Company S sold merchandise to Company P for $40,000. None of that merchandise remains in Company P's inventory as of December 31, 1976.

Preparing Consolidated Statements

In preparing consolidated statements for Company P and Company S, the following steps, characteristic of the consolidation procedure, are illustrated:

A. adjustment of the parent company's Investment account
B. elimination of the parent company's Investment account
C. elimination of intercompany receivables and payables
D. elimination of intercompany sales and purchases
E. elimination of intercompany dividends.

The preparation of consolidated statements illustrated here starts with the single-company balance sheet accounts (from the postclosing trial balances) and the single-company income statements. These data are shown in the first two pairs of columns in Exhibit 13.6. The last pair of columns in Exhibit 13.6 shows the items of the consolidated balance sheet and income statement. The amounts in the last pair of columns are merely the horizontal sum of the other items—Company P items, Company S items, as well as the adjustments and eliminations. The adjusting and eliminating entries are discussed below. The entries are numbered consecutively and correspond to the numbers shown in the adjustments and

EXHIBIT 13.6
Work Sheet to Derive Consolidated Financial Statements for Company P and Company S Based on Data in Postclosing Trial Balances and Income Statements

	Company P		Company S		Adjustments and Eliminations		P and S Consolidated	
	Debit	Credit	Debit	Credit	Debit	Credit	Debit	Credit
Trial Balance Accounts								
Accounts Receivable	200,000		25,000			(3) 12,000	213,000	
Investment in Stock of Company S	650,000		—		(1) 55,000	(2) 705,000	—	
Other Assets	2,150,000		975,000				3,125,000	
Total Assets	3,000,000		1,000,000		55,000	717,000	3,338,000	
Accounts Payable		75,000		15,000	(3) 12,000			78,000
Other Liabilities		70,000		280,000				350,000
Capital Stock		2,500,000		500,000	(2) 500,000			2,500,000
Retained Earnings (Co. P)		355,000				(1) 55,000		410,000
Retained Earnings (Co. S)				205,000	(2) 205,000			—
Total Equities		3,000,000		1,000,000	717,000	55,000		3,338,000
Income Statement and Income Distribution Accounts								
Sales		900,000		250,000	(4) 40,000			1,110,000
Dividend Revenue		13,000		—	(5) 13,000			—
Total Revenues		913,000		250,000	53,000			1,110,000
Cost of Goods Sold	440,000		80,000			(4) 40,000	480,000	
Depreciation Expense	120,000		50,000				170,000	
Administrative Expenses	80,000		40,000				120,000	
Income Taxes	104,000		32,000				136,000	
Total Expenses	744,000		202,000			40,000	906,000	
Net Income	169,000		48,000		53,000	40,000	204,000	
Dividends Declared	50,000		13,000			(5) 13,000	50,000	
Addition to Retained Earnings	119,000		35,000				154,000	
Adjustments and Eliminations Totals					825,000	825,000		

416

eliminations column in Exhibit 13.6. Keep in mind that these entries are recorded only on a work sheet used to prepare the consolidated statements—not in the journal or general ledger of either company.

A. Adjustment of the Parent Company's Investment Account   Because Company P maintains its Investment in Stock of Company S on the cost basis, the Investment account must first be adjusted for P's share of the undistributed income or losses of the subsidiary arising since the date of acquisition. This adjustment restates the Investment account to what it would be if the equity method were used. The procedure is done in four steps, as follows.

A.1.   Determine the retained earnings of the subsidiary applicable to the type of stock held by the parent. In most cases this will be the balance in the Retained Earnings account. In the illustration, the balance in the Retained Earnings account as of December 31, 1976, the date of the consolidated balance sheet, is $205,000.

A.2.   Compute the difference between the retained earnings figure found in **A.1** and the corresponding retained earnings at the date the stock was acquired by the parent. The difference represents the increase (if positive, decrease if negative) in the subsidiary's retained earnings since acquisition. In the illustration this difference is $55,000 (= $205,000 — $150,000).

A.3.   Multiply the change in retained earnings found in **A.2** by the percentage of the subsidiary's outstanding stock held by the parent. In the illustration, Company P owns 100 percent of Company S so that the parent's share of the increase in retained earnings is the total increase, $55,000.

A.4.   Debit the Investment in Stock of Company S account and credit the Retained Earnings account of the parent with the amount found in **A.3**.

(1) Investment in Stock of Company S 55,000
       Retained Earnings (Company P)   55,000
       To adjust P's books from the cost to the equity method.

This entry is entered in Exhibit 13.6. Remember that this entry is not made on the books of either company.

Once entry (**1**) is made, the balance in the Investment in Stock of Company S is the same as it would have been if Company P used the equity method, rather than the cost method, in accounting for its investment in Company S. If Company P were using the equity method, then the preparation of consolidated statements would start with the next step.

B. Elimination of Parent Company's Investment Account   Company P purchased the shares of Company S for their book value at the time of acquisition. Now, after the adjustment from Step **A** above, the parent's investment account plus the amount resulting from the adjustment exactly equals the parent's ownership of the subsidiary's capital stock and retained earnings. Before adding the single-company balance sheet items to determine consolidated totals, the parent's

Investment in Stock of Company S must be eliminated so that both the subsidiary's assets and the parent's investment in those assets are not shown on the consolidated balance sheet.

To eliminate the parent's investment account, debit the subsidiary's Capital Stock (also Additional Paid-In Capital, if any) and Retained Earnings accounts for the parent company's interest. Then credit the Investment account with its balance as adjusted by Step **A**. The entry in Exhibit 13.6 to eliminate Company P's Investment in Stock of Company S is:

(2) Capital Stock (Company S)	500,000	
Retained Earnings (Company S)	205,000	
Investment in Stock of Company S		705,000

To eliminate the adjusted Investment in Stock of Company S
account ($650,000 + $55,000) and the Capital Stock and Retained
Earnings accounts of Company S.

C. Elimination of Intercompany Receivables and Payables A parent may sell goods or buy goods from a subsidiary and treat the resulting obligation as an account receivable or an account payable. The subsidiary will treat the obligation as an account payable or an account receivable. A parent often makes loans to subsidiaries which appear as Notes Receivable, Investment in Bonds, or Advances to Subsidiary on the parent's books. The subsidiary would show Notes Payable, Bonds Payable, or Advances from Parent on its books. A single company would not show Accounts Receivable and Accounts Payable for departments within the company. These transactions must be eliminated from the consolidated balance sheet so that the resulting statement will appear as that of a single company.

In the illustration, Company S's accounts receivable include $12,000 due it from Company P. The entry to record the elimination of the intercompany receivables and payables in Exhibit 13.6 is:

(3) Accounts Payable	12,000	
Accounts Receivable		12,000

To eliminate the intercompany payables and receivables.

This entry completes the adjustments and eliminations for the consolidated balance sheet. The next eliminations are required for the consolidated income statement.

D. Elimination of Intercompany Sales and Purchases Sales between consolidated companies should not be reported in a consolidated income statement, any more than transfers from Work in Process Inventory to Finished Goods Inventory should be reported as sales within a single company. During 1976, Company P acquired $40,000 of merchandise inventory from Company S. To eliminate intercompany sales requires a debit to Sales and a credit to Purchases. In the illustration we are working with, there is no Purchases account. As part of its regular closing entries, Company P computed its cost of goods sold from the inventory equation:

Cost of Goods Sold = Beginning Inventory + Purchases − Ending Inventory.

Therefore the offsetting credit to reduce Purchases, which eliminates intercompany sales, must be to the Cost of Goods Sold account.

(4) Sales	40,000	
Cost of Goods Sold		40,000
To eliminate intercompany sales and purchases.		

Company S sold goods to Company P and Company P sold the goods outside the consolidated pair of companies. In the absence of the elimination of intercompany sales, these sales would be counted twice. The profits on the sales would be computed properly, but the amount of gross sales and purchases would be inflated. To see that profits are computed properly even without the elimination, assume that the goods cost Company S $30,000 and that Company P sold them for $45,000. In the single-company income statements, Company S profits are $10,000 ($=$ $40,000 − $30,000) as a result of the sale to Company P. Company P profits are $5,000 ($=$ $45,000 − $40,000) as a result of its sales to others. Total profits of the consolidated group from these transactions are $15,000, or Company P's revenue of $45,000 less Company S's cost of $30,000. The elimination of intercompany sales does not change the consolidated sales to outsiders or the consolidated cost of goods sold to outsiders.

If either company holds bonds or long-term notes of the other, then there would be a similar elimination of the "borrower's" interest expense and of the "lender's" interest revenue.

E. Elimination of Intercompany Dividends   From the standpoint of Company S, dividend declarations are income distributions. But since the dividends are paid, or payable, to Company P, they represent merely a transfer of funds from one entity within the consolidated group to another. In consolidated statements, intercompany dividends are eliminated so that income distributions to stockholders of the parent are shown correctly. The entry in Exhibit 13.6 to eliminate intercompany dividends is:

(5) Dividend Revenue	13,000	
Dividends Declared		13,000
To eliminate intercompany dividends.		

The adjustments and eliminations for the consolidated balance sheet and income statement are now complete. The last pair of columns in Exhibit 13.6 shows the horizontal sums of each row in the form needed to prepare both the consolidated balance sheet and income statement.

Consolidated Statement of Changes in Financial Position   The consolidated statement of changes in financial position is prepared from consolidated balance sheets for the beginning and end of the period plus additional information from the consolidated income statement. In the illustration, the consolidated statement of changes in financial position is particularly simple. It would start with consolidated net income of $204,000, show an addback for depreciation expense of $170,000, show income distributions of $50,000 for dividends, as well as other details of changes in current asset and current liability items.

Further Complications

The illustration, now complete, for Company P and Company S is simpler than typical consolidations problems in several respects. In particular, notice that all of the adjustments and eliminations had both debit and credit entries either all in the balance sheet accounts or all in the income statement and distribution accounts. No entry had debits in one category and credits in the other. For more complicated problems, where the adjustments or eliminations involve both income statement and balance sheet accounts simultaneously, the work sheet should be based on the preclosing trial balances of the companies being consolidated rather than on the completed single-company balance sheets and income statements.

The following problems, characteristic of consolidations, are discussed in this section.

F.   Acquisition price of subsidiary exceeds book value acquired.
G.   Less than 100 percent of the subsidiary's stock is acquired, resulting in a minority interest.

These further illustrations include the required work-sheet adjusting and eliminating entries, but no corresponding work sheet is presented.

F. Acquisition Price Exceeds Book Value Acquired   Suppose that Company P had paid $700,000, rather than $650,000, for its 100-percent investment in Company S. After Step **B** and entry (**2**) above, the parent's Investment account would still have a debit balance of $50,000. This $50,000 represents the price paid for Company S's assets in excess of their book value, for goodwill, or for both. Assume that $25,000 represents the price paid for buildings, machinery, and equipment in excess of the depreciated cost shown on Company S's books, $5,000 represents the price paid for land in excess of the cost shown on Company S's books, and $20,000 represents the price paid for goodwill. To complete the elimination of the parent's Investment in Stock of Company S, the following entry is required:

(6) Buildings, Machinery, and Equipment	25,000	
Land	5,000	
Goodwill	20,000	
Investment in Stock of Company S		50,000

To complete elimination of parent's Investment account recognizing increased valuation of the consolidated assets.

The consolidated balance sheet will show the building, machinery, and equipment accounts with larger balances than the sum of the single-company accounts. Goodwill, which does not appear in the single-company accounts, will be shown on the consolidated statement. The plant assets, except land, and the goodwill must be amortized, so there will be an adjusting entry to recognize the extra amortization charges on the past and current consolidation income statements. Assume that depreciable plant assets are being amortized over a 10-years' remaining life and that goodwill is being amortized over 40 years, both on a straight-line basis. Company P purchased Company S on January 1, 1973, so the entry to recognize the 3 years of accumulated amortization up to January 1, 1976, would be:

(7) Retained Earnings	9,000	
Accumulated Depreciation		7,500
Goodwill		1,500

To recognize 3 years of depreciation on plant assets with a remaining 10-year life, $7,500 (= 3 × $25,000/10), and 3 years of amortization of goodwill, which is assumed to have a 40-year life, $1,500 (= 3 × $20,000/40), from 1/1/73 to 1/1/76.

The entries to recognize the additional amortization charges for the year of 1976 would be:

(8) Depreciation Expense	2,500	
Accumulated Depreciation		2,500

Depreciation for 1976 on incremental value of plant assets.

Amortization of Goodwill (Expense)	500	
Goodwill		500

Amortization of goodwill for 1976.

When the temporary revenue and expense accounts are closed from the consolidated income summary to the consolidated balance sheet, the debit amounts in entry (8) would be effectively debited to consolidated retained earnings. The December 31, 1976, consolidated balance sheet, ignoring income tax effects, would show $12,000 (= $9,000 + $2,500 + $500) smaller Retained Earnings as a result of entries (7), (8), and the related closing entries.

The consolidated statement of changes in financial position would show add-backs for these extra amortization charges of $3,000 for 1976 which use no working capital.

G. **Recognizing Minority Interest**   Assume that Company P acquired 90 percent of the stock of Company S for a price equal to the book value of 90 percent of Company S's net assets. If Company P purchased only 90 percent of the stock of Company S for its book value of $585,000 (= .90 × $650,000), then the minority shareholders in Company S have a claim on 10 percent of its stockholders' equity. Entry (1) above would instead be:

(1a) Investment in Stock of Company S 49,500
      Retained Earnings (Company P) 49,500
      To adjust P's books from the cost to the equity method (.90 ×
      $55,000).

Entry (**2**) above would eliminate only 90 percent of Company S's stockholders' equity and would instead be:

(2a) Capital Stock (Company S) 450,000
      Retained Earnings (Company S) 184,500
      Investment in Stock of Company S 634,500
      To eliminate the adjusted Investment in Stock of Company S
      account [.90 × ($650,000 + $55,000)] and 90 percent of the
      capital stock and retained earnings of Company S.

The remaining balances in Company S's stockholders' equity accounts are the minority interest. The logical entries to recognize the minority interest would be:

(2b) Capital Stock (Company S) 50,000
      Minority Interest in Company S Capital Stock 50,000
      To recognize the 10 percent minority interest in the capital stock
      of Company S.

      Retained Earnings (Company S) 20,500
      Minority Interest in Company S Retained Earnings 20,500
      To recognize the 10 percent minority interest in the retained
      earnings of Company S.

Then the consolidated balance sheet would show separately the minority interest in capital stock and retained earnings. In practice, however, the credit entries in (**2b**) are seldom made that way. Instead, they are combined to show a single account, Minority Interest, which does not disclose its components. The usual entry to recognize minority interest is:

(2c) Capital Stock (Company S) 50,000
      Retained Earnings (Company S) 20,500
      Minority Interest in Company S 70,500
      To recognize the 10 percent minority interest in the stockholders'
      equity of Company S.

The entry to eliminate intercompany receivables and payables is not affected by the existence of a minority interest. The entry would be the same as the one shown in entry (**3**).

The eliminations of intercompany sales and purchases can be somewhat more complicated when there are unrealized profits on intercompany transactions and a minority interest exists. In our example, we assume that Company P has sold all of the items it purchased from Company S, so there is no special problem and the entry to eliminate intercompany sales and purchases is the same as the one shown in entry (**4**).

When no minority interest exists, we eliminate all $13,000 of the intercompany dividends, because in a consolidated entity they are the equivalent of cash transfers between divisions of a single company. When a minority interest does exist, all of the subsidiary's dividends are also eliminated, but cash of $1,300 (= .10 × $13,000) is distributed outside the consolidated entity to the minority shareholders. This distribution of cash to the minority shareholders reduces the minority interest. The entry to eliminate the subsidiary's dividends would be:

(**5a**) Dividend Revenue	11,700	
Minority Interest	1,300	
Dividends Declared		13,000

To eliminate intercompany dividends ($11,700 is 90 percent of Company S's dividends and represents all of Company P's dividend revenue from Company S) and to show dividends declared on minority stock as a reduction in the minority interest.

The consolidated income statement shows a deduction of $4,800 (= .10 × $48,000) for the minority interest in S's earnings of the year in determining the net income of $199,200 (= $204,000 − $4,800) to the stockholders of Company P. The dividends declared by the consolidated entity consist of $51,300 (Company P's dividends of $50,000 and Company S's dividends of $1,300 declared on the stock owned by the minority interest).

The consolidated statement of changes in financial position starts with the net income of $199,200 to stockholders of Company P. Amounts are added back for the minority interest in S's undistributed earnings of the year (= $3,500 = $4,800 − $1,300) and for depreciation ($170,000), neither of which use working capital. The only use of working capital shown is the $50,000 of dividends declared by the parent. The net increase in working capital for the year is $372,700, exactly $1,300 less than when there was no minority interest. This $1,300 difference represents the funds distributed outside the consolidated entity in the form of dividends declared on S's shares owned by the minority interest.

Concluding Remark

The illustrations in this appendix have all assumed that Company P's acquisition of Company S is accounted for as a purchase. If the pooling of interests method applies, the consolidated balance sheet is merely the sum of the single-company balance sheets with adjustments for intercompany receivables, payables, and stockholders' equity accounts. The pooling method is illustrated in Exhibit 13.4. The pooling of interests consolidated income statement requires adjustments for intercompany sales, purchases, interest, and dividends. There are, of course, no extra amortization charges, because the pooling method does not lead to the recognition of asset revaluations or of goodwill.

QUESTIONS AND PROBLEMS

1. Review the meaning of the following concepts or terms discussed in this chapter.
   a. Minority investment.
   b. Minority interest.
   c. Majority investment.
   d. Marketable securities versus long-term investments.
   e. Cost method.
   f. Equity method.
   g. Parent.
   h. Subsidiary.
   i. Consolidated statements.
   j. Purchase method.
   k. Goodwill.
   l. Pooling of interests method.
   m. Adjustments and eliminations in consolidated work sheet.
   n. Intercompany transactions.
   o. Managing earnings.
   p. Monetary items.
   q. Nonmonetary items.
   r. Exchange rate.

2. The following item appears on a consolidated balance sheet: Minority Interest in Subsidiary Companies. What does it represent?

3. A consolidated balance sheet does not include an item of "goodwill." What are the possible explanations? Consider stock acquired on the market after the subsidiary had been in existence for several years.

4. Why is it impossible to determine from a consolidated balance sheet the amount of retained earnings legally available for dividends, either for the parent company or for the subsidiary company?

5. Indicate some of the types of eliminations which may be necessary in the preparation of a consolidated income statement.

6. Why is the equity method sometimes called a *one-line consolidation*?

7. Company P acquires 100 percent of the stock of Company S at a time when Company S has negative retained earnings, that is, a deficit. P pays more for S than the book value of S's owners' equity. How can this happen?

8. The Annoppers Copper Corporation has, for many years, consolidated the financial position and results of operations of its South American copper mining facility. During the last year, the government of the country in which the mine is located has expropriated the plant of two other U.S. corporations. These two other companies were engaged in manufacturing operations. Should the Annoppers Copper Corporation continue to consolidate the financial statements of its South American facility in its statements issued to stockholders?

9. The exchange rate used in translating accounts from foreign-based books to domestic financial statements can be either the historical exchange rate (the exchange rate in effect when the assets were acquired, liabilities were incurred, common stock was issued, or revenues were recognized) or the current exchange rate (the exchange rate on the date of the balance sheet). Indicate which of these two exchange rates should be used for each of the following accounts.

   a. Cash (Swiss francs).

   b. Accounts Payable (in yen).

   c. Investment in German government bonds.

   d. Discount on German government bonds.

   e. Sales Revenue.

   f. Interest Revenue.

   g. Merchandise Inventory.

   h. Equipment.

   i. Accumulated Depreciation—Equipment.

10. Refer to the items **a–i** in the preceding question. Which of these accounts are "monetary items"?

11. In consolidated statements where the initial acquisition is accounted for with the purchase method, the assets of the acquired firm are revalued to current costs. In consolidated statements where the initial acquisition is accounted for with the pooling of interests method, no assets are revalued.

   a. What would be the effect on consolidated statements if the assets of both acquiring and acquired firms were revalued to current market values?

   b. What would be the logic to consolidations based on revalued assets for both firms?

12. On January 1, Buyer Company acquired common stock of X Company. At the time of acquisition, the book value and fair market value of X Company's net assets were $100,000. During the year, X Company earned $25,000 and declared dividends of $20,000. How much income would Buyer Company report for the year from its investment under the assumption that Buyer Company:

   a. Paid $15,000 for 15 percent of the common stock and uses the cost method to account for its investment in X Company?

   b. Paid $20,000 for 15 percent of the common stock and uses the cost method to account for its investment in X Company?

   c. Paid $30,000 for 30 percent of the common stock and uses the equity method to account for its investment in X Company?

   d. Paid $40,000 for 30 percent of the common stock and uses the equity method to account for its investment in X Company? Give the maximum income that Buyer Company can report from the investment.

13. The CAR Corporation manufactures computers in the United States. It owns 75 percent of the voting stock of Charles of Canada, 80 percent of the voting stock of Alexandre de France (in France), and 100 percent of the voting stock of R Credit Corporation (a finance company). The CAR Corporation prepares consolidated financial statements consolidating Charles of Canada, using the equity method for R Credit Corporation, and using the cost method for its investment in Alexandre de France. Data from the 1976 reports of these companies are given below.

	1976 NET INCOME	1976 DIVIDENDS
CAR Corporation Consolidated	$1,000,000	$ 70,000
Charles of Canada	100,000	40,000
Alexandre de France	80,000	50,000
R Credit Corporation	120,000	100,000

a. Which, if any, of the companies is incorrectly accounted for by CAR according to generally accepted accounting principles?

Assuming the accounting for the three subsidiaries shown above to be correct, answer the next two questions.

b. How much of the net income reported by CAR Corporation Consolidated is attributable to the operations of the three subsidiaries?

c. If all three subsidiaries had been consolidated, what would have been the net income of CAR Corporation Consolidated?

14. During the current year, Buyer Corporation purchased machinery for $20,000, its fair market value, from its wholly owned subsidiary. The machinery had been carried on the books of the subsidiary at a cost of $30,000 and had accumulated depreciation of $16,000. What net book values for this machinery would be shown on:

a. Buyer Corporation's single-company books?

b. Consolidated balance sheet for Buyer and its subsidiary?

c. What adjustments would have to be made on the consolidated income statement because of this intercompany transaction?

15. Company P owns 70 percent of a consolidated subsidiary, Company S. During the year, Company P's sales to Company S amounted to $50,000. The cost of those sales was $35,000. The following data are taken from the two companies' income statements:

	COMPANY P	COMPANY S
Sales	$120,000	$250,000
Cost of Goods Sold	70,000	150,000

a. Compute consolidated sales and consolidated cost of goods sold for the year assuming that Company S sold all the goods purchased from Company P.

b. Compare the consolidated gross margin in sales to the sum of the gross margins of the separate companies.

16. The Roe Company purchased 80 percent of the stock of the Danver Company on January 2 at book value, $480,000. The total capital stock of the Danver Company at that date was $450,000, and the retained earnings balance was $150,000. During the year, the "net income to stockholders" of the Danver Company was $90,000; dividends declared were $36,000. Present adjusting and eliminating entries which would be necessary in the preparation of the December 31 consolidated balance sheet, assuming that Roe Company uses the cost method on its single-company books to account for its investment in Danver Company.

17. A parent company's books show retained earnings of $100,000. The consolidated balance sheet shows no goodwill and retained earnings of $160,000. Consider each of the following questions independently of the others.

a. If the parent owns 80 percent of its consolidated subsidiary, what amount of earnings has the subsidiary retained since its acquisition?

b. If the subsidiary has retained $96,000 of earnings since it was acquired by the parent, what fraction of the subsidiary does the parent own?

c. If the subsidiary had not been consolidated but instead had been accounted for by the equity method, how much revenue in excess of dividends received would the parent have recognized from the investment since the time of acquisition?

18. Lesa Corporation purchased most of the capital stock of its subsidiary in 1974. The subsidiary earned $1 million in 1976 but declared no dividends. The following is an excerpt from Lesa Corporation's financial statements issued for 1976.

Lesa Corporation Consolidated Statement of Changes in Financial Position for the Year 1976

Sources of Working Capital:

Consolidated Net Income		$3,000,000
Addback Charges Not Requiring Working Capital:		
Depreciation of Plant	$150,000	
Amortization of Goodwill Arising from Acquisition of Consolidated Subsidiary	10,000	
Minority Interest in Earnings of Consolidated Subsidiary	200,000	360,000
Total Working Capital from Operations		$3,360,000

a. What percentage of the consolidated subsidiary does Lesa Corporation own?

b. Goodwill arising from the acquisition of the consolidated subsidiary is being amortized using the straight-line method to show the minimum charges allowed by generally accepted accounting principles. What was the excess of the subsidiary's market value as a going concern over the market value of the actual assets shown on its books as of the date of acquisition? Assume the acquisition occurred on January 1, 1974.

19. The Hart Company acquired control of the Keller Company on January 2, 1976, by purchasing 80 percent of its outstanding stock for $700,000. The entire excess of cost over book value acquired is attributed to goodwill, which is amortized over 40 years. The stockholders' equity accounts of the Keller Company appeared as follows on January 2, 1976, and December 31, 1976.

	JAN. 2, 1976	DEC. 31, 1976
Capital Stock	$600,000	$600,000
Retained Earnings	200,000	420,000

The accounts receivable of the Hart Company at December 31, 1976, include $4,500 which is due it from the Keller Company. Hart Company carries its investment in Keller Company on its single-company books at cost. Present journal entries for the following adjustments and eliminations in the December 31, 1976, work sheet for the preparation of the consolidated balance sheet:

a. The adjustment of the Investment in Keller Company account at December 31, 1976.

b. The elimination of the Investment in Keller Company account.

c. The amortization of goodwill.

d. The elimination of intercompany obligations.

e. The determination of the minority interest.

20. Miller Company and Gordon Company merge in a pooling of interests. Miller Company issues 12,500 shares with market value of $150,000 for 100 percent of Gordon's shares, which have book value of $125,000. Data for the two companies before the merger are shown below.

	MILLER COMPANY	GORDON COMPANY
Common Stock (at par)	$100,000	$ 20,000
Additional Paid-in Capital	50,000	30,000
Retained Earnings	200,000	75,000
Stockholders' Equity	$350,000	$125,000

Construct the pooled stockholders' equity accounts. Assume that Miller Company's stock has a par value per share of
a. $4.
b. $6.
c. $10.
d. $12.

21. Marmee Company and Small Enterprises agree to merge at a time when the balance sheets of the two companies are as shown below.

	MARMEE COMPANY	SMALL ENTERPRISES
Assets	$700,000	$312,000
Liabilities	$150,000	$100,000
Common Stock ($1 par)	160,000	64,000
Additional Paid-in Capital	120,000	34,000
Retained Earnings	270,000	114,000
Total Equities	$700,000	$312,000

Marmee issues 50,000 shares with market value of $800,000 to the owners of Small in return for their 64,000 shares, which represent equity of $212,000 (= $312,000 of assets − $100,000 of liabilities). The excess of Marmee's cost ($800,000) over the book value of Small's assets acquired ($212,000) results from Small's book value of assets being $448,000 less than their current value and from $140,000 of goodwill ($800,000 − $212,000 = $448,000 + $140,000).

Prepare consolidated balance sheets as of the merger date, assuming that the merger is treated as a
a. Purchase.
b. Pooling of interests.

22. Partial single-company income statements for Marmee Company and Small Enterprises (see Problem **21**) are shown below for the first year after the merger.

	MARMEE COMPANY	SMALL ENTERPRISES
Sales	$2,000,000	$1,500,000
Other Revenues	50,000	10,000
Total Revenues	$2,050,000	$1,510,000
Expenses Except Income Taxes	1,700,000	1,300,000
Pretax Income	$ 350,000	$ 210,000

Make the following assumptions:

(1) The income tax rate for the consolidated firm is 40 percent.

(2) Where necessary, the extra asset costs that must be recognized in the consolidated statement are amortized over 5 years, and the goodwill is amortized over 40 years.

(3) Amortization of asset costs and goodwill arising from the purchase are not deductible from taxable income in calculations for tax returns.

(4) Small Enterprises declared no dividends.

Prepare consolidated income statements and consolidated earnings per share for the first year following the merger. Assume that the merger is treated as a

a. Purchase.

b. Pooling of interests.

23. Sealco Enterprises published the consolidated income statement for the year 1976 which is shown below.

Sealco Enterprises
Consolidated Income Statement for the Year 1976

Revenues:

Sales		$1,000,000
Equity in Earnings of Unconsolidated Affiliate		40,000
Total Revenues		$1,040,000

Expenses:

Cost of Goods Sold (Excluding Depreciation)		$ 650,000
Administrative Expenses		100,000
Depreciation Expense		115,000
Amortization of Goodwill		5,000
Income Tax Expenses:		
Currently Payable	$42,000	
Deferred	10,000	52,000
Total Expenses		$ 922,000
Income of the Consolidated Group		$ 118,000
Less Minority Interest in Earnings of Consolidated Subsidiary		30,000
Net Income to Shareholders		$ 88,000

The unconsolidated affiliate retained 20 percent of its earnings of $100,000 during the year, having paid out the rest as dividends. The consolidated subsidiary earned $200,000 during the year and declared no dividends.

a. What percentage of the unconsolidated affiliate does Sealco Enterprises own?

b. What dividends did Sealco Enterprises receive from the unconsolidated affiliate during the year?

c. What percentage of the consolidated subsidiary does Sealco Enterprises own?

d. Prepare the "working capital provided by operations" section of the Sealco Enterprises Consolidated Statement of Changes in Financial Position for 1976 assuming that

(i) the statement starts with net income to shareholders;

(ii) the statement shows only revenues and expenses that involve working capital.

24. The condensed balance sheets of the Ely Company and the Hill Company at December 31, 1976, are as follows:

ASSETS

	Ely Company	Hill Company
Cash	$ 60,000	$ 5,000
Receivables	120,000	15,000
Investment in Hill Company Stock (cost)	80,000	—
Other Assets	540,000	100,000
	$800,000	$120,000

LIABILITIES AND STOCKHOLDERS' EQUITY

	Ely Company	Hill Company
Current Liabilities	$250,000	$ 30,000
Capital Stock	400,000	50,000
Retained Earnings	150,000	40,000
	$800,000	$120,000

The receivables of the Ely Company and the liabilities of the Hill Company contain an advance from the Ely Company to the Hill Company of $5,500.

The Ely Company acquired 85 percent of the capital stock of the Hill Company on the market at January 2, 1976, for $80,000. At that date, the balance in the Retained Earnings account of the Hill Company was $30,000. Amortize goodwill, if any, over 40 years.

Prepare journal entries for the adjustments and eliminations on the December 31, 1976, consolidated work sheet to:

a. Adjust the Investment in the Hill Company account.
b. Eliminate the Investment in the Hill Company account.
c. Amortize goodwill.
d. Eliminate intercompany obligations.
e. Determine the minority interest.
f. Prepare a worksheet for the consolidated balance sheet.

25.   **a.**   The Little Company is a subsidiary of the Butler Company carried at cost on the single-company books of the Butler Company. Present journal entries for the following selected transactions. Record in one group the entries on the books of the Little Company, and in another the entries on the books of the Butler Company.

   (1) On January 2, 1976, the Butler Company acquired on the market, for cash, 80 percent of all the capital stock of the Little Company. The outlay was $325,000. The total par value of the stock outstanding was $300,000; the retained earnings balance was $80,000. The excess of cost over book value acquired is all attributed to goodwill.

   (2) The Little Company purchased materials from the Butler Company at the latter's cost, $23,000.

   (3) The Little Company obtained an advance of $9,000 from the Butler Company. The funds were deposited in the bank.

   (4) The Little Company paid $19,000 on the purchases in (**2**) above.

(5) The Little Company repaid $7,500 of the loan received from the Butler Company in (3) above.

(6) The Little Company declared and paid a dividend of $24,000 during the year.

(7) The "net income to stockholders" of the Little Company for the year was $40,000. Present only the entry to close the Income Summary account.

b. Prepare the adjustment and elimination entries which would be necessary in the preparation of the December 31, 1976, consolidated balance sheet, recognizing the effects of only the above transactions. Amortize goodwill over 40 years.

26. The condensed balance sheets of Companies R and S on December 31, 1976, are as follows:

ASSETS

	Company R	Company S
Cash	$ 18,000	$ 13,000
Accounts and Notes Receivable	90,000	25,000
Dividends Receivable	—	—
Inventories	220,000	125,000
Investment in Stock of Company S (cost)	300,000	—
Plant Assets	300,000	212,000
Total Assets	$928,000	$375,000

LIABILITIES AND STOCKHOLDERS' EQUITY

	Company R	Company S
Accounts and Notes Payable	$ 55,000	$ 17,000
Dividends Payable	—	12,500
Other Liabilities	143,000	11,000
Capital Stock	600,000	250,000
Capital Contributed in Excess of Stated Value	—	50,000
Retained Earnings	130,000	34,500
Total Liabilities and Stockholders' Equity	$928,000	$375,000

Additional information:

Company R owns 90 percent of the capital stock of Company S. The stock of Company S was acquired on January 1, 1975, when Company S's retained earnings amounted to $20,000.

Company R has not recorded its share of the dividend declared by Company S.

Company R holds a note issued by Company S in the amount of $8,200.

Excess of cost over book value acquired is all attributable to goodwill, to be amortized over 40 years.

a. Present adjustment and elimination journal entries for a consolidated work sheet.

b. Prepare a work sheet for a consolidated balance sheet.

27. The following balance sheets show current data for Quarta Company alone and for Quarta Company consolidated with its subsidiary:

ASSETS

	Quarta	Quarta Consolidated
Current Assets	$220,000	$365,000
Plant	79,000	147,000
Investment in Subsidiary (cost)	152,000	—
	$451,000	$512,000

EQUITIES

	Quarta	Quarta Consolidated
Current Liabilities	$ 78,000	$145,000
Minority Interest	—	29,200
Capital Stock	320,000	320,000
Retained Earnings	53,000	17,800
	$451,000	$512,000

Several years ago, Quarta purchased 80 percent of the subsidiary for its book value. Quarta accounts for the investment using the cost method. The subsidiary issued $100,000 of capital stock at the time of its incorporation and has not changed that amount over the years. Assume that there are no intercompany transactions.

a. What would be the current balance in Quarta's Investment account had it accounted for the subsidiary using the equity rather than the cost method? (It is possible to answer this question without the calculations called for below. If you cannot, then do the other parts and come back to this one.)

b. Reconstruct the subsidiary's current balance sheet.

c. What was the balance in the subsidiary's retained earnings account at the time that it was purchased by Quarta?

d. What is the current stockholders' equity in the subsidiary?

28. General Products (G.P.) Company manufactures heavy-duty industrial equipment and consumer durable goods. In order to enable its customers to make convenient credit arrangements, G. P. Company organized General Products Credit Corporation several years ago. G. P. Credit Corporation is 100 percent owned by G. P. Company. On occasion, G. P. Company advances funds to G. P. Credit Corporation. G. P. Company accounts for its investment in G. P. Credit Corporation using the *equity method*, and shows the investment on its books at equity plus *advances*. G. P. owns stock in many companies, and consolidates several of them in its financial statements. Refer to the comparative balance sheets and income statements for the two companies in answering the following questions.

a. What was the balance of advances from G. P. Company to G. P. Credit Corporation at the end of 1975?

b. Given that G. P. Company accounted for its investment in G. P. Credit Corporation on the equity method, identify for 1975, the components of G. P. Company's income that are attributable to the Credit Corporation's dividends and undistributed earnings.

c. Assume that G. P. Company had accounted for its investment in the Credit Corporation using the *cost method*.

    (i) Show the components of G. P. Company's income from the Credit Corporation and compute how much larger or smaller G. P. Company's income would have been for 1975 than was reported.

(ii) Identify any G. P. Company balance sheet accounts that would have different balances, and calculate the differences from what is shown in the actual statements and what would be shown had the alternative treatment been used.

d. Assume that G. P. Company had accounted for its investment in the Credit Corporation by *consolidating* it. Perform the same computations as required in (i) and (ii) of part c above for 1975.

General Products Company and Consolidated Affiliates

FINANCIAL POSITION

	(In Millions of $) December 31		
	1977	1976	1975
Current Assets	$ 3,979.3	$3,639.0	$3,334.8
Investments[a]	754.9	714.3	630.9
Other Assets	2,667.6	2,534.5	2,232.8
Total Assets	$ 7,401.8	$6,887.8	$6,198.5
Total Current and Long-Term Liabilities	$ 4,273.8	$4,043.6	$3,603.6
Minority Interest in Equity of Affiliates	$ 43.4	$ 42.4	$ 41.3
Common Stock	$ 463.1	$ 462.3	$ 460.9
Capital Contributed in Excess of Par Value	396.6	368.8	330.0
Retained Earnings	2,371.4	2,096.2	1,874.1
Less: Common Stock Held in Treasury	(146.5)	(125.5)	(111.4)
Stockholders' Equity	$ 3,084.6	$2,801.8	$2,553.6
Total Equities	$ 7,401.8	$6,887.8	$6,198.5

CURRENT AND RETAINED EARNINGS

	For the Year		
	1977	1976	1975
Sales	$10,239.5	$9,425.3	$8,726.7
Net Earnings of Credit Corporation	41.1	30.9	19.9
Other Revenues	148.1	121.1	86.9
Total Revenues	$10,428.7	$9,577.3	$8,833.5
Expenses	(9,895.6)	(9,102.3)	(8,499.8)
Minority Interest in Earnings of Affiliates	(3.1)	(3.2)	(5.2)
Net Earnings	$ 530.0	$ 471.8	$ 328.5
Less: Dividends	254.8	249.7	235.4
Earnings Retained for year	$ 275.2	$ 222.1	$ 93.1
Retained Earnings at January 1	2,096.2	1,874.1	1,781.0
Retained Earnings at December 31	$ 2,371.4	$2,096.2	$1,874.1

[a] Investments in G. P. Credit Corporation are carried on the books at equity plus advances in the following amounts . . . . $ 275.8 $ 232.7 $ 200.7

General Products Credit Corporation

FINANCIAL POSITION

	1977	1976	1975
	(In Millions of $) December 31		
Cash and Marketable Securities	$ 120.9	$ 80.0	$ 73.2
Receivables (net)	2,648.3	2,262.0	2,068.9
Other Assets	20.3	16.7	14.9
Total Assets	$2,789.5	$2,358.7	$2,157.0
Total Liabilities	$2,529.5	$2,126.8	$1,967.0
Capital Stock	$ 110.0	$ 90.0	$ 55.0
Retained Earnings	150.0	141.9	135.0
Stockholders' Equity	$ 260.0	$ 231.9	$ 190.0
Total Equities	$2,789.5	$2,358.7	$2,157.0

CURRENT AND RETAINED EARNINGS

	For the Year		
	1977	1976	1975
Revenues	$ 319.8	$ 280.0	$ 247.5
Less: Expenses	278.7	249.1	227.6
Net Income	$ 41.1	$ 30.9	$ 19.9
Less: Dividends	33.0	24.0	15.0
Earnings Retained for Year	$ 8.1	$ 6.9	$ 4.9
Retained Earnings at January 1	141.9	135.0	130.1
Retained Earnings at December 31	$ 150.0	$ 141.9	$ 135.0

e. Compute the following ratios for G. P. from the annual report as published for 1975. (Refer to Table 7.1 if you have forgotten how to compute these ratios.)

   (i) Rate of return on total capital. (Insufficient information is given to allow an addback to the numerator for interest payments net of tax effects; ignore that adjustment to net income which is ordinarily required. Be sure, however, to add back to the numerator the minority interest in earnings of affiliates. Use the year-end balance of total assets for the year's average.)

   (ii) Debt equity ratio.

f. For 1975, compute the two ratios required in e, assuming that G. P. had consolidated the Credit Corporation, rather than accounting for it with the equity method. Use the information derived in d.

g. Compare the results in e and f. What conclusions can you draw from this exercise about comparing financial ratios for companies consolidating their sub-sidiaries with those of companies that do not?

29. Repeat Problem **28** for 1976.
30. Repeat Problem **28** for 1977.
31. Company A owns 51 percent of the voting stock of Company B. Company B owns 51 percent of the voting stock of Company C. Company C owns 51 percent of the voting stock of Company D. Company D owns 51 percent of the voting stock of Company E. Notice that Company A effectively controls Companies B, C, D, and E. Company A decides that it wishes to control Company Z. Company Z has $30 million of assets and $24 million of liabilities. Company Z's outstanding vot-ing stock sells in the market place for $10 million. Suppose that Company A acquires control of Company Z by having Company E purchase 51 percent of the voting stock of Company Z. Company E "raises" the cash needed to acquire voting control of Company Z by not declaring dividends that would otherwise be declared. Companies D, C, and B ordinarily add to their dividend declarations the amounts received in dividends from their own investments. What cash re-ceipts does the management of Company A forego by having Company E purchase the stock of Company Z in this fashion? Ignore income tax effects.
32. Refer to the financial statements of Ford Motor Company: the income statement in Exhibit 6.4, the balance sheet in Exhibit 6.3, the statement of changes in finan-cial position in Exhibit 12.3, and the statement of stockholders' equity in Ex-hibit 12.2.
   a. How much income did Ford recognize during 1974 from using the equity method for its investments in *un*consolidated subsidiaries and affiliates?
   b. How does Ford classify minority interest on the balance sheet?
   c. What was the minority interest in earnings of Ford's consolidated subsidiaries during 1974?
   d. Assume that the only cause of change in the balance sheet amount for the "Minority Interests in Net Assets of Consolidated Subsidiaries" is earnings retentions. What dividends were declared during 1974 on the stock held by the minority interest in Ford's consolidated subsidiaries?

Chapter Fourteen

Accounting for the Effects of Changing Prices

The conventional accounting model presented in previous chapters rests on the assumption that a *common* or *uniform monetary measuring unit* is employed in recording the results of transactions and events in the accounts. That is, the measuring unit (the dollar) applied in recording the acquisition of a machine costing $10,000 5 years ago is of the same dimension as the measuring unit applied in recording the purchase of merchandise inventory 1 week ago for $10,000. By using a common measuring unit over time, the amounts assigned to individual assets can be more meaningfully summed to obtain a measure of total assets. Likewise, the portion of the acquisition cost of various assets reported as an expense of the current period (depreciation expense, cost of goods sold) can be more meaningfully matched with revenues recognized during the period.

The traditional accounting model also rests on the *realization convention*: increases in the market prices of individual assets are generally not recognized as gains in determining net income until the assets are sold. Only at the time of sale is the determination of the amount of the gain considered to be sufficiently objective to warrant recognition in the accounts.

During periods when the price of each good and service in the economy is relatively stable, the common monetary measuring unit assumption and realization convention are not of particular concern in the analysis and interpretation of financial statements. Market prices of goods and services seldom remain stable, however. Since 1945, the general level of prices in the United States has increased at a rate of approximately 4 percent per year. In recent years, the rate of inflation has been much higher. Even during periods when prices in general have remained relatively stable, the prices of some goods and services have increased or decreased significantly. Changing prices, either in general or of specific goods and services, raise serious questions about the appropriateness of the common monetary measuring unit assumption and the realization convention.

In this chapter, we consider more fully the effects of changing prices on the conventional accounting measurements of net income and financial condition. Several procedures for measuring and reporting the effects of changing prices in accounting reports are described briefly and illustrated. An assessment of each of these suggested accounting procedures is then presented.

■ IMPACT OF CHANGING PRICES ON CONVENTIONAL FINANCIAL STATEMENTS

The accounting problems associated with changing prices might be separated into those related to *changes in general price levels* and those associated with *changes in prices of specific goods and services*. This distinction might be grasped most easily by considering the manner in which a price index is constructed.

Nature and Construction of Price Indices

A *price index* is a measure of the prices of a group, or "basket," of goods and services between two dates. For example, assume that we wished to construct a price index for foods to measure the change in overall prices between January 1 and December 31 of a particular year. We would begin by constructing a typical market basket for food items. To keep the illustration simple, suppose we specify that a typical market basket includes a meat, starch, vegetable, beverage, and bread product. We would determine the price of a specific commodity in each of these food groupings at the beginning and end of the year. The prices of the individual commodities at each date would be summed to obtain the aggregate market price of the basket of goods. The aggregate market price at one date would then be compared to the aggregate price at another date to obtain a price index. Exhibit 14.1 illustrates the construction of such a price index.

Prices for this group of commodities as a group increased 10 percent between the beginning and end of the year. The prices of the individual commodities, however, changed at widely varying rates. The price of bread remained relatively stable, while the price of rice decreased slightly. The prices of sirloin steak, frozen vegetables, and beer increased significantly, but only that of beer increased more than the 10 percent for the group.

Price indices are constructed by the federal government for many different groupings, or baskets, of commodities. Some of these indices are based on a wide assortment of goods and services and are intended as measures of changes in general. The two most important *general price indices* are the Gross National Product Implicit Price Deflator Index and the Consumer Price Index. Numerous indices are constructed for specific groupings of goods and services such as women's apparel, men's shoes, automobiles, and refrigerators. Even these more *specific price indices*, however, contain an assortment of goods of various qualities, dimensions, and styles within the particular product category.

EXHIBIT 14.1
Illustration of the Construction of a Price Index

Commodity	January 1	December 31	Percentage Change in Market Price of Individual Commodities
Sirloin Steak (pound)	$2.40	$2.60	+8%
Rice (32 ounces)	1.30	1.20	−8
Frozen Vegetable (package)	.40	.44	+10
Beer (six-pack)	1.30	1.75	+35
Bread (loaf)	.60	.61	+2
Total	$6.00	$6.60	
Price index, where January 1 prices equal 100	100	110 (= $6.60/$6.00)	

Accounting Problems Associated with General Price Level Changes

As general price levels change, the purchasing power of the dollar, or its command over goods and services, changes. For example, Exhibit 14.1 indicates that $6.60 was required on December 31, to purchase the same group of commodities as $6.00 would have purchased on January 1. The purchasing power of the dollar for this group of commodities declined during the year. Viewed somewhat differently, the December 31 dollar has the equivalent purchasing power of $.909 January 1 dollars (= $6.00/$6.60 or 100/110).

When the dollar is used as the unit of measurement in preparing financial statements, the purchasing power sacrificed by the firm in acquiring goods and services is not the same over time if prices are changing. The purchasing power sacrificed 5 years ago to acquire a machine costing $10,000 is not equivalent to the purchasing power sacrificed last week to acquire merchandise inventory for $10,000. When assessed in terms of general purchasing power, therefore, the dollar does not represent a common, or uniform, measuring unit.

To gain some perspective on the significance of general price level changes, Exhibit 14.2 presents the values of the Gross National Product Implicit Price Deflator Index for various years since 1953.

The rate of inflation since the late 1960's has been significantly larger than that experienced during the preceding two decades. As a result, serious questions have recently been raised about the validity of the common monetary measuring unit assumption and the impact of general price inflation on accounting reports. A technique for making the measuring unit more comparable over time, by filtering out the effects of the changing purchasing power of the dollar, is described and illustrated later in this chapter.

EXHIBIT 14.2
Gross National Product Implicit Price Deflator Index
For Various Years Between 1953 and 1973
(1958 = 100)

Year	Gross National Product Implicit Price Deflator Index	Average Annual Rate of Increase During 5 Years
1953	88.33	
		2.5%
1958	100.00	
		1.4%
1963	107.17	
		2.7%
1968	122.30	
		4.7%
1973	153.94	

Source: *Economic Report of the President* (Washington, D.C.: U.S. Government Printing Office, 1974).

Accounting Problems Associated with Specific Price Changes

An important question in accounting for changes in the market prices of individual assets concerns the period(s) in which gains and losses arising from changing prices of specific commodities are recognized. Under the conventional accounting model, assets such as inventory, land, plant, and equipment are generally stated at acquisition cost on the balance sheet (net of accumulated depreciation in some cases). Any changes in the market prices of these assets while they are held are normally not recorded in the accounts (an exception is in the treatment of marketable securities and inventories under the lower-of-cost-or-market valuation basis). When the assets are sold, any difference between the selling price of the asset and its book value is reported as a gain or loss in the period of sale. The conventional market exchange approach results in not recognizing any gains or losses due to changes in market prices during periods while assets are held.

Consider the following example. American Merchandising Corporation regularly purchases parcels of land as possible future sites for retail stores. Most of its tracts of land are ultimately used for stores. If a decision is made not to locate in a particular area, the land is sold. On January 1, 1975, two parcels of land, Tract A and Tract B, are acquired in a particular city for $100,000 each. On December 31, 1975, several competent real estate appraisers estimate the market price of Tract A to be $115,000 and of Tract B to be $125,000. Late in 1976, a decision is made to use Tract B for a new store. Tract A is then sold for $140,000.

Under the conventional accounting model, a gain of $40,000 (= $140,000 − $100,000) is reported on the sale of Tract A during 1976. This gain, although reported in 1976, reflects an increase in market price over two accounting periods. Net income for 1975 would not include the effects of the decision to hold the parcel of land during 1975 while its market price increased from $100,000 to $115,000. This increase in market price is reported as part of the gain recognized in 1976. The increase in market price of Tract B will likewise not be reflected in the accounts until the land is sold. In this case, however, the land is to be used in operations, probably over an extended period of years. The extent to which the recognition of gains or losses is postponed is therefore likely to be even more significant.

The conventional accounting model is subject to several criticisms with respect to the treatment of changes in market prices of the firm's individual assets. First, net income during periods when assets are held does not reflect the effects of management's decisions to hold rather than sell assets. Second, assets are not stated on the balance sheet at their current market values, so it is difficult for the statement user to assess the firm's financial position, or condition, as of a particular time. Third, net income during periods when assets are sold reflects a biased measure of performance during that period because gains and losses resulting from decisions in prior periods to continue holding the assets are included in the income of the period when the assets are sold.

Several approaches to accounting for specific price changes are discussed later in this chapter. It is important to emphasize at the outset, however, that the accounting problems created by general price level changes (that is, violation of the common monetary measuring unit assumption) are quite different from the accounting problems associated with specific price changes (that is, recognition of holding gains and losses and asset valuation). The procedures designed to deal with general price level changes are not designed to measure the effects of specific price changes.

■ THE RESTATEMENT PROCEDURE FOR GENERAL PRICE LEVEL CHANGES

The objective of the general price level restatement procedure is to state all amounts in dollars of uniform general purchasing power, thereby obtaining a common, or uniform, monetary measuring unit. The purchasing power of the dollar on the date of the most recent balance sheet is usually recommended as the unit of measurement for all financial statements. General price level indices, such as the Gross National Product Implicit Price Deflator or Consumer Price Index, are used to measure the general purchasing power of the dollar on various dates. The general approach is to convert the number of dollars received or expended at various price levels to an equivalent number of dollars in terms of the price level on the date of the financial statements.

For example, assume that two parcels of land are held on December 31, 1976, at which time an index of the general price level is 155. Tract A was acquired during 1958 for $100,000, when the general price index was 100. Tract B was acquired during 1961, when the general price index was 106. The acquisition cost of these parcels of land would be restated from 1958 and 1961 dollars to an equivalent number of 1976 dollars as shown in Exhibit 14.3.

EXHIBIT 14.3
Illustration of General Price Level Restatement Procedure for Land

Item	Conventionally Reported Acquisition Cost	Conversion	General Price Level Restated Acquisition Cost
Tract A	$100,000	155/100	$155,000
Tract B	$100,000	155/106	$146,226

The sacrifice in general purchasing power made during 1958 when Tract A was acquired for $100,000 is equivalent to sacrificing $155,000 (= 155/100 × $100,000) in general purchasing power on December 31, 1976. Likewise, the sacrifice in general purchasing power made during 1961 when Tract B was acquired for $100,000 is equivalent to sacrificing $146,226 (= 155/106 × $100,000) in general purchasing power on December 31, 1976. The restated amounts in Exhibit 14.3 use a measuring unit of uniform general purchasing power.

Two important aspects of the general price level restatement procedure can be noted in Exhibit 14.3. First, the procedure does not represent a departure from the use of acquisition cost as the principal valuation method in preparing financial statements. As is illustrated later, the restatements to a common dollar basis are made to the items reported in the conventional financial statements. Second, the amounts shown for general price level restated acquisition cost do *not* reflect the current market prices of these two parcels of land. The market prices of the land could have changed in an entirely different direction and pattern from that of the general price level change. The focus of the general price level restatement procedure is on making the measuring unit used in acquisition cost-based accounting systems more comparable over time and not on reflecting current market prices of individual assets and equities.

Restatement of Monetary and Nonmonetary Items

An important distinction is made in the general price level restatement procedure between monetary items and nonmonetary items, a distinction that was also made in Chapter Thirteen in the discussion of foreign currency translation.

A *monetary item* is a claim receivable or payable in a specified number of dollars regardless of changes in the general purchasing power of the dollar.[1] Examples of monetary items are cash; accounts, notes, and interest receivable; accounts,

---

[1] For purposes of translating foreign financial statement items into dollars, a monetary item was defined in Chapter Thirteen as a claim receivable or payable in a specified number of units of foreign currency regardless of changes in the exchange rate. The principal difference between the two definitions of monetary items relates to receivables or payables of the foreign unit denominated in dollars. Such items are nonmonetary for purposes of foreign currency translation and monetary for purposes of general price level accounting.

notes, and interest payable; income taxes payable; and bonds. In preparing a general price level restated balance sheet, the valuation of monetary items at the number of dollars due on the date of the balance sheet automatically states them in terms of the general purchasing power of the dollar at that time. No restatement is therefore necessary, and the conventionally reported and restated amounts are the same. For example, assume that a firm has $30,000 of cash on hand on December 31, 1976. On the conventionally prepared balance sheet, this item would be stated at $30,000, the amount of cash on hand. On the general price level restated balance sheet, this item would also be reported at $30,000, representing $30,000 of December 31, 1976, general purchasing power. Since monetary items are receivable or payable in a specified number of dollars rather than in terms of a given amount of general purchasing power, holding monetary items over time while the general purchasing power of the dollar changes gives rise to *monetary gains and losses*. During a period of inflation, a holder of monetary assets loses general purchasing power. For example, a firm with outstanding accounts receivable incurs a monetary loss, since the dollars loaned out are worth more in terms of general purchasing power than the dollars to be received when the account is collected. Likewise, a holder of monetary liabilities gains in general purchasing power during periods of inflation, since the dollars required to repay the debt represent less purchasing power than the dollars originally borrowed. The gain or loss from holding monetary items is reported as an element of general price level restated net income but is not included in conventionally reported net income.

A *nonmonetary item* is an asset or equity that does not represent a claim to or for a specified number of dollars. That is, if an item is not a monetary item, then it must be nonmonetary. Examples of nonmonetary items are inventory, land, buildings, equipment, capital stock, revenues, and expenses. In conventionally prepared financial statements, nonmonetary items are stated in terms of varying amounts of general purchasing power depending on the date the nonmonetary assets were acquired and nonmonetary equities arose. As illustrated in Exhibit 14.3 with the two parcels of land, the conventionally reported amounts of these items must be restated to an equivalent number of dollars as of the date of the balance sheet. The amount of this restatement does not represent a gain or loss to be included in net income, but merely an adjustment to equalize the measuring unit.

Illustration of the Restatement Procedure

On January 1, 1976, The Aliber Corporation was formed to operate a retail business. A general price index (GPI) on this date was 100. During 1976, the general purchasing power of the dollar declined (prices increased), resulting in a GPI on December 31, 1976, of 110. The Aliber Corporation engaged in the transactions listed below during the year (income tax effects are ignored). Notice that each transaction is dated, that the value of the GPI on the date of the transaction is shown, and that all accounts are marked as monetary (M) or nonmonetary (N) in the accompanying journal entry.

January 1, 1976: GPI = 100. The Aliber Corporation is formed with the issuance of 500 shares of $10 par value common stock for $7,000 cash.

(1) Cash (M) 7,000
      Common Stock (N) 5,000
      Additional Paid-in Capital (N) 2,000

January 1, 1976: GPI = 100. A store building is rented for 1 year with 12 months' rent of $600 paid in advance.

(2) Rent Expense (N) 600
      Cash (M) 600

January 1, 1976: GPI = 100. Store equipment is purchased for $500 cash. The equipment has a 5-year life and is to be depreciated on a straight-line basis.

(3) Store Equipment (N) 500
      Cash (M) 500

April 1, 1976: GPI = 103. Merchandise inventory is purchased for $6,000 cash.

(4) Merchandise Inventory (N) 6,000
      Cash (M) 6,000

July 1, 1976: GPI = 105. Merchandise inventory purchased on April 1, 1976, for $5,000 is sold for $8,000 cash.

(5) Cash (M) 8,000
      Sales Revenue (N) 8,000
(6) Cost of Goods Sold (N) 5,000
      Merchandise Inventory (N) 5,000

October 1, 1976: GPI = 108. Salaries for the year ending December 31, 1976, of $800 are paid in cash.

(7) Salaries Expense (N) 800
      Cash (M) 800

December 31, 1976: GPI = 110. Depreciation expense for the year is recorded.

(8) Depreciation Expense (N) 100
      Accumulated Depreciation (N) 100

December 31, 1976: GPI = 110. The revenue and expense accounts are closed and the financial statements are prepared.

(9) Sales Revenue (N) 8,000
      Cost of Goods Sold (N) 5,000
      Rent Expense (N) 600
      Salaries Expense (N) 800
      Depreciation Expense (N) 100
      Retained Earnings (N) 1,500

Both the conventional and the general price level restated balance sheet as of December 31, 1976, as well as the income statement for the year 1976 are presented in Exhibit 14.4.

Notice that cash is the only monetary item appearing on the balance sheet. Since this account is already stated in terms of December 31, 1976, dollars, it is extended in the general price level balance sheet at the same amount as is reported in the conventional balance sheet. The merchandise inventory, store equipment, and accumulated depreciation accounts are nonmonetary items. The conversion restates the acquisition cost of these items to an equivalent number of December 31, 1976, dollars. The common stock and additional paid-in capital accounts are also nonmonetary, and are restated in a manner similar to the merchandise inventory and store equipment. General price level restated retained earnings is the amount necessary to equate general price level restated total assets and total equities. As shown in Exhibit 14.4, this amount can be determined independently by restating net income and calculating the monetary gain or loss.

Revenue and expense accounts are nonmonetary, and must be restated. The approach, as with other nonmonetary accounts, is to convert each item from the price level when revenues were generated and costs were incurred to an equivalent number of December 31, 1976, dollars. Particular notice should be taken of the restatement of cost of goods sold and depreciation expense. The price index when the inventory items and store equipment were originally acquired is used, and not the price index when the inventory items were sold and depreciation expense was recorded. The transaction giving rise to the valuation of merchandise inventory and cost of goods sold occurred on April 1, 1976, when the price index was 103. Likewise, the transaction giving rise to the valuation of the store equipment and depreciation expense occurred on January 1, 1976, when the price index was 100. These dollars amounts must therefore be restated.

A "two-T-account" approach, as shown at the bottom of Exhibit 14.4, is used in calculating the monetary gain or loss. The T-account at the left presents the effects of the various transactions during the period on the monetary accounts. To simplify the example, we have assumed that all monetary transactions affect cash directly, so there are no accounts receivable or monetary liabilities. The numbers in parentheses refer to the journal entries presented earlier in this section. The actual balance in the monetary account (cash in this illustration) on December 31, 1976, is $7,100. The middle column presents the conversion of each monetary transaction from the general price level when the transaction occurred during the year to the general price level on December 31, 1976. The T-account at the right shows the number of December 31, 1976, dollars which are equivalent to the general purchasing power received or expended when the monetary transactions took place. The balance in this second T-account serves as a standard, or criterion, for determining the nature and amount of the monetary gain or loss. If the general purchasing power of the dollar amounts of monetary items received and expended during 1976 had been maintained during the period, the monetary accounts would have a balance of $7,654 at year-end. The actual balance in the monetary account is only $7,100, so a monetary loss of $554 is recognized. During periods of inflation, holders of net monetary assets recognize monetary losses, and holders of net monetary liabilities report monetary gains. During deflationary periods, the opposite results occur.

The general price level restatement procedure for the balance sheet and income statement can be summarized as follows:

1. The balance sheet at the end of the period is segregated into monetary and nonmonetary accounts. Monetary accounts, claims receivable or payable in a specified number of dollars regardless of changes in the general price level, are already expressed in terms of the desired general purchasing power; they are therefore extended in the restated balance sheet as the same amounts as reported in the conventional balance sheet. The remaining balance sheet accounts, except

EXHIBIT 14.4
Restatement of the Financial Statements of
The Aliber Corporation for General Price Level Changes

BALANCE SHEET AS OF DECEMBER 31, 1976	Historical Dollars	(Date for Denominator of Conversion Factor) ×	Conversion Factor: Price Index Values for Conversion[a] =	Common Dollars
Assets:				
Cash	$7,100	(12/31/76) ×	110/110 =	$7,100
Merchandise Inventory	1,000	(04/01/76) ×	110/103 =	1,070
Store Equipment	500	(01/01/76) ×	110/100 =	550
Less: Accumulated Depreciation	(100)	(01/01/76) ×	110/100 =	(110)
Total Assets	$8,500			$8,610
Equities:				
Common Stock	$5,000	(01/01/76) ×	110/100 =	$5,500
Additional Paid-In Capital	2,000	(01/01/76) ×	110/100 =	2,200
Retained Earnings	1,500	(see Income Statement)		910
Total Equities	$8,500			$8,610

INCOME STATEMENT FOR 1976

	Historical Dollars	(Date for Denominator of Conversion Factor) ×	Conversion Factor: Price Index Values for Conversion =	Common Dollars
Sales Revenue	$8,000	(07/01/76) ×	110/105 =	$8,400
Less Expenses:				
Cost of Goods Sold	$5,000	(04/01/76) ×	110/103 =	$5,350
Rent Expense	600	(01/01/76) ×	110/100 =	660
Salaries Expense	800	(10/01/76) ×	110/108 =	816
Depreciation Expense	100	(01/01/76) ×	110/100 =	110
Total Expenses	$6,500			$6,936
Net Income in Historical Dollars	$1,500			
Income Before Monetary Gain or Loss				$1,464
Monetary Gain or (Loss) (see computations below)				(554)
Net Income in Common Dollars				$ 910

EXHIBIT 14.4 (continued)   447

COMPUTATION OF THE MONETARY GAIN OR LOSS FOR 1976

Monetary Items In Historical Dollars (Monetary transactions expressed in the general purchasing power of the dollar at the time of the transaction)	×	Price Index Values for Conversion[a]	=	Implied Common Dollar Amounts (Monetary transactions expressed in an equivalent number of December 31, 1976, dollars)
(1) 7,000	×	110/100	=	(1) 7,700
600 (2)	×	110/100	=	660 (2)
500 (3)	×	110/100	=	550 (3)
6,000 (4)	×	110/103	=	6,420 (4)
(5) 8,000	×	110/105	=	(5) 8,400
800 (7)	×	110/108	=	816 (7)

Implied Common Dollar
Amounts Balance . $7,654

Balance   7,100   × 110/110 = Actual Dollar
Balance   7,100

Monetary Loss ..... $ 554

[a] In these calculations, conversion factors are rounded to two decimal places. Thus, $110/103 = 1.07$; $110/105 = 1.05$; $110/108 = 1.02$.

retained earnings, are restated from the general price level when the assets were acquired or capital stock was issued to an equivalent number of year-end dollars. General price level adjusted retained earnings at the end of the period is the amount necessary to equate restated total assets and restated total equities.

2. The amount determined in Step 1 as restated retained earnings is reconciled or "proved" by restating all transactions affecting retained earnings during the period. For a firm in its first year of operations, as illustrated for The Aliber Corporation, this reconciliation generally involves restating the revenue and expense accounts and calculating the monetary gain or loss. After the first year of operations, the balance in retained earnings at the beginning of the period must also be restated. This amount is determined by repeating Step 1 for the balance sheet at the beginning of the period but stating each item in terms of the purchasing power of the dollar at the end of the period. This latter step is necessary in any case when comparative balance sheets are presented.

Exhibit 14.5 presents the Statement of Changes in Financial Position of The Aliber Corporation before and after restatement for general price level changes. The principal difference between the statements is in the amount of working capital provided by operations. The general price level restated amount for working capital provided by operations of $1,020 includes the monetary loss recognized during the year on current monetary accounts. As was the case with the conventional statement discussed in Chapter Five, the general price level restated statement of changes in financial position is most easily prepared after the restated balance sheet and income statement have been prepared.

EXHIBIT 14.5
Restatement of the Statement of Changes in Financial Position for The Aliber Corporation

Sources of Working Capital:	Historical Dollars	Conversion Factor[a]	Common Dollars
Net Income	$1,500	See Income Statement	$ 910
Add Back Depreciation Expense Not Using Working Capital	100	110/100	110
Working Capital Provided by Operations	$1,600		$1,020
Issue of Common Stock	7,000	110/100	7,700
Total Sources of Working Capital	$8,600		$8,720
Uses of Working Capital:			
Purchase of Store Equipment	500	110/100	550
Increase in Working Capital	$8,100		$8,170

ANALYSIS OF INCREASES (DECREASES) IN WORKING CAPITAL ACCOUNTS

Cash	$7,100	110/110	$7,100
Merchandise Inventory	1,000	110/103	1,070
Increase in Working Capital	$8,100		$8,170

[a] See note a to Exhibit 14.4 for rounding of conversion factors.

In practice, a firm would not restate every transaction using the price index in effect on the day of the transaction. At the present time, general price indices are prepared only on monthly and quarterly bases. Also, since there are thousands of transactions during the year, gathering data on price indices and restating each transaction would be expensive. Instead, various averaging techniques are used. For example, sales for the year might be restated using the average price index for the year. Firms experiencing seasonal sales patterns during the year might use the index for each month or quarter. Our illustration effectively uses an averaging technique by assuming that all sales occur on July 1. Averaging of price indices is also effectively employed under our assumption in the example that all inventory is acquired on April 1, and all salaries are accrued and paid on October 1. In practice, inventory and labor services are acquired at many different times during the year. Average price indices for the period are used, however, in restating these financial statement items for general price level changes.

This illustration has been deliberately kept simple to demonstrate the basic mechanics of the general price level restatement procedure. More extensive treatment of the procedure is beyond the scope of this text. In the next section, the major arguments for and against general price level restated financial statements are presented.

■ ASSESSMENT OF GENERAL PRICE LEVEL RESTATED FINANCIAL STATEMENTS

In 1975, the Financial Accounting Standards Board issued an exposure draft of a proposed Statement of Financial Accounting Standards titled "Financial Reporting in Units of General Purchasing Power." In this exposure draft, the Board proposed that general price level restated financial statements be prepared and presented as supplements to the conventional financial statements for periods beginning after December 31, 1975.[2] There is still considerable controversy, however, as to whether or not these statements provide information that is worth the cost of gathering and reporting it.

The Case for Restatement

Proponents of restating financial statements for general price level changes argue that the annual rate of inflation in the United States is now sufficiently large as to seriously violate the common monetary measuring unit assumption. When the annual rate of inflation averaged between 2 and 3 percent, as was the case during the 1950's and early 1960's, the violation of the common monetary measuring unit assumption was considered tolerable. Most assets, other than land and buildings, were not held for a sufficiently long period of time for the cumulative changing general purchasing power of the dollar to distort seriously the conventional measures of earnings and financial position. With an average rate of inflation now substantially higher than had been experienced earlier, serious distortions in accounting measurements can occur over periods of just a few years.

A second argument favoring restatement concerns the highly objective nature of general price level restated financial statements. The same valuation methods are used as in the conventional financial statements. The general price indices used are prepared by governmental agencies and are widely available. The restated financial statements, therefore, are objective, or verifiable, and hence are easily audited.

A third argument favoring restatement concerns the usefulness of information on the monetary gain or loss recognized during the period. This gain or loss provides a measure for assessing management's decisions to hold cash, extend credit to customers, and obtain capital from short- and long-term creditors. Firms which do not use long-term debt financing are likely to report small or moderate monetary losses during inflationary periods, assuming monetary assets exceed current monetary liabilities. Firms making heavy use of long-term debt financing (that is, highly levered firms) will report monetary gains during periods of inflation. Information concerning the monetary gain or loss is not available in the conventional financial statements.

---

[2] As this book goes to press, it is not yet certain whether the proposals in the exposure draft will be officially adopted by the Board as a Financial Accounting Standard.

The Case against Restatement

Critics of restatement argue that the monetary gain or loss reported is of limited usefulness because the price index used to calculate the gain or loss covers too wide a variety of goods and services. Of more importance, it is suggested, is the firm's success or failure in maintaining the purchasing power of its capital for the types of goods and services it normally acquires (that is, merchandise inventory, land, plant, equipment). These items are given relatively little weight in the general price indices, which place heavy weight on the prices of consumer goods and services.

A second argument advanced by critics of restatement concerns the possibly significant measurement biases in the general price indices employed. The general price indices have been criticized for (**1**) failing to filter out properly the portion of price changes attributable to changes in the quality or other aspects of goods and services; (**2**) using posted prices for some goods and services (particularly industrial goods) rather than the actual invoice prices, which may include discounts and other price reductions; and (**3**) failing to update the goods and services included in the market basket on a sufficiently frequent basis, with the result that the price indices do not adequately reflect the items currently being purchased.

Critics of restatement also argue that financial statement users do not understand general price level restated financial statements, and that an extensive educational effort will be required before the statements can be used in investment decisions. An illustration of the misunderstanding concerning general price level statements is the belief by some persons that the general price level restated amounts for nonmonetary assets, particularly land, buildings, and equipment, represent the current values of these individual assets.

Critics of restatement also point out that several surveys of financial analysts, bankers, and other potential users of the restated accounting reports have indicated that a large proportion of these individuals would not find the statements particularly useful.[3] There is some question, then, as to whether financial statement users would find general price level adjusted statements helpful in their decisions even after an extensive educational program.

The Impact of Restatement on Net Income

One means of assessing the desirability of restatement is to determine if the earnings results would be significantly different than as conventionally reported. During periods of rising prices, one important factor causing restated net income to be *less* than conventional net income is the upward restatement of depreciation expense for cumulative inflation since the fixed assets were acquired.

---

[3] For a summary of the results of these surveys, as well as other arguments against general price level restated financial statements, see Clyde P. Stickney and David O. Green, "No Price Level Adjusted Statements, Please (PLEAS)," *The CPA Journal* (January 1974), 25–31.

A larger difference between conventional and restated earnings would be expected for manufacturing and merchandising firms than for firms in service industries. The most important factor causing restated net income to be *larger* than conventional net income is the monetary gain recognized from outstanding long-term debt during periods of inflation. As discussed earlier, highly levered firms, particularly public utilities, would probably report significant monetary gains. In assessing the impact of restatement on net income of a particular firm, attention should center on the types and relative age of various assets and the extent to which long-term debt is used as a source of capital.

■ ALTERNATIVE APPROACHES TO ACCOUNTING FOR SPECIFIC PRICE CHANGES

Several approaches to accounting for specific price changes have been suggested. One approach adheres to acquisition cost but suggests the use of the last-in, first-out (LIFO) inventory cost-flow assumption and accelerated depreciation methods rather than the first-in, first-out (FIFO) cost-flow assumption and the straight-line depreciation method. Another alternative approach abandons acquisition cost as the valuation basis and substitutes a current valuation basis, either current replacement cost or net realizable value. Each of these approaches is described more fully and evaluated in the sections which follow.

Acquisition Cost with LIFO Inventory and Accelerated Depreciation Methods

The use of the LIFO inventory cost-flow assumption and accelerated depreciation methods (double-declining-balance and sum-of-the-years'-digits) are commonly suggested as procedures for giving effect to price changes in financial statements while continuing to adhere to acquisition cost.

LIFO Inventory Cost-Flow Assumption   The LIFO inventory cost-flow assumption results in cost of goods sold being based on the most recent purchases of inventory items. Net income, therefore, reflects the matching of current selling prices with relatively current costs of acquiring the merchandise. It is suggested that using LIFO provides approximately the same gross profit as if cost of goods sold had been measured by the cost of replacing the goods at the time of sale. The use of LIFO, however, is based on actual inventory purchases and is not subject to the measurement problems inherent in an accounting system based on replacement costs.

As a basis for reflecting changing prices, LIFO is subject to several criticisms. First, while the income statement may reflect more current price information under LIFO than other inventory cost-flow assumptions, the balance sheet valuation of inventory reflects prices paid during earlier periods which, as explained in Chapter Nine, can be substantially different from the current prices of inventory items on hand. Second, during periods of a decrease in the quantity of inventory, cost of goods sold under LIFO will reflect prices paid when inventory layers were added during previous periods. Under these conditions, net income reflects current selling prices and perhaps very old inventory acquisition costs. Use of LIFO is, at best, only a partial solution to accounting for changing prices.

Accelerated Depreciation Methods   The more rapid write-down of depreciable assets using the double-declining-balance or sum-of-the-years'-digits depreciation methods rather than the straight-line method is also suggested as a means of recognizing the effects of changing prices. During periods of inflation, the replacement costs of many fixed assets are likely to increase. If depreciation during the period is determined using the replacement costs of the services of fixed assets consumed, depreciation expense would likely be larger than straight-line depreciation on acquisition cost. It is suggested that current replacement cost depreciation can be approximated by using accelerated depreciation methods while remaining on the acquisition-cost basis of valuation.

As with LIFO inventory cost-flow assumption, accelerated depreciation methods are subject to several criticisms as approaches for giving effect to specific price changes. First, even in the early years of an asset's depreciable life, only by coincidence will depreciation expense based on acquisition cost and accelerated depreciation methods equal the amount that would be obtained from determining depreciation using current replacement costs or some other type of current value. Second, since the total amount of depreciation taken on an asset over its life will not exceed acquisition cost, extra depreciation claimed in early years using accelerated depreciation methods means that less depreciation must be charged in later years. Depreciation expense during the later years will probably seriously misstate the current replacement cost of the asset services consumed during those periods. Third, the rapid write-down of depreciable assets using accelerated depreciation methods results in balance sheet valuations which are likely to be significantly different from the current replacement costs for these assets. Use of accelerated depreciation methods is, at best, only a temporary solution to accounting for changing prices. Even at that, accelerated depreciation methods make only the income statement more current. The balance sheet amounts for depreciable assets can be significantly different than the current values of those assets.

Current Valuation Basis

Several approaches to accounting for specific price changes have been suggested which depart from the use of acquisition cost. Among these alternative approaches are proposals for using current replacement cost (entry value) or net realizable value (exit value) as the valuation basis. It should be noted that, in perfectly competitive markets, the spread, or difference, between the current replacement cost and net realizable value of an asset should be relatively small, essentially representing transaction costs. In less active markets, as characterizes the market for many used assets, the spread between entry and exit values could be much larger, reflecting not only transaction costs but also trading advantages by the buyer or the seller.

Current Replacement Cost Valuation Method   When current replacement cost is used as the valuation basis, nonmonetary assets are stated on the balance sheet at the cost of replacing the assets in their current condition. (Monetary assets and liabilities are, by definition, stated at their current cash-equivalent values). Changes in the replacement cost of assets held during the period and not sold by the end of the period are reported as holding gains and losses in the income statement. Expenses are stated at the cost of replacing the asset services which are consumed during the period.

An example might be helpful in illustrating the use of current replacement cost. Assume that a construction company purchases a crane in new condition on January 1, 1976, for $50,000. The estimated service life of the crane is 5,000 hours. During 1976, the crane is used for 1,000 hours. On December 31, 1976, a similar crane in new condition could be purchased for $60,000, while a similar 1-year-old crane could be acquired for $48,000. The crane would be stated at $48,000 on the December 31, 1976, balance sheet under the current replacement cost valuation basis. The difference between the acquisition cost on January 1, 1976, of $50,000 and the valuation at the end of the year of $48,000 would be reflected in net income for 1976. The $2,000 difference could be disaggregated into a holding gain of $10,000 (= $60,000 − $50,000) and depreciation expense on a replacement cost basis of $12,000 (= $60,000/5).[4]

In determining the replacement cost of various financial statement items, several sources of price data might be used. For merchandise inventory, suppliers' catalogs could be consulted. For manufacturing firms with work in process and finished goods inventories, it would be necessary to identify the various factor inputs into production (for example, raw material used, direct labor services consumed, depreciation recorded on factory equipment) and determine the replacement cost of each. There is likely to be greater difficulty establishing the replacement costs of manufacturing overhead components than of direct material and direct labor because of the numerous indirect cost elements involved in the determination.

In cases where established second-hand markets exist for fixed assets, such as automobiles, furniture, and standardized equipment, replacement cost can be determined from dealers in those markets. In some cases, the federal government prepares specific price indices for certain types of fixed assets. These indices provide information concerning the change in the price of specific assets in a new condition. Some adjustment is necessary to reflect the used condition of the assets on hand. For example, the specific price index for cranes might have increased from 100 to 120 between the beginning and end of 1976. A new crane purchased for $50,000 on January 1, 1976, would have a current replacement cost in new condition of $60,000 at year-end. This amount must be adjusted downward, how-

---

[4] There are other procedures for determining the holding gain and depreciation expense on a current replacement cost basis. The procedure illustrated above has the advantage of being simple and should be satisfactory for this introductory discussion of current replacement cost. The calculation of holding gains on inventory items is illustrated in Chapter Nine.

ever, to reflect the replacement cost of services consumed during 1976. The reduction might be based on the replacement cost of the estimated total capacity of the crane which was consumed during the year or on the cost of renting assets that provide similar services.

The current replacement cost of specially designed equipment and buildings is perhaps the most difficult to determine. A combination of suppliers' catalogs, specific price indices, and real estate appraisals is probably required.

Perhaps the major criticism of using current replacement cost in accounting for specific price changes is the high degree of subjectivity involved in determining replacement cost. Several persons attempting to determine the replacement cost of a specific asset could arrive at widely different replacement cost amounts. Many of these valuations would be difficult to audit effectively, and therefore might not be covered by the opinion of the independent accountant.

While there are difficulties in measuring replacement cost for fixed assets, there is apparently much less difficulty in the case of marketable securities and inventories. Marketable securities and inventories are written down to replacement cost when the lower-of-cost-or-market valuation basis is used. If replacement cost can be determined in a sufficiently objective manner to make downward adjustments, then replacement cost is also objective enough to be used for upward adjustments (that is, holding gains as well as holding losses should be recognized on marketable securities and inventories). Holding gains on marketable securities and inventories are not recognized in practice, however, until the assets are sold.

Net Realizable Value Valuation Basis   Another approach to accounting for changing prices which departs from the use of acquisition cost is to state nonmonetary assets at the net amount at which they could be sold at the end of the year after deducting selling costs (the so-called net realizable value). Any difference in the valuation of the asset between the beginning and end of the year would be reflected in the determination of net income for the period.

The net realizable value of assets such as marketable securities and inventories, for which active markets exist, should be relatively easy to determine. Likewise, the net realizable values of some fixed assets are easily determinable if active markets for used machinery, fixtures, and other items are present. Real estate agents might be consulted in determining the net realizable value of land and buildings. For specially designed equipment and similar assets, no second-hand market may exist from which to determine net realizable values.

The use of the net realizable value basis of valuation is subject to the same criticisms as using current replacement cost. The valuations tend to be more subjective than using acquisition cost, and therefore more difficult to audit. The use of net realizable values is subject to several additional criticisms, however. One criticism attacks the rationale for using exit prices. It is argued that assets are acquired so they can be used in operations. In many cases, selling the assets is not even considered as an alternative. Yet management's performance would be judged on an earnings measure which includes changes in exit prices. A second and somewhat related criticism of using net realizable values is that there may be some specially designed assets which have a significant *value in use* to the firm but which would be stated at zero or relatively small amounts because their *value in exchange* is minimal due to the lack of any interested buyers for the assets or because they are so integrated into permanent structures that their removal costs would be very high.

Except for the manner of determining the current replacement cost or net realizable value of each asset, the procedures employed in preparing financial statements based on these current valuation approaches are quite similar. As an illustration of these procedures, the procedures for preparing financial statements based on current replacement costs are discussed next.

■ ILLUSTRATION OF FINANCIAL STATEMENTS BASED ON REPLACEMENT COST

To illustrate the preparation of financial statements based on the replacement cost valuation method, the information regarding the transactions of The Aliber Corporation for 1976 considered earlier in this chapter will be used. Rather than restating the financial statements for general price level changes, in this case the statements will be adjusted to reflect the current replacement cost valuation method. Assume that the amounts paid for rent and salaries reflect the current replacement costs of these services at the time they were consumed. When the inventory was sold on July 1, 1976, it had a current replacement cost of $7,000. On December 31, 1976, the merchandise inventory could be replaced for $1,500. The store equipment could be replaced in new condition at the end of 1976 for $600.

Exhibit 14.6 presents balance sheets and income statements based on acquisition costs and current replacement costs for The Aliber Corporation. Under both valuation methods, cash is stated at the amount of cash on hand or in the bank. The merchandise inventory is stated at its acquisition cost of $1,000 on the conventional balance sheet and at its current replacement cost on December 31, 1976, of $1,500 on the balance sheet based on replacement costs. The store equipment is stated at a book value of $400 on the acquisition cost valuation method, reflecting $500 historical cost and 1 year's depreciation using the straight-line method and a 5-year life. The current replacement cost of the store equipment is estimated to be $480. This valuation is based on the current replacement cost of similar equipment in new condition of $600 but adjusted downward by $120 (= $600/5) for the 1 year of use. Since The Aliber Corporation does not have liabilities outstanding at year end, the stockholders have a full claim or interest in the total assets of $9,080. The manner in which this interest is disclosed is not of particular significance. In Exhibit 14.6, the contributed capital accounts are stated at the amount of the proceeds from issuing the common stock on January 1, 1976, for $7,000. The remainder of total equities is included in retained earnings.

EXHIBIT 14.6
An Illustration Showing the
Financial Statements of The Aliber Corporation
Based on Acquisition Cost and Replacement Cost

BALANCE SHEET AS OF DECEMBER 31, 1976

Assets:	Acquisition Cost	Replacement Cost
Cash	$7,100	$7,100
Merchandise Inventory	1,000	1,500
Store Equipment		
—at acquisition cost	500	—
—at current replacement cost	—	600
Less: Accumulated Depreciation	(100)	(120)
Total Assets	$8,500	$9,080
Equities:		
Common Stock	$5,000	$5,000
Additional Paid-In Capital	2,000	2,000
Retained Earnings	1,500	2,080
Total Equities	$8,500	$9,080

INCOME STATEMENT FOR 1976

Sales Revenue	$8,000	$8,000
Less Cost of Goods Sold		
—at acquisition cost	(5,000)	—
—at current replacement cost	—	(7,000)
Gross Margin or Operating Margin	$3,000	$1,000
Less Expenses:		
Rent Expense	(600)	(600)
Salaries Expense	(800)	(800)
Depreciation Expense	(100)	(120)
Net Income—As Conventionally Reported	$1,500	
Net Loss Before Holding Gains and Losses		$ (520)
Realized Holding Gain on Inventory Sold		2,000
Unrealized Holding Gain on Inventory Not Sold		500
Unrealized Holding Gain on Store Equipment Held		100
Net Income—Based on Replacement Cost		$2,080

The income statement based on replacement cost is significantly different from the statement based on acquisition cost. Each expense is stated at the replacement cost of the services consumed during the year. When the merchandise inventory was sold on July 1, 1976, it had a replacement cost of $7,000. The excess of the selling price of $8,000 over the $7,000 cost of replacing the merchandise sold represents the *operating margin* realized by the firm on the sale. The firm also realized a *holding gain* on the inventory as a result of holding the inventory during a period (April 1, 1976, to July 1, 1976) when the replacement cost increased from $5,000 to $7,000. The income statement based on replacement cost distinguishes between operating and holding gains and losses. In the conventional income statement based on acquisition cost, the operating margin and realized holding gain are merged into a single amount—gross margin on the sale. Users of conventional financial statements have no information for distinguishing which part of the gross margin is attributable to operating advantages in the market and which part is attributable to holding inventory which must be replaced at currently higher prices. The amounts paid for rent and salaries during the year are assumed to be the current replacement costs of the services consumed. The determination of the $120 depreciation expense was discussed above. The final items of difference between the income statements based on acquisition cost and replacement cost are the recognition of holding gains on the merchandise inventory and store equipment which were held during a period while their replacement costs increased. These gains have not been realized as a result of a market transaction and therefore are not yet reported in the conventional income statement.

The journal entries to integrate the replacement cost valuation method into the regular accounting system based on acquisition cost are as follows:

Merchandise Inventory	500	
Unrealized Holding Gain on Merchandise Inventory		500

To record a holding gain on merchandise inventory resulting from an increase in replacement cost during the year from $1,000 to $1,500.

Store Equipment	100	
Unrealized Holding Gain on Store Equipment		100

To record a holding gain on store equipment resulting from an increase in replacement cost during the year from $500 to $600.

Depreciation Expense	20	
Accumulated Depreciation		20

To record additional depreciation expense for the year resulting from an increase in the replacement cost of the store equipment.

Exhibit 14.7 presents a Statement of Changes in Financial Position for The Aliber Corporation for 1976 based on acquisition cost and current replacement cost. The principal differences between these two statements are (**1**) the amount of depreciation added back to net income and (**2**) the subtraction of the unrealized holding gain on the store equipment from income based on replacement cost because it did not provide working capital. Note, however, that the unrealized holding gain on merchandise inventory did increase working capital for the year. Unlike general price level restated financial statements, net income and working

EXHIBIT 14.7
Statement of Changes in Financial Position of The Aliber Corporation
Based on Acquisition Cost and Current Replacement Cost

	Acquisition Cost	Replacement Cost
Sources of Working Capital:		
Net Income	$1,500	$2,080
Add Back Depreciation Expense Not Using Working Capital	100	120
Subtract Unrealized Holding Gain on Store Equipment Not Providing Working Capital		(100)
Working Capital Provided by Operations	$1,600	$2,100
Issue of Capital Stock	7,000	7,000
Total Sources of Working Capital	$8,600	$9,100
Uses of Working Capital:		
Purchase of Store Equipment	500	500
Increase in Working Capital	$8,100	$8,600

ANALYSIS OF INCREASES (DECREASES) IN WORKING CAPITAL ACCOUNTS

Cash	$7,100	$7,100
Merchandise Inventory	1,000	1,500
Increase in Working Capital	$8,100	$8,600

capital provided by operations under replacement cost based statements do not include a gain or loss on monetary items.

The Securities and Exchange Commission (SEC) now requires that certain large manufacturing and retailing companies disclose some replacement cost data in notes to the financial statements. The required disclosures include:

(1) replacement cost of inventory at the balance sheet dates,
(2) replacement cost of goods sold computed at the time of sale,
(3) replacement cost of plant assets at the balance sheet dates, and
(4) depreciation expense based on replacement costs.

The SEC does not currently require publication of financial statements based on replacement costs, such as those shown in Exhibit 14.6. Nevertheless, the disclosures would be sufficient to enable the reader to construct such statements.

■ INTEGRATION OF ACCOUNTING PROCEDURES FOR GENERAL AND SPECIFIC PRICE CHANGES

In this chapter, we have considered independently the accounting problems associated with general and specific price changes. Changes in the general price level influence the validity of the common monetary measuring unit assumption.

Changes in specific prices have consequences for the valuation of assets and the recognition of holding gains and losses. It has been suggested by some accountants that the effects of both general and specific price changes should be recognized in accounting reports and that, consequently, the accounting procedures designed for each type of price change should be integrated.

In preparing financial statements adjusted for both general and specific price changes, the general price level methodology would be applied to monetary assets and liabilities and a monetary gain or loss recognized. Nonmonetary assets would be stated using either current replacement costs or net realizable values at the end of the period. The difference between the valuation of nonmonetary assets between the beginning and end of the year would not be entirely reported as a holding gain or loss, however. The replacement cost at the beginning of the period of these assets would be restated to the general purchasing power of the dollar at the end of the period. A distinction would therefore be made between *real* and *nominal* holding gains and losses. For example, reconsider the treatment of the store equipment in Exhibit 14.6. The difference between the replacement cost of $500 at the beginning and $600 at the end of the year was recognized as a holding gain of $100. Now assume that an index of the general price level increased from 100 to 115 between January 1, and December 31, 1976. The real holding gain is $25. This amount is determined by restating the replacement cost of $500 at the beginning of the year to dollars of equivalent general purchasing power at the end of the year, obtaining $575 (= $500 × 115/100). The difference between the replacement cost at the end of the year of $600 and the general price level restated replacement cost at the beginning of the year of $575 represents the real holding gain. The remaining $75 (= $575 — $500) is a nominal holding gain.

■ SUMMARY

This chapter has described the effects of changing prices on conventional accounting measurements of net income, financial position, and changes in financial position. A distinction has been made between changes in the general price level and changes in the prices of specific assets and equities. Changes in the general price level were shown to influence the validity of the common monetary measuring unit assumption. Changes in specific prices have consequences for the valuation of assets and the recognition of holding gains and losses. The distinction between these types of price changes and the associated accounting problems should be clearly understood. The techniques for restating financial statements for general price level changes are not designed to reflect changes in the prices of specific assets and equities.

Suggested accounting procedures for general and specific price changes have been briefly described and illustrated. More extensive treatment of these accounting procedures is beyond the scope of this book. These topics are considered further in advanced accounting courses.

QUESTIONS AND PROBLEMS

1. Review the meaning of the following concepts or terms discussed in this chapter.
   a. Common monetary measuring unit assumption.
   b. Realization convention.
   c. General price level changes.
   d. General price index.
   e. General purchasing power of the dollar.
   f. Specific price changes.
   g. Specific price index.
   h. Monetary item.
   i. Nonmonetary item.
   j. Monetary gain or loss.
   k. Holding gain or loss.
   l. Current replacement cost.
   m. Net realizable value.
   n. Inventory profit.
2. The accounting problems associated with changing prices have been described as *general* and *specific*. Explain.
3. Distinguish between the pair of terms listed in each of the following cases.
   a. General price index and general price level.
   b. General price index and general purchasing power of the dollar.
   c. General price index and specific price index.
4. "Financial statements prepared under the conventional accounting model reflect dollars of mixed purchasing power." Explain the meaning of this statement in relation to the balance sheet, income statement, and statement of changes in financial position.
5. When general price level restated financial statements are prepared, under what conditions will a firm recognize:
   a. A monetary gain?
   b. A monetary loss?
6. For which types of asset and equity structures would you expect:
   a. Significant differences between earnings as conventionally reported and as restated for general price level changes?
   b. Insignificant differences between the two earnings measures?
7. Why is there no nonmonetary gain or loss in general price level restated financial statements?
8. Why is there no monetary gain or loss in financial statements based on replacement costs?
9. In financial statements prepared under the conventional accounting model, some items are stated in terms of the current general purchasing power of the dollar while other items are stated in terms of the general purchasing power of the dollar during prior periods. Give several examples of each type.
10. "The LIFO inventory cost-flow assumption and accelerated depreciation methods are not comprehensive means of accounting for specific price changes." Explain.
11. What significant differences would be expected in the balance sheets based on

acquisition cost, acquisition cost restated for general price level changes, and replacement cost?

12. What significant differences would be expected in the income statements based on acquisition cost, acquisition cost restated for general price level changes, and replacement cost?

13. What significant differences would be expected in the statement of changes in financial position based on acquisition cost, acquisition cost restated for general price level changes, and replacement cost?

14. Refer to the amounts of the Gross National Product Implicit Price Deflator Index in Exhibit 14.2. What is the general purchasing power of the dollar in 1973 relative to its general purchasing power in 1953? 1963?

15. Indicate whether each of the following accounts is a monetary item (M) or a non-monetary item (N). State any assumptions which you feel are necessary.
    a. Certificate of Deposit.
    b. Land.
    c. Investment in U.S. Treasury Notes.
    d. Deferred Income Taxes.
    e. Notes Receivable.
    f. Bonds Payable.
    g. Patents.
    h. Common Stock.
    i. Investment in Unconsolidated Subsidiaries.
    j. Allowance for Uncollectible Accounts.

16. Southside Development Corporation acquired two parcels of land on July 1, 1975, for $50,000 each. On December 31, 1975, professional appraisers estimated the current market value, or selling price, of Tract A to be $60,000 and of Tract B to be $45,000. Tract B was sold on July 1, 1976, for $38,000. On December 31, 1976, Tract A had a market value of $65,000.

    An index of the general price level on various dates is determined to be as follows:

    July 1, 1975: 100;
    December 31, 1975: 115;
    July 1, 1976: 125; December 31, 1976: 140.

    a. Determine the amount of gain or loss recognized during 1975 and 1976 relating to these properties under the acquisition cost and current market value, or selling price, valuation methods assuming that changes in the general purchasing power of the dollar are ignored.
    b. Restate the gain or loss recognized during 1976 on the sale of Tract B under the acquisition cost valuation method to the general price level on December 31, 1976.

17. The merchandise inventory of Scoggin's Appliance Store on January 1, 1976, consists of 1,000 units acquired for $250 each. During 1976, 2,500 units of merchandise are purchased at a unit price of $300, while 2,400 units are sold for $400 each. The average replacement cost per unit during 1976 is $300, while the replacement cost on December 31, 1976, is $360 per unit.
    a. Using the acquisition cost valuation method and ignoring general price level

changes, determine the gross margin (sales less cost of goods sold) recognized during 1976 using the FIFO and LIFO cost-flow assumptions.

b. Using the replacement cost valuation method and ignoring general price level changes, determine the amount of the operating margin and holding gain recognized during 1976 using the FIFO and LIFO inventory-costing methods.

18. United Manufacturing Corporation purchased a new machine on January 1, 1976, for $500,000. The machine is to be depreciated using the straight-line method over a 10-year life. Estimated salvage value is zero. An index of the general price level on January 1, 1976, is 160 and on December 31, 1976, is 176.

a. Determine the amount of depreciation expense for 1976 and the book value of the machine on December 31, 1976, using (**1**) the acquisition cost valuation model as conventionally reported and (**2**) as restated for general price level changes.

b. The replacement cost on December 31, 1976, of a similar new machine is $560,000 and of a similar 1-year old machine is $504,000. If the replacement cost valuation method is used and changes in the general purchasing power of the dollar are ignored, what is the amount of depreciation expense and holding gain or loss for 1976?

c. Disaggregate the holding gain determined in **b** into the real gain and the nominal gain.

19. Jones Manufacturing Corporation depreciates its machinery using the straight-line method over a 10-year life with zero estimated salvage value. A full year depreciation is taken in the year of acquisition and none in the year of disposal. Acquisitions, which took place evenly over the appropriate years, were as follows: 1974, $500,000; 1975, $100,000; 1976, $200,000. An index of the average general price level during 1974 was 120, during 1975 was 160, and during 1976 was 180. The general price index on December 31, 1976, is 200.

a. Determine the amount of depreciation expense for 1976 and the book value of the machinery on December 31, 1976, using the acquisition cost valuation method as conventionally reported.

b. Repeat **a**, using the acquisition cost valuation method restated for general price level changes. Round conversion factors used to two decimal places (for example, $200/120 = 1.67$).

20. The Whitley Hardware Store had a net monetary asset position of $200,000 on January 1, 1976, at which time an index of the general price level was 100. Transactions during 1976 and associated indices of the general price level (GPI) are listed below.

(1) Purchases, all on account, totaled $300,000 (GPI = 120).
(2) Sales, all on account, totaled $500,000 (GPI = 120).
(3) Collections from customers for sales on account, $350,000 (GPI = 125).
(4) Payments to suppliers for purchases on account, $200,000 (GPI = 125).
(5) Declaration of a dividend, payable during January, 1977 (GPI = 150). The general price index on December 31, 1976, is 150.

a. Using the two-T-account approach, determine the amount of the monetary gain or loss for 1976.

b. Repeat **a**, assuming a net monetary liability position of $200,000 on January 1, 1976.

21. On January 1, 1976, the Robert Pratt family had $1,200 in its checking account and $5,000 in a savings account. The unpaid balance on the mortgage on their home totaled $20,000, while unpaid bills relating to purchases during December 1975 amounted to $1,000. An index of the general price level on January 1, 1976, was 150. During 1976, the following transactions occurred (general price index is shown in parentheses):

(**1**) Robert Pratt's take-home salary during 1976 was $15,000 (average GPI = 160).

(**2**) The unpaid bills of $1,000 on January 1, 1976, were paid (GPI = 152).

(**3**) Principal repayments of $2,500 were made during 1976 on the home mortgage loan (average GPI = 160).

(**4**) Food, clothing, interest, and other costs incurred by the family during 1976 totaled $10,100, of which $9,300 were paid in cash (average GPI = 160).

(**5**) Interest earned and added to the savings account totaled $250 (average GPI = 160).

(**6**) In addition to the interest earned in (**5**), $2,500 was transferred from the checking to the savings account during 1976 (GPI = 158). The general price index on December 31, 1976, is 170.

Using the two-T-account approach, determine the monetary gain or loss for the family during 1976. Round conversion factors used to two decimal places $(170/150 = 1.13)$.

22. The financial statements of the Hargrave Corporation for 1976, its first year of operations, are presented below.

Hargrave Corporation
Balance Sheet
December 31, 1976

ASSETS

Cash	$ 50,000
Accounts Receivable	180,000
Merchandise Inventory	300,000
Store Equipment	300,000
Less Accumulated Depreciation	(30,000)
Total Assets	$800,000

EQUITIES

Accounts Payable	$ 50,000
Common Stock	500,000
Additional Paid-in Capital	100,000
Retained Earnings	150,000
Total Equities	$800,000

Hargrave Corporation
Income Statement
For the Year 1976

Sales Revenue		$500,000
Less Expenses:		
Cost of Goods Sold	$250,000	
Depreciation Expense	30,000	
Selling and Administrative Expenses	70,000	
Total Expenses		$350,000
Net Income		$150,000

Hargrave Corporation
Statement of Changes in Financial Position
For the Year 1976

Sources of Working Capital:

Net Income	$150,000	
Add Back Depreciation Expense Not Using Working Capital	30,000	
Working Capital Provided by Operations	$180,000	
Issuance of Common Stock	600,000	
Total Sources of Working Capital		$780,000

Uses of Working Capital:

Purchase of Store Equipment	300,000
Net Increase in Working Capital	$480,000

ANALYSIS OF INCREASES (DECREASES) IN WORKING CAPITAL

Cash	$ 50,000
Accounts Receivable	180,000
Merchandise Inventory	300,000
Accounts Payable	(50,000)
Net Increase in Working Capital	$480,000

Indices of the general price level on various dates were as follows (round conversion factors to two decimal places; for example, $200/180 = 1.11$).

(1) On January 1, 1975, when common stock was issued 160
(2) When store equipment was acquired 165
(3) When merchandise inventory was acquired 170
(4) When sales were made 180
(5) When selling and administrative costs were incurred 175
(6) On December 31, 1976 200

a. Restate the balance sheet on December 31, 1976, to the general purchasing power of the dollar on December 31, 1976.

b. Restate the income statement for the year 1976 to the general purchasing power of the dollar on December 31, 1976. Include a separate calculation of the monetary gain or loss.

c. Restate the statement of changes in financial position for the year 1976 to the general purchasing power of the dollar on December 31, 1976.

23. The financial statements of the Hargrave Corporation (see Problem **22**) for 1977, its second year of operations, are presented below.

Hargrave Corporation
Balance Sheet
December 31, 1977

ASSETS

Cash	$ 90,000
Accounts Receivable	190,000
Merchandise Inventory (based on FIFO)	450,000
Store Equipment	400,000
Accumulated Depreciation	(70,000)
Total Assets	$1,060,000

EQUITIES

Accounts Payable	$ 70,000
Mortgage Payable	90,000
Common Stock	500,000
Additional Paid-in Capital	100,000
Retained Earnings	300,000
Total Equities	$1,060,000

Hargrave Corporation
Income Statement
For the Year 1977

Sales Revenue	$750,000
Less Expenses:	
Cost of Goods Sold	$400,000
Depreciation Expense	40,000
Selling and Administrative Expenses	110,000
Total Expenses	$550,000
Net Income	$200,000

Hargrave Corporation
Statement of Changes in Financial Position
For the Year 1977

Sources of Working Capital:

Net Income	$200,000	
Add Back Depreciation Expense Not Using Working Capital	40,000	
Working Capital Provided by Operations	$240,000	
Mortgage Liability Assumed in Acquiring Store Equipment	100,000	
Total Sources of Working Capital		$340,000

Uses of Working Capital:

Dividends Paid	$ 50,000	
Mortgage Liability Partial Payment	10,000	
Store Equipment Acquired	100,000	
Total Uses of Working Capital		160,000
Net Increase in Working Capital		**$180,000**

ANALYSIS OF INCREASES (DECREASES) IN WORKING CAPITAL

Cash	$ 40,000
Accounts Receivable	10,000
Merchandise Inventory	150,000
Accounts Payable	(20,000)
Net Increase in Working Capital	**$180,000**

Additional Information Store equipment costing $100,000 was acquired during the year. The acquisition was financed by long-term borrowing, with the equipment serving as collateral. The equipment is depreciated using the straight-line method over a 10-year life with zero estimated salvage value. A full year's depreciation is taken in the year of acquisition.

Indices of the general price level on various dates were as follows (round conversion factors to two decimal places; for example, 225/200 = 1.13).

(**1**) On January 1, 1976 200
(**2**) When store equipment was acquired 202
(**3**) When merchandise inventory was acquired 204
(**4**) When sales were made 215
(**5**) When selling and administrative costs were incurred 212
(**6**) When mortgage payments were made 225
(**7**) When dividend was declared and paid 225
(**8**) On December 31, 1977 225

a. Restate the balance sheet on December 31, 1977, to the general purchasing power of the dollar on December 31, 1977.

b. Restate the income statement for the year ending December 31, 1977, to the general purchasing power of the dollar on December 31, 1977. Include a separate calculation of the monetary gain or loss.

    c. Prepare an analysis of changes in retained earnings for the year ending December 31, 1977, before and after restatement for changes in the general purchasing power of the dollar. The January 1, 1977, balance in retained earnings, restated to the general purchasing power of the dollar in December 31, 1977, is $120,600.

24. The Whitmyer Corporation was formed on January 1, 1976, to conduct an office rental business. Listed below are various transactions and other events of the firm during 1976. An index of the general price level at the time of each transaction is also shown.

    (1) January 1, 1976 (GPI = 100): Capital stock is issued for $1,000,000.

    (2) January 2, 1976 (GPI = 100): Land costing $100,000 and a building costing $1,500,000 are acquired. A cash payment of $900,000 is made, with a long-term, 10-percent mortgage assumed for the remainder of the purchase price.

    (3) January 2, 1976, to December 1, 1976 (average GPI = 106): Rentals of $300,000 are collected in cash.

    (4) January 2, 1976, to December 31, 1976 (average GPI = 106): Operating costs incurred evenly over the year total $60,000, of which $50,000 are paid in cash and the remainder are on account. All of these costs expired during 1976.

    (5) January 2, 1976, to December 31, 1976 (average GPI = 106): Interest costs are accrued monthly on the mortgage payable and were paid on December 31, 1976.

    (6) December 31, 1976 (GPI = 110): Depreciation on the building is calculated using the straight-line method, a 30-year life, and zero salvage value.

    (7) December 31, 1976 (GPI = 110): A cash dividend of $75,000 is declared and paid.

    a. Set up T-accounts as needed and enter the transactions during the year based on the conventional accounting model.

    b. Prepare a balance sheet as of December 31, 1976, and an income statement and statement of changes in financial position for 1976 using the conventional accounting model.

    c. Repeat **b**, but restate the conventional financial statements for general price level changes. Round conversion factors to two decimal places (for example, 110/106 = 1.04).

    d. On December 31, 1976, the land had a current replacement cost of $150,000. A similar new office building had a replacement cost at the end of 1976 of $1,560,000, while a similar 1-year-old office building had a replacement cost of $1,508,000. The amounts reported as operating and interest expenses in the income statement as conventionally prepared represent reasonably close approximations to the replacement cost of the goods or services consumed during the year. Repeat **b**, using the current replacement cost valuation model (ignore changes in the general purchasing power of the dollar).

Part 4

Synthesis

Chapter Fifteen

Significance
and Implications
of Alternative
Accounting Principles

The independent accountant expresses an unqualified opinion on a firm's financial statements by stating that the statements were prepared in accordance with "generally accepted accounting principles." In previous chapters, we have described and illustrated most of the important accounting principles currently employed in preparing financial statements. In this chapter, we focus on the following questions:

1. What criteria should a firm employ in selecting its accounting principles from among those that are considered "generally acceptable"?
2. What are the effects of using alternative accounting principles on the principal financial statements?
3. What are the effects of using alternative accounting principles on investors' decisions to invest their capital resources?
4. What is the process through which principles in accounting have been developed in the past and might be developed in the future?

An understanding of the significance and implications of alternative generally accepted accounting principles should make you a more effective reader and interpreter of published financial statements. Throughout this chapter, we use the terms *accounting principles*, *methods*, and *procedures* interchangeably.

■ SUMMARY OF GENERALLY ACCEPTED ACCOUNTING PRINCIPLES

A list of major currently acceptable accounting principles, most of which have been discussed in previous chapters, is presented in this section. These accounting principles might be classified into three broad groups based on the flexibility permitted to firms in selecting alternative methods of accounting for a specific item. In some instances, the firm has wide flexibility in choosing between alternative methods, such as in the selection of depreciation methods. In other instances, the specific conditions associated with a transaction or event dictate the method of accounting which must be used. For example, the method of accounting for investments in the common stock of other firms depends on the ownership percentage. The use of the purchase and pooling of interests methods of accounting for corporate acquisitions depends, among other factors, on the form of the consideration given by the acquiring firm. In a third category are instances where the firm has wide flexibility in selecting accounting principles for purposes of preparing its income tax return but limited flexibility in selecting methods for its financial statements. For example, a retail merchandising firm selling goods or services on an installment basis is permitted to use the installment basis of recognizing revenue in its tax return but generally cannot use this method in its financial statements. While a list of major currently acceptable accounting principles is given below, it should be remembered that a particular firm does not have wide flexibility in selecting its accounting methods in all instances.

Revenue Recognition Revenue may be recognized at the time goods are sold or services are rendered, as is typically done under the accrual basis of accounting, at the time cash is collected (installment basis), or as production progresses (percentage of completion method for long-term contracts).

Uncollectible Accounts A provision for uncollectible accounts can be made in the period when revenue is recognized (allowance method) or, if the amount of uncollectibles is not material, in the period when specific accounts are determined to be uncollectible (direct write-off method).

Inventories Inventories can be valued on one of several bases: acquisition cost, lower-of-acquisition-cost-or-market, standard cost, and, in the case of some by-products and precious minerals, net realizable value. When the cost of the specific goods sold cannot be, or is not, determined, a cost-flow assumption must be made. The cost-flow assumption may be FIFO, LIFO, or weighted-average, although LIFO must be used for financial reports if it is used for income tax returns.

Investments in Securities Investments in the common stock securities of other firms are accounted for using either the cost method or the equity method, or else consolidated statements are prepared. The method employed depends primarily on the percentage of outstanding shares which are held.

Machinery, Equipment, and Other Depreciable Assets These fixed assets may be depreciated using the straight-line, double-declining-balance, sum-of-the-years'-digits, or units-of-production method. Estimates of services lives of similar assets may differ among firms.

Intangible Resources Development Cost The costs incurred in creating intangible resources, such as a well-trained labor force or a good reputation among customers, can be treated as an expense in the year the costs are incurred, or capitalized and amortized over some period of years. Research and development costs, however, must be recognized as an expense in the year in which the costs are incurred.

Mineral Resources Exploration and Development Costs   The costs incurred in exploring for and developing potentially productive mineral deposits that are subsequently found to be nonproductive may be recognized as an expense in the period in which the site is determined to be nonproductive (successful efforts costing), or capitalized as part of the cost of productive sites and later recognized as an expense as minerals are extracted from the productive sites (full costing). The amount capitalized, however, cannot exceed the net realizable value of the minerals, or reserves, in the productive sites. These methods of accounting were not discussed earlier in this book. The distinction between successful efforts and full costing relates to whether exploration at each site is considered to be a separate accounting unit or "project," or whether it is part of a comprehensive exploration program resulting in a few productive sites and numerous unproductive ones.

Corporate Acquisitions and Goodwill   Corporate acquisitions may be accounted for using the purchase method or the pooling of interest method, depending on the type of consideration given by the acquiring company, the percentage of outstanding common stock acquired, and other factors. Any goodwill purchased in such acquisitions subsequent to October 31, 1970, must be amortized over a period not exceeding 40 years.

Leases   Rights to the use of property acquired under lease may be set up as an asset and subsequently amortized (financing method), or no recognition can be given to the lease except at the time that lease payments are made each period (operating method). Likewise, the lessor can set up the rights to receive future lease payments as a receivable at the inception of the lease (financing method), or no recognition can be given to the lease except to the extent that lease payments are received each period (operating method).

Premium or Discount on Receivables and Payables   Premium or discount on receivables and payables is amortized using the effective-interest method, although the straight-line method can be used if the results are not materially different.

Investment Tax Credits   A credit, or reduction, in income taxes is permitted for investments in certain depreciable assets, such as equipment, furniture, automobiles, and similar property. The credit is currently 10 percent of the cost of the property, although the rate has been changed several times by Congress. The credit reduces the amount of income tax which the firm must pay in the year the assets are acquired. For financial reporting purposes, the firm can recognize the credit as an immediate reduction in income tax expense (flow-through method), or the credit can be deferred and amortized over the life of the property which gave rise to the credit (deferral method).

Compensation in the Form of Stock Options   When options to purchase shares of stock are granted to officers and employees under qualified stock option plans in lieu of additional cash compensation, no compensation expense is reported. In contrast, firms that provide only cash compensation (no stock options) recognize the full amount paid or accrued as an expense of the period.

The preceding list of acceptable accounting principles is not intended to be exhaustive. Also, it should be remembered that a firm does not always have a choice in the methods which can be used. The factors which a firm might consider in selecting its accounting principles are discussed next.

■ THE FIRM'S DECISION TO SELECT ACCOUNTING PRINCIPLES

The methods of accounting used for income tax and financial reporting purposes generally do not have to be the same. (An exception is the requirement that if LIFO is used for income tax purposes, it must also be used for financial reporting.) Since the firm might pursue different objectives for financial and tax reporting, we discuss separately the selection of accounting principles for the two types of reports.

Financial Reporting Purposes

Accurate Presentation One of the criteria suggested in Chapter One for assessing the usefulness of accounting information was *accuracy in presentation* of the underlying events and transactions. This criterion might be used by the firm as a basis for selecting its methods of accounting. For example, assets have been defined as resources having future service potential and expenses as a measurement of the services consumed during the period. In applying the accuracy criterion, the firm would select the inventory cost-flow assumption and depreciation method which most accurately measured the pattern of services consumed during the period and the amount of services still available at the end of the period. As a basis for selecting accounting methods, this approach has at least one serious limitation. The notions of service potential and services consumed are seldom observable and therefore difficult to measure. Without this information, it is virtually impossible to determine which accounting principles lead to the most accurate presentation of the underlying events. This criterion might serve as a normative criterion toward which the development and selection of accounting principles should be directed.

Fair Presentation The standard, unqualified opinion of the independent accountant indicates that the financial statements "present fairly the results of operations, financial position, and changes in financial position" for the period. *Fair presentation* might also be used, and supposedly is used, as the reporting objective in choosing accounting methods. The fair presentation criterion suffers from the same limitation as the criterion of accurate presentation. Since flows of past and future benefits are difficult to measure, there are likely to be differences of opinion regarding which accounting principles provide a fair presentation for a particular firm. The independent accountant's opinion that the statements "present fairly . . . in conformity with generally accepted accounting principles" in effect means that a "fair presentation" results, by definition, so long as the methods used are in the list of those currently deemed acceptable. "Present fairly" is, then, merely a statement that the accounting methods used are generally accepted and appropriate in the circumstances.*

Conservatism   In choosing between alternative, generally acceptable, methods, the firm might select the set which provides the most conservative measure of net income. Considering the uncertainties involved in measuring benefits received as revenues and services consumed as expenses, others have suggested that a conservative measure of earnings should be provided, thereby reducing the possibility of misleading users of financial statements. As a criterion for selecting accounting principles, *conservatism* implies that methods should be chosen which minimize cumulative reported earnings. That is, expenses should be recognized as quickly as possible, and the recognition of revenue should be postponed as long as possible. This reporting objective would lead to selecting the double-declining-balance or sum-of-the-years'-digits depreciation method, selecting the LIFO cost-flow assumption if periods of rising prices are anticipated, and expensing of intangible development costs in the year incurred. The rationale for conservatism as a reporting objective has been challenged. To the extent that net income of earlier periods is smaller, earnings of later periods will tend to be larger. Also, it is conceivable that some statement users may be misled by earnings reports based on conservative reporting principles. Consider, for example, an investor who sells shares because he or she feels that the firm is not operating in a sufficiently profitable manner with the resources available, when earnings reported in a less conservative manner would not have induced the sale.

Profit Maximization   A reporting objective having the opposite effects to conservatism might be employed in selecting between alternative generally accepted accounting principles. Somewhat loosely termed *reported profit maximization,*[1] this criterion suggests the selection of accounting methods which maximize cumulative reported earnings. That is, revenue should be recognized as quickly as possible, and the recognition of expense should be postponed as long as possible. For example, the straight-line method of depreciation would be used and, when periods of rising prices were anticipated, the FIFO cost-flow assumption would be selected. Costs incurred in developing intangible resources would be capitalized as assets and amortized over some period of years. The use of profit maximization as a reporting objective is an extension of the notion that the firm is in business to generate profits and the firm should present as favorable a report on performance as possible within currently acceptable accounting methods. Profit maximiza-

---

* The AICPA released Statement on Auditing Standards No. 5 in July 1975. This statement is titled *The Meaning of "Present Fairly in Conformity With Generally Accepted Accounting Principles" in the Independent Auditor's Report.* It is too early to tell whether or not this Statement will have a substantial impact on firms' choices between alternative generally accepted accounting principles.

[1] The concept of profit maximization as a reporting objective is not the same as the profit maximization dictum of microeconomics.

tion is subject to a similar, but mirror-image, criticism as the use of conservatism as a reporting objective. Reporting income earlier under the profit maximization criterion tends to mean that less income will be reported later.

Income Smoothing   A final reporting objective which might be used in selecting accounting principles is referred to as *income smoothing*. This criterion suggests the selection of accounting methods which result in the smoothest earnings trend over time. As will be discussed later in this chapter, empirical research has shown that a relationship exists between changes in earnings and changes in stock prices. Advocates of income smoothing suggest that if a company can minimize fluctuations in earnings, then the perceived risk of investing in shares of its stock will be reduced and fluctuations in its stock price will be minimized. Note that this reporting criterion suggests that net income, not revenues and expenses individually, is the object of smoothing. As a result, the firm must consider the total pattern of its operations before selecting the appropriate accounting methods. For example, the straight-line method of depreciation may provide the smoothest amount of depreciation expense on a machine over its life. If, however, the productivity of the machine declines with age so that revenues decrease in later years, net income using the straight-line method may not provide the smoothest net income stream. In this case, perhaps the double-declining-balance or sum-of-the-years'-digits method should be used.

Summary   The principal message of this section is that accurate and fair presentation, while perhaps desirable reporting objectives, are not operational as bases for selecting accounting principles. As a result, firms are free to select from among the methods included in the set of generally acceptable accounting principles, using whatever reporting criterion they choose.

Where does this flexibility permitted in selecting accounting principles leave the user of financial statements? Accounting Principles Board Opinion No. 22[2] requires firms to disclose the accounting principles employed in preparing financial statements, either in a separate statement or as a note to the principal statements. An example of such disclosure for Ford Motor Company is presented in Exhibit 15.1. The effect of alternative accounting principles on investment decisions is discussed later in the chapter.

Income Tax Reporting Purposes

In selecting accounting procedures for income tax purposes, the corporation's objective should be to select those methods which minimize the present value of the stream of income tax payments. The operational rule, sometimes called the *least and latest rule*, is to pay the least amount of taxes as late as possible within the law. The desirability of this rule was discussed at somewhat greater length in Chapter Ten. The least and latest rule generally translates into a policy of recognizing expenses as quickly as possible and postponing the recognition of revenue as long as possible. This policy might be altered somewhat if income tax

---

[2] Opinion No. 22, Accounting Principles Board, AICPA, April 1972.

EXHIBIT 15.1
Ford Motor Company and Consolidated Subsidiaries
Note Describing Accounting Policies

Note 1. Accounting Policies

The following is a summary of certain significant accounting policies followed in the preparation of these financial statements. The policies conform to generally accepted accounting principles and have been consistently applied.

Principles of Consolidation: the consolidated financial statements include the accounts of the Company and all of its domestic and foreign subsidiaries, except for the financing, insurance, real estate and dealership subsidiaries, which are included on an equity basis.

Foreign Currency Translation: the general policy followed in the translation of foreign currency items is to state assets (except net property), liabilities and reserves at rates of exchange prevailing at the end of the period. Net property is translated at the rates in effect on the dates of acquisition of the related assets. Earnings are translated at rates of exchange in effect during the period, adjusted to reflect depreciation and amortization based on historical dollar costs. When more than one exchange rate for a particular currency exists, the rate applicable to remittance of dividends is used to translate foreign currency items. Normal gains and losses on exchange adjustments are included in current income; abnormal gains or losses may be charged or credited, as appropriate, to the reserve for foreign operations.

Depreciation and Amortization: depreciation is computed substantially by use of accelerated methods that result in accumulated depreciation of approximately two-thirds of asset cost during the first half of the assets' estimated useful lives.

The costs of special tools are amortized over periods of time representing the short productive use of such tools.

Pre-production operating costs incurred in connection with new facilities are expensed as incurred.

Advertising and Sales Promotion: advertising and sales promotion costs are expensed as incurred.

Retirement Plan Costs: current service costs are accrued and funded currently. Prior service costs are amortized and funded over periods of not more than 30 years from the dates such costs were established.

Product Warranty Costs: anticipated costs related to product warranty are expensed at the time of the sale of the products.

Research and Development Costs: costs of research and development activities are expensed as incurred.

Investment Tax Credits: investment tax credits are deferred and amortized over the useful lives of the related assets.

Inventory Valuation: inventories are stated at the lower of cost or market, with cost determined substantially on a first-in, first-out basis.

Excess of Cost of Investments in Consolidated Subsidiaries Over Equities in Net Assets: the excess of cost of investments in consolidated subsidiaries over equities in net assets acquired, all of which originated prior to 1965, is not being amortized because, in the opinion of management, there has been no decrease in value.

rates are expected to change, if the firm had losses in earlier years, or if the firm is a sole proprietorship or partnership where earnings are subject to graduated income tax rates.

The desire to recognize expenses as quickly as possible suggests the adoption of the LIFO inventory cost-flow assumption, accelerated depreciation methods (either double-declining-balance or sum-of-the-years'-digits), and immediate expensing of research and development, advertising, and similar costs. Using the installment basis of recognizing revenue is generally desirable for income tax purposes where permitted by the Internal Revenue Code and Regulations, since it results in postponing the recognition of revenue and the resulting income tax payments until cash is collected.

■ AN ILLUSTRATION OF THE EFFECTS OF ALTERNATIVE ACCOUNTING PRINCIPLES ON A SET OF FINANCIAL STATEMENTS

In this section, we illustrate the effects of using different accounting principles on a set of financial statements. The illustration has been constructed so that the accounting principles employed create significant differences in the financial statements. Therefore, inferences should not be drawn about the usual magnitude of the effects of alternative methods from this example.

The Scenario

On January 1, 1976, two corporations are formed to operate merchandising businesses. The two firms are alike in all respects except for their methods of accounting. Conservative Company chooses the accounting principles that will minimize its reported net income. High Flyer Company chooses the accounting principles that will maximize its reported net income. The following events occur during 1976.

1. Both corporations issue 2 million shares of $10 par value stock on January 1, 1976, for $20 million cash.
2. Both firms acquire equipment on January 1, 1976, for $14 million cash. The equipment is estimated to have a 10-year life and zero salvage value.
3. Both firms make the following purchases of merchandise inventory.

DATE	UNITS PURCHASED		UNIT PRICE	COST OF PURCHASES
January 1	170,000	@	$60	$10,200,000
May 1	190,000	@	$63	11,970,000
September 1	200,000	@	$66	13,200,000
Total	560,000			$35,370,000

4. During the year, both firms sell 420,000 units at an average price of $100 each. All sales are made for cash.
5. During the year, both firms have selling, general, and administrative expenses, excluding depreciation and officers' compensation, of $6.6 million.
6. At the end of the year, both companies provide bonuses of $240,000 to officers in addition to the $700,000 salary paid to them during the year. Conservative Company pays cash bonuses of $240,000, while High Flyer Company awards qualified options for purchasing shares of common stock to its officers. Comparable options have a market value of $240,000.

Accounting Principles Employed

The methods of accounting used by each firm in preparing its financial statements are described below.

Inventory Cost-Flow Assumption Conservative Company makes a LIFO cost-flow assumption, while High Flyer Company makes a FIFO assumption. The method chosen by each firm is used for both its financial reports and income tax returns. Since the beginning inventory is zero, the cost of goods available for sale by each firm is equal to the purchases during the year of $35,370,000. Both firms have 140,000 units in ending inventory. Conservative Company therefore reports a cost of goods sold of $26,970,000 [= $35,370,000 − (140,000 × $60)], while High Flyer Company reports a cost of goods sold of $26,130,000 [= $35,370,000 − (140,000 × $66)]. Income tax regulations require a firm to use LIFO in its financial reports if it uses LIFO for its tax return. High Flyer Company desires not to use LIFO in its financial reports and therefore foregoes the tax savings opportunities from using it for tax purposes.

Depreciation Conservative Company decides to depreciate its equipment using the double-declining-balance method on both its tax return and in its financial statements. High Flyer Company decides to use the straight-line method in reporting income to stockholders but the double-declining-balance method in its tax return. Conservative Company therefore reports depreciation expense of $2.8 million (= 2 × 1/10 × $14,000,000), while High Flyer Company reports depreciation expense of $1.4 million (= 1/10 × $14,000,000) to stockholders and $2.8 million on its tax return.

Officers' Bonuses Conservative Company reports the $240,000 cash bonus paid as an expense during 1976, while High Flyer Company reports no expense for the stock options granted. Under generally accepted accounting principles, the fair market value of qualified stock options granted to employees is not shown as an expense.

Investment Tax Credit Since both firms purchased long-term, depreciable equipment costing $14 million, each is entitled to a tax reduction or credit of $1.4 million (= .10 × $14,000,000) in the taxes otherwise payable for 1976. On its financial statements to stockholders, Conservative Company chooses to report the benefits of the tax reduction over the 10-year life of the equipment that gave rise to the tax reduction (deferral method), while High Flyer Company reports the entire benefit of the tax reduction in determining net income reported to stockholders (flow-through method) for 1976.

Comparative Income Statements

Exhibit 15.2 presents comparative income statements for Conservative Company and High Flyer Company for the year ending December 31, 1976. Because Conservative Company reports the same revenues and expenses on both its financial statements and income tax return, its taxable income is the same as reported income before taxes. High Flyer Company reports larger deductions from revenues on the income tax return than it reports to stockholders, and one of these differences—for depreciation on equipment—is viewed as a timing difference. A portion of the income tax expense shown on the income statement of High Flyer Company is not payable currently, and therefore a deferred tax liability will appear on the balance sheet. In this illustration, net income and earnings per share of

EXHIBIT 15.2
Comparative Income Statements Based on Different
Accounting Principles
For the Year Ending December 31, 1976
(dollar amounts shown in thousands except for per-share amounts)

	CONSERVATIVE COMPANY		HIGH FLYER COMPANY	
	Financial Statement	Tax Return	Financial Statement	Tax Return
Sales Revenue	$42,000	$42,000	$42,000	$42,000
Expenses:				
Cost of Goods Sold	$26,970	$26,970	$26,130	$26,130
Depreciation on Equipment	2,800	2,800	1,400[b]	2,800[b]
Officers' Compensation:				
Salaries	700	700	700	700
Cash Bonuses	240	240	—	—
Stock Options	—	—	0	0
Other Selling, General, and Administrative . . .	6,600	6,600	6,600	6,600
Expenses Before Income Taxes	$37,310	$37,310	$34,830	$36,230
Net Income Before Income Taxes	$ 4,690	$ 4,690	$ 7,170	$ 5,770
Income Tax Expense[a]	2,105		2,035	
Net Income	$ 2,585		$ 5,135	
Earnings per Share (2,000,000 Shares Outstanding)	$1.29		$2.57	

[a]Computation of Income Tax Expense:

Income Before Taxes	$ 4,690	$ 4,690	$ 7,170	$ 5,770
Income Tax on Current Income (22 percent of first $25,000 plus 48 percent of remainder)	$ 2,245	$ 2,245	$ 3,435	$ 2,763
Less: Tax Credit for Investment in Equipment	140	1,400	1,400	1,400
Income Tax Expense	$ 2,105		$ 2,035	
Income Tax Currently Payable		$ 845		$ 1,363
Deferred Investment Tax Credit ($1,400 — $140) .	$ 1,260			

[b]Income Taxes Deferred by Timing Differences for Depreciation [.48 $\times$ ($2,800 — $1,400)] . . . . . $ 672

High Flyer Company are almost double the amounts shown for Conservative Company.

Comparative Balance Sheets

Exhibit 15.3 presents comparative balance sheets for Conservative Company and High Flyer Company as of December 31, 1976. The individual asset accounts as well as total assets of Conservative Company are stated at lower amounts than

EXHIBIT 15.3
Comparative Balance Sheets Based on Alternative
Accounting Principles
December 31, 1976

ASSETS

	(amounts shown in thousands)	
	Conservative Company	High Flyer Company
Cash	$ 4,245	$ 3,967
Merchandise Inventory	8,400	9,240
Equipment (at acquisition cost)	14,000	14,000
Less: Accumulated Depreciation	(2,800)	(1,400)
Total Assets	$23,845	$25,807

EQUITIES

Deferred Investment Tax Credits	$ 1,260	—
Deferred Income Taxes	—	$ 672
Common Stock	20,000	20,000
Retained Earnings	2,585	5,135
Total Equities	$23,845	$25,807

those of High Flyer Company. The only real difference between the economic positions of each company is the amount of cash. The difference in the amount of cash is attributable to the payment of different amounts of income taxes by the two firms and to Conservative Company's payment of a cash bonus to officers rather than giving stock options. The differences in the amounts at which the remaining assets are stated are attributable to the different accounting methods used by the two companies. The amounts shown for merchandise inventory and equipment net of depreciation of Conservative Company are smaller than the corresponding amounts for High Flyer Company because a larger portion of the costs incurred during the period by Conservative Company is recognized as an expense.

In the equities portion of the balance sheet, Conservative Company shows deferred investment tax credits, reflecting its decision to recognize the current reduction in income taxes payable as an element of income over the life of the property. Each year $140,000 (= $1,400,000/10) will be amortized and shown as a reduction in income tax expense. (Income taxes *payable* in future years are not affected). High Flyer Company used the flow-through method and recognized the full $1.4 million of tax savings in the determination of net income for 1976. High Flyer Company also reports deferred income taxes on the balance sheet resulting from differences in the timing of depreciation on equipment in the financial statements and income tax return.

Note the effect of using alternative accounting principles on the ratio, rate of return on total assets. Conservative Company reports a smaller amount of net income and also a smaller amount of total assets. One might expect the rate of return on total assets of the two firms to more closely approximate each other than either net income or total assets individually. Significant differences in the ratio for the two firms are still observable, however. The rate of return on total assets of Conservative Company is 11.8 percent [= $2,585,000/($20,000,000 + $23,845,000/2)] and of High Flyer Company is 22.4 percent [= $5,135,000/ ($20,000,000 + $25,807,000/2)].

Comparative Statements of Changes in Financial Position

Exhibit 15.4 presents comparative statements of changes in financial position for Conservative Company and High Flyer Company. The amount of working capital provided by operations of High Flyer Company is larger than for Conservative Company. The difference is more than accounted for by the difference in

EXHIBIT 15.4
Comparative Statements of Changes in Financial Position
For the Year Ending December 31, 1976

	(amounts shown in thousands)	
	Conservative Company	High Flyer Company
Sources of Working Capital:		
Net Income	$ 2,585	$ 5,135
Add Depreciation Expense Not Using Working Capital	2,800	1,400
Add Excess of Investment Tax Credit Reducing Current Taxes Payable Over Credit Recognized in Determining Net Income ($1,400 — $140)	1,260	—
Add Portion of Income Tax Expense Not Payable Currently	—	672
Working Capital Provided by Operations	$ 6,645	$ 7,207
Issuance of Common Stock	20,000	20,000
Total Sources of Working Capital	$26,645	$27,207
Uses of Working Capital:		
Purchase of Equipment	14,000	14,000
Increase in Working Capital	$12,645	$13,207

ANALYSIS OF INCREASES IN WORKING CAPITAL

Cash	$ 4,245	$ 3,967
Merchandise Inventory	8,400	9,240
Increase in Working Capital	$12,645	$13,207

inventory cost-flow assumptions employed. High Flyer Company, using FIFO, reported a smaller amount for cost of goods sold and thereby used a smaller amount of working capital in generating revenues. The remaining difference between the amounts reported as working capital provided by operations of the two firms is attributable to the cash bonus paid by Conservative Company and the differing amount of income taxes paid. Unlike the income statement and balance sheet, the accounting principles which create differences between the amounts of working capital provided by operations and in the increases or decreases in working capital for the year are only those principles affecting working capital accounts (for example, inventory valuation method and cost-flow assumption treatment of uncollectible accounts). The effects of using different accounting principles for nonworking capital accounts are eliminated from this statement through the process of adding and subtracting amounts to net income to obtain working capital provided by operations. The use of alternative accounting principles generally creates smaller differences in the amounts of working capital provided by operations than in the amounts reported as net income.

Moral of the Illustration

In order to interpret published financial statements, you must be aware of which accounting principles from the set of alternative generally accepted accounting principles are used. When reports of several companies are compared, the amounts shown should be adjusted where possible for the different accounting methods used. The notes to the financial statements will disclose the accounting methods used, but not necessarily the data required to make appropriate adjustments.

■ ASSESSING THE EFFECTS OF ALTERNATIVE ACCOUNTING PRINCIPLES ON INVESTMENT DECISIONS

In previous sections of this chapter, emphasis has been given to the flexibility which firms have in selecting accounting procedures and to the possible effects of using different accounting procedures on the financial statements. We now focus briefly on a related and important question: do investors accept financial statement information as presented, or do they somehow filter out all or most of the differences in the financial statements of various firms resulting from differences in the methods of accounting employed? If investors accept financial statement information in the form presented without adjustments for the methods of accounting used, then two firms otherwise identical except for the accounting procedures employed might receive a disproportionate amount of capital funds. Thus, the use of alternative accounting principles could lead to a misallocation of resources in the economy. On the other hand, if investors make adjustments for the different accounting procedures in analyzing the financial statements of various firms, then perhaps the concern over the variety of acceptable accounting principles is excessive. If investors do make such adjustments, then increased disclosure of the procedures followed may be more important than greater uniformity in accounting principles.

The question as to the effect of alternative accounting principles on investment decisions has been the subject of extensive debate among public accountants, academicians, personnel in government agencies, and financial statement users.

Those who believe that investors can be misled point to examples where the market prices of particular firms' shares of stock have decreased dramatically after the effects of using specific accounting procedures have been carefully analyzed and reported in the financial press.[3] In these examples, however, it is often difficult to determine if the price change is attributable to the disclosure of the effects of using particular accounting procedures or to other, more temporary factors affecting the specific firm, its industry, or all firms in the economy. Also, it is difficult to generalize on the effects of using alternative accounting principles on investment decisions from several, perhaps isolated and anecdotal, examples.

An expanding number of empirical research studies, on the other hand, have provided support for the view that investors at the aggregate market level are not misled by the accounting methods employed. This research has developed from the theory and empirical evidence that the stock market is efficient, in the sense that market prices adjust quickly and in an unbiased manner to new information.[4] Unlike the examples supporting the view that investors are misled, these empirical studies have been based on data for a large number of firms spanning long time periods. Also, an effort is made in these studies to control for the effects of economy-wide and industry effects on market price changes.

Several studies have shown that changes in earnings and changes in market prices are associated and, therefore, indicate that information contained in the financial statements is used by investors in making their resource allocation decisions.[5] Several studies have examined the effects of *changes* in the methods of accounting on market prices. Changes in accounting methods which have no real or economic effects have been shown to have little influence on market prices.[6]

---

[3] For several examples, see Abraham Briloff, *Unaccountable Accounting* (New York: Harper & Row, 1972).

[4] See Eugene F. Fama, "Efficient Capital Markets: A Review of Theory and Empirical Work," *Journal of Finance* (May 1970), 383–417.

[5] See, for example, Raymond J. Ball and Philip Brown, "An Empirical Evaluation of Accounting Income Numbers," *Journal of Accounting Research* (Autumn 1968), 159–173; William H. Beaver, "The Information Content of Annual Earnings Announcements," *Empirical Research in Accounting: Selected Studies, 1968*, Supplement to Vol. 6, *Journal of Accounting Research*, pp. 67–92; Robert G. May, "The Influence of Quarterly Earnings Announcements on Investor Decisions as Reflected in Common Stock Price Changes," *Empirical Research in Accounting: Selected Studies, 1971*, Supplement to Vol. 9, *Journal of Accounting Research*, pp. 119–163.

[6] See, for example, Raymond J. Ball, "Changes in Accounting Techniques and Stock Prices," *Empirical Research in Accounting: Selected Studies, 1972*, Supplement to Vol. 10, *Journal of Accounting Research*, pp. 1–38; Robert S. Kaplan and Richard Roll, "Investor Evaluation of Accounting Information: Some Empirical Evidence," *Journal of Business* (April 1972), 225–257; Shyam Sunder, "Relationships Between Accounting Changes and Stock Prices: Problems of Measurement and Some Empirical Evidence," *Empirical Research in Accounting: Selected Studies, 1973*, Supplement to Vol. 11, *Journal of Accounting Research*.

A third group of studies looked at *differences* in the methods of accounting across firms to assess the effects on investment decisions. The results of this last group of studies have been mixed, with several studies supporting the position that investors are misled and several studies supporting the position that they are not misled.[7] The methodology employed in most studies in this third group has been extensively criticized, so the full implications are not clear, at least to us.

Research into the question regarding the effects of alternative accounting principles on investment decisions has not progressed sufficiently for any consensus to have been reached. We have briefly described some of the research that has been conducted to emphasize an important point. It is not obvious, as it might first appear, that the current flexibility permitted firms in selecting accounting principles necessarily misleads investors and results in a misallocation of resources. In fact, there is an impressive and growing amount of evidence to the contrary.[8]

■ DEVELOPMENT OF PRINCIPLES IN ACCOUNTING

In previous sections of this chapter, we have (**1**) provided a summary of currently acceptable accounting principles, (**2**) described the factors which a firm might consider in selecting its methods of accounting, (**3**) illustrated the effects of alternative methods on a set of financial statements, and (**4**) considered briefly the question of whether investors correct for earnings differences between firms attributable to the accounting principles used when making investment decisions. In this final section, we discuss briefly the process through which principles are developed in accounting, and suggest some directions for their future development.

Nature of Principles in Accounting

Principles in accounting differ from those in fields such as physics and mathematics. In physics and other natural sciences, the criterion for evaluating a principle is the degree to which the predictions indicated by the principle or theory correspond with physically observed phenomena. In mathematics, a principle (or theorem) is judged on its internal consistency with the structure of definitions and underlying axioms. In accounting, principles are judged on their general acceptability by preparers and users of accounting reports. Unlike the physical sciences, principles in accounting do not naturally exist awaiting discovery. Unlike

[7] See, for example, Robert E. Jensen, "An Experimental Design for Study of Effects of Accounting Variations in Decision Making," *Journal of Accounting Research* (Autumn 1966), 224–238; Thomas R. Dyckman, "On the Investment Decision," *The Accounting Review* (April 1964), 285–295; John L. O'Donnell, "Relationships Between Reported Earnings and Stock Prices in the Electric Utility Industry," *Accounting Review* (January 1965), pp. 135–143.

[8] For a description of the theoretical framework and a summary of the empirical work behind this position, see Nicholas J. Gonedes and Nicholas Dopuch, "Capital Market Equilibrium, Information-Production, and Selecting Accounting Techniques: Theoretical Framework and Review of Empirical Work," *Studies on Financial Accounting Objectives: 1974*, Supplement to Vol. 12, *Journal of Accounting Research*, pp. 48–129.

mathematics, there is no structure of definitions and concepts in accounting that can be unambiguously used in developing accounting principles.

These observations suggest that the development of principles in accounting is essentially a political process.[9] Various persons or groups have power, or authority, in the decision process which yields generally accepted accounting principles. Some of the more important participants are described below.

Congress   In the Securities Act of 1933, the Congress accepted the ultimate legal authority to prescribe the methods of accounting used in preparing financial statements for stockholders of publicly held corporations. Congress has delegated its authority to the Securities and Exchange Commission (SEC), an agency of the federal government. While the SEC has legal authority to prescribe accounting principles, since 1936 it has delegated most of the responsibility for developing accounting principles to the accounting profession.[10] In most cases, the SEC serves as an advisor or consultant on proposed accounting procedures. In a few instances, the SEC has effectively exerted its legal authority by disagreeing with positions taken within the accounting profession.

Accounting Profession   The accounting profession is composed of practicing accountants, financial managers, controllers, academicians, and others. Each of these groups has its own professional organization or association (American Institute of Certified Public Accountants, National Association of Accountants, Financial Executives Institute, American Accounting Association). The professional organizations sometimes express positions, or opinions, on proposed accounting principles. Most of the specification of accounting principles has been carried out, however, by officially appointed committees or boards within the accounting profession. Between 1938 and 1959, the Committee on Accounting Procedure of the American Institute of Certified Public Accountants issued Bulletins on various topics. Between 1959 and 1973, the Accounting Principles Board (APB) of the American Institute of Certified Public Accountants issued Opinions. These Bulletins and Opinions were considered to constitute generally accepted accounting principles. The APB was composed of individuals from within the accounting profession, with heavy representation from public accounting firms.

Since mid-1973, the Financial Accounting Standards Board (FASB) has been the principal agency outside of the federal government responsible for developing accounting principles. The FASB differs from the APB in two important respects. First, the FASB includes substantial representation from several groups of statement users in addition to members from the public accounting profession. Second, the members of the FASB are employed on a full-time basis and have severed all relations with their previous firms or universities. This severance of relations increases the independence of Board members, and reduces chances for undue

---

[9] For an elaboration on this viewpoint, see Charles T. Horngren, "The Marketing of Accounting Standards," *Journal of Accountancy* (October 1973), 61–66.

[10] Accounting Series Release No. 4, Securities and Exchange Commission, 1938. The SEC reaffirmed its delegation of responsibility by recognizing the Financial Accounting Standards Board in Accounting Series Release No. 150, December 1973.

influence by their previous employers. The FASB periodically issues Statements on Financial Accounting Standards which have the authority of being considered generally accepted accounting principles.

Financial Statement Users   The FASB seeks representation from those doing security analysis and thus some representation from user interests. Professional organizations of financial statement users, such as the Financial Analysts Federation and the Investment Bankers Association, frequently comment on proposed accounting principles to the FASB and SEC. Any individual can, of course, comment on existing or proposed accounting principles to the FASB, SEC, or a member of Congress.

Illustration of the Political Process   The SEC and the FASB both play an important role in the current power structure for developing accounting principles. The amount of authority which the SEC exercises and the amount which is delegated to the FASB varies with the problem area under consideration and with the pressure exerted on the SEC by Congress and others.

An example of the manner in which the political process functions in developing generally accepted accounting principles is described by Horngren,[11] a former member of the Accounting Principles Board. The accounting principle of concern in his discussion is the valuation of marketable securities using current market prices.

> The heart of the issue concerning marketable securities deals with when portfolio gains and losses should be recognized. There is a variety of views ranging from predominant present practice (whereby only realized gains and losses are included in income) to some version of spreading (whereby all gains and losses from changes in market prices are included in income but on some three- to ten-year moving-average, long-term yield basis) to a flow-through approach (whereby all gains and losses are included in income as the prices of marketable securities fluctuate from quarter to quarter).
>
> Another set of issues concerns whether portfolio losses or gains belong in an income statement in the first place. Instead, some accountants believe that a two-statement approach is needed. If adopted, a separate statement of realized and unrealized gains would be used.
>
> An intensive study of this topic was begun in September 1968. Heavy interaction persisted between the APB and all interested parties, particularly representatives of the insurance industry, whose income statements would be dramatically affected by any new accounting standards. In May 1971, there was a two-day public hearing on the issues.
>
> After about three years of spasmodic deliberations, the APB was ready to issue an exposure draft of an Opinion. The Board had narrowed its preferences to two methods using one income statement: either flow-through or spreading. In September 1971, the Board approved a draft

---

[11] Horngren, pp. 63–64.

favoring flow-through. The draft was to be "mini-exposed" to the SEC, the insurance industry and others who had been actively involved. The intention of the Board was to have full public exposure of the Opinion after the October APB meeting.

The insurance companies were bitterly opposed to flcw-through. They blitzkrieged Washington. The SEC, armed with its own preferences and buttressed by industry reactions, informed the APB that it could not support flow-through. At this point, flow-through was a dead duck because higher management (the SEC) had, in effect, overruled the APB.

At its October meeting, the APB again discussed the topic. Because flow-through was no longer an acceptable alternative, the Board changed its preferences to either spreading or a two-statement approach. The Board voted in favor of a two-statement approach, although strong voices were raised in support of spreading. In November, these alternatives were explored with the SEC and the insurance industry. At its December meeting, the Board was informed that the fire and casualty companies had also strongly objected to the spreading method. One potent spokesman for the SEC found some merit in the spreading method, but he informed the Board that the SEC would not impose it or any solution on an industry that was adamantly opposed to it. So spreading was dead.

The Board then discussed two alternatives: (1) some version of a two-statement method and (2) a modification of predominant current practice whereby all companies in all industries would show marketable securities at market value in the balance sheet, unrealized gains and losses in stockholders' equity, and only realized gains and losses in the income statement. However, the fire and casualty companies also vigorously opposed the two-statement method.

Note how the feasible alternatives changed in response to the likelihood of acceptability. The constraints became more binding as the months wore on:

1. *September—flow through or spreading*
2. *October—spreading or two-statement*
3. *December—two-statement or slight modification of status quo.*

Discussions of various versions of the December alternatives were renewed in early 1972. But the Board could not resolve the issues and the SEC was noncommittal on anything except "no flow-through." During the course of the discussions, the top managements of 15 or 20 large insurance companies met together about the issue more than once and also with the SEC commissioners at least once.

The marketable securities scenario was concluded by an APB report to the SEC in March 1972 that summarized the APB deliberations and the alternatives. However, the report offered no preferred solution.

Future Development of Accounting Principles

Unless Congress or the SEC unexpectedly decides to exert its legal authority, we see little reason for the future development of accounting principles to differ materially from that in the past. The process will continue to be a political one, with opposing viewpoints attempting to exert influence on the decision process. Positions taken or opinions rendered by participants in this process must be not only carefully developed but also effectively marketed if the positions are to become generally acceptable to the persons involved in preparing and using financial statements.

To provide some guidance or direction to persons involved in developing accounting principles, we feel that a broad set of financial statement objectives is desirable. Several efforts have been made to enunciate such a set of objectives.[12] It must be recognized, however, that developing a set of financial statement objectives is also a political process.

■ SUMMARY

The structure of accounting principles might be depicted as shown in Figure 15.1. The *universe* of possible accounting principles is encircled by a dashed line because of the difficulty in determining the relative size, or boundaries, of circle **A**. The process of specifying the principles which are designated as *generally acceptable* (the subset of principles from circle **A** represented by circle **B**) is political in nature. Congress and the Securities and Exchange Commission have the legal authority to make the selection, but most of the responsibility for doing so has been delegated to the Financial Accounting Standards Board. The individual firm's selection of accounting principles (the subset of principles from circle **B** represented by circle **C**) might be based on a criterion of accurate or fair presentation. However, since benefits received and services consumed are seldom observable events and are therefore difficult to measure, consensus on which generally accepted accounting principles provide an accurate or fair presentation is difficult to obtain. This chapter suggests that firms might pursue a specific reporting ob-

FIGURE 15.1
Structure of Accounting Principles

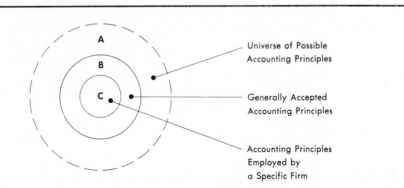

12 Accounting Principles Board Statement No. 4, "Basic Concepts and Accounting Principles Underlying Financial Statements of Business Enterprises," (AICPA, 1970); Study Group on the Objectives of Financial Statements, "Objectives of Financial Statements," (AICPA, 1973).

jective, such as conservatism, profit maximization, or income smoothing, in selecting its accounting principles.

Before we can know whether circle **B** should be widened or narrowed, we must learn whether investors accept financial statement information as presented or whether investors make adjustments to recognize the effects of using alternative accounting principles. This question has been and continues to be the subject of extensive research.

QUESTIONS AND PROBLEMS

1. Review the meaning of the following concepts or terms discussed in this chapter.
   a. Generally accepted accounting principles.
   b. Full costing.
   c. Successful efforts costing.
   d. Investment tax credit.
   e. Flow-through method.
   f. Deferral method.
   g. Accurate presentation.
   h. Fair presentation.
   i. Conservatism.
   j. Profit maximization.
   k. Income smoothing.
   l. Least and latest rule.
   m. Statement of accounting policies.
   n. Development of accounting principles is a political process.

2. Indicate the generally accepted accounting principle, or method, described in each of the following statements.
   a. This inventory cost-flow assumption results in reporting the largest net income during periods of rising prices.
   b. This method of accounting for uncollectible accounts recognizes the implied income reduction in the period of sale.
   c. This method of accounting for long-term investments in the securities of unconsolidated subsidiaries or other corporations usually requires an adjustment to net income to determine working capital provided by operations in the statement of changes in financial position.
   d. This method of accounting for long-term leases by the lessee gives rise to a noncurrent liability.
   e. The presence of goodwill expense on the income statement indicates that a corporate acquisition has been accounted for using this method.
   f. This inventory cost-flow assumption results in approximately the same balance sheet amount as the FIFO flow assumption.
   g. This method of amortizing bond premium or discount provides a uniform annual rate of interest revenue or expense over the life of the bond.
   h. During periods of rising prices, this inventory valuation basis produces approximately the same results as the acquisition-cost valuation basis.
   i. When specific customers' accounts are deemed uncollectible and written off, this method of accounting results in a decrease in the current ratio.
   j. This method of depreciation generally provides the largest amounts of depreciation expense during the first several years of an asset's life.

k. The method of recognizing income from long-term contracts generally results in the least fluctuation in earnings over several periods.

l. When specific customers' accounts are deemed uncollectible and are written off, this method of accounting has no effect on working capital.

m. When used in determining taxable income, this inventory cost-flow assumption must also be used in determining net income reported to stockholders.

n. Under this method of accounting for long-term leases of equipment by the lessor, an amount for depreciation expense on the leased equipment will appear on the income statement.

o. This method of amortizing bond premium or discount provides a uniform annual amount of interest revenue or expense over the life of the bonds.

3. Indicate the accounting principle, or procedure, apparently being used to record each of the following independent transactions.

a.	Losses from Uncollectible Accounts	X	
	Accounts Receivable		X
b.	Cash	X	
	Dividend Income		X
c.	Income Taxes Payable—Current	X	
	Deferred Investment Tax Credits		X
d.	Loss from Price Declines in Marketable Securities	X	
	Marketable Securities		X
e.	Goodwill Amortization Expense	X	
	Goodwill		X
f.	Cash	X	
	Investment in Unconsolidated Subsidiary		X
	Dividend declared and received from unconsolidated subsidiary		
g.	Sales, Uncollectible Accounts Adjustment	X	
	Allowance for Uncollectible Accounts		X
h.	Lease Expense	X	
	Cash		X
i.	Advertising Expense	X	
	Deferred Advertising Costs		X
j.	Investment in Unconsolidated Subsidiary	X	
	Equity in Earnings of Unconsolidated Subsidiary		X
k.	Allowance for Uncollectible Accounts	X	
	Accounts Receivable		X
l.	Loss from Price Decline of Inventories	X	
	Merchandise Inventories		X
m.	Income Taxes Payable—Current	X	
	Income Tax Expense (from Investment Credit)		X
n.	Liability under Long-Term Lease	X	
	Interest Expense	X	
	Cash		X

4. Indicate the accounting principle that provides the most conservative measure of earnings in each of the following cases.

a. FIFO, LIFO, or weighted-average cost-flow assumption for inventories during periods of rising prices.

b. FIFO, LIFO, or weighted-average cost-flow assumption for inventories during periods of declining prices.

c. Cost or equity method of accounting for long-term investments in the securities of unconsolidated subsidiaries where dividends declared by the subsidiary are less than its earnings.

d. Sum-of-the-years'-digits or straight-line depreciation method during the first one-third of an asset's life.

e. Sum-of-the-years'-digits or straight-line depreciation method during the last one-third of an asset's life.

f. The deferral or flow-through method of accounting for the investment tax credit in the year qualifying assets are acquired.

g. The valuation of inventories at acquisition cost or lower-of-cost-or-market.

h. Cost or equity method of accounting for long-term investments in the securities of unconsolidated subsidiaries where the investee realizes net losses and does not pay dividends.

i. The purchase or pooling of interests method of accounting for corporate acquisitions where the market value of the consideration given by the acquiring company exceeds the book value of the acquired company's net assets.

j. The effective interest or straight-line method of amortizing bond premium in the first year that bonds are outstanding.

k. The effective interest or straight-line method of amortizing bond discount in the first year that bonds are outstanding.

5. The summary of significant accounting policies appearing in recent annual reports of Anheuser-Busch, Incorporated, and Fuqua Industries, Incorporated, are presented below. Which firm appears to be using accounting methods resulting in the more conservative measure of earnings? Explain.

■ ANHEUSER-BUSCH, INCORPORATED SUMMARY OF SIGNIFICANT ACCOUNTING POLICIES

This summary of significant accounting principles and policies of Anheuser-Busch, Inc., and its consolidated subsidiaries is presented to assist in evaluating the company's financial statements included in this report. These principles and policies conform to generally accepted accounting principles and have been consistently followed by the company in all material respects.

Principles of Consolidation

The consolidated financial statements include the company and all its subsidiaries. Certain subsidiaries which are not an integral part of the company's primary operations are included on an equity basis.

Sales and Accounts Receivable

Sales and income are recognized at the time the product is shipped and accounts receivable are recorded at that time.

Inventories and Production Costs

Inventories are valued at the lower of cost or market. Cost of raw materials and supplies is determined under the last-in, first-out and average cost methods. Cost of work in process and finished goods is based principally on standard costs, which approximate actual manufacturing and raw material cost, adjusted for last-in, first-out valuation of certain raw materials. Approximately one-half of total inventories (principally brewing raw materials) are valued under the last-in, first-out method.

Plant and Equipment

Plant and equipment is carried at cost and includes expenditures for new facilities and those which substantially increase the useful lives of existing plant and equipment. Maintenance, repairs and minor renewals are expensed as incurred. When properties are retired or otherwise disposed of, the related cost and accumulated depreciation are removed from the respective accounts and any profit or loss on disposition is credited or charged to income.

The company provides for depreciation of plant and equipment on methods and at rates designed to amortize the cost of such equipment over its useful life. Depreciation is computed principally on the sum-of-the-years'-digits method for property acquired after December 31, 1953, and on the straight-line method for property acquired prior to that date.

A portion of the land held by the company is for investment purposes and is not an integral part of the company's primary operations. This land has been classified in the balance sheet as investment properties.

Income Taxes

The provision for income taxes is based on elements of income and expense as reported in the Statement of Income. The company has elected to utilize certain provisions of federal income tax laws and regulations to reduce current taxes payable, the primary item being the calculation of depreciation for tax purposes on the basis of shorter lives permitted by the Treasury Department. The resulting tax benefit has been deferred and will be recognized in the provision for income taxes at such time as depreciation reported in the Statement of Income exceeds that taken for income tax purposes.

The company follows the practice of adding the investment tax credit to income over the productive lives of the assets generating such credit, rather than in the year in which the assets are placed in service. Accordingly, benefits realized from the investment tax credit have been deferred and will be recognized as reductions in the provisions for income taxes in the appropriate years.

Expenditures Which Provide Possible Future Benefits

Plant start-up, research and development, advertising and promotional costs are charged against earnings in the year in which such costs are incurred.

Net Income per Share of Common Stock

Net income per share of common stock is based on the average number of shares of common stock outstanding during the respective years, adjusted for stock splits and stock dividends. Shares issuable upon the exercise of stock options are excluded from the average number of shares for the computation of net income per share since their effect is not significant.

■ FUQUA INDUSTRIES, INCORPORATED
SUMMARY OF SIGNIFICANT ACCOUNTING POLICIES

The accompanying financial statements have been prepared in accordance with generally accepted accounting principles applied on a consistent basis. Operating results of discontinued operations have been reclassified in the statement of income for [last year] to conform with changes in accounting rules regarding such transactions.

Principles of Consolidation

The consolidated financial statements include the accounts of Fuqua and its subsidiaries. All significant inter-company transactions and accounts have been eliminated in consolidation.

Currency Translation

The amounts recorded for Canadian assets and liabilities have been translated into United States dollars generally at exchange rates prevailing at year-end. Fixed and other assets not subject to exchange fluctuations have been reflected at the exchange rates prevailing when acquired. Operating results, other than depreciation of fixed assets, have been translated at rates of exchange during the year. Translation adjustments which are included in income when they occur are not material.

Inventories

Inventories of finished goods, work in process and raw materials are stated at the lower of cost or market, generally on the first-in, first-out method (FIFO). Condominium units and land under development are valued at the lower of specific cost of land, development and construction (including interest and overhead during development or construction) or market.

Property and Depreciation

Property, plant, and equipment are recorded at cost at the time of purchase. For financial reporting purposes depreciation is computed over the expected useful service lives of depreciable assets using the straight-line method. For income tax reporting purposes, depreciation is generally computed under various methods approved by the Internal Revenue Service which allows certain assets to be depreciated at a higher rate during the early part of the useful lives of these assets.

Intangibles

Motor carrier operating rights and broadcast licenses, which are fundamental to the operation of the respective businesses, are not being amortized. Such franchises are not considered to decrease in value as may be the case for depreciable assets.

The excess of the purchase price over net assets of businesses acquired prior to 1971 is not being amortized because, in the opinion of management, they represent assets with continuing value. For acquisitions since 1971, new accounting rules require that such excess or "goodwill" be amortized on the straight-line method not to exceed 40 years.

Research and Development Costs

Research and development costs are substantially all charged to operations as expense when incurred.

Income Taxes

Taxes are provided for all items in the statement of income regardless of the period when such items are reported for Federal income tax purposes. Fuqua elects to utilize certain provisions of the Federal income tax laws to reduce current taxes payable. Taxes which are postponed as a result of these elections are recorded as deferred income taxes. Investment tax credits are used to reduce the provision for income taxes the year in which the related assets are placed in service.

Real Estate Accounting

Interest and other costs associated with the acquisition and development of land and the construction of condominium units for sale are capitalized until development or construction is completed or when the property is committed to productive use or made available for sale. Capitalized costs are included in the cost of sales when the property is sold.

Revenues at Arizona Valley Development Corporation are recognized from the sale of property after the time has elapsed in which the buyer can cancel his contract with a full refund (up to 1 year). When the cancellation period elapses the sale is recorded and reserves are established for the estimated cost of future development work. Also, a portion of the gross profit is deferred until the Company's development obligations (such as streets, water and sewer facilities) have been completed. Appropriate reserves are also established for possible failure by customers to make full payment of the purchase contracts.

At the Haft-Gaines development, "Inverrary," sales of condominium units are recognized when title is passed to the buyer and full cash payment is received (Fuqua does not finance the purchase of condominiums). Sales of land to other builders, resulting in net income of approximately $854,000 in [this year], are recognized when it is determined that the buyer has made sufficient down payment to reasonably assure full payment for the property.

6. South Company and North Company incur $50,000 of advertising costs each year.

South Company expenses these costs immediately, while North Company capitalizes the costs and amortizes them over 5 years.

   a. Determine the amount of advertising expense and deferred advertising costs each firm would report beginning in the first year that advertising costs are incurred and continuing for 6 years.

   b. For this part, assume that the amount of advertising costs incurred by each firm increases by $10,000 each year. Repeat **a**.

   c. Comment on the differences noted in **a** and **b**.

7. On January 1, 1976, two corporations are formed to operate merchandising businesses. The firms are alike in all respects except for their methods of accounting. Ruzicka Company chooses the accounting principles that will minimize its reported net income. Murphy Company chooses the accounting principles that will maximize its reported net income but, where different procedures are permitted, will use accounting methods that minimize its taxable income. The following events occur during 1976.

(1) Both companies issue 500,000 shares of $1 par value common stock for $6 per share on January 2, 1976.

(2) Both firms acquire equipment on January 2, 1976, for $1,650,000 cash. The equipment is estimated to have a 10-year life and zero salvage value. An investment tax credit of 10 percent is applicable to this equipment.

(3) Both firms engage in extensive sales promotion activities during 1976, incurring costs of $400,000.

(4) The two firms make the following purchases of merchandise inventory.

DATE	UNITS PURCHASED	UNIT PRICE	COST OF PURCHASES
January 2	50,000	$6.00	$ 300,000
April 1	60,000	6.20	372,000
August 15	40,000	6.25	250,000
November 30	50,000	6.50	325,000
Total	200,000		$1,247,000

(5) During the year both firms sell 140,000 units at an average price of $15 each.

(6) Selling, general, and administrative expenses during the year other than advertising total $100,000.

The Ruzicka Company uses the following accounting methods (for both book and tax purposes): LIFO inventory cost-flow assumption, sum-of-the-years'-digits depreciation method, immediate expensing of the costs of sales promotion, and the deferral method of accounting for the investment credit.

The Murphy Company uses the following accounting methods: FIFO inventory cost-flow assumption for both book and tax purposes, the straight-line depreciation method for book and the double-declining-balance method for tax purposes, capitalization and amortization of the costs of the sales promotion campaign over 4 years for book and immediate expensing for tax purposes, and the flow-through method of accounting for the investment credit.

a. Prepare comparative income statements for the two firms for the year 1976. Include separate computations of income tax expense. The income tax rate is 22 percent of the first $25,000 of taxable income and 48 percent of the remainder.

b. Prepare comparative balance sheets for the two firms as of December 31, 1976. Both firms have $1 million of outstanding accounts receivable on this date and a single current liability for income taxes payable.

c. Prepare comparative statements of changes in financial position for the two firms for the year 1976.

8. The Langston Corporation is formed on January 2, 1976, with the issuance at par of 100,000 shares of $10 par value common stock for cash. During 1976, the following transactions occur.

(**1**) The assets of the Dee's Department Store are acquired on January 2, 1976, for $800,000 cash. The market values of the identifiable assets received are as follows: accounts receivable, $200,000; merchandise inventory, $400,000 (200,000 units); store equipment, $150,000. The acquisition is accounted for as a purchase.

(**2**) Merchandise inventory is purchased during 1976 as follows:

DATE	UNITS PURCHASED	UNIT PRICE	COST OF PURCHASE
April 1	30,000	$2.10	$ 63,000
August 1	20,000	2.20	44,000
October 1	50,000	2.40	120,000
Total	100,000		$227,000

(**3**) During the year, 210,000 units are sold at an average price of $3.20.

(**4**) Extensive training programs are held during the year to acquaint previous employees of Dee's Department Store with the merchandising policies and procedures of Langston Corporation. The costs incurred in the training programs total $50,000.

(**5**) Selling, general, and administrative costs incurred and recognized as an expense during 1976 are $80,000.

(**6**) The store equipment is estimated to have a 5-year useful life and zero salvage value.

(**7**) The income tax rate is 22 percent of the first $25,000 of taxable income and 48 percent of the remainder. Goodwill arising from a corporate acquisition is not deductible in determining taxable income. Ignore investment tax credit provisions in this problem.

The management of Langston Corporation is uncertain about the accounting methods which should be used in preparing its financial statements. The choice has been narrowed to two sets of accounting methods, and you have been asked to determine net income for 1976 using each set.

a. Set A consists of the following accounting methods (for book and tax purposes): LIFO inventory cost-flow assumption, double-declining-balance depreciation method, immediate expensing of the costs of the training program, amortization of goodwill over 10 years.

b. Set B consists of the following accounting methods: FIFO inventory costing assumption, straight-line depreciation for book and double-declining-balance for tax purposes, capitalization and amortization of the costs of the training program over 5 years for book and immediate expensing for tax purposes, amortization of goodwill over 40 years.

9. Refer to Problem **8.** Determine working capital provided by operations under both Set A and Set B accounting principles. Prepare a separate analysis explaining the difference in the amount of working capital provided by operations under Set A and Set B.

10. Net income of Miller Corporation for the year ending December 31, 1976, is $600,000 based on the accounting methods actually used by the firm. You have been asked to determine the amount of net income that would have been reported under several alternative accounting methods. The income tax rate is 40 percent, and the same accounting methods are used for financial reporting and income tax purposes unless otherwise indicated. The investment tax credit provisions should be ignored in this problem. Each of the following questions should be considered independently.

a. Miller Corporation acquired a machine costing $300,000 on January 1, 1976. The machine was depreciated during 1976 using the straight-line method based on a 5-year useful life and zero salvage value. What would net income have been if the sum-of-the-years'-digits depreciation method had been used?

b. Miller Corporation used the cost method of accounting for its 20-percent investment in the common stock of General Tools Corporation. During 1976, General Tools Corporation earned $200,000 and paid dividends of $50,000. What would net income have been during 1976 if Miller Corporation continued to account for the investment under the cost method for income tax purposes but used the equity method for financial reporting purposes?

c. Miller Corporation used the FIFO inventory cost-flow assumption. Under FIFO, the January 1, 1976, inventory was $300,000 and the December 31, 1976, inventory was $320,000. Under LIFO, the January 1, 1976, inventory would have been $240,000 and the December 31, 1976, inventory would have been $230,000. What would net income have been if the LIFO inventory costing assumption had been used?

11. Refer to Problem **23** in Chapter Seven. Illinois Corporation and Ohio Corporation are in an industry which experienced a 10-percent increase in prices during 1976. Illinois Corporation uses the LIFO inventory cost-flow assumption and straight-line depreciation method. Ohio Corporation uses the FIFO inventory cost-flow assumption and the double-declining-balance depreciation method. Reassess the relative profitability and liquidity of the two firms in light of the information concerning their accounting procedures.

12. The following data are taken from the adjusted trial balances of the Hickory Merchandising Company as of December 31, 1975 and 1976. The brackets indicate amounts to be determined in the solution of the problem.

	DECEMBER 31, 1975		DECEMBER 31, 1976	
Accounts Payable		$ 97,320		$ 98,715
Accounts Receivable—Net ..	$ 580,335		$ 617,530	
Accrued Expenses and				
Withholdings Payable ...		99,800		99,700
Administrative Expense				
Control	449,160		447,260	
Bonds Payable (6%)		300,000		300,000
Cash	114,080		149,485	
Common Stock		100,000		[ ]
Cost of Goods Sold	3,207,840		3,220,390	
Depreciation Expense	45,710		48,825	
Discount on Bonds	25,000		[ ]	
Dividends on Common				
Stock—Cash	50,000		[ ]	
Dividends on Preferred				
Stock—Cash	6,000		6,000	
Dividends Payable		—		[ ]
Federal and State Income				
Tax Expense	104,975		122,675	
Federal and State Income				
Taxes Payable		104,975		111,675
Gain on Sale of Plant		—		[ ]
Interest Expense on Notes ..	2,900		3,100	
Interest Expense on Bonds ..	20,000		[ ]	
Interest and Dividend				
Revenue		16,010		18,070
Inventories	616,120		633,690	
Investments in Subsidiaries ..	162,000		162,000	
Notes Payable		51,500		53,400
Notes Receivable	65,600		68,400	
Plant and Equipment—				
Net	391,880		[ ]	
Preferred Stock		100,000		100,000
Premium on Common				
Stock		700,000		[ ]
Prepaid Insurance	8,240		7,640	
Retained Earnings		[ ]		[ ]
Royalties Revenue		37,020		44,285
Sales		4,552,320		4,605,275
Selling Expenses	642,530		656,230	
	$6,492,370	$6,492,370	$6,662,860	$6,662,860

Additional data:

(1) Preferred stock: 6-percent, cumulative, $100 par value, 2,000 shares authorized.

(2) Common stock: $1 par value, 150,000 shares authorized.

(**3**) On January 10, 1976, a 10-percent stock dividend was declared on common stock, issuable in common stock. The dividend was capitalized at $10 per share.

(**4**) On March 31 and September 30, 1976, dividends of 25 cents per share were declared payable on April 20 and October 20, 1976, respectively. On December 31, 1976, an extra dividend of 12½ cents per share was declared payable on January 20, 1977.

(**5**) Plant and equipment items having a cost of $39,240 and accumulated depreciation of $32,570 were retired and sold for $15,000. Acquisitions during 1976 amounted to $71,500.

(**6**) The bonds were issued on June 30, 1958, and mature on June 30, 1988. All bonds issued remain outstanding; straight-line amortization is used.

    a. Prepare a well-organized comparative statement of income and retained earnings.

    b. Prepare a well-organized comparative balance sheet.

    c. Prepare a well-organized statement of changes in financial position.

13. The principal objective of this book has been to help you develop a sufficient understanding of the accounting process that generates financial statements for external users so that the resulting statements can then be (**1**) interpreted, (**2**) analyzed, and (**3**) evaluated. This problem has been designed partly as a review of the material covered in the book and partly as a means of assessing your progress toward this objective. A partial set of financial statements of Calmes Corporation for 1976, including consolidated comparative balance sheets at December 31, 1975 and 1976, and a consolidated statement of income and retained earnings for the year 1976 is presented on the following pages. A series of discussion questions and short problems relating to the financial statements of Calmes Corporation are then presented. It is suggested that you study the financial statements before responding to these questions and problems.

■ PART I—FINANCIAL STATEMENT INTERPRETATION

For each of the accounts or items listed below and appearing on the consolidated balance sheets and income statement of the Calmes Corporation, describe (**1**) the nature of the account or item (that is, the transaction or conditions that resulted in its recognition) and (**2**) the valuation method used in determining its amount. Respond in descriptive terms rather than using specific numbers from the financial statements of the Calmes Corporation. The first one is provided as an example.

a. Accumulated Costs Under Contracts in Progress in Excess of Progress Billings—

The Calmes Corporation is providing services of some type to specific customers under contract. All costs incurred under the contracts are accumulated in this current asset account. When customers are periodically billed for a portion of the contract price, this account is credited. The account therefore reflects the excess of costs incurred to date on uncompleted contracts over the amounts billed to customers. Since the account does not include any income or profit from the contracts (that is, "accumulated costs"), the firm is apparently using the completed contract rather than the percentage of completion method of recognizing revenues.

b. Investment in Calmes Finance Corporation.

c. Property Rights Acquired Under Lease.
d. Goodwill.
e. Rent Received in Advance.
f. Discount on Bonds Payable.
g. Deferred Income Taxes (Balance Sheet).
h. Minority Interest in Subsidiary (Balance Sheet).
i. Treasury Stock.
j. Estimated Uncollectible Accounts (Income Statement).

Calmes Corporation
Consolidated Statement of Income and Retained Earnings
For the Year Ended December 31, 1976

Revenues

Sales		$6,000,000
Less Estimated Uncollectible Accounts		60,000
Net Sales		$5,940,000
Gain on Sale of Machinery and Equipment		100,000
Income from Contracts in Process		960,000
Equity in Earnings of Unconsolidated Subsidiaries:		
Calmes Finance Corporation	$900,000	
Richardson Company	50,000	
Anthony Company	50,000	
		1,000,000
Total Revenues		$8,000,000

Expenses

Cost of Goods Sold		$2,500,000
Employee Payroll		1,500,000
Depreciation of Plant and Equipment and Amortization of Leased Property Rights		500,000
Amortization of Intangibles		100,000
Interest		300,000
General Corporate		100,000
Income Taxes—Current		700,000
Income Taxes—Deferred		100,000
Total Expenses		$5,800,000
Net Income Before Minority Interest		$2,200,000
Minority Interest in Earnings		200,000
Net Income		$2,000,000
Less: Dividends on Preferred Stock		60,000
Dividends on Common Stock		840,000
Increase in Retained Earnings		$1,100,000
Retained Earnings, January 1, 1976		1,400,000
Retained Earnings, December 31, 1976		$2,500,000
Primary Earnings per Common Share		
(based on 1,000,000 outstanding shares)		$1.94
Fully Diluted Earnings per Share		
(assuming conversion of preferred stock)		$1.25

Calmes Corporation
Consolidated Balance Sheets
December 31

ASSETS

Current Assets	1976	1975
Cash	$ 50,000	$ 100,000
Marketable Securities (at cost)	150,000	—
Accounts Receivable (net of estimated uncollectibles of $80,000 in 1976 and $50,000 in 1975)	300,000	250,000
Merchandise Inventory	700,000	600,000
Accumulated Costs Under Contracts in Process in Excess of Progress Billings	200,000	150,000
Prepayments	100,000	100,000
Total Current Assets	$ 1,500,000	$1,200,000
Investments (at equity)		
Calmes Finance Corporation (100% owned)	$ 2,000,000	$1,100,000
Richardson Company (50% owned)	500,000	450,000
Anthony Company (25% owned)	100,000	50,000
Total Investments	$ 2,600,000	$1,600,000
Property, Plant, and Equipment		
Land	$ 250,000	$ 200,000
Building	2,000,000	2,000,000
Machinery and Equipment	4,000,000	3,650,000
Property Rights Acquired Under Lease	750,000	750,000
Total	$ 7,000,000	$6,600.000
Less Accumulated Depreciation and Amortization	(2,000,000)	(1,900,000)
Total Property, Plant, and Equipment	$ 5,000,000	$4,700,000
Intangibles (at net book value)		
Patent	$ 200,000	$ 250,000
Goodwill	700,000	750,000
Total Intangibles	$ 900,000	$1,000,000
Total Assets	$10,000,000	$8,500,000

Additional Information

(1) Machinery and equipment costing $500,000 and with a book value of $100,000 were sold for cash during 1976.

(2) The only transaction affecting common or preferred stocks during 1976 was the sale of treasury stock.

LIABILITIES AND STOCKHOLDERS' EQUITY

Current Liabilities	1976	1975
Notes Payable	$ 250,000	$ 200,000
Accounts Payable	350,000	330,000
Salaries Payable	150,000	120,000
Income Taxes Payable	200,000	150,000
Rent Received in Advance	50,000	—
Other Current Liabilities	200,000	100,000
Total Current Liabilities	$ 1,200,000	$ 900,000

Long-Term Debt		
Bonds Payable (net of discount of $176,000 in 1976 and $200,000 in 1975)	$ 1,824,000	$1,800,000
Equipment Mortgage Indebtedness	176,000	650,000
Capitalized Lease Obligations	500,000	550,000
Total Long-Term Debt	$ 2,500,000	$3,000,000

Deferred Income Taxes	$ 800,000	$ 700,000

Minority Interest in Subsidiary	$ 500,000	$ 300,000

Stockholders' Equity		
Convertible Preferred Stock	$ 1,000,000	$1,000,000
Common Stock	1,000,000	1,000,000
Additional Paid-In Capital	1,000,000	900,000
Retained Earnings	2,500,000	1,400,000
Total	$ 5,500,000	$4,300,000
Less Cost of Treasury Stock	(500,000)	(700,000)
Total Stockholders' Equity	$ 5,000,000	$3,600,000
Total Liabilities and Stockholders' Equity	$10,000,000	$8,500,000

■ PART II—FINANCIAL STATEMENT ANALYSIS

a. Determine the amount of specific customers' accounts written off as uncollectible during 1976, assuming that there were no recoveries during 1976 of accounts written off in years prior to 1976.

b. The Calmes Corporation used the LIFO cost-flow assumption in determining its cost of goods sold and beginning and ending merchandise inventory amounts. If the FIFO cost-flow assumption had been used, the beginning inventory would have been $900,000 and the ending inventory would have been $850,000. Determine the actual gross profit (net sales less cost of goods sold) of the Calmes Corporation for 1976 under LIFO and the corresponding amount of gross profit if FIFO had been used (ignore income tax effects). Calmes Corporation used the periodic inventory method.

c. Refer to part b. What can be said about the quantity of merchandise inventory at the beginning and end of 1976 and the direction of price changes during 1976? Explain.

d. The Calmes Corporation accounts for its three intercorporate investments in unconsolidated subsidiaries under the equity method. The stock in each of these companies was acquired at book value at the time of acquisition. What were the total dividends declared by these three companies during 1976? How can you tell?

e. The Calmes Corporation accounts for its three intercorporate investments in unconsolidated subsidiaries under the equity method. The stock in each of these companies was acquired at book value at the time of acquisition. Give the journal entry (entries) which was (were) made during 1976 in applying the equity method.

f. The building was acquired on January 1, 1975. It was estimated to have a 40-year useful life and zero salvage value at that time. Determine the amount of depreciation expense on this building for 1976 assuming that the double-declining-balance method is used.

g. Machinery and equipment costing $500,000 and with a book value of $100,000 were sold for cash during 1976. Give the journal entry to record the disposition.

h. The bonds payable carry 6-percent annual coupons. Interest is paid on December 31 of each year. Give the journal entry made on December 31, 1976, to recognize interest expense for 1976 and to amortize the bond discount, assuming that Calmes Corporation uses the effective interest method of amortizing the bond discount.

i. Refer to part h. What was the effective or market interest rate on these bonds on the date they were issued? Explain.

j. The only timing difference between net income and taxable income during 1976 was in the amount of depreciation expense. If the income tax rate was 40 percent, determine the difference between the depreciation deduction reported on the tax return and the depreciation expense reported on the income statement.

k. Give the journal entry that explains the change in the treasury stock account, assuming that there were no other transactions affecting common or preferred stocks during 1976.

l. Was the acquisition of the consolidated subsidiary accounted for as a purchase or as a pooling of interests? How can you tell?

m. If the original amount of the patent acquired was $500,000 and the patent is being amortized on a straight-line basis, when was the patent acquired?

n. The stock of the Anthony Company was acquired on December 31, 1975. If the same amount of stock in the Anthony Company were held during the year, but the amount represented only 15 *percent* ownership of the Anthony Company, how would the financial statements have differed? Disregard income tax effects.

o. During 1976, Calmes paid $85,000 to the lessor of property represented on the balance sheet by "Property Rights Acquired Under Lease." Property rights acquired under lease have a 10-year life and are being amortized on a straight-line basis. What was the total expense reported by Calmes Corporation during 1976 from using the leased property?

p. How would the financial statements have differed if the Calmes Corporation accounted for marketable securities on the lower-of-cost-of-market basis and the market value of these securities had been $130,000 at the end of 1976? Disregard income tax effects.

q. If the Minority Interest in Subsidiary represents a 10-percent interest in Calmes Corporation's only consolidated subsidiary, what was the *total* amount of dividends declared by this subsidiary during 1976? How can you tell?

r. Refer to the earnings-per-share amounts in the income statement of Calmes Corporation. How many shares of common stock would be issued if all of the outstanding shares of preferred stock were converted into common stock?

s. Insert the missing items of information numbered (1)–(17) in the following statement of changes in financial position of the Calmes Corporation. Be sure to include both descriptions of the missing items and their amounts. Provide supporting calculations for each of the missing items in the statement. You may assume that there is no discount or premium on the Equipment Mortgage Indebtedness (See the Exhibit on page 506).

t. As indicated in the statement of changes in financial position, working capital provided by operations of Calmes Corporation during 1976 was $1,824,000. Convert this figure to cash flow provided by operations.

u. On January 2, 1977, the Calmes Corporation requested its bank to grant a 6-month loan for $300,000. If approved, the loan would be granted on January 10, 1977. As the bank's senior credit analyst, you have been asked to assess the liquidity of the Calmes Corporation and present a memorandum summarizing your conclusions. Include any ratios and any other information from the financial statements which you feel are relevant. Also include a summary of information not disclosed in the financial statements which you feel the loan officer should consider before making a final decision.

■ PART III—FINANCIAL STATEMENT EVALUATION

a. The treasurer of the Calmes Corporation recently remarked, "The value or worth of our company on December 31, 1976, is $5,000,000, as measured by total stockholders' equity." Describe briefly at least three reasons why the difference between recorded total assets and recorded total liabilities on the balance sheet does not represent the firm's value or worth.

b. The accounting profession has been criticized for permitting several "generally accepted accounting principles" for the same or similar transactions. What are the major arguments for (1) narrowing the range of acceptable accounting methods and (2) continuing the present system of permitting business firms some degree of flexibility in selecting their accounting methods?

Calmes Corporation
Statement of Changes in Financial Position
For the Year Ended December 31, 1976

Sources of Working Capital

Operations

(3) _____ .... $ _____

Add Back Expenses and Deductions Not
Using Working Capital for Operations:

(4) _____ .... _____

(5) _____ .... _____

(6) _____ .... _____

(7) _____ .... _____

(8) _____ .... _____

Subtract Revenues and Additions Not
Providing Working Capital for Operations:

(9) _____ .... (_____)

(10) _____ .... (_____)

Working Capital Provided by Operations $1,824,000

Other Sources of Working Capital:

(11) _____ .... _____

(12) _____ .... _____

Total Sources of Working Capital .... (2) $ _____

Uses of Working Capital

(13) _____ .... $ _____

(14) _____ .... _____

(15) _____ .... _____

(16) _____ .... _____

(17) _____ .... _____

Total Uses of Working Capital $2,324,000

Net Change in Working Capital .... (1) $ _____

Compound Interest,
Annuity,
and Bond Tables

TABLE 1
Future Value of $1

$$F_n = P(1 \times r)^n$$

r = interest rate; n = number of periods until valuation; $P = \$1$

Periods = n	¼%	½%	⅔%	¾%	1%	1½%	2%	3%	4%	5%	6%	7%	8%	10%	12%	20%
1	1.00250	1.00500	1.00667	1.00750	1.01000	1.01500	1.02000	1.03000	1.04000	1.05000	1.06000	1.07000	1.08000	1.10000	1.12000	1.20000
2	1.00501	1.01003	1.01338	1.01506	1.02010	1.03023	1.04040	1.06090	1.08160	1.10250	1.12360	1.14490	1.16640	1.21000	1.25440	1.44000
3	1.00752	1.01508	1.02013	1.02267	1.03030	1.04568	1.06121	1.09273	1.12486	1.15763	1.19102	1.22504	1.25971	1.33100	1.40493	1.72800
4	1.01004	1.02015	1.02693	1.03034	1.04060	1.06136	1.08243	1.12551	1.16986	1.21551	1.26248	1.31080	1.36049	1.46410	1.57352	2.07360
5	1.01256	1.02525	1.03378	1.03807	1.05101	1.07728	1.10408	1.15927	1.21665	1.27628	1.33823	1.40255	1.46933	1.61051	1.76234	2.48832
6	1.01509	1.03038	1.04067	1.04585	1.06152	1.09344	1.12616	1.19405	1.26532	1.34010	1.41852	1.50073	1.58687	1.77156	1.97382	2.98598
7	1.01763	1.03553	1.04761	1.05370	1.07214	1.10984	1.14869	1.22987	1.31593	1.40710	1.50363	1.60578	1.71382	1.94872	2.21068	3.58318
8	1.02018	1.04071	1.05459	1.06160	1.08286	1.12649	1.17166	1.26677	1.36857	1.47746	1.59385	1.71819	1.85093	2.14359	2.47596	4.29982
9	1.02273	1.04591	1.06163	1.06956	1.09369	1.14339	1.19509	1.30477	1.42331	1.55133	1.68948	1.83846	1.99900	2.35795	2.77308	5.15978
10	1.02528	1.05114	1.06870	1.07758	1.10462	1.16054	1.21899	1.34392	1.48024	1.62889	1.79085	1.96715	2.15892	2.59374	3.10585	6.19174
11	1.02785	1.05640	1.07583	1.08566	1.11567	1.17795	1.24337	1.38423	1.53945	1.71034	1.89830	2.10485	2.33164	2.85312	3.47855	7.43008
12	1.03042	1.06168	1.08300	1.09381	1.12683	1.19562	1.26824	1.42576	1.60103	1.79586	2.01220	2.25219	2.51817	3.13843	3.89598	8.91610
13	1.03299	1.06699	1.09022	1.10201	1.13809	1.21355	1.29361	1.46853	1.66507	1.88565	2.13293	2.40985	2.71962	3.45227	4.36349	10.69932
14	1.03557	1.07232	1.09749	1.11028	1.14947	1.23176	1.31948	1.51259	1.73168	1.97993	2.26090	2.57853	2.93719	3.79750	4.88711	12.83918
15	1.03816	1.07768	1.10480	1.11860	1.16097	1.25023	1.34587	1.55797	1.80094	2.07893	2.39656	2.75903	3.17217	4.17725	5.47357	15.40702
16	1.04076	1.08307	1.11217	1.12699	1.17258	1.26899	1.37279	1.60471	1.87298	2.18287	2.54035	2.95216	3.42594	4.59497	6.13039	18.48843
17	1.04336	1.08849	1.11958	1.13544	1.18430	1.28802	1.40024	1.65285	1.94790	2.29202	2.69277	3.15882	3.70002	5.05447	6.86604	22.18611
18	1.04597	1.09393	1.12705	1.14396	1.19615	1.30734	1.42825	1.70243	2.02582	2.40662	2.85434	3.37993	3.99602	5.55992	7.68997	26.62333
19	1.04858	1.09940	1.13456	1.15254	1.20811	1.32695	1.45681	1.75351	2.10685	2.52695	3.02560	3.61653	4.31570	6.11591	8.61276	31.94800
20	1.05121	1.10490	1.14213	1.16118	1.22019	1.34686	1.48595	1.80611	2.19112	2.65330	3.20714	3.86968	4.66096	6.72750	9.64629	38.33760
22	1.05647	1.11597	1.15740	1.17867	1.24472	1.38756	1.54598	1.91610	2.36992	2.92526	3.60354	4.43040	5.43654	8.14027	12.10031	55.20614
24	1.06176	1.12716	1.17289	1.19641	1.26973	1.42950	1.60844	2.03279	2.56330	3.22510	4.04893	5.07237	6.34118	9.84973	15.17863	79.49685
26	1.06707	1.13846	1.18858	1.21443	1.29526	1.47271	1.67342	2.15659	2.77247	3.55567	4.54938	5.80735	7.39635	11.91818	19.04007	114.47755
28	1.07241	1.14987	1.20448	1.23271	1.32129	1.51722	1.74102	2.28793	2.99870	3.92013	5.11169	6.64884	8.62711	14.42099	23.88387	164.8447
30	1.07778	1.16140	1.22059	1.25127	1.34785	1.56308	1.81136	2.42726	3.24340	4.32194	5.74349	7.61226	10.06266	17.44940	29.95992	237.3763
32	1.08318	1.17304	1.23692	1.27011	1.37494	1.61032	1.88454	2.57508	3.50806	4.76494	6.15339	8.71527	11.73708	21.11378	37.58173	341.8219
34	1.08860	1.18480	1.25347	1.28923	1.40258	1.65900	1.96068	2.73191	3.79432	5.25335	7.25103	9.97811	13.69013	25.54767	47.14252	492.2235
36	1.09405	1.19668	1.27024	1.30865	1.43077	1.70914	2.03989	2.89828	4.10393	5.79182	8.14725	11.42394	15.96817	30.91268	59.13557	708.8019
38	1.09953	1.20868	1.28723	1.32835	1.45953	1.76080	2.12230	3.07478	4.43881	6.38548	9.15425	13.07927	18.62528	37.40434	74.17966	1020.675
40	1.10503	1.22079	1.30445	1.34835	1.48886	1.81402	2.20804	3.26204	4.80102	7.03999	10.28572	14.97446	21.72452	45.25926	93.05097	1469.772
45	1.11892	1.25162	1.34852	1.39968	1.56481	1.95421	2.43785	3.78160	5.84118	8.98501	13.76461	21.00245	31.92045	72.89048	163.9876	3657.262
50	1.13297	1.28323	1.39407	1.45296	1.64463	2.10524	2.69159	4.38391	7.10668	11.46740	18.42015	29.45703	46.90161	117.3909	289.0022	9100.438
100	1.28362	1.64667	1.94343	2.11108	2.70481	4.43205	7.24465	19.21863	50.50495	131.5013	339.3021	867.7163	2199.761	13780.61	83522.27	828×10⁵

TABLE 2
Present Value of $1

$$P = F_n (1 + r)^{-n}$$

r = discount rate; n = number of periods until payment; P = $1

Periods = n	¼%	½%	⅔%	¾%	1%	1½%	2%	3%	4%	5%	6%	7%	8%	10%	12%	20%
1	.99751	.99502	.99338	.99256	.99010	.98522	.98039	.97087	.96154	.95238	.94340	.93458	.92593	.90909	.89286	.83333
2	.99502	.99007	.98680	.98517	.98030	.97066	.96117	.94260	.92456	.90703	.89000	.87344	.85734	.82645	.79719	.69444
3	.99254	.98515	.98026	.97783	.97059	.95632	.94232	.91514	.88900	.86384	.83962	.81630	.79383	.75131	.71178	.57870
4	.99006	.98025	.97377	.97055	.96098	.94218	.92385	.88849	.85480	.82270	.79209	.76290	.73503	.68301	.63552	.48225
5	.98759	.97537	.96732	.96333	.95147	.92826	.90573	.86261	.82193	.78353	.74726	.71299	.68058	.62092	.56743	.40188
6	.98513	.97052	.96092	.95616	.94205	.91454	.88797	.83748	.79031	.74622	.70496	.66634	.63017	.56447	.50663	.33490
7	.98267	.96569	.95455	.94904	.93272	.90103	.87056	.81309	.75992	.71068	.66506	.62275	.58349	.51316	.45235	.27908
8	.98022	.96089	.94823	.94198	.92348	.88771	.85349	.78941	.73069	.67684	.62741	.58201	.54027	.46651	.40388	.23257
9	.97778	.95610	.94195	.93496	.91434	.87459	.83676	.76642	.70259	.64461	.59190	.54393	.50025	.42410	.36061	.19381
10	.97534	.95135	.93571	.92800	.90529	.86167	.82035	.74409	.67556	.61391	.55839	.50835	.46319	.38554	.32197	.16151
11	.97291	.94661	.92952	.92109	.89632	.84893	.80426	.72242	.64958	.58468	.52679	.47509	.42888	.35049	.28748	.13459
12	.97048	.94191	.92336	.91424	.88745	.83639	.78849	.70138	.62460	.55684	.49697	.44401	.39711	.31863	.25668	.11216
13	.96806	.93722	.91725	.90743	.87866	.82403	.77303	.68095	.60057	.53032	.46884	.41496	.36770	.28966	.22917	.09346
14	.96565	.93256	.91117	.90068	.86996	.81185	.75788	.66112	.57748	.50507	.44230	.38782	.34046	.26333	.20462	.07789
15	.96324	.92792	.90514	.89397	.86135	.79985	.74301	.64186	.55526	.48102	.41727	.36245	.31524	.23939	.18270	.06491
16	.96084	.92330	.89914	.88732	.85282	.78803	.72845	.62317	.53391	.45811	.39365	.33873	.29189	.21763	.16312	.05409
17	.95844	.91871	.89319	.88071	.84438	.77639	.71416	.60502	.51337	.43630	.37136	.31657	.27027	.19784	.14564	.04507
18	.95605	.91414	.88727	.87416	.83602	.76491	.70016	.58739	.49363	.41552	.35034	.29586	.25025	.17986	.13004	.03756
19	.95367	.90959	.88140	.86765	.82774	.75361	.68643	.57029	.47464	.39573	.33051	.27651	.23171	.16351	.11611	.03130
20	.95129	.90506	.87556	.86119	.81954	.74247	.67297	.55368	.45639	.37689	.31180	.25842	.21455	.14864	.10367	.02608
22	.94655	.89608	.86400	.84842	.80340	.72069	.64684	.52189	.42196	.34185	.27751	.22571	.18394	.12285	.08264	.01811
24	.94184	.88719	.85260	.83583	.78757	.69954	.62172	.49193	.39012	.31007	.24698	.19715	.15770	.10153	.06588	.01258
26	.93714	.87838	.84134	.82343	.77205	.67902	.59758	.46369	.36069	.28124	.21981	.17220	.13520	.08391	.05252	.00874
28	.93248	.86966	.83023	.81122	.75684	.65910	.57437	.43708	.33348	.25509	.19563	.15040	.11591	.06934	.04187	.00607
30	.92783	.86103	.81927	.79919	.74192	.63976	.55207	.41199	.30832	.23138	.17411	.13137	.09938	.05731	.03338	.00421
32	.92321	.85248	.80846	.78733	.72730	.62099	.53063	.38834	.28506	.20987	.15496	.11474	.08520	.04736	.02661	.00293
34	.91861	.84402	.79779	.77565	.71297	.60277	.51003	.36604	.26355	.19035	.13791	.10022	.07305	.03914	.02121	.00203
36	.91403	.83564	.78725	.76415	.69892	.58509	.49022	.34503	.24367	.17266	.12274	.08754	.06262	.03235	.01691	.00141
38	.90948	.82735	.77686	.75281	.68515	.56792	.47119	.32523	.22529	.15661	.10924	.07646	.05369	.02673	.01348	.00098
40	.90495	.81914	.76661	.74165	.67165	.55126	.45289	.30656	.20829	.14205	.09722	.06678	.04603	.02209	.01075	.00068
45	.89372	.79896	.74156	.71445	.63905	.51171	.41020	.26444	.17120	.11130	.07265	.04761	.03133	.01372	.00610	.00027
50	.88263	.77929	.71732	.68825	.60804	.47500	.37153	.22811	.14071	.08720	.05429	.03395	.02132	.00852	.00346	.00011
100	.77904	.60729	.51455	.47369	.36971	.22563	.13803	.05203	.01980	.00760	.00295	.00115	.00045	.00007	.00001	.00000

TABLE 3
Future Value of Annuity of $1 in Arrears

$$F = \frac{(1+r)^n - 1}{r}$$

r = interest rate; n = number of payments

No. of Payments = n	1/4%	1/2%	2/3%	3/4%	1%	1½%	2%	3%	4%	5%	6%	7%	8%	10%	12%	20%
1	1.00000	1.00000	1.00000	1.00000	1.00000	1.00000	1.00000	1.00000	1.00000	1.00000	1.00000	1.00000	1.00000	1.00000	1.00000	1.00000
2	2.00250	2.00500	2.00667	2.00750	2.01000	2.01500	2.02000	2.03000	2.04000	2.05000	2.06000	2.07000	2.08000	2.10000	2.12000	2.20000
3	3.00751	3.01503	3.02004	3.02256	3.03010	3.04523	3.06040	3.09090	3.12160	3.15250	3.18360	3.21490	3.24640	3.31000	3.37440	3.64000
4	4.01503	4.03010	4.04018	4.04523	4.06040	4.09090	4.12161	4.18363	4.24646	4.31013	4.37462	4.43994	4.50611	4.64100	4.77933	5.36800
5	5.02506	5.05025	5.06711	5.07556	5.10101	5.15227	5.20404	5.30914	5.41632	5.52563	5.63709	5.75074	5.86660	6.10510	6.35285	7.44160
6	6.03763	6.07550	6.10089	6.11363	6.15202	6.22955	6.30812	6.46841	6.63298	6.80191	6.97532	7.15329	7.33593	7.71561	8.11519	9.92992
7	7.05272	7.10588	7.14157	7.15948	7.21354	7.32299	7.43428	7.66246	7.89829	8.14201	8.39384	8.65402	8.92280	9.48717	10.08901	12.91590
8	8.07035	8.14141	8.18918	8.21318	8.28567	8.43284	8.58297	8.89234	9.21423	9.54911	9.89747	10.25980	10.63663	11.43589	12.29969	16.49908
9	9.09053	9.18212	9.24377	9.27478	9.36853	9.55933	9.75463	10.15911	10.58280	11.02656	11.49132	11.97799	12.48756	13.57948	14.77566	20.79890
10	10.11325	10.22803	10.30540	10.34434	10.46221	10.70272	10.94972	11.46388	12.00611	12.57789	13.18080	13.81645	14.48656	15.93742	17.54874	25.95868
11	11.13854	11.27917	11.37410	11.42192	11.56683	11.86326	12.16872	12.80780	13.48635	14.20679	14.97164	15.78360	16.64549	18.53117	20.65458	32.15042
12	12.16638	12.33556	12.44993	12.50759	12.68250	13.04121	13.41209	14.19203	15.02581	15.91713	16.86994	17.88845	18.97713	21.38428	24.13313	39.58050
13	13.19680	13.39724	13.53724	13.60139	13.80933	14.23683	14.68033	15.61779	16.62684	17.71298	18.88214	20.14064	21.49530	24.52271	28.02911	48.49660
14	14.22979	14.46423	14.62315	14.70340	14.94742	15.45038	15.97394	17.08632	18.29191	19.59863	21.01507	22.55049	24.21492	27.97498	32.39260	59.19592
15	15.26537	15.53655	15.72063	15.81368	16.09690	16.68214	17.29342	18.59891	20.02359	21.57856	23.27597	25.12902	27.15211	31.77248	37.27971	72.03511
16	16.30353	16.61423	16.82544	16.93228	17.25786	17.93237	18.63929	20.15688	21.82453	23.65749	25.67253	27.88805	30.32428	35.94973	42.75328	87.44213
17	17.34429	17.69730	17.93761	18.05927	18.43044	19.20136	20.01207	21.76159	23.69751	25.84037	28.21288	30.84022	33.75023	40.54470	48.88367	105.9306
18	18.38765	18.78579	19.05719	19.19472	19.61475	20.48938	21.41231	23.41444	25.64541	28.13238	30.90565	33.99903	37.45024	45.59917	55.74971	128.1167
19	19.43362	19.87972	20.18424	20.33868	20.81090	21.79672	22.84056	25.11687	27.67123	30.53900	33.75999	37.37896	41.44626	51.15909	63.43968	154.7400
20	20.48220	20.97912	21.31880	21.49122	22.01900	23.12367	24.29737	26.87037	29.77808	33.06595	36.78559	40.99549	45.76196	57.27500	72.05244	186.6880
22	22.58724	23.19443	23.61066	23.82230	24.47159	25.83758	27.29898	30.53678	34.24797	38.50521	43.39229	49.00574	55.45676	71.40275	92.50258	271.0307
24	24.70282	25.43196	25.95319	26.18847	26.97346	28.63352	30.42186	34.42647	39.08260	44.50200	50.81558	58.17667	66.76476	88.49733	118.1552	392.4842
26	26.82899	27.69191	28.28678	28.59027	29.52563	31.51397	33.67091	38.55304	44.31174	51.11345	59.15638	68.67647	79.95442	109.1818	150.3339	567.3773
28	28.96580	29.97452	30.67187	31.02823	32.12910	34.48148	37.05121	42.93092	49.96758	58.40258	68.52811	80.69769	95.33883	134.2099	190.6989	819.2233
30	31.11331	32.28002	33.08885	33.50290	34.78489	37.53868	40.56808	47.57542	56.08494	66.43885	79.05819	94.46079	113.2832	164.4940	241.3327	1181.881
32	33.27157	34.60862	35.53818	36.01483	37.49407	40.68829	44.22703	52.50276	62.70147	75.29883	90.88978	110.2181	134.2135	201.1378	304.8477	1704.109
34	35.44064	36.96058	38.02026	38.56458	40.25770	43.93309	48.03380	57.73018	69.85791	85.06696	104.1838	128.2588	158.6267	245.4767	384.5210	2456.118
36	37.62056	39.33610	40.53556	41.15272	43.07688	47.27597	51.99437	63.27594	77.59831	95.83632	119.1209	148.9135	187.1022	299.1268	484.4631	3539.009
38	39.81140	41.73545	43.08450	43.77982	45.95272	50.71989	56.11494	69.15945	85.97034	107.7095	135.9042	172.5610	220.3159	364.0434	609.8305	5098.373
40	42.01320	44.15885	45.66754	46.44648	48.88637	54.26789	60.40198	75.40126	95.02552	120.7998	154.7620	199.6351	259.0565	442.5926	767.0914	7343.858
45	47.56606	50.32416	52.27734	53.29011	56.48107	63.61420	71.89271	92.71986	121.0294	159.7002	212.7435	285.7493	386.5056	718.9048	1358.230	18281.31
50	53.18868	56.64516	59.11042	60.39426	64.46318	73.68283	84.57940	112.7969	152.6671	209.3480	290.3359	406.5289	573.7702	1163.909	2400.018	45497.19
100	113.44996	129.33370	141.51445	148.14451	170.4814	228.8030	312.2323	607.2877	1237.624	2610.025	5638.368	12381.66	27484.52	137796.1	696010.5	414×10^6

Note: To convert from this table to values of an annuity in advance, determine the annuity in arrears above for one more period and subtract 1.00000.

PV m r PAYMENT
x 28 8% 100
=10.809 = 1,089

TABLE 4
Present Value of an Annuity of $1 in Arrears

$$P_A = \frac{1-(1+r)^{-n}}{r}$$

r = discount rate; n = number of payments

No. of Payments = n	¼%	½%	⅔%	¾%	1%	1½%	2%	3%	4%	5%	6%	7%	8%	10%	12%	20%
1	0.99751	0.99502	0.99338	0.99256	.99010	.98522	.98039	.97087	.96154	.95238	.94340	.93458	.92593	.90909	.89286	.83333
2	1.99252	1.98510	1.98018	1.97772	1.97040	1.95588	1.94156	1.91347	1.88609	1.85941	1.83339	1.80802	1.78326	1.73554	1.69005	1.52778
3	2.98506	2.97025	2.96044	2.95556	2.94099	2.91220	2.88388	2.82861	2.77509	2.72325	2.67301	2.62432	2.57710	2.48685	2.40183	2.10648
4	3.97512	3.95050	3.93421	3.92611	3.90197	3.85438	3.80773	3.71710	3.62990	3.54595	3.46511	3.38721	3.31213	3.16987	3.03735	2.58873
5	4.96272	4.92587	4.90154	4.88944	4.85343	4.78264	4.71346	4.57971	4.45182	4.32948	4.21236	4.10020	3.99271	3.79079	3.60478	2.99061
6	5.94785	5.89638	5.86245	5.84560	5.79548	5.69719	5.60143	5.41719	5.24212	5.07569	4.91732	4.76654	4.62288	4.35526	4.11141	3.32551
7	6.93052	6.86207	6.81701	6.79464	6.72819	6.59821	6.47199	6.23028	6.00205	5.78637	5.58238	5.38929	5.20637	4.86842	4.56376	3.60459
8	7.91074	7.82296	7.76524	7.73661	7.65168	7.48593	7.32548	7.01969	6.73274	6.46321	6.20979	5.97130	5.74664	5.33493	4.96764	3.83716
9	8.88852	8.77906	8.70719	8.67158	8.56602	8.36052	8.16224	7.78611	7.43533	7.10782	6.80169	6.51523	6.24689	5.75902	5.32825	4.03097
10	9.86386	9.73041	9.64290	9.59958	9.47130	9.22218	8.98259	8.53020	8.11090	7.72173	7.36009	7.02358	6.71008	6.14457	5.65022	4.19247
11	10.83677	10.67703	10.57242	10.52067	10.36763	10.07112	9.78685	9.25262	8.76048	8.30641	7.88687	7.49867	7.13896	6.49506	5.93770	4.32706
12	11.80725	11.61893	11.49578	11.43491	11.25508	10.90751	10.57534	9.95400	9.38507	8.86325	8.38384	7.94269	7.53608	6.81369	6.19437	4.43922
13	12.77532	12.55615	12.41303	12.34235	12.13374	11.73153	11.34837	10.63496	9.98565	9.39357	8.85268	8.35765	7.90378	7.10336	6.42355	4.53268
14	13.74096	13.48871	13.32420	13.24302	13.00370	12.54338	12.10625	11.29607	10.56312	9.89864	9.29498	8.74547	8.24424	7.36669	6.62817	4.61057
15	14.70420	14.41662	14.22934	14.13699	13.86505	13.34323	12.84926	11.93794	11.11839	10.37966	9.71225	9.10791	8.55948	7.60608	6.81086	4.67547
16	15.66504	15.33993	15.12848	15.02431	14.71787	14.13126	13.57771	12.56110	11.65230	10.83777	10.10590	9.44665	8.85137	7.82371	6.97399	4.72956
17	16.62348	16.25863	16.02167	15.90502	15.56225	14.90765	14.29187	13.16612	12.16567	11.27407	10.47726	9.76322	9.12164	8.02155	7.11963	4.77463
18	17.57953	17.17277	16.90894	16.77918	16.39827	15.67256	14.99203	13.75351	12.65930	11.68959	10.82760	10.05909	9.37189	8.20141	7.24967	4.81219
19	18.53320	18.08236	17.79034	17.64683	17.22601	16.42617	15.67846	14.32380	13.13394	12.08532	11.15812	10.33560	9.60360	8.36492	7.36578	4.84350
20	19.48449	18.98742	18.66590	18.50802	18.04555	17.16864	16.35143	14.87747	13.59033	12.46221	11.46992	10.59401	9.81815	8.51356	7.46944	4.86958
22	21.37995	20.78406	20.39967	20.21121	19.66038	18.62082	17.65805	15.93692	14.45112	13.16300	12.04158	11.06124	10.20074	8.77154	7.64465	4.90943
24	23.26598	22.56287	22.11054	21.88915	21.24339	20.03041	18.91393	16.93554	15.24696	13.79864	12.55036	11.46933	10.52876	8.98474	7.78432	4.93710
26	25.14261	24.32402	23.79883	23.54219	22.79520	21.39863	20.12104	17.87684	15.98277	14.37519	13.00317	11.82578	10.80998	9.16095	7.89566	4.95632
28	27.00989	26.06769	25.46484	25.17071	24.31644	22.72672	21.28127	18.76411	16.66306	14.89813	13.40616	12.13711	11.05108	9.30657	7.98442	4.96967
30	28.86787	27.79405	27.10885	26.77508	25.80771	24.01584	22.39646	19.60044	17.29203	15.37245	13.76483	12.40904	11.25778	9.42691	8.05518	4.97894
32	30.71660	29.50328	28.73116	28.35565	27.26959	25.26714	23.46833	20.38877	17.87355	15.80268	14.08404	12.64656	11.43500	9.52638	8.11159	4.98537
34	32.55611	31.19555	30.33205	29.91278	28.70267	26.48173	24.49859	21.13184	18.41120	16.19290	14.36814	12.85401	11.58693	9.60857	8.15656	4.98984
36	34.38647	32.87102	31.91181	31.44681	30.10751	27.66068	25.48884	21.83225	18.90828	16.54685	14.62099	13.03521	11.71719	9.67651	8.19241	4.99295
38	36.20770	34.52985	33.47071	32.95808	31.48466	28.80505	26.44064	22.49246	19.36786	16.86789	14.84602	13.19347	11.82887	9.73265	8.22099	4.99510
40	38.01986	36.17223	35.00903	34.44694	32.83469	29.91585	27.35548	23.11477	19.79277	17.15909	15.04630	13.33171	11.92461	9.77905	8.24378	4.99660
45	42.51088	40.20720	38.76658	38.07318	36.09451	32.55234	29.49016	24.51871	20.72004	17.77407	15.45583	13.60552	12.10840	9.86281	8.28252	4.99863
50	46.94617	44.14279	42.40134	41.56645	39.19612	34.99969	31.42361	25.72976	21.48218	18.25593	15.76186	13.80075	12.23348	9.91481	8.30450	4.99945
100	88.38248	78.54264	72.81686	70.17462	63.02888	51.62470	43.09835	31.59891	24.50500	19.84791	16.61755	14.26925	12.49432	9.99927	8.33323	5.00000

Note: To convert from this table to values of an annuity in advance, determine the annuity in arrears above for one less period and add 1.00000.

TABLE 5
Bond Values in Percent of Par:
6-Percent Semiannual Coupons

$$\text{Bond Value} = 6/r + (100 - 6/r)\,(1 + r/2)^{-2n}$$
$$r = \text{yield to maturity}; \quad n = \text{years to maturity}$$

Market Yield % Per Year Compounded Semiannually	Years to Maturity							
	½	5	10	15	19½	20	30	40
3.0	101.478	113.833	125.753	136.024	144.047	144.874	159.071	169.611
3.5	101.228	111.376	120.941	128.982	135.118	135.743	146.205	153.600
4.0	100.980	108.983	116.351	122.396	126.903	127.355	134.761	139.745
4.5	100.734	106.650	111.973	116.234	119.337	119.645	124.562	127.712
5.0	100.488	104.376	107.795	110.465	112.365	112.551	115.454	117.226
5.1	100.439	103.928	106.982	109.356	111.037	111.202	113.752	115.293
5.2	100.390	103.483	106.177	108.262	109.731	109.874	112.087	113.411
5.3	100.341	103.040	105.380	107.181	108.445	108.568	110.458	111.578
5.4	100.292	102.599	104.590	106.115	107.180	107.283	108.864	109.792
5.5	100.243	102.160	103.807	105.062	105.935	106.019	107.306	108.053
5.6	100.195	101.724	103.031	104.023	104.710	104.776	105.780	106.359
5.7	100.146	101.289	102.263	102.998	103.504	103.553	104.288	104.707
5.8	100.097	100.857	101.502	101.986	102.317	102.349	102.828	103.098
5.9	100.049	100.428	100.747	100.986	101.149	101.165	101.399	101.529
6.0	100	100	100	100	100	100	100	100
6.1	99.9515	99.5746	99.2595	99.0262	98.8685	98.8535	98.6309	98.5088
6.2	99.9030	99.1513	98.5259	98.0650	97.7549	97.7254	97.2907	97.0546
6.3	99.8546	98.7302	97.7990	97.1161	96.6587	96.6153	95.9787	95.6364
6.4	99.8062	98.3112	97.0787	96.1793	95.5796	95.5229	94.6942	94.2529
6.5	99.7579	97.8944	96.3651	95.2545	94.5174	94.4478	93.4365	92.9031
6.6	99.7096	97.4797	95.6580	94.3414	93.4717	93.3899	92.2050	91.5860
6.7	99.6613	97.0670	94.9574	93.4400	92.4423	92.3486	90.9989	90.3007
6.8	99.6132	96.6565	94.2632	92.5501	91.4288	91.3238	89.8178	89.0461
6.9	99.5650	96.2480	93.5753	91.6714	90.4310	90.3152	88.6608	87.8213
7.0	99.5169	95.8417	92.8938	90.8039	89.4487	89.3224	87.5276	86.6255
7.5	99.2771	93.8404	89.5779	86.6281	84.7588	84.5868	82.1966	81.0519
8.0	99.0385	91.8891	86.4097	82.7080	80.4155	80.2072	77.3765	76.0846
8.5	98.8010	89.9864	83.3820	79.0262	76.3899	76.1534	73.0090	71.6412
9.0	98.5646	88.1309	80.4881	75.5666	72.6555	72.3976	69.0430	67.6520

TABLE 6
Bond Values in Percent of Par:
8-Percent Semiannual Coupons

$$\text{Bond Value} = 8/r + (100 - 8/r)\,(1 + r/2)^{-2n}$$
$$r = \text{yield to maturity; } n = \text{years to maturity}$$

Market Yield % Per Year Compounded Semiannually	½	5	10	15	19½	20	30	40
5.0	101.463	113.128	123.384	131.396	137.096	137.654	146.363	151.678
5.5	101.217	110.800	119.034	125.312	129.675	130.098	136.528	140.266
6.0	100.971	108.530	114.877	119.600	122.808	123.115	127.676	130.201
6.5	100.726	106.317	110.905	114.236	116.448	116.656	119.690	121.291
7.0	100.483	104.158	107.106	109.196	110.551	110.678	112.472	113.374
7.1	100.435	103.733	106.367	108.225	109.424	109.536	111.113	111.898
7.2	100.386	103.310	105.634	107.266	108.314	108.411	109.780	110.455
7.3	100.338	102.889	104.908	106.318	107.220	107.303	108.473	109.044
7.4	100.289	102.470	104.188	105.382	106.142	106.212	107.191	107.665
7.5	100.241	102.053	103.474	104.457	105.080	105.138	105.934	106.316
7.6	100.193	101.638	102.767	103.544	104.034	104.079	104.702	104.997
7.7	100.144	101.226	102.066	102.642	103.003	103.036	103.492	103.706
7.8	100.096	100.815	101.371	101.750	101.987	102.009	102.306	102.444
7.9	100.048	100.407	100.683	100.870	100.986	100.997	101.142	101.209
8.0	100	100	100	100	100	100	100	100
8.1	99.9519	99.5955	99.3235	99.1406	99.0279	99.0177	98.8794	98.8170
8.2	99.9039	99.1929	98.6529	98.2916	98.0699	98.0498	97.7798	97.6589
8.3	99.8560	98.7924	97.9882	97.4528	97.1257	97.0962	96.7006	96.5253
8.4	99.8081	98.3938	97.3294	96.6240	96.1951	96.1566	95.6414	95.4152
8.5	99.7602	97.9973	96.6764	95.8052	95.2780	95.2307	94.6018	94.3282
8.6	99.7124	97.6027	96.0291	94.9962	94.3739	94.3183	93.5812	93.2636
8.7	99.6646	97.2100	95.3875	94.1969	93.4829	93.4191	92.5792	92.2208
8.8	99.6169	96.8193	94.7514	93.4071	92.6045	92.5331	91.5955	91.1992
8.9	99.5692	96.4305	94.1210	92.6266	91.7387	91.6598	90.6295	90.1982
9.0	99.5215	96.0436	93.4960	91.8555	90.8851	90.7992	89.6810	89.2173
9.5	99.2840	94.1378	90.4520	88.1347	86.7949	86.6777	85.1858	84.5961
10.0	99.0476	92.2783	87.5378	84.6275	82.9830	82.8409	81.0707	80.4035
10.5	98.8123	90.4639	84.7472	81.3201	79.4271	79.2656	77.2956	76.5876
11.0	98.5782	88.6935	82.0744	78.1994	76.1070	75.9308	73.8252	73.1036

Glossary[1]

AAA *American Accounting Association.*

absorption costing The generally accepted method of *costing* which assigns *manufacturing costs*, both *fixed* and *variable*, to units produced. Sometimes called "full costing." Contrast with *direct costing.*

accelerated depreciation Any method of calculating *depreciation* charges where the charges get progressively smaller. Examples are *double-declining-balance* and *sum-of-the-years'-digits* methods.

account Any device for accumulating additions and subtractions relating to a single *asset, liability, owners' equity* item, *revenue, expense,* and so on.

accountancy The British word for *accounting;* in the United States, it is used to mean the theory and practice of accounting.

Accountants' Index A publication of the *AICPA* which indexes, in detail, the accounting literature of the period. Issued quarterly since 1974, but less frequently before then.

accountant's report *Auditor's report.*

accounting An *information system* conveying information about a specific *entity.* The information is in financial terms and is restricted to information that can be made reasonably precise.

accounting conventions Methods or procedures used in accounting. This term tends to be used when the method or procedure has not been given official authoritative sanction by a pronouncement of a group such as the *APB, FASB,* or *SEC.* Contrast with *accounting principles.*

[1] Certain terms in the definitions are *italicized.* The *italicized* terms, or variants of them, are themselves explained in the glossary. This glossary contains terms that are not used in the text. Explanations of such terms are included to make the glossary more useful.

accounting cycle The sequence of accounting procedures starting with *journal entries* for various transactions and events and ending with the *financial statements* or, perhaps, the *postclosing trial balance.*

accounting entity See *entity.*

accounting equation *Assets = Equities. Assets = Liabilities + Owners' Equity.*

accounting errors Arithmetic errors and misapplications of *accounting principles* in previously published financial statements that are corrected with direct *debits* or *credits* to *retained earnings.* In this regard, they are treated like *prior-period adjustments,* but, technically, they are not classified by *APB Opinion* No. 9 as prior-period adjustments.

accounting event Any occurrence that is recorded in the accounting records.

accounting methods *Accounting principles.* Procedures for carrying out accounting principles.

accounting period The time period for which *financial statements* which measure *flows,* such as the *income statement* and the *statement of changes in financial position,* are prepared. Should be clearly identified on the financial statements.

accounting policies *Accounting principles.*

accounting principles The concepts that determine the methods or procedures used in accounting for *transactions* or events reported in the *financial statements.* This term tends to be used when the method or procedure has been given official authoritative sanction by a pronouncement of a group such as the *APB, FASB,* or *SEC.* Contrast with *accounting conventions.*

Accounting Principles Board See *APB.*

accounting procedures See *accounting principles,* but usually this term refers to the methods prescribed by accounting principles.

Accounting Research Bulletin (ARB) The name of the official pronouncements of the former *Committee on Accounting Procedure* of the *AICPA*. Fifty-one bulletins were issued between 1939 and 1959. ARB No. 43 summarizes the first 42 bulletins.

Accounting Research Study One of a series of studies published by the Director of Research of the *AICPA* "designed to provide professional accountants and others interested in the development of accounting with a discussion and documentation of accounting problems."

The Accounting Review Scholarly publication of the *American Accounting Association*, which appears four times a year.

Accounting Series Release See *SEC*.

accounting standards *Accounting principles*.

Accounting Trends and Techniques An annual publication of the *AICPA* which surveys the reporting practices of 600 large corporations.

account payable A *liability* representing an amount owed to a creditor, usually arising from purchase of merchandise or materials and supplies; not necessarily due or past due.

account receivable A claim against a *debtor* usually arising from sales or services rendered; not necessarily due or past due.

accounts receivable turnover *Net sales* on account for a period divided by the average balance of net accounts receivable. See *ratio*.

accretion Increase in economic worth through physical change, usually said of a natural resource such as an orchard, caused by natural growth. Contrast with *appreciation*.

accrual Recognition of an *expense* (or *revenue*) and the related *liability* (or *asset*) that is caused by an *accounting event*, frequently by the passage of time, and that is not signaled by an explicit cash transaction. For example, the recognition of interest expense or revenue at the end of a period even though no explicit cash transaction is made at that time.

accrual basis of accounting The method of recognizing *revenues* as *goods* are sold (or delivered) and as *services* are rendered, independent of the time when cash is received. *Expenses* are recognized in the period when the related revenue is recognized, independent of the time when cash is paid out. Contrast with the *cash basis of accounting*.

accrued Said of a *revenue* (*expense*) that has been earned (recognized) even though the re-lated *receivable* (*payable*) is not yet due. This adjective should not be used as part of an account title. Thus, we prefer to use Interest Receivable (Payable) as the account title, not Accrued Interest Receivable (Payable). See *matching convention*.

accrued payable A *payable* usually resulting from the passage of time. For example, *salaries* and *interest* accrue as time passes. See *accrued*.

accrued receivable A *receivable* usually resulting from the passage of time. See *accrued*.

accumulated depreciation A preferred title for the *contra-asset* account that shows the sum of *depreciation* charges on an asset since it was acquired. Other titles used are *allowance* for depreciation (acceptable term) or *reserve* for *depreciation* (poor term).

accurate presentation The qualitative accounting objective suggesting that information reported in financial statements should correspond as precisely as possible with the economic effects underlying transactions and events. See *fair presentation* and *full disclosure*.

acid test ratio Sum of (*cash, marketable securities*, and *receivables*) divided by *current liabilities*. Some nonliquid receivables may be excluded from the numerator. Often called the *quick ratio*. See *ratio*.

acquisition cost Of an *asset*, the net *invoice* price plus all *expenditures* to get the asset in place for its intended use. The other expenditures might include legal fees, transportation charges, and installation costs.

actual cost (basis) *Acquisition* or *historical cost*.

actuarial Usually said of computations or analyses that involve both *compound interest* and probabilities. Sometimes the term is used if only one of the two is involved.

additional paid-in capital An alternative acceptable title for *capital contributed in excess of par (or stated) value*.

adequate disclosure *Fair presentation* of *financial statements* requires *disclosure* of *material* items. This *auditing standard* does not, however, require publicizing all information detrimental to a company. For example, the company may be threatened with a lawsuit, and disclosure might seem to require a *debit* to a *loss* account and a *credit* to an *estimated liability*. But the mere making of this entry might adversely affect the actual outcome of the suit. Such impending suits need not be disclosed.

adjunct account An *account* that accumulates additions to another account. For example, Premium on Bonds Payable is adjunct to the liability Bonds Payable; the effective liability is the sum of the two account balances at a given date. Contrast with *contra account*.

adjusted acquisition (historical) cost Cost adjusted for *general* or *specific price level changes*. See also *book value*.

adjusted bank balance The *balance* shown on the statement from the bank minus or plus appropriate adjustments, such as for outstanding checks or unrecorded deposits, to reconcile the bank's balance with the correct cash balance.

adjusted basis The *basis* used to compute gain or loss on disposition of an *asset* for tax purposes. See also, *book value*.

adjusted book balance (of cash) The *balance* shown in the firm's account for cash in bank plus or minus appropriate adjustments, such as for *notes* collected by the bank or bank service charges, to reconcile the account balance with the correct cash balance.

adjusted trial balance *Trial balance* taken after *adjusting entries* but before *closing entries*. Contrast with *pre-* and *postclosing trial balances*.

adjusting entry An entry made at the end of an *accounting period* to record a *transaction* or other *accounting event*, which for some reason has not been recorded or has been improperly recorded during the accounting period.

adjustment A change in an *account* produced by an *adjusting* entry. Sometimes the term is used to refer to the process of restating *financial statements* for *general price level changes*.

administrative expense An *expense* related to the enterprise as a whole, as contrasted to expenses related to more specific functions such as manufacturing or selling.

ADR See *asset depreciation range*.

advances from (by) customers A preferred term for the *liability* account representing *receipts* of *cash* in advance of delivering the *goods* or rendering the *service* (that will cause *revenue* to be recognized). Sometimes called "deferred revenue" or "deferred income."

advances to suppliers A preferred term for *disbursements* of cash in advance of receiving *assets* or *services*.

affiliated company Said of a company controlling or controlled by another company.

after closing *Postclosing*; said of a *trial balance*.

agent One authorized to transact business, including executing contracts, for another.

aging accounts receivable The process of classifying *accounts receivable* by the time elapsed since the claim came into existence for the purpose of estimating the amount of uncollectible accounts receivable as of a given date. See *sales, uncollectible accounts adjustment* and *allowance for uncollectibles*.

AICPA American Institute of Certified Public Accountants. The national organization that represents *CPA's*. It oversees the writing and grading of the Uniform CPA Examination. Each state, however, sets its own requirements for becoming a CPA in that state. See *certified public accountant*.

all capital earnings rate Net *income* plus interest charges, net of tax effects, plus minority interest in income divided by average total assets. Perhaps the single most useful ratio for assessing management's performance. See *ratio*.

all financial resources All *assets* less all *liabilities*. Sometimes the *statement of changes in financial position* explains the changes in all financial resources rather than the changes in *working capital*.

all-inclusive concept Under this concept, no distinction is drawn between *operating* and *nonoperating revenues* and *expenses*, and the usual entries to retained earnings are for *net income* and *dividends*. Under this concept all income, gains, and losses are reported in the *income statement*; thus events usually reported as *prior-period adjustments* and as *corrections of errors* are included in net income. This concept is not part of *GAAP*.

allocation of income taxes See *deferred income tax*.

allowance A balance sheet *contra account* generally used for *receivables* and depreciable assets. See *sales* (or *purchase*) *allowance* for another use of this term.

allowance for uncollectibles (accounts receivable) A *contra* to Accounts Receivable that shows the estimated amount of accounts receivable that will not be collected. When such an allowance is used, the actual *write-off* of specific accounts receivable (*debit* allowance, *credit* specific account) does not affect *revenue* or *expense* in the period of the write-off. The revenue reduction is recognized when the allowance is credited; the amount of the credit to the allowance may be based on a percentage of sales on account for a period or determined from *aging accounts receivable*. This contra account enables an estimate to be shown of the amount of receivables that will be collected without identifying specific uncollectible accounts. See *allowance method*.

allowance method   A method of attempting to match all *expenses* of a transaction with its associated *revenues*. Usually involves a debit to expense and credit to an *estimated liability*, such as for estimated warranty expenditures, or a debit to a revenue (*contra*) account and a credit to an asset (*contra*) account, such as for uncollectible accounts. See *allowance for uncollectibles* for further explanation. When the allowance method is used for *sales discounts*, sales are recorded at *gross invoice* prices (not reduced by the amounts of discounts made available). An estimate of the amount of discounts to be taken is debited to a *revenue contra account* and *credited* to an allowance account, shown contra to *accounts receivable*.

American Accounting Association   An organization primarily for academic accountants, but open to all interested in accounting.

American Institute of Certified Public Accountants   See *AICPA*.

American Stock Exchange   AMEX. ASE. A public market where various corporate *securities* are traded.

AMEX   *American Stock Exchange*.

amortization   The general process of allocating acquisition cost of assets to the periods of benefit as *expenses*. Called *depreciation* for *plant assets*, *depletion* for *wasting assets* (natural resources), and amortization for *intangibles*. Also used for the process of allocating *premium* or *discount* on *bonds* and other *liabilities* to the periods during which the liability is outstanding.

analysis of changes in working capital accounts   The *statement of changes in financial position* explains the causes of the changes in *working capital* during a period. This part of the statement, which may appear in footnotes, shows the actual changes in the working capital accounts which have been explained in the main section of the statement.

annual report   A report for stockholders and other interested parties prepared once a year; includes a *balance sheet*, an *income statement*, a *statement of changes in financial position*, a reconciliation of changes in *owners' equity* ac-

counts, a *summary of significant accounting principles*, other explanatory *notes*, the *auditor's report*, and, perhaps, comments from management about the year's events. See *10–K*.

annuitant   One who receives an *annuity*.

annuity   A series of payments, usually made at equally spaced time intervals.

annuity certain   An *annuity* payable for a definite number of periods; contrast with *contingent annuity*.

annuity due   An *annuity* where the first payment is made at the start of period one (or at the end of period zero). Contrast with *annuity in arrears*.

annuity in advance   An *annuity due*.

annuity in arrears   An *ordinary annuity* where the first payment occurs at the end of the first period.

antidilutive   Said of a *potentially dilutive security* which will increase *earnings per share* if it is *exercised* or *converted* into common stock. In computing *primary* and *fully diluted earnings per share*, antidilutive securities may not be assumed to be exercised or converted, and hence do not affect reported earnings per share.

APB   Accounting Principles Board of the *AICPA*. It set *accounting principles* from 1959 through 1973, issuing 31 *APB* Opinions during that period. It was superseded by the *FASB*.

APB Opinion   The name given to pronouncements of the *APB* that make up much of *generally accepted accounting principles*; there are 31 APB Opinions, issued from 1962 through 1973.

APB's   An abbreviation used for opinions of the APB.

APB Statement   The *APB* issued four Statements between 1962 and 1970. The Statements were approved by at least two-thirds of the Board, but they are recommendations, not requirements. For example, Statement No. 3 (1969) suggested the publication of *general price level adjusted statements* but did not require them.

application of funds   Any transaction that reduces *working capital*. A *use of funds*.

appraisal   The process of obtaining an amount for an *asset* or *liability* that involves expert opinion rather than explicit market transactions.

appreciation   An increase in economic worth caused by rising market prices for an *asset*. Contrast with *accretion*.

appropriated retained earnings   See *retained earnings, appropriated*.

ARB   *Accounting Research Bulletin*.

arm's length   Said of a transaction negotiated by

unrelated parties, each acting in his or her own self interest; the basis for a *fair market value* determination.

arrears Said of *cumulative preferred stock dividends* that have not been declared on time. See *annuity in arrears* for another context.

ARS *Accounting Research Study.*

articles of incorporation Document filed with state authorities by persons forming a corporation. When the document is returned with a certificate of incorporation, it becomes the corporation's *charter.*

articulate Said of the relationship between any operating statement (for example, *income statement* or *statement of changes in financial position*) and *comparative balance sheets*, where the operating statement explains (or reconciles) the change in some major balance sheet category (for example, *retained earnings* or *working capital*).

ASE *American Stock Exchange; AMEX.*

asset A future benefit or service potential, recognized in accounting only when a transaction has occurred. May be *tangible* or *intangible, short-term* (current) or *long-term* (noncurrent).

asset depreciation range (ADR) The range of *depreciable lives* allowed by the *Internal Revenue Service* for a specific depreciable *asset.*

asset turnover Ratio of net sales to average assets. See *ratio.*

at par Said of a *bond* or *preferred stock* issued or selling at its *face amount.*

attest Rendering of an *opinion* by an auditor that the *financial statements* are fair. This procedure is called the "attest function" of the CPA. See *fair presentation.*

audit Systematic inspection of accounting records involving analyses, tests, and confirmations. See *internal audit.*

audit committee A committee of the board of directors of a *corporation*, usually consisting of outside directors who nominate the independent auditors and discuss the auditors' work with them.

auditing standards A set of ten standards promulgated by the *AICPA*, including three general standards, three standards of field work, and four standards of reporting. According to the AICPA, these standards "deal with the measures of the quality of the performance and the objectives to be attained," rather than with specific auditing procedures.

auditor One who checks the accuracy, fairness, and general acceptability of accounting records and statements and then *attests* to them.

audit program The procedures followed by the *auditor* in carrying out the *audit.*

auditor's opinion *Auditor's report.*

auditor's report The auditor's statement of the work done and an opinion of the *financial statements*. Opinions are usually unqualified ("clean"), but may be *qualified*, or the auditor may disclaim an opinion in the report. Often called the "accountant's report."

authorized capital stock The number of *shares* of stock that can be issued by a corporation; specified by the *articles of incorporation.*

average The arithmetic mean of a set of numbers; obtained by summing the items and dividing by the number of items.

average-cost flow assumption An *inventory flow assumption* where the cost of units is the *weighted average* cost of the *beginning inventory* and purchases. See *inventory equation.*

bad debt An *uncollectible account receivable*; see *sales, uncollectible accounts adjustment.*

bad debt expense See *sales, uncollectible accounts adjustment.*

bad debt recovery Collection, perhaps partial, of a specific account receivable previously written off as uncollectible. A *revenue*, or if the *allowance method* is used, a credit to the allowance account.

balance The difference between the sum of *debit* entries minus the sum of *credit* entries in an *account*. If positive, the difference is called a debit balance; if negative, a credit balance.

balance sheet Statement of financial position which shows *total assets = total liabilities + owners' equity.*

balance sheet account An account that can appear on a balance sheet. A *permanent account*; contrast with *temporary account.*

bank balance The amount of the balance in a checking account shown on the *bank statement*. Compare with *adjusted bank balance* and see *bank reconciliation schedule.*

bank prime rate See *prime rate.*

bank reconciliation schedule A schedule that shows how the difference between the book balance of the cash in bank account and the bank's statement can be explained. Takes into account the amount of such items as checks issued that have not cleared or deposits that have not been recorded by the bank as well as errors made by the bank or the firm.

bankrupt Said of a company whose *liabilities* exceed its *assets* where a legal petition has been filed and accepted under the bankruptcy law. A bankrupt firm is usually, but need not be, *insolvent*.

bank statement A statement sent by the bank to a checking account customer showing deposits, checks cleared, and service charges for a period, usually 1 month.

basis *Acquisition cost*, or some substitute therefor, of an asset used in computing gain or loss on disposition or retirement.

basket purchase Purchase of a group of assets for a single price; *costs* must be assigned to each of the assets so that the individual items can be recorded in the accounts.

beginning inventory Valuation of *inventory* on hand at the beginning of the accounting period.

betterment An *improvement*.

bid An offer to purchase; or the amount of the offer.

Big Eight The eight largest *public accounting (CPA)* partnerships; in alphabetical order: Arthur Andersen & Co.; Coopers & Lybrand; Ernst & Ernst; Haskins & Sells; Peat, Marwick, Mitchell & Co.; Price Waterhouse & Co.; Touche Ross & Co.; and Arthur Young & Company.

bill An *invoice* of charges and *terms of sale* for *goods and services*. Also, a piece of currency.

board of directors The governing body of a corporation elected by the stockholders.

bond A certificate to show evidence of debt. The *par value* is the *principal* or face amount of the bond payable at maturity. The *coupon rate* is the amount of interest payable in 1 year divided by the principal amount. Coupon bonds have attached to them coupons which can be redeemed at stated dates for interest payments. Normally, bonds are issued in $1,000 units and carry semiannual coupons.

bond conversion The act of exchanging *convertible bonds* for *preferred* or *common stock*.

bond discount From the standpoint of the issuer of a *bond* at the issue date, the excess of the *par value* of a bond over its initial sales price; at later dates, the excess of par over the sum of (initial issue price plus the portion of discount already amortized). From the standpoint of a bondholder, the difference between par value and selling price when the bond sells below par.

bond indenture The contract between an issuer of *bonds* and the bondholders.

bond premium Exactly parallel to *bond discount* except that the issue price (or current selling price) is higher than *par value*.

bond redemption Retirement of *bonds*.

bond refunding To incur *debt*, usually through the issue of new *bonds*, intending to use the proceeds to retire an *outstanding* bond *issue*.

bond sinking fund See *sinking fund*.

bond table A table showing the current price of a *bond* as a function of the *coupon rate*, years to *maturity* and effective *yield to maturity* (or *effective rate*).

bonus Premium over normal *wage* or *salary* paid to employees, usually for meritorious performance.

book As a verb, to record a transaction. As a noun, usually plural, the *journals* and *ledgers*. As an adjective, see *book value*.

book inventory An *inventory* amount that results, not from physical count, but from amount of initial inventory plus *invoice* amounts of purchases less invoice amounts of *requisitions* or withdrawals; implies a *perpetual method*.

bookkeeping The process of analyzing and recording transactions in the accounting records.

book of original entry A *journal*.

book value The amount shown in the books or in the *accounts* for any *asset*, *liability*, or *owners' equity* item. Generally used to refer to the net amount of an *asset* or group of assets shown in the accounts which record the asset and reductions, such as for *amortization*, in its cost. Of a firm, the excess of total assets over total liabilities.

book value per (common) share Common *stockholders' equity* divided by the number of shares of *common stock outstanding*.

boot The additional money paid or received along with a used item in a trade-in or exchange transaction for another item. See *trade-in transaction*.

borrower See *loan*.

branch A sales office or other unit of an enterprise physically separated from the home office of the enterprise but not organized as a legally separate *subsidiary*. The term is not usually used to refer to manufacturing units.

budget A financial plan that is used to estimate the results of future operations. Frequently used to help control future operations.

business combination The bringing together into a single accounting *entity* of two or more incorporated or unincorporated businesses. The *merger* will be accounted for either with the *purchase method* or the *pooling of interests method*.

business entity *Entity. Accounting entity.*

bylaws The rules adopted by the stockholders of a corporation that specify the general methods for carrying out the functions of the corporation.

CA *Chartered accountant.*

callable bond A *bond* for which the issuer reserves the right to pay a specific amount, the call price, to retire the obligation before *maturity* date. If the issuer agrees to pay more than the *face amount* of the bond when called, the excess of the payment over the face amount is the call premium.

call premium See *callable bond.*

call price See *callable bond.*

Canadian Institute of Chartered Accountants The national organization that represents *chartered accountants* in Canada.

cancelable lease See *lease.*

capital *Owners' equity* in a business. Often used, equally correctly, to mean the total assets of a business. Sometimes used to mean *capital assets*.

capital asset Properly used, a designation for income tax purposes which describes property held by a taxpayer except inventoriable *assets*, goods held primarily for sale, most depreciable property, *real estate, receivables*, certain *intangibles*, and a few other items. Sometimes this term is used imprecisely to describe *plant* and *equipment*, which are clearly not capital assets under the income tax definition. Often the term is used to refer to an *investment* in *securities*.

capital contributed in excess of par (or stated) value A preferred title for the account that shows the amount received by the issuer for *capital stock* in excess of *par* (or *stated*) *value*.

capital expenditure (outlay) An *expenditure* to acquire long-term *assets*.

capital gain The excess of proceeds over *cost*, or other *basis*, from the sale of a *capital asset* as defined by the Internal Revenue Code. If the capital asset is held more than 6 months before

sale, then the tax on the gain is computed at a rate lower than is used for other gains and ordinary income.

capitalize To record an *expenditure* that may benefit a future period as an *asset* rather than to treat the expenditure as an *expense* of the period of its occurrence. Whether or not expenditures for advertising or for research and development should be capitalized is controversial, but *FASB Statement* No. 2 requires expensing of *R & D* costs. We believe that expenditures should be capitalized if they lead to future benefits and thus meet the criterion to be an asset.

capital loss A negative capital gain; see *capital gain.*

capital stock The ownership shares of a corporation. Consists of all classes of *common* and *preferred stock*.

capital structure The composition of a corporation's equities; the relative proportions of *short-term debt, long-term debt,* and *owners' equity*.

carrying value (amount) *Book value.*

CASB Cost Accounting Standards Board. A board of five members authorized by the U.S. Congress to "promulgate cost-accounting standards designed to achieve uniformity and consistency in the cost-accounting principles followed by defense contractors and subcontractors under federal contracts." The *principles* promulgated by the CASB are likely to have considerable weight in practice where the *FASB* has not established a standard.

cash Currency and coins, negotiable checks, and balances in bank accounts.

cash basis of accounting In contrast to the *accrual basis of accounting*, a system of accounting in which *revenues* are recognized when *cash* is received and *expenses* are recognized as *expenditures* are made. No attempt is made to *match revenues* and *expenses* in determining *income*.

cash collection basis The *installment method* for recognizing *revenue*. Not to be confused with the *cash basis of accounting.*

cash cycle The period of time that elapses during which *cash* is converted into *inventories*, inventories are converted into *accounts receivable*, and receivables are converted back into *cash*. *Earnings cycle.*

cash disbursements journal A specialized *journal* used to record *expenditures* by *cash* and by *check*. If a *check register* is also used, the cash disbursements journal records only expenditures of currency and coins.

cash discount A reduction in sales or purchase price allowed for prompt payment.

cash dividend See *dividend*.

cash equivalent value A term used to describe the amount for which an *asset* could be sold. *Market value*.

cash flow Cash *receipts* minus *disbursements* from a given *asset*, or group of assets, for a given period.

cash flow statement A statement similar to the typical *statement of changes in financial position* where the flows of cash, rather than of *working capital*, are explained.

cash receipts journal A special *journal* used to record all *receipts* of *cash*.

central corporate expenses General *overhead expenses* incurred in running the corporate headquarters and related supporting activities of a corporation. These expenses are treated as *period expenses*.

certificate The document that is the physical embodiment of a *bond* or a *share* of *stock*. A term sometimes used for the *auditor's report*.

certificate of deposit Federal law constrains the *rate of interest* that banks can pay. Under current law banks are allowed to pay a higher rate than the one allowed on a *time deposit* if the depositor promises to leave funds on deposit for several months or more. When the bank receives such funds, it issues a certificate of deposit. The depositor can withdraw the funds before maturity if a penalty is paid.

certified financial statement A financial statement attested to by an independent *auditor* who is a *CPA*.

certified public accountant (CPA) An accountant who has satisfied the statutory and administrative requirements of his or her jurisdiction to be registered or licensed as a public accountant. In addition to passing the Uniform CPA Examination administered by the *AICPA*, the CPA must meet certain educational and moral requirements that differ from jurisdiction to jurisdiction. The jurisdictions are the 50 states, the District of Columbia, Guam, Puerto Rico, and the Virgin Islands.

change fund Coins and currency issued to cashiers, delivery drivers, and so on.

changes in financial position See *statement of changes in financial position*.

charge As a noun, a *debit* to an account; as a verb, to debit.

charge off To treat as a *loss* or *expense* an amount originally recorded as an *asset*; usually the term is used when the charge is not in accord with original expectations.

charter Document issued by a state government authorizing the creation of a corporation.

chartered accountant (CA) The title used in Australia, Canada, and the United Kingdom for an accountant who has satisfied the requirements of the institute of his or her jurisdiction to be qualified to serve as a *public accountant*.

chart of accounts A list of names and numbers of *accounts* systematically organized.

check The Federal Reserve Board defines a check as "a *draft* or order upon a bank or banking house purporting to be drawn upon a deposit of funds for the payment at all events of a certain sum of money to a certain person therein named or to him or his order or to bearer and payable instantly on demand." It must contain the phrase "pay to the order of."

check register A *journal* to record *checks* issued.

CICA *Canadian Institute of Chartered Accountants*.

clean opinion See *auditor's report*.

clean surplus concept The notion that the only entries to the *retained earnings* accounts are to record net earnings and dividends. Contrast with *current operating performance concept*. This concept, with minor exceptions, is now controlling in *GAAP*.

close As a verb, to transfer the *balance* of a *temporary* or *contra* or *adjunct* account to the main account to which it relates; for example, to transfer *revenue* and *expense* accounts directly, or through the *income summary* account, to an *owners' equity* account, or to transfer *purchase discounts* to purchases.

closed account An account with equal debits and credits. See *ruling an account*.

closing entries The entries that accomplish the transfer of balances in temporary accounts to the related balance sheet accounts.

closing inventory *Ending inventory*.

CMA Certificate in Management Accounting. Awarded by the Institute of Management Accounting of the *National Association of Accountants* to those who pass a set of examinations and meet certain experience and continuing education requirements.

collateral Assets pledged by a *borrower* that will be given up if the *loan* is not paid.

collectible Capable of being converted into cash; now, if due; later, otherwise.

commercial paper *Short-term notes* issued by corporate borrowers.

commission Remuneration, usually expressed as a percentage, to employees based upon an activity rate, such as sales.

Committee on Accounting Procedure Predecessor of the *APB*. The *AICPA's* principle-promulgating body from 1938 through 1959. Its 51 pronouncements are called *Accounting Research Bulletins*.

common-dollar accounting General *price level adjusted* accounting.

common monetary measuring unit For U.S. corporations, the dollar. See also *stable monetary unit assumption*.

common-size statement A *percentage statement*.

common stock *Stock* representing the class of owners who have residual claims on the assets and earnings of a corporation after all debt and preferred stockholders' claims have been met.

common stock equivalent A *security* whose primary value arises from its ability to be exchanged for *common shares*; includes *stock options, warrants*, and also *convertible bonds* or *convertible preferred stock* whose cash *yield* for any year within 5 years of issue is less than two-thirds the *prime rate* at the time of issue.

comparative statements Financial statements showing information for the same company for different times, usually 2 successive years. Nearly all published financial statements are in this form. Contrast with *historical summary*.

compensating balance When a bank lends funds to a customer, it often requires that the customer keep on deposit in his or her checking account an amount equal to some percentage, say 20 percent, of the loan. The amount required to be left on deposit is the compensating balance. Such amounts effectively increase the *interest rate*. The amounts of such balances must be disclosed in *notes* to the *financial statements*.

completed contract method Recognizing *revenues* and *expenses* for a job or order only when it is finished, except that when a loss on the contract is expected, revenues and expenses are recognized in the period where the loss is first forecast.

completed sales basis See *sales basis of revenue recognition*.

compound entry A *journal entry* with more than one *debit* or more than one *credit*, or both. See *trade-in transaction* for an example.

compounding period The time period for which *interest* is calculated. At the end of the period the interest may be paid to the lender or added (that is, converted) to principal for the next interest-earning period, which is usually a year or some portion of a year.

compound interest *Interest* calculated on *principal* plus previously undistributed interest.

comptroller Same meaning and pronunciation as *controller*.

conglomerate *Holding company*. This term is used when the owned companies are in dissimilar lines of business.

conservatism A *reporting objective* that calls for anticipation of all *losses* and *expenses* but defers recognition of *gains* or *profits*. In the absence of certainty, events are to be reported in a way that tends to minimize current income.

consignee See *on consignment*.

consignment See *on consignment*.

consignor See *on consignment*.

consistency Treatment of like *transactions* in the same way in different periods so that financial statements will be more comparable than otherwise. The reporting policy implying that procedures, once adopted, should be followed from period to period by a reporting *entity*.

consolidated financial statements Statements issued by legally separate companies that show financial position and income as they would appear if the companies were one legal *entity*. Such statements reflect an economic, rather than a legal, concept of the *entity*.

Consumer Price Index (CPI) A *price index* computed and issued monthly by the Bureau of Labor Statistics of the U.S. Department of Labor. The index attempts to track the price level of a group of goods and services purchased by the average consumer. Contrast with *GNP Implicit Price Deflator Index*.

contingent annuity An *annuity* whose number of payments depends upon the outcome of an event whose timing is uncertain at the time the annuity is set up; for example, an annuity payable for the life of the *annuitant*.

contingent liability A potential *liability*; if a specified event were to occur, such as losing a lawsuit, a liability would be recognized. Until the outcome is known, the contingency is merely disclosed in notes rather than shown in the balance sheet accounts. A *material* contingency may lead to a qualified, *"subject to,"* auditor's opinion.

continuing operations See *income from continuing operations.*

continuity of operations The assumption in accounting that the business *entity* will continue to operate long enough for current plans to be carried out. The *going-concern assumption.*

contra account An *account,* such as *accumulated depreciation,* that accumulates subtractions from another account, such as machinery. Contrast with *adjunct account.*

contributed capital The sum of the balances in *capital stock* accounts plus *capital contributed in excess of par (or stated) value* accounts. *Owners' equity* less *retained earnings.* Contrast with *donated capital.*

contributory Said of a *pension plan* where employees, as well as employers, make payments to a pension *fund.* Note that the provisions for *vesting* are applicable to the employer's payments. Whatever the degree of vesting of the employer's payments, the employee typically gets back his or her payments, with interest, in case of death, or other cessation of employment, before retirement.

control (controlling) account A summary *account* that shows totals of entries and balances that appear in individual accounts in a *subsidiary ledger.* Accounts Receivable is a control account backed up with accounts for each customer. The balance in a control account should not be changed unless a corresponding change is made in the subsidiary accounts.

controlled company A company, a majority of whose voting stock is held by an individual or corporation. Effective control can sometimes be exercised when less than 50 percent of the stock is owned.

controller The title often used for the chief accountant of an organization. Often spelled *comptroller.*

conversion The act of exchanging a convertible security for another security.

conversion period *Compounding period.*

convertible bond A *bond* that may be converted into a specified number of shares of *capital stock.*

convertible preferred stock *Preferred stock* that may be converted into a specified number of shares of *common stock.*

copyright Exclusive right granted by the government to an author, composer, playright and the like for 28 years (renewable for another 28 years) to enjoy the benefit of a piece of written work. The *economic life* of a copyright may be considerably less than the legal life as, for example, the copyright of this book.

corporation A legal entity authorized by a state to operate under the rules of the entity's *charter.*

correction of errors See *accounting errors.*

cost The sacrifice, measured by the *price* paid or required to be paid, to acquire *goods* or *services.* See *acquisition cost* and *replacement cost.* The term "cost" is often used when referring to the valuation of a good or service acquired. When "cost" is used in this sense, a cost is an *asset.* When the benefits of the acquisition (the goods or services acquired) expire, the cost becomes an expense. Some writers, however, use cost and expense as synonyms. Contrast with *expense.*

cost accounting Classifying, summarizing, recording, reporting, and allocating current or predicted *costs.*

Cost Accounting Standards Board See *CASB.*

cost effective Among alternatives, the one whose benefit, or payoff, divided by cost is highest. Sometimes said of an action whose expected benefits exceed expected costs whether or not there are other alternatives with larger benefit/cost ratios.

cost-flow assumption See *flow assumption.*

cost flows Costs passing through various classifications within an entity. See *flow of costs* for a diagram.

costing The process of determining the cost of activities, products, or services. The British word for *cost accounting.*

cost method (for investments) Accounting for an investment in the *capital stock* of another company where the investment is shown at *acquisition cost,* and only *dividends* declared are treated as *revenue.* Used if less than 20 percent of the voting stock is held by the investor.

cost method (for treasury stock) The method of showing *treasury stock* as a *contra* to all other items of *stockholders' equity* in an amount equal to that paid to reacquire the stock.

cost of goods manufactured The sum of all costs allocated to products completed during a period; includes materials, labor, and *overhead.*

cost of goods purchased Net purchase price of goods acquired plus costs of storage and delivery to the place where the items can be used productively.

cost of goods sold Inventoriable *costs* that are expensed because the units are sold; equals beginning inventory plus cost of goods purchased or manufactured minus ending inventory.

cost or market, whichever is lower See *lower of cost or market.*

cost principle The *principle* that requires reporting *assets* at *historical* or *acquisition cost*, less accumulated *amortization*. This principle is based on the assumption that cost is equal to *fair market value* at the date of acquisition.

coupon That portion of a *bond* redeemable at a specified date for *interest* payments. Its physical form is much like a ticket; each coupon is dated and is deposited at a bank, just like a check, for collection or is mailed to the issuer's agent for collection.

coupon rate Of a *bond*, the amount of annual coupons divided by par value. Contrast with *effective rate.*

covenant A promise with legal validity.

CPA See *certified public accountant.* The *AICPA* suggests that no periods be shown in the abbreviation.

CPI *Consumer price index.*

cr. Abbreviation for *credit.*

credit As a noun, an entry on the right-hand side of an *account.* As a verb, to make an entry on the right-hand side of an account. Records increases in *liabilities, owners' equity,* and *revenues;* records decreases in *assets* and *expenses.* See *debit and credit conventions.* Also the ability or right to buy or borrow in return for a promise to pay later.

credit loss The amount of *accounts receivable* that is, or is expected to become, *uncollectible.*

creditor One who lends.

cross-section analysis Analysis of *financial statements* of various firms for a single period of time, as opposed to time-series analysis, where statements of a given firm are analyzed over several periods of time.

cumulative dividend Preferred stock *dividends* that if not paid, accrue as a commitment which must be paid before dividends to common stockholders can be declared.

cumulative preferred stock *Preferred* stock with *cumulative dividend* rights.

current asset *Cash* and other *assets* that are expected to be turned into cash, sold, or consumed within the normal operating cycle of the firm, usually 1 year. Current assets include *cash, marketable securities, receivables, inventory,* and current *prepayments.*

current cost *Cost* stated in terms of current market prices rather than in terms of *acquisition cost. Current replacement cost.* See *net realizable value, current selling price.*

current funds *Cash* and other assets readily convertible into cash.

current (gross) margin See *operating margin (based on replacement costs).*

current liability A debt or other obligation that must be discharged within a short time, usually 1 year, normally by expending *current assets.*

current operating performance concept The notion that reported *income* for a period ought to reflect only ordinary, normal, and recurring operations of that period. A consequence is that *extraordinary* and nonrecurring items are entered directly in the Retained Earnings account. Contrast with *clean surplus concept.* This concept is no longer acceptable.

current ratio Sum of *current assets* divided by sum of *current liabilities.* See *ratio.*

current replacement cost Of an *asset*, the amount currently required to acquire an identical asset (in the same condition and with the same service potential) or an asset capable of rendering the same service at a current *fair market price.* If these two amounts differ, the lower is usually used. See *reproduction cost.*

current selling price The amount for which an *asset* could be sold as of a given time in an *arm's length* transaction.

current-value accounting The form of accounting where all assets are shown at *current replacement cost* (*entry value*) or *current selling price* or *net realizable value* (*exit value*) and all *liabilities* are shown at *present value.* Entry and exit values may be quite different from each other, so there is no general agreement on the precise meaning of current-value accounting.

DDB *Double-declining balance depreciation.*

debenture bond A *bond* not secured with *collateral.*

debit As a noun, an entry on the left-hand side of an *account.* As a verb, to make an entry on the left-hand side of an account. Records increases in *assets* and *expenses*; records decreases in *liabilities*, *owners' equity*, and *revenues*. See *debit and credit conventions*.

debit and credit conventions The equality of the two sides of the *accounting equation* is maintained by recording equal amounts of *debits* and *credits* for each *transaction*. The conventional use of the *T-account* form and the rules for debit and credit in *balance sheet accounts* are summarized as follows.

ANY ASSET ACCOUNT

Opening Balance Increase + Dr. Ending Balance	Decrease − Cr.

ANY LIABILITY ACCOUNT

Decrease − Dr.	Opening Balance Increase + Cr. Ending Balance

ANY OWNERS' EQUITY ACCOUNT

Decrease − Dr.	Opening Balance Increase + Cr. Ending Balance

Revenue and expense accounts belong to the owners' equity group. The relationship and the rules for debit and credit in these accounts can be expressed as follows.

OWNERS' EQUITY

Decrease − Dr.	Increase + Cr.
EXPENSES	**REVENUES**

Dr.	Cr.	Dr.	Cr.
+	−	−	+
*			*

* Normal balance prior to closing.

debt An amount owed. The general name for *notes*, *bonds*, *mortgages*, and the like which are evidence of amounts owed.

debt-equity ratio Total *liabilities* divided by total *equities*. See *ratio*. Sometimes the denominator is merely total *stockholders' equity*. Sometimes the numerator is restricted to long-term *debt*.

debt financing Raising *funds* by issuing *bonds* or *notes*. Contrast with *equity financing*. *Leverage*.

debtor One who borrows.

debt ratio *Debt-equity ratio*.

debt service requirement The amount of cash required for payments of *interest*, current maturities of *principal* on outstanding *debt*, and payments to *sinking funds* (corporations).

declaration date Time when a *dividend* is declared by the *board of directors*.

declining-balance depreciation The method of calculating the periodic *depreciation* charge by multiplying the *book value* at the start of the period by a constant percentage. In pure declining balance depreciation the constant percentage is $1-\sqrt[n]{s/c}$, where n is the *depreciable life*, s is *salvage value*, and c is *acquisition cost*. See *double-declining-balance depreciation*.

defalcation Embezzlement.

default Failure to pay *interest* or *principal* on a *debt* when due.

deferral method See *flow-through method* (of accounting for the *investment tax credit*) for definition and contrast.

deferred annuity An *annuity* whose first payment is made sometime after the end of the first period.

deferred charge *Expenditure* not recognized as an *expense* of the period when made but carried forward as an *asset* to be *written off* in future periods, such as for advance rent payments or insurance premiums.

deferred cost *Deferred charge*.

deferred credit Sometimes used to indicate *advances from customers*. Also sometimes used to describe the *deferred income tax liability*.

deferred debit *Deferred charge*.

deferred expense *Deferred charge*.

deferred income *Advances from customers*.

deferred income tax (liability) An *indeterminate-term liability* that arises when the pretax income shown on the tax return is less than what it would have been had the same *accounting principles* been used in tax returns as used for financial reporting. *APB Opinion* No. 11 requires that the firm debit income tax *expense* and credit deferred income tax with the amount of the taxes delayed by using different accounting principles in tax returns from those used in financial reports. See *timing difference* and *permanent difference*. If, as a result of timing differences, cumulative taxable income exceeds cumulative reported income before taxes, the deferred income tax account will have a *debit* balance and will be reported as a *deferred charge*.

deferred revenue Sometimes used to indicate *advances from customers*.

deferred tax See *deferred income tax*.

deficit A *debit balance* in the Retained Earnings account; presented on the balance sheet as a *contra* to stockholders' equity.

defined benefit plan A *pension plan* where the employer promises specific benefits to each employee. The employer's cash contributions and pension expense are adjusted in relation to investment performance of the pension *fund*. Sometimes called a "fixed-benefit" pension plan. Contrast with *money-purchase plan*.

defined contribution plan A *money-purchase (pension) plan*.

deflation A period of generally declining prices.

demand deposit *Funds* in a *checking account* at a bank.

depletion *Amortization* of a *wasting asset*, or natural resource. See also *percentage depletion*.

depletion allowance See *percentage depletion*.

deposit, sinking fund Payments made to a *sinking fund*.

deposits in transit Deposits made by a firm but not yet reflected on the *bank statement*.

depreciable cost That part of the *cost* of an asset, usually *acquisition cost* less *salvage value*, that is to be charged off over the life of the asset through the process of *depreciation*.

depreciable life For an *asset*, the time period over which *depreciable cost* is to be allocated. For tax returns, depreciable life may be shorter than estimated *service life*.

depreciation *Amortization* of *plant assets*; the process of allocating the cost of an asset to the periods of benefit—the *depreciable life*. Classified as a *production cost* or a *period expense*, depending upon the asset and whether *absorption* or *direct costing* is used.

depreciation reserve An inferior term for *accumulated depreciation*. See *reserve*. Do not confuse with a replacement *fund*.

dilution A potential reduction in *earnings per share* or *book value* per share by the potential conversion of securities or by the potential exercise of *warrants* or *options*.

dilutive Said of a *security* that would reduce *earnings per share* if it were exchanged for common stock.

dipping into LIFO layers See *LIFO inventory layer*.

direct costing The method of allocating costs that assigns only variable *manufacturing costs* to product and treats fixed *manufacturing costs* as *period* expenses. Sometimes called "variable costing."

disbursement Payment by *cash* or by a *check*. See *expenditure*.

disclosure The showing of facts in *financial statements*, *notes* thereto, or the *auditor's report*.

discontinued operations See *income from discontinued operations*.

discount In the context of *compound interest*, *bonds*, and *notes*, the difference between *face* or *future value* and *present value* of a payment. In the context of *sales* and *purchases*, a reduction in price granted for prompt payment.

discount factor One plus the *discount rate*.

discounting a note See *note receivable discounted* and *factoring*.

discount rate *Interest rate* used to convert future payments to *present values*.

discounts lapsed (lost) The sum of *discounts* offered for prompt payment that were not taken (or allowed) because of expiration of the discount period. See *terms of sale*.

discovery-value accounting In exploration for natural resources, there is the problem of what to do with the expenditures for exploration. Suppose that $10 million is spent to drill ten holes ($1 million each) and that nine of them are dry while one is a gusher containing oil with a *net realizable value* of $40 million. Dry-hole, or successful-efforts, accounting would *expense* $9 million and *capitalize* $1 million to be *depleted* as the oil was lifted from the ground. Full costing would expense nothing, but capitalize the $10 million of drilling costs to be depleted as the oil is lifted from the single productive well. Discovery-value accounting would capitalize $40 million to be depleted as the oil is lifted, with a $30 million *credit* to *income* or *contributed capital*.

Discussion Memorandum A neutral discussion of all the issues concerning an accounting problem of current concern to the *FASB*. The publication of such a document usually implies that the FASB is considering issuing a *Statement of Financial Accounting Standards* on this particular problem. The discussion memorandum brings together material about the particular problem to facilitate interaction and comment by those interested in the matter.

dishonored note   A *promissory note* whose maker does not repay the loan at *maturity* for a term loan, or on demand, for a *demand loan*.

distribution expense   *Expense* of selling, advertising, and delivery activities.

dividend   A distribution of *earnings* to owners of a corporation; it may be paid in cash (cash dividend), with stock (stock dividend), with property, or with other securities (dividend in kind). Dividends, except stock dividends, become a legal liability of the corporation when they are declared. Hence, the owner of stock ordinarily recognizes *revenue* when a dividend, other than a stock dividend, is declared. See also *liquidating dividend* and *stock dividend*.

dividend in kind   See *dividend*.

dividends in arrears   Dividends on *cumulative preferred stock* that have not been declared in accordance with the preferred stock contract. Such arrearages must usually be cleared before dividends on *common stock* can be declared.

dividend yield   *Dividends* declared for the year divided by market price of the stock as of a given time of the year.

divisional reporting   *Line of business reporting*.

dollar sign rules   In presenting accounting statements or schedules, place a dollar sign beside the first figure in each column and beside any figure below a horizontal line drawn under the preceding figure.

donated capital   A *stockholders' equity* account credited when contributions, such as land or buildings, are freely given to the company. Do not confuse with *contributed capital*.

double-declining-balance depreciation (DDB). *Declining-balance depreciation*, which see, where the constant percentage is $2/n$ and n is the *depreciable life* in periods. Maximum declining-balance rate permitted in the *income tax* laws.

double entry   The system of recording transactions that maintains the equality of the accounting equation; each entry results in recording equal amounts of *debits* and *credits*.

double-T-account   *T-account* with an extra horizontal line showing a change in the account balance to be explained by the subsequent entries into the account.

double taxation   Corporate income is subject to the corporate income tax, and the aftertax income, when distributed to owners, is subject to the personal income tax.

doubtful accounts   *Accounts receivable* estimated to be *uncollectible*.

dr.   The abbreviation for *debit*.

draft   A written order by the first party, called the drawer, instructing a second party, called the drawee (such as a bank), to pay a third party, called the payee. See also *check*.

drawee   See *draft*.

drawer   See *draft*.

drawing account   A *temporary account* used in *sole proprietorships* and *partnerships* to record payments to owners or partners during a period. At the end of the period, the drawing account is closed by crediting it and debiting the owner's or partner's share of income or, perhaps, his or her capital account.

drawings   Payments made to a *sole proprietor* or to a partner during a period. See *drawing account*.

dry-hole accounting   See *discovery-value accounting* for definition and contrast.

dual transactions assumption (fiction)   In presenting the *statement of changes in financial position*, some transactions not involving *working capital* accounts are reported as though working capital was generated and then used. For example, the issue of *capital stock* in return for the *asset*, land, is reported in the statement of changes in financial position as though stock were issued for *cash* and cash were used to acquire land. Other examples of transactions that require the dual transactions fiction are the issue of a *mortgage* in return for a *noncurrent* asset and the issue of stock to bond holders in return for their *bonds*.

earned surplus   A term once used, but no longer considered proper, for *retained earnings*.

earnings   *Income*, or sometimes *profit*.

earnings cycle   The period of time that elapses for a given firm, or the series of transactions, during which *cash* is converted into *goods* and *services*, goods and services are sold to customers, and customers pay for their purchases with cash. *Cash cycle*.

earnings per share (of common stock)   *Net income* to common stockholders (*net income* minus *preferred dividends*) divided by the average number of *common shares* outstanding; but see also *primary earnings per share* and *fully diluted earnings per share*. See *ratio*.

earnings per share (of preferred stock) *Net income* divided by the number of *preferred shares* outstanding. This ratio indicates how well the preferred dividends are covered or protected; it does not indicate a legal share of *earnings*.

earnings, retained See *retained earnings*.

economic entity See *entity*.

economic life The time span over which the benefits of an *asset* are expected to be received. *Service life*.

effective interest method A systematic method for amortizing *bond discount* or *premium* that makes the *interest expense* for each period divided by the amount of the net *liability (face amount* minus *discount* or plus *premium*) at the beginning of the period equal to the *yield* rate on the bond at the time of issue. Interest expense for a period is yield rate (at time of issue) multiplied by the net liability at the start of the period. The *amortization* of discount or premium is the *plug* to give equal *debits* and *credits*. (Interest expense is a debit and the amount of coupon payments is a credit.) The bond holder makes a similar calculation.

effective (interest) rate Of a bond, the *yield to maturity* at the time of issue. Contrast with *coupon rate*. If the bond is issued for a price below *par*, then the effective rate is higher than the coupon rate; if it is issued for a price greater than par, then the effective rate is lower than the coupon rate.

eliminations *Work sheet* entries to prepare *consolidated statements* that are made to avoid duplicating the amounts of *assets, liabilities, owners' equity, revenues,* and *expenses* of the consolidated *entity* when the accounts of the *parent* and *subsidiaries* are summed.

employee stock option See *stock option*.

employer, employee payroll taxes See *payroll taxes*.

ending inventory The *cost of inventory* on hand at the end of the *accounting period*, often called "closing inventory." The cost of inventory to be carried to the subsequent period.

enterprise Any business organization, usually defining the accounting *entity*.

entity A person, *partnership, corporation,* or other organization. The *accounting entity* for which accounting statements are prepared may not be the same as the entity defined by law. For example, a *sole proprietorship* is an accounting entity, but the individual's combined business and personal assets are the legal entity in most jurisdictions. Several affiliated corporations may be separate legal entities, while *consolidated financial statements* are prepared for the group of companies operating as a single economic entity.

entity theory The view of the corporation that emphasizes the form of the *accounting equation* that says *assets = equities*. Contrast with *proprietorship theory*. The entity theory is less concerned with a distinct line between *liabilities* and *stockholders' equity* than is the proprietorship theory. Rather, all equities are provided to the corporation by outsiders who merely have claims of differing legal standings. The entity theory implies using a *multiple-step* income statement.

entry value The current *cost* of acquiring an asset or service at a *fair market price. Replacement cost*.

equities *Liabilities* plus *owners' equity*.

equity A claim to *assets*; a source of assets.

equity financing Raising *funds* by issuance of *capital stock*. Contrast with *debt financing*.

equity method A method of accounting for an *investment* in the stock of another company in which the proportionate share of the earnings of the other company is debited to the investment account and credited to a *revenue* account as earned. When *dividends* are received, *cash* is debited and the investment account is credited. Used in reporting when the investor owns 20 percent or more of the stock of an unconsolidated company. One of the few instances where revenue is recognized without a change in *working capital*.

equity ratio *Stockholders' equity* divided by total *assets*. See *ratio*.

ERISA Employee Retirement Income Security Act of 1974. The federal law that sets *pension plan* requirements.

estimated liabilities The preferred terminology for estimated costs to be incurred for such uncertain things as repairs under *warranty*. An estimated liability is shown in the *balance sheet*. Contrast with *contingent liability*.

estimated salvage value Synonymous with *salvage value* of an *asset* before its retirement.

except for Qualification in *auditor's report*, usually caused by a change, approved by the auditor, from one acceptable accounting principle or procedure to another.

exchange The generic term for a transaction (or more technically, a reciprocal transfer) between one entity and another. In another context, the name for a market, such as the New York Stock Exchange.

exchange gain or loss The phrase used by the FASB for *foreign exchange gain or loss.*

exchange rate The *price* of one country's currency in terms of another country's currency. For example, the British pound might be worth $2.30 at a given time. The exchange rate would be stated as "one pound is worth two dollars and thirty cents" or "one dollar is worth .4348 (= £1/$2.30) pounds."

excise tax Tax on the manufacture, sale, or consumption of a commodity.

ex-dividend Said of a stock at the time when the declared *dividend* becomes the property of the person who owned the stock on the *record date.* The payment date follows the ex-dividend date.

exercise When the owner of an *option* or *warrant* purchases the security that the option entitles him or her to purchase, he or she has exercised the option or warrant.

exercise price See *option.*

exit value The proceeds that would be received if assets were disposed of in an *arm's-length transaction. Current selling price. Net realizable value.*

expenditure Payment of *cash* to obtain *goods or services.* Virtually synonymous with *disbursement,* except that disbursement is a broader term and includes payments to discharge *liabilities.*

expense As a noun, the *cost* of *assets* used up in producing *revenue.* A "gone" asset; an expired cost. Do not confuse with *expenditure* or *disbursement,* which may occur before, when, or after the related expense is recognized. Use the word cost to refer to an item that still has service potential and is an asset. Use the word expense after the asset's service potential has been used. As a verb, to designate a past or current expenditure as a current expense.

expense account An *account* to accumulate *expenses;* such accounts are closed at the end of the accounting period. A *temporary owners' equity* account. Also used to describe a listing of expenses by an employee submitted to the employer for reimbursement.

expired cost An *expense.*

exposure draft A preliminary statement of the FASB (or APB between 1962 and 1973) which shows the contents of a pronouncement the Board is considering making effective.

external reporting Reporting to stockholders and the public, as opposed to internal reporting for management's benefit. See *financial accounting* and contrast with *managerial accounting.*

extraordinary item A *material expense* or *revenue* item characterized both by its unusual nature and infrequency of occurrence that is shown along with its income tax effects separately from ordinary income and *income from discontinued operations* on the *income statement.* A *loss* from an earthquake would probably be classified as an extraordinary item. Gain (or loss) on retirement of *bonds* is treated as an extraordinary item under the terms of *FASB Statement* No. 4.

face amount (value) The nominal amount due at *maturity* from a *bond* or *note.* The corresponding amount of a stock certificate is best called the *par* or *stated value,* whichever is applicable.

factoring The process of buying *notes* or *accounts receivable* at a *discount* from the holder to whom the debt is owed; from the holder's point of view, the selling of such notes or accounts. When a single note is involved, the process is called discounting a note.

factory Used synonymously with manufacturing as an adjective.

factory cost *Manufacturing cost.*

factory expense *Manufacturing overhead.*

factory overhead Usually an item of *manufacturing cost* other than direct *labor* or direct *materials.*

fair market price (value) Price (value) determined at *arm's length* between a willing buyer and a willing seller, each acting rationally in his or her own self-interest. May be estimated in the absence of a monetary transaction.

fair presentation (fairness) When the *auditor's report* says that the *financial statements* "present fairly . . . ," the auditor means that the accounting alternatives used by the entity are all in accordance with *GAAP.* In recent years, however, courts are finding that conformity with *generally acceptable accounting principles* may be insufficient grounds for an opinion that the statements are fair.

FASB Financial Accounting Standards Board. An independent board responsible, since 1973, for establishing *generally accepted accounting principles*. Its official pronouncements are called "Statements of Financial Accounting Standards" and "Interpretations of Financial Accounting Standards." See *Discussion Memorandum*.

FASB Interpretation An official statement of the *FASB* interpreting the meaning of *Accounting Research Bulletins*, *APB Opinions*, and *Statements of Financial Accounting Standards*.

federal income tax *Income tax* levied by the U.S. government on individuals and corporations.

Federal Unemployment Tax Act See *FUTA*.

FEI *Financial Executives Institute*.

FICA Federal Insurance Contributions Act. The law that sets *"Social Security" taxes* and benefits.

FIFO First-in, first-out; an *inventory-flow assumption* by which *ending inventory* cost is determined from most recent purchases and *cost of goods sold* is determined from oldest purchases including beginning inventory. See *LISH*. Contrast with *LIFO*.

finance As a verb, to supply with *funds* through the *issue* of stocks, bonds, notes, or mortgages, or through the retention of earnings.

financial accounting The accounting for *assets*, *equities*, *revenues*, and *expenses* of a business. Primarily concerned with the historical reporting of the *financial position* and operations of an *entity* to external users. Contrast with *managerial accounting*.

Financial Accounting Standards Board See *FASB*.

Financial Executives Institute An organization of financial executives, such as chief accountants, *controllers*, and treasurers, of large businesses.

financial position (condition) Statement of the *assets* and *equities* of a firm displayed on the *balance sheet* statement.

financial ratio See *ratio*.

financial statements The *balance sheet, income statement, statement of retained earnings, statement of changes in financial position*, and *notes* thereto.

financial structure *Capital structure*.

financing lease A *lease* treated by the lessee as both the borrowing of funds and the acquisition of an *asset* to be *amortized*. Both the *liability* and the asset are recognized on the balance sheet. Expenses consist of *interest* on the *debt* and *amortization* of the asset. The lessor treats the lease as the sale of the asset in return for a series of future cash receipts. Contrast with *operating lease*. Note that the same lease may, in some cases, be treated as a financing lease by the lessor and an operating lease by the lessee.

finished goods Manufactured product ready for sale; a *current asset (inventory) account*.

firm Informally, any business entity. (Strictly speaking, a firm is a *partnership*.)

first-in, first-out See *FIFO*.

fiscal year A period of 12 consecutive months chosen by a business as the *accounting period* for annual reports. May or may not be a *natural business year* or a calendar year.

FISH An acronym, conceived by George H. Sorter, for *first-in, still-here*. FISH is the same cost-flow assumption as *LIFO*. Many readers of accounting statements find it easier to think about inventory questions in terms of items still on hand. Think of LIFO in connection with *cost of goods sold* but of FISH in connection with *ending inventory*. See *LISH*.

fixed assets *Plant assets*.

fixed-benefit plan A *defined benefit (pension) plan*.

float *Checks* that have been *credited* to the depositor's bank account, but not yet *debited* to the *drawer's* bank account.

flow The change in the amount of an item over time. Contrast with *stock*.

flow assumption When a *withdrawal* is made from *inventory*, the cost of the withdrawal must be determined by a flow assumption if *specific identification* of units is not used. The usual flow assumptions are *FIFO*, *LIFO*, and *weighted-average*.

flow of costs *Costs* passing through various classifications within an *entity*. See the diagram on the next page for a summary of *product* and *period cost* flows.

flow-through method Accounting for the *investment tax credit* to show all income statement benefits of the credit in the year of acquisition, rather than spreading them over the life of the asset acquired, called the "deferral method." The *APB* preferred the deferral method in Opinion No. 2 (1962) but accepted the flow-through method in Opinion No. 4 (1964).

FOB Free on board some location (for example, FOB shipping point; FOB destination); the *invoice* price includes delivery at seller's expense to that location. Title to goods usually passes from seller to buyer at the FOB location.

footing Adding a column of figures.

footnotes More detailed information than that provided in the *income statement, balance sheet, statement of retained earnings,* and *statement of changes in financial position;* these are considered an integral part of the statements and are covered by the *auditor's report.* Sometimes called "notes."

forecast An estimate or projection of costs or revenues or both.

foreign exchange gain or loss Gain or loss from holding *net* foreign *monetary items* during a period when the *exchange rate* changes.

Form 10-K See *10–K.*

franchise A privilege granted or sold, such as to use a name or to sell products or services.

free on board *FOB.*

freight-in The *cost* of freight or shipping in acquiring *inventory,* preferably treated as a part of the cost of inventory.

freight-out The *cost* of freight or shipping in selling *inventory,* treated as a selling *expense* in the period of sale.

full costing *Absorption costing.* See *discovery-value accounting* for another definition in the context of accounting for natural resources.

full disclosure The reporting policy requiring that all significant or *material* information is to be presented in the financial statements. See *fair presentation.*

fully diluted earnings per share Smallest *earnings per share* figure on *common stock* that can be obtained by computing an earnings per share for all possible combinations of assumed *exercise* or *conversion* of *potentially dilutive securities.* Must be reported on the *income statement* if it is less than 97 percent of earnings available to common stockholders divided by the average

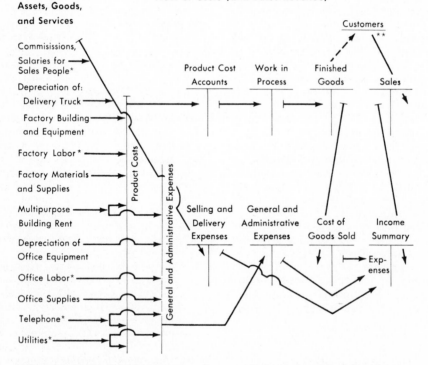

Flow of Costs (and Sales Revenue)

*The credit in the entry to record these items is usually to a payable; for all others, the credit is usually to an asset, or to an asset contra account.

**When sales to customers are recorded, the Sales account is credited. The debit is usually to Cash or Accounts Receivable.

number of common shares outstanding during the period.

fully vested Said of a *pension plan* when an employee (or his or her estate) has rights to all the benefits purchased with the employer's contributions to the plan even if the employee is not employed by this employer at the time of retirement.

functional classification *Income statement* reporting form in which *expenses* are reported by functions, that is, cost of goods sold, administrative expenses, selling expenses; contrast with *natural classification*.

fund An *asset* or group of assets set aside for a specific purpose.

funded Said of a *pension plan* or other obligation when *funds* have been set aside for meeting the obligation when it becomes due. The federal law for pension plans requires that all *normal costs* be funded as recognized. In addition, *past and prior service costs* of pension plans must be funded over 30 or 40 years, depending upon the circumstances.

funding Replacing *short-term* liabilities with *long-term* debt.

funds Generally, *working capital*; current assets less current liabilities. Sometimes used to refer to *cash* or to cash and *marketable securities*.

funds provided by operations An important subtotal in the *statement of changes in financial position*. This amount is the total of revenues producing *funds* less *expenses* requiring funds. Often, the amount is shown as *net income* plus expenses not requiring funds (such as depreciation charges) minus revenues not producing funds (such as revenues recognized under the *equity method* of accounting for a long-term investment).

funds statement An informal name often used for the *statement of changes in financial position*.

FUTA Federal Unemployment Tax Act, which provides for taxes to be collected at the federal level, to help subsidize the individual states' administration of their unemployment compensation programs.

GAAP *Generally accepted accounting principles*. A plural noun.

gain Excess of *revenues* over *expenses* from a specific transaction. Frequently used in the con-

text of describing a transaction not part of a firm's typical, day-to-day operations.

general expenses *Operating expenses* other than those specifically assigned to cost of goods sold, selling, and administration.

general journal The formal record where transactions, or summaries of similar transactions, are recorded in *journal entry* form as they occur. Use of the adjective "general" usually implies that there are also various *special journals*, such as a *check register* or *sales journal*, in use.

general ledger The name for the formal *ledger* containing all of the financial statement accounts. It has equal debits and credits as evidenced by the *trial balance*. Some of the accounts in the general ledger may be *controlling accounts*, supported by details contained in *subsidiary ledgers*.

generally accepted accounting principles (GAAP) As previously defined by the APB and now by the *FASB*, the conventions, rules, and procedures necessary to define accepted accounting practice at a particular time; includes both broad guidelines and relatively detailed practices and procedures.

generally accepted auditing standards The standards, as opposed to particular procedures, promulgated by the AICPA, which concern "the auditor's professional qualities" and "the judgment exercised by him in the performance of his examination and in his report."

general partner Member of *partnership* personally liable for all debts of the partnership; contrast with *limited partner*.

general price index A measure of the aggregate prices of a wide range of goods and services in the economy at one time relative to the prices during a base period. See *consumer price index* and *GNP Implicit Price Deflator*. Contrast with *specific price index*.

general price level adjusted statements See *price level adjusted statements*.

general price level changes Changes in the aggregate prices of a wide range of goods and services in the economy. These price changes are measured using a *general price index*. Contrast with *specific price changes*.

general purchasing power of the dollar The command of the dollar over a wide range of goods and services in the economy. The general purchasing power of the dollar is inversely related to changes in a general price index. See *general price index*.

GNP Implicit Price Deflator (Index) A *price index* issued quarterly by the Office of Business Economics of the U.S. Department of Commerce. This index attempts to trace the price level of all *goods and services* comprising the *gross national product.* Contrast with *Consumer Price Index.*

going-concern assumption For accounting purposes a business is assumed to remain in operation long enough for all its current plans to be carried out. This assumption is part of the justification for the *acquisition-cost* basis, rather than a *liquidation* or *exit-value* basis, of accounting.

goods Items of merchandise, supplies, raw materials, or finished goods. Sometimes the meaning of "goods" is extended to include all *tangible* items, as in the phrase "goods and services."

goods available for sale The sum of *beginning inventory* plus all acquisitions, or purchases, during an *accounting period.*

goods in process *Work in process.*

goodwill The excess of cost of an acquired firm or operating unit over the current or *fair market value* of *net assets* of the acquired unit. Informally used to indicate the value of good customer relations, high employee morale, a well-respected business name, and so on, which are expected to result in greater than normal earning power.

graded vesting Said of a *pension plan* where not all employee benefits are currently *vested.* By law, the benefits must become vested according to one of several formulas as time passes.

gross Not adjusted or reduced by deductions or subtractions. Contrast with *net.*

gross margin *Net sales* minus *cost of goods sold.*

gross margin percentage $100 \times (1 - cost\ of\ goods\ sold/net\ sales) = 100 \times (gross\ margin/net\ sales).$

gross national product (GNP) The market value within a nation for a year of all goods and services produced as measured by final sales of goods and services to individuals, corporations, and governments plus the excess of exports over imports.

gross price method (of recording purchase or sales discounts) The purchase (or *sale*) is recorded at its *invoice price,* not deducting the amounts of *discounts* available. Discounts taken are recorded in a *contra* account to purchases (or sales). Information on discounts lapsed is not made available, and for this reason, most firms prefer the *net-price method* of recording purchase discounts.

gross profit *Gross margin.*

gross profit method A method of estimating *ending inventory* amounts. *Cost of goods sold* is measured as some fraction of sales; and then the *inventory equation* is used to value ending *inventory.*

gross profit ratio *Gross margin* divided by *net sales.*

gross sales All *sales* at *invoice* prices, not reduced by *discounts, allowances, returns,* or other adjustments.

group depreciation A method of calculating *depreciation* charges where similar assets are combined rather than depreciated separately. No gain or loss is recognized on retirement of items from the group until the last item in the group is sold or retired.

historical cost *Acquisition cost; original cost.*

historical summary A part of the *annual report* to stockholders that shows important items, such as *net income, revenues, expenses, asset* and *equity* totals, *earnings per share,* and the like, for five or ten periods including the current one.

holding company A company that confines its activities to owning *stock* in, and supervising management of, other companies. A holding company usually owns a controlling interest in, that is more than 50 percent of the voting stock of, the companies whose stock it holds. Contrast with *mutual fund.* See *conglomerate.*

holding gain or loss Difference between end-of-period price and beginning-of-period price of an asset held during the period. Ordinarily, realized holding gains and losses are not separately reported in financial statements. See *inventory profit* for further refinement, including *gains* on *assets* sold during the period.

human resource accounting A term used to describe a variety of proposals that seek to report and emphasize the importance of human resources—knowledgeable, trained, and loyal employees—in a company's earning process and total assets.

IIA *Institute of Internal Auditors.*

imprest fund *Petty cash fund.*

improvement An *expenditure* to extend the useful life of an *asset* or to improve its performance (rate of output, cost) over that of the original asset. Such expenditures are *capitalized* as part of the asset's cost. Contrast with *maintenance* and *repair*.

imputed cost A cost that does not appear in accounting records, such as the *interest* that could be earned on cash spent to acquire inventories rather than, say, government bonds. Or, consider a firm that owns the buildings it occupies. This firm has an imputed cost for rent in an amount equal to what it would have to pay to use similar buildings owned by another.

imputed interest See *interest, imputed*.

income Excess of *revenues* over *expenses* for a period. Sometimes used with an appropriate modifier to refer to the various intermediate amounts shown in a *multiple-step income statement*. Sometimes used to refer to revenues, as in "rental income."

income accounts *Revenue* and *expense accounts*.

income distribution account *Temporary account* sometimes debited when *dividends* are declared; closed to *retained earnings*.

income from continuing operations As defined by *APB Opinion* No. 30, all *revenues* less all *expenses* except for the following: results of operations, including income tax effects, that have been or will be discontinued; *gains* or *losses*, including income tax effects, on disposal of segments of the business; gains or losses, including income tax effects, from *extraordinary items*; and the cumulative effect of accounting changes.

income from discontinued operations *Income*, net of tax effects, from parts of the business that have been discontinued during the period or are to be discontinued in the near future. Such items are reported on a separate line of the *income statement* after *income from continuing operations* but before *extraordinary items*.

income statement The statement of *revenues*, *expenses*, *gains*, and *losses* for the period ending with *net income* for the period. The *earnings per share* amount is usually shown on the income statement; the *reconciliation* of beginning and ending balances of *retained earnings* may also be shown in a combined statement of income and retained earnings. See *income from continuing operations, income from discontinued operations, extraordinary items, multiple-step, single-step*.

income summary An *account* used in problem solving that serves as a surrogate for the *income statement*. All *revenues* are closed to the Income Summary as *credits*, and all *expenses* as *debits*. The *balance* in the account, after all other *closing entries* are made, is then closed to the retained earnings or other *owners' equity* account and represents *net income* for the period.

income tax An annual tax levied by the federal and other governments on the income of an entity. An *expense*; if not paid, a *liability*.

income tax allocation See *deferred income tax liability* and *tax allocation: intrastatement*.

indenture See *bond indenture*.

independent accountant The *CPA* who performs the *attest* function for a firm.

indeterminate-term liability A *liability* lacking the criterion of being due at a definite time. This term is our own coinage to encompass the *deferred income tax liability*.

individual proprietorship *Sole proprietorship*.

inflation A time of generally rising prices.

information system A system, sometimes formal and sometimes informal, for collecting, processing, and communicating data that are useful for the managerial functions of decision making, planning, and control, and for financial reporting under the *attest* requirement.

insolvent Unable to pay debts when due. Said of a company even though *assets* exceed *liabilities*.

installment Partial payment of a debt or collection of a receivable.

installment contracts receivable The name used for *accounts receivable* when the *installment method* of recognizing revenue is used.

installment sales Sales on account where the buyer promises to pay in several separate payments, called *installments*. Sometimes are, but need not be, accounted for on the *installment method*. If installment sales are accounted for with the *sales basis of revenue recognition* for financial reporting but with the installment method for income tax returns, then a *deferred income tax liability* arises.

installment (sales) method Recognizing *revenue* and *expense* (or *gross margin*) from a sales transaction in proportion to the fraction of the selling price collected during a period.

Institute of Internal Auditors The national association for accountants engaged in internal auditing employed by business firms.

insurance A contract for reimbursement of specific losses; purchased with insurance premiums. Self-insurance is not insurance but merely the willingness to assume risk of incurring losses while saving the premium.

intangible asset A nonphysical, *noncurrent* asset such as a *copyright, patent, trademark, goodwill*, and *capitalized* advertising cost.

intercompany elimination See *eliminations*.

intercompany profit If one *affiliated company* sells to another, and the goods remain in the second company's *inventory* at the end of the period, then the first company's *profit* has not been realized by a sale to an outsider. That profit is called "intercompany profit" and is eliminated from net *income* in *consolidated income statements* or when the *equity method* is used.

interest The charge or cost for using money; frequently expressed as a rate per period, usually 1 year, called the interest rate.

interest factor One plus the *interest* rate.

interest, imputed If a borrower merely promises to pay a single amount, sometime later than the present, then the *present value* of the promise is less than the *face amount* to be paid at *maturity*. The difference between the face amount and the present value of a promise is called imputed interest. See also *imputed cost*.

interest rate See *interest*.

interim statements Statements issued for periods less than the regular, annual *accounting period*. Most corporations are required to issue interim statements on a quarterly basis.

internal control The procedures used by a business in attempting to ensure that operations are carried out or recorded as planned. Particularly in the context of cash transactions, often referred to as an "internal check."

Internal Revenue Service (IRS) Agency of the U.S. Treasury Department responsible for administering the Internal Revenue Code and collecting income, and certain other, taxes.

International Accounting Standards Committee An organization that promotes the establishment of international accounting standards.

in the black (red) Operating at a profit (loss).

inventoriable costs *Costs* that "attach" to products. *Product costs* (*assets*) as opposed to *period expenses*.

inventory As a noun, the *balance* in an asset *account* such as raw materials, supplies, work in

process, and finished goods. As a verb, to calculate the *cost* of goods on hand at a given time or physically to count items on hand.

inventory equation *Beginning inventory + net additions − withdrawals = ending inventory.* Ordinarily, additions are net purchases and withdrawals are *cost of goods sold*. Notice that ending inventory, to be shown on the balance sheet, and cost of goods sold, to be shown on the income statement, are not independent of each other. The larger is one, the smaller must be the other. In valuing inventories, beginning inventory and net purchases are usually known. In some inventory methods, cost of goods sold is measured and the equation is used to find the cost of ending inventory. In most methods, cost of ending inventory is measured and the equation is used to find the cost of goods sold (withdrawals).

inventory holding gains See *inventory profit*.

inventory layer See *LIFO inventory layer*.

inventory profit This term has several different meanings. Consider the following data:

	Number of Units	Total Acquisition Cost of Units
Beginning Inventory	100	$ 1,000
Purchases During Period (at various prices)	1,000	12,000
Sales During Period at $16 per Unit	900	10,500*
Ending Inventory	200	2,500*

*These two costs require a cost-flow assumption for inventory. FIFO is assumed.

Assume, further, that the average selling price during the period has been $16 per unit and that the replacement cost of a unit at the end of the period is $13. Then the following calculations can be performed.

Goods Available for Sale During Period Valued at Replacement Cost (1,100 × $13)	$14,300
Aquisition Cost of Goods Available for Sale During Period	13,000
Holding Gains During Period	$ 1,300

The total of holding gains during the period are split into realized and unrealized portions, using the *cost-flow assumption*, as follows:

Revenues from Sales (900 × $16)	$14,400
Less Replacement Cost of Goods Sold (900 × $13)	11,700
Operating Margin	$ 2,700
Replacement Cost of Goods Sold (900 × $13)	$11,700
Less Acquisition Cost of Goods Sold (FIFO)	10,500
Realized Holding Gain	$ 1,200
Replacement Cost of Ending Inventory (200 × $13)	$ 2,600
Less Acquisition Cost of Ending Inventory (FIFO)	2,500
Unrealized Holding Gain	$ 100

The *gross margin* on sales as reported in the *income statement* is revenues from sales less *acquisition cost of goods sold*. In the example, gross margin is $3,900 (= $14,400 − $10,500). This gross margin is always equal to the *operating margin* plus the realized holding gains ($2,700 + $1,200 = $3,900).

The *SEC*, in its *Accounting Series Releases*, uses the term "inventory profit" to refer to the realized holding gain, $1,200 in the example. The SEC requires that this inventory profit be disclosed in *notes* to the *financial statements* if the amount is *material*. The amount will usually be material in periods of rising prices when a *FIFO* cost-flow assumption is used, as in the example.

The computations can be somewhat more complex than shown in the example here. The replacement cost of goods sold can be computed as of the times of sale, rather than at the end of the period. This requires *perpetual inventory* records and, for that reason, we suspect that most firms which report "inventory profit" do so approximately as we show here.

Others use the term "inventory profit" to refer to the unrealized holding gain—the excess of current replacement cost of ending inventory over its acquisition cost. Still others use the term "inventory profit" to refer to the total holding gains, whether realized or not. Total holding gains can always be computed as the replacement cost of goods available for sale (which is beginning inventory plus purchases valued at replacement cost) less the acquisition cost of goods available for sale.

inventory turnover Number of times the average *inventory* has been sold during a period; *cost of goods sold* for a period divided by average inventory for the period. See *ratio*.

invested capital *Contributed capital*.

investment An *expenditure* to acquire property or other assets in order to produce *revenue*; the *asset* so acquired; hence a *current* expenditure made in anticipation of future income. Said of *securities* of other companies held for the long term and shown in a separate section of the *balance sheet*; in this context, contrast with *marketable securities*.

investment tax credit A reduction in income tax liability granted by the federal government to firms that buy new equipment. This item is deducted from the tax bill, not from pretax income. The tax credit has been a given percentage of the purchase price of certain assets purchased. The actual rules and rates have changed over the years. See *flow-through method*.

invoice A document showing the details of a sale or purchase transaction.

issue When a corporation exchanges its stock (or bonds) for cash or other assets, the corporation is said to issue, not sell, that stock (or bonds). Also used in the context of withdrawing supplies or materials from inventory for use in operations and of drawing a *check*.

issued shares Those shares of *authorized capital stock* of a *corporation* that have been distributed to the stockholders. See *issue*. Shares of *treasury stock* are legally issued but are not considered to be *outstanding* for the purpose of voting, *dividend declarations*, and *earnings-per-share* calculations.

job development credit The name used for the *investment tax credit* in the 1971 tax law on this subject.

journal The place where transactions are recorded as they occur. The book of original entry.

journal entry A recording in a *journal*, of equal *debits* and *credits*, with an explanation of the *transaction*, if necessary.

journalize To make an entry in a *journal*.

Journal of Accountancy A monthly publication of the *AICPA*.

Journal of Accounting Research Scholarly journal containing articles on theoretical and empirical aspects of accounting. Published three times a year by the Graduate School of Business of the University of Chicago.

journal voucher A *voucher* documenting a transaction, leading to an entry in the *journal*.

land An *asset* shown at *acquisition cost* plus the *cost* of any nondepreciable *improvements*. In accounting, implies use as a plant or office site, rather than as a *natural resource*, such as timberland.

lapse To expire; said of, for example, an insurance policy or discounts made available for prompt payment that are not taken.

last-in, first-out See *LIFO*.

layer See *LIFO inventory layer*.

lease A contract calling for the lessee (user) to pay the lessor (owner) for the use of an asset. A cancelable lease is one the lessee can cancel at any time. A noncancelable lease requires payments from the lessee for the life of the lease and usually has many of the economic characteristics of *debt financing*. A noncancelable lease meets the usual criteria to be classified as a *liability* but sometimes under *GAAP*, need not be shown as a liability. The SEC requires disclosure in notes to the financial statements of the commitments for noncancelable leases. See *financing lease* and *operating lease*.

leasehold The *asset* representing the right of the *lessee* to use leased property. See *lease* and *leasehold improvement*.

leasehold improvement An *improvement* to leased property. Should be *amortized* over *service life* or the life of the lease, whichever is shorter.

least and latest rule Pay the least amount of taxes as late as possible within the law to minimize the *present value* of tax payments for a given set of operations.

ledger A book of accounts. See *general ledger* and *subsidiary ledger*. Contrast with *journal*.

legal capital *Par* or *stated value* of issued *capital stock*. The amount of *contributed capital* that, according to state law, must remain permanently in the firm as protection for creditors.

legal entity See *entity*.

lender See *loan*.

lessee See *lease*.

lessor See *lease*.

leverage Refers to the use of *long-term* debt, in addition to *equity*, securities for raising *funds*.

liability Usually, a legal obligation to pay a definite or reasonably certain amount at a definite or reasonably certain time in return for a current benefit.

LIFO An *inventory* flow assumption where the *cost of goods sold* is the cost of the most recently acquired units and the *ending inventory* cost is determined from costs of the oldest units. Contrast with *FIFO*. In periods of rising prices and increasing inventories, LIFO leads to higher reported expenses and therefore lower reported income and lower balance sheet inventories than does FIFO. See also *FISH* and *inventory profit*.

LIFO inventory layer The *ending inventory* for a period is likely to be larger than the *beginning inventory*. Under a *LIFO cost-flow assumption*, this increase in physical quantities is given a value determined by the prices of the earliest purchases during the year. The LIFO inventory then consists of layers, sometimes called "slices," which typically consist of relatively small amounts of physical quantities from each of the past several years. Each layer carries the prices from near the beginning of the period when it was acquired.

limited liability Stockholders of corporations are not personally liable for debts of the company.

limited partner Member of a *partnership* not personally liable for debts of the partnership; every partnership must have at least one *general partner* who is fully liable.

line of business reporting Reporting of income, and sometimes assets, by *segments of a business*, usually classified by nature of products sold but sometimes by geographical area where goods are produced or sold. Sometimes called "segment reporting."

liquid Said of a business with a substantial amount (the amount is unspecified) of *working capital*, especially *quick assets*.

liquid assets *Cash, marketable securities*, and, sometimes, *current receivables*.

liquidation Payment of a debt. Sale of assets in closing down a business or a segment thereof.

LISH An acronym, conceived by George H. Sorter, for *last-in, still-here*. LISH is the same cost-flow assumption as *FIFO*. Many readers of accounting statements find it easier to think about inventory questions in terms of items still on hand. Think of FIFO in connection with *cost of goods sold* but of LISH in connection with *ending inventory*. See *FISH*.

list price The published or nominally quoted price for goods.

list-price method See *trade-in transaction*.

loan An arrangement where the owner of property, called the lender, allows someone else, called the borrower, the use of the property for a period of time that is usually specified in the agreement setting up the loan. The borrower promises to return the property to the lender and, often, to make a payment for use of the property. Generally used when the property is *cash* and the payment for its use is *interest*.

long-lived (term) asset   An asset whose benefits are expected to be received over several years. A *noncurrent* asset, usually includes *investments*, *plant assets*, and *intangible assets*.

long-term (construction) contract accounting   The *percentage of completion method* of *revenue* recognition.

loss   Excess of *cost* over net proceeds for a single transaction; negative *income* for a period. A cost expiration that produced no *revenue*.

lower of cost or market   A basis for *inventory* valuation where the inventory value is set at the lower of *acquisition cost* or *current replacement cost* (market), subject to various constraints.

maintenance   *Expenditures* undertaken to preserve an *asset's* service potential for its originally intended life; these expenditures are treated as *period expenses* or *product costs*. Contrast with *improvement*. See *repair*.

maker (of note) (of check)   One who signs a *note* to borrow. One who signs a *check*.

management   Executive authority that operates a business.

Management Accounting   Monthly publication of the *National Association of Accountants*.

management (managerial) accounting   Reporting designed to enhance the ability of management to do its job of decision making, planning, and control; contrast with *financial accounting*.

manufacturing cost   Costs of producing goods, usually in a factory.

manufacturing overhead   General manufacturing *costs* incurred in providing a capacity to carry on productive activities but which are not directly associated with identifiable units of product.

margin   *Revenue* less specified *expenses*. See *contribution margin*, *gross margin* and *current margin*.

markdown   The reduction below an originally established retail price.

marketable securities   *Stocks* and *bonds* of other companies held that can be readily sold on stock exchanges or over-the-counter markets and that the company plans to sell as cash is needed. Classified as *current* assets and as part of *working capital*.

market price   See *fair market price*.

market rate   The rate of *interest* a company must pay to borrow *funds* currently. See *effective rate*.

markon   An amount originally added to *cost* to obtain *list price*. Usually expressed as a percentage of cost. Further increases in list price are called *markups*; decreases are called *markdowns*.

markup   An amount originally added to cost. Usually expressed as a percentage of selling price. Also refers to an increase above an originally established retail price. See *markon*.

markup percentage   *Markup* divided by selling price.

matching convention   The concept of recognizing cost expirations (*expenses*) in the same accounting period when the related *revenues* are recognized.

material   As an adjective, it means relatively important. See *materiality*. Currently, no operational definition exists. As a noun, *raw material*.

materiality   The concept that accounting should disclose separately only those events that are relatively important (no operable definition yet exists) for the business or for understanding its statements.

maturity   The date at which an obligation, such as the *principal* of a *bond* or a *note*, becomes due.

maturity value   The amount expected to be collected when a loan reaches *maturity*. Depending upon the context, the amount may be *principal* or principal and *interest*.

merchandise   *Finished goods* bought by a retailer for resale. Contrast with finished goods of a manufacturing business.

merchandise turnover   *Inventory turnover* for merchandise; see *ratio*.

merchandising business   As opposed to a manufacturing or service business, one that buys *finished goods* for resale.

merger   The joining of two or more businesses into a single *economic entity*.

minority interest   A *balance sheet account* on *consolidated statements* showing the *equity* in a *subsidiary* company allocable to those who are not part of the controlling (majority) interest. May be classified either as stockholders' equity or as a liability of *indeterminate term* on the consolidated balance sheet. On the *income statement*, the minority's interest in current income must be subtracted to arrive at consolidated *net income* for the period.

minority investment   A holding of less than 50 percent of the voting stock in another corporation. Accounted for with the *cost method* when less than 20 percent is held, and with the *equity method* otherwise. See *mutual fund.*

modified cash basis The *cash basis of accounting* with long-term assets accounted for with the *accrual basis of accounting.*

monetary assets, liabilities See *monetary items.*

monetary gain or loss The *gain* or *loss* in general purchasing power as a result of holding *monetary assets* or liabilities during a period when the *general purchasing power of the dollar* changes. During periods of *inflation*, holders of net monetary assets lose, and holders of net monetary liabilities gain, general purchasing power.

monetary items Amounts fixed in terms of dollars by statute or contract. *Cash, accounts receivable, accounts payable,* and *debt.* The distinction between monetary and nonmonetary items is important for general *price level adjusted statements* and for *foreign exchange gain or loss* computations. In the foreign exchange context, account amounts denominated in dollars are not monetary items, while amounts denominated in any other currency are monetary.

money A word seldom used with precision in accounting, at least in part because economists have not yet agreed on its definition. See *cash* and *monetary items.*

money-purchase plan A *pension plan* where the employer contributes a specified amount of cash each year to each employee's pension fund. Benefits ultimately received by the employee are not specifically defined but depend on the rate of return on the cash invested. Sometimes called a "defined-contribution" pension plan. Contrast with *defined-benefit plan.* As of the mid-1970's, most corporate pension plans were defined-benefit plans because both the law and *generally accepted accounting principles* for pensions made defined-benefit plans more attractive than money-purchase plans. The federal pension law of 1974 makes money-purchase plans relatively more attractive than they had been. We expect the number of money-purchase plans to increase. See *ERISA.*

mortgage A claim given by the borrower (mortgager) to the lender (mortgagee) against the borrower's property in return for a loan.

moving average method *Weighted-average method.*

multiple-step Said of an *income statement* where various classes of *expenses* and *losses* are sub-

tracted from *revenues* to show intermediate items such as *operating income*, income of the enterprise (operating income plus *interest* income). income to investors (income of the enterprise less *income taxes*), net income to shareholders (income to investors less interest charges), and income retained (income to stockholders less dividends).

municipal bond A *bond* issued by a village, town, city, county, state, or other public body. *Interest* on such bonds is generally exempt from federal *income taxes* and from some state income taxes. Sometimes referred to as "tax exempts."

mutual fund An investment company that issues its own stock to the public and uses the proceeds to invest in securities of other companies. A mutual fund usually owns less than 5 or 10 percent of the stock of any one company and accounts for its investments using current market values. Contrast with *holding company.*

National Association of Accountants (NAA) A national society generally open to all engaged in activities closely associated with *managerial accounting.* Oversees the administration of the CMA Examinations through the Institute of Management Accounting.

natural business year A 12-month period chosen as the reporting period so that the end of the period coincides with a low point in activity or inventories. See *ratio* for a discussion of analyses of financial statements of companies using a natural business year.

natural classification *Income statement* reporting form in which *expenses* are classified by nature of items, that is materials, wages, salaries, insurance, and taxes, as well as depreciation. Contrast with *functional classification.*

natural resources Timberland, oil and gas wells, ore deposits, and other products of nature that have economic value. The cost of natural resources is subject to *depletion.*

net Reduced by all relevant deductions.

net assets *Owners' equity*; total *assets* minus total *liabilities.*

net current assets *Working capital* = *current assets − current liabilities.*

net income The excess of all *revenues* and *gains* for a period over all *expenses* and *losses* of the period.

net loss The excess of all *expenses* and *losses* for

a period over all *revenues* and *gains* of the period. Negative *net income*.

net of tax reporting Reporting, such as for *income from discontinued operations*, *extraordinary items*, and *prior-period adjustments*, where the amounts presented in *financial statements* have been adjusted for all income tax effects.

net price method (of recording purchase or sales discounts) The purchase (or *sale*) is recorded at its *invoice* price less all *discounts* made available under the assumption that nearly all discounts will be taken. Discounts lapsed through failure to pay promptly are recorded in an *adjunct account* to purchases (or sales) or in the purchasing context, to an *expense* account. In the context of purchases, management usually prefers to know about the amount of discounts lost because of ineffecient operations, not the amounts taken, so that most managers prefer the net price method to the *gross price method*.

net realizable value Selling price of an item less reasonable further costs to make the item ready for sale and to sell it.

net sales Sales (at gross invoice amount) less *returns*, *allowances*, freight paid for customers, and *discounts* taken.

net working capital *Working capital*; the "net" is redundant in accounting. Financial analysts sometimes mean *current* assets when they speak of working capital, so for them the "net" is not redundant.

net worth A misleading term, to be avoided, that means the same as *owners' equity*.

New York Stock Exchange (NYSE) A public market where various corporate *securities* are traded.

nominal accounts *Temporary accounts* as opposed to *balance sheet accounts*. All nominal accounts are *closed* at the end of each *accounting period*.

noncancelable See *lease*.

noncontributory Said of a *pension plan* where only the employer makes payments to a pension *fund*. Contrast with *contributory*.

noncurrent Due more than 1 year hence.

noninterest-bearing note A *note* which bears no explicit interest. The *present value* of such a note at any time before *maturity* is less than the *face value* so long as *interest rates* are positive.

nonmonetary items All items that are not monetary; see *monetary items*.

nonoperating In the *income statement* context,

said of revenues and expenses arising from transactions incidental to the company's main line(s) of business. In the *statement of changes in financial position* context, said of all sources or uses of *working capital* other than working capital provided by operations.

nonprofit corporation An incorporated *entity*, such as a hospital, with no owners who share in the earnings. Such corporations usually emphasize providing services rather than maximizing income.

no par Said of *stock* without a *par value*.

normal cost *Pension plan expenses* incurred during an *accounting period* for employment services performed during that period. Contrast with *past* and *prior service cost* and see *funded*.

note An unconditional written promise by the maker (borrower) to pay a certain amount on demand or at a certain future time. See *footnotes* for another context.

note receivable discounted A *note* assigned by the holder to another. If the note is assigned with recourse, it is the *contingent liability* of the assignor until the debt is paid. See *factoring*.

number of days sales in inventory (or receivables) Days of average inventory on hand (or average collection period for receivables). See *ratio*.

NYSE *New York Stock Exchange*.

OASD(H)I *Old Age, Survivors, Disability, and (Hospital) Insurance.*

objective See *reporting objective* and *objectivity*.

objectivity The reporting policy implying that formal recognition will not be given to an event in financial statements until the magnitude of the events can be measured with reasonable accuracy and is subject to independent verification.

obsolescence A decline in *market value* of an *asset* caused by improved alternatives becoming available that will be more *cost-effective*; the decline in market value is unrelated to physical changes in the asset itself.

off balance sheet financing A description often used for a *long-term*, *noncancelable lease* accounted for as an *operating lease*.

Old Age, Survivors, Disability, and (Hospital) Insurance The technical name for Social Security under the Federal Insurance Contribution Act (FICA).

on consignment Said of goods delivered by the owner (the consignor) to another (the consignee) to be sold by the other person; the owner is entitled to the return of the property or payment of an amount agreed upon in advance.

open account   Any *account* with a nonzero debit or credit *balance.*

operating   An adjective used to refer to *revenue* and *expense* items relating to the company's main line(s) of business.

operating accounts   *Revenue, expense,* and *production cost accounts.* Contrast with *balance sheet accounts.*

operating cycle   *Earnings cycle.*

operating expenses   *Expenses* incurred in the course of ordinary activities of an *entity.* Frequently, a narrower classification including only *selling, general,* and *administrative expenses,* thereby excluding *cost of goods sold, interest,* and *income tax* expenses.

operating lease   A *lease* accounted for by the *lessee* without showing an *asset* for the lease rights (*leasehold*) or a *liability* for the lease payment obligations. Rental payments of the lessee are merely shown as *expenses* of the period. The lessor keeps the asset on his or her *books* and shows the rental payments as *revenues.* Contrast with *financing lease.*

operating margin (based on replacement costs)   *Revenues* from *sales* minus current *replacement cost* of goods sold. A measure of operating efficiency that is independent of the *cost-flow assumption for inventory.* Sometimes called "current (gross) margin." See *inventory profit* for example computations.

opinion   The *auditor's report* containing an attestation or lack thereof. Also, APB *Opinion.*

option   The legal right to buy something during a specified period at a specified price, called the *exercise* price. Employee stock options should not be confused with put and call options traded in various public markets.

ordinary annuity   An *annuity in arrears.*

ordinary income   For income tax purposes, reportable *income* not qualifying as *capital gains.*

organization costs   The *costs* incurred in planning and establishing an *entity;* example of an *intangible* asset. Often, since the amounts are not *material,* the costs are treated as *expenses* in the period incurred even though the *expenditures* clearly provide future benefits and should be treated as *assets.*

original cost   *Acquisition cost.* In public-utility accounting, the acquisition cost to the *entity* first devoting the asset to public use.

original entry   Entry in a *journal.*

outlay   The amount of an *expenditure.*

out-of-pocket   Said of an *expenditure* usually paid for with cash.

output   Physical quantity or monetary measurement of *goods* and *services* produced.

outstanding   Unpaid or uncollected. When said of *stock,* the shares issued less *treasury stock.* When said of checks, it means a check issued that did not clear the *drawer's* bank prior to the *bank statement* date.

overhead costs   Any *cost* not specifically or directly associated with the production of identifiable goods and services.

owners' equity   *Proprietorship; assets* minus *liabilities; paid-in capital* plus *retained earnings* of a corporation; partners' capital accounts in a *partnership;* owner's capital account in a *sole proprietorship.*

paid-in capital   Sum of balances in *capital stock* and *capital contributed in excess of par* (or *stated*) *value* accounts. Same as *contributed capital* (minus *donated capital*).

parent company   Company owning more than 50 percent of the voting shares of another company, called the subsidiary.

partially funded   Said of a *pension plan* where not all earned benefits have been funded. See *funded* for funding requirements.

partially vested   Said of a *pension plan* where not all employee benefits are *vested.* See *graded vesting.*

partner's drawing   A payment to a partner to be charged against his or her share of income or capital. The name of a *temporary account* to record such payments.

partnership   Contractual arrangement between individuals to share resources and operations in a jointly run business. See *general* and *limited partner* and *Uniform Partnership Act.*

par value   *Face amount* of a *security.*

past service cost   *Present value* at a given time of a *pension plan's* unrecognized, and usually unfunded, benefits assigned to employees for their service before the inception of the plan. A part of *prior service cost.* See *prior service cost* for disclosure rules. See *funded.* Contrast with *normal cost.*

patent   Exclusive rights granted by the government to an inventor for 17 years to enjoy the fruits of an invention. An asset if acquired by purchase. If developed internally, the development costs are *expensed* when incurred under current *GAAP*.

payable Unpaid but not necessarily due or past due.

payee The entity to whom a cash payment is made or who will receive the stated amount of money on a check. See *draft*.

payout ratio *Common stock dividends* declared for a year divided by net *income* to common stock for the year. A term used by financial analysts. Contrast with *dividend yield*.

payroll taxes Taxes levied because salaries or wages are paid; for example, *FICA* and unemployment compensation insurance taxes. Typically, the employer pays a portion and withholds part of the employee's wages for the other portion.

pension fund *Fund*, the assets of which are to be paid to retired ex-employees, usually as a *life annuity*. Usually held by an independent trustee and then is not an *asset* of the firm.

pension plan Details or provisions of employer's contract with employees for paying retirement *annuities* or other benefits. See *ERISA, funded, vested, normal cost, past service cost, prior service cost, money-purchase plan,* and *defined-benefit plan*.

percent Any number, expressed as a decimal, multiplied by 100.

percentage depletion (allowance) Deductible *expense* allowed in some cases by the *federal income tax* regulations; computed as a percentage of gross income from a *natural resource* independent of the unamortized cost of the asset. Since the amount of the total deductions for tax purposes is usually greater than the cost of the asset being *depleted*, many people think the deduction is an unfair tax advantage or "loophole."

percentage of completion method Recognizing *revenues* and *expenses* on a job, order, or contract (a) in proportion to the *costs* incurred for the period divided by total costs expected to be incurred for the job or order, or (b) in proportion to engineers' estimates of the incremental degree of completion of the job, order, or contract during the period. Contrast with *completed contract method*.

period *Accounting period*.

period cost An inferior term for *period expense*.

period expense (charge) *Expenditure*, usually based upon the passage of time, charged to operations of the accounting period rather than *capitalized* as an asset. Contrast with *product cost*.

periodic inventory A method of recording *inventory* that uses data on beginning inventory, additions to inventories, and ending inventory in order to find the cost of withdrawals from inventory.

periodic procedures The process of making *adjusting entries, closing entries,* and preparing the *financial statements*, usually by use of *trial balances* and *work sheets*.

permanent account An account which appears on the *balance sheet*; contrast with *temporary account*.

permanent difference Difference between reported income and taxable income that will never be reversed and, hence, requires no entry in the *deferred income tax (liability)* account. An example is the difference between taxable and reportable income from interest earned on state and municipal bonds. Contrast with *timing difference* and see *deferred tax liability*.

perpetual inventory Records on quantities and amounts of *inventory* that are changed or made current with each physical addition to or withdrawal from the stock of goods; an inventory so recorded. The records will show the physical quantities and, frequently, the dollar valuations that should be on hand at any time.

personal account *Drawing account*.

petty cash fund Currency maintained for expenditures that are conveniently made with cash on hand.

plant *Plant assets*.

plant assets Buildings, machinery, land, and natural resources. The phrase "property, plant, and equipment" is, therefore, a redundancy. In this context, "plant" means buildings.

plug In making a *journal entry*, often all *debits* are known, as are all but one of the *credits* (or vice versa). Since *double-entry* bookkeeping requires equal debits and credits, the unknown quantity can be determined by subtracting the sum of the known credits from the sum of all the debits (or vice versa). This process is known as *plugging*. The unknown found is called the plug.

pooling of interests method Accounting for a *business combination* by merely adding together the *book value* of the *assets* and *equities* of the combined firms. Contrast with *purchase method*.

post   To record entries in an *account* in a *ledger*; usually the entries are copied from a *journal*.

postclosing trial balance   *Trial balance* taken after all *temporary accounts* have been closed.

potentially dilutive   A *security* which may be converted into, or exchanged for, common stock and thereby reduce reported *earnings per share*. *Options, warrants, convertible bonds*, and convertible preferred stock.

preclosing trial balance   *Trial balance* taken at the end of the period before *closing entries*. In this sense, an *adjusted trial balance*. Sometimes taken before *adjusting entries* and then is synonymous with *unadjusted trial balance*.

preferred stock   *Capital stock* with a claim to income or assets after bondholders but before *common stock*. *Dividends* on preferred stock are income distributions, not expenses.

premium   The excess of issue (or market) price over *par value*. For a different context, see *insurance*.

premium on capital stock   Alternative but inferior title for *capital contributed in excess of par (or stated) value*.

prepaid expense   An *expenditure* that leads to a *deferred charge* or *prepayment*; strictly speaking, a contradiction in terms for an *expense* is a gone asset and this title refers to past *expenditures*, such as for rent or insurance premiums, that still have future benefits and are *assets*.

prepaid income   An inferior alternative title for *advances from customers*. An item should not be called *revenue* or *income* until goods are delivered or services are rendered.

prepayments   *Assets* representing expenditures for future benefits. Rent and insurance premiums paid in advance are usually classified as *current* prepayments.

present value   Value today of an amount or amounts to be paid or received later, discounted at some *interest rate*.

price   The quantity of one *good* or *service*, usually *cash*, asked in return for a unit of another good or service. See *fair market price*.

price-earnings ratio   At a given time, the market value of a company's *common stock*, per share, divided by the *earnings per* common *share* for the past year. See *ratio*.

price index   A series of numbers, one for each period, that purports to represent some *average*

of prices for a series of periods, relative to a base period.

price level   The number from a *price index* series for a given period or date.

price level adjusted statements   *Financial statements* expressed in terms of dollars of uniform purchasing power. *Nonmonetary items* are restated to reflect changes in general *price levels* since the time specific *assets* were acquired and *liabilities* were incurred. A *gain* or *loss* is recognized on *monetary items* as they are held over time periods when the general *price level* changes. Conventional financial statements show *historical costs* and ignore differences in purchasing power in different periods.

primary earnings per share   Net *income* to common *stockholders* plus *interest* (*net of tax* effects) or *dividends* paid on *common stock equivalents* divided by (weighted average of common shares outstanding plus the net increase in the number of common shares that would become *outstanding* if all common stock equivalents were exchanged for common shares with cash proceeds, if any, used to retire common shares).

prime rate   The rate for loans charged by commercial banks to their most preferred risks.

principal   An amount on which *interest* is charged or earned.

principle   See *generally accepted accounting principles*.

prior-period adjustment   A *debit* or *credit* made directly to *retained earnings* (that does not affect *income* for the period) to adjust retained earnings for such things as lawsuit settlements and changes in *income tax expense* of prior periods.

prior service cost   *Present value* at a given time of a *pension plan's* unrecognized benefits assigned to employees for their service before that given time. Includes *past service cost*. Such obligations are not recognized as liabilities in the accounting records, but must be disclosed in the notes to the financial statements. Contrast with *normal cost*. See *funded*.

proceeds   The *funds* received from disposition of assets or from the issue of securities.

product   *Goods* or *services* produced.

product cost   Any *manufacturing cost* that can be inventoried. See *flow of costs* for example, and contrast with *period expenses*.

production cost   *Manufacturing cost*.

production cost account A *temporary account* for collecting *manufacturing costs* during a period.

production method (depreciation) The depreciable asset is given a *depreciable life* measured, not in elapsed time, but in units of output or perhaps in units of time of actual use. Then the *depreciation* charge for a period is a portion of depreciable cost equal to a fraction determined by dividing the actual output produced during the period by the expected total output to be produced over the life of the asset.

profit Excess of *revenues* over *expenses* for a *transaction*; sometimes used synonymously with *net income* for the period.

profit and loss statement *Income statement.*

profit margin Sales minus all expenses as a single amount. Frequently used to mean the ratio of sales minus all *operating* expenses divided by sales.

profit maximization The doctrine that a given set of operations should be accounted for so as to make reported *net income* as large as possible. Contrast with *conservatism*. This concept in accounting is slightly different from the profit-maximizing concept in economics, where the doctrine states that businesses should be run to maximize the present value of the firm's wealth, generally by equating *marginal costs* and *marginal revenues*.

promissory note An unconditional written promise to pay a specified sum of money on demand or at a specified date.

proprietorship *Assets* minus *liabilities* of an *entity*; equals *contributed capital* plus *retained earnings*.

proprietorship theory The view of the corporation that emphasizes the form of the *accounting equation* that says *assets − liabilities = stockholders' equity.*

provision Often the exact amount of an *expense* is uncertain, but must be recognized currently anyway. The entry for the estimated expense, such as for *income taxes* or expected costs under *warranty*, is

    Expense (Estimated) X
        Liability (Estimated) X

In American usage, the term "provision" is often used in the expense account title of the above entry. Thus, Provision for Income Taxes is used

to mean the estimate of income tax expense. (In British usage, the term "provision" is used in the title for the estimated liability of the above entry, so that Provision for Income Taxes is a balance sheet account.)

public accountant Generally, this term is synonymous with *certified public accountant*.

public accounting That portion of accounting primarily involving the *attest* function, culminating in the *auditor's report*.

PuPu An acronym for *purchasing power unit*. Some, including the Chief Accountant of the SEC, who think *general price level adjusted* accounting is not particularly useful, poke fun at it by calling it "PuPu accounting."

purchase allowance A reduction in sales *invoice price* usually granted because the *goods* received by the purchaser were not exactly as ordered. The goods are not returned to the seller, but are purchased at a price lower than that originally agreed upon.

purchase discount A reduction in sales *invoice price* granted for prompt payment. See *sales discount* and *terms of sale*.

purchase method Accounting for a *business combination* by adding the acquired company's assets at the price paid for them to the acquiring company's assets. Contrast with *pooling of interests method*.

qualified report (opinion) *Auditor's* report containing a statement that the auditor was unable to complete a satisfactory examination of all things considered relevant or that the auditor has doubts about the financial impact of some item reported in the financial statements. See *except for* and *subject to*.

qualified (stock) option (plan) Said of a compensation scheme in which *options* to purchase *stock* are granted to employees and in which the implicit compensation is neither tax deductible as an *expense* by the employer nor taxable *income* to the employee.

quantity discount A reduction in purchase price as quantity purchased increases. Not to be confused with *purchase discount*.

quick assets *Assets* readily convertible into *cash*; includes cash, *marketable securities* and *receivables*.

quick ratio *Acid test* ratio. See *ratio*.

R & D   See *research and development*.

rate of return (**on total capital**)   See *ratio* and *all capital earnings rate*.

ratio   The number resulting when one number is divided by another. Ratios are generally used to assess aspects of profitability, solvency, and liquidity. The commonly used financial ratios are of essentially two kinds: (1) those that summarize some aspect of operations for a period, usually a year, and (2) those that summarize some aspect of *financial position* at a given moment—the moment for which a balance sheet has been prepared. Table 7.1, p. 205, lists the most common financial ratios and shows separately both the numerator and denominator used to calculate the ratio.

For all ratios that require an average balance during the period, the average is most often derived as one-half the sum of the beginning and ending balances. Sophisticated analysts recognize, however, that when companies use a fiscal year different from the calendar year, this averaging of beginning and ending balances may be misleading. For example, the all capital earnings rate for companies who choose a fiscal year-end to coincide with low points in the inventory cycle is likely to be larger than if a more accurate estimate of the average amounts of total assets were used.

raw material   Goods purchased for use in manufacturing a product.

reacquired stock   *Treasury stock*.

real accounts   *Balance sheet accounts*; as opposed to *nominal accounts*. See *permanent accounts*.

real estate   *Land* and its *improvements*, such as landscaping and roads but not buildings.

realizable value   *Market value* or, sometimes, *net realizable value*.

realization convention   The accounting practice of delaying the recognition of *gains* and *losses* from changes in the market price of *assets* until the assets are sold. However, unrealized losses on *inventory* and *marketable securities* are recognized prior to sale when the *lower-of-cost-or-market* valuation basis is used.

realize   To convert into *funds*. See *recognize*.

realized holding gain   See *inventory profit* for definition and an example.

receipt   Acquisition of *cash*.

receivable   Any *collectible* whether or not it is currently due.

receivables turnover   See *ratio*.

recognize   To enter a transaction in the books. Some writers use "recognize" to indicate that an event has been *journalized* and use "realize" only for those events that affect the *income statement*.

reconciliation   A calculation that shows how one balance or figure is derived systematically from another, such as a *reconciliation of retained earnings* or a *bank reconciliation schedule*. See *articulate*.

record date   *Dividends* are paid on payment date to those who own the stock on the record date.

recourse   See *note receivable discounted*.

redemption   Retirement by the issuer, usually by a purchase or *call*, of *stocks* or *bonds*.

redemption premium   *Call premium*.

redemption value   The price to be paid by a corporation to retire *bonds* or *preferred stock* if called before *maturity*.

refunding bond issue   Said of a *bond* issue whose proceeds are used to retire bonds already *outstanding*.

register   Collection of consecutive entries, or other information, in chronological order, such as a check register or an insurance register, which lists all insurance policies owned. If entries are recorded, it may serve as a *journal*.

Regulation S-X   The *SEC*'s regulation specifying the form and content of financial reports to the SEC.

rent   A charge for the use of land, buildings, or other assets under *lease*.

repair   An *expenditure* to restore an *asset*'s service potential after damage or after prolonged use. Treated as an *expense* of the period when incurred. Because repairs and maintenance are treated similarly in this regard, the distinction is not important. Contrast with *improvement*.

replacement cost   For an asset, the current fair market price to purchase another, similar asset (with the same future benefit or service potential). *Current cost*. See *reproduction cost*.

report   *Financial statement*; *auditor's report*.

reporting objectives (**policies**)   The general doctrines underlying accounting. These include *full disclosure, objectivity, consistency, conservatism*, the assumption of *continuity of operations*, and *materiality*.

reproduction cost   The *cost* necessary to construct an *asset* similar in all important respects to another asset for which a *current value* is wanted but not readily available from market prices. See *replacement cost*.

requisition A formal written order or request, such as for withdrawal of supplies from the storeroom.

resale value *Exit value. Net realizable value.*

research and development Research is activity aimed at discovering new knowledge in hopes that such activity will be useful in creating a new product, process, or service or improving a present product, proccess, or service. Development is the translation of research findings or other knowledge into a new or improved product, process, or service. The *FASB* requires that costs of such activities be *expensed* as incurred on the grounds that the future benefits are too uncertain to warrant *capitalization* as an asset. This treatment seems questionable to us, because we wonder why firms would continue to undertake R & D if there were no expectation of future benefits; if future benefits exist, then the costs should be assets.

reserve When properly used in accounting, the term refers to an account that appropriates *retained earnings* and restricts dividend declarations. Appropriating retained earnings is itself a poor and slowly vanishing practice, so the word should seldom be used in accounting. In addition, used in the past to indicate an asset *contra* (for example, "reserve for depreciation") or an *estimated liability* (for example, "reserve for warranty costs"). In any case, reserve accounts have credit balances and are not pools of *funds* as the unwary reader might infer. If a company has set aside a pool of *cash* (or *marketable securities*), then that cash will be called a *fund*.

residual security A *potentially dilutive security*. *Options, warrants, convertible bonds*, and *convertible preferred stock*.

residual value At any time, the estimated, or actual, *net realizable value* of an *asset*, usually a depreciable *plant asset*.

retail inventory method Ascertaining *inventory* amounts for financial statements by using ratios of cost to selling price.

retained earnings Net *income* over the life of a corporation less all income distributions (including capitalization through stock dividends); *owners' equity* less *contributed capital*.

retained earnings, appropriated An *account* set up by crediting it and debiting *retained earnings*. Used to indicate that a portion of retained earnings is not available for dividends. The practice of appropriating retained earnings is misleading unless all capital is earmarked with its use, which is not practical. Use of formal retained earnings appropriations is declining.

retained earnings statement *Generally accepted accounting principles* require that whenever *comparative balance sheets* and an *income statement* are presented, there must also be presented a *reconciliation* of the beginning and ending balances in the *retained earnings account*. This reconciliation can appear in a separate statement, in a combined statement of income and retained earnings, or in the balance sheet.

retirement plan *Pension plan*.

return A schedule of information required by governmental bodies, such as the tax return required by the *Internal Revenue Service*. Also the physical return of merchandise.

return on investment (capital) *Income* (before distributions to suppliers of capital) for a period. As a rate, this amount divided by average total assets. *Interest*, net of tax effects, should be added back to *net income* for the numerator. See *ratio*

revenue The monetary measure of a service rendered. Do not confuse with *receipt* of funds which may occur before, when, or after revenue is recognized.

reversal (reversing) entry An *entry* in which all *debits* and *credits* are the credits and debits, respectively, of another entry, and in the same amounts. It is usually made on the first day of an *accounting period* to reverse a previous *adjusting entry*, usually an *accrual*. The purpose of such entries is to make the bookkeeper's tasks easier. Suppose that salaries are paid every other Friday, with paychecks compensating employees for the 2 weeks just ended. Total salaries accrue at the rate of $5,000 per 5-day work week. The bookkeeper is accustomed to making the following entry every other Friday:

(1) Salary Expense 10,000
    Cash 10,000
    To record salary expense and
    salary payments.

If paychecks are delivered to employees on Friday, December 26, 1975, then the *adjusting entry* made on December 31 (or perhaps later) to record accrued salaries for December 29, 30, and 31 would be:

(2) Salary Expense 3,000
    Salaries Payable 3,000
    To charge 1975 operations
    with all salaries earned in
    1975.

The Salary Expense account would be closed as part of the December 31 *closing entries*. On the next payday, January 9, the salary entry would have to be:

(3) Salary Expense	7,000	
Salaries Payable	3,000	
Cash		10,000

To record salary payments split between expense for 1976 (**7** days) and liability carried over from 1975 (**3** days).

To make entry (**3**), the bookkeeper must look back into the records to see how much of the debit is to Salaries Payable accrued from the previous year so that total debits are properly split between 1976 expense and the liability carried over from 1975. Notice that this entry forces the bookkeeper both (**a**) to refer to balances in old accounts and (**b**) to make an entry different from the one customarily made, entry (**1**).

The reversing entry, made just after the books have been closed for 1975, makes the salary entry for January 9, 1976, the same as that made on all other Friday paydays. The reversing entry merely *reverses* the adjusting entry (**2**):

| (4) Salaries Payable | 3,000 | |
| Salary Expense | | 3,000 |

To reverse the adjusting entry.

This entry results in a zero balance in the Salaries Payable account and a *credit* balance in the Salary Expense account. If entry (**4**) is made just after the books are closed for 1975, then the entry on January 9 will be the customary entry (**1**). Entries (**4**) and (**1**) together have exactly the same effect as entry (**3**). Also used to describe the entry reversing an incorrect entry before recording the correct entry.

reverse stock split A stock split in which the number of shares *outstanding* is decreased. See *stock split*.

right The privilege to subscribe to new *stock* issues or to purchase stock.

risk A measure of the variability of the *return on investment*. For a given expected amount of return, most people prefer less risk to more risk.

Therefore, in rational markets, investments with more risk usually promise, or are expected to yield, a higher rate of return than investments with lower risk.

royalty Compensation for the use of property, usually copyrighted material or natural resources, expressed as a percentage of receipts from using the property or as an amount per unit produced.

rule of 69 An amount of money invested at r percent per period will double in $69/r + .35$ periods. This approximation is accurate to one-tenth of a period for interest rates between ¼ and 100 percent per period. For example, at 10 percent per period, the rule says that a given sum will double in $60/10 + .35 = 7.25$ periods. At 10 percent per period, a given sum doubles in 7.27+ periods.

rule of 72 An amount of money invested at r percent per period will double in $72/r$ periods. A reasonable approximation but not nearly as accurate as the *rule of 69*. For example, at 10 percent per period, the rule says that a given sum will double in $72/10 = 7.2$ periods.

ruling an account The process of summarizing a series of entries to an *account* by computing a new *balance* and drawing double lines to indicate the information above the double lines has been summarized in the new balance. The process is illustrated below. The steps are as follows. (**1**) Compute the sum of all *debit* entries including opening debit balance, if any—$1,364.16. (**2**) Compute the sum of all credit entries including opening credit balance, if any—$13.57. (**3**) If the amount in (**1**) is larger than the amount in (**2**), then write the excess as a credit with a check mark: $1,364.16 − $13.57 = $1,350.59. (**4**) Add both debit and credit columns, which should both now sum to the same amount, and show that identical total at the foot of both columns. (**5**) Draw double lines under those numbers and write the excess of debits over credits as the new debit balance with a check mark. (**6**) If the amount in (**2**) is larger than the amount in (**1**), then write the excess as a debit with a check mark. (**7**) Do steps (**4**) and (**5**), except that the excess becomes the new credit balance. (**8**) If the amount in (**1**) is equal to the amount in (**2**), then the balance is zero and only the totals with the double lines beneath them need be shown. This process is illustrated below.

An Open Account, Ruled and Balanced
(steps indicated in parentheses correspond to steps described under ruling an account)

Date		Explanation	Ref.	Debit	Date		Explanation	Ref.	Credit	
1976					1976					
Jan.	13		VR	1 2 1 37	Sept.	15		J	42	
Mar.	20		VR	5 6 42	Nov.	12		J	1 3 15	
June	5		J	1 1 3 8 09	Dec.	31	Balance	V	1 3 5 0 59	(3)
Aug.	18		J	1 21						
Nov.	20		VR	3 8 43						
Dec.	7		VR	8 64						
(4)				1 3 6 4 16					1 3 6 4 16	(4)
(5) 1977					1977					
Jan.	1	Balance	V	1 3 5 0 59						

salary Compensation earned by managers, administrators, professionals, not based on an hourly rate. Contrast with *wage*.

sale A *revenue* transaction where *goods* or *services* are delivered to a customer in return for cash or a contractual obligation to pay.

sales allowance A reduction in sales *invoice* price usually given because the goods received by the buyer are not exactly what was ordered. The amounts of such adjustments are often accumulated by the seller in a temporary *revenue contra account* having this, or a similar, title.

sales basis of revenue recognition *Revenue* is recognized, not as goods are produced nor as orders are received, but only when the sale (delivery) has been consummated and cash or a legal receivable obtained. Most revenue is recognized on this basis. Compare with the *percentage of completion method* and the *installment method*. Identical with the *completed contract method* but this latter term is ordinarily used only for *long-term* construction projects.

sales discount Reduction in sales *invoice* price usually offered for prompt payment. See *terms of sale* and *2/10, n/30*.

sales return The physical return of merchandise; the amounts of such returns are often accumulated by the seller in a temporary *revenue contra account*.

sales, uncollectible accounts adjustment The preferred title for the *contra-revenue account* to recognize estimated reductions in income caused by accounts receivable that will not be collected.

Called *bad debt expense* and treated as an expense, rather than as an adjustment to revenue, when the write-off method is used. See *allowance for uncollectibles* and *allowance method*.

salvage value Actual or estimated selling price, net of removal or disposal costs, of a used *plant asset* to be sold or otherwise retired. See *residual value*.

schedule Supporting set of calculations which show how figures in a statement or tax return are derived.

scrap value *Salvage value* assuming item is to be junked. A *net realizable value*.

SEC Securities and Exchange Commission, an agency authorized by the U.S. Congress to regulate, among other things, the financial reporting practices of most public corporations. The SEC has indicated that it will usually allow the *FASB* to set accounting principles, but it reserves the right to require more disclosure than required by the FASB. The SEC's accounting requirements are stated in its *Accounting Series Releases* (ASR) and *Regulation S-X*. See *10–K*.

Securities and Exchange Commission SEC.

security Document that indicates ownership or indebtedness.

segment (of a business) As defined by *APB Opinion* No. 30, "a component of an *entity* whose activities represent a separate major line of business or class of customer. . . . [It may be] a *subsidiary*, a division, or a department, . . . provided that its *assets*, results of *operations*, and activities can be clearly distinguished, physically and operationally for financial reporting purposes, from the other assets, results of operations, and activities of the entity."

segment reporting   *Line of business reporting.*

self-balancing   A set of records with equal *debits* and *credits.*

selling and administrative expenses   *Expenses* not specifically identifiable with, nor assigned to, production.

serial bonds   An *issue of bonds* that mature in part at one date, another part on another date, and so on; the various *maturity* dates usually are equally spaced.

service life   Period of expected usefulness of an asset.

service potential   The future benefits embodied in an item that cause the item to be classified as an *asset.* Without service potential, there are no future benefits and the item should not be classified as an asset.

services   Useful work done by a person, a machine, or an organization. See *goods and services.*

share   A unit of *stock* representing ownership in a corporation.

short-term   Current; ordinarily, due within 1 year.

shrinkage   An excess of *inventory* shown on the *books* over actual physical quantities on hand. Can result from theft or shoplifting as well as from evaporation or general wear and tear.

simple interest   *Interest* calculated on *principal* where interest earned during periods before maturity of the loan is neither added to the principal nor paid to the lender. *Interest = principal × interest rate × time.* Seldom used in economic calculations except for periods less than 1 year. Contrast with *compound interest.*

single-entry accounting   Accounting that does not rely on equal *debits* and *credits.* No *journal entries* are made. *Plugging* is required to derive *owners' equity* for the *balance sheet.*

single proprietorship   *Sole proprietorship.*

single-step   Said of an *income statement* where all *ordinary revenue* and *gain* items are shown first and totaled. Then all ordinary *expenses* and *losses* are totaled. Their difference, plus the effect of *income from discontinued operations* and *extraordinary items,* is shown as *net income.* Contrast with *multiple-step.*

sinking fund   *Assets* and their earnings earmarked for the retirement of bonds or other long-term obligations. Earnings in sinking fund investments are taxable income of the company.

skeleton account   *T-account.*

Social Security taxes   Taxes levied by the federal government on both employers and employees to provide *funds* to pay retired persons (or their survivors) who are entitled to receive such payments. See *Old Age, Survivors, Disability, and (Hospital) Insurance.*

sole proprietorship   All *owner's equity* belongs to one person.

solvent   Able to meet debts when due.

source of funds   Any *transaction* that increases *working capital.*

SOYD   *Sum-of-the-years'-digits depreciation.*

special journal   A *journal,* such as a sales journal or cash disbursements journal, to record *transactions* of a similar nature that occur frequently.

specific indentification method   Method for valuing *ending inventory* and *cost of goods sold* by identifying actual units sold and in inventory and summing the actual costs of those individual units.

specific price changes   Changes in the market prices of specific *goods and services.* Contrast with *general price level changes.*

specific price index   A measure of the price of a specific good or service, or a small group of similar goods or services, at one time relative to the price during a base period. Contrast with *general price index.*

split   *Stock split.* Sometimes called "splitup."

stabilized accounting   General *price level adjusted accounting.*

stable monetary unit assumption   In spite of *inflation* that appears to be a way of life, the assumption that underlies *historical cost* accounting—namely that current dollars and dollars of previous years can be meaningfully added. No specific recognition is given to changing values of the dollar in the usual *financial statements.* See *price level adjusted statements.*

standard cost   Anticipated *cost* of producing a unit of output; a predetermined cost to be assigned to products produced.

stated capital   Amount of capital contributed by stockholders. Sometimes used to mean *legal capital.*

stated value   A term used for *capital stock,* only if no *par value* is indicated. Where there is a stated value per share, it may be set by the directors (in which case, capital *contributed in excess of stated value* may come into being).

statement of changes in financial position   A

statement which explains the changes in *working capital* (or cash) balances during a period and shows the changes in the working capital (or cash) accounts themselves. Sometimes called the "funds statement."

Statement of Financial Accounting Standards See *FASB*.

statement of financial position *Balance sheet.*

statement of retained earnings (income) A statement that reconciles the beginning-of-period and end-of-period balances in the *retained earnings account*. It shows the effects of *earnings*, *dividend declarations*, and *prior-period adjustments*.

Statements on Auditing Standards No. 1 of this series (1973) codifies all statements on auditing standards previously promulgated by the *AICPA*. Later numbers deal with specific auditing standards and procedures. Statement No. 5 (1975) may in practice lead to more restricted choices between alternative *GAAP* for a given transaction; at this time, it is too early to tell.

stock *Inventory. Capital stock.* A measure of the amount of something on hand at a specific time; in this sense, contrast with *flow*.

stock dividend A so-called *dividend*, where additional *shares* of *capital stock* are distributed, without cash payments, to existing shareholders. It results in a *debit* to *retained earnings* and a *credit* to *capital stock* accounts in the amount of the market value of the shares issued. Contrast with a *stock split*.

stockholders' equity *Proprietorship* or *owners' equity* of a corporation.

stock option The right to purchase a specified number of shares of *stock* for a specified price at specified times, usually granted to employees.

stock split Increase in the number of common shares outstanding resulting from the issuance of additional shares to existing stockholders without additional capital contributions by them. Does not increase the total *par* (or *stated*) *value* of *common stock* outstanding because par (or stated) value per share is reduced in inverse proportion. A three-for-one stock split reduces par (or stated) value per share to one-third of its former amount. Stock splits are usually limited to distributions that increase the number of shares outstanding by 20 percent or more. Compare with *stock dividend*.

stores *Raw materials*, parts, and supplies.

straight-line depreciation If the *depreciable life* is *n* periods, then the periodic *depreciation* charge is $1/n$ of the *depreciable cost*. Results in equal periodic charges and is sometimes called "straight-time depreciation."

subject to Qualifications in an *auditor's report* usually caused by a *material* uncertainty in the valuation of an item, such as future promised payments from a foreign government or outcome of pending litigation.

subsidiary Said of a company more than 50 percent of whose voting stock is owned by another.

subsidiary ledger The *ledger* that contains the detailed accounts whose total is shown in a *controlling account* of the *general ledger*.

subsidiary (ledger) accounts The *accounts* in a *subsidiary ledger*.

successful-efforts accounting In petroleum accounting, the *capitalization* of the drilling costs of only those wells which contain oil. See *discovery-value accounting* for an example.

summary of significant accounting principles APB Opinion No. 22 requires that every *annual report* summarize the significant *accounting principles* used in compiling the annual report. This summary may be a separate exhibit or the first *note* to the financial statements.

sum-of-the-years'-digits depreciation An *accelerated depreciation* method for an asset with *depreciable life* of *n* years where the charge in period i $(i = 1, \ldots, n)$ is the fraction $(n + 1 - i)/[n(n + 1)/2]$ of the *depreciable cost*.

S-X See *Regulation S-X*.

SYD *Sum-of-the-years'-digits depreciation.*

T-account Account form shaped like the letter T with the title above the horizontal line. *Debits* are shown to the left of the vertical line; *credits*, to the right.

tangible Having physical form.

tax A nonpenal, but compulsory, charge levied by a government on income, consumption, wealth, or other bases for the benefit of all those governed. The term does not include fines or specific charges for benefits accruing only to those paying the charges, such as licenses, permits, special assessments, admissions fees, and tolls.

tax allocation: interperiod See *deferred income tax liability*.

tax allocation: intrastatement The showing of income tax effects on *extraordinary items, income* *from discontinued operations*, and *prior-period adjustments* along with these items, separately from income taxes on other income. See *net of tax reporting*.

tax avoidance See *tax shelter*.

tax credit A subtraction from taxes otherwise payable, contrast with *tax deduction*.

tax deduction A subtraction from *revenues* and *gains* to arrive at taxable income.

tax evasion The fraudulent understatement of taxable revenue or overstatement of deductions and expenses or both. Contrast with *tax shelter*.

tax shelter The legal avoidance of, or reduction in, *income taxes* resulting from a careful reading of the complex income tax regulations and the subsequent rearrangement of financial affairs to take advantage of the regulations. Often the term is used pejoratively, but the courts have long held that an individual or corporation has no obligation to pay taxes any larger than the legal minimum. If the public concludes that a given tax shelter is "unfair," then the laws and regulations can be changed. Sometimes used to refer to the investment that permits *tax avoidance*.

temporary account *Account* that does not appear on the *balance sheet*. *Revenue* and *expense* accounts, their *adjuncts* and *contras*, *production cost accounts, income distribution accounts*, and purchases-related accounts (which are closed to the various inventories). Sometimes called a "nominal account."

temporary difference See *timing difference*.

temporary investments Investments in *marketable securities* that the owner intends to sell within a short time, usually 1 year, and hence classified as *current assets*.

10-K The name of the annual report required by the *SEC* of nearly all publicly held corporations. This report contains more information than the *annual report* to stockholders. Corporations must send a copy of the 10-K to those stockholders who request it.

term bonds A *bond issue* whose component bonds all mature at the same time.

terms of sale The conditions governing payment for a sale. For example, the terms *2/10, n(et)/30* mean that if payment is made within 10 days of the invoice date, a *discount* of 2 percent from *invoice* price can be taken; the invoice amount must be paid, in any event, within 30 days or it becomes overdue.

time deposit Cash in a bank earning interest; contrast with *demand deposit*.

time-series analysis See *cross-section analysis* for definition and contrast.

times-interest earned Ratio of pretax *income* plus *interest* charges to interest charges. See *ratio*.

timing difference A difference between taxable income and pretax income reported to stockholders that will be reversed in a subsequent period and requires an entry in the *deferred income tax* account. For example, the use of *accelerated depreciation* for tax returns and *straight-line depreciation* for financial reporting.

trade discount A *discount* from *list price* offered to all customers of a given type. Contrast with a *discount* offered for prompt payment and *quantity discount*.

trade-in Acquiring a new *asset* in exchange for a used one and perhaps additional cash. See *boot* and *trade-in transaction*.

trade-in transaction The accounting for a trade-in depends upon whether or not the asset received is "similar" to the asset traded in and whether the accounting is for *financial statements* or for *income tax* returns. Assume that an old asset cost $5,000, has $3,000 of *accumulated depreciation* (after recording depreciation to the date of the trade-in), and hence has a *book value* of $2,000. The old asset appears to have a market value of $1,500, according to price quotations in used-asset markets. The old asset is traded in on a new asset with a list price of $10,000. The old asset and $5,500 cash (*boot*) are given for the new asset. The generic entry for the trade-in transaction is:

New Asset	A	
Accumulated Depreciation (old asset)	3,000	
Adjustment on Exchange of Asset	B or B	
Old Asset		5,000
Cash		5,500

(1) The *list-price* method of accounting for trade-ins rests on the assumption that the list price of the new asset closely approximates its market value. The new asset is recorded at its list price (A = $10,000 in the example); B is a *plug* (= $2,500 credit in the example). If B requires a *debit* plug, the Adjustment on Exchange of Asset is a *loss*; if a *credit* plug is required (as in the example), the adjustment is a *gain*.

(2) Another theoretically sound method of accounting for trade-ins rests on the assumption that the price quotation from used-asset markets gives a more reliable measure of the market value of the old asset than is the list price a reliable measure of the market value of the new asset. This method uses the *fair market value* of the old asset, $1,500 in the example, to determine B (= $2,000 book value − $1,500 assumed proceeds on disposition = $500 debit or loss). The exchange results in a loss if the book value of the old asset exceeds its market value and in a gain if the market value exceeds the book value. The new asset is recorded on the books by plugging for A (= $7,000 in the example).

(3) For income tax reporting, no gain or loss may be recognized on the trade-in. Thus the new asset is recorded on the books by assuming that B is zero and plugging for A (= $7,500 in the example).

(4) *Generally accepted accounting principles* require a variant of these methods. The basic method is (1) or (2), depending upon whether the list price of the new asset (1) or the quotation of the old asset's market value (2) is the more reliable indication of market value. If, when applying the basic method, a debit entry, or loss, is required for the Adjustment on Exchange of Asset, then the trade-in is recorded as described in (1) or (2) and the full amount of the loss is recognized currently. If, however, a credit entry, or gain, is required for the Adjustment on Exchange of Asset, then the amount of gain recognized currently depends upon whether or not the old asset and the new asset are "similar." If the assets are not similar, then the entire gain is recognized currently. If the assets are similar and cash is not received by the party trading in, then no gain is recognized and the treatment is like that in (3); that is, B = 0, plug for A. If the assets are similar and cash is received by the party trading in—a rare case—then a portion of the gain is recognized currently. The portion of the gain recognized currently is the fraction *cash received/market value of old asset*. (When the list price method (1) is used, the market value of the old asset is assumed to be the list price of the new asset plus the amount of cash received by the party trading in.)

The results of applying GAAP to the example can be summarized as follows:

More Reliable Information as to Fair Market Value	Old Asset Compared with New Asset	
	Similar	**Not Similar**
New Asset List Price	A = $7,500	A = $10,000
	B = 0	B = 2,500 gain
Old Asset Market Price	A = $7,000	A = $ 7,000
	B = 500 loss	B = 500 loss

turnover The number of times that *assets*, such as *inventory* or *accounts receivable*, are replaced on average during the period. Accounts receivable turnover, for example, is total sales on account for a period divided by average accounts receivable balance for the period. See *ratio*.

two-T-account method A method for computing *monetary gains* and *losses* for *general price level adjusted statements*. The left-hand T-

trademark A distinctive name, sign, or symbol. Exclusive rights to use a trademark are granted by the federal government for 28 years and can be renewed for another 28 years.

transaction An exchange between the accounting *entity* and another party, or parties, that leads to an accounting entry. Sometimes used to describe any event that requires a *journal entry*.

translation gain (or loss) *Foreign exchange gain (or loss)*.

transportation-in *Freight-in*.

treasury bond A bond issued by a corporation and then reacquired; such bonds are treated as retired when reacquired and an *extraordinary gain* or *loss* on reacquisition is recognized. Also, a *bond* issued by the U.S. Treasury Department.

treasury stock *Capital stock* issued and then reacquired by the corporation. Such reacquisitions result in a reduction of *stockholders' equity*, and are usually shown on the balance sheet as *contra* to stockholders' equity. Neither *gain* nor *loss* is recognized on transactions involving treasury stock. Any difference between the amounts paid and received for treasury stock transactions are debited (if positive) or credited (if negative) to *additional paid-in capital.*

trial balance A listing of *account balances*; all accounts with *debit* balances are totalled separately from accounts with *credit* balances. The two totals should be equal. Trial balances are taken as a partial check of the arithmetic accuracy of the entries previously made. See *adjusted, pre-closing, post-closing, unadjusted trial balance. account* shows actual net balances of *monetary items*, and the right-hand T-account shows implied *common dollar* amounts.

2/10, n(et)/30 See *terms of sale.*

unadjusted trial balance *Trial balance* before *adjusting* and *closing entries* are made at the end of the period.

unappropriated retained earnings *Retained earnings* not appropriated and therefore against which *dividends* can usually be charged.

uncollectible account An *account receivable* that will not be paid by the *debtor.* If the preferable *allowance method* is used, the entry on judging a specific account to be uncollectible is to *debit* the allowance for uncollectibles account and to *credit* the specific account receivable. See *sales, uncollectible accounts adjustment.*

unconsolidated subsidiary A *subsidiary* not consolidated and, hence, accounted for on the *equity method.*

unemployment tax See *FUTA.*

unexpired cost An *asset.*

unfunded Not *funded.* An obligation or *liability*, usually for *pension costs*, exists but no *funds* have been set aside to discharge the obligation or liability.

Uniform Partnership Act A model law, enacted by many states, to govern the relations between partners where the *partnership* agreement fails to specify the agreed-upon treatment.

unissued capital stock *Stock* authorized but not yet issued.

units of production method The *production method of depreciation.*

unlimited liability The liability of *general partners* or a sole proprietor for all debts of the *partnership* or *sole proprietorship.*

unqualified opinion See *auditor's report.*

unrealized holding gain See *inventory profit* for definition and an example.

unrecovered cost *Book value* of an *asset.*

useful life *Service life.*

use of funds Any *transaction* that reduces *working capital.*

value Monetary worth; the term is usually so subjective that it ought not to be used unless most people would agree on the amount; not to be confused with *cost.* See *fair market value.*

variable costing *Direct costing.*

vendor A seller. Sometimes spelled "vender."

verifiable A qualitive *objective* of financial reporting specifying that items in *financial statements* can be checked by tracing back to supporting *invoices*, canceled *checks*, and other physical pieces of evidence.

vested Said of *pension plan* benefits that are not contingent on the employee continuing to work for the employer.

voucher A document that serves to recognize a *liability* and authorize the disbursement of cash. Sometimes used to refer to the written evidence documenting an *accounting entry*, as in the term *journal voucher.*

voucher system A method for controlling *cash* that requires each *check* to be authorized with an approved *voucher.* No cash *disbursements* are made.

wage Compensation of employees based on time worked or output of product for manual labor.

warrant A certificate entitling the owner to buy a specified amount of stock at a specified time(s) for a specified price. Differs from a *stock option* only in that options are granted to employees and warrants are sold to the public. See *right.*

warranty A promise by a seller to correct deficiencies in products sold. When warranties are given, good accounting practice recognizes an estimate of warranty *expense* and an *estimated liability* at the time of sale.

wasting asset A *natural resource* having a limited *useful life* and, hence, subject to *amortization* called *depletion.* Examples are timberland, oil and gas wells, and ore deposits.

weighted average An *average* computed by counting each occurrence of an item, not merely the number of different items. For example, if one unit is purchased for $1 and two units are purchased for $2 each, then the simple average of the transaction prices is $1.50 but the weighted average cost of the three items is $5/3 = $1.67.

weighted-average inventory method Valuing

either *withdrawals* or *ending inventory* at the *weighted average* purchase price of all units on hand at the time of withdrawal or of computing ending inventory. The *inventory equation* is used to calculate the other quantity. If the *perpetual inventory* method is in use, often called the "moving-average method."

window dressing The attempt to make financial statements show *operating* results, or *financial position*, more favorable than would be otherwise shown.

withdrawals *Assets* distributed to an owner. *Partner's drawings. See inventory equation* for another context.

withholding Deductions from *salaries* or *wages*, usually for *income taxes*, to be remitted by the employer, in the employee's name, to the taxing authority.

working capital *Current assets* minus *current liabilities*. The *statement of changes in financial position* usually explains the changes in working capital for a period.

working capital provided by operations See *funds provided by operations*.

work in process Partially completed product; an *asset* which is classified as *inventory*.

work sheet A tabular schedule for convenient summary of *adjusting* and *closing entries*. The work sheet usually begins with an *unadjusted trial balance*. Adjusting entries are shown in the next two columns, one for *debits* and one for *credits*. The horizontal sum of each line is then carried to the right into either the *income statement* or *balance sheet* columns, as appropriate. The *plug* to equate the income statement column totals is the income, if a debit plug is required, or loss, if a credit plus is required, for the period. That income will be closed to retained earnings on the balance sheet. The income statement credit columns are the revenues for the period and the debit columns are the expenses (and revenue *contras*) to be shown on the income statement.

An example of a work sheet is shown here for Caralex Stores, Inc., for the quarter ending September 30, 1976. The Company last closed its books on June 30, 1976. The Expense Control Account is used to record various expenses not shown in separate accounts (see *control account*). The numbers in parentheses on the work sheet correspond to the adjusting entries explained below.

(1) A deposit of $1,250 was made up, journalized, and posted on September 30, but actually was not deposited in the bank until October 1.

Undeposited Cash	1,250	
Cash in Bank		1,250

To reverse entry prematurely recorded.

(2) The net debit balances of accounts receivable from customers is $94,000. A review of individual customers' accounts reveals that several individual accounts have credit balances totaling $650. Thus, the gross amount of accounts receivable is $94,650.

Accounts Receivable	650	
Advances by Customers		650

To set up advances by customers who have made payments on accounts or returned goods for credit.

(3) The merchandise inventory on hand at September 30 is $130,000.

Cost of Goods Sold	246,000	
Merchandise Inventory		246,000

To record reduction in inventory as cost of goods sold. $376,000 − $130,000 = $246,000.

(4) The insurance policies all expire on January 1, 1978. No payments on insurance policies were made this quarter.

Expense Control Account	260	
Prepaid Insurance		260

The insurance policies provide 18 months' coverage as of June 30, 1976. To record insurance expired for 3 months; $3/18 \times \$1,560 = \$260$.

Caralex Stores, Inc.
Work Sheet—Quarter Ending September 30, 1976

	Unadjusted Trial Balance		Adjustments		Income Statement		Balance Sheet	
	Dr.	Cr.	Dr.	Cr.	Dr.	Cr.	Dr.	Cr.
Accounts Payable		32,400						32,400
Accounts Receivable	94,000		(2) 650				94,650	
Accumulated Depreciation		17,000		(7) 500				17,500
Advances by Customers				(2) 650				650
Allowance for Uncollectible Accounts		1,400		(6) 3,200				4,600
Bonus Expense			(12) 752		752			
Bonus Payable				(12) 752				752
Capital Stock		160,000						160,000
Cash in Bank	8,270			(1) 1,250			7,020	
Cost of Goods Sold			(3) 246,000		246,000			
Expense Control Account	62,960		(4) 260 (7) 500 (9) 1,680	(5) 1,200 (8) 1,400	62,800			
Furniture and Fixtures	25,000						25,000	
Income Tax Expense			(13) 2,160		2,160			
Income Tax Payable				(13) 2,160				2,160
Interest Expense	620		(11) 100		720			
Interest Revenue				(10) 240		240		
Interest Payable		400		(11) 100				500
Interest Receivable	80		(10) 240				320	
Merchandise Inventory	376,000			(3) 246,000			130,000	
Notes Payable		24,000						24,000
Notes Receivable	9,600						9,600	
Payroll Taxes Payable		360		(9) 1,680				2,040
Prepaid Insurance	1,560			(4) 260			1,300	
Prepaid Rent	1,200		(5) 1,200				2,400	
Retained Earnings		13,860						13,860
Sales		326,000				326,000		
Sales Returns and Allowances	6,000				6,000			
Sales Tax Payable		9,600						9,600
Sales, Uncollectible Accounts Adjustment			(6) 3,200		3,200			
Supplies Inventory	1,200		(8) 1,400				2,600	
Undeposited Cash	500		(1) 1,250				1,750	
Withheld Income Tax		1,970						1,970
Column Totals	586,990	586,990	259,392	259,392	321,632	326,240	274,640	270,032
Net Income for Quarter					4,608			4,608
					326,240	326,240	274,640	274,640

(5) The rent is $1,200 per month and has been paid through November 30, 1976. When the rent was paid, it was debited to Rent Expense, a component of the Expense Control Account.

Prepaid Rent	1,200	
Expense Control Account		1,200

To set up 2 months' prepaid rent as of September 30. Prepaid rent was $1,200; as a result of this entry, it is $2,400.

(6) The estimated uncollectibles to arise from sales of the quarter are 1 percent of sales net of returns and allowances.

Sales, Uncollectible Accounts Adjustment	3,200	
Allowance for Uncollectible Accounts		3,200

.01 × ($326,000 − $6,000) = $3,200.

(7) Depreciation on furniture and fixtures is 8 percent of cost per year.

Expense Control Account	500	
Accumulated Depreciation		500

3/12 × .08 × $25,000 = $500.

8) The cost of all supplies purchased was debited to Supplies Expense, a competent of the Expense Control Account. The Supplies Inventory at September 30 is $2,600.

Supplies Inventory	1,400	
Expense Control Account		1,400

To set up supplies inventory at $2,600.

(9) The employer's share of payroll taxes has been paid through September 1. The employer's share for September is calculated to be $1,680.

Expense Control Account	1,680	
Payroll Taxes Payable		1,680

To record Payroll Tax Expense for September as a component of the Expense Control Account.

(10) The Notes Receivable account contains a 10-percent note for $9,600 dated June 1, 1976, and due December 1, 1976.

Interest Receivable	240	
Interest Revenue		240

3/12 × .10 × $9,600 = $240.

(11) The Notes Payable account contains a single 10-percent note for $24,000 dated July 15, 1976, and due January 16, 1977. Interest has been accrued on the 15th of each month.

Interest Expense	100	
Interest Payable		100

Interest expense per month is $200 (= 1/12 × .10 × $24,000). The balance of Interest Payable on the note should be $500 (= 2½ × $200). To adjust interest expense for the quarter and interest payable as of September 30.

(12) The manager is to be paid a bonus of 10 percent of the pretax income of the enterprise exclusive of the bonus.

Bonus Expense	752	
Bonus Payable		752

From Income Statement columns:
.10 × ($240 + $326,000 − $246,000 − $62,800 − $2,160 − $720 − $6,000 − $3,200) = $752.

(13) The income tax for the quarter is estimated to be $2,160.

Income Tax Expense	2,160	
Income Taxes Payable		2,160

To record income tax expense for quarter.

Work sheet is also used to refer to *schedules* for determining other items appearing on the *financial statements* that require adjustment or compilation.

write off   *Charge* an *asset* to *expense* or *loss;* that is, *debit* expense (or loss) and *credit* asset.

write-off method   A method for treating *uncollectible accounts* that charges *bad debt expense* and credits accounts receivable of specific customers as uncollectible amounts are identified. May not be used when uncollectible amounts are significant and can be estimated. See *sales, uncollectible accounts adjustment* and the *allowance method* for contrast.

yield   The rate of return on a stream of cash flows; usually said of a *bond.* Sometimes called the "effective rate."

zero salvage value   If the *salvage value* of a *depreciable asset* is estimated to be less than 10 percent of its *cost,* then the tax regulations permit an assumption of zero salvage value in computing *depreciation* for federal *income tax* purposes. This convention is often used in *financial reporting* as well.

Index

(See also Glossary on pages 515-558)